Phenomenology and Indian Philosophy

Published under the auspices of
INDIAN COUNCIL OF PHILOSOPHICAL RESEARCH
New Delhi
and
CENTER OF ADVANCED RESEARCH IN PHENOMENOLOGY
Boca Raton

Phenomenology and Indian Philosophy

EDITED BY

D. P. Chattopadhyaya
Lester Embree
Jitendranath Mohanty

State University of New York Press

First published
in U.S.A. by
State University of New York Press
Albany

For information, address State University of New York Press,
State University Plaza, Albany, N.Y., 12246

Library of Congress Cataloging-in-Publication Data

Phenomenology and Indian philosophy / edited by D.P. Chattopadhyaya, Lester Embree, Jitendranath Mohanty.
p. cm.
Published under the auspices of: Indian Council of Philosophical Research, New Delhi; and, Center of Advanced Research in Phenomenology, Boca Raton.
Includes bibliographical references and index.
ISBN 0–7914–0662–8

1. Phenomenology. 2. Philosophy, Indic. I. Chattopadhyaya, D. P. (Debi Prasad), 1933- . II. Embree, Lester E. III. Mohanty, Jitendranath, 1928-.
B829.5.P452 1991 90-42910
142'.7' 0954–dc20 CIP

10 9 8 7 6 5 4 3 2 1

For
The Pioneers of Phenomenology
in India and
Their Euro-American Colleagues

Contents

My First Trip to India : A Personal Introduction
Lester Embree 1

Phenomenology and Indian Philosophy : The Concept of Rationality
J.N. Mohanty 8

Husserl and Indian Thought
Karl Schuhmann 20

Phenomenology and Indian Philosophy
Sibajiban Bhattacharyya 44

Advaita Vedānta on the Problem of Enworlded Subjectivity
R. Balasubramanian 77

An Indian Interaction with Phenomenology : Perspectives on the Philosophy of K.C. Bhattacharyya
Kalyan Kumar Bagchi 94

Phenomenology and Philosophy of History
David Carr 103

Freedom, Interpretation and Meaning in Human Sciences
D.P. Chattopadhyaya 113

Husserlian Foundations of Sartre's Treatment of Time Consciousness
V.C. Thomas 126

Analysis of I-Consciousness in the Transcendental Phenomenology and Indian Philosophy
Anindita Niyogi Balslev 133

Phenomenology and the Transcendent : Which Way Does One Transcend?
Paulos Mar Gregorios 141

The Paradox of Subjectivity and the Idea of Ultimate Grounding in Husserl and Heidegger
Thomas M. Seebohm 153

Experiment as Fulfilment of Theory
Patrick A. Heelan 169

'Merleau-Ponty's Thesis of the Primacy of Perception and the Meaning of Scientific Objectivity'
John J. Compton 185

The World as the Ontological Project of Man
Ramakant Sinari 198

Technology as Cultural Instrument
Don Ihde 207

Nature and Life World : Towards a Hermeneutics of Nature
R. Sundara Rajan 216

Unity and Plurality of Cultures in the Perspectives of Edmund Husserl and Ernst Cassirer
Ernst Wolfgang Orth 233

Human Scientific Propositions
Lester Embree 247

Phenomenology of Human Relations : Some Reflections
S.P. Banerjee 253

Object, Objective Phenomenon and Objectivating Act According to the 'Vijñaptimātratāsiddhi' of Xuanzang (600–664)
Iso Kern 262

Last Philosophy : Ideas for a Transcendental Phenomenological Metaphysics—Eugen Fink with Edmund Husserl, 1928–38
Ronald Bruzina 270

Hermeneutics in Indian Philosophy
Krishna Roy 290

Reading the Ṛigveda : A Phenomenological Essay
J.L. Mehta 303

Speech and Writing in Heidegger's Philosophy
S. IJsseling 318

Towards a Hermeneutic of Centrality in Indian Art
Margaret Chatterjee 332

Reflections on Papers
D.P. Chattopadhyaya 341

Contributors 366

Index 369

My First Trip to India: A Personal Introduction

LESTER EMBREE

'I feel I have been living many fairy tales on this trip.'
SAM IJSSELING

Some people probably still believe that phenomenology is about particular events individually felt. If the literature is actually reviewed, of course (and one could do worse than look over the essays contained in the present volume), it will be seen that phenomenology typically aims at knowledge that is universal and intersubjectively confirmable. The present introduction may confirm this through contrast, for it shows what a reflective description of subjectivistic and particularistic or, more concisely, a personal life is actually like and thus how unphenomenological it can be. In part, however, it is also intended to show, albeit onesidedly, something of the origins, the course, and the hope for repetition of the first major meeting of Western and Indian philosophers on the thematics of phenomenology and Indian philosophy. Since the following narrative is personal (and thus has the advantage of letting me ramble and jump about, just as memory and fantasy do), the first person form may as well be employed.

In January 1988 I led a delegation of fourteen Westerners to New Delhi to meet with a comparable number of Indian philosophers. I did this in my capacity as President of the Centre for Advanced Research in Phenomenology, Inc. I am aware of four factors behind this meeting on the side of the Western delegation. The oldest and strongest was fellow CARP director Jitendranath Mohanty's long-standing wish to bring a group of phenomenologists back to his home country. He went to the West in the 1950s, first to Germany then back to India and later to America, but never forgot where he came from.

The second and precipitating factor was Dr Krishna Roy of the Jadavpur University, Calcutta. She came to the Summer Programme in Phenomenology held by CARP with the University of Ottawa in August 1985. I remember coming out to enjoy the cool evening after hot day, and finding Jiten and Krishna and others sitting about and talking, and joining them. At some point, Krishna said something like 'You ought to organize a group of phenomenologists to come to India for a conference.' I replied with something like 'That would be wonderful, lots of people we know would love to go, but how could this be done?' Jiten said he thought that there might be people in India who would invite us. We talked about people and timing but beyond that my recollection fades. Many possibilities in the mode of 'Wouldn't it be great if...' arise for our little Center but do not work out because of 'ifs' that cannot be fulfilled.

Krishna went back to India and spoke to Professor D.P. Chattopadhyaya, Chairman of the Indian Council of Philosophical Research, an institution funded entirely by the Government of India. Later, when Jiten went in fall 1986 to give his Presidential Address to the Indian Philosophical Congress, he and D. P. also spoke. By the way, Indians use initials to refer to people and institutions a bit more than I was used to. Perhaps this is derived from British habits, but then again, since I was twice told by Indians with considerable glee of a columnist in India who has argued for years that the British got cricket just like polo from India, perhaps naming by initials went the other way!

Let me jump ahead and mention that I went to India expecting things British to have been widely rejected in a long exploited former colony and, as a phenomenologist, I know that expectations, frustrated or fulfilled, co-constitute what we perceive. I had been taught in school about all the gold that English pirates like Drake took from the Spanish but I had only recently learned that England capitalized herself over centuries even more with wealth taken from India. Among my many happy surprises was how many good things British were not rejected in India. The boys play cricket madly and I saw school for girls let out in knee socks and blazers.

Anyhow, when J. N. came back he told me that he thought something was going to develop and hence it was not totally a surprise when the first letter came to me from D. P. Organizing such affairs is largely a matter of writing letters. I have rather a pile of these but more important here are two things, the impression I quickly got and how something I did automatically was received. These show the third factor for the event called 'Phenomenology and Indian Philosophy' which is the ICPR–CARP interaction. Firstly, the impression I quickly got was that I was dealing with very competent people, which is to say that once both sides were committed, we got down to the administrative details.

Secondly, I do not know whether to be more proud of successes that result from careful research and planning or those that arise by themselves from a well established outlook. The case in point is my automatic expectation that approximately equal numbers from each side would have equal participation in the programme. Through the letters I gathered that this is not what the other side originally had in mind but the reaction to my assumption was not consternation but delight, which I did not quite understand. Only when we were finally there and got to know people and talked personally did I gather that we were different because we wanted at least as much to meet Indian philosophers and hear what they thought as to express our own ideas. I do not know whether it is something particularly American to presume equality, but I do know this was not just my view. It was clearly shared by our delegation from the beginning and manifest at the preparatory session we held. There we had read Jiten's article in the *Encyclopaedia Britannica* on 'Indian Philosophy' and then, when he sketched its history and present state, the rest of us took notes and asked questions like good undergraduates. We knew little, but we knew that, and were going to start making up for our deficiency.

The fourth and final factor was, as just intimated, the group of people who went. In many ways, India was far. All of us had travelled in the West, the Europeans to America and the Americans to Europe, but India is not in the West. People had to find help from their universities for travel costs. There were health considerations in some cases. But there had also recently been an huge show on India at the Smithsonian, the presentation of *The Jewel in the Crown* on television and in paperback books, the films *Gandhi* and *A Passage to India*, etc. But, still, India was far away, like China and Japan. It may not have helped when I insisted we would not all go on one plane and thus risk setting the history of phenomenology back a generation. Two dozen were contacted, at one point nineteen were going, in the end fourteen went. The group that went was a fine one. Perhaps two suffered culture shock without knowing it, the non-psychological sufferings were also manageable, and all were ecstatic about India.

So we went. Again, since the essays are here to speak for the philosophy that was done, I will continue my narrative in personal terms and focus not on the meeting of the philosophies so much as the encountering of India by myself and by the other Westerners I was with at different times. I wish I could believe that we looked so good to India as India looked to us. On New Year's Eve I went out to JFK airport in New York to catch my 747. I was about four hours early and would soon learn that if one passes one's bag in so early it will be about the last one to come back out. Somebody said the plane was larger than the ship on which Columbus went West to find the East. I was seated between an expatriate grandmother from Arizona wracked with ambivalences over re-contracting herself for three more years in public medicine in Saudi Arabia and an Indian computer scientist returning home for the first time since leaving as practically a boy. As travelling strangers who expect they will never meet again tend to do, we talked as if old friends except we had to fill in our backgrounds.

I had a friend who was becoming an 'expat' and was thus prepared to appreciate somebody for whom the country and society, i.e., the United States, in which she had lived most of her life, had become only a place to visit and about which to have rather romantically implausible ideas. I wish her well, this person more of the future than of the past, a citizen of Earth more than American or any other locality.

The story of my other new friend was more familiar, except I was not especially aware such things still happened. He had come to America some twenty years before with $30 in his pocket and an uncle who gave him $100 a month for a year to live on, attended an American state university, washed many dishes, won scholarships, gained a doctorate in computer science, and came to head a department with a budget in the millions. On the other hand, he was not so forthcoming about his mixed feelings upon returning to India. We talked about how the West was continuing centuries of behaviour by skimming the cream of talent from what I tried to call 'the third world, but he suggested we simply call poor countries'. Later, on the way back from India, I sat with another Indian, whose business was in California. The same topic came up. He described how a group he belonged to was attempting to persuade people educated in India to send money back after making their fortunes elsewhere. The final stage of their plan involved monthly telegrams with one word: 'Cheat!'

It took 22 hours to fly from New York to New Delhi in January 1988.

The talk was great. I slept little. Frankfurt airport, where we could stretch our legs, has glass, stainless steel, and cleanliness like a huge science laboratory. Then on to Riyadh (no pictures out the windows please), where the expatriat deplaned. In New Delhi, everybody was met but me. Somebody forgot to put 'a.m.' on my telegram. After waiting for my bags forever, I went through passport control, but none of the little signs on sticks had my name on them. It was about 04.00 a.m. local time. I went outside, where it was remarkably dark and cold and the porters all had blankets over their heads, and I could not figure out how people were getting their cabs.

Then the magic started. Out of the dark came a man who inquired whether I was Professor Embree. But he was not from the ICPR. Instead he had heard me give a paper in Canada years ago. When he heard why I was standing there in the dark (where philosophers of course hate to be), he took charge, organized the cab, he delivered me to the hotel. Thus was proven in one shot not only my international reputation but also the practicality of philosophy! The cab had three wheels, a motorcycle engine, and a cloth top like a huge baby carriage (I came to love riding in them). We zipped down the dark and empty superhighways. He told me over the engine and wind, how he was a Christian but formerly a Muslim and returning for the first time since most of his family was killed in a communal conflict years ago. He would sell his mother's property and then get out of India immediately. I lost the card with his name and address and hope he reads this and writes.

Everything had been thoroughly prepared by the ICPR for our arrival and I was gratefully asleep two hours after the plane landed. Eventually, I awoke and watched the vultures in the tree outside my window awhile. Then I went down to find food. In the lobby I found J. N. and met, finally, D. P. They were coming from the airport, where I had not arrived at 04:00 p.m. For the next week I was under the care of the ICPR: we were let to worry about things about as much as children are when visiting their grandparents. Because of the drought and budget cutbacks that almost caused the cancellation of our meeting, we had the additional adventure of a people's hotel, the Ashok Yatri Niwas. We had rooms; we signed little chits for meals. ICPR people were stationed there, buses took us about, everything. None of us will forget the care and kindness of Dr V. C. Thomas and Mr Satish Bhushan. I wrote the Prime Minister after we got back to praise Chairman Chattopadhyaya and his staff for this treatment and D. P. was appreciative but also made it clear that nothing more than the usual had been done for us. The 'usual' that we experienced would be easy to get used to!

We gathered for the sessions at the Nehru Memorial Library. Perhaps, George Washington's Mt. Vernon would be the symbolic if not functional equivalent. Behind us when we spoke was a picture showing Nehru's face and profile in at least five different sizes, ages, and angles, e.g., in 'adumbrations', a phenomenologist would say. The Indian colleagues are very much like Western academics. Typically, their presentations were solid, well challenged, and ably defended. These colleagues we now know personally often showed much knowledge of phenomenology.

Jiten's Indian clothing was a delight to his Western friends, who had never seen him dressed that way and his first smile showed he knew that. I enjoyed being interviewed by *The Times of India* and had the further fun of being misquoted on the first page. At the breaks we went for tea in a very large Hindu wedding tent made of blue, white and yellow silk that was set up on the lawn. In my snapshots everybody obviously liked everybody else as we chatted there. Outside the tent we saw ravens after scraps in the cooking area behind and also kites and once even eagles, who were after the ravens. During one of these sessions, D. P. was presented with the B. C. Roy Memorial Award, India's highest for a philosopher.

There were about 30 papers presented and discussed at the four-day conference. The brain can become numb. The third afternoon was free so that we could do other things and recoup our energies. Jiten had a list from his wife for spices only available in India and he also needed to get her a sari. I went along for the ride, which was of course by tricab. The most famous sari store, which is called Ramchandra Krishanchandra has a padded platform all around the large room and shelves to the ceiling holding thousands and thousands of saris. There is enormous variety in such things, with designs and colours and materials relating to many places in this country of 800,000,000 people. I think we were told that it took two men a month to weave one by hand. The customer sits in a soft chair or couch and the salesman sits cross-legged on the platform with young assistants ready to scurry for various saris to show.

We were greeted by what we learned was the eldest son of the owner. We were seated, and we were brought tea. The son then sat and began. Sari showing has a rhythm to it. First the seller ascertains something about price range, colour, etc. Then he sends his assistant scurrying for one. And then he casually pulls it out of the plastic and flicks it open like an instantly blossoming flower about the size of the desk I am writing this at. From something the size of a book came this explosion of stunning colour. Then the process is repeated. Jiten laughed at my awe but I think he was taken similarly. I had not agreed to my daughter's request that I bring her one, but did. I saw that the prices crept up gradually but could not care. I now really know what a charming voice is.

After the conference the Westerners were taken to an entertainment of music and traditional dancing of Hindu myths with gods and all. It is not clear how many gods there are in India. In my wonderful *Insight Guides* tour book it is told that some estimate 3,000,000 gods. Others tell me that these are merely aspects or manifestations of one god who is in everything. The count of gods does not, however, seem to be a matter of great concern to the Indians I talked about this with, who were Hindu. The majority of the planet's Muslims live in India, however, and are monotheistic. The dance remains a clear memory of statuesque ladies stamping caloused feet, little bells, music and chant.

We went to India for more than just to meet Indian philosophers and talk philosophy with them. During the conference Jiten took us to a Hindu temple; somehow the pictures Compton and I took of each other with paint on our foreheads did not come out. After the conference the ICPR also arranged a day trip for us to visit Agra and see the Taj Mahal and another around New Delhi. The Taj is about eight stories high and hits you harder as you come out of the tunnel before it than a blossoming sari. The day I saw it was my 50th birthday.

Is there a more beautiful place for my 100th? Along the road coming and going in our air-conditioned bus we saw something of agricultural life, people who worked hard and were poor (but nowise the poorest), and several troups of wild monkeys wandering unafraid among people. We saw a huge plume of smoke from some installation the Soviet Union had given India. India also received a nuclear submarine from the same source while we were there.

Back in New Delhi we saw Gandhi's tomb, which did not hush people as I expected. Maybe respectful silence is a Western trait. We also saw the Red Fort, which is enormous and certainly was intimidating in its time. Most impressive was the memorial made from Indira Gandhi's home. One moves through the rooms in an intimate way and sees pictures of her growing up with her father, then coming to lead the country herself, and finally outside a glass case over an outline on the walk where she was shot down. We also went to the the National Museum and saw much (mostly weapons) from the British period, also much from before (by one story today's Sikhs descend from soldiers who came with Alexander in 326 B.C.), including a replica of a stone with laws from Ashoka (269–232 B.C.) and even something of contemporary Indian painting. Finally, we passed through a Moslem part of Delhi and the smell was different, for many Hindus are vegetarians while Moslems eat meat.

After that, we began to split up. Iso Kern went off to see the birthplace of the Buddha and I did not see him again until just before I left India. Because of the White Huns, there are very few Buddhists in India. Mohanty had already left to visit his mother in Calcutta. I am not sure just where Lanigan and Pietersma went, but I know they had friends or inlaws in India. The next day two cars arranged by the ICPR had drivers who politely controlled us like English bobbies and hardly even slowed down for the road blocks. Indians drive on the left, like the English. I got pretty disoriented riding tri-cabs in traffic the first few days. Oddly, however, I saw no car crashes and no dented fenders—the drivers were actually that polite. Nevertheless, riding to Jaipur at 130 kph on the left side of a two lane highway and passing strings of heavily loaded camels on the *right* while I was discussing Berkeley on perception with Patrick Heelan, while Seebohm and Bruzina behind me looked more ashen every time I looked back, and while the relaxed driver just smiled and smile is another indelible memory.

After awhile we came to Amber. The cars stopped and our choice was to walk or ride elephants up to the fairy tale castle. Elephants move incredibly smoothly and their skin is soft and cool. The one Don Ihde, Sam IJsseling, and I were on was called Jenny. On the way out of Jaipur the drivers said we would now look at a factory. It did not sound like much but we trouped over and went in and saw how carpets are woven and trimmed by hand and then we were taken into another room to be shown jewels. Having had my experience of Indian salesmanship at the sari store, I quickly decided to spend no more than $50, went with a junior salesman to a side room, and soon settled on an opal for Deirdre. Then I could watch the owner himself help half a dozen of the world's phenomenological philosophers spend lots of money (all charge cards accepted) for what they still assure me were terrific buys.

The next day Heelan went off to visit some Jesuit missions and Compton went off to visit the college his uncle had headed even after Independence. The rest of us followed E. W. Orth to Khajuraho (which name he does a great job pronouncing) to inspect the sculpture. Ron Bruzina explained the architecture. An English tiger hunter found the ruins in the 19th Century (the place had been abandoned during the Moslem conquest). They are reconstructed and impressive. So is the contemporary Jain temple. And we saw Japanese tourists in large numbers, including young women as individually stylish in dress and coiffure as Parisian models. The flight on a domestic line was smooth enough, but the plane back was late and Orth had to surrender a rather small pocket knife to the security forces. During the wait, Tom Seebohm, who knows something about the Slavs as well as the Germans, got quite excited reading a book from the newsstand on Indian mythology. The plane landed somewhere on the way back to New Delhi and who walked in but brother Compton full of stories of his pilgrimage!

To make myself stop this yarn, let me tell what happened just before Jiten and I flew back to New York. While we were waiting inside the modernist glass and steel international airport I saw some birds that looked like sparrows flying around. I had seen monkeys and cattle freely moving in cities and towns. Actually, I had previously noticed small birds living inside most of the buildings with nobody paying them any more mind than the cows chewing cud on traffic islands paid the passing cars and trucks. This comfortable mingling of humans and other animals, wild as well as tame, is odd for Western eyes. I mentioned to Jiten that an American airport would have somebody responsible for exterminating any birds that got in. He said instantly that that was terrible. So another pleasant surprise in my first trip to meet philosophical India was a new issue to ponder.

This was my first trip. It does not require deep reflections to recognize how provincial one can be even if one is specialized in so-called 'continental philosophy'. Perhaps phenomenologists are more open to alternative cultural perspectives than the devotees of other philosophical tendencies. I do feel strongly obliged in this era of globalization to become familiar with at least one so-called non-Western culture. (Is mine a non-Eastern culture?) I am too old to learn to speak Chinese or Japanese. The lingua franca of India is English. The people are great. The culture is rich and deep. And there is a great deal of philosophy done. Yes, I will go back to benefit more from India philosophically. And even though we have nothing like the elephants at Amber or Silken tents for coffee breaks, CARP will find a way to invite the ICPR to organize a delegation of our Indian friends to visit us in America. Perhaps they have same fairy tales about us to verify.

Phenomenology and Indian Philosophy: The Concept of Rationality

J.N. MOHANTY

There are philosophers, admittedly great, whose works challenge you endlessly to focus on them—interpreting their thoughts takes hold of you as an unending philological and philosophical task. Aristotle and Kant are such philosophers. There are others, also admittedly great philosophers, whose work releases you to go your own way, whose demand upon you is not to interpret their texts but to follow a path laid down, in an exemplary manner, in their writings. Husserl is such a philosopher.

I began reading Husserl in 1949—picking up a copy of the Boyce Gibson translation of *Ideas* from the library of that indefatigable scholar Rash Vihary Das. Almost forty years of preoccupation with Husserl has—as I look back, I find—set me free to relate to other traditions and other schools of philosophy. Being a 'Husserlian' of a sort, I have not found my access to other philosophies blocked. On the contrary, what is distinctive about the Husserlian path—this being: an openness to phenomena, to the given *qua* given, to the intended meanings precisely as they are intended—challenges you to face up to the task of understanding the other, the other culture, the other philosophical school, the other person. While it has been a long and arduous process trying to understand and appropriate the Husserlian *opus*, the more I have succeeded in it, the freer I have felt to relate myself to the thoughts of the others. I would like to amplify this, on some other occasion, with reference to other modes of philosophizing within the western tradition. On this occasion, I will briefly outline how Husserlian thinking has helped me to understand and interpret the Indian philosophical tradition—in this case, not an other, but I myself.

Had I set out then to explore the 'similarities' and the 'differences' between phenomenology and Indian philosophy, I would have found such features with no great effort, but that finding would have been of no greater value than instituting similar comparisons of Indian philosophy with some other philosophical systems—even if we leave out of consideration the fact, often lost sight of, that Indian philosophy itself, not unlike western philosophy, is a large field containing highly differentiated internal structure. What Husserlian mode of thinking provides us with is not an effective tool for doing what is called 'comparative philosophy', but rather for understanding the other's point of view as a noematic structure and then to go behind it in order to lay bare the experiential phenomenon that is embodied in this structure. The same holds good of phenomenology itself.

I. SKETCH OF A THEORY TO OVERCOME RELATIVISM

Let me begin by formulating my general approach against the background of what may be called the problem of relativism.[1] The all too familiar cultural relativist, if he is a westerner, tells us that the oriental, the Indian or the Chinese, or for that matter, any other 'radically different' community does not do 'philosophy' *in that sense* in which the idea of philosophy was originally instituted by the Greeks. 'Philosophy', along with its implied concept of rationality, is typically western. If the Hindus or the Buddhists did something they today call philosophy, that is not philosophy in the standard western sense; their concept of rationality is radically different from the western. What they call 'their' 'logic' is not 'ours', these 'logics' differ not as Aristotelian from that of the *Principia Mathematica*, but so radically that the same word 'logic' can only be used at the risk of equivocation. It is not uncommon to say that the orientals did not *think*, that they did not raise their intuitions to the level of 'concepts', that their philosophies are in fact religions (and that their religions are intuitive, aesthetic, not conceptual), and so on and so forth.

This raises the large epistemological problem: how can we have access to their thought world save by 'translating' them to ours, which would entail 'transforming' them into our 'constructs' or 'interpreting' them in our terms? As soon as one poses this question, one realizes that the extreme relativism of 'radically different' conceptual frameworks leads, by its internal dialectic, to the denial of such relativism and to the position, argued for by Davidson[2] that there is but our home language and other languages translatable into ours. If we are to understand the other, we must share his framework; if there are different frameworks, different 'worlds', different concepts of 'rationality', we cannot understand them. Could there be a middle ground between these extremes? Could it be that there are *other* worlds, *other* modes of thinking, others in the genuine sense, which are yet accessible to us, not because we all are the same, but because (i) we can also transcend our own 'worlds', (ii) our 'worlds' howsoever different nevertheless have overlapping contents, and (iii) a common identical world is in the process of being constituted by such overlapping contents and by the reflective process of trying to make sense of each other.

Husserl deals with this situation at the level of the ego problematic in the Fifth Cartesian Meditation, and moves on, briefly in sections 56 and 58, to the constitution of higher levels of other cultural worlds. Taking my cue from these and other ideas of Husserl, let me suggest—somewhat briefly and seemingly dogmatically here that (i) although each of us and each culture has its own 'world', it is possible philosophically to reflect on one's world, and thereby to transcend one's world-boundedness and to assume, in the Husserlian jargon, the stance of a transcendental ego; (ii) as a transcendental ego, I can 'apperceive' the other ego as existing there in the mode 'such as I should be *if I were there*'[3]; (iii) I can now understand his world as a sense-structure, constituted by subjective experiences of an eidetic sort, i.e., can establish an eidetic correlation between a noematic achievement and noetic acts, both on eidetic levels; and (iii) finally realize that to say that these 'world-noemata' are *of* one and the same world is equivalent to saying that the identity of the world is an identity in and through these differences, in the process of being constituted through (iv) intercultural understanding, translation and communication, which always rests upon (v) the increasingly recovered *overlapping contents*, but always preserving the otherness of the other.

II. THE INDIAN CONCEPT OF RATIONALITY

Confronted with the historicist-relativistic pronouncements of much of modern thinking, one is left wondering if the Indian concept of rationality was radically different from the western or not. A concept of rationality of a culture is a highly stratified concept, and in any case a higher order concept whose field consists in lower order concepts of various levels. To determine a concept of rationality, one needs to consider: first, what makes, for a culture, a belief acceptable; secondly, what makes a course of action commendable, and, finally, what makes a work of art beautiful. The criteria and principles involved in these operate first of all in the life-world of the community concerned, then in the higher order decisions by the scientists, law-givers and artists, finally in the theoretical discourse of the philosophers. It is to the last that I turn here.

For a brief sketch, the following structure may suffice. For almost all Indian philosophers, the ultimate ground for all evidence, the source for all 'establishment' (*siddhi*), is consciousness (*cit*)—without which no 'being' or 'non-being' could be asserted or denied and there would be 'universal darkness' (*jagadāndhyaprasaṅga*). However, this consciousness is 'neutral' as against truth and falsity; it establishes both. Though a necessary condition, it is not sufficient for establishing truth. For this latter purpose, the Indian philosophers, in different ways, take recourse to a theory of '*pramāṇa*' meaning *both* the specific *cause* of true cognition and also the means of validating or justifying cognitive claims. Every philosophical system in the Indian tradition developed a theory of *pramāṇa* to begin with, which is, at the same time, (a) a theory of *causal* genesis of true cognition and (b) a theory of *justification* of cognitive claims.[4] It appears, then, as though these thinkers solved the problem that has led to much quandary in western thinking: the problem, namely, of how to relate the two spaces—the causal space and the logical space.[5]

To put it this way is to clearly highlight a fundamental difference between Husserlian thinking and Indian philosophy—a difference to which I propose to return later in this essay. For the present, let me continue with the general structure of the Indian concept of rationality. To complete this schematic account, I must add a third component (besides the theory of consciousness and the theory of *pramāṇa*), the theory of action. For all Indian thinkers, cognition issues in a practical, actional response, and the ultimate *guarantee*, for most of them, of the truth of a cognition is practical *success*. A rational belief is one that is appropriately caused, justified by an appropriate *pramāṇa* and leads to successful practice—all three testified by self-evidencing consciousness.

(A) *Theory of Consciousness*

Hussserlian phenomenology guided my search into Indian thinking about consciousness. There are three major components of Husserlian thinking about consciousness: intentionality, temporality and the absolutely foundational—evidencing and constitutive—role of consciousness. Accordingly, I looked at the Indian thinking on these matters from these three perspectives.

(i) *Intentionality.* The thesis of intentionality has itself two parts: that consciousness is always directed towards an object, and—since the intentional object may or may not exist—that every conscious state has a correlative sense or meaning. The first has been a matter of great disputation amongst Indian philosophers (the realists such as the Naiyāyika and the Mīmāṃsā ascribing to consciousness an intrinsic object-directedness (*svābhāvika viṣayapravaṇatva*) and the 'spiritual' (*ādhyātmika*) philosophies insisting on the intrinsic object-lessness (*nirviṣayakatva*) of consciousness. It could at least be said that the Brentano thesis would not have been accepted by the Indian philosophers as though it were a self-evident truth. That the empirical states of consciousness are object-directed was not the point at issue. The issue was: whether the same, or similar, object-directedness could also be ascribed to consciousness even when the latter is 'purified', in Husserlian terms, from all 'naturalistic' adjuncts (*upādhi*). Here one finds a whole array of views in between the two extremes mentioned above, of which at least one is worth mentioning: this is the yogācāra Buddhist view that the *ālambana* (or 'the objective-causal support') of perception is not the so-called external reality, but an internal, cognizable form (*antarjñeya-rūpa*), so that the cognitive act has its own internal objective form.[6]

As regards the theory of sense, the Indian philosophers have by and large preferred a theory of direct reference, their theory of meaning being generally speaking a *referential* theory. In such a theory, as is easy to appreciate, the mediation by sense is uncalled for. However, looking for a theory of sense, one discovers it at unsuspected corners: at those places where the concept of reference is called into question (as in Buddhist *apoha*-theory) or where belief in the eternity of 'word' led them to posit eternal meanings (as in some versions of the *sphoṭa* theory).

In addition to these two questions, Indian philosophers came to focus on two other related issues: does consciousness have a form (*ākāra*) of its own, or does its apparent form really derive from that of its object? The Buddhist who held that the 'objective support' (*ālambana*) is an internal cognizable form of a state of consciousness was, in fact, saying that consciousness has its own intrinsic form (a sensation of blue is 'blue', blue belongs to this sensation not as its colour but as its form).[7] The realists such as the Naiyāyikas and the Mīmāṃsakas defended the opposite view that consciousness of blue and consciousness of yellow differ, not with respect to any intrinsic form of each, but only with respect to their objects which squarely and entirely fall outside them. Consciousness as such is formless (*nirākāra*). Thus you have either a complete realism (the object is totally independent of consciousness which only 'reveals' it) or an idealism (for which the object is but a form internal to consciousness)[8]—but is there a theory of constitution? It is true that consciousness provides the ultimate *evidence* for all cognitive claims, but this evidencing role does not amount to the constituting role as it does with Husserl. To this last point I will return soon.

(ii) *Temporality*. That our conscious life is caught up in time is a truism. Husserl's thesis regarding the temporality of consciousness should not be identified with this truism. It rather consists in the much more significant contention that even after the entire natural world with its spatiality and temporality is placed under brackets, consciousness as the 'phenomenological residuum' and so as 'purified' and as transcendental, is still temporal, and, furthermore, that this latter temporality of consciousness is the constitutive source of all other conceptions of time—of the objective time of nature and of the time of history. Does Indian thought, with its large concern with the inner life of consciousness, come to recognize the temporality of consciousness in this sense? This is a question which is very difficult to answer. There is no doubt that the Indian conception of time is heavily cosmological, and that by and large, consciousness, in its pure, non-empirical nature, is kept outside of the sphere of temporality. Whether there are no places, possibly in the Yoga or in Buddhism, where consciousness's intrinsic, non-objective temporality comes to the forefront is a question which I am not now in a position to answer.[9]

(iii) *Consciousness as absolute, constituting transcendental foundation.* One immediate reason why some of us found Husserl's *Ideas I* (in Boyce Gibson translation) so captivating—and I read the *Ideas* before I came to read the *Logical Investigations*—is that, trained mainly as I was in the overwhelmingly Vedāntic tradition of the University of Calcutta,[10] the idea of transcendentally purified consciousness as a self-enclosed, absolute realm of being had immediately a familiar ring. But it also became increasingly questionable whether the pure consciousness (called *Brahman*) of Vedānta, absolute and foundational though it is conceived to be, can be said to be constitutive of the domains of empirical realities as well as of abstract idealities. Especially in the Advaita Vedānta tradition, consciousness does nothing, it simply manifests, reveals, illuminates or evidences. The domain of objects—real or ideal, the mundane order, that is to say, is neither created by a Godhead nor an emanation of *Brahman*, but an unreal other for which *avidyā* or ignorance (or Māyā, in the standard usage, cosmic ignorance) is held responsible. A non-intentional, non-temporal, non-actional consciousness cannot constitute. It is the foundation (*adhiṣṭhāna*) of the world-appearance, but it does not bring the world about in any sense—theological or phenomenological. Those who rejected the Advaita theory of a non-actional consciousness, and wanted *Brahman* to be the source of the world, resorted either to the theory of creation of a sort (*sṛṣṭi*) or to a theory of emanation. This meant construing consciousness as a force, as an energy, i.e., *cit* as *cit-śakti* (as, e.g., in Śaivism and, in modern times, by Sri Aurobindo)—which does inject a certain intentionality into the texture of consciousness, but still stops short of a constitution theory for reasons that lie deep within the structure of Indian thinking.

As far as I understand the issues now, these reasons lie in (i) the non-availability of a theory of *sense* (as distinguished from reference), and (ii) an ontologically oriented mode of thinking. Phenomenological constitution is constitutions of *sense*, not constitution of the thing itself (but certainly of the sense 'thing itself'). With a theory of sense not around, theory of constitution would become either a theory of evidence (that is to say, of how things are evidenced, known, manifested) *or* a theory of real origination (that is to say, of how things come into being). The former gives epistemology (i.e., a theory of *pramāṇa*), the latter a causally oriented ontology (i.e., a theory of *prameya*). Phenomenology is also a theory of evidence, phenomenological constitution is also a theory of evidence, an account of how *senses* come to givenness, and through senses things, but this evidencing function is not simply epistemological but also transcendental (in the Kantian sense of being the condition of the possibility of transcendent reference). Consciousness as an absolute domain of being, also as the foundational being, is recognized, but not as the constitutive source of all transcendence.

Thus Indian philosophical literature abounds in a descriptive phenomenology of consciousness (recall the Buddhist classification of cognitions, the Sāṅkhya-Yoga theory of the various kinds of mental states (*citta-vṛtti*), the Vedānta theory of the various (real or apparent) modalities of consciousness; but these do not—save possibly in certain Buddhist theories—amount to transcendental-constitutive phenomenology. They oscillate between descriptive psychology and metaphysics of consciousness.

(B) *Theory of Pramāṇa*

I have already noted that the theory of *pramāṇa* incorporates into its body the causal and the logical orders in one. This limits the ideality of the logical and the contingency of the causal—as it must, if the two orders are to coincide. In this again, as in the theory of consciousness, ontology prevails. Husserlian phenomenology begins with rescuing the logical from being submerged in the flow of mental life: the ideality of the logical is made to stand out in contrast with the causal order of the psychological. It ties in with the theory of *sense* at one end and the conception of pure form on the other—both essential possibilities within western thought. On both counts, Indian thought moves along a different path.

(i) *Perception (Pratyakṣa).* In the theory of *pramāṇa*, one *pramāṇa* occupies an undisputed place: perception (*pratyakṣa*). Perception is the beginning of cognition, other forms of cognition are founded on it. As the logician Gaṅgeśa put it, it is 'not caused by any other *cognition*' (*jñānākaraṇakaṃ jñānam*), the *first* in the cognitive hierarchy. Though initially it is sought to be defined in terms of the causality of sense-organs, that definition becomes less and less important. The Jainas want to characterize perception by the 'immediacy' and 'clarity' (*vaiśadya*) of the cognition; both these concepts however are vague. Immediate perceptions are mediated by relational structures of varying degrees of complexity (as *Uddyotakara*, the great Naiyāyika, first showed). In effect, the scope of perceptual cognition was much larger than it has been in the western tradition. While visually perceiving this blue pencil as this blue pencil—i.e., while having a perceptual cognition that is verbally articulated as 'this blue pencil'—I am—on the Nyāya theory which was largely taken over by many other schools—seeing not only (i) this yonder object, but also (ii) the this-ness inhering in it; not only (iii) the blue colour but also (iv) the blueness inhering (not in the pencil but in the blue colour-particular); not only (v) the pencil, but also (vi) the generic property 'pencil-ness'; and not only these relate (i) through (vi) but also relations that tie them together into one complex entity. Thus, on this theory, the universals are perceived (not by any sort of intellectual, rational intuition) but precisely by the instrumentality of the same sense-organs which mediate perception of the particular instance. So also are relations. Recall the suspicions and criticisms that were evoked by Husserl's extension of the concept of 'seeing' to eidetic insight. The Nyāya theory would have been more receptive to such an extension.

Let me take up one particular aspect of the theory of perception which is amenable to an interestingly phenomenological reading. The Buddhists held that our ordinary perceptions are really inferences, because not all the parts of a physical object are presented. On the Buddhist view, a physical object is nothing but an aggregate of parts, and since not all the parts are ever presented, their aggregate is also not presented. What passes as perception, in that case, is really inference from what is given to what is not given. We can really perceive, then, only what is absolutely simple, the pure particular; in effect, true perception is an ineffable experience. The Naiyāyikas argued against this position by asserting (i) that a physical object is not a mere aggregate of parts but a new object that is founded upon the putting together of parts; (ii) that it is not necessary for perceiving this *new* whole that one must be perceiving all its parts, and (iii) consequently, that we may be truly perceiving a whole even when not all its parts are presented. One may read here a phenomenological thesis that perception of a part may serve as the basis for arousing expectations of having the other parts presented,that as this perceptual process unfolds each perspectival presentation contains the intention that there is a determinable whole that is being presented through it and that further exploration of the whole clarifies and progressively fulfils that intention, while all along the same whole that was originally intended is being brought to more adequate givenness. What is perceived in any case is a whole—but always *through* some of its parts (and perspectives[11]).

(ii) *Inference (anumāna).* The Indian *interest* in inference has been cognitive—i.e., as a mode of knowing the world. This has two aspects each of which contrasts sharply with the western logic. On the one hand, inference is studied as a cognitive process consisting in an ordered series of cognitive episodes. This seemingly psychologistic account contrasts with the western understanding of inference in term of propositions as ideal entities (defended by Husserl in the *Prolegomena*). On the other hand, inference is studied as a means of knowing an item in the world, as a consequence of which its truth or falsity, rather than its formal validity or invalidity, is what comes to the forefront—which makes it appear as though Indian logic of inference does not quite raise itself to the level of 'formal logic'.

Husserl's philosophy of logic enables us to have surer grip on the nature of Indian logic—firstly, by locating it in the context of the issue about psychologism, and secondly, by seeing how empty formalism and the cognitive interest go together. The Indian theory of *anumāna* does tell a story about how inferential cognition takes place, the story is in terms of a rule-governed sequence of cognitive episodes. This story thus appears to be psychologistic. But each cognitive episode was assigned a content, in terms of which its linguistic expression was structured, which is not subjective in the sense in which the episode itself is. It is this content, shareable by numerically distinct episodes, that is relevant for determining which sequence of episodes can result in a true inferential cognition. If the reaction against psychologism led, in the *Prolegomena*, to a Platonism of ideal entities, the Indian thinkers, rather than detach the content from the act and assign it a distinct ontological status, construed the mental itself in a non-psychologistic manner[12]—such that (i) the content of the mental retains an identity across acts and (ii) the temporal sequence of acts, under appropriate causal conditions, leads to an inferential cognition that is 'true'. Thus the rapproachment between psychology and logic was done by logicizing psychology as much as by psychologizing logic: the former by assuming that the psychological process of reasoning conforms to the logical (any seeming deviance, as in supposedly fallacious reasoning, being due to misconstrual of the premises), and the latter by making logic a logic of cognitions rather than of propositions.

It was again the Husserl of *Formal and Transcendental Logic* who showed the way to embed the formal within an originally cognitively oriented interest. It is not that the Indian theory of *anumāna* does not know of formal validity. In fact, a formally valid mood can be abstracted from a valid Nyāya *anumāna*. But since the interest was in cognitions (and not in either sentences or in propositions), and in *anumāna* as a *pramāṇa*, i.e., as a source of *true* cognition, the merely formally-valid inference, as in *tarka* or counterfactuals, was left out of consideration.

(iii) *Word (śabda).* I will only make some brief remarks about this unique component of the theory of *pramāṇa*: the theory, namely, that there is a variety of cognition that is entirely word-generated (*śabda-janya*). The latter includes not only knowledge of moral rules, spiritual goals and practices, which are derived from reading, interpreting and understanding the scriptural texts, but also such empirical knowledge of the world as is derived from *listening* to the utterances of competent—intellectually and morally competent—speakers (and derivatively from *reading* the writings of competent authors). I will not go into the reasons advanced by the Nyāya and Mīmāṃsā authors as to why such cognition cannot be reduced to either perception or inference and deserves to be recognized as a mode of cognition *sui generis*. I will not also discuss the theory of meaning that underlies this claim—clearly, it is a referential theory of meaning. What I intend to make a few remarks on is the suspicion that the theory of word-generated cognition, and the important status accorded to it, might undermine the critical nature of the theory of *pramāṇa*. At worst, it appears to be a device to justify scriptures, at its best it amounts to stopping the process of critical enquiry by appealing to the competence, and noble intentions, of the speaker or of the author. In the context of Husserlian phenomenology, the theory would appear to drive a wedge between the claim to know and the need for fulfilling the meaning intention, such that merely *understanding* the sense of the speaker (if accompanied by belief in his competence) is taken in this case to amount to knowing that something is the case.

If strictly Husserlian phenomenology fails to be of help here, it is hermeneutic phenomenology which comes to our aid. If what is crucially at stake is not so much our knowledge of empirical facts which are perceptible, and so inferable in ordinary manner (so that the belief generated by the speaker's utterance is capable of being confirmed or disconfirmed by ordinary perception and inference), but our knowledge of moral rules and spiritual goals and means—then the theory of *śabda* has a pretty good case. But, first, let us bear in mind that the charge of uncritically yielding to testimony is superficial and does not cut deep. The theory of *pramāṇa* provides the critical norms, and the question, whether a cognitive claim is valid or not is to be judged in the light of these norms. If *śabda* is a *pramāṇa* (under appropriate conditions), then one cannot challenge word-generated cognition as uncritical; that would amount to importing a critical norm that is not in consonance with those of the theory itself. Thus one cannot *prima facie* rule out *śabda*, but has to question, *from within the tradition of Indian philosophy*, if it deserves a place in the list of *pramāṇas*.[13]

While the logico-epistemological issue unavoidably is: whether we need to distinguish between *sense* (which is grasped in mere understanding of a sentence) and *reference* (which is grasped in knowing), there are domains such as moral rules where it is through *interpreting* linguistic discourse (and not through any further empirical verification) that one determines what one ought or ought not to do. The point underlying this claim is *not* that one ought to do *because* S (a competent speaker or text) says one ought to do (for that would be to say that moral rules are inferred from the fact that S has uttered sentences embodying those rules). It is rather the point that we learn the rules only from hearing/reading and interpreting verbal instructions. Note that if an accepted set of moral rules is given up, it is given up by imbibing another set of moral rules on the basis of another set of verbal instructions. In this case, *śabda* corrects *śabda*—as a perceptual error is corrected by another perception. It is through these accepted texts that a tradition is built up, but the tradition is not a monolithic interpretation of the basic texts but leaves room for interpretive differences as well as for new possibilities for interpretation. Thus although the different schools of Indian philosophy moved within the space opened up by the *śruti* texts, these schools realized quite different interpretive possibilities.

(C) *Theory of Action*

Husserl wanted to overcome scepticism entirely on theoretical-cognitive grounds (although he includes actional elements within the overall structure of theoretical constitution-analysis of certain kinds of objectivities) by founding knowledge on a stratum of self-evidencing cognitive experience (such as inner time-consciousness or, possibly, the *lebendige Gegenwart*). This is what accounts for its characterization as a variety of 'foundationalism'. Indian thinking also is anti-sceptical[14] and anti-relativistic. While *theoretically* cognitive claims are justified with one or more of the *pramāṇas*, the *pramāṇas* themselves owe their 'power' to their ability to generate successful action (*saphalapravṛttijanakatva*). Scholars of Indian thought have been so much impressed by the presence of this idea of 'ability to generate successful action' that at least one notable and perceptive scholar has proposed that here in this notion possibly one may locate the *original* Indian understanding of truth,[15] which the different systems conceptualized differently. While this thesis in this form is controversial[16], it nevertheless remains uncontroversial that the idea of successful action is central, not peripheral, to Indian thinking on cognition. The minimal thesis, in this regard, I think, is stated by Udayana: universal scepticism is limited by contradiction with practice.[17] There is no merely theoretical doubt. Doubt eventually tells in practice,[18] it will arrest the originally unhesitating mode of acting and transform it into either hesitant action or inaction.

III. CONCLUDING REMARKS ON THE INDIAN CONCEPT OF RATIONALITY

With this highly schematic outline of the concept of rationality in Indian thought, we are in a position to make a few concluding remarks on it in the light of the theory sketched in I as well as against the general background of Husserl's phenomenology.

One point stands out clearly: the Indian philosophies are *not* philosophies in a sense that is *radically* different from the sense that was instituted for the western world by Greek thought. If the idea of pure theory was denied by insisting on the bearing of cognition upon practice, that does not mean—as critics and lovers alike of Indian thought have been prone to insist—that Indian philosophy did not contain theoretical thinking. It was theoretical thinking with an eye on practice—at a certain level, on a possible transformation of life, but, to be sure, without ever sacrificing the rigour of thinking. The Hegelian thesis that Indian thinking remained at the level of immediacy and did not rise to the level of conceptual meditation, is equally wrong. The conceptuality of the Indian philosophies, in its sheer conceptuality, parallels that of western thought. It never mistook immediacy of experience for thinking. However, the two thought-worlds—the Western and the Indian—intersect and overlap: they are neither coincident nor mutually exclusive. The relativist may so sunder them that it would seem impossible to understand the one from the perspective of the other: I have come to the firm conviction that that is just not the case. The absolutist commits the opposite error: he mistakes the task of understanding as simply being one of translation.

After setting aside such general misunderstandings, let me turn to phenomenology. Indian philosophy shares with Husserl the basic thesis that all evidence, and so the ultimate ground of all 'establishment', is consciousness. But Husserl sought after a most radical insight to the effect that all mundane formations, all scientific and everyday structures can, in principle, be shown to be rooted in the structures of consciousness such that the reflecting philosopher can, within his own ego, bring this rootedness to intuitive clarity. This radical thesis of transcendental phenomenology has never showed up in the Indian thought world. As emphasized by me earlier, the foundational consciousness, for Indian thought, is an evidencing and/or grounding consciousness, but not quite a universal-constituting subjectivity.

Thus the laying bare of the rationality of our beliefs and cognitions, of moral rules and artistic creations, confronts, in Indian thought, an absolute limit. The *pramāṇas* 'establish' them, the consciousness evidences this act of establishment, but the judicative authority of the *pramāṇas* is not, and cannot be, traced back to their origin in the structure of that consciousness. What, then, is the source of their authority?

It is at this point that the absolutistic feature of Indian thought exhibits its limits. By 'absolutistic feature' I mean its claim to deliver the nature of reality unaffected by the perspectival character of human thinking or by the temporality and situatedness of the thinker. Philosophy was a science, differing from the empirical sciences only in the order of generality. However, as soon as we turn to the highly differentiated—internally divided—world of Indian thought—characterized by endless confrontations and mutual rapproachments between parallelly developing schools, each with its own theory of *pramāṇa*, one cannot but ask a question, which the classical philosophers, no matter of which school, never asked: wherefrom does a school, Nyāya or Sāṅkhya or Vedānta or any other, derive its basic concepts, its list of *pramāṇas* which it so vehemently defends? One cannot trace them back to the *sūtras*, for the *sūtras* only summarized a conceptualization which was already in operation. Perhaps one has to appeal to an anonymous tradition of interpreting the texts! Thus there is an ultimate relativism, an 'either-or', a choice of interpretive tradition. The only absolute behind all this is the tradition with its texts, endowed with a plasticity of meaning which allows such diverse interpretations. This limit to rationality was operative, but never thematized by the philosophers. Now is the occasion to thematize it, and thereby to press relentlessly towards the ground that supports the alternate conceptualizations. I have doubts, however, whether this ground would be anything like the Husserlian transcendental subjectivity—whether we can find anything but the text, the words of *apauruṣeyaśruti* (the heard but not composed text).

NOTES AND REFERENCES

1. I have developed this idea in 'Phänomenologische Rationalität und die Überwindung des Relativismus' in: E. W. Orth (ed), *Vernunft und Kontingenz*, München: Karl Alber Varlag, 1986.
2. Davidson, D., 'On the very Idea of Conceptual Scheme', in: Proceedings of the American Philosophical Association, 17, 1973/74, pp. 5–20.
3. Husserl, E., *Cartesian Meditations*, trans, by D. Cairns, The Hague: M. Nijhoff, 19, p. 119.
4. Professor B. K. Matilal has emphasized this dual role of the *pramāṇas* in his *Perception: An Essay on Classical Indian Theories of Knowledge*, Oxford: Clarendon Press, 1986, esp. pp. 35–37.
5. The problem goes back to Kant's distinction between *quaestio factis* and *quaestio juris*, and has preoccupied such modern authors as W. Sellars, D. Davidson and R. Rorty.
6. Cp. Matilal, *Perception*, p. 362.
7. Cp. M. Hattori, *Dignāga on Perception*, Cambridge, Mass.: Harvard University Press, 1968.
8. For more on this, see my 'Consciousness and Knowledge in Indian Philosophy', *Philosophy East and West*, 29, 1979, pp. 3–10.
9. For my on-going research into the concept of time in Indian thought, I am indebted to conversations with Anindita N. Balslev as well as to her own work on that topic.
10. This tradition was built up by such fine scholars as K. C. Bhattacharyya, N. K. Brahma, S. K. Das, Kalidas Bhattacharyya, A. K. Rai Chaudhuri—but most importantly by the incomparable Sanskrit Pandit, Mahāmahopādhyāya Yogendranath Tarkavedāntatīrtha.
11. I proposed this reading first in 'Reflections on the Nyāya theory of *Avayavipratyakṣa*', *Journal of the Indian Academy of Philosophy*, I, No. 1, pp. 30–41 [later reprinted in my *Phenomenology and Ontology*, The Hague: M. Nijhoff, 1970]. Cp. Karl Potter's comments on it in Potter (ed), *Indian Metaphysics and Epistemology*, Princeton: Princeton University Press, 1977, p. 79.
12. For more on this, cp. my 'Psychologism in Indian Logical Theory', in: Matilal and Shaw (eds.), *Analytical Philosophy in Comparative Perspective*, Dordrecht, Reidel, 1985.
13. I devoted my Presidential Address at the 61st session of the Indian Philosophical Congress, Calcutta, 1986, to this theme. The lecture entitled 'A Critique of the theory of *śabdapramāṇa* and the concept of tradition' has not yet been published.
14. On sceptical trends in Indian thought, see B. K. Matilal, *Logic Language and Reality: An Introduction to Indian Philosophical Studies* (Delhi: Motilal Banarsidass, 1985), Ch. 1 ('Logic and Dialectic in Ancient and Medieval India'); also his *Perception*, chapter 2 ('scepticism'). Also see K. N. Jayatilleke, *Early Buddhist Theory of Knowledge*, London, 1963.
15. Karl H. Potter, *Journal of Indian Philosophy*, 12, 1984.
16. Cp. J. N. Mohanty, 'Prāmāṇya and Workability - Response to Potter', *Journal of Indian Philosophy* 12, 1984, 329–338.
17. 'Vyāghātāvadhirāśaṅkā', *Nyāyakusumāñjali*, 3.7.
18. Cp. my 'Nyāya Theory of Doubt', *Visva-Bharati Journal of Philosophy*, III, 1966, pp. 15–35. Reprinted in *Phenomenology and Ontology*.

Husserl and Indian Thought[1]

KARL SCHUHMANN

1. SOME BACKGROUND NOTES

The decades after 1830 were a period of disintegration and uncertainty in German philosophy. For almost half a century idealist philosophies, culminating in Hegel's grandiose system, had dominated the philosophical scene, revolving around such spiritual notions as *transcendental ego, consciousness, presentation (Vorstellung), idea, mind* , and *spirit (Geist)*. The rapid collapse of German Idealism—that 'gigantic mountain-range' of creative thought, as Husserl called it in 1917,[2] was due to a combination of causes. There was, in the first place, accelerated progress in the natural sciences, ranging from physiology (Johannes von Müller, Ernst Weber) to physics (Robert Mayer, Hermann Helmholtz) and chemistry (Justus von Liebig, Friedrich Wöhler). The success of the experimental approach visibly demonstrated the futility of all idealistic speculation about nature. Secondly, there was the rapid growth of technology (especially the construction of railways and the invention of the telegraph), combined with the process of industrialization (resulting in tensions between capital and labour which led to radical changes in the economic system). Moreover, new political ideas concerning popular participation in government led first of all to the abortive revolution of 1848 and resulted finally in the unification of Germany after the war of 1866.

Next to philosophical idealism, the other great loser in this course of events was Christianity, especially protestant Christianity, a long-standing ally of idealism. The vacuum thus produced was often filled by vulgar materialist ideas along the line of Louis Büchner's *Kraft und Stoff* (1855). The more educated classes, however, had needs of a more refined nature, and they turned instead to Schopenhauerianism. Schopenhauer stood firmly in the great European tradition of idealism extending from Plato to Kant, but he nevertheless resolutely rejected post-Kantian, and more specifically Hegelian, idealism. Schopenhauer combined the scientist's conviction of a blind causality reigning in the world of nature with a view according to which this world is none the less rooted in a subjective bestowal of sense. He combined the democratic feeling of compassion for all mankind with an elitist view on art, and a belief in the ultimate meaninglessness of history with an ontology in which the will is fundamental. But above all his philosophy, while rating Christianity rather low, made room for religion of a better sort: the religion of India.

The view of Indian thought current among educated circles in the second half of the nineteenth century in Germany was strongly influenced by Schopenhauer.[3] Not only did he give popular currency to expressions such as '*nirvāṇa*' and 'the veil of *māyā*', but he may also be held responsible for the then current amalgamation of all ideas which blew in to Europe from the East. Neither Hinduism and Buddhism nor Brahmanism and Vedānta philosophy were clearly distinguished by Schopenhauer. On one point, however, he was particularly firm: Buddhism is the highest religion in the world, because it is an 'atheistic religion'.[4] Thus it not only surpasses Christian theism, but also comes close to Schopenhauer's own conception of the absolute. Schopenhauer's followers in Germany were therefore able to look down on the parochial Christian rituals practised in their country, while upholding the claim that they, too, were directed toward some higher entity, however vaguely conceived. Moreover, they could feel themselves close to the Vedas and Upaniṣads, considered to be the oldest and most venerable documents of human thought, while at the same time feeling superior to these Indian 'myths' as a result of their own rootedness in the *purely* philosophical ideas of the Schopenhauerian system.

2. HUSSERL AS A STUDENT

To illustrate all this, I want to quote from a document which not only exemplifies this widespread attitude, but also deviates from it in a significant way. It will moreover display the typical framework of Husserl's own understanding of Indian thought. The document in question is a letter written by Thomas Masaryk (1850–1937) in 1876, while Masaryk (who later was to rise to fame as the founder and first President of the Czechoslovakian state) was still a student of philosophy. The letter is addressed to Franz Brentano who had been for some years Masaryk's teacher at the university of Vienna, the capital of the Austro-Hungarian Empire. It was written from Leipzig in Germany where Masaryk moved in order to continue his studies. On 23 November 1876, he writes to Brentano:[5]

> Zöllner is giving a lecture course on Plato's theory of cognition; he swears by Schopenhauer . . . I am personally acquainted only with Dr. Avenarius . . . I met him at the Philosophical Association during a lecture on Budhism[6] given by a Hindu[7] from Caletta;[8] this gave rise to a debate on the value of Christianity which, the lecturer declared, was inferior to Budhism. Avenarius considered Budhism to be more sublime, because it would give up personal immortality. . . . After the assembly had vividly applauded the Budhists, I requested that I be allowed to speak and inquired with the lecturer after the actual state of Budhist doctrine, and there we were told that today's Budhists are in fact no Budhists at all, but an inert and superstitious mass. When he confessed this, the assembly was startled. Then I urged the concept of nirvana which the Hindu did not, as is usually and erroneously done, explain as a complete dissolution, but as a change; I tried to show that Budhism is not that much opposed to the dogma of immortality as is otherwise supposed. Finally, I pointed to the lack of clarity among philosophers and non-philosophers on the issue of pantheism . . . I believe my victory was complete . . . I myself promised to give at a later date a lecture, too, and as a theme I chose to speak on suicide.

First, some information. Johann Zöllner (1834–1882) was a professor of astronomy (he is still remembered as the founding father of astrophotometry).

He also gave lectures on philosophy in which he defended his own peculiar brand of Schopenhauerianism (incorporating metageometrical speculations concerning a possible fourth dimension of space). Richard Avenarius (1843–1896) was a major representative of the so-called empiriocriticist branch of positivism.[9] The Academic Philosophical Association was the official students' club at the Philosophical Faculty in Leipzig, though its sessions were attended by the younger professors also.

Now to the incident reported by Masaryk. It is characteristic of the intellectual atmosphere of the time that an Indian—apparently someone who happened to be travelling through Leipzig on his way to somewhere else[10]—had been invited by the town's *philosophers* to lecture on Buddhist *religion*. Maybe Avenarius had arranged this lecture. It is also significant that Masaryk apparently was the only philosopher in the audience who disagreed with what was said. Although he seems to have won out in the discussion, and although his knowledge of Buddhism seems to have surpassed that of his colleagues, I doubt whether this knowledge was based on a better acquintance with the Indian texts and translations then available in Germany. It seems much rather that in his remarks on immortality he was drawing on his knowledge of *Schopenhauer*, and above all on Schopenhauer's distinction between an exoteric Buddhist doctrine of metempsychosis, destined for the great mass, and an esoteric doctrine of 'palingenesis'.[11]

This is suggested also by Masaryk's book on suicide of 1881, which grew out of his own lecture at the Association. He there explicitly refers to Buddhist metempsychosis, adding: 'It is known that Schopenhauer praised Buddhism highly because of its atheism, but I do not believe that the Buddhist popular religion was ever atheistic. . . . Positively it consisted in a new doctrine of ethics and a more sublime pantheism which in the course of time led to that superstition which we find among today's Buddhists'.[12] The very wording of this note (pantheism, superstition, today's Buddhists) shows that it goes back to the aforementioned Leipzig discussions. And the vagueness of Masaryk's opposition to Schopenhauer ('I do not believe . . . ') suggests that the source of his affirmations is not to be looked for in a better acquaintance with the relevant facts, but rather in his own strong conviction of the superiority of Christianity, a conviction that is displayed throughout this book. Indeed, Masaryk was a life-long adherent of a type of Christian faith which, though broad-minded and liberal, was nevertheless distinctively Protestant in outlook: something not too common in his time. And religion he considered to be the indispensable means for mankind to achieve a truly moral life.

What, now, of Edmund Husserl? Husserl was born in 1859 to an enlightened Jewish family which, though officially still adhering to Mosaic law, had no connections with any sect or church. Husserl's father wanted his children to become part of the educated (and enlightened) class and he therefore saw to it that they received a good school education. In the autumn of 1876 Husserl, after having completed his secondary school, went to Leipzig University to study astronomy. This he did, of course, under Zöllner, and he also attended Zöllner's philosophy lectures, where he no doubt imbibed a good deal of

Schopenhauerianism. It was there, too, that he met Masaryk, who was to become his life-long friend.[13] Masaryk also took him along to the sessions of the Philosophical Association, and it is very likely that Husserl was present at the session described in Masaryk's letter. It is doubtful, however, whether he would have supported the Christian views expressed by Masaryk in the ensuing discussion (as Masaryk reports, he himself was the only one to oppose the 'Hindu'). It seems more plausible to imagine him watching the discussion with a certain interest, but without taking a stand of his own.

Several years later Masaryk was none the less to play a decisive role in this respect in Husserl's life. In 1881 Husserl, who in the meantime had switched from astronomy to mathematics, went to Vienna to take his Ph.D. There he met once more his Leipzig friend, who insisted that Husserl, too, should now join him in studying philosophy under Franz Brentano. Moreover, Masaryk induced his friend to read the New Testament. This resulted in Husserl's being baptised as a Portestant a couple of years later, and from this time on he, too, became a Protestant of the typical Masarykian brand, as he was to remain for the rest of his life.

Before moving on to Husserl's later life, however, let me still add that Husserl in this period was in close contact with what could have been a much more authentic source of information on India. For he made friends in Leipzig with a student of mathematics, Hermann Ernst Grassmann (1857–1922), son of the famous mathematician Hermann Günther Grassmann (1809–1877). The elder Grassmann had been a man of some considerable talent. In the last years of his life he had published an important *Wörterbuch zum Rig-Veda* (1873–75, 5th edition Wiesbaden 1976), and during Husserl's and the younger Grassmann's stay in Leipzig he had published also a translation of the Ṛgveda.[14] It is, however, doubtful whether Husserl saw these works.

In 1887 Husserl habilitated in Halle, where he taught philosophy for some fourteen years. The younger Grassmann was there too—he was a teacher of mathematics at the Latin School of Halle—and he and Husserl continued to be on close terms. But their scientific interests centred around mathematics, the field in which they both had specialized. Husserl's first major publication, the *Philosophy of Arithmetic* (1891), shows that he valued highly the elder Grassmann's work on formal arithmetics and even goes so far as to call him 'the genius Grassmann'.[15] Though Husserl was undoubtedly aware of his work on Sanskrit literature,[16] he had clearly read only his mathematical writings. It is significant that the smattering of remarks on Indian number words and on the invention of the zero-sign contained in the *Philosophy of Arithmetic* all seem to go back to a then current handbook on the history of mathematics.[17] Husserl clearly had not seen any more specific work or sources of Indian thought.

3. HUSSERL IN GÖTTINGEN

Only after Husserl had gone to Göttingen in 1901, where he was to stay until 1916, did Indian themes and ideas again enter into his horizon of thought.

Husserl here made the acquaintance, first of all, of the famous indologist Hermann Oldenberg (1854–1920), his colleague on the Faculty of Philosophy, with whose family the Husserls over the years developed cordial personal relations.[18] That the two men may also have talked indology together is perhaps suggested by a postcard Oldenberg wrote to Husserl from Delhi on 4 December 1912: 'I look forward to being able to give you an extensive account of the attitudes current here (*die hier geübten Einstellungen*).'[19] Oldenberg's employment of the word 'attitude' here, a technical term of Husserl's phenomenology (in his *Ideas I* written precisely at this time, Husserl contrasts the 'natural' and the 'phenomenological' attitudes), suggests at all events that Oldenberg intended to do more than just tell Husserl of his Indian adventures. But it is impossible to establish what exactly Husserl may have learned from his colleague and friend about Indian philosophy and religion.

Husserl, we know, owned a copy of the first edition (1881) of Oldenberg's famous *Buddha. Sein Leben, seine Lehre, seine Gemeinde*,[20] but there are reasons for supposing that he had not received it from the author himself. It is first of all unlikely that Oldenberg should have presented Husserl, who was his colleague only since 1901, with a copy of this long sold-out edition, instead of offering him one of the later editions (the fourth appeared in 1903, the fifth in 1906). Secondly, a good deal of the reading marks in this copy are definitely not Husserl's own. Moreover, the work seems to belong to a series of other books in Husserl's library all of which were published around 1880. I have in mind the four volumes of F. Max Müller's *Essays* (2nd edition of the German translation, published in Leipzig in 1879), the first of which contains some articles on the Vedas,[21] Müller's lecture *India. What Can it Teach Us*? (London 1883),[22] and Paul Deussen's *Das System des Vedanta nach den Brahma-Sutra's des Badarayanas* (Leipzig 1883).[23] The publication date and place of Müller's *Essays* might suggest a connection between these works and the aforementioned debates in the Leipzig Association, but it is also possible that Husserl bought these books because of his broader interest in anthropology—attested, for example, by his discussions of the counting and numbering practices of various peoples in Chapter XII of the *Philosophy of Arithmetic*.

But it may also be that (at least some of) these books belonged originally to Husserl's youngest and very gifted son Wolfgang (1895–1916), who had learned Hebrew and Arabic while still at school. In the spring of 1914, Wolfgang Husserl began his university studies in the department of Oriental Languages, a department which included both the Semitic and the Indo-Iranian languages. Already in the autumn of the same year, however, when World War I broke out, he volunteered for the army and was killed in action two years later. About his last year at school, we have this report by his sister Elisabeth:[24]

We were surprised when Wolfgang introduced into our house a new friend, Mr. Siddiqi, a dark-skinned Indian of about thirty years who for his studies lived in Göttingen, and about whose Mohammedan food regulations he informed us with precision. It turned out that with the money Wolfgang had earned by regularly giving extra lessons to shaky pupils, he had taken Arabian lessons with Mr. Siddiqi. These studies he continued until war broke out. Later Mr. Siddiqi regularly came to ask for news from the battlefront.

It seems almost certain however that Husserl would have had little chance to profit from Siddiqi's visits as a means of obtaining a more reliable picture of Indian thought.[25]

4. HUSSERL AND THE SUTTAPIṬAKA

As far as is known, Siddiqi was the only native from the Indian subcontinent whom Husserl ever got to know in person.[26] Already in his Göttingen days, and especially after he had moved to Freiburg in 1916, he began to attract an increasing number of students from abroad. Kitaro Nishida for example, Japan's leading philosopher, who was sympathetic to Husserlian phenomenology, sent a number of his students to Freiburg, and Husserl published several articles in Japanese journals. Nothing comparable occurred in relation to India, however, and Husserl's knowledge of the great traditions of India as well as of recent developments there had to remain restricted to what he happened to read.

Husserl's only major occasion for getting more thoroughly acquainted with Indian thought occurred in the Christmas vacation of 1924/25. In 1922, the Munich publisher Piper initiated a series of reprints of German translations of various parts of the *Suttapiṭaka* which had been made around the turn of the century by the Viennese Schopenhauerian Karl Eugen Neumann (d. 1915).[27] Somehow these volumes found their way into Husserl's study—it may be presumed that the publisher had sent them to him in order to elicit a judgment which might be used for the sake of publicity. And Husserl did indeed study a good deal of the work and wrote something of a review, which was published in *Der Piperbote*, an advertisement journal of the Piper Publishing House, in the spring of 1925. Husserl's remarks figured there under the general heading 'Über die Reden Gotamo Buddhos' sandwiched between those of the poets Ina Seidel and Jakob Wassermann. I give here a full translation of Husserl's somewhat pathetic text.[28]

I have now read the greatest part of Karl Eugen Neumann's German translation of main parts of the Holy Writings of Buddhism.[29] Once I had started, and in spite of other urgent tasks,[30] I could not pull myself away. Indeed, what a marvellous treasure has here accrued to German translation literature. The publisher has performed an outstanding service by undertaking this in all respects perfect and most tastefully produced re-edition of the immortal life-work of K. E. Neumann.[31] What is probably the highest flower of Indian religiosity, a religiosity which looks purely inward in vision and deed—which, I should say, is not 'transcendent', but 'transcendental'—enters the horizon of our religious and ethical as well as of our philosophical consciousness only with these translations, and it is without doubt destined to contribute to that which effectively shapes this consciousness. The linguistic perfection of this re-creation of the canonical Buddhist writings[32] offers the perfect chance to experience afresh and with true understanding a way of looking at the world which is the complete opposite of our European one, of getting to know it, of taking a stand with regard to it, and of overcoming it religiously and ethically—and to experience, by thus understanding it, its living efficacy. For us and for everyone who, in this time of collapse of our culture—a culture which has become superficial and decadent[33]—looks around yearningly to see where there might be found spiritual purity and integrity, a peaceful overcoming of the world, this becoming visible of the Indian way of overcoming the world is a great experience. For to any sympathetic reader it must soon become clear that Buddhism, as it speaks to us out of its pure original sources,[34] is concerned with a religious and ethical method of the highest dignity for spiritual purification and pacification, a method thought through and carried out with an internal consistency, an energy and a nobility of mind that are almost unmatched. Buddhism can be paralleled only with the highest formations of the philosophical and religious spirit of our European culture. From now on it will be our destiny to blend that Indian way of thinking which is completely new for us, with the one which for us is old, but which in this confrontation becomes alive again and strengthened.

Thanks to the richness of a tradition faithfully upheld, Buddha himself and his most outstanding disciples become concrete in the present writings in an almost palpable way, as the representatives of a novel type of human 'holiness'. It is very much to be regretted that the religion which, for historical reasons, lives in us and which should be in no way sacrificed to this Buddhism, no longer has with regard to its original writings a German translation comparable to this Neumannian one of the *Suttapiṭakam*, as far as understanding from nearby[35] is concerned. For the German language has fatefully departed from the language of the Lutheran translation of the Bible;[36] its 'church language' lacks that spiritual efficacy which would flow directly from a living sense of language. It may, however, be that the breakthrough of Indian religiosity into the horizon of our present will have its beneficial consequences in this respect, too. At any rate it will evoke new powers of religious intuition, and already thereby it will contribute to a new vivification and deepening of the Christian intuition, and will assist our ability to understand Christian religion genuinely and from within. These magnificent Neumannian reproductions are surely invaluable for anyone who participates in the ethical, religious, philosophical renewal of our culture.[37]

I eagerly await the publication of the last parts of the Neumannian translations.[38]

This little text is of course no more than an aside in Husserl's overall production. One should neither overestimate its significance nor expect too much from it, and I will here simply ignore Husserl's somewhat bombastic style, his call for a new Bible translation, and his rather Masarykian view according to which Christianity is on the one hand nothing but a historical accident, while on the other hand it should not be allowed to be superseded by any other religion. The Neumann review nevertheless contains some interesting statements. Two main theses can be distilled from it: Indian religion is transcendental, and its world-view (or rather: that of Buddhism) is the very opposite of that which prevails in Europe.

The first thesis seems to repeat the old Schopenhauerian characterization of Buddhism as an atheistic religion. Buddhism, Husserl says, is not transcendent—not directed towards some deity who would dwell behind the world (as the Christian God is often believed to do)—but transcendental, i.e. it looks inward and assigns to subjectivity the constitutive principles of reality. But there is more, as is already indicated by the fact that Husserl here takes over and makes his own the Kantian distinction between *transzendent* and *transzendental*. Transcendentality is indeed one of the more noble predicates Husserl usually reserves for his own phenomenology.[39] The fact that he is here ready to share it with Buddhism amounts to nothing less than putting Buddhism and phenomenology on a par. Buddhism, Husserl says, can be compared only to 'the highest formations of the philosophical... spirit of our European culture'—a barely veiled periphrasis for transcendental phenomenology.

It is no objection to the intimate relation of the two styles of thought to point out that the one is a religion while the other is a philosophy. For on the one hand it is part of Schopenhauer's heritage that European philosophy and Buddhism could be conceived as close allies (one should bear in mind what had happened in the Leipzig *Philosophical* Association). And on the other hand there is in fact no clear-cut distinction between religion and philosophy in Husserl. Never does he assign a specific place to religion (as Kant for example does) within the limits of which it would be confined. This is why, especially in some of his more elevated moments, Husserl is prone to colour his phraseology with expressions borrowed from the Bible.[40] This applies also to his Neumann review. The notion of an 'overcoming of the world' which Husserl here introduces, ascribing it both to Buddhism and to Christian ethics and religion, is visibly akin to his own more technical operation of 'bracketing' the world's existence in a phenomenological *epoché*.

The message of Indian and European thought is, therefore, one and the same. Both inquire into the world's mode of being, and both see that this is not an absolute being. This world must therefore be overcome, and we must turn towards the inner life of subjectivity. Still, however, their methods in reaching this goal are 'completely opposed'. This last statement may seem to testify to the initial strangeness experienced by someone brought up exclusively in the European tradition when confronted for the first time in his life with a way of thought developed in some other culture. To be content with such a psychological explanation would however be to underestimate the forces which are here at work. Husserl, in this little piece of text, does not develop any argument concerning the issue. It should however be clear that he himself had at all events been able 'to experience afresh and with real understanding' (to quote his own words) the ideas that had become accessible to him via the Neumann translations. If, now, he judged that the *Suttapiṭaka* displayed a method opposed to his own, he must have based this view on a comparison of these texts with his own phenomenological project.

5. A COMPARISON OF SOCRATES AND BUDDHA

There is no evidence that Husserl studied any other works of the Indian tradition in his later life. His image of Indian thought seems, rather, to have been determined by those parts of Neumann's translation of the main texts of the *Suttapiṭaka* which he had read. Husserl in fact identified these texts with Buddhism in general, and moreover he identified (in the traditional Schopenhauerian way) Buddhism with Indian thought as a whole. In reading Neumann he had recognized that Indian thought moved in an important sense on the same level as his own philosophy. The exact relation between the two remained, however, to be spelled out, and an occasion to do this was offered to Husserl as early as the winter semester of 1925/26, when he gave for his advanced students a seminar which, at least according to the title by which it had been announced, was to deal with 'Selected Logical Problems'.

Given the importance of the step taken by Husserl in this seminar for his working out of a definite picture of Indian thought in its relation to phenomenology, it is regrettable that, at this stage at least, the seminar in question can be documented only in a fragmentary and unsatisfactory way. Thus I must ask of the reader more than the usual indulgence in relation to the following somewhat complicated and cumbersome discussion. Of the four months Husserl's seminar lasted, only the last was more or less devoted to the theme that had been announced. The remaining time was spent on preliminary discussions, mainly on how a motivation could arise in natural life for man to develop the idea of philosophy, understood as a type of knowledge that would be self-guaranteeing. At present, we know the names of seven students who participated in this seminar, but the Husserl Archives dispose of the sketchy and sometimes hardly intelligible notes of only one of them.[41] Thus we lack a reliable clue for the adequate interpretation of the manuscripts Husserl himself wrote in connection with the sessions of this seminar.

I shall try, first of all, to sketch the framework of Husserl's discussion of Buddhism in this seminar. In the first days of December 1925 there was discussed the 'theoretical in relation to the mythical attitude'. This concerned the contrast between the goal of an exhaustive, rational explanation of the world as this is achieved by (phenomenological) philosophy, and that way of understanding things which is current in pre-scientific modes of thought.[42] Husserl goes on to distinguish two paths leading to the 'rationalism' of phenomenology. The first starts from the sciences as they are actually given, i.e. from a partial realization of the idea of philosophy, and radicalizes their demand for rationality; the second sets out from those occurrences in practical life which are apt to lead to a universal reflection upon life, and thus to the conception of the idea of philosophy.[43] Husserl here gives a first hint as to how to understand the goal of life as proposed by Buddhism. In his naive practical existence, man lives as it were in 'practical positivity'; that is, he acts in a world of unquestioned basic certainties. But cleavages in this certainty, even universal ones, may occur at any given moment, and are therefore, at least as possibilities, part and parcel of the 'essentialities of human existence'. Such are, for example, moments of desperation, where man suddenly feels the impulse to raise fundamental questions like 'What can I still do, what is left to be hoped for, can I go on living? Would not a voluntary death be the best thing, or a complete renunciation of the world after the manner of Buddhist salvation?'[44] This shows that for Husserl the Buddhist goal of bringing about a universal reflection upon the world flows from the experience of a crisis in the practical existence of man—a conception clearly influenced by the familiar stories about the Buddha's own experiences, experiences which induced him to leave behind his initial pattern of life.

Which brings us to the last session of the seminar before the Christmas break. Here Husserl once more contrasts two alternative ways into phenomenology: (1) through 'a critique of the sciences', and (2) through the 'mythical-practical world-view' to which 'the world-view of theoretical interest' becomes opposed.[45] In January, too, the seminar continued to work out these two ways in which a philosophy in the sense of a universal science might be reached.[46] In the session of 13 January 1926 the opposition between the mythical-practical and the theoretical views is put into historical perspective. This opposition is held to be somehow connected with 'the difference between European and Indian philosophy: we [in Europe] have a well-ordered science, not only isolated pieces of theory'.[47] Indian philosophy, that is to say, is in the last instance motivated by the goal of salvation, and develops its theories only in so far as they are subservient to this *practical* aim. European philosophy, in contrast, pursues the goal of *pure* theory, theory for no external purposes and without any ancillary function being assigned to theory as a whole. This, then, might be considered as a first step in determining the 'complete opposition' between European and Indian thought which Husserl had alluded to in the Neumann review.

In the subsequent session of 20 January Cairns notes that Socrates—the founder of European philosophy, according to Husserl—'as far as his attitude[48] is concerned, could have developed a science, but this science would have been restricted to practical life in the factually existing world'. 'Indian philosophy', Cairns' notes go on, is in contrast 'always a means towards salvation, but is often quite systematic and offers a *purely theoretical* consideration [of the world] as a preparative for salvation in the same way in which this would occur in a Socratic philosophy. In Plato, too, theoretical life is nothing independent [of the practical goal of life]. [Only] in Aristotle is theoretical life [itself] called the most blissful one'.[49]

Is this a recantation of Husserl's position as worked out a week earlier? Husserl seems to affirm that science, in Socratic as well as in Indian philosophy, is carried out in the service of a practical goal (be it life or salvation). Moreover, science is now even said to be both systematic and purely theoretical in Indian thought, and this in contradistinction to what Socrates had achieved. Even Plato did not advance beyond this stage, and only with Aristotle do we have a clear conception of philosophy as such. Cairns' notes, however, unquestionably render Husserl's train of thought in only a somewhat telescoped way. Socrates is brought too close to Indian thought and separated too much from Plato and Aristotle. This is shown above all by Husserl's *Erste Philosophie*, a lecture course he had given two years earlier, namely in 1923/24, and which contains one of Husserl's most elaborate treatments of the Greek origin of the idea of philosophy. Here it is stated that Socrates was 'the first to recognize the necessity of a *universal* method of reason'.[50] According to Husserl, 'Plato and Aristotle paved the way for this idea'[51] by applying it to all areas of knowledge (where Socrates had treated only questions of ethics). Thus, although Husserl had unequivocally recognized the theoretical character of Indian philosophy, he sees reasons to accentuate the universal character of European theory and therefore will remain convinced of its superiority.

This is also brought out by a manuscript Husserl wrote in the two days following the seminar session of 20 January 1926.[52] Under the title 'Socrates—Buddha' he sets out to compare European and Indian thought. His conclusion is that both are motivated by the fact that in our natural life both rational and irrational factors are intertwined. The Greek project of rationalism, on the other hand, is to eliminate all irrationalities by building up a universal science. The Indian, in contrast, who is motivated by the same experience, is more sceptical about the chances for realizing such a project and opts instead for 'a way out in transcendentalism'.[53] He gives up all world-directed willing, and he does so in favour of the categorical imperative of world-renunciation. Yet even this clearly presupposes some reliable diagnosis with regard to how the world *essentially* is, i.e. it presupposes some lasting truths about the world and therefore also science. Under this aspect Socratic and Buddhist thought both aim at a purely theoretical, in itself valuable and autonomous, cognition of things.

In Indian thought, however, the incentive for erecting such a science is the striving for bliss which, according to Buddhism, is obtainable only via salvation (from this world). No matter how universal Buddhist science may become, it will forever be overshadowed by this practical aim of establishing a certain blissful style of life, albeit as something universally justified. Socratic science, in contrast—though one is to concede that 'Socrates himself was not aware of this'[54]—goes beyond this practical interest by adopting 'an interest in truth purely for the sake of truth' (to quote an expression Husserl had used some years earlier).[55] In order to achieve this goal of pure theory, Socratism was to develop a method by which from given truths other ones could be inferred. This means that Socratic science had to develop a logic of the discovery and verification of true propositions. Husserl therefore in the end reaches the conclusion that the superiority of Socratic thought lies in the logic it applies, or more precisely in the *universal logical form* it bestows upon knowledge.

Summarizing his overall position, Husserl writes:[56]

What is the position of cognition in Indian thought? How is this thought related to Socratic thought? Indian thought aims at salvation, at bliss by means of ruthless (*rücksichtslos*) cognition.[57] It assumes therefore also that there are truths which are valid in themselves.[58] Indian cultural life, too, therefore leads to autonomy—to autonomous cognition, by which a true way[59] to bliss can be won, and thereby also truth in itself for just deeds, an autonomous truth in the cognition of ethical and religious norms. In Socrates, too, theory, i.e. knowledge in the sense of genuine knowledge, has the function of being intuitive knowledge about true practice and its norms.... Has Indian thought produced a science of what is, or at least envisaged its possibility, in the same sense in which this has been achieved concerning the science which leads to bliss? But even the way of thought which is part of the doctrine of salvation is for the Indians not distinguished from natural thought as to its form (and logic, so to speak), but only as to the consistency of its knowledge,[60] its freedom from prejudice, its resolute elimination of the natural life-interest,[61] its disinterested evaluation[62] of such interests, and its formulation of those evaluations in general judgments. In Greek philosophy, in contrast, positive scientific thought and knowledge depart radically from the knowledge of [daily] life, and they do so by means of a form and method which are in principle logical.

What is the upshot of all of this? Already in the Neumann review, i.e. prior to his discussion of the peculiarities of Indian thought, Husserl had been convinced that it was the complete opposite of European thought, and moreover that the manner in which it contrasted with European thought somehow made it only second best—notwithstanding the communality of intention toward pure cognition which is manifestly shared by both. To make this general intuition more concrete, however, presented considerable difficulties. Husserl initially tried to conceive this difference in purely quantitative terms. Indian science, being a mere function of the goal of 'overcoming the world', would be developed only as far as is necessary for this purpose.[63] It must remain fragmented, where European science is universal, aims at true knowledge of the world *in its totality*. But this solution failed, for Indian thought aims at overcoming the world *as a whole*, and this presupposes some knowledge of the relativity of this whole—a science of the world which is then as comprehensive as is European science. Moreover, Socrates himself in fact never pressed for such a universal science. The closeness of the Socratic and the Buddhist conception could be seen in the fact that the Socratic maxim—virtue is knowledge, vice results from lack of knowledge—holds for Buddhism, too. Knowledge is in both cases a value in its own right, and both strive after pure theory. Would Socrates, then, forever remain in this sphere of 'pure theory', where Buddhism would at some given moment step out of it in order to garner consequences for practical life? This, too, cannot be upheld. The *ethical* tendency of Socratism militates as much against a view of this sort as does the transcendental, world-renouncing character of Buddhism.

In the end, therefore, Husserl transfers the difference separating the two out into the domain of logic. Where Buddhist thought reaches its results in a natural, straightforward way Socrates does so by way of a specific method. Socrates' affirmations pretend not merely to truth, but also to coherence and consistency, they hang together systematically and universally. They are of a rational *form* that is recognized as such.[64]

6. INDIA—AN ANTHROPOLOGICAL TYPE

Husserl's view was to remain such for the rest of his life, and I am ready to concede that he could not have changed it even if for some reason he had wanted to do so. For the view in question was narrowly tied to his more general views on philosophy, and fitted precisely into a pre-established pattern that had developed over several decades. Husserl therefore in later years saw no special reason to plunge again into Indian texts or to re-elaborate his view on Indian thought in a way different from the results he had already achieved.[65] He came back to these results only when he once more began to reflect on *European* thought in its totality, and he then introduced the Indian way of looking at the world as a useful contrast. This occurred in the last years of Husserl's life when he wrote *The Crisis of European Sciences and Transcendental Phenomenology* (1936). It is in this work that he solemnly declared European mankind to be the bearer of an absolute idea, where India or China represent 'only an empirical anthropological type'.[66] Can one explain away this remark as an old man's slip of the pen? In any event, I will try to make it clear that this view is firmly anchored in Husserl's overall conception of the origin and development of the 'idea' of philosophy, and can only be understood as such.

The ultimate foundation of Husserl's idea of philosophy lies in the rather uncontroversial 'definition of man as *animal rationale*',[67] a definition familiar already to the Greeks. Man of course frequently uses his 'innate' faculty of reason in the practice of his natural, world-directed life—for example in reflecting on what to do or on how to carry out his projects. Thanks to his reason, man can judge both his own actions and those of his fellow-men, all of whom are thinking beings like himself. All men have reason. They therefore know that they can communicate with each other about the world and about worldly affairs. This then makes possible larger communities of thought, cultures, whose communality is arrived at through the elimination of the particularities and discrepancies which are proper to the experiences of the individual and to his personal situation. But now, the presence of reason in all men makes possible even a transcending of the limitations inherent in any given culture. All men inside as well as outside my own culture are 'like me or like us'.[68] It is true that we can talk or think about them only 'in our language and our way of thinking',[69] but this will not lead to cultural relativism. All world-views imply certain general features, thanks to which the world is for all men a 'necessary system of invariant elements'.[70] There are generalities in which indeed 'normal Europeans, normal Hindus,[71] Chinese etc. agree, notwithstanding all relativities'.[72]

Having thus secured his right to pass pertinent judgments about what is going on in other cultures, Husserl now introduces into his concept of reason an element of teleology. Man not only applies his reason in fact; it is even the case that he cannot but try to apply it, wherever possible. This is so because man strives to be man through and through—and reason, as was said, is his most distinctive and therefore his most human attribute. To follow one's reason, is to actualize one's humanity.[73] This is true both of man's individual and of his social existence. Man's development is in all cases to be understood as 'a progressive development toward reason'; thus also 'each culture is of itself directed toward 'true' culture'.[74]

Such a 'true' culture, a culture aiming at a complete actualization of reason as it exists in man, Husserl calls a 'philosophical culture'. For to realize exhaustive rationality is to accomplish philosophy. Husserl's idea of philosophy has been hinted at already above. It may be summarized briefly as follows. Philosophy is universal knowledge and a cognition that is clear and evident under all its aspects. Sufficient reasons can without exception be given for each of its theses. Philosophy is apodictic and fully evident; it is knowledge that has undergone all possible critique. The idea of philosophy, in short, is the idea of absolute omniscience, i.e. of all possible knowledge about whatever is knowable, and knowledge of a sort that is *known* to be absolute and irrevocable. To possess philosophical knowledge is (as Spinoza would have it) to know and at the same time to know that one knows. That type of cognition which is involved in practical life as well as in science is, by contrast, of necessity naive in the sense that it concentrates exclusively on its object, where in philosophy there is added a dimension of reflection, a clarification of a methodical or 'logical' order. Scientific knowledge, to be sure, is theoretical. But philosophy alone is a theory which at the same time is 'the theory of all theories'.[75]

With this ideal of philosophy as self-transparent omniscience in hand, Husserl now looks around in history in order to see which among the thought-formations of the past might best correspond to it. His first result is devastatingly negative. Philosophy thus far has never and nowhere been brought to realization. Not only does it not exist in a finished version, it even has not been undertaken in the only way in which finite man can reach this infinite goal, i.e. by way of an endless progression toward, an approximation to, such knowledge. Philosophy as we know it, Husserl says, is not somehow an imperfect science, but 'as yet no science at all; as a science, it has not even yet begun'.[76] For this reason phenomenology was destined to become the '*true* beginning',[77] and Husserl was proud to be 'the *real* beginner'.[78]

Husserl's guiding idea of philosophy did not appear but of the blue however. Even if this idea had never before been put into action, it had still been *conceived of* long ago. Husserl in fact only intended 'to restore the most original idea of philosophy which, since its first precise formulation by Plato, underlies our European philosophy and science'.[79] It is Plato's (and Socrates') immortal merit to have laid the foundation for the *idea* of a purely rational life in a philosophical culture. One could call it a mere matter of fact and a sheer historical accident that this idea had arisen on European, and more specifically on Greek (Athenian), soil at a certain time. But once this had occurred, and in view of the fact that this idea has ever since determined the highest formations of European culture, one must conclude that this idea is the distinctive mark of 'Europe', a mark which raises this culture above all others on our planet.

Husserl's next step consists in investigating whether this idea might have also been developed by other, extra-European cultures.[80] The result is once more negative. 'All philosophies of the pre-Platonic era as well as all comparable cultural formations of other peoples and cultures', he concludes, can be called philosophy 'only in a loose sense'.[81] Even India and China, the most plausible candidates, do not qualify. Even cultures like theirs represent 'nothing but an empirical anthropological type', to be investigated as such by empirical anthropological methods, but not able to claim any absolute or insuperable value.[82] It is therefore only an equivocation, brought on by certain superficial but misleading similarities, to apply the term 'philosophy' to both European and non-European cultural formations. Today, Husserl observes, 'we dispose of a good many works on Indian, Chinese etc. philosophies, in which these are put on a par with Greek philosophy and are taken as merely different historical shapings within the framework of one and the same cultural idea. Of course, they all have something in common'. One should not however allow 'mere morphological generalities' to hide 'the intentional depths' which separate European from non-European speculations. The former aim at the realization of an absolute idea, no matter how imperfect and distorted the factual result may be; the latter, on the other hand—and notwithstanding even their most brilliant results—have never claimed to be concerned by the explicit idea of philosophical omniscience.[83] This is why, in his 1926 seminar, Husserl had concluded that Buddhism, though in fact operating on the same level as Husserlian phenomenology, could not be identified with philosophy as such. It lacks the genuine logical form—and this comes down to stating that it is no philosophy at all. There exists therefore 'a fundamental difference between Greek or European science (or, to put it universally: philosophy), and those oriental "philosophies" which are said to be its peers'.[84] In other words, it is 'to mistake the meaning of the term, and to tamper with it... if one speaks of Indian and Chinese philosophy and science.'.[85]

To be sure, Plato had, according to his own estimate, done more than just outline the *idea* of philosophy, and the same is true of his successors throughout the centuries up till Husserl's time. Husserl does not intend to underestimate the importance, validity and greatness of the results they had reached, and the same may be said of non-European philosophy also. But when measured by the absolute yardstick of philosophy as a *rigorous* science, all these undertakings sink into insignificance. They are no philosophies at all, but simply world-views (or, to use a term popularized by Marx, ideologies). 'An imperfect science... is no science at all'.[86] such was Husserl's maximalist device. On this view, it was the prerogative of European thought to have stuck firmly to at least the *idea* of philosophy, while all other thought-formations, however close they might have come to real philosophy, must be said to have been simply unphilosophical.

Now if the European idea of philosophy is indeed nothing but the overall fulfilment of man's most fundamental aspiration to humanity, it will follow that the spread of this idea over the earth is inevitable and in fact the most salutary thing that can happen to mankind. To put it in other terms: as man differs from the animals by his reason, so philosophical reason differs from the pre-philosophical, i.e. non-European use of this faculty.[87] 'Europe', that is to say, is something unique and incomparable in the history of mankind. 'All other groups of mankind are aware of this', Husserl maintains, and this motivates them, 'notwithstanding their unbroken will to spiritual self-preservation, to Europeanize themselves, whereas we, as long as we understand ourselves properly, would never Indianize ourselves'.[88]

'The spectacle of the Europeanization of all other cultures'[89] is as empirical fact no sufficient proof of the rightness of Husserl's conception. It may nevertheless be taken to bear some witness to the fact that the European idea of philosophy is of absolute significance for mankind as a whole, in the sense that this spectacle corresponds to what Husserl feels he has reason to expect. In the last analysis this will no doubt imply that all thought-systems approximating to philosophy in other cultures, and especially the Chinese and the Indian ones, are doomed to be abandoned and to disappear, in order to be superseded by (Husserlian) phenomenology.

7. SOME DIFFICULTIES IN HUSSERL'S CONCEPTION

One cannot avoid being deeply impressed by the humanist motivation, the high spirit and the grandeur of Husserl's vision. He succeeds in creating an integrated picture in which non-European thought as well as the Socratic impulse are allotted their proper place; a pattern in which European philosophy from Plato to Kant is powerfully reinterpreted as a struggle—between transcendentalism and object-directed knowledge—which finally become reconciled in phenomenology. The appearance of phenomenology on the scene of thought is the culmination of all prior efforts and the apotheosis of mankind and of reason. But as contrasted with Hegel's in part similar conception, the arrival of phenomenology does not announce the end of history, but rather opens up an endless future for the work of philosophy. The one single force nourishing this whole process is man's effort to realize humanity by instituting reason everywhere—by instituting a philosophical culture.

History is the 'rational animal's becoming effectively rational: this is, in short, the Husserl message. Husserl's philosophy of history therefore coincides with his view of the history of philosophy (for philosophy is the exercise of reason). And here does Husserl indeed come very close to Hegel, for whom, too, the spirit's 'becoming itself' was the motor of history. Because of this similarity it is no great surprise to see that both Hegel and Husserl relegated Indian thought not to the *history*, but rather to the prehistory of thought.

In Husserl this at first seemed not to be so clear. In the 1920's, he had kept open the possibility that Buddhism and phenomenology both produce pure theory in a universal way and therefore that both should be transcendental. Only in the *Crisis* was Indian thought restricted to a level where it would be equated to, e.g., the Papuan's use of reason in handling his daily affairs. Both are 'philosophies' only by equivocation, i.e. they are no philosophies at all. This is however not, I think, a simple reversal of his earlier position; it is rather a difference in accentuation. Buddhism is surely 'philosophical' in Husserl's sense, but it could be recognized as such only by Husserl himself, with *his* idea of philosophy in mind. Buddhism did not establish itself *as* transcendental; this lable had to be attached to it by Husserl and from the outside. Thus Buddhism was a philosophy *malgré lui*, it did not work out the idea which in fact, and in fact alone (but not in essence), was hidden in it.

To continue the search for unconscious antecedents of philosophy in Indian thought is a superfluous literary exercise in the same way that a closer study of the Presocratics is to no avail: since Plato's discovery of the idea of philosophy, it is no longer necessary to trouble oneself with such immature creations of the human mind. To Husserl, as to Hegel, philosophy has now finally reached the stage of full-grown Science, and an occupation with the finer points of Indian thought could therefore be dispensed with.[90]

Husserl's attitude is a typical example of what Halbfass called 'the exclusion of India from the historiography of philosophy'.[91] To Husserl this was not so much a question of factual or practical considerations, but a matter of principles. Husserl's argument can be summarized as follows. His major premiss consisted of an *a priori* analysis of the concept of philosophy as founded on the concept of reason in general. His minor premiss was of an empirical nature. He tested pertinent thought-formations in order to see which ones would meet his requirements, and in which way. The conclusion has been reported above: there was no philosophy outside Europe, and in Europe only Plato had conceived its idea, and only Husserl had begun to work it out.

Husserl's argument is of course vulnerable especially in its minor premiss. Had his examination of other systems indeed been sufficient, both as to quantity as well as to quality and method? The answer must clearly be in the negative, and not only with regard to Indian philosophy (of the richness of which Husserl was completely unaware), but also in Plato's case and in that of European philosophy in general. But is a painstaking collection of counter-examples really of any help? One should not forget that Husserl, like Hegel, had sought to immunise his position by declaring that the only legitimate basis from which to judge his own views—and also to judge all other thought—was his own philosophy (on the base of which he himself had achieved precisely the results in question). The true value of these philosophies could be recognized by phenomenology alone, and therefore 'the truth of such a teleological consideration of history cannot be refuted in any decisive way by citing the documented testimonies of earlier philosophers.'[92] The erudite scholar's digging up of historical facts which do not fit into the Husserlian conception does not invalidate Husserl's scheme, but rather fixes forever the insignificance of this activity and of the facts it is supposed to uncover—and this insignificance had already been affirmed, as the case of Indian philosophy shows, by Husserl himself.

But can Husserl's view really be so water-tight in all respects? Daily experience, as well as the history of science, seem to suggest that certain *general* views can be upheld only as long as they are not outweighed by instances contradicting them. A shift of paradigm may at some stage become inevitable. And Husserl's phenomenology, too, in so far as it concerns itself with historical fact, cannot dwell completely outside the realm of what can be refuted or confirmed by fact. It must entertain at least *some* ties with empirical reality.

Husserl's interpretations, it is true, for the most part stand far removed from the results of scholarly work. But it redounds to his credit that he candidly admits having neglected the question of the precise relation between his own aprioristic definition of philosophy and the *corpus* of texts which goes under this name both inside and outside Europe. His own historical reflections, he admits, are nothing but 'his "poetry of the history of philosophy"' and 'the construction of the "novel" of history'. He frankly concedes that their main function is to assist him in articulating his own ideas. They serve to allow him 'to understand himself and his own intention', and their sole 'purpose is to take stock of himself'.[93] Although these affirmations, as is suggested by the inverted commas Husserl places around 'poetry' and 'novel', should be taken with a grain of salt, they are nevertheless a case of *ridendo dicere verum*. Husserl's views, that is, are even in his own judgment not beyond all doubt and contestation. Indeed they risk falling behind the very standards of science he uncompromisingly upheld, e.g., *vis-à-vis* Indian thought. For according to his own words they serve an eminently *practical* goal: that of Husserl's own self-reflection. One cannot therefore escape the conclusion that, if not Indian philosophy itself, then at any rate what Husserl has to say about it, falls under the category of a practical, maybe even a half-mythical understanding of (thought-formations occurring in) the world.

Another difficulty concerns the effects the Husserlian conception of philosophy is to have on mankind. Are there sufficient reasons for supposing that they will indeed be as salutary as Husserl assets them to be? Here, too, I will not insist on external counter-instances which could falsify Husserl's view. I prefer to confront his claims with his own results. According to Husserl, non-European cultures did not lead to man's overall bliss, because they never devised the idea of philosophy. On the other hand, it is not these cultures, but precisely the European one that, according to Husserl's diagnosis, is faced with 'the existential misery of European mankind'[94] and with 'the crisis of European existence'.[95] The ideal superiority and factual inferiority of European culture are, according to Husserl, demonstrably connected, since the history of philosophy was always but a history of failures, whereas that of world-directed science was one of growing success—but a success which, in the last instance, meant nothing to men. This counterproductive effect was brought about, to be sure, not by this idea as such, but by its wrong application. The important point now is that, in Husserl's view, this wrongness could not have been avoided. 'It is part of the very essence of reason that philosophers can in the first instance understand and work out their infinite task only with a one-sidedness which as such is absolutely necessary'.[96] But if, from Plato's time on, this distortion or (to put it as sharply as possible) the unscientific character of historical philosophies was unavoidable, what then about the second stage which follows Husserl's inauguration of his own phenomenology? Can any warranted assurance be given that the old misery will not repeat itself, albeit on a higher level?

And finally, does the Europeanization of mankind indeed confirm the rightness of Husserl's conception? Is it indeed the dissemination of philosophical rationality that is at stake here? Or is Husserl merely fooled by the undeniable export of European technology—a world-directed practical rationality which is the very opposite of his idea of pure theory?

Such reflections should not be taken to prove the invalidity of Husserl's conception. It should be clear, however, that his idea of philosophy radically transcends the life-styles and philosophies we are acquainted with. The gigantic efforts of thought carried out over millenia, both in India and in Europe, fall prey to it straightaway. But it seems that Husserl's phenomenology enjoys a similar fate. In this case, then, the dialogue between phenomenology and Indian philosophy is to be renewed—this time, on the basis of equality. In Husserlian terms this is to say that, in the same way reason is present in all men, so it is at work also in all cultures. In this sense one should subscribe to Husserl's own affirmation: 'Reason—this is a *broad* title'.[97] It bears witness to Husserl's keen eye that the only time in his life he ever exposed himself (albeit in a mediated way) to the 'bodily presence' of Indian thought, he unfailingly perceived its kindred and congenial nature.

NOTES AND REFERENCES

1. My thanks go to Barry Smith for his invaluable help in the preparation of this paper. Special thanks are due also to Professor S. IJsseling, the Director of the Husserl Archives in Louvain, for his kind permission to quote extensively from the materials preserved at the Archives, and especially for his permission to include in this paper a translation of Husserl's Neumann review.
2. 'Fichtes Menschheitsideal', Husserliana XXV, 267.
3. On Schopenhauer's image of India see Helmuth von Glasenapp, 'Schopenhauer und Indien', reprinted in von Glasenapp's *Ausgewählte kleine Schriften* (ed. by H. Bechert and V. Moeller), Wiesbaden 1980, 487–503, and the chapter on Schopenhauer in Wilhelm Halbfass, *Indien und Europa. Perspektiven ihrer geistigen Begegnung*, Basel—Stutgart 1981, 122–136.
4. Arthur Schopenhauer, *Die Welt als Wille und Vorstellung*, vol. I, Bk. IV, § 68.
5. This letter has been published by Josef Jirásek, 'Z korespondence Franze Brentana a T. G. Masaryka', *Sbornik praci filosofické fakulty brnênske university*, Rada filosofická 18, B. 16 (1969), 95f. The editor manifestly had some difficulties in deciphering Masaryk's handwriting, as is shown by certain errors the publication contains.
6. This is Masaryk's spelling throughout, it has been preserved here (Schopenhauer's variant, by the way, was 'Buddhaism').
7. Though it is surely not excluded that a Hindu should have lectured on Buddhism (maybe the Leipzig Philosophical Association had asked him to do so?), it could also be that, instead of 'Hindu' (*Hindu*), Masaryk had 'Indian' (*Inder*) in mind.
8. Probably the editor's misreading for Calcutta.
9. In later years he was to exert a certain influence upon Husserl. See, e.g., Husserl's lecture course of winter 1910/11, published in Husserliana XIII, 131–138.
10. I did not manage to identify this person.
11. See Schopenhauer, *Die Welt als Wille und Vorstellung*, vol. II, Supplements, ch. 41; *Parerga und Paralipomena*, vol. II, ch. X.
12. Thomas G. Masaryk, *Der Selbstmord als sociale Massenerscheinung der modernen Civilisation*, Munich—Vienna 1982 (= reprint of the edition Vienna 1881), 224 n. 2.
13. See my 'Husserl and Masaryk', in J. Novák (ed.), *On Masaryk*, Amsterdam 1988, 129–156. In what follows I draw in part on this paper. In Leipzig Husserl and Masaryk were in close contact with still another positivist with Schopenhauerian leanings, Carl Göring (1841–1879).
14. *Rig-Veda, übersetzt und mit kritischen und erläuternden Anmerkungen versehen*, Leipzig 1876/77. These two volumes are, however, of less scientific interest than is Grassmann's *Wörterbuch*. See Moriz Winternitz, *Geschichte der indischen Literatur*, vol. I, Stuttgart 1968 (= reprint of the 1908 edition), 63 n. 1 and 2.
15. 'Der geniale Grassmann': Husserliana XII, 96.

16. This is borne out by an anecdote reported by Husserl's wife Malvine in her text *Skizze eines Lebensbildes von Edmund Husserl*, written in 1940. About Husserl's Halle period, Malvine Husserl says with regard to the younger Grassmann: 'He was the son of a famous mathematician who was also a well-known Sanskritist. Our friend was repeatedly asked when giving his name: "Are you the son of the great mathematician Grassmann or the son of the Indologist Grassmann?' To which Grassmann junior answered with a modest look: "I am the son of both"' (Quoted from the publication of this text in my 'Malvine Husserls "Skizze eines Lebensbildes von E. Husserl"', *Husserl Studies* 5 (1988), 115).
17. See Husserlianna XII, 273ff. The work referred to is Hermann Hankel, *Zur Geschichte der Mathematik im Alterthum und Mittelater*, Leipzig 1874. Hankel was a professor at Leipzig University, but Husserl attended only one of his courses (on physics).
18. Under the signature BA 1260, Husserl's library contains a copy of Oldenberg's *Aus Indien und Iran. Gesammelte Aufsätze*, Berlin 1899. The work—which bears no reading marks-contains the following handwritten dedication: 'To my esteemed and dear friends Husserl in memory of the nice and unforgettable days which I spent with them. Bab. Oldenberg. 12.6.26.' Thus even in 1926, six years after Hermann Oldenberg's death and ten years after Husserl had left Göttingen for Freiburg, contacts between the families were still sufficiently close to make Hermann's widow Babette Oldenberg stay for some days with the Husserls. Husserl's library, by the way, also contains a copy of Oldenberg's posthumously published *Das Mahabharata. Seine Entwicklung, sein Inhalt, seine Form* of 1922 (signature BA 1261, no reading marks). This work, too, was probably sent to Husserl on Babette Oldenberg's initiative.
19. Postcard kept under the signature R II Oldenberg at the Husserl Archives. This file contains only one other item from Oldenberg's hand, an official letter addressed to Husserl in 1918 (Husserl had gone to Freiburg two years earlier) on behalf of the Göttingen Philosophical Faculty.
20. Signature BA 1259 of the Husserl Archives. On the significance of this work, the thirteenth edition of which was published in 1959, see J.W. de Jong, *A Brief History of Buddhist Studies in Europe and America*, Varanasi 1976, 28–32, and Guy Richard Welbon, *The Buddhist Nirvana and Its Western Interpreters*, Chicago—London 1968, ch. VI: 'Hermann Oldenberg and the Silent Buddha'.
21. Signature BQ 320. This book bears several reading marks.
22. Signature BA 1205. No reading marks.
23. Signature BA 354. No reading marks.
24. 'Wolfgang Husserl', unpublished MS written by Elisabeth Husserl Rosenberg. Copy at the Husserl Archives.
25. I could not identify this Mr. Siddiqi who must have been born around 1885 (none of the Siddiqi's mentioned, e.g., in the *Who's Who of Indian Writers*, compiled by the Sahitya Akademi, 2nd ed., Honolulu—New Delhi 1964, 336, qualifies). When Elisabeth Husserl Rosenberg calls him an 'Indian', one is to bear in mind that around 1910 India meant British India, not today's state of Bharat.
26. In the first months of 1921 Husserl participated in a collective gift of books bestowed upon Rabindranath Tagore who, as a Nobel prize winner, was quite renowned in Germany. But Husserl of course did not know Tagore in person, and it is doubtful that he ever read one of his books.
27. The titles of the Neumann translations which had been published before 1925 are as follows: *Die Reden Gotamo Buddhos aus der Mittleren Sammlung; Die Reden Gotamo Buddhos aus der Sammlung der Bruchstücke; die letzten Tage Gotamo Buddhos; Die Lieder der Mönche und Nonnen Gotamo Buddhos; Der Wahrheitspfad.*
28. *Der Piperbote für Kunst und Literatur*, 2. Jahrgang, 1. Heft, Frühling 1925, 18f.—Re-edited in *Husserliana* XXVII, 125f.

29. Husserl's review is not detailed enough to allow us to specify which volumes of the Neumann translations he had read. But it seems safe to assume that he had seen the translations of the Majjhima-Nikāya and of the Theri-and Theragāthā, maybe also of the Dhammapada.
30. During the Christmas vacation of 1924/25 Husserl tried to work out for publication two courses of lectures he had given in the last two years (this attempt failed). See my *Husserl-Chronik*, The Hague 1977, 287.
31. Maybe this echoes the preface of the half-anonymous editor E.R. of the third edition of the *Mittlere Sammlung* in which the thanks the publisher 'for having printed the work completely anew and in a noble type, and for having spared no sacrifice in order to reach this goal' (K. E. Neumann, *Die Reden Gotamo Buddhos aus der Mittleren Sammlung*, vol. I, Munich 1922, XXII).
32. Neumann's translations are of undeniable stylistic quality. They were highly praised by leading German poets at the time, including Gerhart Hauptmann, Hugo von Hofmannsthal, Thomas Mann and Stefan Zweig, and were even said to equal the famous Shakespeare translation of the Romantics Schlegel and Tieck. The indologists were however much more reserved in their comments. See, e.g., the critical review by Hermann Oldenberg, 'K. E. Neumanns letzte Arbeit', reprinted in his *Kleine Schriften*, ed. by K. Jauert, vol. II, Wiesbaden 1967, 1532f.
33. Husserl has in mind the consequences which the First World War had had on German intellectual life.
34. In his preface to vol. II of the *Mittlere Sammlung*, Neumann had declared that in these speeches we 'often hear the Master's own words, purely preserved as they had been spoken' (XI). In general, Neumann tends to devalue the two other Baskets of the Tripiṭaka in favour of the Suttapiṭaka out of which, he believes, they would have developed. The Suttapiṭaka is, according to him, a superior source for 'the knowledge of authentic Buddhism' (*Mittlere Sammlung*, vol. I, XXVIII).
35. By 'understanding from nearby' I translate the printed *Nahverstehbarkeit* which could be opposed to *entfernt* (departed from) in the next sentence. But it is more likely that *Nahverstehbarkeit* is simply a printer's error for *Nachverstehbarkeit* (capacity to be understood afresh), a term which lines up with other Nach-words in this Husserlian text like *Nachschöpfungen* or *Nachgestaltungen*.
36. The parallel between Neumann's and Luther's translations is not Husserl's own. E.R.'s preface to vol. I of the *Mittlere Sammlung*, XIV, had stated that 'by his amalgamation of the most noble contents of the Indian language and of German, Neumann has opened up new and unheard-of beauties of the German language, just as Luther had considered it to be his merit to have transmuted the Latin sound of the Vulgate into German.'
37. This expression clearly alludes to the articles on 'The Idea of a Philosophical Culture' (see Husserliana VII, 203–207) and 'Renewal: Its Problem and Its Method' (see *Kaizo* Tokyo 1923, 84–92) which Husserl had published in 1923.
38. There are no signs that Husserl also read Neumann's *Die längere Sammlung der Reden Gotamo Buddhos*, i.e. his translation of the *Dīgha-Nikāya*, which in any case appeared only in 1926.
39. As Husserl declared about a decade after he had written the Neumann review, transcendentality in his philosophy was another name for 'questioning back to the ultimate source of all cognitive formations, for the cognizer's self-reflection upon himself and upon his cognitive life' (*Die Krisis der europäischen Wissenschaften*, Husserliana VI, 100).
40. The best-known case for this procedure is Husserl's comparison of his transcendental reduction—which leads to his phenomenology—to a religious conversion (Husserliana VI, 140). Closer in time to the Neumann review is a letter Husserl wrote on 21 February 1926, where he affirms that 'a systematic phenomenology of world-constitution

shows from below, how God, in eternal creation, creates the world' (quoted in my *Husserl-Chronik*, 295).

41. These sets of notes were written down by the American Dorion Cairns (signatures N I 24 and N I 25 of the Husserl Archives). Cairns' command of German was rather limited and it is doubtful whether he could follow all the details of Husserl's exposition. Certainly he did not manage to commit them to paper in a satisfactory way.
42. MS B I 21/71–82 of the Husserl Archives, written on 2 and 3 December 1925 (see the entry under this date in my *Husserl-Chronik*, 298, where, however, the relation of this text to Husserl's seminar had not been recognized, because Cairns' notes were acquired by the Archives only after the *Chronik* was published).
43. MS B I 21/69–70. In my *Husserl-Chronik*, 294, I suggested that this manuscript might have been written in October 1925. Now, however, I prefer to date it December 1925, thereby relating it to Husserl's seminar.
44. MS B I 21/69a. The phrase 'renouncing the world' comes close to the 'overcoming of the world' which Husserl had ascribed to Buddhism in the Neumann review.
45. Husserliana VIII, 251f. When this manuscript was published, it was not yet known that it belonged to the context of Husserl's seminar.
46. MS A IV 2/9–15. See *Husserl-Chronik*, 300, where, however, the affiliation of this text to the seminar is not yet indicated.
47. N I 25 (Cairns' seminar notes of 13 January 1926).
48. Cairns' text has *Stellung* (position) which I emend to *Einstellung* (attitude).
49. N I 25. The additions are mine. Husserl alludes to Aristotle's *Nicomachean Ethics*, Bk. X, ch. 7.
50. Husserliana VII, 11 (my italics).
51. I expressly draw this quote from a text (published in Husserliana VII, 296) which was later dated by Husserl 'probably 1925'. Indeed, I surmise that this manuscript is part of the complex of texts which he wrote in connection with the seminar of 1925/26. Husserl's descrpition of the fact that men share a common world (so that we may converse with Kaffirs or Tibetans), and are aware of this already in the relativities of natural practical life—relativities that contrast with the absolute character of scientific knowledge—all this is very close to Husserl's other manuscripts of December 1925. The very phrase 'Plato . . . has paved the way for theoretical cognition' reappears in MS B I 21/88b which will be treated next: one more confirmation of the dating I have proposed.
52. MS B I 21/88–94, dated '21 and 22 January 1926' (see my *Husserl-Chronik*, 301). According to Husserl's indications, this (still unpublished) manuscript originally consisted of some eleven pages—of these, however only the first seven are to be found in convolute B I 21 (I did not manage to trace the missing ones). For our present purposes however this is not a problem, since Husserl in fact goes beyond the theme of confronting European and Indian philosophy already after his opening page, in order to disucss the broader issues of science and reason in general. This manuscript has already been analysed by Debabrata Sinha, 'Theory and Practice in Indian Thought: Husserl's Observations', *Philosophy East and West* 21 (1971), 255–264.
53. Cf. Husserl's affirmation in the Neumann review that Buddhism is a *transcendental* religion.
54. This is the grain of truth in Cairns' note of 20 January 1926 that Socratic science had been restricted to practical life in the world as it factually exists. According to Husserl Socrates indeed did not work out the idea of pure theory in all its aspects and consequences.
55. This is how Husserl had described the idea of philosophy in his 1923 article 'Die Idee einer philosophischen Kultur' (Husserliana VII, 203).
56. MS B I 21/88.
57. Maybe this affirmation was inspired by the repeated statement in various *suttas* of the

Majjhima-Nikāya that to acquire knowledge is to overcome suffering, and that man's overall aim is knowledge and salvation, i.e. salvation by knowledge. More important could be that in Husserl's copy of Oldenberg's *Buddha* (1881) the statement that, for pre-Buddhist doctrine as well as for Buddhism itself, 'to cognize or not to cognize is the decisive factor with regard to the definitive destiny of the mind' (51) has been underlined in pencil. But even this does not seem enough to explain why Husserl here uses the adjective *rücksichtslos* to characterize knowledge from the Buddhist point of view (I find this adjective, by the way, also in Schopenhauer's 'Preface to the Second Edition' of his *Die Welt als Wille und Vorstellung*, where it is used to qualify Schopenhauer's own philosophy).

58. This is to say that Buddhism has overcome the temptation of radical scepticism in the same way in which Socrates, against the Sophists of his time, had secured the existence of truths in themselves. See Husserliana VII, 8f.
59. *Ein an sich wahrer Weg*: could this be an allusion to the *Dhammapada*, whose title, as was said above (n. 27), had been translated by Neumann as *Wahrheitspfad*?
60. This echoes the notion of 'internal consistency' which, according to the Neumann review, is a distinctive mark of Buddhism.
61. The *Ausschaltung des natürlichen Lebensinteresses* which is here ascribed to Buddhism, comes close to Husserl's own phenomenological reduction. Already in his *Ideas* I he had called this an *Ausschaltung* of the 'thesis of the natural attitude' (Husserliana III/I, 56).
62. The corresponding notion in Husserl's own phenomenology is that of the 'disinterested spectator' (see, e.g., Husserliana VIII, 106–108).
63. This is why Husserl had raised the question whether Indian thought ever 'produced a science of what is'. Or, as Cairns noted more bluntly in the seminar session of 27 January 1926, 'the Indian attitude is one of willed renunciation... So one can understand why the Indians never have developed a science of the world.' (N I 24).
64. The factual incorrectness of this view is shown by J. N. Mohanty in his 'Phenomenology and Indian Philosophy: The Concept of Rationality', *Journal of the British Society for Phenomenology* 19 (1988), 269–281.
65. One of the few reminiscences of Indian themes in Husserl is a manuscript he wrote in October 1932 where in passing he refers to Buddha's fig-tree. But this is nothing but an example displaying some not too exact erudition: Husserl believes that Buddha 'taught' under this tree (Husserliana XV, 241).
66. Husserliana VI, 14.
67. Husserliana VI, 337; cf. Husserliana VI, 13: 'Man is a rational being (animal rationale)'.
68. Husserliana VII, 291 (about 1925). In what follows, I prefer to quote, giving their dates, not only texts deriving from the manuscripts which are part of the *Crisis* complex of 1936/37, but also texts spread over the last decade (and more) of Husserl's life. This is in order to underline the continuity of Husserl's thought about these themes.
69. Husserliana VII, 297 (about 1925).
70. Husserliana VII, 253 (1925).
71. Husserl's enumeration makes it clear that, instead of 'Hindu', he should have said 'Indian'. For a comparable case see n. 7 above.
72. Husserliana VI, 142.
73. Cf. Husserliana VII, 204 (1923) and Husserliana VI, 13: Man is 'virtually directed toward reason'.
74. Husserliana VIII, 241f. (about 1921).
75. Husserliana VIII, 195 (about 1924).
76. Husserliana XXV, 4 (1911).
77. Husserliana VIII, 328 (1925).
78. Husserliana V, 161 (1930).
79. Ibid., 139. More exactly speaking, the idea of philosophy had been first devised by

'the incomparable double star: Socrates—Plato' (Husserliana VII, 8).

80. This implies that Husserl first had to determine which specific cultures would fall under his concept of 'Europe'. This, then, is what he has to say about it: 'The English Dominions, the United States etc. belong to Europe, whereas the Eskimos or Red Indians at our fairs, or the Gypsies who constantly wander about Europe, do not' (Husserliana VI, 318f.) All groups who have imbibed the (European) idea of philosophy and have thereby become assimilated to European culture, are therefore Europeans.
81. Husserliana XVII, 5 (1929).
82. Husserliana VI, 14.
83. *Ibid.*, 325.
84. *Ibid.*, 329. Husserl could have levelled this accusation, e.g., against F. Max Müller who, in vol. I, 66 of his *Essays* of 1879 had said: 'The early Hindus were a people of philosophers', which phrase is underlined with pencil in Husserl's copy.
85. Husserliana VI, 331.
86. Husserliana VIII, 323f. (1925).
87. Cf. Husserliana VI, 338. Is this really to degrade non-European thought? I am not so sure about this, as this play with proportionalities may be continued further. As non-philosophical reason in Husserl's sense (e.g., Indian thought) is to philosophical (i.e. European) reason, so phenomenology is to pre-phenomenological (European) philosophy—and non-Husserlian phenomenology (e.g., of the Pfänder, Scheler, or Heidegger variety) is to Husserl himself (cf. Husserliana VI, 170n. and 439). I would even venture to suggest a last link to this chain: in the same way Husserl's own early (pre-phenomenological, in the sense of pre-transcendental) thought is to his mature transcendentalism. In all these cases, the dismal result is obtained by applying Husserl's maxim of everything-or-nothing.
88. Husserliana VI, 320. Husserl's conditional clause 'as long as we understand ourselves properly' seems to hint at a hidden circle in this argument.
89. Husserliana VI, 14.
90. I cannot help quoting here at some length Wilhelm Halbfass' judgment about Hegel: 'He looks at Indian philosophy from the summit of his time and of his system, in which Western thought is cumulated together. To him, the European context has grown beyond the Asian traditions, it comprehends and cancels them, and they can and must be understood on this basis. The question is superfluous how a standpoint could be reached for a judgment and a just "comparison": it has, so to speak, been answered, before it could be raised, and this by the historical development itself, which has led Europeans to the height of their reflection and has made them the discoverers and historians also of the non-European traditions.' ('Indien und die Geschichtsschreibung der Philosophie', *Philosophische Rundschau* (1976), 109). All this can without the slightest exception be transferred to Husserl.
91. Wilhelm Halbfass, *Indien und Europa*, ch. IX (165–182).
92. Husserliana VI, 74. One must however concede that Husserl was aware of the fact that he had construed 'an untrue Plato etc'. (Husserliana VI, 512). But he did not try to solve the problems this entails.
93. Husserliana VI, 513 and 556. For a less prosaic interpretation of these statements see Rudolf Boehm, *Vom Gesichtspunkt der Phänomenologie*, The Hague 1968, 242–249.
94. Husserliana VI, 200.
95. *Ibid.*, 347.
96. *Ibid.*, 338. This statement reminds one once more of the Hegelian 'theodicy' of reason in its historical development.
97. *Ibid.*, 337 (italics mine).

Phenomenology and Indian Philosophy

SIBAJIBAN BHATTACHARYYA

I. Introduction

Phenomenology, specially as a philosophical method, has developed, in the last 50 years or so, in various ways which exhibit a sort of family resemblance. In this paper I shall use 'phenomenology' in a wider sense to include also what is usually known as 'existential phenomenology'. Indian philosophy, which has developed for more than 2000 years in a geographical area as vast as a continent, includes so many schools and sub-schools that they do not exhibit any family resemblance. Although it is customary to characterize philosophical movements by their geographical limits—Polish logic, German idealism, French existentialism, British analytical philosophy, contemporary Australian or American philosophy, and so on, it is clear that Western philosophical thinking does not observe national boundaries. Dummett, Davidson, McDowell, for example, have freely been commenting on each other's positions. Indian philosophy is Indian in a more special sense, for although Indian philosophical theories have sometimes been exported to neighbouring countries, there is no evidence that Indian philosophy was ever influenced by foreign philosophies. Even now those who are developing Indian philosophy are, in general, ignorant of English or any philosophical tradition which is non-Indian. As Indian philosophy has developed in total seclusion, it is difficult to decide how to interpret it to Western scholars who have not been exposed to it. Modern scholars of Indian philosophy, therefore, use all sorts of methods—analytical, logical, phenomenological, in order to recapture the richness of philosophical thought for non-Indian readers. As it is impossible to cover, even briefly, all areas and all schools of Indian philosophy, I shall take up, rather arbitrarily, some problems of the philosophies of the self as presented in Sāṅkhya (dualism) and in different forms of Advaita (monism) to exhibit their relation to phenomenology.

We may classify Indian theories of the self into four different types: (1) according to I-philosophies the self is what is primarily meant by 'I'; (2) according to You–philosophies, the self is really what is meant by 'you'; (3) according to We-philosophies the self is what is meant by 'we'; (4) according to Impersonal theories, the self is really impersonal, universal consciousness which is neither I, nor you, nor we. I shall now explain these four types of theories of the self.

II. I–Philosophies

According to this type of philosophies, everyone is a particular individual, epistemically different from everyone else,—from 'you' or 'he' or 'they'.

Every individual knows himself as 'I', yet the ontological structure and content of this I-sense ('I') is not thereby determined. The 'I' may be the immediate being of a self-conscious monad; it may be just a series of ontologically momentary mental states experienced wrongly as permanent; it may be that consciousness is ontologically impersonal and the I-sense, the sense of one's being a person, is a mis-conception. The body which is *my* body may be experienced as I; even a very different object, mental or material, may be fused with, directly felt as, I; even the entire universe may be so felt. This I-sense means experiencing oneself as a being, an identity. Attachment, i.e., emotional involvement, love, empathy and other similar processes are processes of identifying, (fusing, confusing) oneself with, being affirming oneself as something that is ontologically different. It does not matter if what I have fused myself with is, to others, a material object. I have direct experience of what others call a physical object as myself. There is also the reverse process of psychological distancing, detachment, experiential separation of 'I' from what was previously experienced as 'I'. I shall now explain some of the Indian theories.

A. SELF-IDENTITY, SELF-IDENTIFICATION, SELF-SURRENDER

Problems of self-identity may be viewed in two ways—horizontally, as problems of referring thoughts, feelings, emotions, attitudes etc., to the same person over time, and vertically, as problems of identifying the self with a not-self. This difference in points of view is not the same as that between 'the third-person version' and 'the first-person version' in the sense in which Shoemaker uses these terms,[1] for even the first-person version of the problem is that of ascribing past and present experiences to me, and is thus the problem of self-identity across time. This is the usual point of view of Western philosophers, while Indian philosophers are concerned with the problem of explaining how the self can identify itself whatever it is identified with. To explain this Indian point of view, I begin with a quotation from William James:

'The following vivid account of a fit of hasheesh-delirium has been given me by a friend:

> ... I next enjoyed a sort of metempsychosis. An animal or thing that I thought of could be made the being which held my mind. I thought of a fox, and instantly, I was transformed into that animal. I could distinctly feel myself a fox, could see my long ears and bushy tail, and by a sort of introversion felt that my complete anatomy was that of a fox, ... I was next transformed into a bombshell, felt my size, weight, and thickness, and experience the sensation of being shot up out of a giant mortar, looking down upon the earth, bursting and falling back in a shower of iron fragments'.[2]

The following points about this report may be noted.

(i) That the experience of this self-identification with anything that came to the mind was hallucinatory cannot detract from not merely its logical possibility, but also from the reality of the experience. It has now become fashionable in philosophy to examine imaginary cases to refute a philosophical theory of self-identity; there ought not to be any objection to using a hallucination, a vivid experience, for the purpose. We shall, however, see that there are other more common types of experience of self-identification.

(ii) One may identity oneself with anything whatsoever; hence self-identification is radically different from personal identity for which either physical continuity, or memory or both are necessary. Robert Nozick's theory of closest continuer[3] is as out of place here as the other theories of criteria of self-identity.

(iii) This is because here there is no question of knowing oneself as the same person over time. I may identify myself with a fox at some time but in this self-identification there is no awareness of myself continuing over time. The question, of course, could be raised, but is not raised at all.

(iv) Identity as a relation is reflexive, symmetrical and transitive. Consciousness is always directed to something, and to be directed to itself, it has to reflect on itself, to turn itself upon itself, to be related to itself. This is why self-consciousness involves a reflexive relation and Nozick formulates his theory of self-identity on the basis of a special kind of reflexive relation. In identifying myself with an object, say, a fox, I do not have to be reflexively aware of myself, although when I have identified myself with a fox, I know myself as a fox, and *then* this reflexivity comes in. But the problem here is not how I know myself, but how I can possibly identify myself with a fox or whatever. Self-identification is also not symmetrical; there is no question of the bombshell identifying itself with me when I identify myself with it. Nor is it transitive. *A* may identity with *B* with and *B* with *C* but from this it does not follow that *A* identifies himself with *C*. This is because when *A* identifies himself with *B*, he identifies himself with *B* as he knows him. This is common in love; when *A* loves *B* it so often happens that he loves his own image of *B*. Later on, these points will be discussed in detail.

(v) There is also a dis-identification which is presupposed in every act of self-identification. It is necessary to cease to identify myself with this person that I am now in order that I may identify myself with the bombshell. There must be total forgetfulness of my previous identification.

The exclusive concern with the expression of identification is not the same as the concern with the first person identity over time. Moreover, this experience does not amount to a philosophical theory about what I am. The difference in the point of view becomes clear by contrasting it with Derek Parfit's analysis of his Branchline case. 'My Replica thinks that he is me, and he seems to remember living my life up to the moment when I pressed the green button. In every other way, both physically and psychologically, my Replica is just like me'.[4] The question that is important but is not asked here is *not* whether my Replica or everyone else thinks that he is me, but whether *I* think (experience) that I am the Replica. This question is important because self-identification, as we have seen, is not symmetrical. If I do not experience this identity then my death due to cardiac failure will be *my* death. What is necessary to believe (experience) that I continue to live in 'my' Replica is to dis-identify myself from myself and experience myself existing on Earth as another person. It is only by this psychological and experiential distancing from my former self and identifying myself with 'my' Replica that I can be 'consoled' not 'just a little' but can avoid death when my former self dies.

There is, however, a further point. I presumably do not identify myself with my Replica because I know how by pressing the green button I can cause my Replica to appear on the Mars. But, then, this knowledge which I have before pressing the button is shared by my Replica. If this knowledge prevents me from identifying myself with my Replica, it will prevent him, too, from identifying himself with me. If, on the other hand, in spite of this knowledge, my Replica can think that he is me, there is no difficulty in my thinking that I am the Replica. As a matter of fact, in self-identification I may identify myself with what is known by others and was previously known by me to be other than myself. This point will be explained in detail later.

The difference in the points of view appears also in the manner of talking. Parfit continually talks of the Replica 'thinking that he is me'. But I do not 'think' that I am myself, I do not 'believe' that I am myself—I am just myself; my whole being is myself, and as my being is also partly conscious being, I am consciously myself. Even when I identify myself with what I knew, and others know, to be other than myself, the identification requires cancellation or suspension or total forgetfulness of the experience of identity with my previous self and I have direct experience of myself *being that*; I do not just *think* that I am that.

(vi) The difference between the usual problem of self-identity and self-identification becomes clear if we realise that in self-identification, the self that identifies itself with anything whatever, may be *ontologically* just the living body (behaviourism), or a self-substance (*spiritualism*), a momentary idea or perception (a self-less person); whatever *be* the ontological status of the self, it is the I-sense that is transferred from it to that with which the self identifies itself. The ontological self does not enter into this transference of I-sense. 'The third-person version' and 'the first-person version' do not differ in the same way as self-identity differs from self-identification; for even in the 'first person version' there is a question of myself remaining the same person over time and appropriate criteria, perhaps memory etc., will be relevant for explaining this identity and sense of identity. In the case of self-identification only the experience of self-identification suffices, no other criteria are needed.

(vii) Yet we should note here that when I thus identify myself with anything, that thing does not remain that thing, but becomes 'ensoulded'. When I identify myself with a bombshell, I do not become an inanimate object, but import my feeling into it, ('felt my size. . . .' 'experienced the sensation of being shot up . . .' etc.).

Advaita Vedānta explains this type of phenomenon as a case of fusing or confusing of myself with any person or object. This confusion or fundamental unclarity about the real nature of myself[5] is also a confusion about the nature of the object. This is the cause of emotional involvement with, or attachment to, a not-self. This attachment admits of degrees; in its initial stage the attachment expresses itself in the form of desire for a person or object. This desire makes us take pleasure in the thought of the desired object, wanting to *possess* it, i.e., to have it as mine. When attachment grows, the object, whether attained or not, is felt as mine, and at the most intense state, it is felt as *I*. We have a glimpse of this self-identification in empathy. But it is easier to identify oneself with the object of desire in dream. I may dream that I *am* a child, an old man, an angel, a giant or an animal. I may even dream that I am dead, but I retain consciousness and am aware of my dead body. I do not dream that I am an inanimate object, a stick or a table. In dream this identification is total, for then there is no memory of myself as I am in the waking state; if the memory persisted, it would have rankled and interfered with my identifying myself anew. That attachment admits of degrees is obvious; it is clear, for example, in the story of 'Tom Canty':

> By and by Tom's reading and dreaming about princely life wrought such a strong effect upon him that he began to *act* the prince, unconsciously . . . but at last his thoughts drifted away to far, romantic lands, and he fell asleep in the company of jeweled and gilded princelings who lived in vast palaces, and had servants salaaming before them, of flying to execute their orders. And then, as usual, he dreamed that he was a princeling himself'.[6]

According to Advaita Vedānta, I identify myself only occasionally with my son, friends or desired objects, for attachment to them is not as intense as it can be; most of the time they are experienced as mine. I usually identify myself with my body in the waking state, for my attachment to my body is more intense and intimate. In dream I may forget this identification. My attachment to my ego is closest, because even in dream I continue to have the I-sense although I may be a child or whatever. It is only in deep dreamless sleep that I transcend this identification, for then I lose my I-sense totally; I have no sense of *being* the person that I am in the waking state or in dream. If one can go beyond this state of dreamless sleep, then one can realise the true nature of the self. Only at that stage is the self known with clarity and certainty; at all other stages, the self remains as an unclear, elusive over-receding background which, however vaguely felt, remains the hidden foundation of my being in all my activity. As I become conscious of myself when engaging in activities of life, this self-consciousness cannot be regarded as involving a reflexive relation. I am conscious of myself only when involved in cognitive acts or practical activities. In introspection myself as the owner of my mental states or as that to whom the states are ascribed eludes my grasp. The owner or the subject himself cannot be brought to the focus of attention.

There is another type of self-identification, i.e., self-realization. I have already stated that self-awareness during waking state is of the vaguest kind and is confused with awareness of objects. But there is a deepening of awareness of the self and at the deepest level there is immediate, indubitable, clear awareness of one's ownself which is self-realization. According to Advaita Vedānta, this realization is of impersonal consciousness which is the foundation not only of the psycho-physical complex of the individual which is me, but of the whole world. So by identifying oneself with that impersonal consciousness one identifies oneself with the world. This type of self-realization requires total surrender of one's individual self, its dissolution in the universal consciousness.

Self-surrender, like self-awareness, has many levels. Self-surrender at the superficial level is just relaxation,[7] but when it is total, it is effacement, annulment of my being. The metaphor used here is of a doll of salt that goes to fathom the sea; it melts without residue and loses its being totally. In this type of self-surrender, one can surrender oneself only to a superior person, not to any inferior being or inanimate object. If self-surrender is total, there is no I-consciousness, one experientially identifies oneself with the impersonal universal consciousness. As this self-identification is self-realization, it can be objectively verified by others. Christian saints meditating on Jesus have been reported to develop stigmata. Sri Ramakrishna is reported to have felt unbearable pain when people walked on the grass. People saw marks on his body when one boatman slapped another in a boat.[8] One may identify oneself in this sense not merely with a Supreme Person, but also with the entire universe.

There are different kinds of self-surrender. Self-surrender may admit of degrees, may be temporary or permanent, may be the result of effort or may be spontaneous or automatic. Thus one may have even a knack of temporarily putting oneself to sleep or blotting oneself out, as when a medium vacates his mind and hands it over to an invited or sometimes uninvited spirit; The medium does not identify himself or herself with the alien spirit: self-surrender is not self-identification. In this type of self-surrender, when one comes to, one does not have any memory of what happened through oneself. But in other types of cases of temporary relinquishing of charge, one still remains in the background, has memory of what happens to oneself during the interval, as for example, when a poem gets composed a dream and one remembers it on waking.

Psycho-analytic explanations of the process of becoming conscious of the unconscious urges is not really relevant here. For it is the living experience of being suspended or totally cancelled that matters, and not the experience of being swept off one's feet, of being brushed aside, by an inner force. For the power that engulfs one is felt as welling up from within as well as coming in waves from outside. In 'die to live', the person who dies is not the person who lives, but he is that to whom the person dying surrenders.

B. THE SELF AS I

Everyone is a unique individual, but this ontological uniqueness, unlike the uniqueness of, say, a grain of sand, is identical with the I-sense, an awareness of being a unique individual. I am *myself*, not you, he or she. Thus 'I' in this sense is opposed to 'you', 'he' or 'she'. Often this 'I' is explained in terms of private ownership. The 'I' is the unique owner of thoughts, feelings, emotions, desires and actions; they are thus *mine*—no one else can own them.

This explanation of the I-sense in terms of ownership is an inadequate explanation, for I do not own thoughts in the same way as I own emotions or as I own actions. In deep, concentrated thinking, it is the object that determines the process of thinking and not the subject. In rigorous logical thinking, in the syntax of propositional logic, for example, the subject has to follow the rules almost mechanically, cannot read any meaning into the defined terms other than what has been stated in the definitions. In logical thinking the subject has no role at all. In emotion man sees the object as deeply suffused by subjective colours. The emotions are not merely determined by the subject, but affect the subject also a consequence—my emotions *move me* in a way in which my thoughts do not. My actions reveal what I am now and determine what I shall be in future in a way which neither my thoughts nor my emotions can do.

It may be argued here that from the fact that my emotions affect me, move me, while my thoughts do not, it does not follow that I own my emotions in a different way than I own my thoughts. My emotions move me, while my thoughts do not, not because they are *my* emotions, but because they are my *emotions*, and not *thoughts*. It is the very nature of emotions to affect me more strongly than thoughts, but this does not mean that they are *my* emotions in a special sense.

This argument misses entirely the fact that I get more deeply involved in emotions than in thoughts; that is why emotional disturbance may lead to problems of identity. So also action, i.e., voluntary, purposive behaviour, flows from my very being. Success in action tends to promote self-confidence, while failure tends to undermine it. This is why in Indian philosophy we have a law of *karma* (interpreted to mean both action and intention to act) as determining what I shall be and become. My thoughts are important only in so far as they may lead to attachment to the objects I think about and, eventually, to action, or failing that, to desire to act in order to obtain them.[9]

Robert Nozick has advocated a 'creative act' of reflexive self-reference from inside to explain the origin of I-sense.[10] This act of synthesis is the same for the 'components of action, intention, causal production' (p. 88). But this fails to account for the felt difference between the relations of 'I' with my thoughts, my emotions and my actions. The 'I' is not related to all these in the same way—a fact which Nozick's theory fails to explain.

C. THE SELF AS SUCCESSION OF MENTAL STATES

Hume, in a well-known passage, writes: 'When I enter most intimately into what I call *myself*, I always stumble on some particular perception or other, of heat or cold, light or shade, love or hatred, pain or pleasure. I never can catch *myself* at any time without a perception and can never observe anything but the perception.... I may venture to affirm... of mankind that they are nothing but a bundle or collection of different perceptions, which succeed each other with an inconceivable rapidity and are in perpetual flux and movement'.[11]

I examine this theory in some detail from the standpoint of Sāṅkhya, Advaita Vedānta and Kāśmīra Śaivism which put forward indentical views on this point. If mental states, 'perceptions', succeed one another with 'inconceivable rapidity', then it is not clear how 'a bundle' of them is to be conceived. It will be appropriate to talk here of a succession of mental states, rather than a bundle, unless, of course, one brings in the modern idea of logical construction to understand 'a bundle or collection of different perceptions'. The second point is that our experience of ourselves is of the most direct kind imaginable; yet Hume asserts that we are a victim of illusion when we think of ourselves as permanent, enduring selves. Now if we are mistaken about our very being, there does not seem to be anything of which we can have true perceptions. This leads to an unmitigated form of scepticism which Hume has been interpreted by many to have come very close to. Indian philosophers generally assert that we have a wrong belief about the nature of the self but they do not, with the exception of the Buddhists, question the validity of awareness of an abiding self. However, they differ in their explanations of this awareness. I shall now try to show why Hume's theory of self is essentially inadequate.

Hume's theory is that the self is not merely not a permanent substance but is also ontologically discontinuous. This ontological discontinuity must also imply discontinuity in experience. Between any two perceptions there is a temporal gap, and as there is nothing in the gaps, there can be neither ontological nor experiential personal identity. Hume seems to be aware of this difficulty, but tries to cover it up, and not solve it, by his theory of perceptions succeeding each other 'with inconceivable rapidity'. The rapidity must be not only 'inconceivable' but also 'inexperienceable', for there will be nothing during the gaps which can be an experiencing subject then. The preceding perception cannot experience it as the gap is still to come, the succeeding perception cannot experience it as the gap has ceased to exist when it has come into being. This being the case there is no reason for Hume to hold on to the theory of inconceivable rapidity of succession; for even if the perceptions do not succeed each other with 'inconceivable rapidity' and the intervening gaps are lengthened, still the gaps will not be experienced as there will be nothing to experience them. The gaps are actually there, whether inconceivably short or very long—all incapable of being experienced; and if the existence of long gaps makes the unity of the self inconceivable, the inconceivably short gaps cannot solve this difficulty. To explain the immediately felt unity of the self it is necessary to deny the *existence* of gaps in consciousness, not merely their experience or conceivability. Hume's reason for assuming 'inconceivable rapidity' seems to be that then one would not *notice* these gaps. But then 'one' has to be a transcendent subject witnessing the succession, just as in a movie still pictures of a certain sort projected, not with inconceivable rapidity, but with sufficient rapidity, will be seen by a person as moving continuously. But what is important is to note here that the subject has to be a transcendent subject distant from the projected pictures. The pictures themselves, if they were conscious, would not be able to see the continuity; even if the gaps were widened the pictures themselves would not be aware of them; only the transcendent subject can experience the gaps.

In order to explain the ontological and experiential continuity of the self, philosophers of the Sāṅkhya, Advaita Vedānta and Kaśmīra Śaivism schools postulate the existence of a deeper level of permanent consciousness without perceptions or representations. This contentless consciousness which lies beneath the lair of representations succeeding each other in a discontinuous series, shines through the split-second temporal gaps, just as light shines through cracks in a wall. This contentless shining consciousness is not involved in the personal life of the individual and is, therefore, regarded as mere witnessing consciousness revealing itself not merely through the temporal gaps between the successive representations, but also revealing the inner states themselves. The empirical subject knows only representations of the external objects but the representations themselves have to be known directly without representations; for if representations were needed to know representations this would lead to infinite regress. This witnessing consciousness which reveals all internal states reveals also the state of deep dreamless sleep. This experience is the only evidence of deep sleep, for when one is in deep sleep, one does not know any external objects, does not have any contents of empirical consciousness which the witness can reveal. That one was asleep cannot be inferred from anything one may know when one wakes up. This direct experience of sleep during sleep is the only evidence of it.

The philosophers of Advaita Vedānta and Kāśmīra Śaivism point out that in ordinary introspection we can know ourselves only through perceptions or representations. But if we are very attentive and alert we find the split-second gap in the series of perceptions through which the contentless consciousness shines. The easiest way to self-realisation is to identify oneself with the contentless pure consciousness peeping through the gaps. It is not to contemplate or mediate on this consciousness, but to identify oneself experientially with it, to fall from the covering of representations into the depth of consciousness through the split-second gap. This experience of being the contentless deeper consciousness is the experience of nothingness contrasted with the objective, discontinuous, surface consciousness. As this split-second experience of deeper consciousness is the experience of peace, pure freedom from constraints of objects, this tends to make the experience stay longer, with the gaps between representations in objective consciousness becoming longer and longer. With practice in staying beneath the objective consciousness, the pure subjectivity asserts itself and the surface consciousness is wholly suspended without any effort at self-control. When this is achieved one has transcended the world of objects and has achieved self-realization. We shall later explain this concept of witnessing consciousness in detail.

D. THE BODY AS I

There are various sorts of problems connected with the notion of the body, i.e., the living body of a man. In the Western philosophies of the body, three basic questions are usually discussed. (1) Can the concept of the body be defined without a prior presupposition of the concept of a person? It is generally agreed that this is not possible. (2) Is the relation between body and mind an extraneous or a necessary, logical, relation? This question relates to the problem of explaining the reason for the union of a particular body with a particular mind. This problem is important for deciding issues of transmigration of souls, or doctrines of 'metamorphosis' or 'metempsychosis'. Thus the problem of the body is basically the problem of the relation between body and mind. (3) Another major problem of the relation between the human body and the human soul is found in Wittgenstein's *Philosophical Investigations*—'The human body is the best picture of the human soul' (*Der menschliche korper ist das beste Bile der Menschlicha Seels*). Some have translated 'korper' as face, thereby rendering Wittgenstein's sentence, 'The human face is the best picture of the human soul.'[12] But this seems to be a falsification of Wittgenstein's theory. Implicit in the sentence is the question: Is soul such that it is necessarily revealed, correctly and adequately, through the body?

In Indian philosophy, the body of any living being is regarded as belonging to a *jīva*, which may be very roughly and inadequately *regarded as corresponding* to the Western concept of 'person'. Thus there is no question of regarding the body as extraneous to the *jīva*. The reason for a particular *jīva* assuming a particular physical body is both causal and moral. The problems of *mind-body relation* become, at their deepest level, problems of incarnation (i.e., associating consciousness with a body) and liberation (i.e., dissociating consciousness from the body). Problems of incarnation, again, may be of two types—(i) general problems of how consciousness can have a body at all; and (ii) special problems of how a particular self or centre of consciousness can have the particular body which is his body. Problems of liberation are problems of explaining how the reverse process of dissociation from a body can be made significant and shown to be possible. In both the types of incarnation, and in liberation, the crucial problem is to understand the meaning of 'consciousness having a body'.

At another level the problem of a person assuming a body and discarding it is the problem of birth and death—i.e., the problem of a *jīva* assuming a physical body and giving it up. I shall discuss the problem of birth and death after explaining the problem of incarnation.

I have stated that according to Indian philosophy one can identify oneself with anything, living or non-living, through intense attachment, love or empathy. There is, however, a sense in which one is naturally identified with what one *calls* one's body. I shall now explain this sense.

A new born child does not distinguish its body from the environment. As sensations gradually crystallize into a sense of its body, its conception of itself, too, crystallizes to that extent. The first point to be noted here is that all individual selves are not at the same level of perfection—spiritual, moral, intellectual or emotional; therefore, all selves do not have their bodies in the same sense. This is because their bodies do not have the same value, the same importance, the same function for them. For ordinary men, i.e., *men living a life* of self interest, *having* a body is to be *identified with* it. This is the case with children, for they are openly, unabashedly, selfish. So we may say that every man is born with this attitude, that this is the *original*, natural, attitude of men. Many men never grow out of it in their lives. A man at this level of life is just conscious, self-conscious, living body, which is felt as one with his ego, with himself.

Our immediate awareness of our selves is awareness of our selves as bodies. The empirical subject 'knows' itself as identical with the body. This 'knowledge' however, is really a false belief. I 'know' what is actually my body as myself even though I say 'my body'. The *expression*, 'my body' implies a distinction between *myself* as the owner and the body as the owned, yet I am not clearly aware of this distinction.[13] My body is felt as myself, at the empirical level the body *is* the self; yet no one can say 'I am the body', unless one has at least the concept of a body different from the self, a concept which one can acquire only from the *śāstras*. The expression 'my consciousness' is also impossible, because at all stages of subjectivity, I *am* myself, 'myself' is not 'my self' if it implies a distinction between me and myself; 'my self', therefore is the same as 'myself' i.e., 'I'. That the whole of the individual's existence is bodily existence is shown not merely in his attributing the so-called M-predicates to his body like 'reclining', 'six feet tall', but also in attributing the so-called P-predicates like 'honest', 'wise', etc. For even the P-predicates are not applied to a non-bodily entity, for at this stage, the individual is incapable of thinking, imagining, feeling himself except in terms of what we (at a superior level of conception or of existence) call his body. (He himself does not call it his body, for it is he himself). At this level of existence, I act in this world with 'my body'; I know things by means of 'my body' (sense-organs, brain, etc.); I satisfy my desires by means of 'my body'. It is only by being in the body, i.e., *by being identical with it*, that the self, i.e., myself, is in effective communion with the world, is in the world. 'To contemplate this truth is to realise that the body is not a prison house but a living link of the individual with the universe'.[14] 'The feeling that the body is integral to the universe, creates a sense of wholeness that can help the body to attain perfect health'.[15] 'So we can understand how I can exclusively own the body, and yet go far beyond it. As the body is limited to superficial view, so am I. But as the body is really one with the universe, so am I, too ... The second view would be the view of those who care to look deeper and wider into fact'.[16] It is necessary to explain here more fully what we mean *by identifying the ego with the body*. First, it is not the *whole* body, not even everything in the body, which is immediately experienced as 'I'. Leaving aside such outer growths as hair and nails with which the ego does not identify itself,[17] there are millions of living organisms within the body like the blood corpuscles which are not felt as 'I' or as part of myself. These organisms, though essential for the very existence of the body, still have their separate *lives; they live* and propagate, fight and die, within the body, yet they are never felt as myself. The ego identifies itself with the body only *through* the nervous system—central, sympathetic, and parasympathetic; consciousness spreads itself all over the body through the afferent and efferent nerves. The blood cells have *their own cell structure, their own bodies, their own lives*. They are not felt as 'I' or as a part of 'I', simply because the nervous system, though sustained by blood circulation and various functions of the blood cells, does neither pervade them, nor control their lives.

Secondly, although consciousness is felt as spread all over the body, i.e., it is the body as a whole which is felt as 'I', yet the ego, at this stage of human existence, is located or *rooted* in the lowest part of the spinal cord. The ego is felt as *being there*, and views the entire world from there. The point of view of the ego is that of the lowest form of self-consciousness. That there is such a thing as the *location* of the ego in some portion of the nervous system which becomes its *stand-point* is experienced in suitable circumstances. Thus when one trips and has a sense of suddenly being supportless, one has a feeling of emptiness in the pit of one's stomach. This sickening feeling of emptiness, of being supportless, also comes when one unexpectedly confronts a very grave personal danger for which one is not all prepared, when one's very existence is threatened. Only in such times of crisis do we have immediate and overwhelming experience of ourselves as being located in a part of the body.

The ego may get located in the higher centre of the nervous system. When this happens, consciousness gets deepened and broadened. 'The Vedas speaks of seven planes where the mind dwells. When the mind is immersed in worldliness it dwells in the three lower planes—at the navel, the organ of generation, and the organ of evacuation. In that stage, the mind loses all its higher visions—it broods only on 'woman and gold'. The fourth plane of the mind is at the heart. When the mind dwells there, one has the first glimpse of spiritual consciousness. One sees light all around. Such a man, perceiving the divine light, becomes speechless with wonder and says: 'Ah! what is that? What is this? His mind does not go downward to the objects of the world. The fifth plane of the mind is at the throat. When the mind reaches this plane, the aspirant becomes free from all ignorance and illusion. He does not enjoy talking or hearing about anything but God. If people talk about worldly things, he leaves the place at once. The sixth plane is at the forehead. When the mind reaches it, the aspirant sees the form of God day and night. But even then a little trace of ego remains. At the sight of that incomparable beauty of God's form one becomes intoxicated and rushes forth to touch and embrace it. But one does not succeed. It is like the light inside a lantern. One feels as if one could touch the light, but one cannot on account of the pane of glass.

'In the top of the head is the seventh plane. When the mind rises there, one goes into *samādhi*. Then the *Brahmajñānī* directly perceives *Brahman*. But in that state his body does not last many days. He remains unconscious of the outer world. If milk is poured into his mouth, it runs out. Dwelling on this plane of consciousness, he gives up his *body in twenty-one days*. That is the condition of the *Brahmajñānī*.[18]

E. THE SĀṄKHYA THEORY OF THE EMPIRICAL SUBJECT

In order to explain the Indian conceptions of incarnation it is necessary to explain first the conception of the body. As men are embodied selves, one would have expected more or less the same type of experience everywhere and the same type of theory of the body in all philosophies; it is, therefore, strange to find the Indian conceptions of the body radically different from Western conceptions. The main reason for this fundamental difference seems to be that while the problem of transmigration or reincarnation is the central problem in Indian theories of the body, Western philosophers have not seriously considered this problem in their theories. In what follows I shall explain the Sāṅkhya theory of the empirical subject, i.e., the self as embodied, as this theory has been widely accepted with modifications to suit the general metaphysical theories of different schools.

The Sāṅkhya philosophy may be regarded as a sort of dualism, postulating as many selves as there are living beings and a primordial matter which is the source of the material world. The self in Sāṅkhya is not conscious, but consciousness; it is 'pure' consciousness in the sense (i) that it is above all change, motion or modification, (ii) that, therefore, there can be no contents in it, neither pleasure nor happiness nor suffering nor pain; (iii) that it is not personal, not 'myself'. It is matter which is the principle of all change and becoming. Thus this theory is the oppositive of Western theories which regard matter as inert and spirit as active, and God as pure activity. In its traditional interpretation, the Sāṅkhya system does not admit the existence of God.

The empirical subject is that which knows objects (real or unreal), performs actions (moral or immoral), feels pleasure or pain. It is the principle of unity running through all types of objective knowledge, actions and feelings of an individual. That which knows objects is also that which acts and feels. The question which often arises in Kant's philosophy about the relation between the Pure Theoretical Reason and the Pure Practical Reason does not arise here. There are not three subjects in one individual—one for knowing, one for acting and one for feeling; there is just one subject which knows, acts and feels.

The ego is an essential constitutive factor of the empirical subject; it manifests itself in the form of 'I-consciousness'. Every knowledge must be someone's knowledge, every act someone's act, every feeling someone's feeling. To *express* one's knowledge, etc., one says 'I know', 'I act', 'I feel': one's introspective awareness always involves one's *awareness* of the ego. Hence all introspective reports are in the first person singular. Of the empirical subject as knower the ego is *one* of its constitutive factors. The empirical subject in the context of knowledge reveals, on analysis, a composite structure of six elements—(i) consciousness, (ii) presentation, (iii) the ego, and (iv) an instrument of deliberation, (v) sense-organs, (vi) the body.

(*i*) *Consciousness*

The first element is consciousness. That the empirical subject involves consciousness should be obvious, whatever the relation between the empirical subject and consciousness. By itself this *element* of consciousness is not, however, 'I-consciousness' but consciousness pure and simple. This pure consciousness is simple (without any structure), unchanging and unaffected by any change. There is no content in it; contents of consciousness are not contents *in* consciousness. This element of pure consciousness is not an act either; it is *not* intentional, does not refer to anything.

Pure consciousness is not a substance and cannot be a substratum of qualities. When the *empirical subject* feels pain, this pain is *not* a *quality* of the consciousness; it is a *conscious experience*, but is not consciousness. All mental states and acts are *conscious* states and acts, but are not *consciousness*. The mental states themselves are non-conscious—*different from consciousness*, but somehow *related* to consciousness. We now explain the nature of this relation.

Pure consciousness involved in empirical consciousness is the transcendental consciousness which is separate and distinct from every thing other than consciousness. It *ought to be felt* (known) as such, but it is not *actually* felt as separate and distinct from the other non-conscious elements constituting the empirical subject. This is due to a transcendental non-discrimination (lack of discrimination, or ignorance of the real nature of the real) between reals of separate nature which makes all empirical experience, cognitive, conative and affective, transcendentally confounded. Because of this non-discrimination, pure consciousness feels (knows) itself as identical with the principle of presentation, although it is *not* really so. Consciousness falsely *identifies itself* with the principle of presentation.

(*ii*) *Buddhi*

The very basic feature of *empirical* consciousness is that it can have presentations, that things and objects can be presented to it. Consciousness at this level is always consciousness of objects which are presented to it. Objects can be presented to consciousness only through mental states. The capacity to have states is thus the fundamental feature of empirical consciousness and, because of this capacity, empirical consciousness is intentional, is capable of referring to objects. This capacity is due to a non-conscious ontological element in the very structure of the empirical subject, called the *buddhi*. This ontological element is material in nature, being the mirror on which objects, on the one hand, and pure consciousness, on the other, are *reflected*. But pure consciousness and the objects do not get reflected in the *buddhi* in the same way. Pure consciousness *identifies* itself with the *buddhi*, but objects are *represented* in *buddhi* by images or ideas. Knowledge of objects is not possible unless consciousness *and* the object are somehow related. This relation is ontologically possible because of the false identification of pure consciousness with the *buddhi*. Hence the empirical subject *knows* consciousness only as *reflected* in the *buddhi*, this reflection being a metaphorical way of saying that pure consciousness has *falsely* identified itself with the *buddhi*.

(*iii*) *Ego*

The ego is the ontological reality producing the I-sense. This I-sense cannot be produced by the *buddhi* which is the principle of unrelated representations of objects. Even though ontologically all these representations belong to the *buddhi* as their material cause, still this ontological relation of belonging to the the same substance cannot produce the I-sense which unites and organises all representations and their traces. This ego, according to Sāṅkhya, is a material substance evolved from the *buddhi* and is ontologically dependent upon it. Yet because the *buddhi* is illumined by borrowed light of the self, the ego, evolving from it, also enjoys this borrowed consciousness. The ego, which is ontologically material, is nonetheless experienced (wrongly) as the centre of consciousness. If there were no representations there could be no unity of them.

(i) The ego as the principle of ownership: The principle of presentation, the *buddhi*, is a substance—the images or ideas of the objects are modifications of this substance. Yet the *buddhi* is not the epistemic owner of its own modifications. The ego is the epistemic owner of all representations and their unconscious traces. I have already explained that the ego does not own different types of mental states in the same way.

(ii) The ego as the usurper: The empirical subject as the composite structure of the three non-conscious factors of consciousness is dominated by the ego. This domination has to do with the relation of the ego with pure consciousness present in empirical consciousness. Pure consciousness in its turn cannot be ascribed to something else or owned by someone else because it is the *ultimate owner*. So phrases like 'my consciousness' must be misleading, for consciousness is the *basis* of the 'I-consciousness' and this consciousness cannot be mine. The ego is ontologically dependent upon and derived from the principle of presentation; it is *not* consciousness, but a mode of the material principle—the *buddhi*. Once the ego emerges, it *masquerades* as the owner of all conscious states and acts, *usurps* all functions of *pure consciousness* as the real basis of all conscious phenomena. It is the ego which deludes pure transcendental consciousness present in empirical consciousness and makes it *wrongly* think and feel that consciousness is the doer, knower, enjoyer etc. But this ego is ontologically derivative, because it is dependent upon the *buddhi*. If there were no mental states, either of cognition, or of conation, or of affection, there would be nothing which the ego could own; but as the ego is the principle of ownership, of appropriation, it is logically and ontologically dependent upon the *buddhi* which produces the mental states which are to be owned. This ownership, again, introduces a stable and enduring unity among different mental states. Mental states are unified as states owned by *the same person*, as states of the same person; with the ego is born the *person*. But if the ego is regarded as the *owner* of mental states, this *ownership* must be of a very special type. This ownership is not anything like legal ownership; for example, I do not own my mental states, or my body, in the same way as I own my horse. To say 'I *have* knowledge' is to say 'I know', a feeling is *mine* if and only if I *feel* it, and so on. 'My' here is not a derivative of 'I'—it is *another way* of saying the same thing.

(iii) The ego is the principle of unification, and, as the principle of unification, it is also the principle of restriction and limitation. The ego delimits empirical consciousness and differentiates one empirical subject from another.

(iv) Paradoxically, the ego endows not merely the empirical subject with independence, making it the doer of its own deeds and the enjoyer of its own feelings, but endows the object, too, with the same degree of independence. This is because the ego, while turning the empirical consciousness into the subject of knowledge, makes the subject the owner of its own knowledge. Thus the distinction is made between an act of knowing which the subject performs and owns, the act which is subjective, and the object of knowledge which the subject cannot own, or in any way modify by an act of knowing, i.e., an object which is totally independent of the *empirical subject*, not merely of its *act of knowing*. Thus the ego delimits the empirical consciousness as the knowing subject by the independent object.

The world is experientially the correlative of the ego and if the world vanishes, so does the ego. The world thwarting the senses gives stability to the ego. A person standing on a precipice and looking down when no objects thwart his vision, has a sickening feeling of being supportless. In the *tāntric* text, *Vijñānabhairavam*, a method of dissolving and transcending the ego is recommended; it consists simply in experiencing that nothing is solid, neither the body, nor the ground on which I stand; nor are the objects I see and touch—they do not support *me*. This experiential feeling of being totally unsupported *at once* dissolves the ego, and the individual is liberated.

(v) The ego, again, becomes the *centre* of all the states and the acts of the subject. If becomes the point of view in knowing—the only point of view that a person can have i.e., that personal point of view of all interests, motives etc., which remain tied to the ego. Whenever a person acts, the *prime consideration* remains the furthering of his *own* interests. The entire mental life of a person *revolves* round the ego. He always thinks not merely of himself, but also *in* his own way, acts not merely to gain personal objectives but also forms his character by thus acting, and reveals the systematization or ordering of his interests. This systematization is the work of the ego.

The ego, therefore, has the following functions—it (i) is the source of 'I-consciousness'; (ii) is the owner of all the mental states and the acts of the individual; (iii) organizes, systematizes, *all the contents* of the *buddhi* into a unity; (iv) restricts the person and separates him from other persons and the world of objects, (v) is the centre around which all thoughts, actions revolve; (vi) usurps all functions of pure consciousness as the foundation of the person; (vii) is the principle of identity and, in ordinary mortals, identifies itself with the body-mind complex. This is why everyone *feels* himself to be the body-mind complex.

(*iv*) *Manas*

The fourth element in the empirical subject is that which is responsible for deliberation. Sometimes there is conscious vacillation as in a state of doubt which is resolved only by a deliberate act. This activity is different from mere presentation; there cannot be any doubt unless conflicting descriptions of the same object are simultaneously presented to consciousness. The activity of resolving the doubt by deliberation is due to an ontological element called *manas*. The *manas* is derived from the ego and is dependent, logically and ontologically, upon it. For conflicting descriptions of the same object can give rise to a state of doubt only if the descriptions are presented simultaneously to the same object. Without personal identity there can be no conflict among presentations. Thus if Mr Z knows something as B, and if Mr Y knows that something as not-B, there is no state of doubt even though B and not-B are contradictory. The law of contradiction as a law of thought cannot be stated simply as: A cannot be thought to be B and not-B at the same time. It has to be stated as: A cannot be thought to be both B and not-B at the same time by the same person. And because without the ego there cannot be any person, doubt and its resolution are dependent upon its function, and so also is the *manas*. Thus *manas*, being ontologically dependent on the ego, is different in different persons. As the principle of doubt and supposition, of determination and ascertainment, it is the determining factor of logical and philosophical theories. Thus there is always the possibility that philosophical theories will be different for different types of persons, and even for different persons. This is true not merely of philosophical theories, but of all theories, theorizing being an activity of the *manas*. In the case of empirical theories, too, there is always the possibility of different theories explaining the same set of facts. Their difference is not, for this reason, merely linguistic; for, the question whether they all explain the same facts equally satisfactorily or not, can be raised and answered only if the attitude, purpose and interest of the persons involved are taken into consideration.

(*v*) *Sense-organs*

The theories of sense-organs evolved in India are completely different from those evolved in the West. Western philosophy, by and large, holds the sense-organs as identical with different parts of the body—the eyes, i.e. eye-balls, for example, are regarded as the sense-organs of vision. But in Indian philosophy sense-organs are never identified with their bodily locations. They are conceived as imperceptible powers. With the exception of the materialists, other schools are unanimously of this view.

According to Sāṅkhya, the organs are eleven in number—five sense-organs, five motor-organs and the *manas*. These organs exist and operate as the manifested forms of the ego (ahaṅkāra) which has the three elements of *sattva*, *rajas* and *tamas*. The organs are manifestations of the *sattva* element in the *ahaṅkāra*. This means that the ego in order to manifest itself needs to evolve these organs. Thus these organs are ontologically independent of the gross physical body and therefore cannot be identified with anything in this body. It is true that no other form of the real emerges from these organs so that these organs are, in that sense, final evolutes. The five *tanmātras* or subtle sensory qualities like colour, taste smell, sound and touch, give rise to the five gross elements of fire, water, earth, *ākāśa*, air, which ordinarily are regarded as substances possessing those qualities. But according to Sāṅkhya, the so called sensory qualities of colour, touch etc., are ontologically prior to the so-called substances. Thus it is the ego which gets transformed into the organs as also into the *tanmātras* in order to realize its potentialities.

Of these eleven organs five are external sense-organs, the *manas* is the internal sense organ and the rest are motor organs. These motor organs again are five in number—*vāk* (the motor organ of speech) hands, (the motor organ for doing things) legs (the motor organ for movement), the motor organ of excretion and the genitals. As all these organs are ontologically independent of the gross physical body, they cannot be identified with the parts of the body their locations. These organs belong to what is known as the subtle body which is constituted by the *buddhi*, the *ahaṅkāra* and these eleven organs and the five *tanmātras*. This subtle body survives the death of the physical body and so the organs cannot be identified with anything in the physical body.

These eleven organs are called 'indriyas' for they are the means of inferring the self which is called 'Indra'. The inner-sense (*antaḥkaraṇa*) consists of three elements e.g., *buddhi*, the *ahaṅkāra* and the *manas*. Thus the inner-sense is that which has representations belonging to the person and is capable of thinking alternatives and resolving doubt.

The reason for regarding the motor organs as *organs* found in the *Sāṅkhya* is that there cannot be any instrument without an agent, and in the case of all the organs, the agent is the self. Thus all these organs serve as marks for the presence of the self. If anything speaks we infer there is a speaker (the self) just as from the fact that something perceives we infer that there is a perceiver, a knower, i.e., the self. Thus the motor organs are organs, instruments, justifying the inference of an agent who uses these instruments to achieve his end.

(*a*) *External sense organs.* According to *Sāṅkhya*, sense organs produce perceptual knowledge only by reaching out and grasping objects. The sense organ of vision, for example, goes out to grasp the object. This theory of vision is advocated by all schools of Indian philosophy, except Cārvāka and Buddhism. It is based upon our direct experience of objects *out there*. The scientific theories which hold that we see objects when light rays are reflected from them on the retina cannot explain the visual perception, illusory or veridical, of objects out there. As the sense-organs are conceived in Indian philosophy as powers located in the appropriate parts of the body, there is no difficulty in holding that the sense-organs reach out to objects, instead of stimuli from objects reaching the sensory nerves. According to Vācaspati Miśra, the sense organs copy the objects vaguely and indefinitely. This apprehension is called *ālocana* or *nirvikalpaka pratyakṣa*. The sense organs themselves can copy objects, i.e., apprehend them because all the sense organs are evolutes of the *Śattvika ahaṅkara* and *sattva guṇa* has the power of manifestation.

The sense organs then present the copies of the objects which they receive to the inner sense. Thus the external sense organs have two functions—to copy objects and to present them to the internal sense.

(*b*) *Function of the Inner Sense.* According *Sāṅkhya*, the inner sense is really three-fold, being constituted by the *manas*, the *ahaṅkāra* and the *buddhi*. According Vācaspati Miśra, when external senses present the objects apprehended vaguely and indefinitely to the inner sense, the *manas* 'supervenes on this material, analyses it, explicates what is implied, distinguishes between substance and attributes... and makes clear what was before vague.'[19] According to Vācaspati, therefore, the *manas* explicates what is indeterminate; 'it does not add to the given material.' This function of the *manas* is called *saṅkalpa*.

The *manas* is an organ of both cognition and action. Gauḍapāda takes *saṅkalpa* of *manas* in the sense of intending the functioning of both sets of organs; 'this intention is *saṅkalpa* and thus mind (*manas*) has a function common to both sets of organs.

We have already explained the functions of the *buddhi* and the *ahaṅkara* in detail. The distinctive functions of the three factors of the inner sense are to have determinate presentation (the *buddhi*), to have I-sense or self-consciousness (*ahaṅkāra*) and to explicate (*manas*). 'The common function is the *circulation of the five forms* of vital air.... They exist when the internal organs exist, and when those cease to be, they also cease to be'. There is, however, a difference between Gauḍapāda and Vācaspati Miśra on this point. While according to Gauḍapāda the circulation of the vital airs is the function of all the thirteen organs, internal and external, taken collectively, Vācaspati holds that this is the function of the internal organs only.

Thus in the production of a perception the external sense organ and the three factors of the inner sense must co-operte. The problem now is whether they all act simultaneously or successively. The *Sāṅkhya* theory is that in some cases of external perception all these factors function simultaneously and in other cases successively. 'An example of simultaneous functioning is the recognition of a tiger or cobra revealed by a flash of lightning and the instantaneous flight consequent thereon. The stages of the intermediate perception, the explication thereof, the reference of it to the self and the determination to act in this or that way' are instantaneous. 'An instance of successive functioning would be the doubt followed by a recognition of that as a human being, the reference of that to the self, and determination to meet and talk to the man'. Where cognition is non-perceptual like inferring or remembering, the internal organs operate without the aid of the external organs. But their functioning necessarily presupposes a prior perceptual cognition.

As the inner sense involves three different factors, it is necessary to postulate a directive principle organizing and controlling them for their harmonious cooperation to produce one single result. This is necessary because these three different factors do not by themselves co-operate in this way. It is the empirical subject and his purpose which alone makes the *buddhi*, the *anaṅkāra* and the *manas* function harmoniously.

The *manas* and also the sensory and motor organs evolve out of the ego. It is the ego which evolves itself through an inner urge into the sense-organs. Hence the sense-organs are ontologically the creations of the ego. Parallel with this creation of the *manas* and the sense-organs, the ego also evolves out of itself the sensory qualities of sound, touch, colour, taste and smell. These sensory qualities are the ontological material cause of the five gross elements *akāśa* (ether?) air, fire, water and earth. This shows that the pure sensory qualities demand to be embodied in gross matter and hence they evolve them. The body is composed of the gross five elements, that is why it is called the gross body. It comes into existence at the time of conception and goes out of existence at the time of death. Therefore this body is known as changing and impermanent. But the complex consisting of the *buddhi*, the ego, the *manas* and ten sense-organs constitute, according to Sāṅkhya, the subtle body of the individual. Thus all the psychological states, drives and emotions of Western philosophy belong to the subtle body. The reason for this is that the self which is pure consciousness can have no contents in it and hence all contents of consciousness are contents of the material substance, the *buddhi*, organized by the material ego. This body transmigrates and carries all the traits of the character of the individual. The ego ensures the identity of the person through deaths and births. Only in rare cases can a person have memories of his own past lives but generally one does not have this memory. In the next section we shall explain in detail the concepts of birth, death and reincarnation.

F. BIRTH, DEATH, REINCARNATION

Indian philosophy in general, except the materialist Cārvāka, does not believe in the first birth. An individual has been existing from beginningless time and is caught in the cycle of births and deaths. Thus every birth is a rebirth.

Although this succession of births and deaths of an individual requires the identity of the individual across different births, this is guaranteed by the identity of the subtle psychical body. The idea of rebirth is necessary as much causally as ethically. It is only because of the presence of unfulfilled desires that one is born again, has a body appropriate for realising the dominant desires, and also the physical and social environment. A person having a pronounced violent temper and other base propensities may be born as an animal in which state he can best fulfil his latent propensities. Yet in this animal existence the individual merely works off his propensities without accumulating any more evil *karma*. It is only a human being who can accumulate new *karma* by performing good or bad actions, because only a man bears moral responsibilities for his actions. Thus when an animal dies, his animal propensities are thoroughly exhausted and he may be born a man again. The ethical principle involved here is that all the evil deeds that a person can perform in his life-time cannot condemn him to *eternal* punishment in hell. His punishment will be commensurate to the sum-total of his evil deeds and after this punishment the person necessarily gets another chance of being moral by being born again as a man. Thus the particular body that a person has is not accidentally related to his moral nature. As the destiny of all creatures is to attain fulfilment, all creatures must be eventually liberated.

According to Indian philosophy in general, a person lives a life only to achieve what is to be achieved in this life and, after he has done that the term of his life comes to its end. Death is the dissolution of the physical body but not of the subtle body which carries the propensities, the desires, the emotions and the thoughts of the individual. The identity of the individual is constituted by the subtle body which contains the ego, the I-sense, of the individual.

Boredom does not result from satisfying the same sort of bodily desires by the same sort of objects. One generally does not get bored of eating, though not necessarily the same kind of food, three or more times a day to satisfy one's hunger; or of quenching one's thirst many times a day all through one's life. So also with other bodily desires. When Williams talks of 'such a thing as justified but necessary boredom', he gives examples of non-bodily, intellectual, attachment 'to the radical cause' the boredom is by 'rhetoric', or 'sentry-duty'.[20] But generally one does not get bored of bodily desires.

Now when a person lives he has a mass of desires, not perhaps all well-formed, or even consistent—in some situations one talks of a 'conflict of desires'. So also a person has an enormous mass of beliefs, some rational, many irrational, some conscious, many unconscious; some even inconsistent—consciously or unconsciously. Still, in so far as the person is *one* person, there must be a system, even though a very loose one, of his desires and his beliefs. His craving for the satisfaction of bodily desires remains even when he dies. This is the reason or cause of his being born again with a body in an environment which will best satisfy his *dominant* desires. If a person has committed suicide, his assumption of a new body is not only delayed but comes after much suffering and turmoil in the subtle body. A disembodied person gets a new body only when he yearns after it with his whole being in the subtle body. But a person who has committed suicide, has deliberately destroyed his body, cannot yearn for a new body with his whole being even though his unsatisfied desires torment him, goad him, to cry out for getting an appropriate body. This is because his consciousness, his decision to destroy his old body, conflicts with his yearning for a new body. This new body he gets only by sincerely repenting his action and the will that prompted that action. This repentance does not totally erase the stains his suicidal act has left on his subtle body, but it can weaken their force. Unless this weakening of the will to destroy his old body is brought about through repentance, he cannot get his new body. Thus suicide, or even *a desire to commit suicide*, is the cause of unbearable pain and suffering in the subtle body and, hence, is regarded as the gravest sin that any one can commit.

Now through the series of births and deaths, a person is led to moral and spiritual perfection through pain and suffering. When one attains a state of desirelessness, one is liberated and transcends the cycle of births and deaths. The state of desirelessness is not again a state of desiring desirelessness; not to desire anything is not to desire something, not even to desire not to desire anything. Thus the main motive of attaining liberation, of getting rid of one's subtle body, one's ego, one's I-sense, is to attain a state which will be eternally free of all suffering. Suffering is directly caused by unfulfilled desires, and desires by ignorance of the nature of the subject desiring and of the object desired. If this ignorance is removed, all desires are rooted out for good. This leads to immortal existence of the pure self.

III. You–Philosophies

Philosophies of the self of this type emphasize that consciousness is always directed to something other than itself. Even in the case of the so-called self-consciousness there is a distinction between the self as the subject and the self as the object. Consciousness is not complete in itself but requires something else for its existence. (i) We may realize this dependence of the notion of *I* on that of *you* if we note how children learn to use 'I'. Many children say 'you are hungry' when they mean 'I am hungry' because they themselves are addressed by others as 'you'.[21] Some children use proper nouns, i.e., names by which others address them, when they should use 'I'. Instead of saying, for example, 'I am hungry', a child something says 'John is hungry'. The awareness of myself as 'I', as an individual is a later development from awareness of myself as '*you*'. (ii) The concept of soliloquy or monologue is parasitic on the concept of dialogue. (iii) So also the subjective act of judgement is merely an internalization of the act of speaking. Thought may even be identified with subvocal speech. Speech or using language is the essence of consciousness, at least of human consciousness. But speaking necessarily involves the existence and presence of a hearer, i.e., another person. Use of demonstratives like 'this', 'that', etc., will be impossible if there were no other persons to address—as Frege pointed out. (iv) So also, as the existentialists argue, the subjective feeling of shame is not possible in the absence of other persons. (v) The moral values like truth, nonstealing etc., will be impossible without the presence of others. (vi) In religion, too, God is regarded as the indwelling spirit controlling everything thought, felt and willed by the individual. The sense of *I* is really due to ignorance. Self-surrender to God is the only way to attain liberation. 'Thy will be done', is the attitude of the devotee. The individual merely reflects the glory of God, the individual self is nothing *without its relation* to God who is addressed as 'Thou'.

Vaiśṇava philosophers distinguish between five different types of devotion to God. (i) Master–servant relation: This relation between a devotee and God is possible only when God is realised as infinite in glory and grandeur. The devotee serves God with no ulterior motive of personal gain or even of pleasing God. It is absurd to imagine that a finite individual can ever please God even by his whole-hearted service. The devotee serves God only because he cannot help it; in service he finds his own fulfilment, the satisfaction of his innermost urge. (ii) Friendship: This relation is possible only when the devotee forgets God's grandeur, and treats Him more or less as his equal. Yet this friendship is much more than between two kindred spirits; this is the relation of the devotee *with his own innermost* being; God is realised as the inalienable partner.[22] (iii) Tenderest feeling to God as that of a mother to her child: The devotee feels as if God is his child, much in the way the Selfish Giant of Oscar Wilde felt towards the divine child or as Mother Mary felt towards the child

Jesus. Mother Mary must have known her child to be Jesus from the fact of immaculate conception, from the visit of three wise men of the East to honour the child, from the divine advice to Joseph to take the child away to Egypt and from many other indications. Thus although the child was the son of God and known to be so, still Mother Mary felt motherly affection for Jesus. Sometimes the roles are reversed, as in Śākta philosophies, where God becomes the mother and the devotee the child. (iv) Love of a wife for her husband: The devotee loves God as a lover loves her beloved. (v) Total merging: This is merging of one's personality with God. This comes as the culmination of self-effacement in the presence of God. This is the state of perfect calmness.

In all these attitudes the devotee finds his true being only in God who is addressed as 'Thou'. There are two conceptions of liberation—self-realization and God-realization. In Sāṅkhya philosophy, for example, the liberated self is the individual self; self-realization means realization of the individual self as separate from the body, mind, etc. Liberation as God-realization is the realization that God alone is real, the individual is essentially dependent on Him. There are systems like Yoga which have conceptions of both self-realization and a type of God-realization, but God-realization is regarded as a means to self-realization which is the *summum bonum*. But devotees, specially Vaiśṇavas, regard desire for self-realization as an impediment to God-realization.

The two conceptions of liberation have different practical consequences. To attain liberation in the sense of self-realization, one has to purge the mind of impurities to make it calm. One who has attained liberation in this sense is at peace with himself and with the world. It is inconceivable that such a person would indulge in violence or start a war. But there are many instances of men who have surrendered themselves to God, of God-intoxicated men, who have started wars on a large scale. Even God has been conceived as incarnating himself in order to destroy sinners. Any one who has surrendered himself to God, has surrendered his reasoning, his sense of morality and his will to God. He will do whatever God asks Him to do, and as God's ways are inscrutable we cannot be sure that a God-man will not start a war at the command of God. Thus while it is unthinkable of a Buddha or a Mahāvīra starting a war and destroying people and even animals, Rāma and Kṛṣṇa are revered for destroying sinners wholesale.

IV. We–Philosophies

We–philosophies emphasize the basic nature of We–consciousness, I–consciousness being an abstraction from it. 'We' the plural of 'I' cannot mean just a plurality of I's, i.e., a plurality of individuals each of whom knows himself as an I. For the concept of a plurality of I's contains a contradiction. Any individual knowing himself as I emphasises his individuality, isolates himself conceptually and experientially from all other individuals; hence a plurality of individuals all knowing themselves as so many I's will be so many different individuals—all isolated from each other. The plurality which is *we* must not be serverally many, but a collection, a group, and isolated I's resist being herded together into even a loose unity. The concept of I is the result of conceptual or existential individuation which must be undermined in the concept of we. I consider other individuals as 'you', 'he', 'they' and so on. But *I* and *you* and *he* or *they* cannot be collected together into *we*.[23] This shows that We-consciousness cannot result from broadening, widening, of I-consciousness to encompass *others*, *you*, *he* or *they*, and also that the we-concept cannot be a logical construction from a plurality of I-concepts; it is not a construction or a summation.

This impossibility of attaining We-consciousness starting from I-consciousness, either by logical construction or by broading of I-consciousness, should make. clear the basic character of We-consciousness which encompasses many individuals who, however, are seen or felt to be on one side. United we stand, divided we fall; and the essential unity is a basic experience. 'We', being grammatically the plural form of the first person pronoun, cannot encompass all individuals, but is essentially opposed to *you* and *them*. The felt unity of *we* is built into the very concept, so much so that 'we' *simpliciter* is only elliptical. This semantical incompleteness of 'we' is different from the systematic ambiguity of 'I'. The ambiguity of 'I' is resolved by knowing who the speaker is, perhaps in an extralinguistic context. But the semantic incompleteness of 'we' cannot be solved by knowing who the speaker is. The complete form of expression has to have the principle of unity built into it—'we Bengalis', 'we Hindus', 'we artists', 'we, men of this earth' (as opposed to beings from some other planets). This shows that we-consciousness is a group-consciousness which also opposes the group to other groups. This incompleteness of '*we*' *contrasts* with the lack of incompleteness of 'I' or 'you'. To say, 'I, the son of Abraham . . .' or 'I, Mr. so and so . . .' is to give additional information just as in 'you, Mr. A'. Here we may distinguish between two types of expectancy. Expectancy arising from incomplete expression is of one type, and expectancy which can be raised about something said is of another type. Thus we do not understand the meaning of 'we' unless it is further explained; but we may ask for further information about the person spoken to when the second person pronoun is used. Use of the third person pronoun 'he' or 'they' almost robs the individual(s) spoken of, of their individuality, turns persons into nameless, amorphous, substances.[24] Hence using this pronoun indicates contempt on the part of the user of the expression who deliberately wants to humiliate the person thus spoken of. Use of the second person pronoun 'you' indicates due recognition of the personality almost on par with the personality of the speaker. Hence 'you and I' can be combined into 'we', while 'he and I' or even 'you and he and I' can never be so combined. There is a corresponding semantic incompleteness of the plural 'you'. The singular 'you' is systematically ambiguous and this ambiguity can be resolved by knowing the person addressed, perhaps in an extra-linguistic context. But the plural 'you' is like 'we' in that it is semantically incomplete and its meaning remains incomplete unless the principle of unity is built into the expression: 'you men', 'you Bengalis', 'you artists' and so on. The third person singular 'he' or plural 'they' can be used only when some person or persons have already been referred to by the use of nouns or other descriptive *expressions*.

We can now see that starting from the we-concept we arrive at the I-concept by a sort of limiting process. We may progressively reach the I-concept thus: 'we three...' 'we two...' and then 'I'. But this I-concept is still fundamentally different from the I-concept of I-philosophies, for this I-concept is essentially a we-concept although vacuously so in the absence of others, but I-concept of I–philosophies is one of *self-containment* and *self-sufficiency*.

The primacy of we-consciousness becomes evident more clearly in the sphere of practical activity as, for example, in team spirit. Even in theoretic consciousness, use of language is essentially to communicate to other speakers of the language. Psychologically, too, a person isolated from all others, as in solitary imprisonment, feels disturbingly lonely, showing the essential reality of man in communality and not in individuality. For the Greeks and the Romans, the individual was a *zoon palitikon* having no reality apart from the *palis*. The importance of the community and even of ancestors is prominent in all primitive cultures. 'The ancestors provide more than a personal and ethnic immortality. The hierarchical ancestral community is the repository of the accumulated knowledge of successive generations, and in this sense it is the memory of the ethnic groups.[25] All members of the ethnic group constitute the meaning of 'we'. Thus even anthropologically the sense of the community is prior to the Cartesian *cogito* or the Leibnizian *monad*.

Self-realization is also different in We–philosophies. One cannot attain individual liberation. Liberation will be either for all or for none. According to *Sir Aurobindo*, no one has so far been liberated because all are not liberated. Gopinath Kaviraj, distinguishes between Yoga and *Akhaṇḍa-Mahāyoga*. Yoga liberates individuals, but *Akhaṇḍa-Mahāyoga* will liberate all. This liberation of all is different from the Catholic conception of a kingdom of heaven. According to Sri Aurobindo, liberation in the sense of individual liberation is the ascent of the individual to the supra-consciousness level. But Sri Aurobindo's Yoga will involve a descent of the supra-consciousness to this world which will then totally transform it into a divine reality. The transformation of matter by the descent of the supra-consciousness is the ultimate aim of Sir Aurobindo's Yoga.

V. Impersonal Philosophies

Impersonal philosophies, unlike You–philosophies and We–philosophies, do not deny but rather affirm that out initial experience of ourselves is of personal selves. Yet this initial experience, however basic and direct, is not, for that reason, incorrigible. According to Impersonal philosophies like Advaita Vedānta there are deeper levels of consciousness of which one is not directly aware at the surface level. Ordinary experience of the self as personal is an experience of the surface level of consciousness. According to Advaita Vedānta the core of impersonal, pure, universal consciousness is covered with five exterior sheaths which are material. The outermost sheath is the gross body, the second sheath is the vital, the third sheath is the mental, the fourth is of thoughts, and the fifth is of enjoyment. Within this fifth sheath the pure impersonal consciousness which is universal remains hidden; to reach this inner reality one has to make an inward journey and experientially dissociate oneself from one's body, life, mind, thoughts and enjoyment. This process of psychological distancing may be gradual or may be achieved at one stroke.

The reason why this universal pure consciousness lies hidden from view at the surface level is that *māyā* which ontologically is the stuff of the world epistemically blinds us. Really it is more than mere blindness for *māyā* has two functions that of concealment of the real and that of the projection of the unreal. This dual function of *māyā* is often explained by an analysis of ordinary illusion. When we mistake a piece of rope for a snake, our ignorance of the piece of rope conceals it from our vision and projects the snake out there. When we see the real piece of rope we realize not merely that there is no snake now but also that there was never any, not even when we perceived it; we also realize not merely that there is no perception of snake now, but also we could never have perceived it. Thus knowledge cancels illusion in the sense that the object of an illusory perception as well as the illusory perception is cancelled with retrospective effect. So also a person who has realized his innermost impersonal consciousness realizes that he was never a finite, restricted being, not even when he had a direct experience of it. In Indian philosophies liberation is either identified with, or leads to, the ceassion of all pain and suffering for all time to come. In Nyāya–Vaiśeṣika philosophy it is argued that pain that we have already experienced cannot be undone, so what liberation achieves is the avoidance of all *future* pain. But according to Advaita Vedānta the pain that we experience now, or that we experienced in the past, being an illusory appearance will be cancelled by realization with retrospective effect. We shall realize not merely that we shall have no pain in the future but also that we never had any in the past. The liberated person while living in this body experiences the world in time, although he 'does not consider it as real' '*kaumāṇi bhujyamānāni bādlhitatvāt paramarthato na paśyati, Vedantasāra*, 219. Liberation according to Advaita Vedānta, is the realisation of total identity with impersonal consciousness. This universal impersonal consciousness is eternally there without any content in it, transcending all relations; to identify oneself with it is to see that one could never have existed at all as a separate individual.

A person who attains liberation while living in this body does not experience himself as an embodied being. He lives mechanically very much as the potter's wheel continues to move with its own momentum even when the potter is no longer moving it. The world is not experienced as real, for, as we have already explained, the body and the world are correlatives in experience. The world is seen as transparent covering, not concealing, the inner reality of the universe which is the same as the inner reality of the self. The liberated person sees the world as unsubstantial. He does not see the essences (*Wesensschau*) of particular objects but sees them as if they were reflections in a mirror. The liberated person has no naturalistic attitudes. Every thing predicated of existence *may be* said to have been 'bracketed'. Yet this seeing of the world-show is not like phenomenological reduction of Husserl because there is no eidetic reduction, no seeing of essences. Moreover, Husserl scholars are usually agreed that the phenomenological reduction is merely methodological and does not involve a real transformation of the person. Yet the Indian point of view is completely different. Unless there is a total transformation of personality one cannot realize or directly experience the world without existence. Indian philosophers point out that it is not possible for anyone who is deeply attached to worldly objects—his body, good food, money, fame and so on—to even methodologically bracket out objects. There will be no genuine phenomenological reduction, but only a mock reduction. Husserl himself at one stage envisaged phenomenological reduction *as existential conversion*.[26]

Thus the experience of the liberated soul and Husserl's phenomenological reduction differ fundamentally as the world the liberated soul sees consists of particular objects although experienced as non-existing. 'A man', says Vedāntasāra, 219, 'who is conscious that a magical performance is being given does not consider it real even though he sees it.'

VI. Theories of Consciousness

In Indian philosophy these are four types of theories of consciousness. These theories, however, do not concern themselves with the same level of consciousness. Consciousness has been conceived (i) as purely intentional; (ii) as witness; (iii) as the foundation of my embodied existence or of the whole world; (iv) as reflection.

(i) Consciousness as intentional

Empirical consciousness is purely intentional in the sense that consciousness is constitutively tied up with objects, internal or external. Consciousness is always consciousness *of* something; there cannot be any consciousness pure and simple. This means that consciousness is to be identified with cognition or thought. For it is not immediately clear that our feelings and emotions have objects, refer to objects as cognitions do. Emotions are, of course, directed towards some objects; love, for example, must be *for* some object. Still the objects of emotions are really objects of thought involved, causally or otherwise, in emotions.

(ii) Consciousness as witness

The concept of witenessing consciousness is contrasted with the concept of the enjoyer or suffer, that is, of the consciousness involved in action and its consequences. The outward-looking consciousness is involved in actions which it performs because of desires and aversions, and hence enjoys or suffers pleasure or pain. The witnessing consciousness is a disinterested on-looker, not a performer of actions, and hence not an enjoyer or suffer. Witnessing consciousness knows, although without modes of the inner sense, all internal as well as external objects directly. The external objects are known either *as* already known, or *as* unknown. This concept of knowing an external object *as* unknown is peculiar to Advaita Vedānta. The concept is necessary for understanding that knowing an object for the first time means *knowing a previously unknown* object. This *knowing* is really *recognizing* i.e., knowing what was already known, although *as* unknown. There cannot be any emotional involvement in objects *known thus*; this kind of knowledge is *bare* knowledge— knowledge of witnessing consciousness. Although an individual is, most of the time, *involved in* actions still the underlying witnessing consciousness reveals all that the individual feels, does, thinks, all the time. That is, witnessing consciousness is all-seeing and always. This is why there can be no unconscious states, desires etc., in the individual of which he is unaware. This inner consciousness is aware of everything that goes on within an individual.

This theory has an important consequence. Ordinarily, an individual passes through three different types of states of consciousness—waking, dream and deep, dreamless sleep. Witnessing consciousness witnesses not merely what the individual does in his waking state, but also the dream state and also the dreamless sleep. The consciousness that is aware of the 'blank' of dreamless sleep, cannot be ordinary experience of objects. Witnessing consciousness, which cannot go to sleep, is there to 'know' the state of sleep.

(*iii*) *Consciousness as the foundation*

This theory is propounded in those philosophies which do not regard individual selves and/or the entire world as we know them as self-supporting. These theories may take the form of an extreme monism according to which all plurality whether of the finite selves or of the objects of the universe is an unreal appearance of the one reality. The relation between appearance and reality, therefore, receives a close attention and scrutiny. The entire world, according to Advaita Vedānta, is illusory, and like all illusory objects need to be supported by something real. It is of the view that illusory objects can masquerade as real only by borrowed reality. So the world–show has to be supported by an underlying reality.

The difference between Vijñānavāda school of Buddhism and Advaita Vedānta is fundamental on this point. According to Vijñānavada the world is a hallucination, and hence there is no underlying reality to support it. According to Advaita Vedānta, the world is not a pure hallucination, for it has reality itself for its basis. A creation of mind cannot *appear to be real*, cannot be an object of belief, unless it derives its apparent reality from an underlying reality. Thus according to Advaita Vedānta objects of the so-called hallucination derive their reality from the subject, from consciousness which experience, them. Otherwise an unreality, which is really an impossibility, cannot even appear to be real.

(*iv*) *Consciousness as reflection*

The empirical subject is introspectively known to be finite. The finitude of the subject is not so much its exposure to pain and suffering as its essential limitations—its very much limited powers of cognitions, affection and conation. The finite individual is a particular person having a body, and is, consequently, limited by things and persons. The finite person is not all-comprehensive; he is not everything that is there; he is not the universe. He is not omnipotent, omniscient or omnipresent. This limitation is due primarily to the ego which circumscribes consciousness, and ties the mental states into a knot as it were; the body is only the external manifestation of the ego. So long as the ego remains, finitude, in the sense of limitations of personality, remains. Liberation is liberation from the ego and its limitations. The individual is liberated by transcending the ego. Thus, liberation is not primarily a permanent relief from all types of suffering; it is not even the realization of an abstract undifferentiated consciousness, but rather transcendence beyond the ego and its restrictions. By cutting the knot of the ego, consciousness ceases to be personal, it is spread out infinitely, and becomes identical with the world which is a content of the transcendental consciousness—arising from it and again withdrawing into it. So long as consciousness is egocentric, all thoughts, feelings and actions are directed towards furthering the interests of the ego. But when consciousness is universe-centric, thoughts and actions no longer serve the interests of a single individual, they become disinterested. As there can be no sense of want there is no longer any feeling of pleasure or pain; there is only a sense of fullness, unvarying and undying. There is nothing outside this transcendental consciousness, there is nothing to be attained. The actions and thoughts of a man who has attained to this state are unmotivated actions—free from every restriction, even those of logic. Therefore, there is no reason why thoughts and actions should be there; they are there simply because the free transcendental consciousness freely wills them. The problem which arises here is: if this transcendental consciousness be the only reality, how then do objects, the world and individuals, arise? In order to solve this problem we have to explain the nature of transcendental consciousness and the nature of creation.

Transcendental consciousness is self-consciousness; the process of being self-consciousness is reflection. This power of reflection is the power of the transcendental consciousness and is identical with it. This reflective power is also the same as its freedom. We should note here the difference of this theory from the Advaita Vedānta theory. According to Advaita Vedānta, the ultimate reality is the self-shining consciousness which is different from the knower and the known. This consciousness is not *of* anything, for *of* involves a relation, and this consciousness transcends all relations. Thus the transcendental consciousness, according to Advaita Vedānta, is pure knowledge without any reference to any knower and to anything known. So although this consciousness is self-shining, it is not self-consciousness, i.e., consciousness *of* itself; it is not reflective consciousness and there is no power of reflection in the transcendental consciousness. The transcendental consciousness of Advaita Vedānta is consciousness pure and simple; it simply *is*, it is bare existence, but not consciousness in the real sense. For consciousness and reflection are one and the same.

Now let us see how the world can arise from the transcendental consciousness which is reflective consciousness. Through reflection, consciousness becomes conscious of itself; reflecting is not creating. So the world cannot be said to be created. By reflection that which is implicit in consciousness is made explicit; the so-called creation of the world can be nothing but the process of its manifestation, the process of being made explicit. The whole world is in consciousness; the universe is transcendental consciousness; sometimes it is manifest, sometimes not. Transcendental consciousness is implicit when the power of reflection remains dormant or is dispositional; at this stage there is no world, no creation. Such an inactive, i.e., unreflective, state of transcendental consciousness has to be postulated only if we hold that the universe as a whole can cease to be. If the cessation of the universe is not insisted upon, then there is no need to postulate the inactive state of the transcendental consciousness.

The act of reflecting is the act of making explicit what is already there in consciousness, and this is the so-called act of creating. For, the act of making explicit by reflection is to make what is made explicit stand before consciousness as if it were different from, or other than, the reflecting consciousness. The object is not that which stands over against the subject (*Gegenstand*) but 'that which stands before the subject' as if it were different from it. Reflection is the act of creating an *appearance of duality* in the subject, the duality of the subject which reflects and the object which is reflected upon. But in self-consciousness, the self which is conscious and the self of which it is conscious are not really opposites, the object-self is not really an other of the subject self, nor is it felt to be so. To reflect is to hold before consciousness what is in consciousness. So, self-consciousness is altogether different in nature from ordinary, objective consciousness wherein the subject is confronted by an object which is its contradictory, so much so that in ordinary knowledge of objects there *seems* to be a dialectical unity of opposites. In reflective awareness, there is no such felt opposition between the reflecting subject and the subject reflected upon. The world of objects stands before the transcendental subject just as in reflection the subject stands before itself. This explains why without the act of reflecting the world collapses and vanishes into the inactive transcendental consciousness.

We can now see the fundamental difference between this theory and that advocated by Advaita Vedānta. Śaṅkara starts with the opposition of the subject and the object, so much so that their apparent unity becomes an insoluble mystery to him. The realization of this mysterious element in all experience is, for him, the beginning of philosophical thinking. His assumption that the subject and the object are contradictories leads him to postulate *māyā* in order to explain this contradiction, although his explanation amounts merely to an affirmation that the manifestation of the world is essentially an insoluble mystery. Kāśmīr Śaivism, the theory we are trying to explain here, does not start with the assumption that the subject and the object are contradictory in nature. This assumption seems plausible only if we take ordinary objective knowledge as the model of all knowledge, but there is no reason to do this. If we take our stand on reflective self-awareness instead of on objective knowledge, then there is no need to assume that the subject and the object are contradictories, and there is no need for us to acquiesce in a dualism even in a mitigated form. There is nothing but reflective awareness; there is no need to postulate even *māyā* in order to explain the appearance of the world.

(*v*) *Concluding remarks*

It is now necessary to explain the different senses in which consciousness is intentional and is the foundation of the universe. According to Nyāya consciousness is intentional, and there are no levels of consciousness. According to Sāṅkhya and Advaita Vedānta, consciousness is intentional only as empirical consciousness, i.e., consciousness somehow identified with the *antaḥkaraṇa*. But behind empirical consciousness, there is foundational consciousness which is not intentional at all. There is a fundamental difference between what Advaita Vedānta takes to be foundational consciousness and what Kāśmīr Śaivism takes it to be. According to Advaita-Vedānta, pure consciousness is the foundation of the world of which I am a part in the sense in which the rope is foundation of the illusory snake; that is, consciousness as reality is the foundation of the world-appearance. But, according to Kāśmīr Śaivism, pure consciousness is the foundation of the world as the ocean is the foundation of the waves. The world originates in consciousness, endures in it and gets withdrawn into it. The world never gets out of the ambit of consciousness even when it appears as 'out there'. As the metaphor of the ocean and waves on it emphasises, the world is the content of pure consciousness. This is a peculiarity which distinguishes Kāśmīr Śaivism from Advaita Vedānta and Sāṅkhya according to which only empirical consciousness has contents which are really modes of the material *antaḥakaraṇa*. The theory that pure consciousness has contents is a necessary conscequence of the concept of reflective consciousness in Kāśmīr Śaivism; for reflection or 'looking within' will be otiose if there is nothing in consciousness to see. Reflecting on a pure contentless consciousness cannot achieve anything. Pure consciousness is self-shining but not reflective, according to Advaita Vedānta philosophers. The world is not related in any way to consciousness, let alone being contained in it. So in realising Brahman one has necessarily to cross a void, for there is no continuous passage from illusion to reality, from the finite to the infinite. The two realms are ontologically and experientially separated by an unbridgeable gulf.

I shall conclude by pointing out that on Advaita Vedānta and Kāśmīr Śaivism there is no necessary connection between self-realization and inwardness. Although in all systems inwardization is recommended as a way of reaching the innermost being of man, yet both in Advaita Vedānta and Kāśmīr Śaivism this realization is not the mere realisation of myself but also the realization of the foundation of the universe. Thus even in the inward journey, the final goal is the realisation of wideness, of infinite expanse. As 'all is Brahman' it is not necessary to realise it only in the innermost depth of the individual. One may as well travel outwards to experientially identify oneself with the uiverse and then to transcend it. Even on one's journey inwards, one gradually rises above this world and passes through other higher worlds corresponding to concentrated emotional states. There is a hierarchy of worlds corresponding to the levels of experience. The mundane world corresponds to waking experience at the surface level, and at the deeper levels of experience of subjectivity there is a corresponding of a refined world of objects.

This process of outward expansion is stated by one mystic thus: 'At the beginning I began to expand my ego. Then gradually I spread my I-sense all over the world, and directly experienced that I was the world. With this expansion of the ego there was also an ascent through different subtle worlds, as if doors after doors were opened. Ultimately rising beyond all the worlds, I found myself in a realm of light, and I spread myself all over. By expanding myself infinitely in this infinite light, I attained the final goal'[27] (which is transcending the ego and becoming one with the impersonal infinite consciousness.)

NOTES AND REFERENCES

1. Sydney Shoemaker, *Self-Knowledge and Self-Identity*, Calcutta Allied Publishers, Calcutta, 1971.
2. William James, *The Principles of Psychology*, Vol. II New York, Henry Holt & Company, 1983, pp. 121–122.
3. Robert Nozick, *Philosophical Explanation*, Oxford, 1981, pp. 29ff.
4. Derek Parfit, *Reasons and Persons*, Oxford, 1985, pp. 200ff.
5. 'We become something else, without necessarily having understood what we were before '*The Day of the Scorption*, Pual Scott, Panther. London, Granada Publishing, 1984; p. 173.
6. Samuel L. Clemens, *The Prince and the Pauper*, London, Masterpiece Library, Magman Books, 1968, pp. 16–18.
7. William James, *The Varieties of Religious Experience*, New York, Longman, Green and Co., 1929, pp. 110ff.
8. *Sri Sri Ramakrishna-līlā-prasanga* (in Bengali), Swami Saradananda, Vol. 2, Calcutta, Udbodhan, Bengali Year, 1356, pp. 303ff.
9. 'Thinking of objects leads to attachment to them . . .' *Gita*, 2, 62
10. Robert Nozick, *Philosophical Explanations*, Oxford, 1981, pp. 87ff.
11. *A Treatise of Human Nature*, ed. Selby-Bigge, BK1, pt. 4, Sec. 6.
12. *The Philosophy of the Body*, ed. S. F. Spicker, Chicago, Quadrangle Books, 1970, p. 3.
13. This solves the so-called 'paradox' of 'the bonds which unite me to my body', of pure being and pure having; in 'The Phenomenology of the body' by Alphonse de Waelhens, in *Readings in Existential Phenomenology*, ed. N. Lawrence and D. O'Connor, New Jersey, Prentice Hall, 1967, p. 151.
14. D. M. Datta, 'Philosophy of the body' in *Philosophical Perspectives*, Bharati Bhawan, Patna, 1972, p. 48.
15. *Ibid.* p. 49
16. *Ibid.* p. 46
17. It is, of course, quite possible to identify oneself with one's hair. Shaving off hair may be worse than death.
18. *The Gospel of Śri Rāmakrishna*, tr. by Swami Nikhilananda, Mylapore, Madras, Sri Ramakrishna Math, June, 1986, pp. 150–151.

19. All quotations in this section are from *The Sāṅkhyakārika of Iśvara Kṛṣṇa*, ed. & tr. by S. S. Suryanarayana Sastri, University of Madras, 1942, pp. 52ff.
20. 'The tedium of immortality' in *Problems of the self*, Cambridge, Cambridge University Press, 1973, pp. 95–96.
21. For a detailed discussion of the role of addressing in communication, see Ram Chandra Gandhi's *Presupposition of Human Communication*, Oxford University Press, Delhi, 1974.
22. 'The Friend: a Persian expression for God' says Dr. Aziz. *Passage to India* by E. M. Forster, Penguin Books, 1985, p. 273.
23. 'Since there cannot be plural *ego et ego*, nor *tu et tu* without change of person addressed, if follows that *ego* and *tu* have no proper plurals. *Ego et tu* is an inclusive from and is naturally a dual (*we*), while ego *et alii* is exclusive of *tu* and requires a separate plural word (*nos*).'

    William J. Entwistle, Aspects of *Language*, 1953, p. 207, quoted in 'Language of Soial Hierarchy' by Dr. K. Kunjunni Raja, in *Rajasudha*, Madras, 1982, p. 244.
24. This is when further information about the person spoken of is not given earlier or later. The situation is completely different if after describing a person, one uses 'he' in sentences which follow simply as a matter of grammatical propriety.
25. Jullian Ries, "Immortality" in *The Encyclopedia of Religion*, Vol. 7, Macmillan, New York, 1987.
26. 'Perhaps it will even become apparent that the total phenomenological attitude and the corresponding epoche is called upon to bring about a complete personal transformation (*Wandlung*) which might be compared to a religious conversion, but which even beyond it has the significance of the greatest existential conversion that is expected of mankind. (*Husserliana* VI. 140). Quoted in The Phenomenological Movement, Vol. 1, H. Spiegelberg, Martinus Nijhoff, The Hague, 1965, p. 136, f.n.1.
27. Swami Satyananda, *Bhagavān Guru O Jagad Guru* (in Bengali), B.S., 1379, pp. 9–10.

Advaita Vedānta on the Problem of Enworlded Subjectivity

R. BALASUBRAMANIAN

1. AN OVERVIEW

Advaita Vedānta may be characterized as 'transcendental phenomenology' and 'metaphysics of experience'. These two characterizations suggest that Advaita is seized with four issues; a basic problem, a method for analysing the problem, a transcendental principle whose evidence is apodictic, and a metaphysical thesis to which it is commited.

Basic Problem

The basic problem is connected with 'the enworlded subjectivity'. There is, on the one hand, the dichotomy between consciousness and the world of objects presented to consciousness; there is, on the other hand, the involvement of consciousness in the objects of the world. How is it possible, Advaita asks, that consciousness which is essentially different from everything else presented to it as its object, gets itself involved in the objects of the world surrounding it, losing its identity in such a way that it is not even reckoned as an entity in its own right along with other objects? This is the problem of 'enworlded subjectivity'. At the commencement of his commentary on the *Brahma-sūtra*, Śaṅkara invites our attention to this problem of 'enworlded subjectivity'. The dichotomy between consciousness and what is presented to consciousness shows that whatever is presented to consciousness is 'transcendent' to it and, is, therefore, an *object* of consciousness, whereas consciousness which reveals whatever is presented to it is the *subject*. The distinction between consciousness and what is presented to consciousness is what Śaṅkara calls the distinction between '*asmad*' and '*yuṣmad*', the subject and the object, the Self and the not-Self. Absorbed as we are in our day-to-day life under the overwhelming influence of an attitude which is naive and natural, we fail to notice the radical distinction between the subject and the object, and confuse and mix up the one with the other. The naive and natural mode of thinking and its resultant activity are due to our ignorance of the Self, the pure consciousness, the transcendental subjectivity. What Husserl calls the life-world, the world of lived experience (Lebenswelt) is spoken of as '*lokavyavahāra*' (the worldly life, the worldly activity, the world horizon) by Śaṅkara. One could see 'the natural attitude' fully manifest in worldly life (*lokavyavahāra*) comprising all kinds of activities—cognitive, affective, and conative. Śaṅkara states the problem as follows:

It is a matter not requiring any proof that the object and the subject which are signified by the terms '*yuṣmad*' and '*asmad*' (i.e. the not-Self and the Self) and which are opposed to each other like light and darkness, cannot be identified. In the same way, their respective attributes also cannot be identified. Hence, it follows that it is wrong to superimpose upon the subject, which is of the nature of consciousness and which is referred to as *asmad*, the object which is spoken of as *yuṣmad*, and the attributes of the object; it is also to superimpose the subject and the attributes of the subject on the object. In spite of this, it is quite natural, owing to wrong knowledge, not to distinguish the two entities (i.e. object and subject) and their respective attributes, . . . and carry on the worldly life by saying 'That I am', and 'That is mine'.[1]

If 'I' stands for the Self, the transcendental subjectivity, how can it be identified with, or be the owner of, anything that is transcendent to it, be it the mind, or the sense organ, or the body, or any external object outside one's mind-sense-body complex? It means that the Self without remaining aloof becomes worldly and is entangled in the affairs of the world giving rise to the problem of 'enworlded subjectivity'.

Method

The method of Advaita consists in a rigorous inquiry into the given world as presented to consciousness. The given world as presented to consciousness comprises not only the outer world of external objects, but also the inner world of the cogitations of the mind. The inner world of the mind comprising the various mental operations as understood by Hume, or the categories of the understanding as emphasized by Kant, is as much transcendent to the Self, the pure consciousness, as the outer world is. The phenomenological *epoche*, calls for an inquiry into both the outer world and the inner world in order to find out their source, the principle which provides meaning and validity to the inner mental world of perceptions and the outer physical world of daily life, the principle which is the presupposition of all experience, of all knowledge at all levels. Consider the following passage from Husserl, which emphasizes the need for inquiry into the given world to find out its source:

We must never lose sight of the fact that this transcendental phenomenology does nothing but interrogate just that world which is, at all times, the real world for us; the only one which is valid for us, which demonstrates its validity to us; the only one which has meaning for us. Phenomenology subjects this world to intentional interrogation regarding its sources of meaning and validity, from which . . . its true existence (as a horizon of experience) also flows.[2]

Śaṅkara amplifies, in the following passage, the notion of enworlded subjectivity by speaking about the Self which, though one only, appears to be many when it is associated with a plurality of mind-sense-body complexes, the epistemological distinction between the knower and the known, the means of knowing and the experience of the empirical world, the state of ignorance when one does not know the Self and the state of knowledge when one knows it:[3]

The Self within is one only; two inward Selfs are not possible. But owing to its limiting adjunct, the one Self is practically treated as if it were two, just as we make a distinction between the ether of the jar and the universal ether. Hence there is scope for scriptural texts which set forth the distinction between the knower and the known, for perception and other means of knowledge—for the experience of the empirical world and for scripture which contains injunctions and prohibitions. So the scriptural text, 'Where there is duality as it were, there one sees another,' declares that the whole practical wolrd exists only in the state of ignorance; while the subsequent text, 'But when the Self only is all this, how should one see another?'[4] declares that the physical world vanishes in the sphere of true knowledge.

Noticing the outer world of activities, secular and scriptural and the inner world of mental operations, Advaita undertakes a regressive inquiry, from the 'outer world' to the 'inner world' and from the 'inner world' to the 'source' of both. However, it is first of all necessary to understand the 'inner world' of cogitations before one tries to understand the outer world of daily life, as it is nearer to the Self and as it is not, therefore, properly distinguished from the Self.

Apodictic Principle

Advaita holds the view that the evidence of consciousness is apodictic. If we say that something is such-and-such and that something as not such-and-such, it is on the basis of the evidence of consciousness. Advaita maintains that whatever is affirmed by consciousness through its intentional performance can never be rejected and that whatever is denied by consciousness through its intentional performance can never be accepted. There is no other principle than consciousness for the acceptance or rejection of anything.[5] Consciousness by its very nature is revelatory. It reveals objects on its own; it also reveals them through the ego or the mind.[6] It is with reference to the latter that Advaita speaks of the intentionality of consciousness. The intentional performance is not ascribed to the pure Self or consciousness, but only to consciousness associated with the ego or 'I' which is transcendent to consciousness. The distinction which Advaita makes between the pure consciousness and the ego-consciousness (mind-consciousness), which is very subtle, but profound and crucial, is comparable to the distinction between the pure or the transcendental ego and the *epoch*-performing ego accepted by Husserl. Keeping this important distinction between the seeing of consciousness (i.e. the seeing of the pure Self) and the seeing of the ego-consciousness (i.e. the empirical self), Śaṅkara speaks of two kinds of seeing or vision (*dṛṣṭi*) and the distinction between them. To quote Śaṅkara:

> Seeing is of two kinds, ordinary and real. Ordinary seeing is a function of the mind as connected with the visual sense; it is an act, and as such it has a beginning and an end. But the seeing that belongs to the Self is like the heat and light of fire; being the very essence of the witness (Self), it has neither beginning nor end . . . The ordinary seeing, however, is related to the objects seen through the eye, and of course has a beginning. . . The eternal seeing of the self is metaphorically spoken of as the witness and although eternally seeing, is spoken of as sometimes seeing and sometimes not seeing . . .[7]

Metaphysical Commitment

Advaita has a metaphysical position which it seeks to justify on the basis of the apodictic evidence of consciousness. It holds that consciousness, the pure

Self, which is the source and support of everything that is presented to it, is the sole reality, which is worthy of seeing. To know this Self, the transcendental subjectivity, is to know everything which derives its meaning from it. It is for this reason that the *Upanaiṣad* speaks of the 'knowledge of all' from 'the knowledge of the one' transcendental reality,[8] which is called by different names—Ātman (the Self), *Brahman* (the Infinite), *Sat* (Being).

2. THE TRANSCENDENTAL CONSCIOUSNESS AND THE TRANSCENDENT EGO

Distinction between the Self and the Ego

Though the Self is different from the ego just as it is different from the senses, the body, and the external objects, it is difficult to distinguish the one from the other. The conceptual as well as the practical difficulty in this regard should not stand in the way of keeping them separate. Conceptually many philosphers stop with the ego and do not proceed inwardly behind the ego. To these philosophers, the ego cogito seems to be the final stage in the analysis of subjectivity. Our day-to-day language also is not practically helpful in distinguishing the Self from the ego, since the word 'I' is used to refer to both of them. For example, when we say, 'I know this', 'I remember that object', 'I recognise this person', 'I desire this', 'I resolve to do that', and so on, the 'I', the first person singular, in all these statements refers to the ego which performs various mental operations. Also, we do say sometimes, 'I know myself', 'I know my mind', 'I am aware of my thinking', 'I know my likes and dislikes', and so on. In these cases the 'I' which knows the mind and its states and its mental operations refers to something which is different from the ego or the mind for the simple reason that they are related as the subject and the object, the knower and the known. The 'I' in these cases stands for the Self, the inward consciousness, which is a witness to the ego and its functioning. Since the linguistic usage in our daily discourse permits the usage of the word 'I', in the sense of both the Self and the ego, there is the practical difficulty in distinguishing the one from the other. The Husserlian phenomenology which has gone through descriptive, transcendental, and egological stages in its development is aware of the distinction between the Self and the ego in so far as it speaks of 'the transcendental I' and 'the empirical I', 'the pure ego' and 'the psychological ego', and so on. But this distinction, it appears, is not scrupulously adhered to; and so scholars are of the view that the tension between the two 'I's, the transcendental 'I' and the empirical 'I', has not been resolved in the Husserlian phenomenology.[9] The use of the word 'ego', with different qualifications such as 'pure' and 'empirical', 'transcendental' and 'factual', and so on, complicates the problem. Critics like Sartre who have been inspired by the programme and method initiated by Husserl are of the view that Husserl went back to the Cartesian ego in the final stage of his phenomenology in spite of Husserl's insight into the pure consciousness as the 'phenomenological residuum', that which stands on its own providing meaning and validity to every aspect of our experience, outer as well as inner, our experience of the life-world as well as our experience of the cogitations of the ego. The difficulty that one notices in the phenomenology of Husserl does not arise in the transcendental phenomenology of Advaita which devotes considerable attention not only to the elucidation of the distinction between the Self and the ego, as it is difficult to comprehend this distinction, but also in justification of this distinction which is ignored by others like Rāmānuja. Though the linguistic usage of the word 'I' (*aham*) may be ambiguous and misleading, Advaita takes advantage of the availability of the different words for the purpose of referring to the Self and the ego. The word '*cit*' signifies the Self, the pure consciousness, whereas the word '*antaḥkaraṇa*', which literally means the 'internal organ', is used to refer to the ego/mind.

Husserl's Ego cogito cogitata

A brief reference to Husserl's view of consciousness is necessary at this stage. The phenomenological method guarantees to Husserl the *ego*, the *cogito*, and the *cogitata*. Though the earlier Husserl did not believe in the existence of the absolute, pure consciousness, the later Husserl frankly admitted in his *Ideen* that his earlier scepticism with regard to the ego, an identical subject, was untenable. The later Husserl held the view that there is a transcendental ego, 'standing behind' or 'presiding over' the intentional consciousness. Consciousness must be understood not as 'empty' consciousness, but as ego-endowed consciousness. The cogitations of the ego would include all intentional acts—doubting, understanding, affirming, denying, willing, feeling, and so on. The cogitata are the referents or intentional objects of the cogitations. So the tripartite formula adopted by Husserl was *ego cogito cogitata*. According to Husserl, the intentional act of consciousness is something 'directed towards an object' outside it. Consciousness, therefore, is always consciousness of something. Though this is the central idea of the theory of the intentionality of consciousness, Husserl has introduced other features in the theory, which contribute to its complexity. The ego-endowed consciousness which is intentional is related to the object outside it not directly, but only through the *hyletic data* which are contained in consciousness and which represent the intentional objects. The intentional act relates the data which are in consciousness to an object which is transcendent to it. This amounts to the work of construction of an object by interpreting the given data. And this work of the intentional act is known as objectivation. The intentional act not only objectivates, but also establishes the identity between two objects which are transcendent to it. Further, it connects one aspect of the intentional object with its other aspects through 'fulfilment'. Finally, it 'constitutes' the intentional object. As a result of these features introduced by Husserl, the intentional object, we have to say, is known only as what the intentional act makes it: it becomes something constituted by the intentional consciousness. Phenomenology thus becomes a study of the principles governing the intentional act by which an object is 'constituted' out of the hyletic data. It may be mentioned here that the way in which the later Husserl developed phenomenology was not acceptable to Sartre who treats consciousness as something which confronts an object transcendent to it and not as something which it itself constitutes. Sartre repudiates Husserl's transcendental ego, but retains the intentional acts and the intentional objects of consciousness.

Intentionality of Consciousness

The theory of the intentionality of consciousness which plays an important part not only in the phenomenology of Husserl but also in the phenomenological ontology of Sartre deserves a careful consideration. Husserl assigns to consciousness not only an important place in his system, but also makes it the starting point of philosophical investigation. Sartre does not disagree with Husserl on this issue, though he was thoroughly unhappy with the latter's formula of 'turn to the subject' which replaced the earlier formula of 'turn to the object'. To both Husserl and Sartre, consciousness is intentional. However, the theory of intentionality of consciousness takes a new dimension in the Sartrean phenomenological ontology; for, Sartre, unlike Husserl, rejects the transcendental I, but clings to the intentional consciousness and the intended objects, and makes of consciousness a non-substantial and impersonal being, a 'free spontaneity', a 'great emptiness', a 'wind blowing towards objects'. Consciousness, Sartre says, is always consciousness *of* something. It is always pointing toward that which is beyond it. There is no consciousness, according to Sartre, which is not related to a transcendent, object. Following Husserl, Sartre maintains that intentionality is essential to consciousness; consciousness, that is to say, is defined by intentionality. He considers this to be 'the fruitful definition'[10] of consciousness. Sartre thus accepts Husserl's theory of the intentionality of consciousness. There is, however, an important difference between Husserl and Sartre even here: while for Husserl intentionality is *one* essential feature of consciousness, for Sartre intentionality is consciousness. For the present we can ignore this difference between them, as it does not in any way affect the problem of the intentionality of consciousness which we are now considering.

Advaita Vedānta which is transcendental phenomonology is also interested in the question of the intentionality of consciousness. Keeping to the distinction between the pure consciousness and ego-consciousness, Advaita raises the question whether consciousness *per se* is intentional or whether the ego-consciousness is intentional. This question is important in the context of Husserl inasmuch as the distinction between 'the pure I' and 'the empirical I', is accepted by him. Is it the pure consciousness, 'the phenomenological residuum', that is intentional? Or, is it the *epoche*-performing ego that is intentional? This question need not be asked in the case of Sartre because he not only holds that consciousness *per se* is intentional, but also accounts for the origin of the ego in terms of the intentionality of consciousness. Advaita maintains that consciousness *per se* is not intentional, but it becomes intentional because of the ego. Is there any evidence to say on the basis of a thoroughgoing application of the phenomenological method that consciousness is always and necessarily consciousness *of* something? Advaita answers this question in the negative. I shall argue this point on the basis of the phenomenological analysis as given in Advaita Vedānta which undoubtedly throws a new light on this problem.

It is a basic mistake to restrict phenomenology to the study of consciousness and what it reveals only from the standpoint of waking experience. We have not only waking experience, but also dream experience and dreamless sleep experience as well. Advaita may be characterized as radical empiricism inasmuch as it studies experience at all the three levels—waking, dream and dreamless sleep. It accepts the nature of consciousness as known at these levels.

It is undoubtedly true that consciousness in our waking experience is always consciousness *of* something. In our waking experience we do not have access to consciousness as such apart from the object which it reveals and to which it is related. When we reflect on our consciousness, we know it to be intentional; we know it as the consciousness of this or that object. The intended object at this level may be physical like a table or a tree. Or, it may be a psychical state like pleasure or pain. In short, waking-consciousness is intentional. It needs must have transcendent objects related to it at this level. Being awake means being awake *to*.

As in the case of waking experience, in dream experience also consciousness is intentional, because here it is always related to 'objects'. My reflection on dream experience tells me that I was aware of many 'objects' at that time.

As distinguished from waking and dream experience there is the experience of sleep which is free from dream. When a person wakes up from dreamless sleep and reflects on the nature of experience he had, he says that at that time he was not conscious of anything whatsoever, objective or subjective. Nevertheless, there was consciousness at that time, though there were no objects, no phenomena, related to it. If consciousness were also absent at that time, recollection to the effect, 'I was not conscious of anything then' would be impossible. The point is that consciousness reveals objects if they are present; and when there are no objects to be revealed, consciousness remains alone. It is, therefore, wrong to say that intentionality, as Sartre would put it, is consciousness, or that consciousness by its very nature is intentional. According to Advaita, consciousness becomes intentional only as a result of its association with the mind; and it has this connection with the mind in waking and dream experience. But in deep sleep experience, mind as mind is absent with the result that consciousness remains alone without being intentional. Advaita maintains that intentionality is not essential (*svābhāvika*), but only adventitious (*aupādhika*), to consciousness. While it is true that there is no phenomenon without consciousness, there is no phenomenological evidence to say that there is no consciousness without the phenomenon.

On the basis of the distinction between consciousness and the ego, Advaita holds that not only the intentional act, but also the work of objectivation, identification, fulfilment, and constitution mentioned by Husserl belong to the ego or the mind, which is transcendent to consciousness. It justifies this position on the ground that these cogitations are known in the same way as the external objects and their qualities are known, and that what is known must be transcendent to the knower. In other words, since consciousness is aware of these cogitations as they occur from time to time, as they appear and disappear in the mental horizon, they cannot belong to, or be part of, consciousness. For example, when someone sees an object, the object seen is transcendent to the seer. When someone perceives the whiteness, or the tallness, or the movement of an object, the quality or the action that is perceived cannot be the quality or the action of the perceiver, but must be the quality or the movement of the object in which it inheres. The same principle holds good in the case of the cogitations which one is aware of. These cogitations or mental operations also are objects of consciousness but are not consciousness itself. It is relevant in this connection to refer to an *Upaniṣadic* text which says: 'Desire, resolve, doubt, faith, want of faith, steadiness, unsteadiness, shame, intelligence, fear—all these are but the mind.'[11] What this text emphasizes, mentioning only a few of the mental operations in a suggestive way, is that all cogitations or mental operations are but states of the mind and that they are not, just because consciousness is aware of them, constitutive of consciousness.

It should be pointed out in this connection that what is commonly called the ego or the 'I' is not consciousness but the object of consciousness. If it were identical with, or part of consciousness, it could not be known by consciousness. We find that the ego or the 'I' appears only during our waking and dream experience. In our waking experience there is the 'I' which functions as knower (*jñātā*), as doer (*kartā*), as experiencer (*bhoktā*); it functions, that is to say, as the subject of knowledge, as the agent of action, and as the experiencer of the consequences of action. In support of this there is the evidence of the statements that we make from time to time with the first person singular such as 'I know this', 'I do this', 'I reap the rewards of my actions', and so on. This is equally true in our dream experience which is very significantly on a par with our waking experience. The 'I' is as much prominent in our dream experience as it is in our waking experience. A person perceives objects, performs deeds and suffers for his action in dream experience, and is also aware of them. The dream world parallels the waking world, though there are also significant differences between them. The 'I' which is present both in the waking and dream experience is absent in the state of sleep. It is well-known that sleep (*suṣupti*) is the state in which one is not conscious of anything, external or internal; and one is not even conscious of oneself in that state. When a person is awake and recollects his experience, he testifies to the fact that he was not aware of anything at that time and also that he was not aware of himself at that time. Just as there is consciousness of the presence or absence of something, even so there is consciousness of the presence or absence of the ego or the 'I' as the case may be. It follows that the ego or 'I' which is known as sometimes present and sometimes absent is transcendent to consciousness.

If the ego or the 'I' were identical with consciousness and not something transcendent to consciousness, then what is it that is aware of it? Is it aware of itself? Or, is there anything else which could be aware of it? The first alternative is untenable, as it amounts to saying that one and the same entity is both the subject and the object at the same time in the same act of cognition. When we say that it is aware of itself, does it mean that this ego which is consciousness divides itself into two parts such that one part of it is the knower and the other part is the known? This is impossible, as consciousness is one and homogeneous and does not admit of division into two parts, the subject-part and the object-part. There is also another difficulty. If the ego which is known is identified with consciousness, then consciousness can never be the knower, or the seer, or the witness, to which everything is presented: that is, not being different from the ego, it becomes the known; if so, there will be no knower at all. Nor can it be said, with a view to overcome the above difficulties, that consciousness which is the knower at one time becomes the known at another time. A thing is what it is, and it cannot become something different. It is impossible for a thing to change its nature. Consciousness by its very nature is the seer all the time. And to say that it becomes the known is to assume a knower other than consciousness. And what is that which knows it? This question will now take us to the second alternative.

If the ego which is identical with consciousness is known by something else, that 'something else' cannot be the 'object', for an 'object' is always what is known by, and what derives its meaning from, consciousness. On the contrary, that 'something else' must be consciousness and not an object. It follows from this that one consciousness is known by another consciousness. If we persist in the same kind of questioning, we have to say that the second consciousness is known through a third one, and so on, leading to the fallacy of infinite regress. This difficulty apart, there is the unwarranted assumption that there is a plurality of consciousness. What is the evidence to show, Advaita asks, that there is more than one consciousness? To establish the existence of a plurality of consciousness, we require not only the differentiating features in terms of which we could say that one consciousness is different from another consciousness, but also a consciousness as the witnessing principle of these differentiating features. The features which help to distinguish one object from another are configuration (*avasthā*), place (*deśa*), time (*kāla*), and qualities (*guṇa*). Two objects, we say, are different from each other because of their difference in configuration, because of their location in different places, because of their existence in different periods of time, and because of the difference in their qualities. The question is whether differentiating features such as configuration, place, time, and qualities can be associated with consciousness for the purpose of proving the existence of a plurality of consciousness. Every differentiating feature, it must be borne in mind, has to be noticed by consciousness. In that case it becomes what is seen or witnessed to (*sākṣya*) by consciousness, and so it cannot belong to the latter. On the contrary, it must be transcendent to consciousness for the simple reason that it is seen or noticed by consciousness. It means that the existence of more than one consciousness cannot be proved. Therefore, the ego or the 'I' which is transcendent to consciousness should not be identified with consciousness. There is nothing *in* consciousness, no content, no structures, no qualities, no parts, by which it can be identified and marked off from other things. All that can be said about consciousness is that it is revelatory of things presented to it; and it is by this nature that it is differentiated from the objects which it is aware of and which are, therefore, transcendent to it.

Sartre's Theory of Non-egological Consciousness

It will be helpful in this connection to consider the non-egological theory of consciousness which Sartre formulates by placing the ego outside consciousness. According to Sartre, consciousness is non-substantial. Consciousness is 'all lightness, all translucence.[12] It is not a container; it does not contain anything—no images, no representations, no contents. By its very nature it transcends itself in order to reach an object, and exhausts itself in this transcendence.[13] When there is consciousness of a tree, the tree is not in consciousness—not even in the capacity of a representation. A tree is in space by the side of the house. There is, Sartre says, no content in consciousness which is 'a great emptiness', 'a wind blowing towards the objects'.

In order to understand the impersonal nature of consciousness it is necessary to start with the distinction introduced by Sartre between pre-reflective consciousness and reflective consciousness. The former is also referred to as a non-positional or non-thetic self-consciousness, while the latter is also called positional or thetic consciousness. The consciousness with which we start is the consciousness of something; it is the consciousness which is turned toward something other than itself. There is consciousness of a table, of a portrait and so on. Sartre maintains that consciousness of an object is at the same time consciousness of being consciousness of an object. For example, when there is consciousness of a table, there is consciousness of being aware of the table. Consciousness not only reveals something, but also reveals itself. It means that at the time of the consciousness of the table there is non-reflective awareness of consciousness. If this is not the case, it would be, Sartre argues, a consciousness which is ignorant of itself, that is to say, an unconscious being which is absurd.[14]

It is Sartre's contention that the 'I' or ego arises only at the reflective level. There is, first of all, let us say, consciousness of a tree. By reflecting subsequently on my intentional act and the intended object, I say, 'I am conscious of the tree.' There is no place for the 'I' or ego in the unreflected consciousness. Here is one of the examples given by Sartre supposed to be based on the phenomenological analysis of the problem: 'I was absorbed just now in my reading. I am going to try to remember the circumstances of my reading, my attitude, the lines I was reading. I am thus going to revive not only these external details but a certain depth of unreflected consciousness, since the objects could only have been perceived by that consciousness and since they remain relative to it. That consciousness must not be posited as object of a reflection. On the contrary, I must divert my attention to the revived objects, but without losing sight of the unreflected consciousness, by joining in a sort of conspiracy with it and by drawing up an inventory of its content in a non-positional manner. There is no doubt about the result: while

I was reading, there was consciousness of the heroes of the novel, but then I was not inhabiting this consciousness. It was only consciousness of the object and non-positional consciousness of itself. I can now make these a-thetically apprehended results the object of a thesis and declare: there was no 'I' in the unreflected consciousness.'[15] Just as there is no content in consciousness, even so there is no 'I' or ego in it. Consciousness is, therefore, non-substantial and impersonal.

Sartre's theory of non-egological consciousness is acceptable to the Advaitin. Sartre's explanation of consciousness as impersonal and no-substantial, as 'a great emptiness', is a reiteration of the Advaita view that consciousness is not a substance possessing attributes, that it is not a whole consisting of parts, that it is not an entity which can be specified as such-and-such, as it is free from class feature, qualities, action, and relation. The view that the ego or 'I' which is transcendent to consciousness arises only at the reflective level of consciousness is the echo of the Advaita view which holds that the ego (*aham*) arises when there is *cidābhāsa*, i.e. consciousness reflected in the internal organ; and this consciousness associated with the internal organ, which alone is capable of reflection, may be characterized in the terminology of Sartre as consciousness in the second degree. Sartre does not deny the existence of the ego, but only denies that it is in consciousness. He says that the ego which is transcendent to consciousness is the unity of subjective states and actions known through reflection. There is, Sartre observes, something mysterious, irrational about the ego.[16] We cannot apprehend the ego apart from states and actions. If we take away one by one all the states and actions, the ego would disappear. According to Sartre, spontaneity is what characterizes consciousness. If the ego appears to have spontaneity, it is because consciousness projects its spontaneity into the ego. This account of the ego as a mystery and a problem, as that which functions through the borrowed light (spontaneity) of consciousness, is fully amplified in all the major works of Advaita. The difficulty arises only when Sartre denies the role of the transcendental consciousness as the unifying principle of the intentional acts. Sartre argues that the transcendent object intended by consciousness gives unity to the different intentional acts. His argument is not convincing. It appears that Sartre who banishes the transcendental 'I', the permanent factor underlying all our acts of consciousness, by the front door brings it back inside through the back door. At every stage in his explanation he tacitly assumes the existence of such a permanent consciousness in all our acts of consciousness. Sartre thinks of consciousness as something individualized and particularized by the objects to which it is related. He also thinks in terms of a flux of consciousness.[17] Very often he uses the expression, 'fleeting consciousness'.[18] Though there are innumerable acts of consciousness (i.e., intentional consciousnesses) coming one after another in a regular procession, whether they relate to one object or different objects, it is quite possible, according to Sartre, to connect all of them in reflection as if there were a common identical factor running through them. I shall focus attention on two examples given by Sartre.

Consider the case of my counting the cigarettes in a packet and knowing that they are ten in number. At the time of counting I have, says Sartre, a non-thetic consciousness of my adding activity: that is to say, there is consciousness of the cigarettes which are counted, and also a non-reflective consciousness of what I do. If any one should ask, 'What are you doing?' I reply at once: 'I am counting.' Sartre observes: 'This reply aims not only at the instantaneous consciousness which I can achieve by reflection, but at those fleeting consciousnesses which have passed without being reflected on, those which are for ever not-reflected-on in my immediate past.'[19] If the consciousness which reflects could at a flash connect the fleeting consciousnesses which are no more, it must be because of its being the constant, identical factor persisting in all acts of consciousness.

The point will be clear if another example in which there is sufficient time interval between the different acts of consciousness is examined. Consider the case of destruction to which Sartre alludes. Sartre says that destruction is intelligible only when it is viewed against the act of consciousness. Destruction, according to him, is a 'humanistic' term. A storm, for example, does not destroy; it only brings about a modification in the distribution of masses of beings. But to notice the change of distribution, to perceive the change from one state of affairs to another, we need a witness, an identical element which persists in the interval of time. To say that something is no longer or that there is something else, 'there must be,' observes Sartre, 'a witness who can retain the past in some manner and compare it to the present in the form of no longer.'[20] This observation of Sartre's is significant as it contains a clear refutation of his own position. If there are only fleeting acts of consciousness succeeding one another without an identical element persisting through them, a study of an object at two or more intervals of time to find out what change it has suffered, or a comparison of two states of affairs at two or more intervals of time, is impossible. But inasmuch as Sartre thinks in terms of 'a witness who can retain the past in some manner,' he admits, though unconsciously, the existence of an identical factor persisting through time. This identical factor that runs through the different acts of consciousness is no other than the transcendental I denied by Sartre.

Entanglement of the Journeying Self

The empirical journey of the transcendental subjectivity to the world horizon passes through the landmarks of the mind, the senses, and the body. As it moves from its non-dual, non-relational state, there is progressive entanglement with the objects transcendent to it until it emerges as the enworlded subjectivity in all its completeness. We have seen that there is a need for a rigorous regressive analysis of the objects presented to consciousness for the purpose of catching hold of the inward Self, the transcendental subjectivity, as the phenomenological residuum; and in this regressive analysis the homecoming starts from the outer world to the inner world, and then from the inner world to the Self, which ultimately remains alone.

The internal organ (*antaḥkaraṇa*), what is commonly called the mind, is the first entity with which consciousness comes into relation. The association of consciousness with the internal organ gives rise to the emergence of the 'I' or ego. Though the ego or 'I' is transcendent to it, and is, therefore, different from it, it nevertheless identifies itself and appears as 'I'. In the words of Sureśvara, it is as though it has put on the mask of the 'I'. It is this 'I' that is commonly spoken of as the 'empirical I', as the 'ego-consciousness', as the 'factual I'; it is the *epoche*-performing ego of Husserl. The relation between the transcendental Self and the empirical 'I' is the relation of the revealer and the revealed (*avabhāsaka-avabhāsya-saṃbandha*). Once the ego or 'I' emerges at this level, that is to say, once the transcendental Self puts on the mask of the 'I', then it begins to function through its intentional acts, taking advantage of the senses and the body. In this process it identifies itself with the mind, with the senses, and then with the body. This identification is evident in the claims that we make in our daily life such as 'I am happy', 'I am blind', 'I am stout', and so on. Functioning through the mind-sense-body complex, the 'I' comes into relation with the objects of the external world, develops pragmatic attitude towards them through its intentional acts, considers those objects which are helpful to it as good and those which are not helpful as bad, and behaves as if it were helped or hindered by them. The transcendental subjectivity which provides meaning and validity to the objects is now thrown into the world as the embodied subjectivity as if it were an entity in need of sustenance from the very objects which are 'constituted' or 'accomplished' by it. Nothing is more tragic, more poignant, than this existential situation in which the source bcomes the supported, and the helper, the helped. Such is the entanglement of the Self as the embodied subjectivity functioning as a being-in-the-world overwhelmed by the natural attitude of 'That I am', and 'That is mine'. The journey of the Self is one of progressive 'fall'. Sureśvara sums up, in a language which is terse, the emergence of the enworlded subjectivity as follows.

> The internal organ, being delimited by the 'I'-notion, becomes an object directly to the reflected consciousness (i.e., *cidābhāsa*), of which the immutable, inward Self is the cause. Now, except the relation of the revealer and the revealed, no other relation is tenable between the 'I' and its knower. Appropriating the internal organ as its own and putting on the mask of the 'I', the Self becomes fit enough for the helped-helper relation, and comes to be related to the external objects, helpful or harmful as the case may be, claiming them its own.[21]

The phenomenological reflection through a rigorous regressive analysis helps us to remove the coverings of the Self, including the mask of the 'I' which are external to it and know the Self as it is. If the transcendental subjectivity is the real Self (*mukhyātma*), the 'I', the empirical self, which functions through the mind-sense-body complex, is the false self (*mithyātma*).[22] Since the 'I' brings together the Self and the objects of the world, its role is crucial. So long as there is the 'I', there is the world; and when the 'I' goes away, there is no more the familiar world horizon.

3. METAPHYSICS OF NON-DUALISM—THE CONSUMMATION OF TRANSCENDENTAL PHENOMENOLOGY

Advaita holds that the evidence of consciousness is the only evidence that is certain and apodictic for any claim that we make that we know something or that we do not know something. Every source of knowledge is dependent on consciousness; whatever be the source of knowledge, be it perception, or inference or scripture, it presupposes consciousness as its ultimate source. That which is the presupposition of every kind of knowledge and every source of knowledge cannot be validated by any other principle. When we say that something is the case or that something is not the case, it is on the basis of the evidence of consciousness that we say so. In the language of William James, Advaita may be characterized as 'radical empiricism'. Advaita maintains that whatever is shown or revealed by consciousness cannot be rejected, and that whatever is not shown or revealed by consciousness cannot be accepted. In fact, it goes to the extent of saying that even the claim that something is not known presupposes the evidence of consciousness, just as the claim that something is known presupposes the evidence of consciousness. Earlier, reference was made to two kinds of seeing or vision (*dṛṣṭi*), real (*paramārthikī*) and actual (*laukikī*), mentioned by Śaṅkara.[23] The former is the seeing or vision of consciousness, while the latter is the seeing or vision of the mind or through the mind. This distinction between the two kinds of seeing is of great significance, as it highlights the role of consciousness as the witnessing or the knowing principle. When I say, 'This is a table,' and 'That is a tree,' I have the knowledge of the object through the mind. It is what is called 'modal cognition', i.e., cognition through the mode of the mind (*vṛtti-jñāna*). In these cases, consciousness reveals things through the mind; and in the absence of consciousness, mind by itself, which is material, cannot give us knowledge of anything. It is not the case that every case of seeing or knowing is through the mind. There are cases where consciousness without the medium of the mind or any other medium, directly reveals the object. The case of the ego or 'I' is a standing example in this regard. We have already pointed out that the ego which is revealed by consciousness is transcendent to consciousness. Though the ego or 'I' may appear to be the knower (*jñātā*) in respect of objects external to it, the real position is that it is an object in relation to consciousness. Advaita holds that the ego or 'I' is directly revealed by consciousness (*kevala-sākṣī-bhāsya*) without the intervention of the mind. Similarly, when I say, 'I am ignorant of something,' 'That is unknown to me,' it is on the basis of the direct evidence of the witnessing consciousness. In short, every kind of claim that we make—that something is *known*, or that something is *unknown*—is on the basis of the transcendental consciousness which reveals objects directly or through the intentional performance of the mind. The evidence of the transcendental consciousness is intrinsically valid. It is, therefore, considered to be the principle of all principles, the source of all of our claims—claim to knowledge as well as claim to ignorance.

On the basis of the phenomenological method, Advaita maintains that whatever is cognized must be admitted to be existent. Every cognition has a cognitum. And this is as much true without regard to what is called erroneous cognition as it is true in respect of veridical cognition. In the well-known example of the rope-snake error, a person first of all cognizes the object in front as a snake and gives expression to his cognition by saying, 'This is a snake.' Subsequently on a closer view he cognizes it as a rope, corrects the mistake he has committed and says, 'This is not a snake, but a rope.' While the initial cognition affirms the existence of a snake, the subsequent cognition, which sublates the earlier cognition, denies it by affirming the existence of the rope. Negation presupposes affirmation: that is to say, what is initially affirmed alone can be denied subsequently.[24] The fact is that 'snake' was presented to consciousness as an object, and it was cognized as such by the person concerned at that time, in that place. What is cognized cannot be dismissed as non-existent.[25] At the same time, since the subsequent cognition has sublated it, it cannot be said to be existent.[26] On the basis of the evidence of the intentional acts of consciousness we have to say that the rope-snake has a peculiar ontological existence such that it can be characterized neither as non-existent nor as existent. Advaita, therefore, says that the rope-snake has to be accorded some kind of reality, what it calls phenomenal reality (*pratibhāsika-sattā*), in the world horizon. Advaita examines the objects of the external world such as the table and the tree by applying the same phenomenological method. These objects, like the rope-snake, are not only cognized, but also suffer sublation. While they are affirmed by our waking experience, they are denied by our dream experience, just as what is affirmed by the dream experience is denied by the waking experience. What is seen in the daily waking experience gets sublated when someone is fortunate enough to realize the transcendental Self as the sole reality. As in the case of the rope-snake, the objects of the external world must be accorded some reality, since they have been cognized and sublated. Noticing the difference between an object of erroneous cognition and an object of normal waking consciousness,[27] Advaita says that objects such as table and the tree have empirical reality (*vyāvahārika-sattā*). The transcendental consciousness is not an 'object' like rope-snake or a tree, which can be cognized. Since it is self-luminous, it is always known; or, as Śaṅkara would put it, it does not remain unknown. Nor is there any possibility of its sublation. What is other than consciousness is 'object'—dependent on consciousness for its meaning and validity; and so the question of sublation of consciousness by 'object' does not arise. Consciousness, according to Advaita, possesses absolute reality (*pāramārthika-sattā*). The phenomenological method which Advaita pursues results in the theory of the levels of reality—what is phenomenally real, what is empirically real, and what is absolutely real. The transcendental consciousness which is autonomous, which is absolutely real, is one and non-dual. There is nothing else, similar or dissimilar to it, which is autonomous. It is homogeneous and indivisible. It cannot be seen; nor can it be sublated. It is, therefore, unique. Its nature being what it is, Advaita, following the Upaniṣadic lead characterizes it as 'one only without a second' (*ekameva advitīyam*).[28] The rigorous pursuit of transcendental phenomenology to its logical end consummates in the metaphysics of non-dualism to which Advaita is committed.

NOTES AND REFERENCES

1. At the commencement of his commentary on the *Brahma-sūtra*, Śaṅkara observes that we carry on our worldly life by identifying ourselves with the body as when we say, 'I am stout,' or with the sense-organs, as when we say, 'I am blind,' or with the mind as when we say, 'I am happy'. In all these cases the 'I', the first person singular, signifies the Self, the transcendental consciousness, whereas 'stoutness', 'blindness', and 'happiness' are the characteristics of the body, the visual sense, and the mind respectively. Though the identification of the Self with the characteristics of the mind-sense-body complex is untenable, we do resort to it in our daily life. Similarly, we say 'my body', 'my eye', 'my mind', and so on as if I were the owner of the body and other objects. Once again the 'I' which signifies the Self has no relation whatsoever to anything. Nevertheless, we behave in our daily life as if the Self were in relation with other objects. Śaṅkara says that it is because of our ignorance of the nature of the Self that we wrongly identify the Self and the not-Self, the subject and the object.
2. See Husserl's Berlin lecture on 'Phenomenology and Anthropology,' in McCormick and Elliston (Ed.), *Husserl: Shorter Works* (Notre Dame University Press, 1981), p. 322.
3. Śaṅkara's commentary on the *Brahma-sūtra*, 1.2.20.
4. *Bṛhadāraṇyaka Upanaiṣad*, 4.5.15.
5. Husserl characterizes this principle as 'the principle of all principles'. He observes: 'Every type of first-hand intuiting (*originar gebende Anschauung*) forms a legitimate source of knowledge (*Rechtsquelle*); whatever presents itself to us by 'intuition' at first-hand, in its authentic reality, as it were (*sozusagen in seiner leibhaften wirklichkeit*) is to be accepted simply for the thing as which it presents itself, yet merely within the limits within which it presents itself.' Quoted by Herbert Spiegelberg, *The Phenomenological Movement* (Martinus Nijhoff, The Hague, 1960), Vol. I, p. 128.
6. Advaita holds the view that any 'object', whether known or unknown, must fall within the scope of consciousness. An oft-quoted statement conveys this basic standpoint as follows: '*sarvaṃ vastu jñātatayā vā ajñātatayā vā sākṣicaitanyasya viṣaya eva*'.
7. Śaṅkara's commentary on the *Bṛhadāraṇyaka Upaniṣad*, 3.4.2.
8. See *Chāndogya Upaniṣad*, 6.1.3. Uddālaka tells his son that there is the supreme reality 'by which what is not heard becomes heard, what is not perceived becomes perceived, and what is not known becomes known.'
9. See Debabrata Sinha, *Phenomenology and Existentialism: An Introduction* (Calcutta, Progressive Publishers, 1974), p. 72.
10. Sartre, *The Transcendence of the Ego*, Tr. F. Williams and R. Kirkpatrick (New York, The Noonday Press, 1957), p. 38 and p. 41.
11. *Bṛhadāraṇyaka Upaniṣad*, 1.5.3.
12. Sartre, *The Transcendence of the Ego*, p. 42.
13. Sartre, *Being and Nothingness*, Tr. H. E. Barnes (New York, Philosophical Library, 1956), p. li.
14. *Ibid.*, lii.
15. *The Transcendence of the Ego*, pp. 46–47.
16. The Advaitin tries to bring out the irrationality of the ego as follows. (1) Though by itself, it is material (*jaḍa*), it appears to be non-material, i.e. sentient, when it is

associated with consciousness. '*antaḥkaraṇavṛttiviśeṣasya ahaṅkārasya svato jaḍatvepi citpratibimba-grahītayā bhavati ajaḍatvamiti.*' (2) Though it is only an 'object', it also plays the role of the knower, the subject, when it is with the reflection of consciousness. '*kevala ahaṅkārasya dṛśyatvepi sābhāsāhaṅkārasya draṣṭṛtvaṃ sambhavati.*'

17. *The Tanscendence of the Ego*, p. 60.
18. *Being and Nothingness*, p. liii.
19. *Ibid.*, p. liii.
20. *Being and Nothingness*, p. 8.
21. Sureśvara, *Naiṣkarmyasiddhi*, Saṃbandhokti to III. 60.
22. See Śaṅkara's commentary on the *Brahma-sūtra* 1.1.4 (end-portion).
23. See p. 5.
24. The principle is stated as follows: '*prasaktasya pratiṣedhaḥ.*'
25. *pratīyamānatvāt na asat.*
26. *bādhyamānatvāt na sat.*
27. For example, a dream object is 'private', whereas an object like 'table' seen in the waking experience is 'public'. Gauḍapada mentions other differences as well in his *Māṇḍūkyakārikā*, Chapter II, verses 4, 13, 14, and 15.
28. See *Chāndogya Upaniṣad*, 6.2.1. According to Advaita, the expression, 'one only without a second', implies that the Self or consciousness is free from three kinds of difference—sajātīya, vijātīya, and svagata—and that it is therefore unique.

An Indian Interaction with Phenomenology: Perspectives on the Philosophy of K. C. Bhattacharyya

KALYAN KUMAR BAGCHI

Prefatory. I begin my paper with two quotations, both from Professor K. C. Bhattacharyya. The first quotation brings out Bhattacharyya's view on the nature of metaphysical or ontological enquiry. The second quotation brings out Bhattacharyya's view on *how* one should proceed in one's task in philosophy. The first quotation is from an article of Bhattacharyya's written in 1903. The second quotation is from Bhattacharyya's famous essay on 'The Concept of Philosophy'.

I use the first quotation to show how Bhattacharyya's early ontologial outlook permeates even his later work. *The Subject as Freedom*, (henceforth *SF*), on which I rely heavily to find out how the Advaita Vedāntic mode of philosophising can interact with Husserl's phenomenology and how, on the basis of his understanding of the Advaita Vedānta, Bhattacharyya makes a genuine contribution to the general *philosophical* issue (which is more important than the *historical* study of a school of thought) of the relationship, if any, between phenomenology and ontology.

The second quotation is meant to bring out the *methodological affinity* between Bhattacharyya and Husserl in respect of their philosophical task. Such affinity is only indicated in Bhattacharrya's essay on 'The Concept of Philosophy', but it is elaborated in *SF*. But although this book is phenomenological in method, its ontological motivations are obvious.

However, to describe *SF* in just phenomenological or ontological or even phenomenological-cum-ontological terms is to adopt a jejune view of the matter. It appears to me that *SF* strikes a *unique harmony between ontology and phenomenology*. It shows that (i) the phenomenological method is, motivationally, ontological, so that it must reach its acme, so to say, on ontology and that (ii) *intimations* of ontology are *embedded* in our experience and *demand to be made explicit*.

1. 'Elsewhere what I am does not directly affect what I know; but here in metaphysics, the true theory must rise from my true being: I have no right to call the self known till I am truly myself, i.e., till I am rid, in *life*, of the illusion of the identity between the mind and body . . .' [K. C. Bhattacharyya, 'Mind and Matter', 1906.[1] Ital. author's].

2. 'Philosophy is . . . [a] self-evident elaboration of the self-evident . . .' [K. C. Bhattacharyya, 'The Concept of Philosophy' in *Studies in Philosophy (SP)*, Vol. II, Calcutta, Progressive Publishers, 1958, p. 103.]

The contentions of the present paper are animated by the thought contained in the texts quoted above, the thought that a philosopher is somehow or other involved in a process of self-engagement. Such a process may otherwise be called 'reflection'. If there is anything in Bhattacharyya's thought which brings him close to phenomenological thinking, it is the method of self-engagement which is employed as much by him as by the great Husserl.

'Self-engagement', it should be made clear at the outset, does not smack of any dealing with some imagined self or subject of knowledge absolutely out of the context of human knowledge or experience. Phenomenology, so far as its avowed objective is to 'let experience tell its own tale', begins its enquiry, at least historically, with our knowledge at our daily concerns, such as those involved in collecting information regarding particular persons, places, etc., predicting about the weather, calculating the chances for obtaining a job, deliberating about some plan etc. Phenomenology, in fact, would 'describe', hold before our minds' eye so to say, isolate the structure or the structures *involved* in our knowledge of the world. Phenomenology would only prescribe the method of deepening our knowledge so that this method could discover or *uncover*, those structures overlaid by knowledge in its 'mundane' attitude, to use Husserl's diction. Similarly, K. C. Bhattacharyya, too, advocates the method of self-consciously or reflectively uncovering or abstracting *within* knowledge, not *from* it, its presuppositions, or discovering in a more reflective grade of knowledge the presuppositions of the relatively less reflective grade of knowledge. This is delineated in his essay on 'The Concept of Philosophy' and also elaborated in his book, *SF* decidedly the apex of his philosophic creativity.[2] But whatever the details of the application of the phenomenological method and whatever the terms in which it is described—'reduction' in Husserl, 'negative attention' in Bhattacharyya or again, 'back to experience' in Husserl, 'transcendental method' or 'scaffolding'[3] in Bhattacharyya,—the fact remains that both Bhattacharyya and a philosopher officially of the phenomenologist pursuasion would discover *in* knowledge in its 'mundane' (Husserl) or 'objective'[4] (Bhattacharyya) attitude *knowledge itself* in its 'phenomenological' or 'transcendental' (Husserl) or 'subjective'[5] attitude.

Now, the necessity of employing the phenomenological method arises out of the *distinctive phenomenological understanding* of philosophical problems. Of the two texts quoted, the first gives us an indication of how philosophical problems are to be viewed. Though the specific point of the text is to establish with reference to the self that to *know* it is to be *one* with it, yet lurking within it is the general point that philosophical problems are quite unlike other problems, i.e., problems we encounter in our non-philosophic pursuits. Philosopical problems are unlike problems in other spheres of our lives because the philosopher cannot just rest content with finding out the solution to his problem: problem-solving and solution-finding cannot be just two *separate* events in his psychological history. That is, a philosopher cannot take a retrospective view as to how his problem arose with the attitude of an onlooker reviewing or recounting the events of his past. When his problem is solved, he cannot any longer relapse to his past, but, on the contrary, makes a complete break with the modes of thought which raised the problem for him.

All this is because *lurking in the very problem that a philosopher raises is his solution*. To repeat, to a philosopher there is no one mental slick which raises a problem *and* a clarity of vision or understanding which finds the solution. His problem is an implicit recognition that the mental slick which account for certain appearance needs a *self*-corrective: so that we may say that (i) *in raising the problem and in finding the solution he actually traverses twice on the same straight line* and that (ii) he raises his problem in a reflective attitude. He is *self-engaging*. Self-engagement or reflection, in the specific phenomenological sense, is not a second-order activity (of understanding, a conscious process which might have discovered some fact, i.e., truth about the world). When one is engaged in the second-order activity of understanding a conscious process (that precedes such activity in time), one may, of course, unearth assumptions or presuppositions or postulates of the first-order conscious activity, and, to that extent, may, admittedly, be said to have gained some new enlightenment with reference to the subject that the first-order conscious activity was directed upon. Nevertheless, both the first-order activity and the second-order activity are world-centric in attitude. If the second-order activity reviews the first-order activity, whatever be the way it may adopt for its review—the way, for example, of recording, reassessing, reconstructing, etc., the steps, ideas, postulates, categories, etc., involved in the first-order activity, its aim to the end of the chapter is to *know the world better*. It is not a whit less chained to the world than the first-order activity. But reflection in the distinctive phenomenological sense understands the world as 'meant', a 'noema' constituted in a 'noetic act', to use Husserl's expressions. As Husserl says, '... der gegenstand is gemeint...'[6] Or as Bhattacharyya says, study of the world is the study of how it is constituted immanently in consciousness. Says Husserl: 'The greatest problems of all are... those of the 'constituting of the objective field of consciousness'.'[7]

Compare now Husserl's description of phenomenological study as 'immanent' study of the structural forms of our knowledge of the world with the cluster of statements that Bhattacharyya makes about philosophical study. Observes Bhattacharyya: 'Philosophy is [a] self-evident elaboration of the self-evident.'[8] Again to quote him: 'Philosophy starts in reflective consciousness. Reflection is the awareness of a content *as to* a mode of consciousness.'[9] (Italics author's). He affirms: '...the particular logical method by which Kant obtained his transcendental constants has never been identified or named in logic... The transcendental method is a self-evident transition, a process *in* self-consciousness and not in consciousness and as such should be taken as a kind of introspection which is neither logical mediation nor mere internal perception...'[10] The *methodological affinity* between the two philosophers now becomes immediately evident. Also, an 'immanent' study of consciousness or a 'self-evident transition' is fundamentally different from a logico-presuppositional enquiry into knowledge such as Kant founded. The latter may be formulated in the *Modus Tolleus* 'Unless P. then not Q' (where 'P' = the Kantian transcendental constants and 'Q' = knowledge of the world). Of 'P', however, there is no warrant in Kant: questions have in fact been raised, justifiably so, about its comprehensiveness and uniqueness as interpretative framework of our knowledge. A self-evident or phenomenological elaboration of the noetic-constitutive forms of consciousness, however, does not have to face such question.

We now come to confront two related questions. *First*, are philosophical problems *necessarily* phenomenological? *Secondly*, should the 'noetic act' be the alpha and the omega of philosophical enquiry? From our answers to these questions will emerge the difference between Bhattacharyya and Husserl.

To turn to the first question. For Bhattacharyya philosophical problems arise when we leap over 'the barriers of commonsense' as he says in his essay of 1906, the source of our first quotation. The essay abounds in observations which have metaphysical overtones: e.g., 'commonsense . . . feels itself contradicted'; 'there is the fact of illusion and its correction'; 'our knowledge itself is at every moment based on illusion'; '. . . we have a fundamental illusion on which all our experiential knowledge depends' and so on. These observations of his suggest that for Bhattacharyya philosophical problems concerning commonsense spring from metaphysical commitments. It was, however, no part of Husserl's work to castigate commonsense. His phenomenology, in so far as it is phenomenology, would maintain strict neutrality with regard to metaphysical or ontological questions.

What is, however, of importance in so far as a comparative study of Bhattacharyya and Husserl from the phenomenological viewpoint is concerned is the influence the essay of 1906 casts on even the most elaborate phenomenological work (not avowedly so but according to our interpretation which follows) of Bhattacharyya, viz., his book on *SF*. For here 'Subject or subjectivity . . . conceived after Vedānta'[11] (according to Bhattacharyya's own admission) is the starting-point of enquiry into 'object'. While 'object' is 'meant', according to Bhattacharyya, but 'object as the meant is distinguished from the subject . . . of which we have an awareness other than meaning-awareness.' The contrast with Husserl the phenomenologist for whom the object is a 'noema' constituted in a noetic act is obvious. Here some observations of Bhattacharyya which make the point that we *know* the subject may be quoted. Thus: 'The Subject . . . and the object . . . are the two things that are known'.[12] 'The reality of what is meant can always be doubted and so the object is not known with the same assurance as the subject that cannot be said to be meant'.[13] Referring to Kant's epistemological task of 'deducing' the knowing 'functions', Bhattacharyya observes that epistemological enquiry (into knowing) as such is rooted in the faith 'in the *facthood* of the knowing function'.[14] The 'Subject is believed without being meant'. Bhattacharyya's enquiry into the different forms of subjectivity, 'elaboration' as he calls it, a word that has a phenomenological ring in it, is permeated by the initial or foundational knowledge of subject; the *direction* of his enquiry *from subject* to its different objective forms marks him off from Husserl. From his point of view, the Husserlian noetic acts can be discovered only if we start with the 'belief' in the subject.

We do not, however, *historically*, start with the subject. We *start* with the knowledge of the object, *then* installed in the 'faith in the facthood' of the subject start philosophy—but not *descriptively* or *historically*. We discover the forms of the object or the objectivity of the subject and also discover the subject *in* objectivity, i.e., the different objective forms of the subject.

Thus the Vedāntic metaphysical motivations of Bhattacharyya come out clearly. At the same time, however, his is not the speculative Vedānta that makes a mockery of the object. He discovers the subject in the object. The initial faith in the subject comes to be deepened progressively through the different objective forms of the subject and thereby a *Vedāntic metaphysic of experience* is spelt out. Though we, historically speaking, start with the object, yet *object is, in reflection, retrospectively viewed* by the *subject as its own*: here what is historically the first is philosophically, the last. In so far, then, as Bhattacharyya elaborates the belief in the subject through different objective forms, he presents *a phenomenology of the subject* of the Vedānta for that matter and, thereby, *situates* Vedānta in the context of phenomenology and adds to its corpus. At the same time, he shows how phenomenological or noetical analysis of the object is at bottom rooted in the ontology of the subject. *Vedānta adds* phenomenological methodology to its *corpus* and *phenomenology gains an ontological dimension* in the hands of K. C. Bhattacharyya.

In the last part of this paper, we present a rough sketch of what might be indifferently called Bhattacharyya's Phenomenology of the Subject or the Ontology of objective knowledge following his book *SF* in which his philosophic career reaches its acme.

In the beginning of *SF*, Bhattacharyya distinguishes between the object as 'What is meant' and the subject 'of which there is some awareness other than the meaning awareness'.[15] Later on, he speaks also of 'the positive freedom of the subject'.[16] Subjectivity is initially felt to be distinct, it is 'felt detachment from the object'. Had it not been so felt from he beginning, there would have been 'no theoretic passage from what is meanable or objectively knowable to the subjectively knowable "I".'[17] The subject 'may . . . be said to have a feeling of relating itself to the subject. . . . This felt relating is the positive freedom of the subject having different felt modes like knowing, feeling . . .'.[18] Knowing is described as a 'subjective function'.[19] And the functions 'represent the modes of freedom'.[20]

Of 'Function' it is said that it is to be understood 'as being a metaphor for a positive something which is literally expressed only in the negative way as what the known object is not and being thus not even an accomplished meaning'.[21]

What is important to note is the distinction between function and meaning. Function is no meaning but freely refers to meaning and, what is phenomenologically important, it is freedom from meaning. We have the consciousness of freedom from objectivity and the task of epistemology, according to Bhattacharyya, should be to interpret the different psychological functions truly in line with the suggestion of subjective or spiritual freedom.

Is not Bhattacharyya speaking in Husserlian terminology? Does not Husserl, too, speak of the meaning function and the meant content? We shall discuss the contrast, if any, between the two thinkers in the last section of this essay.

How does Bhattacharyya perform the Phenomenological Reduction to Subjectivity? We can see how 'Freedom' supplies the instrument of such reduction. The problem of phenomenological reduction has two sides, viz., (1) reduction of objectivity to its subjective sources and (2) the phenomenological clarification of subjectivity. And these two studies may be linked up by observing that subjectivity clarifies or distinguishes itself and thereby freely posits the object. Our previous study of Bhattacharrya's epistemology has shown us how 'object is declared in so far as knowledge distinguishes itself, i.e., withdraws itself from object'. 'To say that an object is known is to imply that knowing has freed itself from the object. It is also to imply, at the same time, that object cannot be known, i.e., cannot be declared, unless so distinguished.'[22]

We have now to see how Bhattacharyya would perform a phenomenological clarification of subjectivity. Two requirements have to be fulfilled to that end: first, in accordance with Bhattacharyya's basic notion of freedom, such clarification must consist in withdrawing subjectivity from the object, and, in accordance with Husserl's programme, the motive of such clarification should be to delineate a self-complete realm of subjectivity.

But before the clarification is attempted, one important consideration has to be disposed of. Subjectivity is initially felt to be distinct,—freedom, in other words, is not a new acquisition. Where, then, is the scope of phenomenological clarification such as can delineate a self-complete realm of subjectivity? Is not Bhattacharyya overdoing his task?

We reply he is not. For, phenomenological clarification of subjectivity must consist in freedom from the thraldom of meaning, and not until meaning is outgrown altogether can phenomenological reduction stop.

We can now follow Bhattacharyya in his attempt at phenomenological clarification. The 'steps' in such clarification should correspond to a 'gradation of subjective functions'.[23] Bhattacharyya presents the gradation thus: 'Identified as we are with our body, our freedom from the perceived object is actually realised only in our bodily consciosness. . . . The next stage of freedom is suggested by the distinction of the perceived object including the body from the ghostly object in the form of the image, idea and meaning which may be all designated 'presentation'. . . . The dissociation of the subject or consciousness from this presentation conceived as a kind of object would be the next stage of freedom which may be called non-presentational or spiritual subjectivity'.[24] Along with this it must also be remembered that 'the grades of subjectivity imply grades of objectivity, the terms being conceived in a relative sense. To spiritual subjectivity, the psychical is objective and so to psychic subjectivity, the bodily, and to bodily subjectivity the extra-organic is objective.'[25]

But does not the higher stage of subjectivity *mean* the lower stage of subjectivity? If so, spiritual subjectivity is not the highest stage of subjectivity, and hence, phenomenological reduction should continue *ad infinitum*.

We reply that one and the same stage of subjectivity becomes a meaning-mode and a subjective or functional mode by reflecting upon itself. Each meaning-mode, by its self-deepening, calls forth another mode. As self-deepening, it is subjective, but then what becomes of it as a meaning-mode? Is it illusory? The simple reply is that as meaning-mode it is not subjective, and as subjective it is not a meaning-mode. But how can one and the same mode be a meaning-mode and a subjective-mode at the same time? One way of replying to this is that the same mode becomes a meaning-mode in its attitude to the object, and a subjective-mode by reflecting upon itself. The distinction of the modes is transcendental, not objective. The basis of the distinction of modes is Transcendental or Spiritual subjectivity. At each stage of subjectivity the demand is the same: it is the demand of the 'I' as being in a stage to be free from that stage. Where, therefore, Bhattacharyya says, '. . . I conceive that I can be free successively as body from the perceived object, as presentation from the body, as feeling from presentation . . . ',[26] he should be interpreted as meaning that I can conceive that I as body am free from the perceived object, that the self-same 'I' as presentation am free from the body, that, again, the self-same 'I' as feeling am free from presentation etc. etc. . . If, now, the distinction between the different subjective modes is not objective but transcendental, there must be one-sided identity and other-sided difference as between a higher and a lower subjective-mode: so that while body or presentation or feeling is 'I', I am neither body, nor presentation, nor feeling. This is phenomenological reduction *par excellence*.

Reference may here be made profitably to the Advaita Vedānta notion of subjectivity. Bhattacharyya himself points out that he conceived of subjectivity 'after Vedānta as conscious freedom or felt detachment from the object'.[27]

For, does not the Advaita (non-dualist) also formulate a similar psychology of spiritual life? Does it not also speak of the confusion of the 'I' with bodily subjectivity and psychological subjectivity? Again, does it not speak of the truth of bodily subjectivity and of psychological subjectivity as lying in spiritual subjectivity?[28] What the Vedānta calls '*Adhyasa*' (superimposition, roughly speaking) lies precisely in mistaking the body or the mind for the Self. Śaṅkara begins his commentary on the *Brahma-Sūtras* with a discussion on superimposition. It has been said that the '*Annamaya*' (material) is the body of the '*Prāṇamaya*' (the vital), and the latter is the soul of the former. Similarly, the '*Manomaya*' (the mental) and the '*Vijñānamaya*' (the super-mental) are the souls of the '*Prāṇamaya*' and the '*Manomaya*' respectively, whereas the '*Prāṇamaya*' and the '*Manomaya*' are the bodies of the '*Manomaya*' and the '*Vijñānamaya*' respectively. Now, the '*Ānandamaya*' (the blissful), has been referred to as the indwelling spirit inhabiting the '*Vijñānamayakoṣa*', and the '*Ānandamaya*' has not, in its turn, been referred to as the '*Koṣa*' or the body of any subtler form of the Absolute Self.[29]

We may now summarize what, according to us, is the phenomenological programme of Bhattacharrya. Its task is two-fold, namely, first, to delineate the steps whereby gradually, i.e., consecutively, the freedom of the modes of subjectivity from the corresponding objective modes can be achieved. This is really the reflective detachment of the subjective functions which, as thus detached, are fixed upon by the themselves. Secondly, not only is the freedom of a higher stage of subjectivity from a lower stage to be achieved, but also the truth of an objective mode is to be shown as lying in the subjective mode of the next higher stage.

We have seen that for both Husserl and Bhattacharyya, the object is the 'meant' content. Both speak of subjective function as meaning or intending the object. But we are to remember, first, that Bhattacharyya not only distinguishes function from meaning but also speaks of the freedom of function from meaning; secondly, and this follows from the first, meaning-function must ultimately recoil upon freedom, i.e., freedom from meaning as such.

Husserl, again, speaks of the 'suspension' of the naive, natural, objective or psychological attitude as a prerequisite to the phenomenological attitude. Such suspension, however, is impossible without committing oneself to idealism, i.e., freedom from objectivity. What Bhattacharyya says in his criticism of Kant is well worth quoting in the present context too. 'After the resolution of the objectivity of the object into the knowing function, independence of the object becomes inconceivable... '.[30] Compared to Husserl's philosophy, Bhattacharyya's idealism seems to be more in conformity with the basic requirements of the phenomenological programme.

But once more, a complete, comprehensive, full-fledged assessment of Bhattacharyya's philosophy should not restrict us to the 'ontological and/or phenomenological context'. For a study of this philosophy not only yields insights into the ontological dimensions of phenomenology or the phenomenological methodology implicated in ontology (as our foregoing study has revealed), but, what is more, adds a new dimension to phenomenological thought. The elaboration of a phenomenology of the subject or a metaphysics of our knowledge of the objective or 'meant' world on Vedānta foundations brings out that metaphysics, conceived down the ages as rooted in man's feeling of transcendence,—in whatever way such feeling may be explained, e.g., metaphysically as in Plato or immanently as in Kant—has its intimations in our objective knowledge or experience. Accordingly, objective experience is interpreted by Bhattacharyya as 'symbol' (the expression is used repeatedly in the first two chapters of *SF*) of metaphysical reality, i.e., the subject which is *known*. Thus a phenomenology of the subject or metaphysic of objective knowledge locates the demand for transcendence *within the inner boundary of knowledge* and corrects the mistaken notion that metaphysics fixes the boundary of knowledge in the *outer* dimension. In so far as Bhattacharyya's reconstruction of his native philosophy, i.e., Vedānta, does thus locate the metaphysical demand, he must be credited with having given a new direction to phenomenology that strangely resembles the one given by Heidegger with whose thought he never had any conscious historical interaction.

NOTES AND REFERENCES

1. I discovered this essay among the unpublished manuscripts of the late Professor K. C. Bhattacharyya in 1980. Subsequently, with the permission of his son, Professor Kalidas Bhattacharyya (who died in 1984), I published it in 1981 with my 'Preamble', 'Analysis' and 'Upshot' in the *Journal of Indian Philosophy*, 9 (1981), pp. 19–27, ed., Professor B. K. Matilal.
2. The book is included in the Collected Works of Bhattacharyya. See Bhattacharyya: *Studies in Philosophy*, Vol. II. Calcutta, Progressive Publishers, 1958 (Hereafter referred to as *SP*).
3. *op. cit.*, Bhattacharyya's essay on 'Transcendental Method' in *SP*, Vol. II, p. 360.
4. Bhattacharyya uses these expressions repeatedly in *SF*.
5. *Loc. cit.*
6. *SF* and *SP* Vol. II, p. 19. The statement of Husserl is quoted from Logische Untersuchungen I. TEIL, Funftz Auflage, Max Niemeyer Verlag', Tubingen 1968, p. 333.
7. Husserl, Ideas, (tr. Boyce Gibson), p. 327.
8. Bhattacharyya, 'The Concept of Philosophy', in *SP*, Vol. II, p. 103.
9. Bhattacharyya, 'The Absolute and Its Alternative Forms' in *SP* Vol. II, p. 125.
10. Bhattacharyya, 'Knowledge and Truth' in *SP*, Vol. II, p. 152.
11. Bhattacharyya, Preface to *SF* in *SP*, Vol. II, p. 3.
12. Bhattacharyya, *SF*, *FP*, Vol. II, p. 23.
13. *Ibid.*, p. 23.
14. *Ibid.*, pp. 26, 28.
15. *Ibid.*, p. 1.
16. *Ibid.*, p. 24.
17. *Ibid.*, p. 27.
18. *Ibid.*, p. 25.
19. *Ibid.*, p. 22.
20. *Ibid.*, p. 30.
21. *Ibid.*, pp. 21–22.
22. My essay on 'Notion of Epistemology in Professor K.C. Bhattacharyya', *Philosophical Quarterly*, Amalner, India, July, 1963.
23. *SF* in *SP*. Vol. II, p. 41.
24. *Ibid.*, pp. 41–42.
25. *Ibid.*, p. 43.
26. *Ibid.*, p. 205.
27. *Ibid.*, preface *loc. cit.*
28. cp. The Vedānta Conception of '*Annamayakoṣa*', '*Prāṇamayakoṣa*', '*Manomayakoṣa*' and '*Ānandamayakoṣa*'.
29. *Śāṅkarabhaṣya*, 1/1/12
30. *SF* in *SP*, Vol. II, p. 30.

Phenomenology and Philosophy of History

DAVID CARR

In the English-speaking world it has long been customary to point out that the term 'philosophy of history' is ambiguous. It refers not to one but to two very different sets of philosophical questions and concerns. Some philosophers in the West (Augustine, Vico, Hegel, Spengler, Toynbee) have advanced metaphysical theories about the course of human history itself; this project has come to be called the speculative or substantive philosophy of history. Others, beginning with Dilthey and the Neo-Kantians in the late 19th century, and extending to our own day in the British and American analytic tradition (Hempel, Collingwood, Dray, Danto, White), have turned their attention to historical knowledge or inquiry, and have asked questions belonging more to epistemology or the philosophy of science than to metaphysics. This is usually called the analytical or critical philosophy of history.

Meanwhile, in the European phenomenological tradition extending from Dilthey and Husserl through Heidegger, Gadamer, Sartre, Merleau-Ponty and Ricoeur, we find a recurrent central theme which goes by the name of historicity or historicality (*Geschichtlichkeit* or *historicité*). One thing which to my mind has never been made sufficiently clear is this: to what extent does the notion of historicity, as elaborated by the phenomenologists, contribute to or constitute a philosophy of history in either of the two senses mentioned earlier, or in some third sense yet to be specified. It is to this question that I shall address myself in what follows.

I

I shall begin by discussing some central ideas of Husserl, Dilthey, and Heidegger. The thematic focus of these three thinkers was the same, though they called it by different names. For Husserl it was 'consciousness' (*Bewusstsein*), for Dilthey 'life' (*Leben*), for Heidegger human existence or 'being-there' (*Dasein*). Each came to this thematic focus from a different direction: Husserl in the course of developing his phenomenology; Dilthey in his search for a foundation for the humanistic disciplines; Heidegger in the attempt to work out a new approach to the question of being, or ontology. Their common theme can perhaps be best described as the structure of individual human experience as it is lived; each thought that this theme called for the development of a special set of descriptive concepts; each thought that the key to this structure had something to do with *temporality*.

Though Dilthey was much older than Husserl, the two seem to have worked out the ideas I am interested in at roughly the same time (the first decade of this century), and for reasons which will become evident later I shall begin with Husserl. In his lectures on *The Phenomenology of Internal Time-Consciousness*,[1] Husserl begins his discussion of the experience of time by asking how it is that we are conscious of something that unfolds in time like a melody. He notes the obvious fact that, as the melody progresses, we must continue to be aware of the notes that have passed, but we do not *hear* them as we hear the note that is presently sounding, even weakly, for then we would be hearing the notes all at once. Clearly we do not hear the elapsed notes, for they are gone forever; rather, as we usually say, we *remember* them. But to speak merely of memory, and to describe the hearing of the melody as the combination of a perceptual awareness (hearing proper) with a memory, is not enough. It suggests, correctly enough, that the elapsed notes are non-existent or non-actual, and that they belong to the past, indeed my past—they have been and have been heard by me. But it tells us nothing about the relationship of these remembered notes to the one that is now sounding. I can remember many notes from different points in the past that have nothing to do with what I'm hearing in the present. What must be accounted for is the just-pastness of the previous note, in virtue of which I hear two notes as a succession—or, more precisely, in virtue of which I hear one note *as* succeeding another. We must distinguish, says Husserl, between two radically different sorts of memory or consciousness of the past, one (memory in the usual sense) in which I focus my attention on something which is over and done, and another which attaches itself immediately to the present. This latter sort of memory, which Husserl calls primary remembering or retention, is not something I can indulge in or not, as I choose; it is a necessary part of my experience of something present. I hear the note sound; that is, I hear it as something that happens, that 'takes place'. But to take place means to *take the place* of something else, and in the case of the melody I must be aware both of the note that sounds and of the one whose place it takes. There is no consciousness of the present as present, then, without a consciousness of the just past. But what I retain—in this case the previous note—was likewise heard as taking the place of its immediate predecessor—it involved its own retention, in other words—so that when I retain it I retain its retention as well. Every retention is thus the retention of a retention, and so on.

What emerges from this analysis is a description of the temporality of experience that is in some ways analogous to Husserl's description of the spatiality of visual perception. To see a thing is to see it against a spatial background that extends behind it and away from it and from which it stands out. The notions of focus and background are strictly correlative: no focus without background, no background without focus. Particular objects can shift from focus to background or vice versa, depending on a change in the perceiver's location or direction of attention, but while the content thus changes, the structure remains constant. As for time: if we consider the present as the focus, retention forms its background, its context or horizon which is the condition for its being experienced.[2] Retention is the horizon which extends into the indefinite 'distance'. Whatever 'takes place' in experience takes place within the context of the past; the present carries the past along with it. In recollection, or what Husserl calls secondary remembering, I can turn my attention to this background, delve into it as it were; but I need not be attentive to the past in this sense in order to live in the present. Primary remembering, on the other hand, is a structural feature of present experience which can never be lacking.

Though he does not speak about it at length, Husserl recognizes that the future constitutes a similar horizon or 'background' for present experience. Again we must distinguish between explicitly attending to the future—thinking about it, representing it, etc.—and the immediate horizon-consciousness of the future, which Husserl calls protention. The point to be stressed about this whole analysis is that experienced time, like experienced space, is a complex structure: one can no more experience the present in isolation from its past and future than one can see an object apart from its spatial *entourage*. What I am doing, seeing, feeling *now* is part of a temporal pattern that makes it what it is for me, gives it its meaning. To use Husserl's term, time-consciousness is what *constitutes* the present as present.

The analogy to seeing objects in space suggests something like a temporal field that would be analogous to the visual field, and the use of hearing a melody as an example suggests something of the narrowness of Husserl's descriptive focus. Dilthey, by contrast, talks about 'life', and means by it specifically human and indeed individual life, in the sense of 'living one's life'. Thus his focus is much broader than Husserl's but he deals with it in terms that are very similar.[3] One's life is something that unfolds in time, and while the same temporal predicates that apply to physical objects and events—simultaneity and succession, duration and change—can be applied to life as a series of events, we must speak in different terms if we wish to describe the lived experience of time (*das Erlebnis der Zeit*). As experienced, time is a flux, but it has an articulate structure which Dilthey, like Husserl, describes in terms of the past, present, and future.

Describing the experience of time, Dilthey speaks of 'the ceaseless forward push (*Vorrücken*) of the present, in which what is present forever becomes past and what is future, present. Presence is the filling of a temporal moment with reality . . . This filling with reality, or presence, perdures, whereas what makes for the content of experience is always changing.'[4] To live, then, is always to be 'located' in the present, with a past trailing along behind and a more or less open future ahead of one. But one's 'location' is in another sense always different, since the content of the present is always changing and with it the content of the past and the future. The content of the past is in one sense fixed, of course, though it is constantly being added to; but even what remains the same is always given, so to speak, from a new perspective, that of the changing present. And the future, whose content is forever being robbed as slips into the present and the past, is nevertheless always growing and changing as new possibilities for action, new expectations and the like, emerge.

For Dilthey, the course of life consists of more or less distinguishable parts, which he calls lived experiences (*Erlebnisse*), but these are what they are in virtue of the whole structure to which they belong. We are always engaged in the present in what we are doing or experiencing, but this present stands out against the background of the past and against the partly open horizon of the future. This temporal structure is the form of life, but it does not guarantee what Dilthey calls the 'coherence of life' (*Zusammenhang des Lebens*). This coherence is rather something that has to be achieved, through a particular explicit form of reflection. Dilthey discusses the art of autobiography—particularly those of Augustine, Rousseau, and Goethe—as the attempt to give coherence to the events, actions and experiences of one's life. But autobiography, he says, is only the literary expression of the sort of reflection on one's course of life that goes on in all of us. And, of course, it occurs not just once; the autobiography is constantly being revised. Part of the process of life, then, is the attention that is paid to the coherence of life, placing the present in the context of a temporal whole that gives it a sensible structure.

Dilthey's account is like Husserl's in bringing out the three-dimensional structure of lived temporality, but his focus is broader—'life' rather than particular experiences—he pays more attention to the future than Husserl does, and he introduces the element of 'autobiography' or concern for the coherence of life. If we now take Dilthey's conception of the coherence of life, and use the melody of Husserl, not as an example of a temporal experience, but rather as a metaphor for the temporal structure itself, we can perhaps approximate, in a rather sketchy way, the Heideggerian conception of temporality without becoming too lost in his terminology.[5]

When we listen to a song we have not heard before, each note is heard as part of the song, as a place in the over-all pattern that is the melody. But the melody may develop in unexpected ways, so that the notes previously heard belong to an over-all pattern that is different from the one we originally placed them in. Our grasp of the whole, and thus of the elapsed notes as its parts, may change several times as the song unfolds. But of course this means that our anticipation of the future goes though the same changes as our retention of the past. The place and significance of each note is not settled until we reach the end and have heard it all. But at each stage in its unfolding, we were projecting ourselves to the end, so to speak, taking each note as part of the whole we took the melody to be.

Now if we consider living one's life—Heidegger's *Dasein* as the business of existing in a human way—to be like a melody, we can understand what Heidegger means when he says that *Dasein* is the temporal structure of being always 'ahead of itself' (future), yet also 'already in' the world (past), and alongside or with things (present). But Heidegger adds a further descriptive element to the structure. There is the awareness that hits each of us from time to time, and can be a rather shattering experience—Heidegger calls it *anxiety*—that we are, so to say, writing the song ourself and no one else can write it for us; and yet (barring suicide) we are unable to determine when it will end; and, even if we could so determine its end, we could never just *be* at the end, in the sense of existing there and looking back, for the end is death. The completeness of life is something we are aware of only from within it, i.e. when it is incomplete. This notion of anxiety and the awareness of death leads to what Heidegger calls 'resoluteness', and the distinction between authenticity and inauthenticity. Resoluteness means not necessarily changing one's tune (to continue our earlier metaphor) but rather accepting responsibility for its composition, even if it remains the same. One has this responsibility, whether one accepts it or not. Inauthenticity—avoiding this responsibility—is living one's life as most of us do most of the time, as if it were a song written by someone else, or no one in particular. Resoluteness corresponds in some ways to Dilthey's autobiographical stage, the attentiveness to and concern for the coherence of life.

While Husserl analyses a short-term passive perception like hearing a melody, and Heidegger and Dilthey examine the long-term business of understanding and structuring one's whole life, their analysis is applicable to an intermediate range of phenomena as well. Whether actively or passively, we are always engaged in particular temporal structures of greater or lesser scope. Whatever the focus of the present, whether observing an event or engaging in some course of action, we always make sense of that present by holding in our grasp the past and projecting before us the future which together make sense of that present. Actions in particular, whether tying one's shoe or going shopping or building a house or writing a book, are temporal structures of the sort in which each present phase fits into a temporal pattern we have more or less explicitly in mind. I say 'more or less explicitly' because we occasionally have to remind ourselves what we are doing while we are doing it, and we often revise our conception of what we are doing as we go along. This is what we often call acting reflectively, consciously or self-consciously.

But this self-consciousness or self-awareness, which we occasionally retrieve in the midst of some course of action, is not the isolated awareness of the 'self', or of some instantaneous experience, as if comparable to an object perceived at a glance. Rather, it is the construction or re-construction of a temporally extended *story* in which the present action or experience has a part, plays a role joining past and future. Daily life is full of such stories that fit into one another and overlap; the same events and actions can play roles in different stories, etc.

II

Having sketched the broad outlines of our composite theory of human *temporality*, drawn from the ideas of Husserl, Dilthey and Heidegger, we now turn to *historicity* and the problem of history. We asked whether this theory is relevant to the philosophy of history in either of its traditional forms. First we must ask, in keeping with our original distinction: to which history is it related: the historical process itself or the discipline of describing and understanding that process? The answer is that it is not only related to both, but also enables us to understand the relation between the two.

First, the theory can contribute to our understanding of the historical process. It does this not in the manner of the speculative philosophy of history, suggesting claims about the origin, unfolding and destiny of historical reality as a whole, but rather by making it possible to discern some important features of historical events and human historical existence. The simplest way to affirm this would be to say that the historical process is generally regarded as being made up of individuals' acting and living out their lives, and that our theory is primarily a theory of individual human life and activity. It thus gives us an account of basic units—the atoms, as it were—of which the historical process is composed, whatever else the latter may be. But this would be a minor contribution indeed, and in fact I think the theory, with some adjustments, can do more than this.

We ordinarily think of the historical process in terms of the lives not of individuals but of peoples, of nations, of classes, or of collective endeavours like art or music or science. One of the debates in the philosophy of history and social science has concerned what sort of entities such collectivities are, and in particular whether we are justified in attributing to them the same sorts of properties we attribute to individuals, such as character, purpose and activity. But it is possible to sidestep this issue by saying that in their activity, individuals often *identify* themselves with such a group or collective endeavour, whether as leaders or as participants, such that the individual thinks of the activity he or she is engaged in not as 'my own' but rather as 'ours'. Such collective activity is surely not all there is to the historical process, but it is an important part of it, and it is primarily (though not exclusively) in this sense that the activities, projects and lives of individuals contribute to or figure in the historical process. It is primarily the activities of leaders, of course, that stand out in this way. Caesar's crossing the Rubicon is part of the historical process in the way that his crossing the street for a loaf of bread is not, because his action is at the same time the action of his army and is seen as an event in the life of the Roman Republic.

When I say it is *seen* in this way, I mean it is seen thus by those who participate in it and those who are affected by it, and also, most importantly perhaps, that it is seen this way by Caesar himself. This means that the past out of which his action arises and the future toward which it tends—i.e., the temporal context that gives it its meaning—is the past and future not just of Caesar himself but of the group to which he belongs. To be sure, personal ambition, lust for power, the fulfilment of a certain self-image are also involved in Caesar's action; and to this extent it is an element in his own personal biography. It is unlikely, however, that these elements would figure in his *auto*biography, that is, the manner in which he would account for his action to others or even to himself. The participants in the storming of the Bastille may also have had individual projects into which this particular action could be inserted as part of a coherent *personal* story. But the storming of the Bastille is not just the result of many individual actions converging, as when a bank fails because many people decide, independently of each other, to draw out their money. Individuals act, but each considers himself a participant in an action which is undertaken by the group of as such. This means that, for each individual, the action or event fits into a story not just about himself, but about the *group* which acts; and this story may include other actions and events in which a given individual was not a participant and about which he or she may not even know in detail.

The point, then, is that this context is the 'proper' context of the action or event not somehow in itself, or for some future or ideal historian, but rather *for* the individuals involved. For *them*, the temporal context which makes sense of the present action may be social rather than individual.

There are, of course, differences in the degree to which individuals are aware of the social context of their action. But in the social world there is generally no lack of reminders of this context in case individuals should forget it. Collective existence and action is always surrounded by a certain kind of talk, of which political rhetoric is perhaps the most pervasive example, which interprets events, proposes actions, and explains them after they have happened, and which does this by fitting them into a story which is not that of any individual but that of some group.

Often, the purpose of such rhetoric is the very establishment of such a group, or, more precisely, to persuade people that they belong to such a group and thus to bring about their identification with it. Many of the suprapersonal entities that we think of as being involved in the historical process owe their existence, at least in part, to this kind of identification. Modern nation-states as historical forces could be said to depend on people identifying themselves with those states. The same could be said of those social entities that have been in competition with political units, historically, for the allegiance of individuals: family, religion, race, people, class, linguistic minority, etc. Often, though not always, certain 'facts' about persons are relevant, that is, facts that are independent of their self-consciousness, of the sort that might be known to a historian or social scientist and might figure among the statistics of a given society: the fact of speaking one language rather than another, of practicing one religion rather than another, of being a worker or a capitalist, a woman or a man. Political rhetoric makes use of such facts and tries to persuade individuals that their fate is bound up with some unit like class, religion or state and thus to identify themselves with it, e.g. to consider themselves primarily as members of the international proletariat rather than as French or German.

In any case, it can be argued that individuals always identify themselves with some group or other (and sometimes, of course, with more than one). Assuming such identification, events then happen which are things that happen to *us* rather than *me*, actions are undertaken which are *our* actions rather than *mine*, plans are *ours* to carry out, goals to be achieved are *our* goals. Just as the life of the individual, whose actions and experiences are elements in a personal autobiography which is more or less explicitly in mind, and which on occasions, like Heidegger's moments of anxiety, gets articulated and rearticulated, so the life of the group always implicitly has *its* autobiography, whose articulation and occasional revision falls to the leaders and rhetoricians of the group. Almost invariably, such articulation takes the form of an interpretation of the group's past, sometimes a myth of origin or foundation; a conception of the group's future or its destiny—sometimes alternative destinies—and of course a representation of the present as a decisive moment, sometimes a crisis or turning point. Consider the example of Lincoln's 1863 Gettysburg Address, in the midst of the American Civil War—words that every American child learns in school:

> Four score and seven years ago our fathers brought forth on this continent a new nation, conceived in liberty, and dedicated to the proposition that all men are created equal. Now we are engaged in a great civil war, testing whether that nation, or any nation so conceived and so dedicated, can long endure.

Lincoln's address belongs to the historical process, as everyone would agree, and following our interpretation we can see how and why. It explains the meaning of an event or collective action or endeavour (the war) by placing it in a story with a past and future—or, as we might say, a beginning, middle and end—it articulates that event not only for the speaker, who is also the leader of the nation in this case, but also for his listeners, who are also the participants in the event. In Husserl's terminology we could say that his articulation *constitutes* the event, places it in the temporal horizon that gives it its meaning. For what is the event, we might ask, apart from how it is seen and lived by those involved? (To be sure, a later historian may insist that the event was somehow other than leaders and participants took it to be, but what they took it to be, or rather their taking it to be such, is still part of the historical process with which the historian has to reckon.) Lincoln's address is part of the historical process, then, because the process consists of events and actions that are interpreted as events and actions of a group by the members and the group; or, more radically, the events and actions only exist as historical events to the extent that they are so interpreted and constituted.

But with an example like this it can easily be seen that we are on the borderline between history as process and history as inquiry or knowledge. The life of a social group involves the identification of individuals with events, activities and endeavours that belong to the group itself; this, in turn, requires a more or less explicit *articulation* or *account* of the life of the group involving its past and its future in order that the significance of events and activities of the present can be agreed upon by participants. Common life requires a common and recurrent stock-taking, and this is something that is performed on behalf of the group by one or some of its members. The political leader performs this task rhetorically, usually in order to bring out a particular action or common endeavour; and depending on the nature of the objective to be achieved, his or her account of past and future will be of greater or lesser scope. The success of such a leader's endeavour will usually depend on the degree to which his or her interpretation of events is accepted by others. But a similar sort of stock-taking can be undertaken by individuals whose purpose is not necessarily to achieve some immediate result. They may or may not have a longer-term future conception of their community that they wish to realize, partly through their interpretation of events. In any case, their project, like that of the political leader, involves explaining the significance of the present in terms of a past and a future, and it is something they do on behalf of the community to which they belong.

Obviously what I have in mind here is the activity of historians who write or tell the history of their own people or community. And we can describe their activity as arising out of the temporal structure of communal life, which is individual life 'writ large'. For Dilthey, Husserl and Heidegger, individual life is not just a sequence of events and actions, but a sequence that is experienced in terms of a more or less coherent temporal structure. And it is self-conscious, we said, not in the sense of any momentary self-awareness, but rather in the sense that the very coherence, or lack of it, of the sequence of events is reflected on and articulated in the process of self-clarification and self-justification that makes up the elements of an implicit autobiography. Most of us never write out such an autobiography; all of us are constantly revising it. But it is something we must engage in from time to time; it is not something tacked on and optional. Telling the story of one's life, if only to oneself, is part of living.

Now we can say that such story-telling is part of communal life too. If the community exists through individuals joining in common endeavours and activities, then these must be made sense of by virtue of their place in the life or the community, and not just in the life of each of the individuals who participates. Particular events and actions, then, are experienced and undertaken as belonging in such a context, whose coherence becomes a matter of concern. Such coherence is achieved, or at least attempted, in the telling of a story about the community which makes sense of the present in terms of its past and its future. The existence of such a story, and the concern with 'getting it right', revising it, etc., is as much a part of communal life as the autobiographical element is part of individual life. Elements and versions of the story, as aids in interpreting the events of common life, may figure in the ordinary conversation of members of the community. But usually the responsibility for the telling of the story is taken over by, and ceded to, particular individuals. As story-telling functionaries for the community, historians then belong together with leaders, political speakers and writers, journalists and pamphleteers.

I want to claim that history as inquiry has its *origin* in this story-telling aspect of communal life. Independently of being historians or of being engaged in historical research or even of reading history, we understand the historian's enterprise through the kind of explicit or implicit story-telling that goes with being a member of a community of some sort. And the historian is doing nothing more than expanding and making explicit the kind of story-telling we are all involved with.

Just as our approach to history as process was different from that of the speculative philosophy of history, so our approach to history as inquiry is different from that of the analytic philosophy of history. Phenomenological questions are situated at a different level. Our basic question could best be put this way: to what areas of experience, which lie outside or are prior to the domain of historical inquiry as such, does such inquiry correspond? Our claim is that we are intimately involved with the historical, in the sense of the human past, independently of any theoretical or strictly cognitive interest in it. Life in the family, the city, the larger community whatever its nature, to the extent that the individual identifies with it and participates in its activities, carries with it a communal past that forms part of the background or context for what happens in the present.

Thus the implicit or explicit autobiography of the individual has its counterpart in the account that is given of common experience or common action and endeavour, an account that may be given by one or some individuals on behalf of the community but which is properly an account concerning the community as such and not any individual. Such accounting, stock-taking, story-telling, we have argued, is not extrinsic to community life, added on as if it were optional, but is just as necessary an element of it as autobiographical reflexion is of individual life. The very historical process itself is generated by such accounts, and we can speak of this story-telling function as being at the origin of history as process, just as we have spoken of it as the origin of history as inquiry. We are not attempting to break down the distinction between these two senses of history; we are tracing them to a common origin.[6]

NOTES AND REFERENCES

1. Bloomington, Indiana University Press, 1964. We shall be paraphrasing the ideas of these three authors, and not quoting extensively or restricting ourselves to their terminology. Here the reader is referred especially to the first twenty sections of Husserl's lectures.
2. Cf. *Ibid.*, p. 45.
3. In the case of Dilthey we have drawn on the collection edited by M. Riedel (Wilhelm Dilthey, *Der Aufbau der geschichtlichen Welt in den Geisteswissenschaften*, Frankfurt, Suhrkamp verlag 1970) especially pp. 233–251.
4. *Ibid.*, p. 237.
5. We are limiting ourselves, of course, to *Being and Time* (New York, Harper and Row 1962). The reader is referred especially to sections 41 and 65.
6. An earlier version of this essay appeared in *Philosophia Naturalis*, Band 25, Heft 1–2, 1988.

Freedom, Interpretation and Meaning in Human Sciences

D. P. CHATTOPADHYAYA

I

Prefatory. The nature of human sciences is bound to be intimately related to, if not reflective of, human nature. The subject matter of human sciences, broadly speaking, consists of human actions, dispositions and their societal affiliation. Given the same societal affiliation, different human beings, even the same human being at different times, are/is free to be diversely disposed and can act differently. *Freedom* of action and disposition is a key concept in all human sciences. Situated identically—'identically' from an external point of view—humans *interpret* their relations with the 'situation' in question in different ways.[1] Since the human situation consists largely of human beings themselves, the diversity of man-situation relationship should also be understood as an expression of the diversity of the interhuman relationship. The ability of one and the same man to view and review his relationship with other human beings in widely different ways is evident from the changing and complex texture of the interhuman relationship. For example, the same partners in life, who at one stage love each other, may develop hatred and get finally separated. Comparable change of relation between nations committed to identical ideologies is not unknown either.

In the understanding of social phenomena, the most important role is played by will, action and communication. Phenomenology of will shows *why* human beings cannot remain what they are and *how* the historical thrust of their life makes them different from what they are. The so-called involuntary body, and extension of inanimate nature in us, is an essential, enabling condition, not, a negation, of human volition. A sense of finitude and incompleteness is always at work in human life.[2] Man wants to be qualitatively richer and socially larger than what his present conditions and constraints allow him to be. This consciousness goads him on to set certain goals for himself which, if realised, would enrich and enlarge his existence. Phenomenology of will is intimately related to phenomenology of action. In fact, will is incipient action, and action articulated will. Through action man throws his being forward. He cannot do this in isolation, in a social vacuum. He needs active support and also active opposition to realise his aims. The process of human becoming is not smooth, onesided and unilateral. Unless man ceases to be what he is, he cannot be what he wills to be. Unless he gets out of the rut of his present habits, he cannot authentically initiate new actions. Even before he actually takes up new courses of action, he cultivates within himself the necessary will to act. Before it is found possible for him to execute his plan of action, the plan is infused with, and invigorated by, his resolution or determination. Even while he does not act, he *means* to act. Suspended action is action meant. Even unperformed action has its own meaning. Its meaningfulness is derived from its experiential background and goal-oriented character. This is a dispositional character. It is more than a *state* of body or even of mind. It is tension, preparatory extension, of mind. It is intention, external meaning, of mind. It is mental preparation for action. Reflectivity of consciousness discloses different and refined layers of this unperformed but meant action. Phenomenology of *individual* will and action is in a way *symbolic representation* of the will and action of the concerned milieu. True, in the parallelogram of the social forces one cannot literally represent others. But the truth of symbolic representation can hardly be in doubt. And it owes its existence to more or less free nature of all human beings. It is also partly due to *unintended* consequences of intentionally performed actions. Consequently, we come across some phenomena in social life which nobody intends in isolation but which turns out to be the outcome of the action of the milieu.

What these changing phenomena bring to the focus of our attention is freedom of action and disposition (with or without reference to the attending circumstances). Phenomenological reflection on the nature of human relationship brings another very important concept of our notice; and that is *meaning*. Given a particular disposition of mind, a person may mean *friendship* to me; given another disposition, the same person may mean *hostility* to me. In other words, all things being equal, one is more or less free to interpret the meaning of others' actions and dispositions. Underlying these changing interpretations and meanings of human actions and dispositions is a form of life, which, in turn, is sustained and moulded essentially by human freedom. *Lebensform* and what makes it possible form a growing and creative, i.e., non-vicious circle.

In what follows I propose to try to clarify phenomenologically the ontology of human nature and its bearing on human sciences to be understood basically in terms of *interpretation* and *meaning*.

II

Freedom. That man is free is not really disputed. But philosophers and human or social scientists are not unanimous in their construal of freedom. It has been differently construed, viz., (a) as absence of constraint, (b) as recognition of necessity, (c) as spontaneity and (d) as consciousness. Each one of these views is open to more than one interpretation. In fact, it has been differently interpreted. This is evident from the history of eastern and western philosophies of social thought.

Freedom as absence of external constraints is not a very clear concept. It calls for considerable elucidation. The more we reflect on it, the more seminal appears its meaning.

The distinction often drawn between 'the external' and 'the internal' in naturalistic terms turns out, on scrutiny, to be untenable. A devotee may be more determined or influenced by the presence of the idol or the image of a deity than by the living presence of another person or the deity's priest. To him, the presence of the stone-deity may mean much more than that of all human beings. In contrast, an imprisoned freedom fighter in iron fetters may continue to feel the spirit of freedom in him. To him, the presence or the absence of external constraints may not be a sufficient condition for giving or taking away human freedom. We know of many persons who fear things they do not even know of and cannot assign any convincing reason for their fears. The neurotic feeling of persecution is said to be of this nature. Are not many of us, non-neurotic humans, often afraid of lack of freedom? Curiously enough, even free situations at times put a sense of fear in us. Freedom is like a double-edged knife. It may cut our bond; it may also cut itself.

The pre-reflective view that body curbs our freedom has to be carefully looked into. It seems that there is duality in the role of the body. In a sense my body curbs my freedom. The physical inertia of body, its spatial situatedness, its passions, needs, etc., somehow tie me down to a limited area. To a certain extent, the motion of my body is restricted by its weight and orientation. Viewed thus, my body is an impediment to my freedom.

Implicit in this assertion is the assumption that I have an existence which is non-somatic and non-hedonic and there lies the true seat of my freedom. In other words, the suggestion is: I, as a thing-being (*jada-puruṣa*) or somatic being (*śarīra puruṣa*), am not free and that I, only as a mental being (*manomaya puruṣa*) am free. The philosophers of the dualist or gradualist persuasion often use this argument as a plank of anti-physicalism and anti-hedonism. Both in Sāṅkhya and in Kant one can easily discern this trend of thought. One socio-ethical corollary of this view is to berate the significance of body in the context of freedom. In 'Two Negations' of *The Life Divine* Sri Aurobindo shows the fallacy of this view.[3]

The defenders of the anti-somatic approach to freedom fail to see the sense in which the body is a positive condition, and not an impediment or constraint, of freedom. Even if it is assumed that I have a mental plane of existence, that does not mean that my other plane, the somatic is anti-thetical to it. On the contrary, the body is, phenomenologically speaking, articulative of my so-called inner freedom. It is in and through my body that I articulate, execute and exercise my freedom. So do other humans as well. Words of our mouth, our physical labour and whatever else we do with our bodies bring us in *communion* with each other. In other words, we need a body in order to be aware of our membership of, our belonging to, a community. To dramatize this point one might say: only embodied beings can form a *community*. Physical things or bodies, which know no freedom, cannot form a community. The reason that we, humans, can form it is indicative of the fact that our bodies are expressive and *communicative*, and not physical in the sense of a cold, inanimate and dead thing. Our body-being, even while it performs a *separative* role, does not cease to be communicative.

The question of communication does not arise unless persons aiming at or engaged in communication are effectively separate from each other. Communication is neither soliloquy nor bare repetition. Mechanical repetition diminishes the content of communication. Gradually a stage may come when one's saying gets meaningless and fails to be communicative. Communication is intended to annihilate or, at least, minimise the effects of separation. Two or more persons may talk for a long time without being successful in communicating their views. This often happens in diplomatic discussions. Success in communication lifts discussion to the level of discourse. In discourse we are more interested in communicating rather than in defending our views and in swaying others with our feelings. Interestingly enough, sometimes we succeed in communicating without saying, without discussion or discourse. Silence may be communicative but it presupposes common social milieu, shared experiences, expectations, norms, etc. Somehow, this 'presupposition' needs to be lived (in experience).[4] The notion of shared experience, on phenomenological analysis, is found to be rooted in our bodily being. The social 'presuppositions' that make our experiences, expectations, etc. sharable have somehow to be lived in order to make this sharability possible. This fact brings us back to the notion of the body, without which we cannot belong to a social milieu and share our life with each other.

The double-edgedness or the duality of human freedom may be clarified in another way. My body, without ceasing to be mine, is both subjective and objective. It has a *subjectivity* of its own which is not experientially available to others, unless, of course, we try to explain the concept of experience itself in the language-game-theoretic model of Wittgenstein[5] or in the behavioural model of Skinner.[6] When we speak of the subjectivity of the body we do not even remotely deny its objective availability of what it expresses, articulates, exercises and performs.[7] In this sense, the body has admittedly an *objective aspect*.

Our actions, linguistic as well as (non-linguistic) behavioural are intelligible to others because what we do or what the body does is public, i.e., available both to self and others.

Human will as a phenomenon develops because there is a persistent sense of absence in us from which we *need* to be free. This felt need has two aspects. On the one hand, it is symbolic of negation or non-being in our being and, on the other, it tends to draw us out of our changing bounds of being. As was said earlier, we can neither live nor will as possible discrete, atomic and monadic beings. The normative structure of our will is informed not only by the negation in us but also by what is not there in the milieu to which we belong. When I see my fellow beings, I see them in their finitude, in their incompleteness, as engaged in striving for reaching out to some goals and goods which they need and want but which are not available to them. The seemingly positive perception of the bodies of my fellow human beings is actually normatively loaded. This load is increased through communication and discourse. The more I hear of them, their lives, their weals and their woes, the more I live *with* them. In effect, my being-with-them is symbolic of my positive association and normative identification with them. More than knowledge I am tied to them by *sympathy*. Being-with-others is mainly sustained by a field of sympathies, not cognition or contemplation. Though in our cognitive acts, too, we go beyond ourselves and try to identify ourselves with objects, our success here is limited. It is for this reason—implicit normative reason—that we supplement cognition by *imagination*. It is also a mode of a being's response to what is not there. Images are more constructive than receptive in character. Imagination is nourished more by will than by perception or even cognition.[8] It is with the aid of imagination that we can hope to produce what our milieu is bereft of, and try to get for our fellow beings what they do not have. For it is imagination that enables us to understand their needs and the necessity of satisfying them. Beyond imagination, but partly on the basis of it, work sympathies. In and through sympathies we widen and broaden our scope of life and fulfil its chosen aims. Our bodies enable us not only to know others but also to have their companionship. This is how embodied human beings through their knowledge, imagination and sympathies enlarge and enrich their social forms of existence.

Extending this line of argument it can be shown that once we understand the meaning of somatic freedom, it can serve as a seemingly meagre input of social action and communication. If our social life gradually turns to be larger and larger, the latter i.e., the enlarged output, can be shown to be an expansion of the 'meagre' input.[9] The basic ontology of the social forms of life, smaller and larger, is same. Whether we try to understand the structure and the function of the family, the clan, the tribe, etc., or those of a nation, a confederation of nations, an empire, etc., the basic ontology is provided by embodied human freedom.[10]

III

From Freedom. When we emphasize the embodied aspect of human freedom, we try to show two things, (i) that human freedom is concrete and public, and (ii) that social forms human sciences study have no disembodied or 'spiritual' being. When we thus discount the spiritual ontology of human sciences, we do not mean to deny altogether their invisible or theoretical aspects. The whole of our social life cannot indeed, be translated into observational language. Neither observation itself nor its largest possible outcomes are observationally available. The 'hidden' recesses of our social life are also not empirically available. It is only in and through phenomenological reflection on the nature of human freedom and what is disclosed by it, the smaller forms of life, that we can gradually get into the larger forms of life, their hidden recesses and complexity.

What we call societal facts, e.g., 'national policy climate', 'international currency market', 'global peace' are understandable but not experientially available. One outcome of human freedom is to go ever beyond the given. Phenomenology shows us how to understand the not-given in terms of the given, without any inductive leap as ordinarily understood. Therefore, one who resorts to this approach has no need to give any justification of this method. Phenomenology of social sciences, as conceived in this short paper, is to show how certain basic concepts of phenomenology serve as a key to the understanding of complex social phenomena. It also shows the abstract, anatomical and unconvincing character of the causal approach followed in physics—for example. We can, if we like, construct a social physics, only man will not find a place in its *causal structure*.

The passage from the 'simple' given to the 'complex' not-given, from the 'specious' present to the 'obscure' past or future, proves problematic not only to the sceptics of the Buddhist or the Humean type but to all human beings. It has been understood in very many ways, viz., in terms of (i) laws or regularities, (ii) rational reconstruction in which (i) is implicit, (iii) continuous narration or description in which (i) is denied place, and (iv) intentional exploration or excavation.

Firstly, both inductivists (like Hempel) and anti-inductivists (like Popper) believe in methodological monism. The plausibility of the hypothetico-deductive model of explanation authored by them rests squarely on the testability of the concerned laws and regularities. The description of the initial conditions, covered, backed up and related by laws, are bound to be sketchy. This model of explanation is often known as Covering Law Model (CLM).

Secondly, the logic of rational reconstruction is not quite different from that of CLM. In this case, the model is reconstructed or reenacted, implicitly assuming the validity of certain laws. The particular explanatory statements purport to describe the dispositions and actions of the concerned human beings within the appropriate context. Since the context is spatio-temporally distant and, therefore, not directly surveyable, it has to be reconstructed either on the assumption of *perfect* rationality (in the analogy of the geometrical zero co-ordinate point) or on the assumption of the validity of certain laws of science. Coherence is the most important requirement which needs to be satisfied by the Rational Reconstruction Model (RRM). But the model is open, in principle, to possible testing evidences. For example, a coherent anthropological or historical explanation, is expected to survive possible empirical tests. In some of their works, Weber and Popper have defended RRM, a flexible variant of CLM. Its basic aim is to put the *text* of the action to be understood in the (reconstructed) *context* of its performance so that the meaning of action is better disclosed. RRM is a step beyond CLM, intended to do away with, at least partially, the *structural abstractness* of the latter.

Thirdly, there are some pro-idealists (Croce, Collingwood and Oakeshott) who maintain that socio-historical explanation consists *only* of continuous narration of concrete description and do *not* need any covering law whatsoever. This model seeks to leave behind the abstractness or sketchiness entailed by the laws of CLM. It is generally known as Continuous Series Model (CSM). The important insight that we find in this model is that it recognizes a 'non-external' relation or concrete nexus between events which, taken as a whole, serve as an explanation. According to CSM, social explanation may be viewed as a (dichronical) continuum or a (synchronical) plenum. In their 'spiritual' depth human beings, viewed historically or sociologically, are inseparably interrelated or, as Hegel observes, unified. Unity and continuity of social relations symbolized in, and interpreted by, human beings provide the ontological substructure of CSM. Social forms are said to be expressive of human thought sought to be freely articulated.[11]

Finally, the phenomenologist draws our attention to the 'internal thread' which ties different events, narrated or described, into a continuum or plenum. The actions and dispositions which constitute the stuff of explanation are essentially *human* and, therefore, impregnated with human purpose or projection. Man has been differently described as 'self-exceeding' (Sri Aurobindo), 'being-there' (Heidegger) and 'project' (Sartre). Underlying the formulational difference, there is a common point which highlights the presence of man in what he does or brings about. He is present in his dispositions to act, in the process of his actions and in the resulting products. It is this human root of socio-historical events which makes it possible for us to discover or excavate the internal thread which tie or interweave human events together. This may be called Phenomenological Descriptive Model (PDM). While in Hegelian phenomenology, individual human beings are seen as the manifestations of Spirit (*Geist*) and their actions are interpreted accordingly, in PDM, as conceived here, there is no such metaphysical presuppositions. Human history and society are essentially human products devoid of any metaphysical back-up principle.

Now we will try to see very briefly how in terms of PDM we can move from human freedom to different social forms, smaller and larger.

IV

From Smaller To Larger Human Aggregates. Nobody denies that human aggregates, smaller or larger, from family, clan, commune and tribe to nation, confederation of nations, empire and the world order in the making, are basically rooted in human nature and needs. This 'unanimous' view is sure to sound trivially true. But once we get into different theoretical and practical accounts of the passage from the life of the individual to that of the social aggregates, we see that behind the facade of unanimity there is substantive difference.

The naturalist-causalist tries to show that the dynamics of the passage from the individual to the aggregate is provided by *external* factors like environment and technology. The antinaturalist-teleologist is of the view that the dynamics of the passage is *internal* to the individual and his inexhaustible potentiality. Implicit in the second view is the assumption that the individual is essentially universal or that there is a secret but growing God. The phenomenologist seeks to show that it is within human consciousness and in terms of its intentionality that one has to understand and discover the reason of the passage from the individual form of life to its social forms. Once the true nature of man is understood, the supposed dichotomy between 'the external' and 'the internal' dynamics and the resulting debate between the defenders of the first view like Marx and those of the second view like Sri Aurobindo and Hegel, turn out to be somewhat out of place. The so-called external factors like environment and technology do not work on the life of man, individual or social, in a mechanical-causal or unilateral way. The social role of man has to be rightly understood. He is not a causal creature of his circumstances. The expression 'his circumstances' is important. Because of the discernment of his judgemental competence man can always distinguish between those factors of his environment which are beneficial to him and, those which are not. Both his senses of *episteme* and *techne* are formed accordingly. In fact, power of judgemental discernment, the choice of the place of habitation, and technology are expressive of his freedom. To say this is not to deny that at times causal-natural forces may overwhelm man and frustrate his intention and thinking. If man-environment relation is perceptibly looked into, it becomes clear that man is simultaneously a creator and a creature of his environment. There is a sort of dialectic between the two.

When the human root of knowledge becomes invisible in the mist of abstraction, the paradigm of modern knowledge, science, is accepted as a manipulative mechanism. Neither scientific epistemology nor technology should be interpreted as an external manipulative device. Certainly, tools and techniques have their use-value. Knowledge may also be put to practical use. Literature and fine arts may be used as means of propaganda. But none of these technical or instrumental uses of science, technology and arts should make us blind to their essential human root and inspiration. It can be shown that every technique we invent or employ is purported to fulfil some or other human need. In art-forms, life-experiences are represented to provide aesthetic satisfaction. Through all these *works* we, in a way, express, ourselves, our will, and expand our world.[12]

It is not at all surprising that many existentialists and phenomenologists of the Marxist persuasion are veering round to the view that once we succeed in grasping the human root of the 'dialectics of nature', we will see that in the latter the former is deeply involved. 'Natural thing' is not quite alien to the 'human thing'. If the Kantian dictum, 'man makes nature possible', is one-sided and untenable, the naturalist's pronouncement, 'nature makes man possible', is equally so. Nature is not there out in space-time, complete in itself, to be passively watched. Nor are we complete in ourselves, independent of and separated from nature.[13] Hence the point which the phenomenologist tries to bring out first in his concept of the subjectivity of body, which is a sort of *tertium quid* between nature and self, as to show how it works as a passage from the seemingly 'narrow' confines of individuality to the expanding horizons of social form, existence and meaning. The accounts of the formation of human aggregates provided by the antinaturalist-teleologist may or may not be God-based. Though some thinkers like Samuel Alexander and Teilhard de Chardin start as naturalists, they end up with a type of teleology. Evolutionary transition from naturalism to super-naturalism, from causalism to purposivism, is sought to be rendered plausible in terms of qualitative emergence.[14] There are others like Hegel and Sri Aurobindo who maintain that super-nature itself is dormantly present in nature. Causal forces are essentially the secret handiworks of the Divine purpose.

It is easy to show the phenomenological undertone of the second trend of social thought. Here the individual is taken to be 'the first self-conscious formation of life', as 'our index and our foundation'. The individual has in him a feeling of limitation in and around him, which he wants to do away with. In order to enlarge the horizon of his freedom, to undo the effects of limitation, he tries to internalize these limiting conditions. This process, rightly understood, is phenomenological, neither abstract-logical nor external-technological. It is in and through the living and concrete enlargement of his consciousness that man tries to see the community, if not the unity, of his conscious life with that of his fellow human beings. The gradual self-development, self-enlargement and self-formulation of the individual is partly conscious and partly unconscious. Sri Aurobindo observed: 'The primal law and purpose of the individual life is to seek its own self-development.... In the same way, the primal law and purpose of a society, community or nation is to seek its own self-development'.[15]

In the formation of family, man finds his basic intention of self-development fulfilled. Familial relations may be conjugal and/or parental. The emergence of family is hardly datable. It is therefore taken primarily in a conceptual sense. It is a kin-group; each of its members is a relative of the others. The clan, a further enlargement of the individual life, is a compromised kin-group, compromising the uni-local residence and the unilateral descent. Both family and clan are blood-determined social units. But neither has been found to be suitable for the fulfilment of growing human needs and aspirations. The community is said to be the outcome of the consciousness of the lack of self-fulfilment. Community life is intended to provide its members with increased opportunity to fulfil their needs through social intercourse, adequate food through cooperative food gathering techniques, and security against illness, incapacity, or enemy attack through mutual aid and assistance. At every stage of his life, whether it is familial or communal or tribal or even national, man increasingly feels the needs of certain additional goods and services which cannot be provided by his existing social units or human aggregates. And that, in the main, accounts for the gradual enlargement of the scope of the aggregative life and its increasing complexity, including the multiplication of needs and increase in division and satisfaction of labour.

The above teleological account of anthropological evolution lends itself to both phenomenological and non-phenomenological idealistic interpretations. One can substantiate it by extensively quoting, for example, from Hegel's *Phenomenology of Spirit* and *Philosophy of Right* and Sri Aurobindo's *The Human Cycle* and *The Ideal of Human Unity*. Neither Hegel nor Sri Aurobindo is a phenomenologist in any ordinary sense. But without distorting their substantive theses and forms of reasoning, it can be shown how close their views are to those developed later on by such thinkers as Jaspers, Marcel, Heidegger, Sartre and Ricoeur. While tracing human development, philosophy of history and philosophical anthropology finds two distinct forms, one of enduring *individuality* and other of growing *universality*. Though distinctly discernible, these forms are integrally complementary.

V

Subjectivity and Freedom: True and False. The freedom that finds expression in and through the body knows no boundary and, given will, can see enlarging horizons. The diversity of human aggregates is indicative of the different possible forms of expression of human freedom. Here freedom is to be understood primarily as an ontological phenomenon, a phenomenon which has the potentiality of growth and the actualisation of which depends much upon some attending conditions, physical, vital, psychical and socio-economic. The individual self, as indicated earlier, has been conceived as physical being (*śarīra puruṣa*), vital being (*prāṇa puruṣa*), mental being (*manomaya puruṣa*) and psychical being (*citta puruṣa*). In each of there planes of being there are many sub-planes. The planes and sub-planes of freedom that the individual as subject can possible enjoy are literally endless. The point has been penetratingly analized by K. C. Bhattacharyya.[16]

When we speak of the ontology of freedom, what we want to highlight is its *concrete* expression in the individual, in the social forms consisting of and constituted by individuals. Once the 'ontology of man' is truly grasped, we have reason to prefer the expression 'embodied man' to 'the body of man', 'man is free' to 'man has freedom'. One is here reminded of Heidegger's 'ontology of man' as Being-in-the-world.[17] The worldly character of man cannot be exhaustibly comprehended instantly. It is disclosed in and through time, i.e., historically. The observable physical contexts of human behaviour on their own do not provide us the reliable cues necessary for understanding what human freedom is, what are its free forms of expression. If human body is taken as a natural thing, we are landed in a sort of socio-political behaviourism, as if body has no subjectivity or free interiority of its own. The planes and sub-planes of the subjectivity of human freedom have already been briefly referred to. But the embodied context of freedom is liable to gross misunderstanding. Human body is not a thing that acts. It is, in Marcel's language, a *homo viator*, an active being. It is in his activity, in his ceaseless making or becoming, that man's true identity is to be found. Man is a being-on-the-way. The same point has been made out been made out in a different way but Sartre when he speaks of man as a 'Being which what it is not, and which is not what it is'. This existential-phenomenological insight regarding human nature is captured by Sri Aurobindo in his description of man as a perpetual 'self-exceeding' creature. In philosophical anthropology we see how in and through their creative self- interpretation, use of *logos* and technology, word and work, humans complexity and enlarge their forms of life, imagination and thought, how without losing their *singular* self-identity, they seek *unity* of increasingly larger forms of life.

Man exceeds himself because that is the expression of his inmost nature, i.e., freedom. Man's *self-projection*, self-transcendence, is essentially *evaluative* in nature. By describing its physical and physiological contexts and conditions we will not be able to show the abundance of its inner drift and quality. The reason why the familial man seeks to be a tribal man, why the tribal man wants to be a national man and why the national man seeks his global identity cannot be gathered from the bare description of the surface features of our socio-historical evolution. From the *surface* structure one has to get into the *deep* structure, from *phenomenal* description to *phenomenological* description. The *active* and *sympathetic* inner characters of the social forms and the process of their formation have to be looked into.[18] When we speak of phenomenological description of man's social self-transcendence, what we propose to describe is the enlarging and deepening *meaning-structure* of human action and intercourse. But our aim of excavation or exploration of meaning may be defeated if we get bogged into false subjectivism, a sort of mentalism, or false objectivism, a sort of behaviourism. In fact, we are required to grasp the *dialectical* interaction of physiological, biological and psychological planes of life, motion and action.[19] The point to be additionally noted here is that none of these planes, taken in isolation, nor all these, taken as a totality, can disclose the concreteness of meaning and value of human action and intercourse. This point has been emphasised time and again also by Sri Aurobindo.

Sri Aurobindo draws an important distinction between true subjectivism and false subjectivism. To follow this one has first to realise that 'subjectivity and objectivity are not independent realities, they depend upon each other; [and that] they are the Being, through consciousness, looking at itself as subject on the object and the same Being offering itself to its own consciousness as object to the subject'.[20] If objectivity is construed in the naive naturalistic sense, man is led to believe that even his own body, and integral part of his Being-in-the-world, has something unrelated to his own inner moral and spiritual needs and that the satisfaction of its needs can be pursued in an *exclusive* manner. This is a dangerous belief. It leads to false subjectivism, a false dogma that the somatic being is the true seat of human identity. In ethics it gives rise to hedonism. In politics it provides the ideology of aggressive nationalism, ruthless imperialism and unprincipled hegemonism. Once man forgets his own deeper identity, inner freedom, he seeks freedom in the elimination of the conditions and the beings which appear to him as a threat to his own somatic or narrow egoistic satisfaction. Once he forgets that his own being is *in* the world and as a part of it, he may go berserk in damaging or even destroying the world. The constitutive *other* of his own being. This is the philosophical point underlying Nazism and Fascism of the recent past and new colonialism of the contemporary time.

The individual man commits a grave error of judgment if he identifies himself with his immediate physical and physiological identity, forgetting his deeper and far-reaching spiritual identity. A comparable gravity of error becomes evident in the aggregative life, small and large, when it tries to understand itself, by following an alien-objective method and in terms of external circumstances, institutions and the *static* habits and forms they impress upon our otherwise *dynamic* consciousness. This external-institutional method of human sciences is methodologically inadequate and distortive and substantively, i.e., praxiologically, frustrative of our natural human *projects*. If the individual interprets himself wrongly, the wrong interpretation affects his actions and dispositions accordingly, resulting in the frustration and suspension, if not negation, of his larger aims.

NOTES AND REFERENCES

1. One naturally recalls Vico, who, even in the triumphant days of Newtonian mechanism, had the intellectual courage of writing *New Science* (1725), highlighting the self-interpreting nature of man of all human sciences.
2. Paul Ricoeur. *Freedom and Nature: The Voluntary and the Involuntary*, trans. and Intr. Erazim V. Kohak. Northwestern University Press, 1966. pp. 66–84.
3. Sri Aurobindo, *The Life Divine*, 1 Vol. edn., New York: 1949.
4. Jurgen Habermas. *The Theory of Communicative Competence Reason and the Rationalization of Society*, trans. T. McCarthy. Boston: Beacon Press, 1981. pp. 117–36.
5. Ludwig Wittgenstein. *Philosophical Investigation*, trans. G. E. M. Anscombe. New York: Macmillan, 1968.
6. In this connection, I am reminded of the well-known controversy between Chomsky and Skinner on their argument in 'defence' of freedom.
7. On the objective availability of the body, there is not much of a dispute. It is regarding the ontology of the body that the disputants differ. In this connection, I find the position taken by Merleau-Ponty in such of his works at *The Structure of Behaviour*, *Phenomenology of Perception* and *Primacy of Perception* very instructive.
8. J. P. Sartre. The Psychology of Imagination. London, Metheun, 1972. pp. 154–5.
9. This expression is bound to remind one of Quine's expressions, 'meagre input' and 'torrential output'. *Ontological Relativity and Other Essays*. New York, Columbia University Press. 1969. p. 83. Though Quine's and our perspectives are different, the problematique is basically similar. Consequently, the perceptive scholar can easily discover a similarity of approach in the context.
10. My position on the subject, particularly its application to different social forms, smaller and larger, may be gathered from my History, Society and Polity. Delhi, Macmillan, 1976. About the models of social explanation, see my *Individuals and Societies: A Methodological Inquiry* (2nd edn.). Calcutta, Scientific Book Agency. 1973.
11. Charles Taylor, *Hegel*, Cambridge: Cambridge University Press, 1975. pp. 214–21, 365–88; see also, Michael Oakeshott, *Experience and its Modes*, Cambridge: Cambridge University Press, 1985. Ch.III.
12. Richard E. Palmer. *Hermeneutics: Interpretation Theory in Schleiermacher, Dilthey, Heidegger and Gadamer*, Evanston: Northwestern University Press, 1969, Part II.
13. M. Heidegger. *Being and Time*, New York: Harper & Row, 1962, pp. 247–50.
14. See, for example, D. P. Chattopadhyaya. *Environment Evolution and Values: Studies in Man, Society and Science*. New Delhi: South Asian Publishers, 1983.
15. Shri Aurobindo, *The Human Cycle*, Pondicherry Sri Aurobindo Ashram, 1949, p. 39.
16. 'The Subject As Freedom' in K. C. Bhattacharyya, *Studies in Philosophy*, Delhi: Motilal Banarsidass, 1983, pp. 367–454.
17. M. Heidegger. op.cit. pp. 78–90.
18. See, for example, Max Scheler's *Man's Place in Nature*, Farrar, Straus, New York: Noonday Press, 1963; and Amitai Etzioni's *The Active Society*, New York: Free Press, 1968.

19. This important point has been persuasively argued by Maurice Merleau-Ponty in many of his books, including the ones quoted above.(5).
20. Sri Aurobindo, *The Life Divine*, 1 Vol. edn., New York, 1949, p. 578.

Husserlian Foundations of Sartre's Treatment of Time Consciousness

V. C. THOMAS

Phenomenology and existentialism constitute a search for meaning, the meaning of the most personal and intimate kind. One way of grasping oneself most personally and intimately is to understand oneself from a temporal view point, i.e. to understand oneself as born at a particular point of time, as living here and now and as dying now or about to die. This, in a nutshell, means understanding time to be the very essence of man. The primary question here, in the context of this essay, is: how does Sartre account for the primordial temporal character of man (the for-itself) and to what extent, if any, does he depend on Husserl while elucidating it?

The difference between Husserl and Sartre on a number of phenomenological themes is well known and it has attracted the attention of many scholars. But it is also true that there are similarities between Husserl and Sartre in their approaches to the elucidation of certain phenomenological topics. Among other things, this paper makes an attempt to show that on a number of points, especially in the understanding of time consciousness, a key concept both in phenomenology and existentialism, Sartre not only owes much to Husserl but has also developed further some ideas of the latter.

Sartre makes an extensive use of Husserl's *Phenomenology of Internal Time Consciousness* in elaborating his own ideas on time. But it must be noted here that Sartre does not confine himself to Husserl's treatment of time. Upon the foundations of Husserl's elucidation of time, Sartre formulates and expounds his views on time. Only then could he apply the notion of lived-time to concrete human situations. Sartre's rejection of phenomenological reduction—existential, psychological and transcendental, so dear to Husserl—widens his scope and opens up his eyes to much that is meaningful in human existence, factors which are, in fact, bracketed off[1] in Husserl's phenomenology.

A profound insight that is evident in Husserl's notion of consciousness is that the flow of consciousness is to be grasped always in terms of the temporal structures of 'now', 'retention' and 'protention'. 'Now' is not an unextended mathematical thin-edged moment, rather it is such that it grows into future and past. It is a moment whose thickness encloses within itself both the past and the future, a moment which gnaws both the past and the future. This is expressed, phenomenologically, by stating that the present is given along with its 'horizons'.[2] The now-phase constantly undergoes transformations; for it flows back and sinks in time into the past. This flowing and sinking give rise to 'retention'. The inevitability of retention is such that whatever is an object of perception must correspondingly become an object of retention. Whatever I perceive as the present moment of a temporal event, I perceive as that which will become an object of retention while it is given in the present. The 'now' itself is the crystallization of an expectation. 'Protention', the moment of expectation, is due to the very tending character of consciousness. With the help of a large number of examples, chosen especially from the domain of music, Husserl demonstrates that expectation belongs to the very essence of an impression of the present and this element of expectation is present in every act which is perceived as a temporal event.

In spite of the multiplicity of the modes of temporality, Husserl manifests his philosophical ingenuity by asserting the unity of the modes of temporality.[3] This is because he holds that every act of memory contains intuitions of expectations whose fulfilment is in the present. Husserl's point is this: a manifold of temporal phase intimately united with each other can ever be present in consciousness at one and the same instant.

The claim that Sartre makes in connection with the temporality of consciousness is very radical. Husserl points out that the flow of consciousness is in terms of temporal structures of 'now', 'retention' and 'protention', i.e. he assert the equiprimordiality of both consciousness and temporality such that consciousness is always a temporal consciousness. But Sartre's position seems to be this: we cannot even be conscious unless we are temporal.[4] This means that to be (to exist) is to be temporal. In other words, consciousness cannot but be temporal. Consciousness is the source of time and time, in turn, transforms consciousness to a temporal consciousness for time is the very propulsive heart of consciousness. This highlights that the temporality of consciousness is the existential centre of the latter. Temporality is the being of the for-itself in so far as the for-itself cannot but exist ekstatically. Consciousness (in the present) is not what it is (past), it is what it is not (the future).

Sartre's treatment of the temporality of consciousness centres around the unity of the modes of time consciousness, the discussion of time in and around subjectivity and the ontological relationship of temporal modes. That which unifies the multiplicity of modes of time consciousness in Husserl is the transcendental ego which is central to Husserl's phenomenology.[5] The transcendental ego is the matrix or the source of consciousness. The function of the transcendental ego consists in bestowing meaning and unity to the multiplicity of acts. And without the transcendental ego manifold-directedness of consciousness is reduced to mere stream of impressions devoid of significance. The transcendental ego, due to its intentionality, synthesizes various aspects, perspectives and stages of an object, transforming it into a single unified whole. The elucidation of intentionality in terms of its inborn dynamism and inherent forward thrust is the striking character of Husserl's philosophy.

But Sartre rules out the transcendental ego as the principle of unity[6] and declares that the unity of consciousness is sufficiently accounted for by the unity and thrust of intentionality.[7] This assertion of Sartre, it is interesting to note, is firmly rooted in Husserl's phenomenology.

Husserl in his *Phenomenology of Internal Time Consciousness* speaks of longitudinal and transverse intentionalities. The longitudinal intentionality 'goes through the flux which in the course of the flux is in continuous unity of coincidence with itself' (section 39). But in the transverse intentionality one is 'conscious of the unity in the very act of sensation.' In fact, Sartre makes a mention of transvere intentionality in *The Transcendence of the Ego* (p. 39).

It is on the basis of the longitudinal and transverse intentionalities that Sartre rules out every extraneous source of unity of the flow of consciousness and upholds that unity which prevails in the very flow itself. It is such a unity which, while flowing, unifies the flow with itself, giving to itself an immanent unity and internal self-directedness. In other words, from Sartre's point of view, the multiplicity of experiences *is*, indeed, a multiplicity but it remains a unified multiplicity, that is, a multiplicity which is internally unified. The transverse intentionality unifies every single experience with the totality of experiences, giving a sort of unity in breadth to it, whereas the longitudinal intentionality gives a sort of unity in length; both together constituting the unity of the flow of the stream of consciousness.

When a stream flows every drop of water in it has a *linear relationship* to the drops of water in front of it and behind it. At the very same time, the very same drop of water has a *latitudinal relation* to the drops of water which are on its sides. It is not only the drops of water that have this relation but everything that is in the stream has this linear and latitudinal relation. Husserl's longitudinal intentionality of the stream of consciousness is comparable to the linear relation and his transverse intentionality is parallel to the latitudinal relation.

To express the unity of the three modes of time consciousness, Sartre makes use of the term 'recollecting synthesis'. Recollection, from Husserl's point of view, is inseparable from its horizon; the future.[8] But recollection (retention or the past) itself is the horizon of the present.[9] In other words, recollection synthesizes both the future and the present and thus formulates the recollecting synthesis. That which synthesizes (the various modes) is the for-itself. The for-itself synthesizes these modes because the latter are the self projections of the former.

While using the expression 'recollecting synthesis', the initial assumption of Sartre is that there is a multiplicity of modes and that they are synthesized into a unity by the for-itself. But Sartre uses another expression 'the unity that multiplies itself' to indicate the unity of the modes. But here the assumption is of the reverse kind,—reverse to the one mentioned above. From the initial unity (of the for-itself) there arises a multiplicity. This multiplicity is not a random scatteredness; rather, it is the unity itself that grows into multiplicity. Hence, the multiplicity is the multiplicity of the unity of the for-itself. This is what Sartre designates by diasporatic or ecstatical unity. We find ourselves as already having a multiplicity of experiences. This multiplicity, while remaining a multiplicity, gives rise to the unity of experiences, i.e. in every single present experience the multiplicity or the totality of the past experiences manifests itself. Every single experience, in turn, is a part of the multiplicity (totality) of experience. Hence arises the dialectics between the single and the multiple (totality of) experiences. It is the transverse and the longitudinal intentionalities that unify every single experience with the multiplicity of experience. They, being the principles of unification of the flow of consciousness, move ahead from every particular experience to the multiplicity of experiences and from the multiplicity of experiences to the individual experiences.

If Husserl's examination of time is in and around the transcendental ego, i.e. broadly speaking, subjectivity, Sartre's discussion of time is in and around the for-itself, the Sartrean subjectivity.[10] Indeed, Sartre refuses to assign to the ego the status which Husserl bestows on it. For Sartre, the ego is one among the objects. It is the sedimentation of experiences. As the Husserlian ego assigns meaning, so also the Sartrean for-itself creates meaning. My 'ego', from Sartre's point of view, refers to my past, the 'me' I have become. This amply shows that Sartre's notion of the ego is temporal.

When Sartre speaks of the modes of temporality, he is not discussing any general past, present or future; rather his concern is with *my* past. Hence he elucidates the notion of mineness of temporality. His enquiry into the present as presence shows that the for-itself is the being by which presence enters into the world. Similarly, it is by means of the for-itself that the future arises in the world. What is to be understood from this is that whether it be the past or the present or the future, it is impossible to make any inquiry into any one of them unless they are understood in relation to the for-itself.

The close link between the for-itself and the modes of temporality (which are nothing but the projections of the for-itself) gives rise to an ontological relationship among the modes of temporality. In other words, the ontological relationship among the modes of temporality is built upon the foundation of the for-itself. To put it more concretely, the basis of the ontological relationship between the past and the present is the 'mineness of the past'. What is implicit in this is that the ontological relationship appears to be similar to the notion of horizon. While speaking of the relationship between the past and the future, Sartre does not use the term 'ontological relation'; his preferred expression is 'horizon'. This clearly suggests an affinity between horizon and the ontological relation.

Sartre's ontological commitment is clearly evident in the subtitle of *Being and Nothingness*, viz., 'An Essay on Phenomenological Ontology'. He goes about constructing his ontology under the influence of Heidegger's assertion that ontology is possible only by way of phenomenology. But does his ontology have any relation to Husserl's phenomenology and, finally, is Husserl ontologically committed? Husserl's ontological commitment seems to be nil or thin although this is a matter of debate among the Husserlian scholars. That his phenomenology could be used to arrive at an ontology is very different from saying that Husserl himself has his ontological commitment. The existentialists make use of his phenomenological notions to arrive at an ontology. In other words, if one speaks of ontological commitment in the usual traditional sense, Husserl, to my mind, is not ontologically committed. In fact, his elucidation of phenomenological reduction brackets out existence, the root concept of ontology. If at all any kind on ontology is to be found in

Husserl, it arises from the presence of *isness* in his phenomenology. But we do find in Husserl such notions as consciousness, ego and temporality. If one has a leaning towards ontology, such concepts could be liberally made use of in formulating and articulating it. What strikes us is that Sartre's explicit statement regarding the ontology of temporal modes is, indeed, a development consequent on Husserl's notion of time.

The for-itself which temporalizes itself by existing, i.e. in and through existence, exists in meaningful contexts and significant situations. The totality of such contexts is called the 'world'. The world is the fabric of meaningfulness. It is the significant set of meaningful relations pointing to the horizon of the for-itself. It is the matrix within which the for-itself's relation to others and things spring up, gets sedimented and perishes. Sartre shares Heidegger's insight in stating that the for-itself is ever in the world. While describing his notion of the world, Sartre speaks of the 'this-world' and the 'lived-world'. While measurable, chronometric time is peculiar to the world of physical entities, lived-time is the temporality of the lived-world, the world of the for-itself.

Is Sartre indebted to Husserl when he points out how measurable time originates? It must be said that in his *Phenomenology of Internal Time Consciousness*, Husserl rules out the possibility of measurable time in the sense that by means of the phenomenological treatment no measurable time can be arrived at. For this reason it can be said that Sartre's discussion of measurable time is totally independent of Husserl. It must also be pointed out that a modified and adapted version of Husserl's notion of constitution appears in Sartre as well when he examines the origin of measurable time. The for-itself, as ekstatic temporality, constitutes measurable time by apprehending the 'this' as permanent and by disclosing it as existing in three dimensions of time related to one another by a relation of before and after, i.e. 'a relation of exteriority of indifference'.

Although Sartre stands outside the phenomenological tradition while examining the notion of measurable time, he is well within the domain of Husserl's philosophy, more so within the confines of Heidegger's existentialism, when he elucidates the temporality of the lived-world. For the key phenomenological concepts like retention, protention, horizon and the like are extensively exploited by Sartre in this context. The lived-world manifests itself when the for-itself uses instruments. There is an element of decision on the part of the for-itself while using instruments; and decision takes place in time. The for-itself decides to use instruments in the present in a particular manner because it has learned from the past experiences the various modes of their utility. Again, when the for-itself actually uses instruments, there is always one or the other definite end in view, i.e. the future. Unless there is a goal to be attained and unless one has already experienced it somehow in using an instrument, one would not be using it at all for that particular result. The way in which the notion of retention, protention and horizon are instantiated merit no further explication here.

Another point that reveals the temporality of the lived-world is the idea of awaiting, a notion which has been extensively used by Heidegger. There is, in fact, a striking agreement between Heidegger and Sartre with regard to the understanding of the concept of awaiting. I await a particular result (in the future) while using a tool (in the present) on the basis of what I have learnt from my past experiences. While examining the notion of awaiting in the context of elucidating the temporality of the lived-world both Heidegger and Sartre combine Husserl's notions of horizon of the now (i.e. retention is the horizon of the present) and the horizon of the past (which is the future) into the one single notion of awaiting.

Sartre goes beyond the notion of awaiting to notions like 'decision' and 'in order to' while examining the temporality of the lived-world. This is because Sartre's is an action-oriented philosophy (constitution needs to be understood here as activity); and action involves decision and use of instruments (i.e. in order to). The kind of action which the later Sartre advocates is revolutionary and which undoubtedly points towards the lived-world *praxis*, undoing or destroying the 'useless' practico-inert of yesterdays.

To recapitulate, while Husserl asserts the equiprimordiality of consciousness and time, Sartre insists on the ontological primacy of time, i.e. one cannot be conscious unless one is temporal, and the Sartrean definition of the for-itself follows from the ontological *a priority* of time. While Husserl accounts for the unity of the manifold-directedness of consciousness in terms of the transcendental ego, Sartre rules out the possibility of such an extraneous source of unity and demonstrates how the (internal) unity of consciousness is established in terms of the unity and thrust of intentionality. Sartre's contentions on the ontology of temporality and the temporality of the world are definitely, from a phenomenological and existentialist angle, advances on Husserl's position.

NOTES AND REFERENCES

1. Professor Meszaros' contention in *The Work of Sartre* Vol. 1, *Search For Freedom*, that Sartre is opening the Husserlian brackets does not convey the sense that Sartre is doing away with the Husserlian brackets; for even after opening the brackets the same can still remain. Opening up of a door does in no way mean the elimination of the door itself.
2. From a phenomenological–existential point of view the notion of horizon is very important because it is that towards which we tend; it designates the future which we are in the process of realizing intentionally. When we see an object we 'see' one or the other phase of it. But the truth is that our perception has much more content both in depth and width than what is actually 'seen'. That which is perceived effectively refers to what is not immediately given. This datum not immediately given, but which is always present and inseparably united with what is actually seen, constitutes the horizon. The inexact morphological forms which lie at the fringes of the exact ones gradually become clear as one proceeds towards the horizon.
3. Those who dealt with the notion of the time in the past laboured hard to discover a principle of unity which for them was most often a metaphysical necessity. The need to establish the possibility of such a principle of unity arose because of our experience of the multiplicity of temporal dimensions. But this trend of thinking is reversed by

...the phenomenologists and the existentialists. They also hold that there is a plurality of temporal dimensions. And, this is precisely because there is a primordial principle of unity which is the transcendental ego (Husserl), *Dasein* (Heidegger) or the for-itself (Sartre).... That there is a principle of unity is the only *raison d'etre* for multiplicity.

4. That is, temporality is the *a priori* necessary condition for there being any consciousness at all. This indicates the ontological priority of temporality.
5. We do find radical changes in Husserl's understanding of the ego. In 1901, while publishing the first edition of *Logical Investigation* , Husserl rejected the conception of an identical ego over and above the intentional acts of consciousness. But in 1913, while publishing the second edition, Husserl altered his position stating that 'since then I have learned to find it, or more precisely, I have learned not to be diverted in the pure grasp of the given by the excess of the metaphysical ego.' What we find in *Ideas* is a careful and meticulous exploration of this ego.
6. Sartre does not accept Heidegger's notion of *Dasein* as a principle of unity of (the flow of) consciousness although there are many points of similarities between the for-itself and *Dasein*.
7. By rejecting the notion of the transcendental ego, what Sartre wants to establish is that consciousness does not have a source extraneous to it which can unify it and direct it (to an object). Rather consciousness is unified within itself internally and the flow of consciousness to its objects is a matter of its inherent power.
8. 'Every act of memory contains intuitions of expectations ... ' and 'recollection is not expectation, its horizon' (*Phenomenology of Internal Time Consciousness*, (section 24).
9. 'Retention constitutes the living horizon of the now ... ' (*Phenomenology of Internal Time Consciousness*, (section 18).
10. It may not be easy to speak of subjectivity in Sartre's philosophy as he refuses to accept a subject, an ego, in the domain of consciousness (the for-itself). But he often uses the word 'self' to designate the for-itself and by subjectivity we mean this self or the for-itself. In the place of the term subjectivity, it may be possible for us to use the term 'selfitivity', if such an expression is allowed at all.

Analysis of I-Consciousness in the Transcendental Phenomenology and Indian Philosophy

ANINDITA NIYOGI BALSLEV

The philosophical exploration of I-consciousness has a long history in both Indian and Western thought. Some of the conceptual models and analyses that have emerged in one cultural framework may be profitably reviewed in the light of another. A study of the different levels of the constitution of 'I' in the Transcendental Phenomenology of Husserl is important not only as a remarkable achievement in the context of Western thought regarding this issue but is also useful for an appreciation of the philosophical concern for this question in the Indian philosophical tradition, notably in Advaita Vedānta. This paper is an attempt to understand the nature of the philosophical investigations into the question of ego in the Transcendental Phenomenology of Husserl and in Advaita Vedānta, with special reference to the writings of Madhusūdana Sarasvatī touching upon the methodological devices that are employed as well as the structures of consciousness that are thereby disclosed.

I

Husserl's concern regarding the question of the constitution of 'I' or ego is reflected in his major works, *Logical Investigations* (1900–01), *Ideas* (1913) and *Cartesian Meditations* (1931). The complexity of the Husserlian phenomenological investigation becomes evident as one takes into consideration the development of his theory of ego in these works. In order to retrace the different stages of the complex egology in Transcendental Phenomenology, it may be noted that there are levels of description which point to a gradual delimiting of the study of ego achieved by an employment of the methodological device technically called 'reduction'. The theory of ego unfolds through such notions as the 'empirical ego', the 'phenomenological ego', the 'pure or polar ego' and the 'monad or the transcendental ego'.

For a discussion of what exactly is yielded by following the various steps of reduction, reference may be made to the description of the ego in Husserl's early work, *Logical Investigations*. What is meant by 'empirical ego' in this work is not very different from what is understood by a 'person' in ordinary discourse with his/her mind and body and as having a conscious agency. Agency here is not understood as something in consciousness but simply as the person undergoing experiences. This ego, as he puts it, is a 'thing-like object and can be perceived' just as we perceive an external thing.[1]

Beginning from this, it is interesting to note the three steps of reduction that Husserl successfully employs in order to achieve an understanding which phenomenological reflections alone could yield. This is obtained gradually by bracketing the thesis of natural attitude concerning the question of ego.

Husserl arrives at the notion of a 'phenomenological ego' in his *Logical Investigations* by means of a reduction. This reduction, however, is not yet the transcendental reduction of *Ideas*, but merely a process of abstraction which remains fixed in the natural-psychological domain. What Husserl attained at this point by employing the first reduction, i.e. the phenomenological-psychological, consists in focusing on consciousness and its experiences by turning away from (that is, by not attending to) the various external objects with which consciousness is ordinarily occupied. The ego that is now encountered is nothing unfamiliar; it is the psychologically functioning ego. Even if its focus is on inner experiences, phenomenological psychology is not at this point very remote from the empirical psychology operating with naturalistic assumptions about the ego.

Thus the 'phenomenologically reduced ego', to quote Husserl's own words, 'is nothing peculiar, floating above many experiences; it is simply identical with their interconnected unity.'[2] Husserl's position at this point, as has been noticed by many, is not dissimilar to that of David Hume. Husserl explicitly states that he was unable to find any pure ego enduring as a 'centre of relations' or as a transcendental subject. It is probable that in his understanding of the 'interconnectedness' which accounts for the unity of consciousness Husserl was influenced by Brentano's idea of 'primordial association'. He found it unnecessary to postulate a transcendental ego above or behind the conscious processes since the contents of consciousness have 'their law-bound ways of coming together, of losing themselves in comprehensive unities'.[3] This itself constitutes the phenomenological ego or unity of consciousness without need of any additional ego. In any case, what needs to be noted is that, at this stage, Husserl rejected the notion of an ego-principle 'which supports all contents and unities'.

This position, however, underwent serious revision in his *Ideas*. It is here that the second step of the reduction is employed. Technically called the transcendental reduction, it suspends all empirical or naturalistic assumptions. If the first reduction achieved a rudimentary phenomenology, not totally demarcated from psychology, the second reduction attains what is called 'pure phenomenology'. Now Husserl admitted a 'pure ego' as 'necessary and plainly indubitable'. The transcendental reduction could not suspend it, since it is found as given together with all processes of consciousness. The epoché brackets the empirical elements, enabling one to focus exclusively on the transcendental elements of consciousness. A clear distinction thus emerges between the empirical and the transcendental ego. It now remains to understand what purpose this ego serves and in what sense it cannot be repudiated as a 'corrupt form of ego-metaphysics' which Husserl so consciously sought to avoid in his *Logical Investigations*. It is possible that Husserl was led to this because of his increasingly deeper involvement with the analysis of time-consciousness. In any case, it is clear that, with the introduction of transcendental reduction in *Ideas*, a radically different picture emerges. The empirical ego and the phenomenological ego are now seen as themselves intentional objects, as unities which are results of intentional constitution and 'over and beyond this nothing at all'. The idea of a pure ego that phenomenological inspection now reveals is 'neither experience nor a process', but 'the active and affected subject of consciousness'. Husserl describes it in his *Cartesian Meditations* as that which 'lives in all processes of consciousness and is related, through them, to all object poles'.[4] This is a description of the ego in its transcendental aspect, which does not involve any ontological commitment.

The third or the final step is the eidetic reduction which aims at disclosing universal, *a priori*, necessary structures in the domain where this reduction is carried out. For an investigation into the nature of ego this implies the possibility for 'a study of those transcendental features of the ego and its acts that are universal and necessary.' The eidos ego is the universal structure of any ego whatsoever. This structure would include (a) the mere subject pole of all intentional acts, (b) the genesis of an ego, i.e., an account of how an ego's life unfolds, and (c) the general form of time in which all experiences of an ego come together as one compossible world.

A clearer picture of Husserlian egology appears as one further considers the *Cartesian Meditations*. In the fourth meditation, the problem of the self-constitution of the ego is dealt with. The following is a brief summary of the principal ideas. Under the section 'The ego as the identical pole of subjective processes',[5] it is observed that the ego not only experiences itself as a flow of mental life but also as '*I*'. The I who lives that mental life and the *I* whom I experience as myself are the same I. The mental acts are unified not merely objectively, i.e., as directed to one and the same object, but also as belonging to an identical ego. The ego is the active and passive subject of consciousness.

The section entitled 'The ego as the substrate of habitualities', however, states that the ego is not merely an empty pole of identity. Every intentional act which I perform generates in me a new property which lasts until it is cancelled. Every decision that I take, every belief that I acquire leaves in me a corresponding property. Such a property itself however is not a temporal process. In this manner the ego continuously constitutes itself as a personal ego with a relatively abiding style known as its personal character.

Husserl distinguishes the ego taken in its full concreteness from both the above conceptions of the ego and calls it the monad. As a monad the ego includes not only its flowing intentional life, but also the objects meant in that life. Thus the ego sets up its surrounding world consisting first of those objects with which I am acquainted and then of those which I anticipate as possible objects of acquaintance.

Each of these conceptions of ego may be understood either as an empirical or as a transcendental concept-empirical if understood independently of the transcendental epoché and transcendental if all the concepts involved are understood in the context of the epoché. Thus one arrives at the profound thesis that the empirical and the transcendental are not two, numerically distinct entities, but rather one and the same entity regarded from two standpoints. Husserl is aware that this would give rise to such questions as: Is the transcendental ego born and does it die?[6] Furthermore, if every empirical predicate has a transcendental counterpart, can one ascribe gender predicates, *e.g.*, 'male' or 'female', to a transcendental ego?

II

If constitutive phenomenology has for its goal a systematic exploration of consciousness giving rise to a full-fledged phenomenological egology, the same may be said of Advaita Vedānta. A genuine philosophical appreciation of the Advaitic manner of exploring consciousness involves a radical modification, so to speak, of the metaphysics of the naive standpoint. It does not side with the Indian realism of Nyāya or Mīmāṃsā in maintaining that objects are entirely independent of consciousness and that consciousness, being formless (*nirākāra*), only reveals what is given to it; nor does it side with the Indian idealist tendencies, such as Yogācāra Buddhism, in supporting the position that consciousness projects its own forms, the so-called object being reducible to the latter. The notion of the empirical or the conventional (*vyāvahārika*) acquires a technical significance here. The conceptual frame operates with the key concept of *adhyāsa*, a term which I will leave untranslated in this paper. The import of the notion of the empirical (*vyāvahārika*) in the Advaita analysis is to be grasped within a framework which is not committed to such traditional alternatives of either naive realism or subjective idealism.

It is in this context that I want to examine some aspects of the Advaitic understanding of the 'I' or the ego-principle as being due to *adhyāsa*. The customary understanding of *adhyāsa* and its implication that the result of *adhyāsa* has no ontological reality is to be suspended for the time being. The concern of this paper is precisely to understand analytically in what sense the *adhyasta*, here the 'I', *aham*, is disclosed to the reflective gaze as being constituted in various strata of complexities which form the essential insight of Advaita egology.

Before delving into this question it may be noted briefly that there is a whole variety of philosophical analysis concerning I-consciousness in Indian philosophy. Leaving aside the Buddhist and the Jaina contributions, the Brahmanical tradition alone knows of a wide diversity of views. The philosophical concern for this question especially in the Vedantic tradition has given rise to long controversies among its different schools. One finds detailed treatments, dealing with different aspects of the problem, of such issues as the nature of personal identity, the problem of self-knowledge or the linguistic analysis of the indexical 'I', its meaning and reference.

Now turning directly to the core of the Advaitic analysis, one observes its radical difference from views which consider the I as a metaphysical entity, conceiving the relationship between the I and the flow of consciousness in various ways. Advaita Vedānta unravels the *constitution* of I-consciousness in a unique manner without positing the I as a metaphysical entity. It is especially with reference to this question that the Advaitic notion of *adhyāsa* plays a fundamental role.

The following analytical exposition is based on Madhusudana Sarasvatī's *Advaita-siddhi* and *Siddhāntabindu*.

What is startling in the Advaitic description of I-consciousness is the account of the various stages of *adhyāsa*, which bring to light the different levels of abstraction that an analysis of subjectivity allows for. *Siddhāntabindu*, for example, describes step by step the extension of the I-sense, starting from an empty principle of *ahaṁkāra* which is *a priori* in the sense that it is beginningless and is a condition of the possibility of mundane experience. In our experience the awareness of I is never found in its primordial simplicity. It is mixed up with other predicates and attributes. With the key idea of *adhyāsa* , one can disclose gradually the entire process of constitution of the psychological, corporeal and social layers of subjectivity. This order of *adhyāsa* is described in *Siddhāntabindu*, proceeding from the idea that even the primordial *adhyāsa* of *ahaṁkāra* is a product whose constitution presupposes consciousness tinged with *ajñāna* (nescience).

This is followed by a whole series of steps. All such psychological processes as desire, resolution, etc. (*kāmasaṃkalpādi*) are seen as attributes of the ego—meaning that they cannot take place unless the subjective pole is *already* there characterizing consciousness, i.e., unless consciousness is qualified by *ahaṁkāra*. Likewise, the attributes of the sense organs (*indriyadharmāni*) are also appropriated by the ego. This *adhyāsa* gives rise to such cognitions as 'I am blind' or 'I am deaf'. There is however no direct superimposition of the sense organs on the ego, hence no such cognitions as 'I am the eye' or 'I am the ear'. Next in order is the appropriation of the gross body by the ego, but there is again no such cognition as 'I am the body', but rather as 'I am human'—'being human' being in part a corporeal attribute. From this one may pass on to what is called the *mama-adhyāsa*, accounting for the constitution of the sense of '*mine*'. The ego now gradually appears in its social dimension, extending its reach over a son (*putra*) and property (*vitta*). The order of the various levels of constitution of the ego is said to be manifest in *the degree of closeness that each adhyāsa has to the I*, accounting for the subtle differences of love and attachment (*prema-tāratamya*) that one has for them

A deeper insight into the Advaitic analysis of *ahaṁkāra* or the ego principle would involve a more technical understanding of the different forms of *adhyāsa* (such as *svarupādhyāsa*, *saṃsargādhyāsa*, etc.)—all worked out in the background of a conception of consciousness as absolute and foundational.

The phenomenological description of consciousness which Gurwitsch expresses in the following words, based on the writings of Husserl himself, is also interesting for those familiar with Advaitic thought. He writes:

> Consciousness is not taken as part of the real world and as one reality among others. We have a right to characterize consciousness as absolute only to the extent that we conceive of it exclusively as a medium and, so to speak, as the theatre in which the constitution of all sorts of objects—including psychical and human realities, such as

the soul, the mind, the ego, the personality, our social and historical being, etc.—takes place.[8]

Consciousness is a common subject-matter for both psychology and phenomenology, yet there is a difference, as Gurwitsch succinctly puts it, 'in so far as consciousness in psychology is accepted as one reality among others and is studied in its dependence on extra-conscious data'.[9]

III

A question then may be raised in the context of both Advaita Vedānta and Transcendental Phenomenology, regardless of how they might otherwise differ: In what sense can this transcendental consciousness be philosophically regarded as *human*? Is *nirguṇa*, *nirviśeṣa* (attributeless, free from determination) consciousness, which is unsublatable (*abādhya*) also human consciousness? Or, can the 'consciousness, considered in its purity . . . reckoned as a self-contained system of Being, as a system of Absolute Being, into which nothing can penetrate, and from which nothing can escape . . .'[10] be regarded as human consciousness?

The answer is obviously in the negative in both cases. For Husserl 'being human' is an interpretation, a meaning constituted by transcendental consciousness. In other words, 'I am a human' is not a self-interpretation of a human but like all meanings, 'being human' is also a meaning and so is a constituted noema. It is this which demarcates transcendental phenomenology from every conceivable form of philosophical anthropology. For Advaita, transcendental consciousness *appears* as human (*jīva*) owing to *avidyā* or nescience. The constitution of 'human' presupposes the constitution of 'I', and that involves—as we have seen—different stages. On the other hand, for Advaita thinking *jīva*-consciousness is wider in scope than I-consciousness. Again, saying that *avidyā* is at the root of constitution implies that the genesis of constitution is beginningless (*anādi*).

Finally, I would briefly comment on a remark by Professor Mohanty, that 'Indian philosophical literature abounds in a descriptive phenomenology of consciousness' but that the systems 'oscillate between descriptive psychology and metaphysics of consciousness.'[11] Even if this may generally be a valid observation in the case of other traditional systems of Indian philosophy, it may not hold with regard to the philosophy of consciousness which has developed within the frame of Advaita Vedānta.

It seems to me that the Advaita philosophy of consciousness, notwithstanding its difference from the transcendental constitutive phenomenology, cannot be classified as a species of descriptive psychology. Neither can it be taken as a typical sample of a metaphysics of consciousness which has not abandoned, so to speak, 'the natural attitude'. Thus the ideas that consciousness is the absolute ground and that the world and with it all that is worldly including the ego is *adhyasta* are to be grasped in a philosophical terrain dealing with transcendental problems. '*Mithyātva*' (falsity), a technical term used in the

Advaita description of the object or the objective, is not to be taken as an evaluation or as a judgement using the criteria of natural attitude. Similarly, although the word '*sat*' (being) is used in connection with *cit* (consciousness), the Advaita position must not be confused with any form of metaphysics of consciousness in any naive sense but is to be understood in the light of the fundamental Advaitic philosophical motivation.

It may be observed that in the context of transcendental phenomenology the ideas of 'relative' and 'absolute' also acquire special significance. What does 'relative' signify? Again to quote Gurwitsch, 'any object whatsoever, as concerns its existential sense, is relative—relative to the reduced consciousness, but not to consciousness viewed as human psychical reality and thus embraced by the entire world.'[12] 'The notion of philosophy of consciousness as first philosophy' is to be appreciated precisely in this sense.

The Advaita understanding, not unlike that of Transcendental Phenomenology, abandons the traditional conception of consciousness in the sense that the absolute character of consciousness is disclosed not in relation to mundane realities of which the empirical ego is an example. It is in this sense that the Advaita attitude, like the phenomenological, may be said to stand in contrast to all the natural attitudes presupposed by traditional ontologies. The Advaita analysis is a radical departure from other traditional systems in its understanding of the foundational and absolute character of consciousness.

Here it may be noted that '*adhyāsa*' is commonly translated as 'superimposition'.[13] My point is that this understanding of *adhyāsa* fits the case of rope-snake or shell-silver illusion where one mundane object appears as another. But when it is a question of the very possibility of the empirical order, the application of the same understanding of *adhyāsa* as superimposition has serious shortcomings. It seems to me, therefore, that at such as level of discourse we need to give up the model of one thing being imposed upon another. The concept of *adhyāsa* is more complex and subtle than its translation as 'superimposition' conveys.

This notion of constitution is to be located in between the idea of mere manifestation (*prakāśa*) and the idea of creation (*sṛṣṭi*), so that the constituted (in this case, the empirical world) is neither an independently existing reality that is merely manifested by consciousness nor a subjective production.

The notion of falsity as applied to the empirical order must be radically distinguished from the idea of falsity of natural understanding. Advaita is not a specimen of a metaphysics from the natural standpoint. This is why a phenomenological interpretation that I have suggested seems to me appropriate and even necessary for a deeper understanding of the Advaita Vedānta.

NOTES AND REFERENCES

1. E. Husserl, *Logical Investigations*, E tr. J. N. Findlay, New York: Humanities Press, 1970, Vol. II, pp. 541, 551.
2. *Ibid.*, p. 541.

3. *Ibid.*, p. 51.
4. E. Husserl, *Cartesian Meditations*, E tr. D. Cairns, The Hague: M. Nijhoff, 1960, p. 66.
5. *Ibid.*, 31.
6. Cp. The Husserliana volumes XIII, XIV & XV on 'Intersubjectivity'.
7. Madhusūdana Saraswatī, *Advaita Siddhi*, 2nd Edition, Bombay, 1937. Also his *Siddhāntabindu*, Government Oriental Series, 1962.
8. A. Gurwitsch, *Phenomenology and Theory of Science*, ed. L. Embree, Northwestern University Press, 1974, p. 206.
9. A. Gurwitsch, *loc. cit*, p. 188.
10. J. N. Mohanty, 'Phenomenology and Indian Philosophy' (This volume).
11. E. Husserl, *Ideas* I, E tr. B. Gibson, 49, esp. p. 139.
12. A. Gurwitsch, *loc. cit*, p. 189.
13. Śaṇkara defines '*adhyāsa*' as "*smṛtirūpaḥparatra pūrvadṛṣṭāvabhāsaḥ*."

Phenomenology and the Transcendent: Which Way Does One Transcend?

PAULOS MAR GREGORIOS

Phenomenology has three faces—ontological-metaphysical as in Hegel, epistemological-methodological as in Husserl, and existential-hermeneutical as in Heidegger. In this paper we specifically focus on the phenomenological method as developed by Edmund Husserl (1859–1938), referring only in passing to the two other faces.

Hegel, especially in *Phaenomenologie des Geistes*,[1] works out the phenomenology of the 'self-alienated spirit' (*sich entfremdete Geist*), as it develops dialectically both in the observing subject and in the observed object as well as in the inter-action between consciousness and its object, leading to reflection. But his methodology was speculative, and not grounded in logic—even Hegel's own dialectical logic. For Hegel Spirit (*Geist*) is Reason (*Vernunft*); and Spirit is the world. The pure unity of the *Ich* and the *Seins* will become illuminated within Reason itself, or that is Reason's task—to find that unity. It is basically 'thought-work' or *Denkarbeit* that will reveal that unity between the *Fuersichseins* and the *Ansichseins* which is the ultimate goal of the thinking and knowing process. *Wesen* or Reality is not only ultimately *geistig* (spirit), but also one—and this one is an in-and-for-itself spiritual essence—*anundfuersichseiende geistige Wesen*, which is not yet consciousness itself[2] but a project for consciousness.

For Husserl, this is too speculative and unacceptable. He was looking for a more precise and methodologically exact process for assessing consciousness and the world. His teacher Franz Brentano (1838–1917) had clearly shown him that Hegelian and other forms of German idealism were basically incompatible with the rigorous canons of modern science. But Brentano himself seemed fairly content with a revival of the medieval scholastic notion of *adaequatio* between consciousness and its object. Brentano had been trained as a Roman Catholic priest, and served as one for 9 years (1864–1873), before leaving the priesthood for philosophy and the academy.

Heidegger (1889–1976), on the other hand, found his teacher Husserl's enthusiasm for the alleged preciseness of the natural sciences too dated, having its origin in the optimism of the early 20th century about science. In fact Heidegger reacted to the opposite extreme, and shocked the West by saying 'Science does not think' (later qualified by the addition of the phrase—'in the way thinkers think').[3] For Heidegger, modern science is the culmination and development of the Western metaphysical quest, and that culmination is a disaster. It not only fails to disclose the true meaning of Being, but it in fact forecloses the possibility. It presumes that the human subject and the world as object together constitute the whole of reality—an assumption for which there is no scientific warrant, since it is not empirically demonstrable or logically necessary.

Husserl had to come back and deal with his student's criticism; and in that process gave us a more mature form of phenomenology.

Logical Investigations,[4] in three volumes, appeared from 1899–1901. It was a painstaking and systematic attempt (more or less on the model of Kant's *Critique of Pure Reason* showing the limits of Reason itself) to delineate the limits of empirical science and to prevent empirical science from trespassing into the territory of philosophy where it was incompetent. It was philosophy's job to clarify the nature of science and to provide a proper theoretical basis for it. And this was Husserl's project: 'discovery of the essence of pure consciousness' within which scientific activity takes place. Husserl's student Heidegger also pointed out the paradox of the fact that science is unable by any scientific methodology to show what science is.

However, the credentials of modern science at the beginning of our century stood so high that the main philosophical trend was antispeculative and science-related; the only kind of philosophy that could have any standing was a philosophy of science, providing a fundamental theoretical basis for science.

That is what Husserl set out to achieve in his *Ideas, General Introduction to Pure Phenomenology*,[5] (thirty years after the *Logical Investigations*) in 1931, the centenary year of Hegel's death and the 150th anniversary of the publication of Kant's *Critique of Pure Reason*. Husserl was consciously trying to lay a new foundation for modern philosophy, parallel to and revising radically, both Kant and Hegel, but in fact heavily indebted to both.

In order to avoid misunderstanding Husserl, we have to state here what is well known to phenomenology scholars—namely, that there is an ocean of difference between ordinary or descriptive phenomenology and transcendental phenomenology as Husserl sought to expound. The first is simply describing phenomena as they appear to us, as faithfully as we can. Transcendental phenomenology, on the other hand, demands a radical change in the ordinary or commonsense perspective, as well as the phenomenological *epoche* or provisional bracketing of the external world of objects.

It is the 'bracketing' that induces the transcendental reduction which makes transcendental phenomenology possible. This 'bracketing' or phenomenological *epoche* is a procedure often misunderstood by superficial students of phenomenology. Husserl himself, in his introduction to the English translation (p. 23 ff), refers to this misunderstanding as an assimilation to his teacher Franz Brentano's teaching on the psychology of consciousness—describing psychic processes in consciousness.

THE EPOCHE—THE FIRST REDUCTION

The world 'out there', from the natural or common sense standpoint, is always there, at-hand, present. But is it really out there in the form in which we perceive it? Husserl does not answer this question, but proposes that we suspend our judgment, introducing methodological doubt as Descartes (inspired by Augustine, who in turn was inspired by the ancient Skeptics) did. If they say there are three realities as traditionally held (namely, God, the world and the human self), let us suspend judgement about all that. Let us doubt everything. We have the freedom to do so.[6]

About the world 'out there' which the commonsense view takes for granted, we do not say either that it is real or that it is unreal. We simply suspend judgement about its existence or non-existence; we do not make any judgement, positive or negative, about the external world. But for purposes of more precise knowledge, we leave the world outside of consideration for the time being. That is what we are asked to do in the fundamental epoche or act of bracketing—merely refraining from any judgement about the external world or the things in it. We disconnect from consciousness any thesis whatsoever about the status of the objective or *reell* world. This means also, for the time being, excluding from consciousness all the discoveries of the empirical sciences, because they too relate to this external world.[7]

What emerges after this *epoche* is pure consciousness—particularly my pure individual consciousness to which I have a privileged access. There is now revealed to consciousness a new being—a region of my own consciousness, and we focus attention on this new region, which is not annihilated by the *epoche*. This unique new being is the field which phenomenology studies, not from a commonsense or descriptive viewpoint, but from a transcendental perspective. The theme of enquiry of phenomenology is thus 'the essence of consciousness'.[8] This has been made clear in Husserl's earlier attempt to write an introduction to the phenomenological method—*Philosophy as a Rigorous Science* (1911).[9] It was this work that his brilliant pupil Heidegger so rigorously criticized.

The Heideggerian criticism was taken into account by Husserl in the more elaborate and circumspect *The Crisis of European Sciences and Transcendental Phenomenology*,[10] written in his mid-seventies and posthumously published. For this revised version of phenomenology, Husserl had to borrow Dilthey's *Lebenswelt* (life-world) as a basic concept. First Husserl calls in question the fundamental error of Western thought occurring as early as Galileo: 'The surreptitious substitution of the mathematically substructed world of idealities for the only real world'—the world which we perceive and experience. Geometry itself—the tracing of interconnections between mathematical idealities (point, line, angle, circle)—was formed by dissociation from its original milieu i.e., 'geo-metry', or the measuring of the earth, or simply, surveying. Geometry created a false world of ideal or mathematical realities. And what science in general does is this construction of idealized realities—ahistorical, general, mathematical, ideal, only indirectly related to the particular instance of the here and now.

That is one reason why Wilhelm Dilthey's *Lebenswelt* with a specific methodology for the *Geisteswissenschaften* (human or social sciences) different from that for the *Naturwissenschaften* (natural or physical sciences) appealed to Husserl. Life-world is a world of experiences—not just of discreet things existing in the space world out there. The phenomenological *epoche* lays bare this world of experience in consciousness, quite apart from what is there in the external world.

Once the transcendental viewpoint is reached, that is, when the object of consciousness is no longer the external world, but consciousness intentionally reflecting on consciousness, then we are ready for the second reduction of phenomenology.

THE SECOND REDUCTION

The 'experiencing gaze' of consciousness is now 'intentionally' turned on itself. The first discovery is that though the external world has been temporarily shut out, there appears a new phenomenon—the life-world of consciousness, dynamic, moving in a 'Heraclitean flux' with 'an infinity of actual and possible transcendent experience'.[11] Standing there at the gates of this enormous, complex, unexamined world, one must plan to enter cautiously, so as not to lose one's way, misdirected by habits and prejudices acquired in the process of dealing with the external world. No map of this life-world in consciousness has been charted by previous philosophy.

What Husserl tries to get is 'the transcendental constitution' of this world, in the light of which we can grasp the various realities inside this 'subjective' world of consciousness. The first ordering is a simple one—*ego*, *cogitatio* and *cogitatum*: the experiencer, the experiencing and the experienced.[12] But Husserl is looking for an 'ontology of the life-world', based on a pure *a priori*, unlike Kant's Practical Reason. This life-world-in-consciousness is a strange paradox—it can be subject *vis-à-vis* the world, and also object *vis-à-vis* its own transcendental standpoint. Humanity is at once world-constituting subjectivity and yet is incorporated in that same world,[13]—as an embodied being.

Husserl calls the second reduction the *phenomenological-psychological reduction*[14] (italics in original). This reduction is for the transcendental ego (oneself from the transcendent view-point) to see one's own consciousness as at once a universal phenomenon of consciousness of the world *and* self-consciousness. When my subjectivity by using its intentionality (directed thinking), manages to conceive this consciousness-of-the-world-plus-consciousness as a universal phenomenon and not as particular individual experience one has finally got to the subject-matter of phenomenology. It is this absolute universal present in all human subjectivity that now needs structural analysis—not Kant's Pure Reason and Practical Reason as separately conceived. It is this universal domain of world-and-self-consciousness that is the *a priori*—for all experience in all knowledge. Phenomenology is the analysis of this objective domain within the subjective consciousness and thus becomes the basis for all philosophy and all science.

In analysing this universalized world-and-self-consciousness which includes all knowledge, Husserl uses the two concepts of *noema* and *noesis*. The *noema* is what one finds in consciousness; in my consciousness there is a tree, a cow, a river, a book, all the colours, tastes, textures, contours and flows I can potentially experience in the world. One analyses each of these *noemata* in pure consciousness, without reference to any particular tree or cow or river in the external world. I find that each *noema* is composed of an ideational nucleus and a host of qualities attached to it. When I need to understand any reality I encounter in the external world, what happens is a two-fold process. On the one hand my consciousness turns its intentionality towards it. Secondly from the inexhaustible fund of *noemata* in my consciousness I compose an appropriate *noema* which I presume will fit the externally encountered object or target of my intentionality. This *thetic* or projecting process is what Husserl calls *noesis*. If the one projected does not fit, consciousness can bring out from its store one that fits better.

It is clear here that the noetic process pre-supposes the existence of the appropriate *noemata* already innate in consciousness. This pre-supposition comes from the Platonic tradition of eidetic essences innate in the mind and from the theory of knowledge as remembrance, but Husserl would deny that source and insist that the presence of the *noemata* in consciousness is a fact of observation, apodictically self-evident.

THE PROBLEM OF THE TRANSCENDENT

German philosophy frequently uses the term 'transcendent' to mean something which goes beyond the irreducible subject-object dichotomy of every day experience. The function of the transcendent is then to unite the two—consciousness and world, subject and object. This is so in Hegel, Fichte, Kant, Husserl and others. What Husserl means by 'transcendental phenomenology' is an analysis of the universal self-and-world. Consciousness that comes to light after the first *epoche* brackets out the external world as object, and the second reduction razes off the particularities of the individual consciousness. In this doubly transcended viewpoint, Husserl seems to believe, we transcend the irreducible subject-object duality to come upon the unitary reality of universal self-and-world-consciousness.

Has the problem of transcendence been short-circuited in this process? That is the question we raise in this paper.

Man, I mean the human being, male-female, is a bounded being. To be finite and self-conscious is to be aware of one's *finis*, one's limit. The human being is not infinite. He/she is not only locked into so many boundaries—of time, of space, of limits to knowledge, of gravity, of death, of want and lack, of limits to power, of vulnerability to suffering, of sickness, sorrow and so on—but also consciously and subliminally aware that one is so locked in.

And yet this finite, bounded limited being has within itself an inbuilt impulsion to break through all barriers—to overcome the bounds of gravity and fly, to break the bounds of death by seeking the life that overcomes death. The human being is thus a bounded being in both senses—that he/she is bounded by boundaries and that he/she strives to break through these boundaries.

This is real transcendence—not the Kantian-Husserlian transcendence where the ego shifts its usual stance and looks away from the external world to look inward upon one's own subjective consciousness. Human transcendence then means also not simply going beyond the four dimensions of space-time, but breaking through every barrier, even the barriers imposed by so-called rationality. The permanent tension between the 'is' and the 'ought' to which Ernst Bloch calls our attention in *Das Prinzip Hoffnung* is transcendence only in a partial sense. A human being has the inbuilt impulsion to be perennially moving beyond the 'is' to the 'ought'. But that is not still the essence of transcendence, though it is an indicator of the inner pressure to transcend.

It is of course possible for a human being to accept the limits and bounds and to live within these boundaries without chafing. Some actually manage to do so. But what we regard as outstandingly human is outstandingly boundary-breaking.

Can the Husserlian methodology deal adequately with this transcendence? Only if such transcendence is innate in consciousness. For Husserl, 'only transcendental subjectivity has ontologically the meaning of Absolute Being', because it alone 'is nonrelative, that is relative only to itself'.[15] Transcendence ends, for Husserl, with the Transcendental I: 'I, the Transcendental, absolute I, as I am in my own life of transcendental consciousness; but besides myself, the fellow-subjects who in this life of mine reveal themselves as co-transcendental, within the transcendental society of "Ourselves", which simultaneously reveals itself'.[16]

This is the transcendent Absolute Being that Husserl has to offer us—the inter-subjective community of self-and-world-consciousness, revealed by the epoche and the reduction. In the realm of Being thus revealed, there is 'a separation...between two radically opposed and yet essentially inter-related regions of Being'.[17] One is the world of *reell* objects, the other is the world of consciousness with its *noematic* and noetic *structures*. 'Consciousness-in-general' is an independent realm of Being though it is correlated to the realm of objects of which it is conscious. Both *noemata* and *noeses* are inter-dependent and inseparable; both are eidetic, the former, *noema*, is innate in consciousness; noesis is an intentional act, thetic, directed.

According to Husserl, while the world's external objects can themselves be divided into genera, species, classes etc., all perceptual acts of meaning-generation or *noema-noesis* confirmation belong 'intrinsically to a single supreme genus'.[18] Husserl then goes on to analyze the universal category of a *noema*, as composed of a nucleus 'X' holding together certain predicates. The nucleus 'X' is the nodal point in consciousness around which the predicates are clustered. This is the common structure of all *noemata*.

When we analyse the external object to which the *noema* in consciousness is related, we find the same structure. The *reell* or material object is also composed of a nucleus 'X' holding together certain properties or predicates. The difference between the noematic object in consciousness and the *reell* object in the external world does not lie in the predicates, but in the nature of the two nucleii. Meaning, however, relates only to the predicates, not to the nucleus. And it is Husserl's contention that in the thetic or noematic-noetic act, the whole meaning, without any residue, of the external object is intuited in terms of its set of predicates. What is left unintuited is only the *reell* nucleus 'X' of the external object, and is replaced by a noematic nucleus X which corresponds to the *reell* nucleus. The nucleus without its predicates has no meaning-content and therefore in eidetically intuiting an external object, its whole meaning is intuited. Husserl calls both nucleii an 'empty X' without determinate or specific meaning content, common to all external objects and corresponding noemata.

From this analysis of the simple perception of a single external object, regarded as a 'monothetic' act, Husserl moves on to a consideration of synthetic or polythetic acts, which are constructed on the same basis—a nucleus X which holds together many objects with many predicates and their relationships. Of course, all monothetic or polythetic acts are subject to revision when the external object changes perspective and reveals predicates previously unsuspected, as it often happens in the advancement of the sciences. In that sense every meaning-intake is provisional and incomplete; but as far as the then known properties of the external object are concerned, the *noetic-noematic* act takes in the whole meaning of the object, without any Kantian residue like the 'thing-in-itself'.

But Husserl would also admit:

> ....In principle we (can) only have inadequately appearing (therefore also only inadequately perceivable) objects. But we must not overlook the modifying qualification we made (earlier): inadequately perceivable, we said, *within the finite limits of appearance*. There are objects—and realities (*Realitaeten*) which are included under the rubric of Nature or World are here included—which cannot be given with complete determinacy and with similarly complete intuitability in any limited finite consciousness.[19]

Transcendence, for Husserl, arises also out of this provisional inadequacy and possible revision of all meanings. Especially when the object is not *reell* or thingly.

> When the dator intuition is of a *transcending* character, the objective factor cannot come to be adequately given; what can alone be given here is the *Idea* of such a factor, or of its meaning and epistemological essence, and therewith an *a priori rule for* the well-ordered infinities of inadequate experiences.[20]

For Husserl, however, every 'imperfect givenness contains within itself a rule for the ideal possibility of its perfecting'[21] rules for producing greater givenness.

Towards the end of his *Ideas*, Husserl begins to speak of God—'as the ideal representative of absolute knowledge'.[22] I am not sure whether Husserl conceives of God as a '*reell* object' in the external world or as a noematic construct for which there is no corresponding object in the external world. What Husserl tells us is that even for God the rule 'whatever has the character of a spatial thing, is intuitable only through appearances' is applicable.[23] For him the givenness is only in the appearance, and therefore God also is given through appearances.

The philosophical justification for such an affirmation probably comes from the *noema* of God as an idealized human being. Husserl seems unaware of what is today evident—that the kinds of human minds we know of are always associated with a material human body which plays a decisive role in all mental perceptions. Husserl tries to suggest that the conditions of our space-time body-mind perception must apply to God also. If God is like man—both *res cogitans* and *res extensa*, as well as *res temporalis*, then this may be justified. Husserl's *noema* of God cannot be checked since its external correlate is not readily traceable in the manifold of appearances.

I suggest that the Phenomenological method is intrinsically incapable of apprehending the radically transcendent. It only appears to get around the problem of the transcendence of the Thing, for the nature of the difference between the nucleus X in the eidetic *noema* and that in the *reell* object is too easily glossed over by Husserl. His contention that it is intrinsically impossible for transcendental Being to be given except through appearances, has no philosophical warrant, unless one makes human perception the only kind of perception possible. Husserl's postulate that Transcendental Being is given only in appearances and that appearances are only of individual-temporal beings, led Heidegger to seek the true Being behind the beings. Husserl himself was prepared to move away, in Platonic fashion, to the essences, eternal, unconditioned, which are supposed to lie behind the existences. These essences in turn are innate in consciousness as *noemata*; therefore, the consciousness of self becomes the home of all possible transcendent beings.

On the other hand, in clarifying the distinction between Transcendence and Immanence, he acknowledges the Kantian discovery that the Thing-in-itself cannot be immanent in consciousness[24] in principle, and therefore belongs to the realm of the transcendent. 'Thus, the Thing itself, *simpliciter*, we call transcendent'.[25] This does not mean that perception does not come in touch with the Thing itself. The affirmation is that it does, for the only way Things themselves can present themselves to us is through appearance, and in perception we are in touch with them through their appearances. Husserl, citing the view of 'God, the subject of absolutely perfect knowledge, and therefore also of every possible adequate perception', as naturally possessing 'what to us finite beings is denied, the perception of things in themselves'[26] follow it up with the sentence: 'But this view is non-sensical'. What Husserl wants to affirm seems to be what Sartre picked up from him—namely, that Transcendent being appears to us in two modes, the *en-soi* and the *pour-soi*, the *ensich* and the *fuersich*, the in-itself and the for-itself. What is seen from the Transcendental phenomenological viewpoint after the *epoche* or bracketing of the world and the eidetic reduction of universal ego-consciousness are these two realms—the realm of a self-conscious of its own consciousness (*en-soi*) and the world of things as it presents itself to us (*pour-soi*).

Of these two perceptions, only the first is indubitable. 'Every immanent perception necessarily guarantees the existence (*Existenz*) of its object.'[27] But the certainty relates only to the immanent perception. As far as the external world is concerned: 'every experience (*Erfahrung*)... leaves open the possibility that what is given, despite the persistent consciousness of its bodily selfpresence, does *not* exist.[28] In other words, it is the experience that is self-certifying, not the object of experience.

To put it together again,

> In every way, then, it is clear that everything which is there for me in the world of things is on grounds of principle only a *presumptive reality*: that *I myself* on the contrary, for whom it is there (excluding that which is imputed to the thing-world 'by me'), I my-self or my experience in its actuality am *absolute* Reality (*Wirklichkeit*), given through a positing that is conditioned and simply indissoluble.[29]

Ego-consciousness is thus necessary and absolute. The Thing-world is contingent, changing with perspective variation, always capable of non-Being.

In this consciousness-of-self-and-world, which is for Husserl Absolute Being, and which is the result of two transcendences, first in the *epoche* of change of standpoint, and second in the eidetic reduction of consciousness from its individual peculiarities,—in this consciousness, is there room for further transcendence? We should end this paper with that question, and a qualifying commentary from Diṅnāga, one of the greatest of logical minds produced by the Indian civilization.

The Indian tradition puts the highest emphasis on this 'third' transcendence. In Husserl one brackets the external world, only later to come back to it with better tools with which to handle it. And when one has also reduced the individual particularities of the ego, one is already in the realm of the Absolute—the inter-subjective community of consciousness.

In the Indian tradition the real transcendence occurs only at the point where consciousness as consciousness-of is itself transcended, to become consciousness-in-itself, where all dualities of consciousness and its objects are finally overcome in the unifying vision.

Hegel tried to incorporate this unifying vision as an intellectual exercise or *Denkarbeit*. It is a vision that goes beyond religion for Hegel. Religion appears as 'intuition of the Divine'. But the final vision of the Spirit goes beyond. 'It is not only the intuition of the Divine, but the Divine's intuition of itself,'[30] says the English translator of Hegel in an awkward phrase. The original text says:

> *Sie* (d.h. die Schoene Seele) *ist naemlich Wissen von sich selbst, in seiner reinen durchsichtigen Einheit,—das Selbstbewusstsein, das dieses reine Wissen von dem reinen Insichsein als den Geist weiss, nicht nur die Anschauung des Gottlichen, sondern die Selbstanschauung desselben.*[31]

In other words, for Hegel the ultimate transcendence comes when Pure Consciousness becomes aware in the Great Insight that Consciousness as subject and external world as object are in fact but manifestations of the same Spirit.

The Indian tradition calls a halt to this too easy a jump of the intellect into the intuition of the divine. It asks for a radical revolution in the human consciousness which puts an end to all thinking as such, and recommends *upāsanā*, initiation, and *sādhanā* or discipline leading to realization. When the ultimate realisation finally dawns it is no longer a fruit of thought or

Denkarbeit but an experience that transcends all *aparā-vidyā*, all conceptual-intellectual activity. The way of conceptual knowledge and that of spiritual realization are discontinuous.

There is no provision for this knowledge that transcends all knowledge in Husserl's Phenomenology. In Hegel there is such a provisions, but his great insight is in the ultimate analysis, only an intellectual insight, the end result of going beyond the various levels of dialectical thinking.

Phenomenology, at least as Husserl developed it, conceived the conscious rational human mind as the only instrument of knowledge, and provided, therefore, only for conscious experience of the world of everyday life. By its very focus on the rational conscious, analytical, it rules out the possibility of dealing with the Transcendent. Transcendental Phenomenology as a school of philosophy is dated, precisely because of its failure to take into account the new discoveries in scientific thinking that were coming up in Europe towards the end of Husserl's life[32]—namely, Special Theory of Relativity, Quantum Mechanics, and Uncertainty or Probability theories. His epistemology could not take into account the peculiar problems of conceiving reality in the pictorial fashion of the phenomenological *noema-noesis*. One reason for this situation lay in his failure to follow the developments in scientific theory. For a thinker who claimed to develop a scientific philosophy, this was indeed a strange omission. Hussal was also introducing too many elements from a Platonic theory which had no basis in scientific investigation—like *noemata* innate in consciousness. And if even non-transcendent reality is ultimately non-pictorial, how can pictorial, space-extended noemata deal with it?

In conclusion, one can make the observation that in most of modern Western philosophy, with some exceptions, e.g., that of Martin Heidegger, the reality of the world of phenomena seems to be taken for granted. Most modern Western philosophy shies away from questions of real transcendence, and seeks to play with lower forms of transcendence such as the transcendence of the ego which emerges in consciousness when we seek to make the ego-cum-consciousness an object of observation and analysis. What happens in Husserl is a two-stage sleight-of-mind. In the first stage, there is a bracketing of the status of the world of *reell* objects, which sounds quite profound. We get a feeling that this philosophy takes the problem of the reality of this world in a seriously sophisticated manner. We then move into the magisterial analysis of the universal self-with-consciousness, and consciousness-with-its-noematic-objects, and the intriguing concept of thetic intentionality. All this is done in a brilliant and *nuancé* manner, which inspires confidence, but does not quite convince.

In the second stage, the simple and naive assumption is made that the *reell* object has the same structural composition as the eidetic or noematic object-in-consciousness. The assumption that the external object is made up simply of a different nucleus X but has the same qualities or predicates as we observed in the noematic object has no philosophical warrant whatsoever. It can be characterized, as we have stated, as only a dexterous 'sleight-of-mind', one that dazzles and yet fails to convince. The *reell* or external chair is in fact sittable. The noematic chair, on the other hand, is not at all sittable. And to assert that the difference between the two is only a matter of slight variation in the nature of the nucleus X is, to put it mildly, going beyond the warranted.

It is in this connection that I want to draw our attention to the point made by Diṅnāga (Dignāga),[33] perhaps the greatest of Indian logicians, on a par with Husserl in the subtlety of his thought, though this Indian Buddhist philosopher lived and wrote some 14 centuries before Husserl. His *Pramāna-samuccaya*, to be dated around the 5th century A.D., is a pioneering work in the Indian logic of perception. Diṅnāga's methodology is eminently secular, and rigorously economical (reminding us of Occam) in axiomatic assumptions. He posits only two principles of knowledge or *pramāṇas*—sense-impression or *pratyākṣa* and inference or *anumāna*. Corresponding to the two *pramāṇas* there are only two *pramēyas* or cognizables, namely, the world and thought. This seems to be very much as in Husserl.

Diṅnāga makes an interesting distinction between the nature of sense-impression and that of perception. In the sense-impression, the mind is passively acted upon by the external object or *vastu*. The agent in the sense impression is the *vastu* itself, not the perceiving mind. In perception of the external object, however, the mind is active. When an external object like a cow faces the mind, the cow creates the sense-impression. But we do not perceive the sense-impression itself. By the time our mind has made a judgment: 'this is a cow', *anumāna* or inference has come into operation. There is no one-to-one correlation between the *vastu* which confronted us, and our mental judgment that this is a cow. The 'cow' is a universal which we have produced out of our mind. The *vastu* itself has its own *śvalakṣaṇa* which is a unique particular distinct from everything else (*sarvato-vyāvṛtta*), momentary (*kṣaṇika*), without extension or duration, both of which are supplied by the mind. The *vastu* is a 'point-instant' without any dimension, for dimensions are *anumāna* or inference products.

The *vastu* is by no means illusory or unreal for Diṅnāga; in fact, the point-instant of the *vastu* alone is real, so long as it is a non-illusory perception or *nirvikalpa-pratyakṣa*. The *vastu* is beyond all subject-object modalities, and it is not even true to say that the *vastu* is the subject of the sense impression. The pure *vastu* is also beyond all subject-predicate determination (*viśeṣya-viśeṣaṇa-bhāvanāvagati*).

What Husserl does in more or less identifying or equating the external object and the mental object, Diṅnāga would call an *adhyāvasāya* or false identification. *Diṅnāga* would not be satisfied with the slight difference between the two as consisting in the nature of the nuclei, because for him the *reell* object has neither nucleus nor qualifying predicates. *Diṅnāga*, I believe, would have been happier with the Heideggerian perception that the phenomenon as a *Seiende* is actually a manifestation of the *Sein*. For Diṅnāga, however, there is no way by which thinking can get through the *Seiende* to the *Sein*.

The transcendent is not to be caught in the conceptual net, even the transcendental ego-consciousness-world, it seems.

NOTES AND REFERENCES

1. *Phaenomenologie des Geistes*, Suhrkamp, 1970/1984 p. 324 ff.
2. *Ibid.*
3. On this see my *Science for Sane Societies*, 2nd edition, New York, Paragon, 1987. pp. 177ff.
4. *Logische Untersuchungen*, 1899–1901, 2nd edition 1913, 3 volumes, Halle, M. Niemeyer. English Trans. J. N. Findlay, *Logical Investigations*, 2 vols. (vol. I has German I and II), London, Routledge and Kegan Paul, 1970.
5. *Ideen zu einer reinen Phaenomenologie und Phaenomenologischen Philosophie* 1931. Eng. Tr. London, George Allen & Unwin, New York, Macmillan, 1931. It is interesting to note that two of Husserl's later works have also practically the same sub-title—'Introduction to Phenomenology'.
6. *Ideas*. pp. 107–108.
7. *op. cit.*, p. 111.
8. *see Ideas*. pp. 114 ff.
9. Eng. Tr. Q. Lauer (ed.) *Phenomenology and the Crisis of Philosophy*, New York, 1965.
10. *Die Krisis der europaischen Wissenschaften und die transzendentale Phaenomenologie: Eine Einleitung in die Phaenomenologische Philosophie* ed. Walter Biemel, The Hague; Martinus Nijhoff, 1954; Engl. Tr. Evanston, Northwestern University Press, 1970, 3rd Prtg. 1977.
11. *The Crisis of European Sciences*, p. 153.
12. *Ibid*. 50 pp. 170.
13. *Ibid*., p. 182.
14. *Ibid*., p. 236.
15. E. Husserl, *Ideas*, Author's Preface to the English Edition p. 21.
16. *Ibid*., pp. 21–22.
17. *Ideas*, 128, p. 359.
18. *Ibid*., p. 397.
19. *Ideas*, p. 397, italics original.
20. *Ideas*, p. 398, italics original.
21. *Ibid*., p. 413.
22. *Ibid*., p. 418.
23. *Ibid*.
24. see *Ideas*, pp 133–34.
25. *Ibid*, p. 134.
26. *Ideas*, pp. 135–136.
27. *Ibid*., p. 143.
28. *Ibid*., p. 144.
29. *Ibid*., p. 145.
30. Hegel, *Phenomenology of the Spirit*. Eng. Tr. A. V. Miller, OUP. 1977/1979 p. 483.
31. G.W.F. Hegel, *Phaenomenologie des Geistes*, Frankfurt, Suhrkamp. 1970/1984. p. 580. My translation would be as follows: 'It (i.e., *the beautiful soul*) is therefore its knowing in itself, in its pure transparent unity—the self-consciousness that knows this pure knowing from its own pure being-in-itself as Spirit, not only through the intuition of the Divine (Godly) but by self-intuition itself.'
32. The basic laws of Quantum Mechanics were formulated from 1925–28. Husserl died in 1938.
33. Diṅnāga was formerly studied by foreign scholars like Theodor Stcherbaski, Eric Frauwallner, Hidenori Kitagawa and Masaaki Hattori; Hattori's *Dignāga on Perception, being the Pratyakṣa-paricheda of Dignāga's pramaṇasamuccaya from the Sanskrit fragments and the Tibetan versions*. Cambridge, Mass., Harvard University Press, 1968, provides a major reference.

The Paradox of Subjectivity and the Idea of Ultimate Grounding in Husserl and Heidegger

THOMAS M. SEEBOHM

The paragaraphs preceding the explication of the interplay of psychology and transcendental phenomenology in the *Crisis*[1] develop the formula that, according to Husserl, elucidates the principle of the interplay. It is the formula of the paradox of subjectivity. This formula is supposed to explicate the root problem with which the development of Husserl's phenomenology was infected from its very beginning. It is, however, also the principle of the criticism that has been raised by Martin Heidegger against Husserl's transcendental phenomenology. Before dealing with this criticism it is useful to elucidate the formula of the paradox of subjectivity with the aid of some reminders concerning the problem of psychologism in Husserl.

Husserl's arguments against psychologism[2] in the "Prolegomena" tell us that psychologism is simply a kind of relativism and that relativism can be refuted because it is self-contradictory. It has been said that the argument is spurious because the argument against relativism is spurious.[3] Indeed, the argument was later restated by Husserl himself.[4] According to psychologism, empirical psychology as a science is the final arbitrator in all questions concerning cognitive validity claims. Husserl argued that psychologism implies relativism. Relativism denies that scientific knowledge has universal objective validity. Hence psychologism denies the objective validity of its own judgments concerning cognitive validity claims. Furthermore, Husserl had pointed out already in the "Prolegomena" that there is one type of relativism which cannot be refuted, viz., the individual relativism which claims the relativity of validity claims not for the species but for each individual.[5] In connection with Husserl's later critique of Dilthey and world-view philosophy another type of relativism also entered in, namely historism.[6] Husserl did not offer arguments against historism. He only emphasized its devastating consequences. It is obvious that consequentialist arguments cannot be directed against historism. Like individual relativism and unlike psychologism, historism is not commited to the belief in the objective validity of scientific knowledge. Contrary to the mistaken formulations of the 'Prolegomena', there is, hence, in Husserl, no argument against relativism possible in a mundane phenomenology. There is an argument that points out that the claim of empirical science to function as final arbitrator in questions of epistemology leads to relativism and that relativism contradicts the validity claims of science.

In the later writings Husserl considered the transcendental-phenomenological reduction as the only remedy against psychologism and anthropologism in the broader sense, i.e., the sense that includes historism and other kinds of relativism. This broader sense includes even the phenomenological research offered by the *Logical Investigations*. They are characterized in the first edition as 'descriptive psychology'. Psychologists of the time frequently claimed that descriptive psychology is the basic tool of espistemology.[7] Already in 1903 Husserl rejected this view.[8] Although it was not made clear enough in the first edition, he claimed that the descriptions in the *Logical Investigations* do not refer to empirical persons and psychic facts. Rather as phenomenological they refer to the *a priori* essential structures of the experience in which logical objects are given. A description of inner experience and structures of intentionality is thus not an empirical psychology, although it can still be understood as an naturalistic discipline. Twenty years later[9] Husserl wrote that the *Logical Investigations*, though not an empirical descriptive psychology still represents a subtle psychologism. Indeed, any attempt to justify validiy claims by means of a turn to the subject without explicitly performing the transcendental phenomenological reduction represents a transcendental psychologism of some sort.[10] If only the eidetic reduction were performed in investigations of structures of experience, then the investigation would not be phenomenology proper but rather eidetic psychology. Since in this case there would be no transcendental phenomenological reduction, the being of the subject would still be a being in the world. Thus eidetic psychology is later characterized as a subtle type of transcendental psychologism or even anthropologism.

The relation of the tendencies of descriptive and then eidetic psychology towards either transcendental psychologism or transcendental phenomenology is by no means a negative relation of mutual exclusion. On the contrary, Husserl in his later writings asserts again and again that all the contents of eidetic psychology's descriptions are also without restriction valid in transcendental phenomenology. The only difference is the attitude with which these contents are considered. In eidetic psychology they are still considered in the mundane attitude. In transcendental phenomenology they are considered in the transcendental attitude that is the result of the reduction. Furthermore, in addition to the Cartesian path there is a path to the transcendental phenomenological reduction via psychology. All that is necessary there is a thorough critical phenomenological reflection on the presuppositions of the descriptions of eidetic psychology itself, i.e., an intentional analysis of the cognitive activities of eidetic psychology itself.

The paradox of subjectivity which explicates the interplay can be now formulated as follows: On the one hand, the world and all its contents are given as the correlate of consciousness. On the other hand, we can think of the being of consciousness only as a being in the world. The second part of the paradox explains why anthropologism is a necessary part of the self-apprehension of subjectivity. The 'where' of its being can be apprehended only in the world. This, in turn explains why such a self-apprehension is necessarily infected with relativism. To be in the world is to be in one specific context in the world. Whatever is in the world in a context is in its being determined by this context. But under this presupposition it must be admitted that the way in which consciousness has the world as its correlate it determined by the specific context and, therefore, is different in different contexts. The additional puzzle is that the way in which this determination is thought depends upon the basic structure of the world-view and the different ways in which determinations can be thought in different world-views.

The paradox of subjectivity is helpful in some respects but leads to some other difficulties in the theory of the reduction. Given the paradox, the reduction can be understood as a decision in favour of the first part of the paradox. It is not obvious in the beginning that a full account of the paradox as a whole can be given after the reduction, and thus it is not obvious that the overcoming of relativism is again anything more than the decision to deny the motives for accepting relativistic positions.[11]

A new evaluation of the controversy between Husserl and Heidegger is possible. The existence of this controversy has been neglected in the literature, last but not least because there are very few sources and most of them have been published only recently. There is, in addition, an interesting historical question. The 'paradox of subjectivity' in the *Crisis*, where the being of subjectivity is at least under one perspective characterized as a 'being in the world', was developed by Husserl after he had read the early works of Heidegger. It can be asked, therefore, whether he was influenced by Heidegger in this respect and whether the paradox can be considered as Husserl's own answer to Heidegger. The following considerations are, however, systematic considerations. The historical and biographical aspect is not of significance here.

Husserl tells us in his critical remarks about Heidegger that though Heidegger offers an intentional psychology, he rejects the reduction and therefore does not have a real understanding of the constitution of the object and of reality. His philosophy, like the philosophy of his forerunners Dilthey and Scheler, is thus an anthropologism connected to an objectivism and naturalism. In counterdistinction to the use of this term earlier, e.g. in *Philosophy as a Rigorous Science*, 'Naturalism' here signifies the presupposition of the mundane attitude in which the existence of the world is not bracketed because the reduction is not performed.[12] In a nutshell, this criticism says nothing else but that Heidegger has chosen the priority of the mundane self-apprehension of the subject, i.e., he has chosen the part of the paradox which Husserl considered to be secondary in a sense that needs some clarification.

Heidegger's early conception of phenomenology presented in the lecture course *Grundprobleme der Phänomenologie*[13] confirms this thesis and answers in addition the question why Heidegger preferred the other part of the paradox: Phenomenology is the method of scientific philosophy and must be distinguished from world-view philosophy.[14] The method of scientific philosophy includes the methodical ideal of ultimate grounding (*Letztbegründung*). The development of the idea of ultimate grounding itself is the driving force of Heidegger's criticism of the transcendental-phenomenological reduction and Husserl's transcendental phenomenology in general.[15] Husserl speaks in his theory of the reduction about an absolute and apodictic *being* of the subject and a *being* of the world that is only a *being* relative to this absolute *being* of the subject. What is presupposed here, not asked and not answered, is the question of *being*. If one asks, however, the question of the 'being of subjectivity', then it can only be understood as 'being in the world'. This understanding, however, cancels the transcendental-phenomenological reduction. All said historical questions set aside, it can be said from a systematic point of view that Heidegger turns the paradox of subjectivity against Husserl and his idea of reduction at this point.

Together with this criticism Heidegger proposes a new type of reduction which shall serve the idea of ultimate grounding better than Husserl's reduction. At this point he still calls it 'phenomenological reduction'.[16] It is the reduction of the beings (*Seiendes*) to *being* (*Sein*) in the ontological difference. The ultimate grounding is, hence, an ontological grounding. This idea needs some explications in order to arrive at a proper comparison with Husserl's idea of ultimate grounding. Such an explication can also explain why Heidegger in the subsequent development first drops the term 'phenomenology' and later speaks first about 'hermeneutic phenomenology', then about 'hermeneutics' and finally abandons even this term as characterizing his new way of thinking.

Joseph Kockelmans[17] has shown that the *Grundprobleme* are heavily influenced by Heidegger's interpretation, critique and reformulation of Kant's doctrine of method. The lecture *Phänomenologische Interpretation von Kants Kritik der reinen Vernunft*[18] was given immediately after the *Grundprobleme*. Heidegger's early methodological reflections are, hence, the fruit of his critical considerations of both Husserl and Kant. The significance of the philosophers of classical antiquity and the middle ages shall not be denied with this thesis. Systematically considered they have, however, significance for Heidegger because he thought he succeeded in his criticisms of modern philosophy and first of all of the philosophies of Kant and Husserl.

Heidegger's *ontological* idea of ultimate grounding in the *Grundprobleme* is critical to the extent in which it is grounded in the critical distinction between beings and *being*. It is transcendental because it transcends the realm of beings towards *being*.[19] The ontological structure of existence (*Dasein*) is grounded in the transcendence of *being*.[20] The *a priori* is understood as the form of the pre-ontological understanding of being as beings. An analysis of the *a priori*—i.e., Kant's enterprize—under which beings are given is, hence, in the final instance only possible from the viewpoint of the ontological difference, Heideggers 'phenomenological reduction' in the *Grundprobleme*.

The original intention of Heidegger is, therefore, to replace Kant's transcendental logic with a transcendental ontology,[21] more precisely to show that a transcendental ontology is the ultimate ground for a transcendental logic. At the same time a transcendental ontology is supposed to be the ultimate ground also for phenomenology and its theory of the *a priori*.

Some of the difficulties of Heidegger's idea of an ontological interpretation of the idea of ultimate grounding, which will be discussed in detail later can be foreseen already from a Kantian perspective. The Kantian ultimate *conditions*—it is Fichte who first demanded that they ought to be understood as ultimate determining grounds—are for Kant 'transcendent' in the sense of 'absent.' Neither the subject nor the object can be known 'in themselves.' Heidegger's *being* has the same character with respect to pre-ontological understanding. Ontological understanding still has this character to the extent which *being* cannot be thematized 'in itself' but only in the ontological difference. After abandoning the ideal of ultimate grounding, Heidegger developed a new criticism of Husserl. He says that Husserl's phenomenology is grounded in a 'metaphysics of the present'.[22] It is grounded in the evidence of what is originally given and thus it fails to recognize the priority of the transcendent, the absent, namely *being*.

This criticism has been corroborated later by Derrida.[23] It reveals, however, also the difficulties of the possibility of the idea of an ontologically ultimate grounding of the *Grundprobleme*. *Being* as ultimate ground cannot be 'assumed' like a Neokantian hypothesis. An ultimate ground cannot be represented after ultimate grounding is achieved as something which is not there in some '*aletheia*,' but 'absent' in principle. But if so, then Heidegger himself will still represent some 'metaphysics' of the present'. He can be defended against such charges by pointing out that in the end he himself abandoned the idea of 'ultimate grounding.' This will be explained later. It is clear, however, that if he himself abandons the idea of an ultimate ontological grounding, then his early criticism of Husserl is pointless. He himself could not deliver what he promised to deliver.

Before looking into this matter we have now first to investigate how Husserl's idea of ultimate grounding by choosing the other part of the paradox may prove its mettle against the charges raised by Heidegger. In order to achieve this goal it will, however, be necessary to reject some essential elements of Husserl's own self-understanding. It will be necessary to remove everything which implies ontological theses and, hence, also ontological idealism.

Husserl himself quite frequently mentioned that critical problems still remain after the transcendental phenomenological reduction. If transcendental phenomenology would be guided only by a naive trust in the newly discovered apodicticity without really knowing the nature of this apodicticity, then these problems would indeed remain unsolved. It is neither necessary nor possible to give here a full account of this 'critique of the critique'. What is at stake is the paradox os subjectivity and the problem that it creates for transcendental subjectivity because, according to Heidegger, the *question of being* is not asked *and the nature of transcendence* is not grasped properly. In terms of the paradox, this could be done only by giving priority to the other part of the paradox. In the 'critique of the critique' there are two places in which the problem of *transcendence* surfaces again: (1) the problem of the self-giveness of the subject in the constitution of inner temporality and (2) the problem of 'solipsism', which is actually the problem of the givenness of the other, the alter ego.

With respect to the first problem, three aspects can be distinguished: (a) The unity of consciousness is taken for granted in the analyses following the transcendental phenomenological reduction.[24] Thus, the phenomenology of inner time consciousness and its constitution is an essential part of the 'critique of the critique.' (b) The transcendental phenomenological attitude requires a split between observing and observed consciousness.[25] How such a split is possible in the unity of consciousness can only be understood if the temporal character of consciousness is properly analysed. (c) The apodictic self-giveness is original self-giveness but not an adequate self-giveness and it is restricted in its apodicticity to the present phase of inner temporality.[26] The analysis of inner temporality is, therefore, also of significance for a critique of the proper meaning and the scope of apodictic evidence.

A brief outline of the formal structure of the constitution of time consciousness indicates the answers that can be given to these questions from Husserl's own phenomenological research. The original temporal flux is constituted on the lowest level of passive constitution.[27] The abstract moments that constitute the whole of the flux are: (i) the moments that constitute the form of the flux, i.e., the actual now or *nunc stans* with its protentional horizon and the continuum of retentions in the retentional horizon, and (ii) the contents of the flux, which emerge as primary impressions in the actual now and flow off from there into the continuum of retentions. From the present temporal perspective the contents vanish into the retentional continuum, i.e., they flow off into a temporal realm which is *not* given in original evidence.[28]

An explicit consciousness *of* inner temporality is constituted only on the level of intentional acts of remembering, expectation and immediate reflections on the flux of the living present itself. All these acts occur within the temporality that is constituted on the lowest level—like everything else in consciousness, including the ego. They are themselves temporal and constitute in their original temporality a consciousness of the 'stream of consciousness' that stretches beyond the living present into a past that is *not* originally given. They constitute the consciousness of duration and succession and with it the consciousness of *what is absent from the present.*[29]

We can emphasize three points:

(1) The formal structure of the original flux can be recognized only because it is to be found in every flowed off phase of time that can be an object of reflection. The *nunc stans* of the actual now in the living present *cannot*, however, *be objectified by reflection*. Rather, it is the place in which all objectification occurs. The split that occurs between observing and observed consciousness can thus be explained by the termporal structure of consciousness, which is pregiven for all acts of reflection.

(2) Inner temporality and its unity is not the result of synthetic activity of the ego on active consciousness. On the contrary, all these activities occur in this medium, which is pregiven for them in 'passive' constitution. There are classes of intentional acts in which consciousness and its temporality is given for itself objectifies itself. But the evidence in which it is given to itself, though apodictic, is *not adequate* in several respects. The first and most essential

aspect of the structure which is '*absent*' is *the actual emergence* of inner temporality in form and content itself. It cannot be given in original evidence *for objectifying acts* in the *nunc staus*.

(3) Past phases of consciousness can be selectively thematized by acts of remembering. As past phases they belong to the immanence of consciousness but they are for the acts of remembering a transcendence—a transcendence in immanence, as Husserl says. They are, furthermore, not given in original and apodictic evidence in the same way in which consciousness is accessible to itself in reflections in the living present. Furthermore, the 'past' is there and can even determine the activities of actual consciousness without being thematized by remembering. Indeed, only very few features are thematized and Husserl's analyses admit the recognition not only the unconscious but also of a subconscious realm within and for consciousness, i.e. a realm that is 'absent' in principle and connected with the *nunc stans* which is as well 'absent' for reflection.

The problem of the *transcendence* of the world can only be treated properly in connection with the analysis of intersubjectivity, i.e., the solution for the postponed problem of solipsism.[30] Something can be said about the *transcendence* of the world and objects in the world from the viewpoint of the *transcendence* in immanence mentioned above.[31] Transcendent objects are given as real objects of perception only via intentional acts of consciousness that synthesize disjunct phases of inner time in which the 'same' object was given and may be given. Such intentional acts are the acts of remembering, expectation and the presentification of the present absent—an act of the imagination that already includes the givenness of the other. It is, hence, the 'transcendence in immanence', i.e. in the residuum of the reduction, which in part explicates the nature of the transcendence of identical objects of consciousness and their categorial structure—a point which cannot be pursued here.

Husserl's own account of the givenness of the other and intersubjectivity in the fifth *Cartesian Meditation* is difficult to understand because its background, the transcendental aesthetics of phenomenology, is nowhere explicated in the *Meditations*. It is clear, however, from the Meditations that Husserl recognizes that the *transcendence* of objects of perception presuppose that they are in principle possible objects for another consciousness, i.e. *transcendence in general presupposes intersubjectivity*. The consciousness of the other is, however, itself in a very peculiar sense *transcendent* for my consciousness. The analysis of the givenness of the other is, hence, a key problem for the 'critique of the critique.' We begin with a brief explication of the background that is, as mentioned, missing in the *Cartesian Meditations*.

The hyletic field, i.e. the 'sensuous' contents of consciousness, belongs to the immanence of consciousness. The hyletic contents are not isolated data but rather given in a field that has its own constitution. This constitution is passive and it is pregiven to all intentional activities of the ego. One aspect of this constitution of the field is the form of succession, i.e., the constitution of inner time consciousness. The other forms are the forms determining simultaneous coexistence in the living present, i.e., the field of *localization*.[32] The generally determining structures are *Gestalt*-structures, i.e. contrast/fusion, pairing, foreground/background, etc. They determine, likewise in pure passivity, the associative awakening of past phases of consciousness.[33]

The ego has no active part in this constitution. It is rather affected by it. It is affected primarily by contrast-phenomena, i.e., not by the hyletic contents but by the relations they have with each other. The affections comes (1) from the field of localization in the living present, but also (2) from the past through associative awakening of contents by contents. The ego can respond to such affections with kinesthetic perceiving, remembering and expectations, activities which are closely connected with each other. The relation of affection between the hyletic field and the ego takes place within the field itself. The ego is in the field.[34] The ego's being in the field is determined by the most basic pairing relation through which the field is structured as a whole, namely the 'inside' of my body and the 'outside' of the field that surrounds it. The relation is not only a relation of localization. Temporal structures also play a role.[35]

An absolute here-now 'inside' my body relates to the 'thereoutside' in the following way. A 'there' is a potential 'here' only in the retentional or protentional horizon of kinesthetic activities. That means that the here-now is always unique at every given moment, and it is at every moment confronted with a manifold of simultaneous theres which are potential heres, but never simultaneously actual heres. It should be noted that neither 'here' nor 'there' nor 'here-now' can be understood as 'points'. They are all constituted by contrast-phenomena grounded in qualitative contents of the hyletic field. The 'here-now' has as body a specific 'thickness'. The primordial ego in the field of its ownness, i.e., the ego that is left if one abstracts from the givenness of the other[36] is neither more nor less than the 'pole,' the centre of the embodied here-now in the hyletic field. Its kinesthetic movements are the movements in which 'theres' have been run through, made into here and let drop out the here-now again.

The other is, therefore, primarily experienced as a simultaneously given other here-now, i.e. another body. It is clear from the structure of the field and the nature of kinesthetic movements that *such a simultaneous here-now* can never be brought to *original evidence*, i.e., it can never be presented, it can only be *appresented* in my original here-now. What is given is the outside of another living body. It is appresented as *living* because an inside is associated with it through an associated transfer of the inside/outside structure of my primordial body.[37] The associative transfer happens in the hyletic field in pure passivity, i.e., no activity of consciousness is implied. It 'happens' to it, affects it. It experiences in passivity another 'transcendence in immanence' that, in the dimension of localization, is the counterpart to the 'transcendence in immanence' that confronts consciousness with the past.[38]

The givenness of the other as other living body in purely passive associative constitution is the ground for all higher forms of communicating with others and understanding them. Its first basic function is, however, a function in the representation of *transcendent* objects of perception. In the experience of a *transcendent object* of perception there are always only appresented, but not originally given, aspects of the object. To the extent to which they are appresented as simultaneously existing with the originally given aspect it is also appresented that they can be given simultaneously in original evidence for another consciousness in a here-now that is, seen from my point of view, there. *Thus transcendent objects are from the very beginning transcendent only as intersubjectively given objects.* Their transcendence is constituted in the *double transcendence* in the immanence that is found on the one hand in the flowed off past of consciousness temporally and the transcendence in immanence in the field of localization with the givenness of the other. In both cases such constitutions are not the consequence of intentional acts, spontaneities of the subject. They 'happen' to consciousness in passive constitution.

Some modifications of the concept of 'apodicticity' and of the concept 'transcendence' are necessary after these analyses, which belong to the 'critique of the critique'. First, one has to distinguish between the apodicticity of the self-givenness of the existence of consciousness and the apodicticity in which certain structures of consciousness are given. In both cases apodicticity *qua* impossibility of not being given can be experienced only to the extent to which that which is experienced can be rediscovered in the structure of reflection on this experience. It is, hence, temporality that makes possible, such an experience because iterated reflection is possible only in the framework of temporality.

Apodicticity in the self-givenness of the existence of consciousness taken for itself is 'blind'. Without explicating the structures of consciousness it does not lead to any content of critical knowledge. Having in mind the paradox of subjectivity and Heidegger's criticism, one has from the outset to avoid a serious error Husserl fell into and was, hence, wide open to the objection raised by Heidegger. The apodicticity of the self-givenness of consciousness to consciousness with respect to its existence *ought not to be understood as an ontological statement.* It is simply wrong to say that subjectivity is in any sense an 'absolute' being or '*absoluter Seinsboden*'. The statement about the apodicticity of self-givenness is a purely epistemic statement about a mode of knowing and not an ontological argument concerning existence. It is, therefore, also of interest *only* for a consciousness that has an interest in apodictic evidence and such an interest is an epistemic interest. To ask for the 'being' of the subject has as its immediate consequence that subject and object *are not* considered as correlates of their *being known*. This means, however, that talking about being is impossible inside the reduction. The reduction which is at least in the beginning the decision for one part of the paradox is cancelled if the concern is 'being,'—the 'being' of the subject is 'being in the world'.

The pure apodicticity of self-givenness with respect to existence taken for itself is useless seen from an epistemic point of view. According to Husserl there are apodictically given structures in an 'eidos ego', 'consciousness in general': the general structures of intentionality, temporality, actuality and potentiality, genetic structures and structures of the hyletic field. They serve in further investigations as parametres, frames for variations in which further structures of consciousness can be discovered. Such secondary structures are not given in apodicticity.

Structures of consciousness given in apodictic evidence are given as such only for a consciousness that has an interest in apodictic evidence. Furthermore, it holds that not all of them belong with eidetic necessity to all possible forms of consciousness. To the extent to which apodictic evidence is given with respect to intentional activities of consciousness such structures belong with evidetic necessity only to the type of consciousness that lives in such activities. Thus all the apodictic evidence that can be discovered in a phenomenology of reason belongs with eidetic necessity only to a consciousness which has fully developed reason. Thus there is only one realm in which 'structure given in apodicticity' and 'belongs with eidetic necessity to every type of consciousness' are not separable. *It is the realm of passive constitution.*

Regarding these structures, some further modifications in the concept of 'apodicticity' must be introduced. They have immediate significance for the problem of transcendence. *Prima facie* it can be said that an apodictic evidence is, though not adequate, an original evidence. According to many interpreters and critics of Husserl who have enough textual evidence to support their claims, it could be said that according to Husserl an original evidence is an evidence given 'bodily' in the living present and hence we have a metaphysics of presence. This interpretation does not fit however, the results of the analyses of passive synthesis. The result here is the apodictic evidence that there is for consciousness a necessary transcendence, absence in three dimensions: (a) the *nunc stans* as the place of its emergence is impenetrable, (b) the past of the passively constituted continuum of retentions and its contents as a transcendence in immanence and, (c) finally, the 'there' in the field of localization as a simultaneous other "here-now", as another transcendence in immanence. What is "*originally given*" is *absence as necessary absence*. There should be no surprise about that. Those who find great delight in pointing to the priority of 'absence' nowadays want to tell us as well that this priority is a necessary priority and cannot be cancelled, i.e., they claim to have apodictic evidence about this priority of absence.

Such an interpretation seems not to fit into the strict separation of the experience of the transcendent world from the experience of the transcendental sphere of consciousness that Husserl introduces still in the beginning of the *Cartesian Meditations*. Furthermore, it does not fit any ontological understanding of the so-called phenomenological idealism. There can be no doubt that Husserl himself cherished idealism. There can be no doubt that Husserl himself cherished such a self-interpretation of his phenomenological investigations. But following his own analysis of the experience of the other and applying what he has said about the transcendence in immanence, the only possible conclusion—never drawn explicitly by Husserl and at some places denied—is that the difference of the 'here-now' and the 'there' in the hyletic field (and with it this field as a field of localization) belongs to the sphere of immanence, i.e. the transcendental sphere. That means that there is not only an '*inner temporality*' but also an '*inner spatiality*' left in the residuum of the *epoché*. It seems to me that without such an assumption it is impossible to give a phenomenological account of the givenness of the other as independent from the constitutive activity of my consciousness and hence of transcendence in general.

There will be, however, no difficulty for such an interpretation if the reduction is understood from the outset as only epistemic and not ontological. To 'bracket' the natural attitude does not mean that the transcendence of the world has been bracketed. The reduction only 'brackets' the claim that the world, in whatever understanding it presents itself, is the first evidence underlying all other evidence. The world, including its transcendence, remains as a validity phenomenon. The task is to analyse the meaning of this transcendence, beginning with consciousness as first evidence. If the reduction is understood as having only an epistemic function the following thesis is completely compatible with such a reduction: Transcendence emerges for the subject on the genetically lowest level of constitution in pure passivity. It emerges from the very beginning as something given for consciousness that is prior to all acts of consciousness. Seen under the reduction as an epistemic reduction the priority of the active life of consciousness is epistemic and not genetic. To state that consciousness can strive for evidence only under the genetic presupposition of a transcendence that makes such a striving possible, is itself an epistemic statement and as such even apodictically evident.

It can now be asked what phenomenology can say under these circumstances about the paradox of subjectivity. If the priority of the subject is understood only as an epistemic priority, then there will be no difficulty any more with the very obvious observation that the natural attitude is genetically prior to the transcendental attitude. It is a general 'law' of intentionality, that all intentions of oblique reflective nature are onesidedly founded in intentions directed towards objects. Furthermore, the genetic priority of the natural attitude is—again in genetical investigations—shown to be a necessity. It is a necessity because it emerges out of the 'transcendence in immanence' that determine the structure of subjectivity in passive constitution. It is the natural attitude that represents the other part of the paradox of subjectivity for which the being of subjectivity is a being in the world. The ontological priority of world and transcendence on which this part of the paradox insists is recognized under the reduction in epistemic interpretation. The priority occurs *here as genetic priority*, i.e., it is recognized that the 'question of being' has indeed genetic priority in the genesis of knowing.

Finally, transcendental phenomenology can at least point to the original emergence of the whole context. The '*nunc stans*' was in its actual existence beyond the power and—metaphorically speaking—in the 'back' of phenomenological reflection. It is the common ground of all apprehension and self-apprehension and the source of the emergence of reality—as given with or without the attitude generated by the reduction. Seen from an ontological point of view the urge to say something about it is pressing. Seen from an epistemic understanding of the reduction one has simply to state: in this case the presence is given throughout in absence.

I tried to give a version of transcendental phenomenology under which the objections of Heidegger (and others) in the *Grundprobleme* and later are rendered pointless. There is, however, in the *Grundprobleme* a positive claim which implied another criticism. It is impossible, according to Husserl and his reflections, to achieve ultimate grounding in the natural attitude, i.e., under the part of the paradox that explicates the being of subjectivity as being in the world. Hiedegger, apparently, thought otherwise, at least in the beginning of his career. Let me point out in the last part of this paper that Heidegger's *Denkweg* leads, in its end, precisely to the result which can be foreseen from Husserl's point of view. This is, of course, not something that has been said by Heidegger in the way in which I state it here. Rather it is part of his later universal criticism of transcendental philosophy.

Kockelmans has shown[39] that Heidegger's intention in *Being and Time* and other writings belonging to the same period is still to present an epistemology which has the task of a philosophical grounding of the sciences. Fay[40] has collected material that shows that at this time Heidegger had a similar attitude with respect to formalized logic and mathematics. There is also no hint at this time that the idea of ultimate grounding via the explication of the ontological difference has been abandoned. Careful reading with hindsight, i.e., having in mind the later writings of Heidegger, allows us, however, to determine the problem which later on forced Heidegger to rethink the problem of grounding and ultimate grounding.

We find in *Being and Time* first a 'more profound grounding' in the explication of temporality as the 'ontological meaning of care'. In this explication 'theoretical knowing' occurs in the transition from the second to the third level of temporality.

The first level of grounding is the analysis of the temporality of the being of *Dasein*. Here 'resolutness comes back to itself in the future and posits itself in the present of the situation'.[41] 'Time is originally the timing of temporality and as such the possibility of the constitution of care'.[42]

The second level is the level of the '*abkünftige*' temporality. The word '*abkünftig*' is not an originary German word. It means on the one hand 'grounded', 'secondary', but it has, on the other hand, the connotation of 'turning away from the origin' which is, as mentioned, future, '*Zukunft*' as '*Abkunft*'. On this level of time, temporal beings are given. It is the time of circumspect care in the structure of being-concerned-with. As ecstatic time which has no serial character it has the modes of 'now as', and 'then, when' in the past and in the future. Time is public-time on that level as the work of the days and nights disclosed in circumspect care.[43]

The third level is the level of abstract world time. It can be characterized with Aristotle: 'For time is this: what is counted in the movement in accordance with what is earlier and what is later'. Time on this level is a counted series of nows and instead of 'places' one has the coexistent points of abstract space. Both are indifferent to 'being concerned with' and, hence, meaning.[44]

Heidegger introduced the existential conception of science in the analysis of 'circumspect care'. This existential concept of science is different from the concept of science that understands science as *Begründungszusammenhang*, as connected grounding. Science is understood as a mode of being in the world, in which beings (*Seiendes*) and Being (*Sein*) are discovered or disclosed. The existential conception of science is explicated by asking for the *ontological genesis* of theoretical behaviour and the theoretical history of science.

The relevant point is not the simple vanishing of the practical 'being concerned with', i.e., the theoretical attitude is not reached by simply no longer being involved in things with which we are 'being concerned with'. The origin of the theoretical attitude is rather a 'looking around' that has the character of 'checking what is the case' (*Nachsehen*). It occurs in the 'being concerned with' and thus the 'being concerned with' has its own 'theoretical aspect.' This explains why later on theories always have a practical aspect in their techniques of observation and experimentation.

What happens in the transition of the second to the third level of temporality is the discovery of 'if-then' relations in the 'being concerned with' and 'circumspect care' of the second level. This relation receives the character as a relation between facts (*Vorhandenem*) and with this objective grounding relation we have science understood as '*Begründungs-zusammenhang*'.

This brief reminder is sufficient to illustrate two points. (1) Though the style is different, the whole analysis reminds us of Husserl's theory of the levels of time constitution. One could, indeed, try to understand the whole analysis in a phenomenological framework, add some corrections from the phenomenological point of view, but also enrich the phenomenological analyses given by Husserl with viewpoints taken from Heidegger. An epistemic reflection on the analysis itself would then immediately lead to the reduction. (2) This will be, however, a gross misreading of Heidegger's intentions. The whole analysis of *Dasein* in *Being and Time* has only the function to prepare the question of being which discloses the ontological difference. According to the *Grundprobleme* the ultimate grounding can take place only there.

In 'Der Satz vom Grund'[45] Heidegger finally abandons the self-interpretation of the ontological difference as 'ultimate grounding' in the traditional sense in his criticism of the principle of sufficient reason. Already in *Being and Time* Heidegger points out that the if-then of circumspect care becomes a universal principle if it is applied to pure objects (*Vorhandenes*). The environment is thus changed into nature *qua* nature of the natural science. In its original form the 'principle of sufficient reason' simply states that 'everything has its reason' and 'Nothing is without reason'. It has its time of 'incubation' in the time of metaphysical thinking. In this metaphysical thinking it has, according to Heidegger, a 'double tune' (*doppelte Tonart).* Let us simply say it has a double meaning.

The first meaning is expressed by the '*principium reddendae rationis sufficientis*', the principle of sufficient reason. In this form it leads metaphysics to the '*causa prima*' which is 'deus'.[46] The second, more hidden meaning discloses itself in the 'speaking of being which grounds the beings'. At the end of the time of the incubation the first meaning is the governing meaning that has pushed the second completely into the background. In this governing meaning the principle of reason governs science, mathematics and technology. Reason is understood here as 'reckoning ratio' and logic as the calculus of mathematical logic. The goal is universal rationalization, i.e., the delivery of reasons we can reckon with, count on.[47]

The striving of modern philosophy for 'ultimate grounding' belongs, according to Heidegger, to the unfolding of the first meaning of the principle. Pure reason is in Kant as theoretical and as practical reason *ratio pura*, ground of all grounding and positing of the absolute ground.[48] Kant's method brings the principle of sufficient reason to its ultimate power. 'It reaches its ultimate power in the principle of subjectivity which is nothing else than to claim unlimited power for the principle and its striving for complete rationalisation.[49]

Heidegger criticized Husserl in the *Grundprobleme* for not asking the question of being. Without asking this question one cannot reach ultimate grounding. There is a shift in the '*Satz vom Grund*' which affected this criticism. To ask for 'ultimate grounding' under the first meaning of the principle and thus also turning to the principle of subjectivity is itself the basic mistake. Heidegger does not mention Husserl in the *Satz vom Grund* but it is obvious that the characterization of Kant there is also valid for Husserl. If the 'ultimate ground' is thought as subjectivity, then the '*Entzug*', the vanishing of being and the vanishing of the possibility of speaking being, is the necessary consequence. To ask for 'ultimate grounding' means that the question of being cannot be asked properly.

This verdict can be considered from two sides. It says as well that asking the question of being, asking the question of the being of the subject and answering this question with 'being in the world' does indeed also exclude the possibility of asking meaningfully for ultimate grounding. This is precisely why Husserl bracketed the natural attitude and why I argued in this essay that already an ontological interpretation of the reduction destroys the possibility of reaching the goal that Husserl declared to be this goal: to find a meaningful explication of 'ultimate grounding'. Is it possible that there is an ideal of 'ultimate grounding' that corresponds to the second meaning of the principle of reason. First it has to be said, according to Heidegger, that we still live in the time of incubation in which the 'second tune' cannot be heard.[50] Secondly it is obvious from the hints that Heidegger gives, that the speaking of being, *die Sage des Seins*, has the character of poetical-prophetical discourse in which a mystical experience of the ground as an abyss, the *Grund* as *Abgrund*, speaks. It is difficult, but not impossible, to translate the discourse of ultimate grounding in approximately one-to-one corresponding terms from one language into another. Thus it is an indicator that Heidegger is after something which is still unknown and his hints in this respect in the '*Satz vom Grund*' cannot be translated. They can only be explained with the aid of philological commentary on some peculiarities of German.[51] Thus Heidegger had to abandon the original program of the *Grundprobleme* that was connected with his criticism of Husserl, namely to fulfil Husserl's program of ultimate grounding in asking first the question of the being of the subject and then the question of being.

NOTES AND REFERENCES

1. E. Husserl, *Die Krisis der Europäischen Wissenschaften und die transzendentale Phänmenologie*, Husserliana VI, 1954, §§ 53, 55 (Henceforth KR).
2. E. Husserl, Prolegomena, *Logische Untersuchungen I*, Husserliana XVIII, 1975, §§ 34–38 (Henceforth LU).
3. D. Folleesdal, *Husserl und Frege*, Oslo, 1958. Cf. J. N. Mohanty, *Husserl and Frege*, Indiana U.P., 1982 20 sequ.
4. E. Husserl, 'Philosophy as a Rigorous Science, in: *Phenomenology and the Crisis of Philosophy*, Harper & Row, 1965, esp. 92–105.
5. Prolegomena, § 35.
6. Philosophy as a Rigorous Science, 129—Lauer and others translate 'Historismus' as 'historicism'. I follow the terminology of K. Popper: *The Poverty of Historicism*, Routledge & Kegan Paul, 1960 in distinguishing between *historism* and *historicism*. Historicism is represented by theories—like those of Hegel and Marx—which attempt to give an account of universal history as a whole. Such an account is seen from the viewpoint of historism, which represents a kind of relativism, as nothing else than bad metaphysics.
7. Cf. Spiegelberg, H. *The Phenomenological Movement*, Vol. I, Nijhoff, 1960, esp. 57 (about Stumpf).
8. Cf. the Preface to the Prolegomena, *Logical Investigations* Vol. I. (in the translation of Findlay, Routledge & Kegan Paul, 1970, 47.)
9. *Formal and Transcendental Logic*, Husserliana XVII, §§ 56, 99 (Henceforth FTL).
10. For an account with more references, see Th.M. Seebohm *Die Bedingungen der Möglichkeit der Transzendentalphilosophie* Bonn, 1962, 156–159.
11. For a criticism in this kind, cf. G. Funke, 'Practical Reason in Kant and Husserl', in: *Kant and Phenomenology*, Center for Advanced Research in Phenomenology and U.P. of America, 1984, 1–29.
12. Husserl's notes about Heidegger are published in Diemer, A. *Edmund Husserl, Versuch einer systematischen Darstellung seiner Phänomenologie*, Meisenheim, 1956, 29–30. See also FTL §§ 56, 99.
13. Gesasmtausgabe II. Abteilung, vol. 24, Frankfurt Klostermann, 1975, (Henceforth *GP*).
14. *GP* 1–3.
15. *GP* 255 ff.
16. *GP* 26, 31.
17. For the following cf. J. Kockelmans, 'Kant's Method and Heidegger', in: *Kant and Phenomenology*, Th. M Seebohm & J.J. Kockelmans eds, Center of Advanced Research in Phenomenology & UP and America, 198, 161–183,—see also Kockelmans, *Heidegger and Science*, Center of Advanced Research &c., 1985, 53 sequ.
18. Gesamtausgabe II. Abteilung, Bd. 25, Frankfurt, Klostermann, 1977.
19. *GP* 20 sequ. Cf. Kockelmans, Kant's Method . . ., 165 sequ.
20. Kockelmans, Kant's Method. . . ., 197.
21. Kockelmans, Kant's Method. . . ., 180.
22. 'Die Onto-Theologische Verfassung der Metaphysik' in: *Identität und Differenz*, Pfullingen, Neske, 1957.
23. Derrida, J., *La Voix et le Phenomene*, Presses Universitaires de France, 1967.
24. *Ideen zu einer reinen Phäneomenologie und phänomenologischen Philosophie* Vol. I.

Husserliana III, 1950, 197 f, 209, (Henceforth *ID* I). *Cartesiansische Meditationen und Pariser Vorträge*, Husserliana I, 1950, 81, 109 (Henceforth *CM*).

25. *CM* 73, *Erste Philosophie II*, Husserliana VIII, 1959, 440/441, (Henceforth *EP II*).
26. *CM* 67 f, *EP II* 169.
27. *CM* 49 f.
28. *Zur Phänemonologie des inneren Zeitbewußtseins*, Husserliana X, 42 f.
29. An account with more references is given in Th.M. Seebohm, 'Reflexion and Totality in the Phenomenology of E. Husserl in: Journal of the British Society for Phenomenology, Vol. 4, 1973, 25 sequ.
30. *EP II* 173, *CM* 69, cf. the addendum 239.
31. *CM* 80 see also *Analysen zur Passiven Synthesis*, Husserliana XI, 112 sequ, (Henceforth *APS*), *KR* 189, *CM* 134, 140, 155.
32. *APS* 133.
33. *APS* 120, 205.
34. *APS* 149 sequ.
35. *CM* 137.
36. *CM* 131–136.
37. *CM* 137–145.
38. *KR* 189, *CM* 134, 140, 155.
39. Joseph J. Kockelmans, *Heidegger and Science*, Center for Advanced Research in Phenomenology & UP of America, Washington DC, 1985.
40. Thomas A. Fay, *Heidegger: The Critique of Logic*, The Hague, Nijhoff 1977.
41. Heidegger, M. Sein und Zeit, Max Niemeyer, Tübingen, 1953, 326 (Heceforth *SZ*). The translations are mine.
42. *SZ* 331.
43. *SZ* 406 sequ.
44. *SZ* 421.
45. *Ter Satz vom Grund*, Neske, Pfullingen, 1957, (Henceforth *SG*).
46. *SG* 53 sequ.
47. *SG* 53 sequ, 98 sequ. 65, 166 sequ.
48. *SG* 127.
49. *SG* 138.
50. *SG* 90, 97.
51. *SG* 96, 98.—In German "principle" is '*Grundsatz*' or—as in Heidegger—briefly '*Satz*'. '*Staz*', however, has a second meaning in German, which is disconnected from the first, i.e., 'statement', namely 'leap'. 'Abyss' is in German expressed by using the linguistic root '*Grund*' and called '*Abgrund*'. Thus the German counterpart to 'principle of reason' is 'statement of the ground,' which is rendered by Heidegger in the 'second tune' to '*Satz in den Grund*' and then '*Satz in den Abgrund*', 'leap into the abyss'. The impossibility of translating this 'movement of thought' has no longer anything in common with the difficulties of translating technical philosophical terminology.

Experiment as Fulfilment of Theory*

PATRICK A. HEELAN

Goal of Science is the Study of Phenomena: It is a very common view among scientists and philosophers bolstered by a long and eminent tradition that the purpose of scientific inquiry is theory-making, that is, that the goal and term of scientific research is a good theory.[1] Whatever the cultural and historical reasons for this view, there are weighty reasons—philosophical and empirical—for rejecting it.

Taking the ultimate, i.e., philosophical, goal of scientific research to be to say something about reality, philosophy needs to specify critically where reality is to be found and how it is to be studied philosophically. Now the home of reality is not, as Edmund Husserl correctly argued,[2] the domain of theoretical entities ("idealities," to use his term) but the domain of perceptual phenomena, that is, the world. Science then in this view should regard its task as complete (at least, provisionally) when it has said what it has to say (at least, provisionally) about the worldly phenomena of science.

How (worldly) phenomena are to be understood, how they are to be analyzed is not an easy or trivial matter, but one of the major problems of philosophy. I shall not rehearse here the variety of solution given by different philosophies. The most influential solution among modern philosophies of science is the empiricist one; this takes perceptual phenomena to be composed or constructed out of elementary, primitive, culturally and historically non-relative parts, 'given' exclusively by the world to the sensing knower as fully determinate 'mirror images' of its attributes, and capable of functioning as a secure foundation of theoretical, scientific, and all advanced forms of knowledge. Such a foundation-seeking view bears some resemblance to Husserl's, but for the later Husserl, we find a tension between two mutually antagonistic positions, 1. a *foundational* one that inclines towards *idealism*, that there are ideal transcendental structures normative for all possible worlds and all human subjectivity, and 2. a *historical* one that inclines towards *realism*, that phenomena as 'given' by the world are elicited by a historical culture, that they are never fully determinate, that they do not 'mirror' the world as this is in itself, and that they are not composed of elementary, primitive parts 'given' in a (culturally) non-relative way.[3]

It is important to consider Husserl's view because he was the author of a complex and sophisticated theory about the nature and structure of a phenomenon, which, as I have shown elsewhere[4], was influenced by the scientific milieu of Göttingen where he lived for fifteen years as an *Extraordinarius* in the Faculty of Philosophy. Here he was the colleague and friend of the best theoretical sicentists of his time, the members of the *Erlanger* school of mathematics and the Hilbert school of theoretical physics.[5]

According to Husserl, a *phenomenon* is to be understood as the invariant that underlies the ordered diversity of profiles (or perspectives) the phenomenon manifests to perceivers in the life-world. Such an objective invariant is matched by a subjective (representing) invariant, the bodily 'kinesthesis' (or constituting capacity or agency) through which humans explore this particular unity amid sensible diversity within experience. Both emulate ('represent,' in the mathematical sense) the invariant of a common abstract transformation group. He called the law among the profiles of the object 'the *noema*'; this is matched by a certain agency of the subject capable of actively anticipating and exploring the noematic structure of the object—such an agency he called 'the *noesis*'[6]. Both the *noema* and the *noesis* can be interpreted as emulating ('representing,' in the mathematical sense) a common abstract transformation group, just as the phenomenon and its kinesthesis emulate the invariant of that group. Real worldly kinds—like the 'natural kinds' of a more classical philosophy—are then the *noemata* to which correspond the *noeses* of human cultural and historical being-in-the-world. Phenomenology investigates these *noemata* through a study of their corresponding *noeses*, a central part of such theoretical studies is the positing for each *noesis/noema* pair a common abstract transformation group.[7]

Reinforcement for the conclusion that the goal of science is to give an account of the worldly phenomena of science—scientific *noemata*—comes from the pragmatic and logical inability of scientific theory alone to determine its domain of worldly phenomena. The most frequent response to this discovery, often called the Duhem-Quine-Hesse thesis, is some form of Conventionalism, Instrumentalism, or Relativism.[8] A careful *noetic* analysis reveals that such a conclusion is not well founded since important factors have been overlooked in the former philosophical analysis. The connection between theory and data, the domain of scientific phenomena,[9] is not arbitrary in the way suggested by the Duhem-Quine-Hesse thesis, but *noetic* analysis suggests that it is achieved through the mediations of aesthetic praxis, hermeneutics, and practical phronesis.

Contrary to the prevalent view—and together with Husserl—I argue that the pre-eminent goal and final term of scientific research is the constitution and experimental control of scientific phenomena and the production of new scientific phenomena. Such a goal generally involves theory, but the problematic character of this involvement is something I want to stress. For example, although in the general case 'shaping' scientific phenomena involves theoretical means, it is sufficient as a rule if these means are incorporated in practical procedures and skills; they do not have to be known explicitly as premises for experimental research to be conducted. Many off-the-shelf scientific instruments apply scientific theories not known to—or no longer needed by—the experimentalist within the context of a particular research programme. Moreover, when scientific phenomena eventually become naturalized in the world, e.g., in the case of temperature, the explicit connection with theoretical premises, e.g., with thermodynamics, can and usually is dropped. Fortunately, perhaps, for common folk, one does not need to know thermodynamics and its theoretical entities of temperature, entropy, etc., to be able to recognize within the context of the life-world the *phenomenon* of temperature. Let the phenomenon of temperature be called 'temperature$_x$' and the theoretical entity temperature, 'temperature$_t$'.

The metaphysical or philosophical core of a *worldly* scientific realism is not then in theory, but in the worldly scientific phenomena and data about them which theory 'explains'. To study these in a realistic sense is to approach them, not with a theoretical attitude, but with a phenomenological attitude.[10] Let me explain why this is so and why the consequences are momentous for the philosophy of science.

I will discuss in order the following topics: (1) Scientific research as comprising two different and contrasting roles, experimental and theoretical. (2) The pre-experiment, or the need to 'prepare' scientific phenomena for research. (3) The validity of pure experimental method; scientific phenomena as perceptual, social, and historical. (4) The sense in which theory provides an 'explanation' of phenomena and phenomena come to 'fulfil' theory. (5) Theory not as descriptive of phenomena, but as descriptive of the representing and naming field of phenomena. (6) Experimental and theoretical roles in research as different but complementary. (7) Scientific (Theory) Realism as a residue of mythopoetic thinking and the defense of Scientific (Phenomena) Realism.

1. SCIENTIFIC RESEARCH AS COMPRISING TWO DIFFERENT AND CONTRASTING ROLES

Experimental and Theoretical: Looking at figure 1, S_x represents the experimental (or observational) role of the scientific researcher and O_x is the scientific phenomenon, its measured profiles are the data of the experiment. S_t represents the theoretical role; its aim is to 'explain' O_x, and it does this by focusing on the structure of the preparation and measurement process in which O_x is revealed. O_x is the direct object of the experimental role S_x and the indirect object of the theoretical role S_t; the direct object of the theoretical role S_t is the preparation and measurement process.

In the activities of preparation and measurement in which O_x (together with its measured profiles) is constituted for S_x, the instruments M play a mediating role between S_x and O_x. M contains readable instruments with dials, counters, photographic plates, etc. Events occur in M—typically changes in the dials, counters, photographic plates, etc., of the readable instruments; call these events Q, these are the 'measurement-events' to be interpreted by the experimental and theoretical research roles. *They are not as yet scientific data.*

Putting ourselves in the experimental role S_x, let us try to analyze the *noema* phenomenologically. From the start, the measurement-events Q are not bare naked physical events, but tentative data, i.e., tentative manifestations of the profiles *of* some scientific phenomenon to be prepared or measured.

In either case, S_x seeks to interpret the bare events Q as data, i.e., as profiles $|X>_x$ of the worldly presence (or occurrence) of O_x.[11] Should the experimenter's interpretation be successful, Q cease definitively to be bare physical objects but become profiles of a 'dressed phenomenon' O_x, they become scientific data. That is, for the experimenter S_x, the measurement-events Q lose definitively any possible independent physical presence and they become, as it were, a 'transparent' medium through which the profiles $|X>_x$ of the phenomenon O_x appear. The *noema* is the law characteristic of O_x that orders these profiles.[12]

Putting ourselves now in the theoretical role S_t, let us try to analyze the *noema* of this role phenomenologically. In the theoretical role, the preparation and measurement procedure is viewed outside the experimental act to which and within which it appears as a phenomenon. The measurement-events Q come to be described in the theoretical role as part—the accessible part—of the 'observer's' noetic state $|X'>_x$—the 'observer' being S_x united to the readable technologies of the experiment for the purpose of experiencing the phenomenon O_x. These are also in some still-to-be-analyzed sense scientific data, but they are data of a different sort; they explicitly refer to Q *as readable states of the instrument, i.e., as a source of measure-numbers*. The measure-numbers are, of course, ideal mathematical entities; they are not the theoretical entities of the theory, for these are the vectors $|X>_t$ of the theoretical model, but they enter into the determination for these vectors. Neither the physical states of the instrument nor the measure-numbers read from them—nor even the ideal model vectors $|X>_t$—are *profiles of the scientific phenomenon*, though they are, of course, related to the latter in ways to be discussed below.

The measurement-events Q function differently within the experimental and the theoretical roles of a research program but in neither case are Q independent or independently defined physical events. They are not the data of the experiment, for of themselves and without 'interpretation' they are neither $|X>_x$ nor $|X'>_x$. From the viewpoint of the theoretical role S_t, Q are 'interpreted' as objects of a peculiar kind, as *data about the representing field of the phenomenon*. In contrast, from the viewpoint of the experimental role S_x, Q are 'interpreted' as *data about the phenomenon, i.e., profiles of the phenomenon. Interpretation* is involved in both cases, but clearly in different senses and in different ways.

In the first case, Q are a 'text' to be 'read', i.e., they are physical events possessing normatively the structure of a 'text' or representing field. Here, 'to interpret' Q is 'to read' from Q measure-numbers q_1 that in some way through the theoretical model $|X>_t$ represent (or designate) the profiles of the phenomenon O_x. The 'reader' S_t must know when and how to make such 'readings'.

In the second case, Q are not like a 'text', they do not merely indicate the character and presence of the phenomenon the way a textual sign would, but they present the phenomenon (i.e., exhibit it, manifest it) to the experienced observer S_x. To such 'observation', Q become transparent to a set of its perceptual and worldly profiles $|q_1 \ldots >_x$. Now $|q_1 \ldots >_t$ and $|q_1 \ldots >_x$ are not the same; $|q_1 \ldots >_t$ are model vectors and $|q_1 \ldots >_x$ are data of an experiment, i.e., worldly profiles of a represented phenomenon. Measure numbers q_1 and model vectors $|q_1 \ldots >_t$ can 'represent' the profiles of a phenomenon by serving as *names* for them within a network of names. Data as profiles $|q_1 \ldots >_x$ can be *denominated* by the measure-numbers q_1—just as numbers can be used, e.g., in football, to name and differentiate between participants.

The relationship, however, is stronger than just naming, they are like the digital coding of musical sounds on a compact disk, they denominate the sounds to be heard and they are 'causal' in their production. A symphony is not the same as the digital score for a disk recording (this is a theoretical entity) nor is it the same as the electronic marks on the compact disk (this is an electronic representation of the symphony) but it is what both denominate and what is produced by the electronic representation when this is 'interpreted" by a good player, amplifier, and set of speakers. So, for example, in the scientific case of an electron_x, the set of electron profiles are not themselves theoretical entities (such as the variables of the theory or the vectors $|X>_t$ they help to specify), nor are they the controlling or responding characteristics $|X'>_x$ of the instruments, but they are what both designate and what the latter produce within the praxis of good experimental work.

In neither the experimental nor the theoretical case, are the measurement-events Q independent physical events; they are 'interpreted', and interpreted differently in the two cases. In the theoretical case, Q are *deliberately, consciously, and methodologically* 'read' by S_t to give the measure-numbers q_1, sampling the variables of the theory; they specify the model vectors which name profiles of a phenomenon. In the experimental case, Q are *existentially* interpreted (as in an act of perception) by S_x, i.e., they become transparent to the profiles $|q_1 \ldots >_x$ of a scientific phenomenon O_x. In their transparency, they can be said to show these profiles.[13] In the theoretical role S_t, Q become the accessible part $|q_1' \ldots >_x$ of the existential representing field $|X'>_x$, and in the experimental role S_x, Q become the accessible part $|q_1 \ldots >_x$ of the represented field $|X>_x$, the experimental data. Both $|q_1 \ldots >_x$ and $|q_1' \ldots >_x$ are real, they are in the world. Note how the dual perspective on Q transforms the measurement-events Q into dual vector fields, $|X'>_x$ for S_t, and $|X>_x$ for S_x. The measure-numbers q_1 and the vectors $|q_1 \ldots >_t$ are ideal, they are not in the world. They serve for S_t as an ideal model, like a geometry, that can be used like a language to describe the phenomenon.

The naming of the profiles $|X>_x$ after the theoretical vectors $|q_1 \ldots >_t$, should not obscure the fact that two different and complementary research roles or contexts are involved, viz., the experimental S_x and the theoretical S_t. S_t 'reads' the measure-numbers q_i of $|q_1' \ldots >_x$. S_x uses q_1 not to designate numbers but to designate empirical profiles $|q_1 \ldots >_x$; that is, q_n designates the q_n-th profile $|q_n \ldots >_x$, not the scale number q_n. Like the music of a digital symphonic recording, each note of the music is designated by a digital score, so the profiles of a scientific phenomenon are similarly number coded. The code is established by the standard institutionalized procedure of preparation and measurement.

Scientific research is the outcome of dialectical interplay between two research roles, S_x (the experimenter) and S_t (the theoretical scientist); these are not different individuals but roles that scientists play. Whenever then the processes of preparation/measurement successfully produce for S_x a sequence, say, of related profiles $|q_n \ldots>_x$ of the same phenomenon O_x, the measure-numbers q_n of these profiles are linked numerically for S_t by the equations of the theory T. Under these circumstances, *numerical* theory linkage—or better, the linkage of vectors in the model—implies some sort of *real causal* linkage in the world. The notion of worldly causality invoked here is not just correlational, it expresses the causality appropriate to worldly events, i.e., ontological and efficient. Through their profiles in the world and through their measure-numbers, phenomena 'fulfil' theory in a complex way to be further discussed below.

It may be helpful to make an analogy with vision.[14] M is analogous to the retina and visual cortex, and Q is analogous to the relevant retinocortical excitations that mediate the profiles $|X>_x$ of the visual object to vision and are themselves 'transparent' to the act of vision. The character of the mediating role of Q in relation to O_x is similar to the character of the mediating role of relevant retino-cortical excitation in the case of vision; 'interpretation' in its dual methodological and existential forms transforms the mediating field in both cases. There is a difference, however, between the two cases. A scientist can turn away from the scientific phenomenon and re-focus attention on the instrument. To do this, the scientist has simply to move from the role characteristic of S_x to the role characteristic of S_t. The visual perceiver, however, cannot make this switch, because the eyes are not detachable from the body, while external instruments are detachable.

From what I have said all too briefly, it follows that the mediating role of M—more specifically of Q—must be studied from two standpoints: 1. from the *phenomenological* standpoint of S_x 'inside' the act of recognizing the scientific phenomenon O_x as a worldly phenomenon—such an act of recognition eventually takes on the character of perception—and, 2. from the *theoretical* standpoint of S_t 'outside' of the same act.

2. THE PRE-EXPERIMENT, OR THE NEED TO 'PREPARE' SCIENTIFIC PHENOMENA FOR RESEARCH

In the natural sciences, scientific phenomena are usually—but not always, as I pointed out above—the product of a working theory. The very language of science seems to say so by giving scientific phenomena the same names as theoretical entities. However, there must be a sense in which scientific phenomena (say, $electron_x$, associated with $|X>_x$) are other than just theoretical entities (say, $electron_t$, associated with $|X>_r$), because phenomena can force theories to change. The reverse is also true. Purely theoretical changes can force changes in phenomena by changing the standard institutionalized procedures of preparation and measurement. Phenomena then have a certain independence of theory, and theory of phenomena. There is a certain reciprocal priority between the theoretical entity ('sub-t') and the experimental phenomenon ('sub-x') best understood, as we shall see, in the spirit of the hermeneutical circle.

Scientific phenomena (such as electron_x) are constituted through the skilful use of institutionally standardized technologies of preparation and measurement that can be relied on to produce or to 'corral'—all things being equal—standard exemplifications of the phenomena to be 'explained' or otherwise researched. Standardized technologies used in this way are (what I call) 'readable technologies',[15] they function as somatic extensions of the human body ('detachable sense-organs'—to use the words of M. Merleau-Ponty[16]) conspiring to make possible for the inquirer the range of 'kinaestheses'[17] (Husserl's term for subjective constituting capabilities or agencies) necessary for the *noetic* constitution, by preparation and measurement, of the determinate *noema* of a scientific phenomenon. Preparation and measurement are functions of the experimental role S_x of a researcher. The experimental use of scientific readable technologies M_1 eventually completes the move from theory to phenomena by providing the phenomena ('sub-x') that theoretical entities ('sub-t') 'explain'.

In the S_x role, the observational or empirical judgment, like all perceptual judgments, is both *interpetative* (*hermeneutical*) as outlined above, and *practical* (in the Aristotelian sense, of being normed by a social institutional praxis). The *noetic* constitution of experimental phenomena is also *aesthetic*.

The aesthetic character of experimentation is the unique satisfaction enjoyed by S_x and by S_x's colleagues—though differently—of skilled and excellent performance, something that is not guaranteed by any set of rules, procedures, standards, precedents, instruments, or theories. It is enjoyed by the expert experimenter in the perfection of performance; it is enjoyed by his knowledgeable colleagues as the appreciative witnesses (viewers, auditors, etc.) of the performance.[18]

3. THE VALIDITY OF PURE EXPERIMENTAL METHOD: SCIENTIFIC PHENOMENA AS PERCEPTUAL, SOCIAL, AND HISTORICAL

It is the case that in many sciences today, particularly the medical and biological sciences, the emphasis of research is on those scientific phenomena that are determined directly by the application of powerful technologies such as chromotography, electron microscopy, CATSCAN, Imaging Tomography, etc., to an expanding domain of subject matter. Such research can be taken to exemplify pure (i.e., non-theory-led) experimental methods. Here theory is subsumed by the operating procedures of the technique and by skill, none of which are explicitly part of the theory, and scientific research becomes concentrated on perfecting procedures to prepare and measure scientific phenomena and in interpreting the outcome of the experiment, not for the purpose of making a theory but to establish correlations among data, i.e., to find correlations among the profiles of the revealed phenomenon; for example, to identify and correlate traces of specific proteins in a solution, or take a 3-dimensional model of an organic molecule.

There are many cases even in physics and chemistry of pure experimental method, e.g., in the use of the microscope, the spectrograph, the mass spectrometer, etc., whenever in fact data correlation or the causality among data is the aim of research. Phenomena that are unexpected, exciting, and radically new can also be produced in the pure experimental way, for example, the discovery of X-rays, or penicillin and, more recently, of superconductivity at near-room-temperatures. In the pure experimental method, S_x (the experimental scientist) tries by skilful manipulation and generally without *explicit* recourse to theory to discover correlations among profiles of established phenomena or to constitute new and interesting scientific phenomena using established readable technologies.

In the experimental role S_x, the researcher recognizes the occurrence of an experimental phenomenon O_x under some given noematic profile. The observational or empirical judgment that results is, on the basis of the Husserlean analysis into *noema* and *noesis, a perceptual judgment*. The profiles $|X>_x$ (or $|q_1 \ldots >_x$) of O_x are exhibited to S_x while the representing field $|X'>_x$ (or $|q_1' \ldots >_x$) is laid out before S_t. Both research roles are necessary. $|X>_x$ and $|X'>_x$ are linked in the process of preparation and measurement through dual ways of interpreting Q; Q is interpreted *existentially* as $|q_1 \ldots >_x$ by S_x and *methodologically* as $|q_1' \ldots >_x$ by S_t. In other words, S_t is authorized to '*read*' the measure-numbers q_1 to the extent that S_x experiences the presence of O_x; in that case, the occurrent profile is *denominated* by q_1—or better, by $|q_1 \ldots >_t$—as $|q_1 \ldots >$x. In brief, experimental data are what S_x experiences and S_t denominates.

What is measured—the phenomenon—has no determinate essence outside of (independently of) the norms established by the constitutive processes of institutionally standardized systems of preparation and measurement. This is the practical aspect of preparation/measurement. It is such institutionally standardized praxis which gives the phenomenon its profiles, that is, it 'dresses' the phenomenon to take its place in the world. A scientific phenomenon (such as electron$_x$) does not exist apart from some way of appearing—i.e., manifesting its worldly presence—this is its 'dress', for the phenomenon is the experiential unity that is 'dressed' by the experimental procedure. A phenomenon may appear in many different 'dresses', depending on the variety of standard institutionalized preparation/measurement procedures for the phenomenon. It may also change its 'dress' with time. A sceintific phenomenon then is, like all worldly phenomena, a social and historical entity, a product of human worldly culture.

Successful constitution of a new scientific phenomenon using an experimental procedure without the explicit intervention of theory is, of course, a significant advance for a scientific research program. It is, moreover, an aesthetic achievement of the pure, expert creative activity of the experimentalist. It is like the composition of a new piece of music by a composer—a novel achievement in its creation but one that subsequently can be reproduced by skillful performers and endorsed by an educated audience. However, unless the constitution of the new phenomenon is understood theoretically, the research program is generally regarded as incomplete. Let us look at the reason why.

4. THE SENSE IN WHICH THEORY PROVIDES AN 'EXPLANATION' OF PHENOMENA AND PHENOMENA COME TO 'FULFIL' THEORY

It is one of the functions of S_t—the theoretical scientist—to decipher the worldly causal structure that underlies the repeatable processes of preparation and measurement. This means providing an account of how the phenomenon O_x is related to the measurement-events Q within the process of preparation/measurement. We have noted that the *uninterpreted* bare instrumental responses Q are neither the phenomenon to be explained nor are they profiles of the phenomenon; they are as-yet-indeterminate and merely as-yet-potential in relation to the research project; whatever description is given them, it will be provisional and tentative until Q disappear into $|q_1 \ldots >_x$ for S_x and $|q_1' \ldots >_x$ for S_t.

Let T be the theory that 'explains' the phenomenon O_x; it is a model about theoretical entities and the states $|X>_t$ of such entities as they evolve in time under the functional relationships between them. Then the measurement-events Q 'fulfil' the theory T only under the following conditions: 1. for S_t, the numerical values q_1 which are 'read' from Q satisfy the equations of T, i.e., the sampled measured variables can be taken to specify the theoretical states $|q_1 \ldots >_t$ of the theory and 2. For S_x, Q *can be construed as due to the coming-to-presence (for S_x) of the phenomenon O_x*. The latter condition, so obvious in many ways, has largely been overlooked in the literature about experimentation and measurement. These two 'fulfilment' conditions must be simultaneously satisfied.

1. For S_t, the measurement-events Q 'fulfil' the theory by becoming the accessible part $|q_1' \ldots >_x$ of the representing field $|X'>_x$ of the phenomenon. i.e., the instrumental response Q must be 'readable' by S_t according to some scale,[19], and the measure-numbers q_1 'read' from it as pertaining to the object O_x must satisfy the equations of theory T as a system of equations. This—taken with the second condition—will turn out to be the condition that Q can serve as the accessible part $|q_1' \ldots >_x$ of the existential state $|X'>_x$ that gives S_x perceptual access to $|X>_x$.

2. In addition and simultaneously, for S_x, *the scientific phenomenon O_l and its set of profiles $|X>_x$ must be constituted as lawfully present in the world* through the practical, hermeneutical, and aesthetic agency of S_x within the preparation/measurement process. Q then 'fulfil' the theory by becoming the accessible part $|q_1 \ldots >_x$ of the profiles $|X>_x$ of the phenomenon O_x.

5. IN WHAT WAY IS THEORY DESCRIPTIVE?

We must now face up to an important but counterintuitive consequence of the analysis that has just been given, that *theory as used descriptively by* S_t—the theoretical scientific role—*does not itself formally describe the profiles* $|X>_x$ *of the scientific phenomenon*. Assume that a scientific phenomenon (such as electron$_x$) is present, i.e., it is successfully constituted *noetically* for S_x by the processes of the experiment. Then from the standpoint of theoretical science S_t, what does theory describe in the world? It describes the *representing field* $|X'>_x$ of the phenomenon (say, electron$_x$) as the latter is institutionalized within the experimental scientific community (or that portion of the representing field that is experimentally accessible to S_t). The accessible representing field is not electron$_t$, but is the ontological structure $|X'>_x$ that serves within the experimental activity of preparation and measurement (O_x in figure 1) as an existential hermeneutic for the experimenter S_x (i.e., to be 'interpreted existentially') in so far as S_x actively anticipates, explores, and eventually recognizes the presence of the scientific phenomenon O (i.e., electron$_x$) and its profiles $|X>_x$.

From the point of view of S_t, then, theory describes, *not* O_x or its profiles $|X>_x$, but the representing field $|q_1' \ldots >_x$ *of* the profiles $|X>_x$.

One could, of course, argue that the referent of theory is the mathematical model $|X>_t$ 'fulfilled' by the theoretial variables of which q_1 are sample measured values, that is, for example, the theoretical entity, electron$_t$. Such a referent has no perceptual profiles in the world. It would presumably show its presence in the world through Q just like the phenomenon described above, except that Q would not be profiles of a phenomenon, but independently describable physical events, 'indicators' of the existence and occurrence of the appropriate theoretical entity. Such a view is incoherent for a number of reasons: 1. it leaves intact all the problems that follow from the Duhem-Quine-Hesse thesis and that lead inevitably to Conventionalism; 2. it nevertheless continues to satisfy the noetic-noematic conditions for establishing the existence of a 'dressed' perceptual scientific phenomenon in the world. Without availing of the insight this brings to the understanding of scientific research; 3. it mistakenly claims that Q have definite descriptions within science apart from their use in the two contexts of experimental and theoretical research.

6. EXPERIMENTAL AND THEORETICAL ROLES IN RESEARCH ARE COMPLEMENTARY

In summary, a scientific theory *explains* a scientific phenomenon by specifying (by and for the theoretical role S_t) the representing field of the phenomenon constituted by and for experimental role S_x within the institutionally standardized system of preparation and measurement of the phenomenon. The relationship between the two research roles is a kind of *complementarity*; the object of theoretical inquiry (for S_t) and the object of experimental inquiry (for S_x) *complement* one another in the way, for example, retino-cortical excitation and visual objects complement one another, (as we presume) retino-cortical excitation functions within the existential hermeneutic of vision in the way described above.

Another example of such complementarity is the way a picture and the pictured complement one another. The picture functions within the existential hermeneutic of seeing the picture in the picture—with this difference that, while the processes of preparation and measurement make the scientific phenomenon present as a reality, the picture does not make the pictured phenomenon present as a reality but instead as a kind of visual hallucination. The picture surface contains the representing field $|X'>_x$ of the represented profile $|X>_x$ of the pictured object. Experimental research—compared above with musical composition and performances—can also be compared with painting (as a form of making pictures), and theoretical research with the study of the formal properties $|X'>_x$ of the picture surface that makes picturing possible.

7. SCIENTIFIC (THEORY) REALISM AS A RESIDUE OF CLASSICAL PHILOSOPHY AND THE DEFENCE OF SCIENTIFIC (PHENOMENA) REALISM

It should now be clear that Scientific (Theory) Realism,[20] or Realism in the classical sense makes a fundamental mistake by identifying science exclusively with the work of the theoretical scientific role S_t. The special and peculiar contribution of the experimental scientific role S_x is overlooked. Taking science as exclusively the work of S_t, it makes the mistake of identifying the representing field for the represented object, and of identifying the represented profiles $|q_1 \ldots >_x$ with the ideal set of measure-numbers q_1—or better, with the mathematical vectors of the theoretical model $|X>_t$. The measure numbers q_1, etc., though 'read off' the instruments of preparation/measurement and though normatively satisfying the equations of the theory, nevertheless merely denominate the profiles. As I have pointed out, the represented profiles $|q_1 \ldots >_x$ are not accessible to S_t but accessible only to S_x, while the representing field $|q_1' \ldots >_x$ is not accessible to S_x but only to S_t.

The mistake of Scientific (Theory) Realism is analogous to mistaking the retino-cortical excitation for the objects seen, to mistaking the score for the musical piece, and somewhat analogous (as we have seen) to the mistake of taking the picturing surface for the pictured object. The fact that mistakes of this kind have been elevated into a bandwagon of inspirational dogma for groups of philosophers interested in cognitive science and in artificial intelligence—a movement emulated by some artists and art critics—does not, of course, justify them. It illustrates unfortunately how the difficulties and failures of a philosophical position—I mean the crisis of the classical tradition in philosophy and, particularly, in the philosophy of science—can be used to rally support for a program under attack by converting it into an ideology. This is what, for example, Eliminative Materialism[21] has done. The failure to make the necessary distinction between the functions of S_t and S_x is a philosophical failure rooted mostly in the non-hermeneutical epistemology of the classical tradition.

It is ironic that the classical scientific tradition, which saw itself as rescuing rationality from myth, metaphor, and symbol came to share with myth the confusion characteristic of mythopoetic thinking, namely, the inability to make an adequate distinction between reality and the models, metaphors, and symbols through which we speak about it. The failure of classical Scientific Realism of distinguish properly between the theoretical function of science and the experimental function, between theory and phenomenon, shows wherein this failure lies. The point I want to make, of course, is about a mistaken epistemic theory of science. A better understanding of the experimental nature of the scientific enterprise can have significant consequences for more than the philosophy of science, it could affect the pursuit of scientific inquiry notably in the cognitive and social sciences and enable us to speak more intelligently about the cultural implications of science and technology.

$$S_x \text{———————} |M| \text{———————} > O_x = |X>_x$$

$$Q = |X'>_x$$

$$|X>_t = \text{theoretical model}$$

$$S_t$$

FIGURE 1. EXPERIMENTAL (S_x) AND THEORETICAL (S_t) ROLES.
Note how the two forms of inquiry are inextricably linked!

ACKNOWLEDGEMENTS

* This paper has benefited from discussions with many colleagues. I would like to thank principally, Professors Panjit Nair, Chandra·Gupta, J. J. Compton, J. J. Kockelmans, L. Embree, R. Crease, and B. Babich.

NOTES AND REFERENCES

1. This so-called 'Platonic' view of modern science has often been attributed to Galileo and is characteristic of the rationalist scientific tradition. It is strongly endorsed by the Göttingen school of theoretical physics that set the model for science in this century. Led by F. Klein, D. Hilbert, R. Courant, and H. Minkowski, it influenced the work of A. Einstein, E. Schrördinger, W. Heisenberg, H. Weyl, E. Wigner, C. N. Yang and practically all of the great scientists of our time.
2. In the *Crisis*, Husserl (1970); see also Heelan (1978b and 1987c) for a recent commentary, and the work of J. Compton, e.g., Compton (1983), who has consistently held this view.

3. The tension between two such mutually antagonistic positions about science has been largely overlooked until recently. It has been customary in phenomenology to accept the view as Husserl's that science is *essentially* and *irremedially* 'Galilean' and therefore committed to replacing phenomena by theoretical entities, e.g., Kockelmans and Kisiel (1970), Kockelmans (1985), Gadamer (1975 and 1982), Heidegger (1967, 1977). Recent work acknowledges the tension in Husserl's philosophy of science, for example, Rouse (1987a and 1987b), Seigfried (1980), Zucker (1982), as well as Heelan (1985, 1983, 1987b, 1987c).
4. Heelan (1987b, 1987c).
5. For Klein's *Erlanger Programme*, see Klein (1932/1939). For its application to physics, see, e.g., Courant and Hilbert (1924/1937) and Wigner (1967). For a commentary on Husserl's affirmation and critique of this view in the *Crisis*, Husserl (1970a), see Heelan (1983, 1987b, and 1989c).
6. See Husserl (1950 and 1970), passim.
7. Such a view is at the basis of Piaget's research programme on accommodation and assimilation in the development of perception in children. It is also at the basis of recent computational research about perception, e.g., David Marr's work on vision, which tries to make a 'seeing machine' i.e., one which capable of emulating vision; in these programmes 'algorithm' stands in for abstract transformation group.
8. See Quine (1969), Hesse (1980), and Duhem (1954).
9. *Data* are the measured attributes of occurrences of scientific phenomena, e.g., the energy of an electron$_x$. These are also the occurrent (i.e., measured) profiles of phenomena. An electron$_x$ is an occurrence of an electron as a phenomenon; electron$_t$ is the theoretical entity; see below.
10. Single quotes, as in 'explains,' are used in this paper with terms which from the point of view of this paper become problematic. One of the aims of this paper will be to clarify the ambiguity of such terms.
11. Dirac notation highlights the fact that the Husserl theory of the phenomenon is a *transformation theory* of the phenomenon. The use of vectors for the field of profiles and their representing field (see below) presupposes that they constitute homologous vector spaces in the most flexible sense. This is a presupposition which I have tried to justify elsewhere. In classical science, ket-vectors reduce to contravariant Cartesian vectors in a 3N (or relativistic 4N) phase-space.
12. The usual term 'data' carries with it empiricist overtones which I want to avoid. In my analysis, data correspond to the profiles of a phenomenon, e.g., the energy of an electron as a phenomenon (i.e., of electron$_x$—see below). Much discussion of the relationship between theory and data, even of the more enlightened kind, such as, for example, in Ackermann (1985), is profoundly unsatisfying because the notion of *data* is not adequately analyzed.
13. *Methodological* hermeneutics is the conscious and deliberate work of interpreting a text or a set of signs or symbols. *Existential* hermeneutics, introduced by Heidegger, is that ontological character of all understanding whereby it is—even unconsciously—an act of interpretation. See Heidegger (1962, 1967, 1977), Gadamer (1975), Bleicher, J. (1980), and Heelan (1983, 1986a, 1986b). See also Kockelmans (1985).
14. See Heelan (1986b).
15. See Heelan (1983a) for a discussion of 'readable technologies.' Such a view is similar to views presented by Hanson (1961), Polanyi (1964), and from the phenomenological point of view, Ihde (1979), and others.
16. Merleau-Ponty (1964b), p. 178.
17. See Husserl (1970), and for a commentary, see Heelan (1987b and 1987c).
18. The notion of aesthetic activity used here as related to performance is that studied by Gadamer (1975) in that great work. See Holton (1978), chapter 2 for his study of

Milliken' work on the electronic charge. On p. 64, he reproduces a page of Milliken's laboratory notes inscribed with the words 'Beauty; *Publish* this surely, *beautiful*! See also Heelan (1987a), and, for a readable account of the influence of aesthetic and social factors on recent scientific research in high energy physics, see Crease and Mann (1986).

19. For the nature of *scales* and a criticism of opinions, see the treatment, say, of Duncan (1984).
20. Scientific (Theory) Realism, widely called simply 'Scientific Realism' today, is a view that became very influential through the essays of W. Sellars, cf. Sellars (1963). See Leplin (1984). It has been adopted by many philosophers of science and its most rigorous exponent is C. Hooker (1987).
21. See Sellars (1963), Feigl (1958), Churchland, Paul, (1979), Churchland, Patricia (1986), Uttal (1978).

REFERENCES

Ackermann, Robert, J. 1985. *Data, Instruments, and Theory*. Princeton: Princeton University Press.

Bleicher, John. 1980. *Contemporary Hermeneutics. Hermeneutics as Method, Philosophy, and Critique*. London and Boston: Routledge and Kegan Paul.

Churchland, Patricia Smith (1986). *Neurophilosophy*. Cambridge, MA: MIT Press.

Churchland, Paul. 1979. *Scientific Realism and the Plasticity of Mind*. Cambridge: Cambridge University Press.

Compton. John. J. 1983. 'Natural science and being-in- the-world', paper read at meeting of the Pacific Sect. of the APA, March, 1983.

Courant, Richard, and Hilbert, David. (1924/1937). *Methoden der Mathematischen Physik*.

Crease, Robert, and Mann, Charles. 1986. *The Second Creation*. New York: Macmillan.

Duhem, Pierre. 1954. *Aim and Structure of Physical Theory*. Princeton: Princeton University Press.

Duncan, Otis Dudley. 1984. *Notes on Social Measurement: Historical and Critical*. New York: Russell Sage Foundation.

Fiegl, Herbert. 1958. 'The "mental" and the "physical",' in Feigl H., Scriven, M., and Maxwell, G. (eds.) *Minnesota Studies in the Philosophy of Science*, Vol. 2. (Minneapolis: University of Minnesota Press, 1958), pp. 370–497.

Gadamer, Hans-Georg. 1975. *Truth and Method*. Trans. G. Barden and J. Cumming. New York: Seabury Press.

———, 1982. *Reason in the Age of Science*. Cambridge, MA: MIT Press.

Hanson, N. Russell. 1961. *Patterns of Discovery*. Cambridge and New York: Cambridge University Press.

Heelan, Patrick. 1975. 'Hermeneutics of experimental science in the context of the Life World', in Ihde and Zaner (eds.), pp. 7–50.

———, 1983. *Space-Perception and the Philosophy of Science*. Berkeley and Los Angeles: University of California Press.

———, 1986a. 'Interpretation and the Structures of Space in Scientific Theory and in Perception', in *Research in Phenomenology* Vol. XVI, *Hermeneutics Today*, ed. by J. Sallis. Atlantic Heights, NJ: Humanities Press. pp. 187–199.

———, 1986b. 'Machine perception', in *Philosophy of Technology*, II. *Information Technology and Computers in Theory and Practice*, ed. by C. Mitcham and A. Huning. Boston and Dordrecht: Reidel. pp. 131–156.

———, 1987a. 'A Heideggerian Meditation on Science and Art,' in *Hermeneutic Phenomenology*, ed. J. J. Kockelmans. University Park, PA: Pennsylvania University Press.

———, 1987b. 'Husserl's Philosophy of Science', in *Philosophy of Edmund Husserl: A Textbook*, ed. by J. N. Mohanty and W. McKenna. Pittsburgh and Washington, D.C.: CARP and University Press of America.

———, 1987c. 'Husserl's Later Philosophy of Science,' *Philosophy of Science*, 54 (1987), pp. 368–390.

Heidegger, Martin, 1962. *Being and Time*. Trans by J. Macquarrie and E. Robinson. New York: Harper and Row.

———, 1967. *What Is a Thing?* Trans. by W. B. Barton, Jr. and V. Deutsch. Chicago: Regnery.

———, 1977. *The Question Concerning Technology and Other Essays*. Trans. by W. Lovitt. New York: Harper Colophon.

Hesse, Mary. 1980. *Revolutions and Reconstructions in the Philosophy of Science*. Bloomington: Indiana University Press.

Holton, Gerald. 1978. *The Scientific Imagination: Case Studies*. Cambridge: Cambridge University Press.

Hooker, Clifford 1987. *A Realistic Theory of Science*. Albany, NY: SUNY Press.

Husserl, Edmund. 1950. *Ideen zu einer reinen Phaenomenologie und phaenomenologische Philosophie*, Book I Ed. M. Biemel. Husserliana, Vol. 3. The Hague: Nijhoff.

———, 1952. *Idden zu einer reinen Phaenomenologie und phaenomenologische Philosophie, Book II: Phaenomenologische Untersuchungen zu Konstitution*. Ed. M. Biemel. Husserliana, Vol. 4. The Hague: Nijhoff.

———, 1970. *Crisis of European Sciences and Transcendental Phenomenology*. Trans. by D. Carr. Evanston: Northwestern University Press.

Ihde, Don. 1979. *Technics and Praxis*. Dordrecht and Boston: Reidel.

Ihde, Don and Zaner, R. (eds.) 1975. *Interdisciplinary Phenomenology*. The Hague: Nijhoff.

Kisiel, Theodore. 1977. 'Heidegger and new images of science', *Res. Phenomenology*, 7 (1977), pp. 162–181.

Klein, Felix. 1932/1939. *Elementary Mathematics from an Advanced Standpoint*, 2 vols. New York: Macmillan.

Kockelmans, Joseph J. 1985. *Heidegger and Science*. Pittsburgh and Washington, D.C.: CARP and University Press of America.

———, and Kisiel, Theodore (eds.) 1970. *Phenomenology and the Natural Sciences*. Evanston: Northwestern University Press.

Leplin, Jarrett (ed.) (1984), *Scientific Realism*. Berkeley and Los Angeles: University of California Press.

Merleau-Ponty, Maurice. 1964. *The Primacy of Perception*. Evanston: Northwestern University Press.

———, 1968. *The Visible and the Invisible*. A. Lingis. Evanston: Northwestern University Press.

Polanyi, Michael. (1964). *Personal Knowledge*. New York: Harper and Row.

Quine, W. O. (1969). *Ontological Relativity and Other Essays*. New York: Columbia University Press.

Ricoeur, Paul. 1978. *The Philosophy of Paul Ricoeur: An Anthology of his Work*. Boston: Beacon Press.

———, 1981. *Hermeneutics and the Human Sciences*. Trans. by J. B. Thompson. Cambridge: Cambridge University Press.

Rouse, Joseph. 1987a. 'Husserlian Phenomenology and Scientific Realism', *Philosophy of Science*, 54 (1987), pp. 222–232.

———, 1987b. *Knowledge and Power*. Ithaca: Cornell University Press.

Seigfried, Hans v. 1980. 'Scientific realism and phenomenology', *Zeit. f. Philosophishce Forschung*, 24 (1980), pp. 395–404.

Sellars, Wilfred. 1963a. *Science, Perception, and Reality*. London: Routledge and Kegan Paul.

Ströker, Elizabeth, (ed.). 1979. *Lebenswelt and Wissenschaft in der Philosophie Edmund Husserls*. Frankfurt am Main: Klosterman.

Toulmin, Stephen. 1982 'The construal of reality: Criticism in modern and postmodern science', *Critical Inquiry*, 9 (1982), pp. 93–111.

Uttal, William. 1978. *Psychobiology of Mind*. Hillsdale, NJ: Erlbaum.

Wigner, Eugene. 1967. *Reflections and Symmetries*. Indiana University Press.

Zucker, Francis J. 1982. 'Phenomenological evidence and the "Idea" of physics,' in Bruzian et al. (1982), 269–290.

'Merleau-Ponty's Thesis of the Primacy of Perception and the Meaning of Scientific Objectivity'

JOHN J. COMPTON

One of the central tasks for any philosophy of science is to assess the conditions and limits of scientific objectivity. What should we take this sort of objectivity to mean? How is it to be legitimated? How can it be achieved? Is it even possible in principle, given the human condition? These questions are of perennial concern, of course, but in recent discussion they have become acute. They have been focused within the philosophy of science in the wake of the powerful critiques of Feyerabend and Kuhn and are central to the debates between 'realists' and 'antirealists'. And they have been posed in a more global way within the epistemological and ontological critiques of such thinkers as Gadamer, Foucault, and Rorty. Dealing with such questions obviously takes one back to a consideration of first principles! In this spirit, I would like to show how I have found certain insights from the phenomenological tradition to be useful in reflecting on the meaning of scientific objectivity and, thus, in addressing these central issues. In doing so, I want to offer an explication, in the context of the philosophy of science, of Merleau-Ponty's thesis of the 'primacy of perception.'[1]

I

The focus for a phenomenological philosophy of science is to be found in the relation between *theoretical activity* and the *pre-theoretical situation* within which this sort of activity is carried on. The point of such a philosophy is to allow the significance of science to appear by showing how the scientific, experimental-theoretical way of being with things is a transformation, albeit a well-founded transformation, of our more fundamental, everyday manner of being in and with the world. Martin Heidegger put the task this way in *Being and Time* and Edmund Husserl developed it in his very different direction in *The Crisis of European Sciences*.[2] While much of what follows is inspired by these thinkers, I have found the work of their French descendant, Maurice Merleau-Ponty, to be the most concretely suggestive. As Merleau-Ponty sees it, the most fundamental way in which human beings find themselves in the world is in their bodily perceptual interaction with it. Thus, on this approach, the meaning of natural science should be found to lie in the manner in which science modifies and expresses pervasive features of the pre-scientific life of perception.

It is not that there are no other elements which conspire to constitute the scientific point of view. In fact, there are many—the mythic and poetic consciousness, for example, as well as the mechanical arts, economic production, intellectual playfulness, the forms of language, the drive to mathematical abstraction, and so on. Yet all of these are themselves taken to be ways in which the perceived world is explored, interpreted, and selectively transformed. Thus, scientific activity, as a very special historically developing synthesis of these elements, should be seen, through them, to bear fundamentally upon the world as perceived.

Merleau-Ponty puts his view in the following way:

> The whole universe of science is built upon the world as directly experienced, and if we want to subject science itself to rigorous scrutiny and arrive at a precise assessment of its meaning and scope, we must begin by reawakening the basic experience of the world of which science is the second order expression. Science has not and never will have, by its nature, the same significance *qua* form of being as the world which we perceive, for the simple reason that it is a rationale or explanation of that world.[3]

This view is sometimes called by him the thesis of the 'primacy of perception'. The thesis is, roughly, that the perceptual world constitutes the primary sense of world for us upon which the very notion of the physical world or the biological world, the world for the sciences, is parasitic. The scientifically known world just *is* the perceptual world, refined, interpreted and enriched in special ways for special purposes.

Now if this approach is taken, two things would seem to follow: (1) In so far as natural science can be understood to articulate aspects of the world as directly experienced, it may rightly claim to offer an objective account of it; but (2) that objective account would derive its meaning and limits from the significance which that direct experience of the world is found to have. The first implication underscores the persistent reference of all scientific activities to the world as perceived; the second underscores the crucial importance of subjecting our basic experience of the world to careful analysis if we are to understand the meaning of that reference. The first suggests that whatever scientific objectivity may be it will be parasitic upon perceptual objectivity; the second suggests that perceptual objectivity may be expected to have its own and very special sense.

Merleau-Ponty goes on to interpret his thesis in the following way:

> In speaking of the primacy of perception, I have never, of course, meant to say that science, reflection and philosophy are only transformed sensations or that values are deferred and calculated pleasures. By these words 'primacy of perception,' we mean that the experience of perception is our presence at the moment when things, truths, values are constituted for us; that perception is a nascent *logos*: that it teaches us . . . the true conditions of objectivity itself. . . . Thus, although we are always immersed in the world and perceptually present to it, yet the idea of truth itself is an ideal implied in the least perception.[4]

Now natural science pursues this 'ideal' and its *logos* is founded upon perceptual consciousness. It should follow that an analysis of the perceptual situation would reveal foundations for significant features of the life of science including the meaning of scientific objectivity. Let me offer a quick sketch of Merleau's account as I see it.[5]

Everything depends upon how perceptual life is to be understood. Classical empiricism with its sensations has to be rejected; sensations are abstractions only; perceptual life actually finds a world of things. Merleau-Ponty's distinctive contention was that Husserl's phenomenology and the Gestaltist's psychology could be taken to converge in recognizing the fundamental reciprocity of perception, the embodied conscious activity of engagement and response, through which meaningful features of bodily things are actively disclosed. In perception, the world is constituted as meaningful 'from within'; its characteristic qualities and relations and structures emerge as the way the world is and has been all along, as typical, and, thus, implicitly at least, as the way the world will be at other places and times and for any others like me. In this way, he thought, perceptual life already contains a kind of proto-objectivity.

What is it like? Following Husserl, Merleau-Ponty insists that it is characteristic of perceived things to be disclosed through perspectives. We always encounter a perceived thing with some bodily organ, from a particular point of view (or point of hearing or touching), and in a momentary state or condition. Yet we encounter it also and inseparably as the *same* something which we just before had encountered with another bodily organ or from another point of view (or point of hearing or touching) and in another momentary state, and as the *same* something we can encounter with yet other bodily organs and from other points of vantage and in other momentary states. The perceived thing is what it is in and through these different, but recognizably related, actual, past, and possible perspective variations. This, then, is a nascent principle of objectivity: A perceived thing *can* only emerge through limited perspectives: A perspective discloses a thing, not in spite but *because* of its being limited; a perspective offers *access* to a thing *only* because it is from *some* place and not from 'nowhere', from *this* place and time and point of vantage and not from some other one; it discloses a thing only because at the same time it hides it. But, equally, a perspective hides the thing only in so far as it at the same time discloses it *as* a *thing*, as something more than just this perspective, as that upon which the perspective is taken, as something which is open to yet further, implied and related possible perspectives depending upon what I do. A perceived thing, and the world of perceived things, thus presents an horizon for the active exploration of perspectival unities.

This sort of relational objectivity is also, and inseparably, an intersubjectivity. This feature appears in two ways. In the first place, while the fundamental contours of perceived things emerge relationally, *for* us as percipients, the percipient in this encounter is not the personalized individual that we are, but rather what we are as conscious-bodily-mobile-organisms of a species-specific sort. As such, we find these contours in a generalized and habitual experience of being familiar with the typical features of things, of 'knowing our way about', of 'being able to go on'. We find ourselves 'in the world' in an *im*personal way, as bodily kineastheses; thus, as Merleau-Ponty (and Husserl) put it, perceptual life is, at bottom, 'anonymous'. Things are experienced in perception as open to being viewed, heard, smelled, and touched, as well as moved and used, in typical ways by myself as typical and, thus, implicitly at least, by any others, if there are any others, who may be like me. Their experienced perspectives are emptily imputed, once again implicitly, to be similar to my own. Perspectives which I do not now have might be had by others and they would, once again implicitly, cohere with my own. But, in addition, of course, and this is the second and inseparable element in intersubjectivity, I do in fact come to experience others. The experienced structure of 'being with others' is as fundamental as that of 'being with things'. The implicit possibility of others is, bit by bit, filled out with their presence in various relationships, intimate and distant and with various valences, and thus in various 'modes' of inter-subjective life. With this emerge a more full-blooded sense of self and of inter-personal similarities and differences and, in turn, possibilities for more specialized communities and communal perceptions of things. Throughout, however, the basic structure remains—the perceived world is a world experienced not simply for *me*, but for *us*. And just as I experience myself as *in* the perceived world, so I experience myself as with others *in* that world as well. Objectivity, already in pre-scientific life, is a form of intersubjectivity, and intersubjective experience is inseparable from the encounter with a perspected surrounding world of things.

At this point a third structure of pre-scientifically experienced objectivity can be brought into play. We can recognize that the perceptual world is not only experienced in embodied inter-relations which are essentially perspectival and open to others but which are essentially temporal and historical as well. Things are perspectivally disclosed through a time which is, at least implicitly, a time of common bodily interactivity, of ourselves with others and with things, a 'pre-personal time'.[6] To be sure, we come to recognize that differing things, mountains, plants, animals, and, of course, ourselves, have differing life-times just as we all have differing life-worlds, that we encounter and are encountered according to differing embodied temporalities, some more stable and repetitive, some more individualized and variable, with differing inter-subjectivities too. But we experience these differences within an intersecting, overlapping, inter-communicating network or field of temporality which forms us all as it allows us our variable possibilities of forming ourselves. Merleau-Ponty suggests that the structures of the natural world, of what we call physical entities as well as those of animals and human beings, are contingently established, more or less stable, patterns of meaning-relations, both instituting and instituted by this polymorphous spatial-temporal field.[7] Thus we should be able to see continuities, as well as differences, across the human and nonhuman worlds. We should be able, among other things, to see that human cultural practice, such as language and the sciences, brings into being instituting communities and instituted realities which do not altogether differ from, but can be seen to take up and express aspects of the sense of the natural 'institutions' of meaning which inform the typical beings and processes to be found in the pre-linguistically and pre-scientifically encountered life-world.[8]

So the thesis of the primacy of perception is just this: If we understand perceptual life in this way, if we see its nascent objectivity in these structures of perspectivality, intersubjectivity, and instituting temporality, we might be able to understand how this provides some basis and warrant for, as well as shows some of the limits of, the distinctive meaning of scientific objectivity. Let me suggest three respects in which this might work.

II

In the first place, this view of perception and of the human perceptual situation permits one to understand, in a schematic way at least, why science develops historically as it does: Research traditions may be expected to be context-dependent and perspectival, but in a sense which, far from calling scientific objectivity into question, actually renders it intelligible. That is, science develops as it does, and its strategies of development exhibit the sort of rationality they do, precisely because of the roots of science in the perceptual life-world.

It is significant that many of those like Russell Hanson and Thomas Kuhn who have tried to understand scientists who are at work in differing scientific communities, have constantly made use of analogies between them and the inhabitants of different perceptual worlds. As traditions of research are developed, Hanson and Kuhn speak of these worlds as being refined and extended; as a scientist's theory crumbles under criticism, they speak of the destruction of the scientist's world; as members of divergent orientations seek to understand one another, these writers speak of the difficulties attendant upon an investigator's entry into a world different from his or her own, of a Gestalt switch, and the like.

Now it should be evident that from a phenomenological point of view these locutions are not simply analogies. Scientific activity, as a cognitive style, aims to articulate certain structures of the perceptual world. Science *is* quite precisely an historically instituted and transformed way of living the perceptual world, of engaging ourselves with it. And a particular scientific tradition is a particular way of doing so. The result is that we should expect to find expressed in scientific activity many of the characteristics of our ordinary, embodied perceptual life: For example, in this light, science will quite properly appear to be a skill or, better, a variety of skills and practices, and not a 'science' at all. Scientists will be understood to learn their trade much as artists and artisans do, by apprenticeship to the possibilities and instrumentalities of things, not by learning to apply explicit rules of method. Scientists will be seen as learning how to perform certain experimental tasks, how to formulate and solve certain theoretical problems, and how to try to extend these experimental and theoretical strategies to problems and fields which appear to be similar to ones already mastered. They will be found frequently (inevitably?) overextending themselves and failing in these efforts, simply because of the essential limitations involved in exploring and testing perceived similarities among diverse things. On this basis, we can understand that what is seen by an investigator is not what happens to 'strike his eyeball', but what is suggested to him in terms of the background cues present in his world. So we should *expect* what Kuhn reports to be the case, that different investigators will be likely to find their worlds populated differently.

But the most important point is this: Because differing research traditions are perceptually lived as worlds and not merely intellectually entertained, they cannot be taken up and put down at will. What we should expect is precisely what takes place historically. The common scientific world *can* only emerge dialectically, through conflict and mediation among differing research traditions, as a regulative ideal of inquiry. This is one expression in scientific history of what Merleau-Ponty called the ambiguousness of the perceptual world. The world is given through perceptual perspectives, always both beyond us as a lure and yet relative to our point of view; it can be nothing purer or more transparent than this in scientific investigation. Scientific research traditions, and the theories developed within them, reveal the world to us in the same manner as do perceptual perspectives, and they do so, similarly, only because at the same time they hide it.

This is, it seems to me, the important truth behind Kuhn's account of paradigm-based research. At the same time it suggests that he ought to have been in no doubt, when pressed by critics, that there is always going to be *some* basis for communication across paradigms, if one seeks it, for the very reason that, like perceptual perspectives, scientific research contexts do constitute points of view on a shared, if elusive, perceptual world. To be sure, scientific intersubjectivity *is* always instituted in some particular, contingent, and limited mode of experimental and theoretical practice. But at some point, because such modes of practice are founded within a more generic and fundamental perceptual practice which engages the common perceptual world, disputants must be able to recover the use of some common concepts or experimental techniques from which to move to begin to clarify their differences. Kuhn was surely right, however, to resist the notion that scientific inquiry necessarily envisions a *completely* determinate 'limit' or 'end' to inquiry—a world of perfect consensus not susceptible to further perspectival exploration, possible modification, and even massive reconstruction. Such a world, a *non*-perspectival world, would not be a perceptual world at all and not, in any case, the world within which natural science is actually carried on. However, this result—this essential element of indeterminateness in the regulative ideal—in no way invalidates the notion of objectivity, but rather confirms it. It is not *in spite of* the inevitably perspectival and, in some measure, always indeterminate character of perception that objects are disclosed, but precisely *because* of it. Seeing and handling a thing in *this* limited way and at *this* limited time is just what gives us access to it. And to have *this* limited perspective is inevitably *not* to have others. It is only through a projected (and typically, if precariously realized) convergence of such limited perspectives over time that we identify and use a perceived thing as 'object'. So, similarly, is it bound to be with the objectivity of the fine-structures of perceived things as these are disclosed in experimental and theoretical perspectives over scientific history. Only a dialectical history of partial, often conflicting, and all the more precariously convergent research traditions can allow us (in some measure) to identify and to use the deeper structural features of the same perceived natural world.[9]

III

Now in addition, I believe, Merleau-Ponty's phenomenological approach can 'save the sense' of the usual critical assessment and justification of hypotheses and theories in science as well. That is, we can understand how the pre-theoretical practice through which we engage the perceived natural world provides a necessary warrant for the typical, generic criteria by which we assess explanatory theories and according to which we validate their claims to truth.

Theoretical conjectures in the mature physical sciences inevitably claim more than to be reports of what is directly empirically verifiable. They are usually taken to posit regularities together with various micro and macro-processes and structures which in some sense 'explain' those regularities. All such claims are at best indirectly and incompletely testable. So one has to ask, what justifies this kind of conjecture? Why do we, or should we, consider theories of this sort to be appropriate or 'explanatory' at all? Beyond the clearly variable, material ideals of 'goodness' which separate research programs such as Galileo's from Aristotle's, or that of a corpuscularist from a field-theorist, we seem typically and more generically to require that our theories posit some sort of causal structures; that these theories be internally consistent and, in some systematic sense, simple; and that they provide for comprehensive and extensible empirical application. Why so? Besides these virtues of 'explanatory power', if a theory actually meets these requirements and if it generates new predictions, opens up new areas of phenomena to study, and continues to be successfully tested in these new areas, we are inclined to consider the theory 'empirically adequate'. Again, why so? The traditional answer to these questions is that we require such qualities because theories which satisfy them will disclose the truth about the natural world. But of course the question all along has been just this: What entitles us to infer from a successful theory's explanatory power together with its empirical adequacy to the legitimacy of its claim to represent (something like the) truth?[10]

Obviously, there are many stories about this. One may decline to infer from a theory's explanatory power and empirical adequacy to its truth. But if one *does* make this inference, as our forefathers Kant and Husserl argued long ago, there seems to be only one form in which to offer a convincing justification for it—namely, that we be able to show how the very project of theoretical thinking is, at least in important respects, continuous with and expressive of our pre-theoretical experience, and thus that the generic criteria for 'good' theoretical explanations, as well as those for the empirical adequacy of theories, are already implicit in our perceptive and active encounter with the natural world. In this way natural science could be shown to have a 'purchase' on the world, to have a legitimate claim to disclose it and, in this sense, to have a potential truth-value. One need not take this form of justification to require a complete or strict transcendental argument; rather, one might (and I believe one should) follow Merleau-Ponty in taking it to be an invitation to explore such continuities and motivations between perceptual and theoretical life as may plausibly be found, and to promise no more than an appropriately limited and qualified outcome.[11]

Now, of course, the principles which such an approach takes to be *implicit* in our pre-theoretical experience of the natural world have become *explicit* within the sciences in a distinctive form. They were not already 'written' as such in the book of nature as perceived. Nature, as encountered in ordinary perception, admits of manifold forms of cultural construal, of the symbols and resemblances of the shaman and the alchemist as well as of the chemistry of Lavoisier and Dalton. At the same time, such cultural variations only take place within certain constraints. As we saw earlier, the perceived world has its own distinctive structural features. And, although I can only begin to suggest how it is so, it *does* seem obvious that the generic theoretical and empirical criteria which have come to govern scientific work are well founded in those features.

For example, *pace* Hume, primordial forms of the causal relation—such as conditionality, reciprocity, productivity, praxis, and the like—are in fact to be found in our pre-scientific, perceptual encounter with the world. That encounter presents, not impressions, but a network of dynamic, growing and changing, inter-dependent and inter-active beings, with ourselves included, as the very condition of there being a perceptual world at all. Scientific posits of causal relations are idealized and selective versions of perceptually recognizable ones. Similarly, the ideals of 'unity of system', of 'simplicity' and 'comprehensiveness' in theoretical explanation, coupled with the requirement that any posited structures be empirically faithful and extensible, are evidently expressions, in formal terms, of the structural features we find in the perceptual encounter with things. This is apparent when we reflect upon the fact that perceived things present themselves essentially as perspectival 'unities-within-multiplicity', as embodied simples, instituted in implicit and projected relations with others and with other things. Given a perceptual world of the sort we have, there is given also a presumptive 'horizon' of further and more remote unities and continuities, as well as differences and discontinuities, to be disclosed through shared inquiry. And, again, the entire process of experimental manipulation and observational testing with respect to posited theoretical constructs is a counterpart to our everyday pursuit of a perceptual object's problematic perspectives—with greater risk involved, to be sure, but not different in principle. In both cases, we explore, use, intervene in, identify, interrogate, and re-identify structures of the perceived world through following out the implications and possible convergences of perspectival variations. Both empirically tested theoretical constructs and perceived things are, in their different ways, bodily and historical 'institutions', as Merleau-Ponty put it. It should thus be no surprise that there are comparable principles of determination implicit in each.

From the standpoint of the thesis of the primacy of perception, then, what warrants the truth-claims of natural science, in so far as they can be found to be warranted, is not just the empirical adequacy of its constructs, their continued usefulness for the prediction of phenomena, nor even the explanatory power of those constructs, however strong. It is rather the structural conformity of the fundamental theoretical and empirical demands of science, which lie behind the search for predictability and explanatory power, to the structures of our pre-theoretical, perceptual experience of the world. Or, to put it another way: On this phenomenological view, it is *just* to the extent that we *can* recognize the constructive and inductive strategies of natural science to be continuous with our well-established perceptual practices of exploring, manipulating, and thus of differentiating, identifying and reidentifying perceived natural things and their relations, and *only* to that extent, that we can reasonably assent to the truth-value of the explanatory conjectures of theoretical science which go beyond ordinary perception.[12]

IV

If we follow up this point, I believe, we are led to see how our prescientific, perceptive and active engagement with the world provides the necessary context within which the persistently realistic intentionality of scientific practice may be properly and faithfully explicated.

The problem here is nothing less than that of finding the most adequate account of the ontological import of theoretical understanding generally. Again, there are many stories. How one proceeds, however, depends crucially upon an account of *reference* in theoretical thinking. Naturalisms, as Husserl and Merleau-Ponty saw them, and many 'scientific realisms', as we see them today, take this reference, at least potentially, as transparent. For them, it is as if theoretical representation could, in principle, directly and immediately disclose the natural world—as if it could provide a 'God's Eye View', as Hilary Putnam put it.[13] The flaw in such naturalisms and realisms is just that we simply do not have transparent access to the world. Our scientific access is through a developed cultural practice in which theoretical thinking is essentially constructive, perspectival, and in interplay with what Patrick Heelan has nicely termed 'readable technologies', techniques of experimental control and measurement which give interpretable outcomes.[14] When one emphasizes this context, as a phenomenological standpoint must, quite another view of reference suggests itself. It will be taken to be *indirect*. There is no God's Eye View to be had, but realism of reference can be preserved by taking theoretical understanding to bear essentially upon the lived natural world of pre-theoretical experience. The thesis of the 'primacy of perception' is precisely that *all* reference is finally a lived relationship *in and with the world*, and only derivatively a relation of thought. Theoretical constructions can gain reference *only* when mediated to the lived world because it is only there, in our living interaction with the world, that any sense is given to the existence of a world at all.

Now if one takes that point of view, theoretical representation has to be viewed as an abstract, selective grasp of the very same objects as are presented to us in the pre-theoretical, perceptual life-world. Theoretical explanation transforms the lived-world, to be sure, but it is a transformation which is to be taken as directed to revealing, in a universally communicable way, the things themselves. This is why 'instrumentalist' accounts of theory, while correct as far as they go, are incomplete. The 'ray' theory of light is indeed a metaphorical redescription for special purposes of quantitative law-like regularities in the observed behaviour of visible light; so also, the kinetic theory of matter is a redescription, in a particular theoretical tradition, accompanied by certain analogies, of the observable behaviour of gases, liquids and solids. However, such redescriptions are *not* mere calculational devices for prediction with an addendum of images. These theories, together with the appropriate technologies of observation, are instrumental in a far larger sense. They provide a means of representing the perceived world, of exploring it, interrogating it, and disclosing further 'deep-structure' within it *as* their theoretical models and analogies prescribe. In the process, such theories-cum-technologies permit us both to enrich our perception, by rendering observable certain aspects of the newly discovered structures, and to satisfy intellectual demands, implicit in perception itself, for the conceptual articulation of those structures. Thus, as part of an entire research tradition, tested theory can be understood to have a realistic intentionality—to determine and to express, in selective and special ways, and thus to uncover and to augment, certain of the structures of the world as it is for us.[15]

It has to follow, then, that we will draw a conclusion for which Merleau-Ponty laid the groundwork, but which he did not draw. If we take the 'primacy of perception' seriously, we shall have to treat any tested theoretical concepts, including those which specify or presuppose the existence of theoretical entities, as conceptual articulations of certain aspects of the parts, and relations among the parts of the things of perception—abstract, partial, and experimentally and conceptually mediated articulations to be sure, but articulations nonetheless. The microstructures of things, while, to be sure, being instituted in a way which is more risky than perception and dependent upon it, still have to be seen as being as real as the things of the perceived world with which science begins. No more real, mind you, but real nonetheless—'real' not in the sense of another world behind or causing the world we see, but real in the sense of the refined and enriched significance *of* the world we see, when that world is manipulated experimentally and its significance is expressed in theoretical and typically mathematical terms. As has so often been noted, the pre-scientifically experienced world is like a text to be read, even if there is no way, as Galileo and many others hoped, to read it literally. The scientific reading of the world brings of analytical clarity and to systematic coherence certain hitherto unsuspected meanings—if clearly not all of the meanings—of the text.

V

Let me sum up the argument I have sought to present. The task was to give an account of the meaning of scientific objectivity within a phenomenological account of human being-in-the-world. The thesis of 'the primacy of perception' was developed and extended to suggest that the cognitive style of natural science depends for its intelligibility and legitimacy upon its being an expression of structural features in our ordinary perceptual being-in or being-with the world in pre-scientific life. We saw first that this thesis would permit us to understand why science develops historically as it does, as a dialectic of context-dependent and perspectival research traditions, and how this process is at the same time capable, at least in principle, of a kind of perspectival objectivity. On this basis, in addition, we were able to become clear that scientific practice, while transforming our existential stance in the world into one with a distinctive cognitive and technological character, still bears on the natural world and enables us to make justifiable existence claims about unobserved structures and processes within it.

But the crucial point of such a reflection is conditional: We have been able to warrant our persistent conviction of the objectivity and realism of science only in so far as we have been able to discern convergences between scientific and perceptual life. We have found it possible to warrant scientific understanding of nature *only* in so far as it is possible to warrant taking perceptual life itself to bear on and reveal the world of nature and thus to *give the criteria* for what we could allow natural science to assert. On this view, the practice of science and its implicit norms are parasitic upon perceptual practice and its implicit norms. Natural science does tell us what the natural world is like; it permits us to transcend momentary personal and cultural perspectives to a remarkable degree and, thus, to attain a considerable measure of objectivity; it augments our knowledge of causal structures in deep and unsuspected ways and affords us new powers to intervene in the world and to reconstruct it for our purposes. We may come to view the natural world, theoretically and through our instruments, as it extends indefinitely in time and space, in the small and in the large. But we do so only from a point of view, from a point of view we have institutionalized in the traditions and practices of what we call natural science. We have good grounds for considering these practices as disclosive of the world, however, *only* to the extent and in the sense that they are rooted for their fundamental rationality, in prescientific, perceptual understanding. If there is no understanding of the world in perception, there is no understanding in science either, and the limits of our understanding in perception set comparable limits upon scientific understanding as well.

NOTES AND REFERENCES

1. This essay is drawn in part from an earlier one, 'Some Contributions of Existential Phenomenology to the Philosophy of Natural Science', *American Philosophical Quarterly*, Vol. 25, No. 2, April 1988, pp. 99–113. Related recent studies of importance for this project include those by Joseph Kockelmans, 'On the Problem of Truth in the Sciences', *Proceedings and Addresses* of the American Philosophical Association, Vol. 61, No. 1, Sept. 1987, pp. 5–26, and by Patrick Heelan, 'Hermeneutical Phenomenology and the Philosophy of Science', chap. 4 in *Gadamer and Hermeneutic Phenomenology*, edited by Hugh J. Silverman, forthcoming from Methuen. Also see

Heelan's *Space Perception and the Philosophy of Science*, Berkeley and Los Angeles, University of California Press, 1983, and Kockelmans' *Heidegger and Science*, Current Continental Research, Washington D.C., University Press of America, 1985.

2. Martin Heidegger, *Being and Time*, tr. Macquarrie and Robinson, London, SCM Press, 1962, sec. 69(b), and Edmund Husserl, *The Crisis of European Sciences*, tr. David Carr, Evanston, Northwestern University Press, 1970.
3. Maurice Merleau-Ponty, *The Phenomenology of Perception*, tr. Colin Smith, New York, The Humanities Press, 1962, p. viii.
4. Maurice Merleau-Ponty, 'The Primacy of Perception ', in *The Primacy of Perception*, edited by James Edie, Evanston: Northwestern University Press, 1964, p. 25.
5. Merleau-Ponty's thought developed considerably after the time of the lecture which puts his views in terms of 'the primacy of perception' (i.e., 1947). However, I believe the thesis remains at the core of his thought until the end—i.e., through the time of the last, posthumously published writings which we have. See, e.g., *The Visible and the Invisible*, tr. Alphonso Lingis, Evanston, Northwestern University Press, 1968, section 1, pp. 14–27.
6. *Phenomenology of Perception*, *op. cit.*, p. 453 (French edition, *op. cit.*, p. 517).
7. Maurice Merleau-Ponty, *Themes From the Lectures at the College de France 1952–1960*, translated by John O'Neill, Evanston, Northwestern University Press, 1970, pp. 86–7, 93ff. And see also, *Phenomenology of Perception*, *op. cit.*, pp. 428–33 and *The Visible and the Invisible*, *op. cit.*, pp. 138–44.
8. *Themes From the Lectures*, *op. cit.*, p. 140.
9. For a striking statement of this view, see Marjorie Grene, 'Perception, Interpretation, and the Sciences: Toward a New Philosophy of Science', in *Evolution at the Crossroads: The New Biology and the New Philosophy of Science*, edited by David Depew and Bruce Weber, Cambridge, M.I.T. Press, 1985, pp. 1–20. Also to the point is my 'Marjorie Grene and the Phenomenon of Life', *Proceedings of the Philosophy of Science Association 1984*, Vol. 2, 1985, pp. 354–64.
10. This is about the way van Fraassen puts the issue in *The Scientific Image*, *op. cit.*, pp. 10, 153–57, 197–98. Joseph Kockelmans responds to him directly with a phenomenological view of the meaning of truth in 'On the Problem of Truth in the Sciences', *op. cit.*
11. See Merleau-Ponty's hints, 'The Primacy of Perception', pp. 19–21, and 'Phenomenology and the Sciences of Man', pp. 65–77, in *The Primacy of Perception*, *op. cit.*
12. This is the basis, I think, for the force of the more restricted argument to the effect that the continued effectiveness of certain theoretical models, through various refinements and extensions over scientific history, gives us warrant to believe in their being something like the truth, an argument which Ernan McMullin offers in 'A Case for Scientific Realism', in Jarrett Leplin's *Scientific Realism*, *op. cit.*
13. Hilary Putnam, 'Two Philosophical Perspectives', in *Reason, Truth, and History*, Cambridge, Cambridge University Press, 1981.
14. Patrick Heelan, 'Natural science as a hermeneutic of instrumentation', *The Philosophy of Science*, 50 (1983), pp. 181–204.
15. I should point out that this view, which might be called 'the enrichment thesis', is a direct consequence of taking the reference to perceived things, and the correlative realism of science, all the way. But it is an implication which Heidegger and Husserl seem to have rejected and which Merleau-Ponty did not draw. I believe this is because they failed to see that mathematical natural science is *not* merely a formalizing science like geometry, but one which proposes and tests structural-causal explanations. Thus they failed to see the continuity between structural explanation in science and the identifying and re-identifying of objective structures in perception. And they missed the crucial role of instrumentation, as an extension of the organs of perception, through which new elements and levels of physical reality may become perceptible to

us. These important modifications of the traditional phenomenological theory of science have been forcefully presented by Patrick Heelan in several papers, among them 'Hermeneutics of experimental science in the context of the Life World', in Don Ihde and Richard Zaner, eds., *Interdisciplinary Phenomenology*, The Hague, Nijhoff, 1975, pp. 7–50, and 'Natural science as a hermeneutic of instrumentation', *Philosophy of Science*, *op. cit.*

The World as the Ontological Project of Man*

RAMAKANT SINARI

When Kant, for the first time in the history of epistemology, used the principle of Copernicus to explain how our knowledge of things is determined by the structure of our subjectivity, he bequeathed to subsequent philosophers the task of defining the boundaries of man's existence *vis-à-vis* the world. Kant tried to prove that our experience of the world is governed by the constitution of our mind. The world in knowledge conforms to the 'stuff' human consciousness is made of, i.e., to the constitutive principles of our faculty of knowing. The organizing norms of our reason shape the way we know whatever we know. The problem (which in fact arose with Plato's theory of knowledge) regarding the connection between the idea and the object, the 'understood' and the perceived, the thing known and the thing-in-itself, was given by Kant a new status by placing the subjectivity of the knower at the centre of the whole process of knowledge.

Since Kant the distinction between the subjective and the objective has remained the cornerstone of epistemologies. Science strives to discover the laws of the objective—its goal is to state the 'truth' about the objective structure of the universe. Perhaps the most basic assumption of science is that objective knowledge is the only valid kind of knowledge, for it is definitive, exact, unambiguous, and mathematically determinable. So in order to know a thing reliably, it must be objectified, that is, it must be posited 'outside' by the knowing mind. The ultimate design of all sciences is to build up a single system in which the totality of phenomena, actual and possible, would cohere in accordance with the tacit laws of logic. Science keeps out of its consideration the elements that constitute subjectivity. Its promise is to know the universe purely objectively, to reach reality as it is.

The main thesis of Kant's *The Critique of Pure Reason* leans toward subjectivism and demonstrates mind's inherent incapacity to reach phenomena in themselves. To know something, according to Kant, is to place it within a certain frame of mind, to bring it under the 'categories of the understanding', and by that very process to construct it against mind's natural endowments. Thus the knowing subject is unable to leave off the epistemic enclosure within which he resides and leap out to the essence of the known. He apprehends the world as it is given to him in his innate conceptual setting and not as it in itself is. Things in their absolute objectivity, that is, thing as they are, are called by Kant *noumena* or things-in-themselves. It can be said that for him our knowledge of the world is not, really speaking, the knowledge of the world-in-itself but rather the knowledge of the way or modes by which we perform the act of knowing. His subjectivism is the first forceful attempt to suggest that the scientist's faith and the metaphysician's conviction that conclusive knowledge of Reality is attainable rests on a kind of naiveté.

Kant was sure that in the act of knowledge the mechanism of subjectivity must be regarded as most relevant. Not only does subjectivity organize the given impressions through its *a priori* categories (unity, totality, quantity, necessity, cause-effect, negation, existence, modality, etc.), but it must also be said that without it no experience would be possible. The revolution which Copernicus had caused in astronomy with his hypothesis that the movement of the heavenly bodies is not just passively witnessed by (the man on) the earth but that the earth itself has its own independent movement, seems to have anticipated Kant's epistemological breakthrough in philosophy. Copernicus had made the earth's motion a central factor in the explanation of the scheme of heavenly bodies; Kant made the constitution of the knowing mind the pivot around which knowledge takes place and is systematized.

The subjective and the objective are like two poles implicit in all knowledge. They are the ontological extremities into which almost every knowledge situation is analysable. In empirical knowledge, more than in personal, introspective, or self-knowledge, the subject-pole posits the object 'there'. This only means that the knower intuits this 'there object' as having an autonomous being which he can study and describe and control or change. Thus science has to trust that the knower is capable of discovering the laws that govern the universe, that is, that the subject-pole by applying the principles of reason would one day succeed in establishing a system or hierarchy of systems ready to explain why the object-pole is as it is and how it would behave in the altered circumstances. For the purpose of scientific knowledge, the knowing mind and the knowable (or the known) world are two fundamental substances into which Reality itself can be divided. The statement of the laws regulating their behaviour and the development of an 'absolutely' valid intellectual picture of their total operation are the ultimate programme of science.

Ordinarily it is not the function of science to doubt the objectivity of the universe. In natural sciences, for example, the reality of the physical and biological world is assumed; the world is believed to be there for its disclosure to the rational mind. Through the methods of observation, analysis, hypothesization, and verification these sciences aim at unfolding the 'mystery' of the universe. Thus if the objective existence of the phenomena observed is questioned, that is, if the presupposition that events outside us follow a certain order or uniformity and occur independent of the factors constituting the act of observation is doubted, scientific explanation would cease to have any 'real' reference. They very logic of natural sciences demands our unbiased registering of what goes on there 'outside.' The scientific attitude has to 'throw out' anything that it researches on and claims to know. To a scientist, reality is an organisation of uniformities whose knowledge, inasmuch as it is contained inside descriptive or causal statements totally free from the subjective nuances, must be taken as *the* truth.

Actually the very possibility of scientific knowledge, like that of commonsense knowledge, is due to its reliance on naive realism. The assumption that the structure of the universe is self-governed and fully knowable runs underneath both commonsense and scientific attitudes. That is why both these ways of knowledge are object-anchored, object-organizing and, when applied in the actual world, object-mastering. By their very objectivistic commitment scientific theories do not take into account the agencies that influence the knowing mind in its encounter with what is given to it.

Now, whatever may be its ultimate metaphysical standing, in any knowledge situation it is subjectivity that confers a meaning on the known object. In fact unless a thing enters into the range of human subjectivity it would not stand out as experienced. As Husserl, for whom the direction of Kant's philosophy was of great significance, has pointed out, the unique characteristic of subjectivity is its intentionality, i.e., its directedness toward the given.[1] Husserl maintained that every experience harbours in itself a meaning of some kind, or at times several meanings, in accordance with which it emerges before consciousness as real. The peculiar nature of the object of knowledge is that it is something 'meant' to the knower, lies outside him, and is *there* because of him. Without this curious 'meaning' or 'beholding' function of the subject there would not be anything registered as known. Knowledge, in its essence, is an act of intuiting meaning whose organisation and association with objects outside is one of the most perplexing acts of our consciousness.[2]

Husserl's famous method of phenomenological reduction is an exercise in the suspension of the empirical world from consciousness and in capturing the original consciousness structure. The phenomenologists of the Husserlian persuasion support the possibility of consciousness's attaining what is called the *eidetic* or essential meanings which form the very basic stuff which the human existence is made of. Our experience of the world is the projection of this stuff; it is the realization of what is ontologically innate in the constitution of the self.

No inquiry into science can afford to overlook the fact that in our act of comprehending the world pure objectivity is a chimera. On the face of it it might seem that in scientific observation the constitution of the observing mind is hardly a relevant determinant. A scientific statement is generally looked upon as an absolutely impersonal description of the state of affairs available in the world. Whoever may make such a statement, sciences maintains, the statement can be tested and seen as either mirroring or not mirroring reality as it is. Scientific laws are thus recognized as logical entities corresponding to the perceived and 'public' material entities. Sciences like physics, chemistry and biology claim to show how, by the use of the techniques of analysis, measurement, experimentation, and proof, an objective, materialist explanation of the whole empirical domain is offered.

With one of the strongest defences in our time of what he calls 'epistemology without the knowing subject', Mario Bunge argues in favour of objectivity in scientific knowledge thus:

...(an item of knowledge) is objective because, and to the extent that, there are animals capable of acquiring it and putting it to the test with the help of criteria independent of personal factors such as authority or firmness of conviction. The degree of objectivity of a proposition may be estimated by virtue of the rules of the knowledge game, such as those of logic and empirical testing.[3]

> The sciences that study physical objects, or things, are the factual sciences.... These disciplines try to find the laws of such subjects, in particular their laws of change, such as equations of motion, field equations, chemical reaction equations, social mobility matrices, and historical trends. . . . The law statements that factual scientists are after tell us what the really possible states of things are as well as what the really possible changes of state (i.e., events or processes) of concrete objects are.[4]

Nevertheless such an objectivism, although consistent with the career of science and continuously supported by the spectacular progress made by scientific researchers finds it hard to put up with (what can be called) the rise of the inner man in the present century.

All scientific knowledge is basically creation of man. For an impression to pass as knowledge, it must appear within the field of our awareness. Human consciousness, or its intentionality, runs into objects, so to say, and focuses on them against the background of an infinite number of other objects. While it stays preoccupied with a particular object, the environing objects linger and vacillate as indistinct but ready to come into the zone of the known. Indeed these environing objects may never become distinct and fixed before consciousness, on the other hand, they may eventually disappear into total obscurity, into some unfathomable spatial openness along the nexus between the knower's self and the world. The subjective idealists are serious when they argue that since, metaphysically speaking, it is our subjectivity in which ideas and their interrelations dwell, we should say that the world corresponding to them is *in* us, i.e., it is our own creation.

What must be emphasized here is that the subject-pole encounters the given (a thing, an event, an idea, an impression) in a certain manner, or from its own peculiar vantage point. By granting the world a sense, a form, or a pattern and by selecting a definite aspect of it in observation, man apperceives and anticipates the very ontology of the world. Hence in the whole intercourse between man and the world, or between subjectivity and objectivity, unless what is given in experience satisfies what can be called the 'existential conditions' inherent in the total psychic structure of the experience, it would not be comprehended. The world, in this sense, represents the uncovering of the ontological project of man.[5]

In fact, when we go deep into the very anatomy of knowledge and raise questions like 'how does one know that one knows?' 'how does mind *see* that the knowledge of something given to it is certain or clear?' 'how can we account for the gap between the subject-pole and the object-pole?' and perhaps the most germane question of all, viz., 'what is the state of consciousness of a philosophical inquirer who goes beyond and behind the two poles in knowledge and watches their interaction?' we begin to realize the mystery of consciousness itself.

But natural sciences do not concentrate on the mechanism of knowledge, except by way of finding out its physiological correlates. Since their design is to formulate laws that could account for the origin, the evolution, and the future condition of the entire universe, they take for granted that the laws of knowledge do not fall inside their purview. For them to explain the 'why' and the 'how' of knowledge is to determine the mechanics of the human brain, which, according to them, is nothing more than a highly complex configuration of material constituents.

Because of the most dependable predictive ability and the resultant control natural sciences have come to command over different kinds of spatio-temporal events, it is no wonder that their method is today valued as the most fruitful. Thus, in social sciences, which are basically attempts at understanding man and his life in society, researchers consider the application of this method as incumbent on them. Many social scientists today propose to study human or social materials as objectively as natural scientists treat physical objects. They look for laws of 'behaviour'—thus their nick name 'behavioural scientists'—that would explain everything concerning the individual-and-society interaction.

There is no doubt that the immense credibility that natural sciences have acquired and the fantastic marvels that they have made possible in the spheres of their application are largely due to their method of approaching the universe, presenting and formulating the same. One cannot but admire the wealth of welfare and good that they have generated for mankind by enabling it to develop technologies for facilitating its adjustment to, and control over, the forces of nature. The ground they have prepared in space technology for the penetration of man into the solar system surely contains the possibility of a solution to the rapidly depleting earthly resources. And all this is obviously the result of their trust in the possibility of objective knowledge, i.e., their assumption that all phenomena are basically material, that they are causally determined, and that, therefore, the logic comprising quantification, measurement, analysis, and experimentation must be applied to all of them as uniformly as possible.

The view, sweeping in its scope, states that any happening in the universe is fully reducible to a determinable pattern of change in the material structure of the universe, and that, as soon as this pattern is explained in terms of the laws governing it, other happenings in its set could be accurately predicted. This view is called 'scientific determinism' by Karl Popper.[6] The main thrust of it is that there is no mystery about anything in the universe, including human phenomena, once we come to know the physical and chemical constituents of it and the laws governing them. Subjectivity, the freedom of the human self, the spontaneity and creativity of the mind, even the uniqueness one experiences about his or her being in the world, are all translatable, according to this theory, into material configurations of the brain. The Cartesian dualism is thrown overboard. Hobbes had said that the basic condition of all organic, as of inorganic bodies, is one of motion, i.e., collision, conflict, and war. For Newton, the laws of motion are central to all happenings and it is these laws that can be shown to explain them. Laplace believed that the world is reducible to corpuscles interacting among themselves according to the laws of Newtonian dynamics. Marx and Watson did not see anything in the mental reality of man which does not have for its equivalent man's bodily behaviour.

The use of the laws of science, that is, the laws found in physics, physiology, biology, chemistry, etc., for the purpose of determining 'human' events has reached a stage when any reference to subjectivity, to our 'inner space', is regarded as unwarranted. Efforts of the behavioural scientists to reduce humans and human societies to mathematically mappable systems of behaviour are made unrestrainedly. The assumption is that human beings are complexes of behavioural processes, conglomerations of definite hereditary and environmental factors, and, therefore, fully accountable by means of what B. F. Skinner anticipates as 'a science of behaviour (adopting) the strategy of physics and biology'.[7] So, to understand man is to look upon him as a field of interactions between the organism that he is and his environment, to evolve a mathematical model of his total existence. Like physics and biology and chemistry, social sciences promise to provide a complete model of man-as-a-machine.

The behavioural intrepretation of human existence, despite its occasional protestation, ignores the subjective, the creative, and the existential at its core. The inherent policy of modern science is that it either claims to guarantee the conclusive explainability (in theory, if not in practice) of almost every phenomenon in the universe or, if something does not fit into its compass, refuses to recognise its relevance. The phenomena whose very meaning science thus rejects, usually have a base in the psychic, the intentional, the transcendental, or the inward.

The empirical study of man conducted by behavioural sciences is in tune with their emulation of natural sciences. Phenomena which are anchored in what is called man's subjectivity these sciences would attempt to account for in terms of well-established natural laws. Their account of these phenomena, stated in the language of cause-effect relationship promises to provide us with an exhaustive chart indicating the actual and the possible human responses to different stimuli. Thus, the empirical-analytic approach to subjectivity, to the 'inside' of man, is in every respect identical with the approach of natural sciences to the structure of the universe.

If taken strictly on the ground of its effectiveness, the empirical-analytic explanations of man's behaviour patterns may seem to be flawless. This is because of the materialist and determinist character of such explanations. They make it a point not to construct untestable or transempirical hypotheses and not to confirm any statement unless it reflects observed or observable facts. Their fascination for observational language is boundless and uncritical. So, what has been regarded for centuries as the spiritual foundation of man is here understood through the categories of human behaviour. Our most authentic experiences like feelings, mental acts, self-knowledge, self-identity, meaning-intuition, etc., which are the basic stuff constituting our subjectivity, are not recognised as primordial facts of our 'being', but rather as a variety of compounded behavioural expressions. In the process, man's subjectivity—that is, his 'inner space', or the act of transcendence that he fundamentally is, is lost.

We have already said that however objective an understanding of the world science may claim to have reached, there is necessarily in it an expression of consciousness's unique act of intuiting and organizing meanings. It is this act that both Kant and Husserl recognized as constituting the essence of man. It is because of the presence of man in the world that all meanings, theories and explanations originate. The knowing consciousness *sees* the world to be there, builds up meanings and theories and explanations around it, and develops the technique of controlling it. From the beginning of history, man has not only shown curiosity with regard to his environment but he has also, almost instinctively, applied whatever knowledge he could gain for changing it. In this sense, he has always been technological and subjectivist in his encounter with the world.

One of the shortcomings of the very methodology of natural and behavioural sciences is that their investigation is strictly confined to the causes of phenomena. Any thinking about the purposes and goals of human activity is supposed to fall outside their investigation. However, it is in the planning of science, in its practice for changing the situation on the globe to man's advantage, that scientists cannot forego the question on human subjectivity—human aspirations, hopes, desires, and projects concerning the collective well-being of mankind. In fact, the whole history of scientific-technological civilization represents mankind's decision to pursue certain values, a definite way of life, to seek the fulfilment of its innate 'passions'. Thus, if man is to attain the fullest realisation of his spirit, it is necessary that he not only control his environment, and gain supremacy over the anti-survival forces, but also be aware of the inner dimension of his self.

There is no technique by which the width of human subjectivity can be completely mapped out. It is a domain in which imagination, insights, intuitions, decisions, and one's *Weltanschauung* spring up before they take a concrete shape in one's life, conduct and attitude toward others. The sphere of subjectivity is too elusive to be captured inside language. It is of the nature of a wholesome feeling of one's being real and absolutely unrestrained in one's inner space. In fact, the very sense of being human that lies underneath our experience of living in the world is rooted deeply in our subjectivity. Subjectivity is the core of my existence in the sense that within my inner self I am aware of my personal identity, my unique reality, and my freedom to manipulate my own thoughts, feelings, volitions, attitudes, and so on. The aim of what might be termed as the ontology of the inner man should be to verbalize this transempirical reality at the heart of our existence.[8]

The kind of reach we have *in* us is unlike any intellectual encounter we have with objects and other persons. The most significant characteristic of human consciousness is to intuit itself as the pivot of all that 'goes on' in and out of it. Consciousness is *in* freedom. It is freedom. For all mental acts are seen to arise in it wholly spontaneously as if they flowed out of its open and elusive being. These acts are, of course, occasioned by what may seem to be objectively operating stimuli. I find myself as the seat of all that 'happens' to me—psychic and bodily processes—, I own my impressions, I am an existence *a priori*. I am an absolute authority with regard to my inside in the sense that

I can transcend what I am, have a kind of bird's-eye view of what I am. Śaṅkara, the famous Indian metaphysician of the eighth century A.D., and Husserl and Sartre in our own time, have stressed this when they say that consciousness, as a self-seeing act, self-reflective content, constantly moves in between the transcendental and the phenomenal, the pre-reflective and the reflective, and almost out of its own inertia reveals to itself that it is a world-experiencer. The world-experience is strangely intertwined with the subjectivity of the experiencer.

The whole scientific and technological enterprise of man is the expression of his being. As Heidegger points out, this enterprise must not be looked upon as merely a programme of producing definite situations with techniques, but as the ontological approach of man toward his being-in-the-world.[9] It has made man realize freedom from most atrocious boundaries to his existence. The amount of protection and well-being it has provided to man today has no parallel in history. There is something basically utilitarian about the practice of science. It endeavours to bring to man ease and comfort, emancipates him from the state of suffering generated by the environment factors, and heightens his *joie de vivre*.

But what science has consistently overlooked is the *elan* of man. Human consciousness perpetually stretches itself out into transempirical dimensions. It creates feelings, interests, attitudes, insights, volitions, which are the very *sine qua non* of our existence. Whatever progress the scientific-technological age has brought about must not, therefore, deprive man of his inner being, his search for the meaning of his life out there in the world. Perhaps, the most serious evil that science, when it is rooted totally in objectivity and determinism, has given rise to is the de-humanisation of man. Totally mechanical science has reduced man to a function, to an object, and is attempting to sever him from his primordial ontological base altogether. Man's self-alienation is one of the avoidable but grave maladies of our age.

* Some of the key ideas in this paper have already appeared in my 'Science and the Meaning of Being Human', *Dialectics and Humanism*, No. 3, Poland, 1980, pp. 73–82.

NOTES AND REFERENCES

1. The theory that human subjectivity is intentional (propounded by Husserl and then widely supported by phenomenologists and existentialists) is one of the most revolutionary theories in epistemology. It can definitely be said that it is an attempt to draw philosophers' attention to the complexity of human consciousness as the ultimate 'understander' of the world.
2. See my 'Being, Meaning and Saying' in V. K. Bharadwaja, ed., *Rationality and Philosophy*, New Delhi, Northern Book Centre, 1984, pp. 45–57.

3. Mario Bunge, *Scientific Materialism*, Dordrecht, Reidel Publishing Company, 1981, pp. 152–53.
4. *Ibid.*, pp. 162–63.
5. What R. D. Laing, the famous existential psychologist, says about the being of the world in us is illuminating. He writes: 'We all know from our personal experience that we can be ourselves only in and through our world and there is a sense in which 'our' world will die with us although 'the' world will go on without us.' See his *The Divided Self*, Middlesex, Penguin Books, 1965, pp. 19–20.
6. See Karl R. Popper, *The Open Universe: An Argument for Indeterminism*, London, Hutchinson & Company 1982, pp. 29–33.
7. B. F. Skinner, *Beyond Freedom and Dignity*, Middlesex, Penguin Books, 1973, pp. 180–81.
8. For a fuller treatment of this idea see my 'The Quest for an Ontology of Human Self' in S. S. Rama Rao Pappu and R. Puligandla, ed., *Indian Philosophy: Past and Future*, Delhi, Motilal Banarsidass, 1982, pp. 119–136.
9. See Webster P. Wood's 'The Aristotelian Versus the Heideggerian Approach to the Problem of Technology' in Carl Mitcham and Robert Mackey, ed., *Philosophy and Technology*, New York, The Free Press, 1972, pp. 353.

Technology as Cultural Instrument

DON IHDE

My topic today will be, broadly, *technology transfer*. By that I mean the introduction of some set of material artifacts out of their original context of human praxes or techniques, into some other cultural context. Such transfers overall are commonly recognized as the spread of so-called 'advanced' technologies, such as those common to the northern hemisphere high technology, high industrial nations, to the so-called 'less developed' and largely southern hemisphere nations. On a smaller scale, technology transfer may also mean the adaptation of some single technology of one people by another through means of cultural encounters.

Technology will mean here, as it has in my previous work, some artifact or set of artifacts—material culture—related to a context of human action or praxes (which include techniques of use). I shall be focusing, however, upon the exchange itself and in particular upon its cultural dimensions.

When a 'technology' transfer occurs it has long been known that more than a transfer of some artifact is involved. The steel axe has been the classic example of a simple transfer. The standard analysis usually goes something like this: (a) When a 'technologically advanced' people—with steel axes—come into contact with, say, peoples using only Stone Age tools, there will be an initial flow of artifacts from the advanced to the indigenous people. They will simply adapt and even covet steel axes. (b) The reason, the standard analysis usually holds, is that the steel axe is obviously more efficient and functional—it cuts down trees faster and with less effort. Never mind that this reason is also *ipso facto* already an assumed value within the 'advanced' culture. (c) But, then, at first unknown to the recipient people, more is being received than a steel axe. What, underneath, is being taken in is a new set of relations, primarily economic, which will eventually result in dependency relations for the indigenous people. Thus, because the indigenous people, now accustomed to the steel axe, cannot produce one—they do not have the technological praxis—they must enter trade and other relations (furs for axes) which eventually make them dependent upon the 'advanced' culture.

This standard analysis is not wrong *per se*, but neither is it very penetrating and it is too simply skewed to economic factors. Heidegger, for example, has used the radio as an illustration of a technology transfer which comes closer to what I am after with respect to technology as cultural instrument. It is well known that two artifacts which are immediately fascinating to previously isolated indigenous peoples are wristwatches and radios. Nor is it necessary that the context of understanding which belongs to the watch or the radio be immediately apprehended. Fascination with movement, light and particularly, sound, is sufficient to make the artifact desirable and to start and process of 'culture transfer'. And, indeed, one would probably be hard pressed to isolate two more crucial technologies for this purpose than the clock—which transformed the entire sense of time and public order in Western technological civilization—and the radio—which has transformed the entire communication and embodiment of language presence in that same history. But what the clock and radio transfer, as cultural instruments, is much more than a set of economic relations. Such artifacts are the non-neutral means by which an entire cultural gestalt can be carried.

Although I shall keep the narrative of this analysis concrete by use of cultural variants, there are certain theses which I am arguing which may be placed in the open:

Thesis One: There are no neutral technologies, or, positively put, all technologies are *non-netural.* I use this phrase deliberately to eliminate any tendency to pre-judge technologies as simply 'good' or 'bad'. They are transformational in that they change the quality, field and possibility range of human experience, thus they are non-neutral.

Now in one sense, this is a trivial insight known at least intuitively by most people except for certain philosophers, philosophers of science, social scientists and the older fashioned scientists. Industrialists, engineers, commercial people, pioneers and militarists have long known that technologies are non-neutral, as have some philosophers in certain traditions.

This thesis, however, becomes clearer if one is also aware that technologies must be understood *phenomenologically*, i.e., as belonging in different ways to our experience and use of technologies, as a human-technology relation, rather than abstractly conceiving of them as mere objects. Were technologies merely objects totally divorced from human praxis, they would be so much 'junk' lying about. Once taken into praxis one can speak not of technologies 'in themselves', but as the active relational pair, human-technology. The human with a steel axe is different than the human without one—the transformational effect becomes clear when we regard as the *primitive* of our analysis, this *human-technology pairing*.

Thesis Two: If abstracting technologies as neutral objects is one error, then reifying Technology (with the capital 'T') is an equivalent one. There is no unitary, determined single destiny to technological development. There is a multistable and diverse and ambiguous set of multiple directions whose ends are probably not predicable any more than any historical-cultural development can be adequately predicted. Thus I am arguing against the Elluls, the Marcuses and other thinkers who claim that there is a single, inevitable direction to a Technology which is out of control. The 'power' of technologies, conversely, must be isolated at a more subtle level, that of human social and cultural interchange, examples of which I shall examine.

Thesis Three: The dimensions of 'technology transfers' are never simply economic or productive, but multidimensioned and involve basic cultural and existential interchange. This is therefore a rejection of any foundationalist or reductionist explanation and an opting for a more multidimensional and phenomenological model of understanding. It will involve utilization of a *variational theory* such as originated with Husserl, but now adumbrated into the historical-cultural domain both through interdisciplinary use of historical and anthropological insights and of imaginative variants upon these. In this sense I may be thought of as developing a non-Marxian thesis regarding interpretation, without being anti-Marxist.

Example 1 Gold Prospectors and New Guinean Highlanders

In 1930 the first white colonists from Australia began to penetrate the New Guinean highlands in search of gold—they were totally unaware that they were to encounter multiple tribes of highlanders, now estimated to have been nearly a million in population at that time. Although not with scholarly purposes, the prospectors fortunately took a movie camera with them and recorded these first encounters—a recent, remarkable educational television program played this film and also provided interviews with older highlanders who remembered this first encounter. I shall focus upon certain 'technology transfers' which occurred in these first meetings.

It should be pointed out that at first, most of the highlanders regarded the newcomers as either *gods* or *ghosts*. In the recounts, they emphasized that they had never seen *white* people and that their cultural beliefs held strongly that they (the highlanders) were the *only people* living in the *only world*, the highlands. A plausible notion, then, was that the white newcomers were ghosts or spirits from some 'beyond'. I need not point out that this pattern of shock and interpretations is, far from being unusual, almost typical of first encounters between peoples. It, in fact, echoes some of the first encounters recorded between Spaniards and Incas in Latin America.

Later, of course, they gradually discovered that the newcomers were mortals—interestingly in quite concrete and perceptual ways. Because the colonists wore clothing, the highlanders at first though that ghosts or gods did not defecate, fornicate or urinate—but soon someone spied a newcomer doing his duty and as the film showed, every material leaving was immediately investigated. The highlanders soon discovered that the excrement had the proper *human* smell! One could say, a very 'earthy' discovery!

Now, however, focus upon the technologies: There were, of course, steel axes and knives and these were immediately seized upon as fascinating and desirable. But, I suggest, not simply because they were functional or more efficient—axes and knives were *familiar* and *understandable* artifacts, already there in the indigenous culture. The point of juncture was *familiarity within a known praxical gestalt*. Steel axes and knives were different in material and appearance, but clearly easily recognizable and understandable. Contrarily, even though rifles were clearly much superior in weapon power than axes or knives, there was not much of an initial fascination with guns (until later). To demonstrate their power (again quite aware of the non-neutrality of the human-technology symbiosis) the prospectors killed a pig at close range. There was a shock of fear at the report of the gun, but as the film showed and the reports indicated, such a killing did not at first seem so impressive. Anyone could kill a pig at close range. Later, after the tribesmen came to realize that the whites were mortals like themselves, their *technologies* were perceived as not only fascinating and desirable, but perhaps capturable—so a raid was prepared and occurred with the predicable, disasterous result. Nine islanders were slain by a fusilade of riflefire and only *then*, because this occurred at a distance beyond spear range did the new technology become awesome.

Were I to leave the example here with the axe-gun technologies, the standard analysis might seem not only correct, but sufficient. But that was not exhaustive. The colonists carried tinned goods, for example those old elliptical sardine cans. These they discarded along the way as 'junk'. But the lids were immediately picked up and *incorporated into elaborate headdresses* by the highlanders. Again, there is a pattern of a new artifact first being incorporated into a known praxis, a fashion praxis if you will. And, again, for those who have known all along that fascination and adornment are as good a way into the hearts and minds of humans as any, recall the long history of trading which has involved cheap and gaudy goods in initial encounters. The Spaniards carried vast quantities of hawkbells for trading (shiny and sounding). And, in the cases mentioned, one interesting fact is that the bauble, if it had some original use as a hawksbell, is taken into an entirely new and different use, but one which is familiar to the recipient. It is not far from hawksbells and shiny tin cans to television and, one might add for some fascinated with today's screens, videogames and word processors!

My point is this: empirically, the steel axe and the mirror are simultaneously and equally fascinating and desirable. It takes a peculiar and selective perception to ignore the latter and choose the former as basic, which is to say that a simplistic economic determinism is already a chosen theory which is then self verified. Instead, I am suggesting, there is a structure, a multidimensioned structure, to such interchanges which simultaneously involve a multiplicity of levels and functions.

The interstices which initially occur, take place in certain crucial familiar praxes: axes and knives to familiar functions, mirrors and baubles to other ones. Thus we find the strange anomalies of certain artifacts used in ways entirely different from their designed purposes. Watches, for example, while desired are not at first used to 'tell time' since the whole context of hours, minutes and seconds is initially unfamiliar. Instead, they are used for decoration, prestige, and for a kind of mini-entertainment through their noises and motions. A more functional example comes from the use of a compass by the Puluwatians in Micronesia—although used for steering a straight course (and thereby replacing the more subtle reading of wave patterns of traditional navigation)—it is not used to tell points of direction or degrees (steer 180° course) since this system of navigation remains foreign to the traditional navigators of Puluwat.

There is a deeper significance here than may appear. It is two sided:

(a) first, any technology may be used in a multiplicity of ways, limited only by the individual and cultural imaginations of the people or user. Heidegger's famous hammer is a good example. In use it is not an object-as-such, but the transparent and familiar attainment of a practice. But, equally, it may be used in any number of ways. It could, and perhaps is dominantly used, for its designed purpose—to hammer. But it could be used as a paperweight, an object d'art, a murder weapon, a pendulum weight, a door handle, etc. This ambiguity of uses is, however, not indefinitely extendable. The hammer would not serve well as a rope, a sewing needle or other artifact which in its range would also display some span of multiple uses. Here is a dimension to human-technology uses which is deeply unpredicable and uncontrollable. But it is not something which belongs essentially to modern technology; it has always been a dimension of human-technology relations. The cultural variations alluded to are simply dramatic examples of precisely this possibility structure. Obviously, such possibilities may be trivial, benign or frightening. Even a complex nuclear plant *could* be used in a number of ways—for example as a giant grain silo, converted to coal, taken as a piece of junk or, better, junk sculpture, preserved as a monument. And its products, as we so frightenly know, can be used for making terrorist bombs (nuke packs now come in the fifty pound variety), poisons for the New York Waterworks, or any number of possibilities. No one can control these uses as such!

(b) But if any artifact may be used in multiple ways, one might be tempted to say that it nevertheless 'is', in some ontological sense, this or that thing. This is, however, to misconstrue technological artifacts. Apart from human-technology relations, such *technofacts* as they might be called, would at best be certain conglomerations of material being, for example their physical or chemical properties. But the being of a technofact is more like that of an art object than a natural object, not only by being made, but by its use context. Thus the ambiguity of uncontrolable, multiple uses for any single technofact is balanced by the ambiguity that I may also use any number of technologies to achieve the same purposes.

If I wish to hammer, I may normally use a hammer in it Heideggerian sense—but I could use a crowbar, a piece of steel sculpture, a properly shaped stone. This is not to say that the ambiguity of being able to use a multiplicity of technologies for the same purpose means that technologies are either neutral or irrelevant. To the contrary, it is to say that each varient upon a human-technology symbiosis has related possibilities—while each of the above technofacts could be used to hammer, the use of the palm of my hand or a waterballoon for this purpose would be futile. Yet the range of ambiguity in both multiple uses of a single technology or single purposes utilizing a range of technologies once again exemplifies both the essential unpredictability and ambiguity of the human-technology relation, and the impossibility of 'control'.

It is now time to return to the theme of technology as cultural instrument. In the examples given so far, I have shown how technologies are first taken into recipient cultures through what may be called a recognition of the familiar. The steel axe and knife and the shiny bauble both have immediate, recognizable roles to play in the indigenous culture, even if the recipient has no idea what he or she is 'buying'. The fascination and desire will be enough to insure the giver or bringer of the technology of a wedge into the recipient culture.

However, there is another side to familiarity in the encounter between two alien cultures, and that is strangeness. Strangeness and familiarity are two sides of the single, multidemensioned phenomenon. Strangeness seems at first dramatic and obvious—but it usually lacks comprehension. In the example I have given, the taking of the gold prospectors as ghosts or spirits, there was a dramatic recognition of strangeness, and an attempt to bring it into familiarity—the concept of ghost or spirit. Let us now, however, turn the tables so that the encounter between two people will be seen to be two-sided. The colonist also perceives strangeness and attempts to familiarize it.

When the Colombians first began to explore the New World they recognized the strangeness of the peoples—there are remarks about costume (nakedness or near nakedness), customs (cannibalism and marriage practices among the Carib) and the like. But not unlike the highlanders, this strangeness is accommodated within a persistent familiarity. Not only did Columbus continue to believe that he had discovered the Indies or Orient, but the very category 'Pagan' as an attempt to place the indigenous peoples under a familiar idea, a religious conception not *functionally* unlike ghost or spirit.

What is especially striking is that strangeness is so difficult to perceive that representations of the indigenous peoples frequently remain distorted for long periods of time. For example, the first portrayals of 'Indians' by early Colonial painters frequently look like Michelangelo anatomy drawings. To be sure, the feathers and loincloths are portrayed, but the physical features remain primarily 'European' in appearance even if the bodies represented ones covered with body paint. In North America, for example, it was only in the 19th century that one began to get genuinely realistic representations, as in the extensive painting projects of George Caton. Interestingly, by the time portraits of this quality began to appear, it was already painfully apparent that the Indian way of life was disappearing. There remained, aftersome centuries of interaction, deep misperceptions between people of the different cultures. Yet what of material culture and technological interchange?

We tend to overlook that the exchange is always two-way, without denying that something the exchange is not equal. The Spanish horse and later the rifle, completely changed the lifestyles of plains Indian—in fact the romantic image of the roving hunters and migratory peoples which inhabit our imaginations were already post-exchange social patterns. Similarly at the level of material culture, who are the Irish without the potato, the Italians without the tomato, the New Englander without corn, or the world without tobacco? All these were exchanges which came from New World material cultures. What is different between today and yesterday, is that all these products are now virtually universal in distribution. This fact alone both *diversifies* and *homogenizes* 'World Culture'.

That technology transfers will occur at cultural interstices, and that this exchange will inevitable carry culture change, has been illustrated. Furthermore, that the transfer will occur at some point of familiarity or fascination may also have been demonstrated. Moreover, these exchanges do not necessarily occur between variants upon low or appropriate technologies, but may occur between very high and very low technological contexts. India, for example, is attempting to 'leapfrog' its rural development programme by introducing television rather than a series of other technologies into rural areas. Thus the satellite receiver set up in a field being plowed by oxen becomes a symbol of India's development. The fascination of a village television substitues for the hawksbell.

All this leads us, uncritically, to too frequently assume that there is some kind of overwhelming, even Frankensteinian trajectory to modern Technology conceived of with the capital 'T'. Yet without denying the march of the most recent technological revolution over the globe, two pauses would be taken. Are there modern technologies which are *not* adapted? and, if so, why? By shifting the emphasis, another aspect of transfer may be noted. Again, begin with early explorational examples.

The first European explorers entering the Pacific were amazed at the ship technology of the Islanders. Large catamarans, capable of carrying 200 warriors, rapidly outstepped the clumsy, bulky European craft. These catamarans or multihulls had not only conquered the entire Pacific a millennium before Columbus conquered the Atlantic, but were more manoeuverable, faster, more seaworthy than any European craft. Yet there never was an attempt to capture or copy this technology by the Europeans. (Nor, conversely, did the Islanders feel tempted to copy the European craft.) Only today in the times of now over thirty knot sailing multihulls for transoceanic racing have Westerners perfected the ancient designs. Here was a technology not transferred in spite of its efficiency and functionality.

Similarly, in the twentieth century, there exists a simple technology which would probably do more to help peoples escape poverty and drudgery than any single technology, but it is not adapted and is more ignored than rejected. I refer, of course, to birth control technologies which remain contrary to certain cultural values in spite of their obvious advantage for creating conditions for material wish fulfilment often equally desired by the very rejectors of the technology. Not all technologies are adapted, even when they have obvious advantages. And the resistance is a cultural one, not a difference between technological levels.

I have now examined a very few simple examples of technology transfers with their cultural implications, let us now step back and note a few of the structural features embedded in such transfers:

1. In a transfer, an artifact is transferred. But in its original setting the artifact is paired with a human praxis, a technology is a human-technology relation. What is perceived as *useful*, in the typical transfer, must therefore, make contact with a recognizable praxis, the familiar. Steel axes and knives are

immediately incorporatable. Here would be an example of a technology transferred between recognizable praxes.

2. But transfers may also occur between two entirely different praxes, with again, the artifact being the focal object in the transfer. The use of sardine cans as shiny headpiece centres removes the artifact entirely from its previous field and places it in a new praxis. Here, what determines the new use relates to the already established praxes of the recipient culture. One could illustrate this just as well for early European culture. As Lynn White has shown, technologies such as 'automated prayer wheels' became, once transferred, sources of power, the windmills of early Medieval Europe.
3. Similar praxes may utilize different technologies and remain parallel. The resistance to adapt multihulls by Westerners and the counterpart resistance to monohulls by Pacific Islanders illustrate this phenomenon. Only by changing the context, the cultural trajectory itself, would adaptation occur.

What these variants show—at the social-cultural level—is that just as at the individual level technologies must be understood as human-technology pairings, so much they be conceived at the social-cultural level. Only by understanding such gestalts will we be able to both understand and perhaps better prepare for transfer.

I want to conclude with an imaginative, rather than empirical example to illustrate the often radically different cultural gestalts which nevertheless can find focus in some fascinating technological artifact. I begin with the fascination of the Early Modern Era, from the time of Descartes through even the present. This people is fascinated with automata. Their philosophical puzzles are filled with questions about how we might or might not be fooled by a cleverly contrived automaton. Is that store dummy 'real' or a clever imitation of a person? In fact, I recently twice saw—once in France, again in Germany—a bit of theatre in which, amongst automated dummies, there was a live human imitating the automatons in an inversion of the fascination. The human movements had become 'mechanical' such that one had to look twice to detect the contrivance.

Yet this same people would walk past odd assortments of boxes which would emit human voices and music (speakers and amplifiers) without showing the slightest bit of curiosity. To have a human voice come from a most inhuman artifact was *not* fascinating.

Contrarily, the New Guinean highlanders were, on first hearing a 1930's Victrola, virtually astonished at the voice in the box—and indeed, some tried to find the 'man inside'. Would they have been fascinated to have a masked dancer, similar to oneof the shamen in their own festivals but which was in fact an automaton, speak? I suspect such a phenomenon would have been far less fascinating than the voice in the box.

While the secret to these virtually inverted sets of fascination-to-familiarity lies in the equal different praxes of the two peoples, there is hidden here a deeper clue to the cultural perceptions which both allow and resist the transfers of which I have been speaking.

I have been suggesting that in the complex issue of technology transfer, not only is more involved than the transfer of some artifact, but that entire cultural gestalts are involved. Moreover, in such transfers, there is always an exchange which is itself multidimensional. Those dimensions which range from fashion to force have both points of resistance and of opening which are often and probably endemically unpredicable. This is in no way to deny that there are often assymetrical aspects to such exchanges—patterns of dominant/recessive, of dependency/exploitation—and these are obvious in certain cases. But at the same time, such exchanges are not simply reducible to either economic or political factors. Until we understand the deeper dynamics of such exchanges, we are unlikely to do more than polemicize about the role of variant technologies and the ways they are culturally embedded.

This is also to suggest that technologies in ensemble are probably more like cultures than like tools. And were we to think in these terms the whole problematic of much contemporary thought concerning technology would have to be rephrased. For example, the popular question concerning whether or not we can control technology, if thought of as parallel to a culture, would suddenly appear to be a rather misdirected question. We are rarely concerned with whether we can control a culture (indeed, whenever that question is raised it itself appears with ominous overtones in the light of recent history), yet the question of directions with a culture are in fact crucial to our social and political life. By pairing technologies as human-technology primitives, it may be possible to shift both our understanding of technology transfer and to escape what appears to me to much misdirected questioning currently dominating the debates over such issues.

Nature and Life World: Towards a Hermeneutics of Nature

R. SUNDARA RAJAN

Section I: *Turn towards the Life World*

It is quite well known that Dilthey saw himself as engaged in a continuation of the Kantian critical programme, namely, doing to the historical or cultural sciences what Kant had done to the sciences of nature. In explicit self-consciousness of this intention, Dilthey described his life-work and ambition as working out a critique of historical reason to complement Kant's own Critique of Pure Reason, which, according to him, was concerned only with the exact sciences of nature.[1] Like Kant, Dilthey too gave his programme an epistemological turn—the moving question here was about the condition of possibility of our cognition of human action.

Given that we do grasp the meanings of texts and other expressions of life, the basic question is: what are the conditions of possibility of this discursive understanding and of the correctness or validity of interpretations rather than the strictly technical procedures of understanding and interpretation? And this question of the possibility of understanding is a transcendental question and not an empirical one. The various maxims and procedural rules of right interpretation can no doubt be justified only empirically in the context of and in relation to the specific kinds of materials and the various kinds of texts and discourses they seek to understand, just as, for Kant, specific laws of connection among phenomena can and must be only empirical. But the principle and ground of possibility of such empirical laws itself cannot be empirical. Similarly here also the hermeneutical principle is the supreme principle of the possibility of understanding as such in abstraction from specific cases or forms of understanding. This principle itself cannot be an empirical—in this case, a psychological—principle. In some such way, we may say, Schleirmacher had even prior to Dilthey, opened out the vast field of transcendental hermeneutics.

Dilthey took the next decisive steps along this road. But he also recoiled from some of its implications. There is some irony in this. For Dilthey saw himself in a Kantian image; he wanted to work out a critique of cultural sciences complementary to the critique of the sciences of nature. It is important to note a number of delicate points about this project. Firstly, Dilthey was not, I think, basically contesting the idea or image of science. He was only concerned with showing how scientific, i.e., exact, cognition of human actions and human productions is possible. In their own way, human sciences are forms of exact, methodical knowledge. The point is not to question their epistemic status but to show how such a cognition is possible. In this respect, Dilthey is far removed from a contemporary philosopher like Peter Winch for whom the very idea of a social science is a questionable one.[2] In this, Dilthey was truly Kantian, asking the question of the possibility of knowledge in this domain. But in another respect, Dilthey departs radically from the Kantian programme. For, unlike Kant, Dilthey does not seem to accept fully the *a priori*/empirical, and transcendental/psychological distinctions. He does not, therefore, seek the foundations of human sciences in a transcendental critique but in rather what the calls 'descriptive psychology'.

Kant, of course, severely criticized the view that would found critical enterprise on psychology. For him, psychology, in so far as it is a science at all, presupposes the transcendental conditions of possibility of cognition and hence cannot itself supply those conditions. Kant could maintain this critical stance towards 'psychologism', because, for him, the categorial principles are constitutive of objects and in so far as psychology claims to be objective cognition of phenomena, it too must presuppose such constitutive principles. But in Dilthey, the rejection of the *a priori* carries with it the rejection of the programme of constitution also. This, in turn, has a two-fold consequence for Dilthey. Firstly, Dilthey is left with psychology as the foundational discipline. It is true that the psychology he was thinking of is not to be identified with the causal explanatory psychology of the scientific schools. Dilthey himself described it as a purely descriptive psychology, although he was not very successful in clarifying its nature and scope.[3] Secondly and more importantly, for our purpose, rejection of the constitutive programme leaves Dilthey vulnerable to a hidden positivism, as far as nature and natural objects are concerned. At times he gives the impression that facts and objects are not transcendentally constituted but empirically given. Here he takes descriptive psychology as the foundation of epistemology. In other words, he is, at this level, inclined to disregard the transcendental affiliations of epistemology. Given this orientation both the objects of cognition and the subject are to be understood within the presuppositions of an empiricist-positivistic objectivism. It is within the limits of such an ontology that we have to look for the foundations of human sciences. In other words, the hermeneutical disciplines can be conceived only as an enclave within an over all positivistic framework. Dilthey himself seems to have believed that this would be a viable mode of existence for human sciences; he seems to have believed that nature could be given over to explanation and human action to understanding. But in so far as the framework of nature is not radically questioned, such a separation of objective existence and subjective meaning could not be stable. The domain of nature too must be brought within the possibility of a hermeneutical understanding. In other words, a hermeneutics of nature and not merely a hermeneutics of understanding is what we need to ground human sciences.

The need for widening the scope of our hermeneutical perspectives may be seen in the context of two sets of considerations. Firstly, we may briefly consider the presuppositions of objectivity and inter-subjectivity and secondly, we may approach, on the basis of these reciprocal presuppositions, the notion of a hermeneutical or life-worldly understanding of nature. Recent discussions of the foundations of science, especially in the Kuhnian tradition, have clearly brought out the fact that scientific activity requires an intersubjective context, both for issues of discovery as well as for validation.[4] It is only in terms of this inter-subjective or consensual framework that we can hope to clarify the very sense of truth and objectively valid knowledge. In this sense, it is true that objectivity of our knowledge—claims presupposes a certain inter-subjective consensus. I am not merely saying that a social background or context is a factual or empirical requirement of scientific cognition, but I suggest that the notion of inter-subjective recognizability is conceptually tied to the notion of objectivity. This inner or conceptual connection between our epistemic claims and a social or inter-subjective context can be exhibited by means of a brief analysis of the meaning of cognitive claims such as 'I know P'. The accepted pattern of analysis of epistemic claims such as 'I know P' is as follows:

1. I believe P to be true.
2. I have adequate grounds for my belief.
3. P is true or it is the case that P.

I do not wish to dispute this analysis for what it is worth, but I would like to point out that when I claim to know P, it seems to me that I am, in some sense, implying not merely that I have evidence or grounds for my belief but further that I can and am willing to produce such grounds. Of course, there may be a situation in which I can waive such responsibility but it seems to me that my epistemic claim carries with it a *prima facie* obligation to produce the grounds when called for. In other words, in making the claim, I assume and accept the responsibility for proof. It is a matter for further determination whether this obligation should be incorporated into the meaning of 'knowledge' or whether it should be taken as part of the force of making an epistemic claim. We may call this sense of responsibility epistemic responsibility because here I am assuming a responsibility for proving, or for a complete certification for, what I say.[5]

But against this strong sense of epistemic responsibility, when I judge that P, I am not claiming any such compelling power on my part to demonstrate or prove my claim. But neither am I saying merely that this is what I believe. I am claiming that if I and my interlocutors should enter into a free and unrestricted dialogue, I can persuade them to accept my claim on grounds which are reasonable to be persuaded by. In other words, I am assuming a responsibility for rational persuasion by bringing out aspects of the issue in question and considerations about it in such a manner that in the course of deliberation with others which ensues out of those considerations, a consensus could be arrived at. I claim to have a right to their assent and I also accept a responsibility proportioned to that right, namely, the responsibility for making possible a reflective deliberation about the issues at stake. My judgement opens me out towards a dialogue with others in which I am willing both to persuade and be persuaded by. Judgemental responsibility, like epistemic responsibility, is an assumption of a dialogue with others. My epistemic claims are not therefore only mine; they are made on behalf of others also. They are 'judgement-with', in Aristotle's terms. In Aristotle, judgement (*gnome*) is related to *suggnome* (sympathetic understanding) and *eugnome* (the quality of being considerate).[6] The fact that the faculty of objective cognition is connected with dialogic virtues such as sympathy and consideration places the pursuit of objectivity, i.e., the sciences, in a larger framework of life with others. But what is important for our purpose is the fact that this shared sense of a common life with others is made possible only within the fame of a common environing natural world. In other words, if it is true to say that objectivity presupposes inter-subjectivity, it is equally true to say that inter-subjectivity presupposes objectivity or rather a common natural world. This aspect of the matter can be brought out by means of a brief analysis of Alfred Schutz's phenomenological descriptions of the modes of inter-subjectivity.[7]

Schutz distinguishes several modes of relationship to the other, the chief of which being the mode of fellow man, consociate, functional or impersonal role relationships, and predecessor and successor.[8] But of all these modes it is the immediate face-to-face encounter with the other, where each participant is 'bodily' present to the other, which is the basic mode in the sense that is in terms of this that the other types of inter-personal relations could be explicated, for all of them presuppose, directly or indirectly, the lived presence of the other in the relation of fellowman.[9] Now, as Schutz says, what gives a specific status to this mode of inter-subjective experience is the phenomenon of bodily presence, for here the other is present not merely with me but before me as an embodied being characterized by perceptual immediacy.[10] Now, in so far as all other modes of inter-subjectivity pre-suppose this life-worldly presence of the other, it could be said that the structures of inter-subjectivity, too, in their own way presuppose the framework of a common natural world, for, it is only within this natural framework that we can make sense of the experience of bodily presence.

Husserl brings out this environing natural world which frames both my experiencing physical objects and other ego-subjects in his description of the natural standpoint in the *Ideas*. He writes, 'I am conscious of a world endlessly spread out in space, endlessly becoming and having endlessly become. I am conscious of it; that signifies, above all, that intuitively I find it immediately, that I experience it. By my seeing, touching, hearing and so forth and in the different modes of sensuous perception, corporeal physical things are simply there for me, "on hand" in the literal or figurative sense. . . . Animate beings too—human beings, let us say, are immediately there for me. . . . They also are present as actualities in my field of intuition, even when I do not heed them. . . . In my waking consciousness I find myself in this manner at all times related to the world which remains one and the same, though changing with respect to the composition of its contents. Moreover, this world is there for me not only as a world of mere things, but also with the same immediacy as a world of objects with values, a world of goods, a practical world. This applies not only in the case of "mere physical things" but also in the case of human and brute animals belonging to my surroundings. They are my "friends", or "enemies", my "servants" or "superiors", "strangers" or "relatives", etc.

'But I do not merely find other subjects present in my world, but I experience them as related to the world before me in the same way as I am. All that which holds for me myself holds, as I know, for all other human beings whom I find present in my surrounding world. Experiencing them as human beings, I understand and accept each of them as an ego-subject just as I myself am one and related to his natural surrounding world. But I do this in such a way that their surrounding world and mine are objectively one and the same world of which we are all conscious'.[11]

It is true that this presence of the other subject as not merely an object but as an ego-subject in my life-world creates serious problems for Husserl's constitutional analysis.[12] But what is relevant for us at this point is that there is a pre-theoretical understanding of nature and that it is in terms of this life-worldly perspective that even the exact cognition of nature in the form of the natural sciences have to be situated. The explorations of these structures of the life-worldly understanding of nature may be regarded as the first or primary task of the phenomenological approach to natural sciences. But a phenomenological philosophy of natural sciences has also to describe the modes of constitution by which the theoretical world of the exact sciences have been formed on the basis of the life-world. Husserl has indicated in the *Crisis* the major lines of such a phenomenological theory of science but, as Gurwitsch notes, this has been a rather neglected area of phenomenological concern.[13]

But it is first necessary to indicate more clearly the approach of a phenomenological theory of science. From this point of view, I believe that it is the idea of a pre-theoretical life-worldly understanding of nature that is the distinctive feature of a phenomenological philosophy of science, for it is this which gives us a philosophy of nature and not merely a philosophy of natural science. Since within this life-worldly understanding, natural objects appear meaningful to human subjects, we may call this pre-theoretical understanding the hermeneutics of nature. In the first stage of the argument, I shall, in a general fashion, seek to argue for the strategic importance of such a hermeneutical understanding of nature, and at the second stage, I shall indicate the major categories involved in such a hermeneutics of the life-world.

Section II: *Towards a Hermeneutics of Nature*

Today, it is taken almost as a self-evident truth that it is the natural sciences which are the final arbiters of all possible knowledge of nature. The realm of nature is the object domain of the sciences and any cognitive claim about nature must therefore be consistent with and warrantable by the methods of scientific inquiry. Given this first-order primacy, philosophy of science can, it is held, only be a conceptual clarification and interpretation of the logic of inquiry. Philosophers may analyze the conceptual structures of explanation and the logical stratification of the fundamental concepts of sciences but natural sciences, together with a conceptually articulated interpretation of them, alone give us a complete and closed self-reflective understanding of nature.

Nature is what the sciences disclose it to be, mediated by a philosophical analysis of the discourse of sciences. There does not seem to be either a ***need*** or a *possibility* of a philosophy of nature which would belong to another level or type of discourse altogether. Or, to put it somewhat differently, philosophy's concern with nature must be a mediated concern in the form of a philosophy of natural sciences, rather than in the form of a philosophy of nature.[14]

It may be objected that this conclusion follows only if one accepts the empiricist's concept of science, and that, given the realist's concept, there may be an altogether different conclusion. But I want to suggest that, even on a realistic understanding of science, the prospects of a distinctive and autonomous philosophy of nature are not very bright. On a realistic understanding, natural science is, in itself, an inquiry into the nature of the fundamental entities, processes, powers and structures of the natural world. In this sense, natural science is itself a philosophy of nature, but it is as *science* that it gives us such a knowledge of nature and the question remains whether philosophy can give us an independent understanding of the world. If the empiricistic view too radically separates science from philosophy, the realistic view seems to identify them too closely, and I feel that the possibility of a distinct philosophical understanding of nature is precluded by both. Whatever may be their differences, both realism and empiricism seem to have a common presupposition, namely, that nature is what sciences disclose it to be. It is this presupposition which closes off the possibility of a distinctive philosophy of nature. In the movement towards an autonomous philosophy of nature, it is with this presupposition that one must begin.

In other words, I am suggesting in other words, that we consider the philosophical importance of our pre-scientific knowledge of nature. I am, of course, not merely pointing out that there is such a pre-theoretical understanding of nature. What I want to suggest is the epistemological primacy or cognitive normativeness of such an understanding. If science is a disclosure of the world, it cannot cut itself off permanently from the implicitly governing pre-understanding of reality which is inscribed in our life-worldly experience of nature. This life-worldly understanding includes within itself the sense of reality and the sense of significance of nature for us; i.e. it provides the implicit framework of understanding of what it is to be a real object and what meaning or significance the reality of an object has for human experience. These two aspects of *reality* and *significance*, correspond in a general way, to what Husserl calls the internal and external horizons of our perception of things in the natural attitude. In *Experience and Judgement* Husserl describes the internal horizon as pertaining to the possible characterizations of the object itself and the external horizon as the relations of the object with other objects and ultimately with the world 'as the horizon of all individual real things capable of being experienced'.[15] The structures making up the internal horizon predelineate our sense of reality of natural objects, while the structures of the external horizon contextualize the object in terms of the relational manifolds in which it is experienced. But the two, the internal and the external horizons, are not, however, to be taken in isolation; rather they together constitute our life-worldly understanding of nature and it is these structures which provide the basis for all other objectifications of exact sciences. But these modes of understanding of nature are themselves complex articulations; we may accordingly speak of the archaeology of the life-world, by which we may mean the various levels of articulations of sense by which the sense of reality as well as the significance of that reality for us is made available. It seems to me that it is one of the fundamental tasks of a phenomenological theory of science to explore these structures of sense which are built into our life-worldly understanding of nature. The fundamental method of such an investigation is what Husserl describes as the method of correlational analysis. But as Gurwitsch points out there is a problem which arises at the very beginning of life-world analysis.[16]

In the *Crisis* Husserl had argued that the life-world as it is given in immediate experience has been occluded and concealed under a tissue of constructions belonging to mathematical science of nature. 'Something which is truly a method or rather the result of a method is taken to be true being while the life-world has been taken as a subjective phenomenon.'[17] But when a science becomes oblivious of its 'originating' presuppositions, Husserl tells us, it loses its intelligibility in the philosophical sense. To restore the sense of modern science, we must therefore withdraw from these constructions. This withdrawal does not mean merely not using certain concepts and principles—what is required is fundamentally a new style of thinking. But the life-world to which this new style gives us access is not given merely as a world of nature but as an intrinsically social or cultural world.[18] But if the life-world is given as an intrinsically cultural world, then the deconstruction of scientific interpretability does not lead to the merely perceptual world in its purity but rather to the natural world interpreted in a certain socio-historical way. And this means that the said deconstruction leads us to an interpretation of the world that has been formed by our own history and culture.

The attempt to move away from the Galilean style of thinking leads us paradoxically to or own contemporary interpretation of the life world, which is, historically speaking, the outcome of the very scientific formation we are attemtping to move away from. In this sense, there arises the problem of the possibility of transcending history by way of phenomenological reflection. Furthermore, if different socio-historical periods have their own specific life-worlds, then merely the theme of the life-world by itself cannot overcome relativism. In other words, the theme of the life-world, for all its intrinsic importance, cannot be the ultimate problem of a phenomenological theory of science. On the contrary, it is precisely the theme of the life-world that sets the tasks for a phenomenological reflection on sciences.[19] Given any specific life-world, we must retrace the acts of consciousness by which precisely such a world becomes inter-subjectively formed. These acts, of course, are not simple or elementary; rather they are complex systems and series of acts of different orders—perceptual, memorial, anticipatory, evaluative and so on. It is through these complex noetic structures that a cultural world is presented. The systematic description of these acts and their function in building up a cultural world may be called constitutive anthropology. But it is possible to go beyond the relativistic presuppositions of even such a constitutive anthropology, as Husserl himself suggested in his debate with Dilthey in *Philosophy as a Rigorous Science*.[20] He argued, in effect, that whatever differences there may be in different cultural worlds and in the corresponding cultural mentalities, the correlation between the two is itself *a priori*. However, it appears to me that this response to relativism is excessively formal and abstract. Perhaps we could take a more concrete step if we could describe certain universal structures of consciousness that make possible a cultural world as the life-world of a socio-historical group. If that is possible, we would have described the conditions of the possibility of culture as such. These universal structures would give us an idea of the invariant necessities which each specific cultural world would exemplify in its own specific and characteristic way. In fact, in his *Experience and Judgment* as well as in his *Formal and Transcendental Logic* Husserl himself seems to be suggesting that there is a structure or core common to all life-worlds,[21] but this core cannot be seen as the so-called objective-scientific universe. We may say that what Husserl is seeking to explore in these investigations are the necessary structures of every possible life-world, under the guidance of the fundamental principle of the noetic-noematic correlation. Since this is the regulative *a priori* of his analysis, he calls it the 'Universal Correlations *a priori*'.[22] Husserl's correlational analysis proceeds in two inter-connected steps: firstly, he describes certain basic structural features of the life-world with the intention of showing them to be the invariant aspects of any possible life-world. This may be called the *noematic pole* of the analysis. Secondly, in so far as any and every noematic feature or aspect is presented by way of specific acts which are correlated with it, the analysis turns to the subjective or *noetic pole*. Here he describes the complex connections and combinations of the acts of consciousness by which the invariant structures are constituted.

Since these structures are claimed to be embedded in any possible life-world, they are *a priori* to any such world but the sense in which they are *a priori* is very different from the *a priori* elements in a scientific theory. Husserl calls them 'life-worldly *a priori*'[23] and describes their investigation as 'transcendental aesthetics', in a sense similar to, but not identical with, that of Kant.[24] Transcendental aesthetics in Husserl's sense is concerned with 'the eidetic problem of any possible world as a world given in pure experience' and is to provide 'the eidetic description of the all embracing *a priori*, without which no object could appear as an object'.[25] Husserl further describes its task as 'the disengagement of the logos of the perceptual world'.[26] In commenting upon this programme, Gurwitsch describes this logicality as 'proto-logic' and claims that the various steps which lead from such a proto-logic to logic in the formal and systematic sense is an area seldom explored in phenomenological discussions.[27] I shall use the idea of internal and external horizons as organizing principles in terms of which we may further explore some of the structural features of the logicality pervading our perceptual experiences. As already pointed out, the internal horizon indicates certain dimensions or aspects of our experience of natural objects which constitute our working criteria of reality or objectivity of such experiences. It is in terms of these aspects that we make sense of the concept of physical reality. But it is not these aspects separately but taken together that they predelineate the conception of reality.

THE INTERNAL HORIZON

According to Gurwitsch, spatiality, temporality and habituality are the pre-dominant aspects in terms of which we experience physical objects.[28] Things encountered in the life-world have spatial shapes but these are to be taken as 'physiognomic types' rather than approximations to ideal geometrical figures; similar remarks apply to the temporality of things, their duration, motion and change. By 'habituality' Husserl means the changes which take place in the life-world; things, we may say, have 'habits' of regularly behaving in typical ways under typical conditions, but these regularities are not to be understood as invariant functional relations expressible in the form of mathematical equations. In all these characterizations, the use of natural types of shape, motion and change are involved. As in the social world, so also here in our life-worldly dealing with the natural world, it is by way of types that we make sense of our experiences; in this sense, 'typification' is one of the basic modes of constitution.[29]

It is true that it is within the framework of spatio-temporality that we experience the specific 'reality' or 'objectivity' of physical objects, but this phenomenon of reality within the framework of spatio-temporal principles has yet to be articulated. In other words, I am suggesting that there are certain more specific noetic-noematic clues to the phenomenon of reality or objectivity. We may call such indices or clues the noematic *sinn* of physical objects, for according to Husserl's theory of intentional reference, it is the meaning or *sinn* of the noema that prescribes the object.[30] Hence it may be useful at this stage to have a brief overview of Husserl's theory of noetic-noematic correlation since the clues of objectivity, as we may call them, are part of the noematic *sinn* of a perceptual act. We may represent the phenomenological content of a perceptual act as follows:

Phenomenological Content

- Noesis
  - Real Quality (thetic phase)
  - Real Matter (sinn-giving phase)
- Noema
  - Ideal Quality (thetic component)
  - Ideal Matter (*sinn*)

It is to be noted that the noema is not the intended object itself, but rather that by way of which the object is intended (in scholastic terms, the noema is not an *id quod cogniscitur* but an *id quo cogniscitur*).[31] We may also say that the noema is transcendental, while the object is transcendent (in this characterization, it is to be noted that while the term 'transcendental' has clear Kantian connotations, the term 'transcendent', as used here, departs from the Kantian usage of 'transcendent'). 'The transcendent' here is not something outside experience altogether but precisely that to which experience points. Our question is precisely what are the indications in the noema itself by means of which the transcendency of the object is acknowledged.

If the noema is to serve as a medium of access to the transcendent object, it must be conceived as analogous to the sense of an expression, i.e., somewhat as a sense determines the referent in Frege, so also the noema of an act must be thought of as prescribing the object to which the act is directed.[32] And it is indeed with this analogy in mind that Husserl extends the notion of meaning to acts also. 'Originally these words (i.e. sense, meaning etc.) have reference only to the linguistic sphere, the sphere of expressions. However, it is virtually unavoidable and at the same time an important step forward in knowledge to enlarge the meanings of these words and to suitably modify them whereby they find application to the entire noetic, noematic spheres, that is, in all acts, whether they are bound up with acts of expressions or not'.[33] Accordingly, Husserl speaks of the meaning component of the noema of an act as its noematic *sinn*. This is important for us for it is within the noematic meaning that we can find the indices of the transcendency of the object. In other words, the noema is the means by which we interpret the objectivity of the physical object.

Turning to a more discriminating analysis of the noematic meaning itself, Husserl distinguishes within this nucleus or kernel, two components, the X-component and the component of predicative sense.[34] The predicate senses prescribe the properties an object is intended as having and the X-component prescribes the object to which the properties are ascribed. Taken together, the two components determine a specific object as having various attributes and determinations. The predicate senses are themselves quite complex. They include, among other things, (i) sensuous determinations such as 'green', 'hard', 'soft', etc., (ii) indeterminate characterizations such as 'having a backside', etc., (iii) material-ontological expressions such as 'thing', 'figure', 'cause', etc., and (iv) formal ontological determinations such as 'object', 'attribute', etc.[35] Besides these explicit components in the noematic meaning, there are also certain implicit components of sense which make up what Husserl calls the object-horizon and the act-horizon of the noematic *sinn*.[36] Given any specific perceptual act in which an object is intended in a certain way, the very content of the act itself shows the object as having many more properties and determinations which are given only in a pre-figurative way in the act itself. For example, the object may be perceived as an apple tree but in the perception itself there is, as it were, a pre-figuration of further unspecified properties such as having fruits, on both the front and the back, as harbouring various kinds of birds, etc. These are further determinations of the object and they fill out in explicit detail some of the characteristics included in the meaning of the original act. These further possible properties and characterizations which spell out the implicit content of the original act, Husserl calls the object-horizon, while those further acts which could realize these further possibilities he calls the act-horizon.[37] Both the act and the object horizons give expression to the transcendency of the object of perception.

But it is not only the meaning components of the noema that provide a clue to the experience of reality or objectivity, but the other aspects of the noema such as its thetic correlate are also functional in building up the significance of the experience of reality. By the thetic component we mean the way of givenness of the content of the experience. In the case of a perceptual experience, for example, aspects such as perceptual givenness, its attentional clarity, etc., would be included in the thetic component. These 'adverbial' aspects of the act, so to say, also contribute to the experience of perceptual objectivity.

Apart from the thetic component, we must also keep in mind the role of what Husserl calls the X-component in this context. Unlike the predicate senses, this part of the noematic meaning does not have any descriptive or characterizing function. On the contrary, the role of the X-component is to provide a centre of unification for all the predicate senses. The object is intended, not merely as a collection or sum of its properties and attributes, as Hume would have it, but as an integration or synthetic unity of the properties. It is this idea which is expressed in the X-component in the noematic *sinn*.[38]

But this component of sense has another function also. In every act, the object is intended as having further properties which could be realized in further possible acts. These possible acts make up the act-horizon. Now, these possible acts within the act-horizon are anticipated as bearing upon the same object; they are co-directed acts in the sense of intending the same object but specifying it in different ways. The co-directedness of a set of possible acts is expressed by the fact that all of them have the same X-component in the noematic *sinn*.[39] It is thus that the X-component secures the identity of the object in and through different characterizations of it.

But there is an even more sublte way in which the act and the object-horizons build up our sense of reality of physical objects. The object-horizon includes those further properties and characteristics of the object which are (i) compatible with the presently given perception and (ii) which fill out the indefinite pre-delineations of the present experience.[40] Now (ii) does not include only perceptual characteristics but all forms of characterizations compatible with the present perceptual experience of the object.[41] In other words, the object-horizon indicates the possible situations and ultimately the possible worlds in which the currently given object could occur as a constituent of true characterizations.[42] The object-horizon expresses the sense that this object which here and now I am seeing is yet capable of transcending the act in which it is given to me; its reality or objectivity precisely means the independence of the immanent. I intend the object as transcending not only my current perceptions of it but also in a stronger sense as transcending the boundaries of my experience itself and as being available to others. The object-horizon expresses the inter-subjective accessibility of the perceptual world.

Similarly, within the act-horizon also Husserl includes not merely further possible perceptions but also all other acts bearing upon the same object and even, more importantly, the acts of others co-directed upon this object. Like the object-horizon, the act-horizon, too articulates the sense of a shared reality. But I would like to suggest an even more fundamental way in which Husserl's later theory of horizons in the *Cartesian Meditations*, for example, articulates the sense of an objective reality of nature within the life-world.[43] Within the horizon of sense are included, on the one hand, my very general categorial and conceptual belief systems bearing upon the understanding of nature (i.e. the culturally formed meanings and interpretations of nature which are in the background of my experience) as well as certain purely individual and personal significances and value-tones which the object has for me.[44] For example, I experience this tree as not merely an apple tree but as the last tree my father planted in this garden. In so far as my perceptual experience is thus modulated by my past, the object becomes expressive of my moods, sentiments and sense of life.

This is important for us to note for in the life-world, human beings experience nature not merely as set over against them but also as their 'place' and home, they find as themselves participants in its reality and not merely its observers. The natural world includes the human subjects but not as parts or elements but as perceiving, cognizing and meaning-giving subjects. There is a participatory as well as an expressive relationship, or better still, a bond between consciousness and its world such that that human beings find nature in its lived immediacy a proper support and base for their practical as well as symbolic intentionalities. It is this richly textured experience of nature in the life-world that I am thinking of as the hermeneutics of nature (perhaps such a project would be closer to Merleau-Ponty than Husserl himself in the strict sense). In the next section, I hope to articulate some of the basic interpretative categories of such a hermeneutics of nature.

Section III: *Nature and the Life-World*

In the life-world, human subjects experience natural objects in three modes—firstly, as realities set over against them; but secondly, as the basis and foundation of their common world and, thirdly, as expressive of personal uniqueness and individuality. These three modes may be called the modes of transcendence, participation and intimacy respectively.

THE MODE OF TRANSCENDENCE

Natural entities and powers are experienced as things and forces to be met with or encountered. This sense of offering a resistance as something to be reckoned with is the primordial meaning of 'objectness'. Natural entities are not merely spatial in the sense of having spatial shapes, but they are felt to be things to be met with in space. This may be called the aspect of facticity, in which objects are presented as being there before us, before we arrive on the scene as it were. This aspect of being antecedently there carries with it the sense of perduring or enduring through change. Real objects have an aspect of substantiality about them. But the substantiality of things should not be understood abstractly in the sense of a bare indifferent substratum; the substantiality of concrete objects is not a Lockean 'I know not what' but rather a synthetic unity of properties and powers. The substantiality of things is the symbolic of the dynamic and relational unity of things.

Because of this dynamic and synthetic unity, the various attributes and powers of things conform to certain regularities and types of orderly process. It is this rule-connectedness which is the foundation of what Husserl calls the habituality of things in the life-world.[45] Things, we may say, display characters in the sense of settled dispositions, although, in exceptional circumstances, it may appear that they too, like human subjects, act out of character. This orderliness of things we may call nomological coherence, a certain type of order and pattern that persists in things in different situations or conditions. Like in the human case, consistency or coherence in the sense of a settled pattern of reactions is a mark of reality here also.

Because of this rule-connectedness or nomological coherence, objects are experienced as being the same under different perspectives. As we saw, it is this consistency which is expressed in the possibility of co-directed acts. To be real, we may now say, is to be the referent of co-directed acts. This means that the object is identically the same in different states, conditions or relations into which it may enter. We may call this the aspect of perceptual invariance.

It is these aspects of facticity, subtantial nomological coherence and perceptual invariance, which constitute the experience of transcendence. For Husserl, the sense of transcendence is given in our experience itself, for every perception of a real object is merely a perception of an aspect of it, for no object can be fully characterized in a perceptual act. Its depth is virtually inexhaustible. On the side of experience, there is a feeling of incompleteness, while on the side of the object, there is a compelling indication of its inexhaustibility. This sense of the object always surpassing our experience is an essential note of the reality of things. Thus Husserl writes '... the perception of a physical thing involves a certain inadequacy of necessity; a physical thing can be given only "one sidedly" ... a physical thing is necessarily given in mere "modes of appearance" ... necessarily there always remains a horizon of determinable indeterminateness, no matter how far we go in our experience. No god can alter that no more than the circumstance that $1+2=3$, or that any other eidetic truth obtains."[46]

It is this felt transcendency that interprets a certain experience as the experience of something real. Natural objects, and also nature as a whole, are thus experienced as transcendent. But this surpassing of our experience is not a frustration of cognition; it is not experienced as the intrusion of the random and the arbitrary. Rather, the previous aspects that we mentioned, particularly the aspects of substantiality, nomological coherence and perceptual invariance give the mode of transcendency a positive connotation as the symbol of the depth dimension of our experience of nature. This feeling of being in contact with an inexhaustible source of order and coherence is perhaps the peak moment in the career of science itself. In a sense we could even describe this experience of transcendency as the *telos* of science.

But in the life-world, nature is perceived not merely as transcendent, as something set over against us. Much more primordially, nature is presented as the environing home that supports our shared forms of life; nature is the ontological foundation of being-with. It is in terms of a common natural world that mere co-existence of consciousness is transformed into a co-presence, for it is nature that supports all our communicative practices; the carriers of human sense and meaning are utlimately the objects and events of the natural world. But nature does not merely function as the external mechanism of communication; it is also the ground of possibility of common actions. In this sense, only a natural being could be a social being. All specifically human cultural significations have a natural basis, for culture itself is a specifically human symbolic response to the structures of transcendence that we mentioned a while ago. If science could be seen as a cognitive response to the dimensions of transcendence, art and religion too could be seen as a response to the primordial structure of being in the world. But the life-worldly experience of nature also provides the natural foundation for the sense of history. I find myself living in a world in which the ideas and aspirations of past generations have been sedimented; I live in a world of material productions of the past and I am also conscious that the generations who will come after me would also find themselves in such a sedimented world. It is this material continuity which functions as the effective symbol of continuing history. In this manner, nature in the life-world is also experienced in the mode of participation. And today, we experience the threat to this sense of participation most acutely as the threat to the environment which is the natural basis of that sense of participation.

But human subjects experience nature in a more interior way in the form of the lived immediacy of their own bodies. Existential phenomenologists like Merleau-Ponty have particularly emphasized the crucial role of embodiment in all our acts, symbolic as well as behavioural. It is this mode of presence of nature in the form of the lived body that I call the aspect of intimacy. But 'embodiment' may be taken for our purpose, in a larger extended sense as well as in the strict sense of the term. In a larger sense, even external things like tools and implements to which we have been habituated, our own past and even familiar trees and plants and particularly animals could be appropriated in the mode of intimacy. Polanyi calls this intimate appropriation 'knowing by indwelling'. Human consciousness, in these modes, develops a certain rapport with things and, on the basis of that intimacy, it develops skills of tact and subliminal discrimination and also the capacity to invest natural objects with personal significance. The first, the phenomenon of tact, is at the bottom of all human powers of craftmanship, while the second is the root of the symbolic expressiveness of art and literature. In their developed forms, these traits appear to be exclusive only to the gifted few but these are universal natural human possibilities. Consider, for example, the use of animal fables and stories in all cultures to convey psychological and social insights.

This inwardness and intimate presence of nature functions as a sort of counter-point to the first mode of transcendence. But, in fact, all these three modes reciprocally determine each other such that the understanding of nature that results reflects all the three. In fact, it is precisely this compresence of all the three modes of transcendence, participation and intimacy which distinguishes the life-worldly experience of nature and it is precisely the elucidation of the compresence of all these modes within the life-world that is the fundamental theme of a phenomenological philosophy of nature.

From this point of view, it is somewhat surprising that the theme of the life-world, for all its significance, does not seem to have been used to the full range of its promise in Husserl's *Crisis*. In that text, the life-world functions within a critical horizon, as a contrastive idea to the theoretical constructivism of modern science. It is certainly true that the idea of life-world does have this critical salience but left alone by itself, it may give rise to a certain doubt as to whether science would be possible at all without man's alienation from the life-world. It is, therefore, necessary to use the theme of the life-world more positively as indicating the shapes of alternative configurations of science. From this point of view, I would like to suggest that particularly in the context of our present concern with ecological sciences, the philosophical-phenomenological theme of the life-worldly understanding of nature as sketched above may have some relevance. Today, it is being increasingly realized that merely a causal or correlational understanding of man and environment would not be adequate to deal with the problems that we face in this context; it is also necessary to understand the formation of subjective perceptions and life-styles. For this purpose, environment is to be seen as providing certain themes of orientation which different cultures build up into distinctive life-worlds. The meaning of the environment, the kind of patterned experiences it provides and the subjective aspect of the quality of life which is congruent with that kind of meaning of nature—these are the new issues of the new ecology. Of course, the fact that we are concerned with the role and influence of images of the environment need not in the least imply that the environment is effective only by way of such subjective factors. The objective causal role of the environment, the dominant theme of environmental sciences, need not be denied but what requires to be seen is that the proper understanding of this role is possible only on the basis of a prior phenomenological understanding of the environment. In this sense, the theme of the life-world could be used for developing an ecological hermeneutics.

NOTES AND REFERENCES

1. For a fuller discussion of the Kantian background of Dilthey's hermeneutics, see *Towards A critique of Cultural Reason*, R. Sundara Rajan, Pt. 4, Sec. 2, Oxford University Press, 1987.
2. Peter Winch, *The Idea of Social Science,* London, Routledge & Kegan Paul, 1958.
3. R. Sundara Rajan, op. cit. 117–118.
4. Thomas Kuhn, *The Structure of Scientific Revolutions*, Chicago, Chicago University Press, 1970.

5. For a more elaborate discussion of epistemic and judgemental responsibility, see my *The Primacy of the Political* (forthcoming but available in mimeographed form at the Department of Philosophy, Univesity of Poona, Pune, India).
6. Aristotle, The Nichomachian Ethics, Book Z 1143a 20, tr., H.G. Apostle Dodrecht, D. Reidel Publishing Company, 1975.
7. Alfred Schutz and Thomas Luckman, *The Structures of the Life World*, tr. Richard M. Zaner and H. Tristram Engelhardt, Evanston, North Western University Press, 1973.
8. *Ibid.*
9. *Ibid.*
10. *Ibid.*
11. Edmund Husserl, *Ideas*, tr., F. Kersten, Sec. 27, pp. 51–52.
12. For a critical discussion of this issue, see Tran Duc Thao *Phenomenology and Dialectical Materialism*, tr., Daniel J. Harman and Donald V. Morano Chap. II, Secs. I and II, D. Dordrecht, Reidel Publishing Company, 1986.
13. Aron Gurwitsch, *Phenomenology and the Theory of Science*, Evanston, North Western University Press, 1974, p. 31.
14. For a further discussion of this presupposition, see my *Towards a Critical Philosophy of Nature in Rationality and Philosophy* (ed.) V.K. Bharadwaj, New Delhi, Northern Book Centre, 1984.
15. Aron Gurwitsch notes that while the idea of internal and external horizons is present in the *Ideas* (Sec. 27), yet the theme is most fully treated in *Experience and Judgement* (Secs. 8 and 22) and *Cartesian Meditations.*
16. Aron Gurwitsch, *Phenomenology and the Theory of Science*, pp. 19–20.
17. Edmund Husserl, *The Crisis of the European Sciences and Transcendental Phenomenology* (trans.) David Carr, p. 51, Evanston, North Western 1970.
18. Aron Gurwitsch, *Phenomenology and the Theory of Science*, p. 20, Evanston, North Western Univesity Press, 1974.
19. *Ibid.*
20. Edmund Husserl, 'Philosophy as a Rigorous Science' in *Phenomenology and the Crisis of Philosophy*, (trans.) Quentin Lauer, N.Y., 1965.
21. Aron Gurwitsch, *Phenomenology and the Theory of Science*, p. 25.
22. In the *Ideas* Husserl describes this feature as 'equivalent of consciousness', while in *The Crisis* he describes it as 'universal correlations A priori'.
23. Edmund Husserl, *The Crisis*, Sec. 51.
24. Edmund Husserl, *Formal and Transcendental Logic*, (trans.) Dorion Cairns, The Hague: Martinus Nijhof, 1969.
25. *Ibid.*
26. *Ibid.*
27. Aron Gurwitsch, *Phenomenology and the Theory of Science*, p. 30.
28. *Ibid.*, pp. 48–55.
29. Edmund Husserl, *Experience and Judgement*, Sec. 83, p. 331, (Trans.) James S. Churchill and Karl Ameriks, Evanston, North Western University Press, 1933.
30. Edmund Husserl, *Logical Investigations I* (trans.) J.N. Findlay, Sec. 13, p. 289, Humanities Press, 1970.
31. Theodore De Boer, *The Development of Husserl's Thought*, pp. 43–45, (trans.) Theodore Plantinga, Martinus Nijhoff, 197.
32. Basing Themselves on Falesdal, David Woodruff Smith and Ronald MacIntyre develop an extended comparison of Frege and Husserl on sense and reference in their *Husserl and Intentionality*, chapter IV, Boston, D. Deidel Publishing Co., 1982.
33. Edmund Husserl, *Ideas*, p. 107.
34. *Ibid.*, Secs. 130 and 131.
35. *Ibid.*
36. David Woodruff Smith and Ronald MacIntyre, in *Husserl and Intentionality*, Chapter V

remark that the notion of horizon first emerges seriously in *Ideas* and finds its nature formulation in the *Cartesian Meditations*.

37. Edmund Husserl, *Ideas*, Sec. 47.
38. *Ibid.*, Sec. 131.
39. *Ibid.*
40. *Ibid.*, p. 315.
41. *Ibid.*
42. *Ibid.*, Sec. 135.
43. Edmund Husserl, *Cartesian Meditations*.
44. Edmund Husserl, *Experience and Judgement*, Sec. 25, pp. 122–23.
45. Edmund Husserl, *Ideas*, Sec. 142.
46. *Ibid.*, Sec. 44, pp. 94–95.

Unity and Plurality of Cultures in the Perspectives of Edmund Husserl and Ernst Cassirer

ERNST WOLFGANG ORTH

The themes 'culture' and 'human being,' science of culture and anthropology became increasingly important for philosophy in the nineteen-twenties. The writings of Max Scheler, Martin Heidegger, and Helmuth Plessner bear witness to the importance these themes came to acquire at that time. The thematizing of 'human being' and 'culture' has to be seen together: for man shows up within a culture; and, vice versa culture has to be understood as man's world. Thus there was a need to establish the name 'cultural anthropology' (*Kulturanthropologie*) as the title of a discipline connecting the two features.

The term 'Kulturanthropologie' was introduced in Germany in 1942 by Erich Rothacker.[1] In the English speaking countries, especially in North-America, the term 'cultural anthropology' had been used earlier. It was already an established term in the nineteen–twenties, denoting the empirically oriented discipline of ethnology.

In Germany, cultural anthroplogy was—already before bearing this title—a comprehensive philosophical anthropology. The best example of philosophical anthropology may, perhaps, be found in the works of Helmuth Plessner, whose important work from 1928 '*Die Stufen des Organischen und der Mensch*[2] received far too little attention.

Initially the thematization of human being and culture seems, however, to bring forth a tendency against philosophy, although it is called philosophical anthropology. Instead of being called philosophical, anthropology, it should rather be called '*geisteswissenschaftlich*' or human-scientific anthropology since it is characterized by gathering of empirical knowledge about man and his world, a knowledge which is accumulated by the humanities and social sciences. Empirical knowledge is gathered in order to gain an understanding of the factual human being and of factual culture. And thus this so-called philosophical cultural anthropology often turns against the central disciplines of philosophy itself: against metaphysics which it deems too speculative, against logic which it deems too formal, and against epistemology which it deems too abstract. This new approach is supposed to bring a concretion which nevertheless is often obtained at the cost of relativism or uncritical objectivism.

In this situation it is of specific significance that the interest in cultural-anthropological questions and approaches also emerges in the writings of those philosophers whose genuine domain consists in strictly epistemological interests, and who insist on the necessity of a first philosophy although they reject traditional metaphysics. Here I think of representatives of transcendental philosophy such as Edmund Husserl, the phenomenologist, and Ernst Cassirer, the Neo-Kantian.

With his intentional-analytical phenomenology of consciousness, Husserl develops a transcendental philosophy as first philosophy. Cassirer achieves a comparable result. Starting from the Neo-Kantian philosophy of consciousness, he develops a philosophy of symbolic forms which is not merely the title of his *opus magnum*,[3] but also the general title of all of his philosophical works after 1920. Cassirer himself also characterizes them as works on philosophy of culture.

In this context we have to consider the fact that transcendental philosophy since Descartes has rigorously observed the rule not to confound transcendental questions with psychological or anthropological ones. In Husserl this is manifest in his struggle against psychologism and in Cassirer we can see it in his criticism of anthropomorphism. But, curiously enough, in Husserl one can also find warnings against inappropriate fears in regard to psychologism,[4] and Cassirer even favours a transcendental anthropomorphism in opposition to the usual (psychological) anthropologism.[5] To me this seems due to a peculiar double-motivation which has existed in modern transcendental philosophy from the very first. *On the one hand*, transcendental philosophy presupposes a decided thematizing of the human being, i.e., of human subjectivity; it counts on—to speak in Dilthey's terms—the 'principle of phenomenality' (*Satz der Phänomenalität*) which means that every knowledge about the world is knowledge within human consciousness, and that this consciousness is itself the only entity which the human being can be sure of authentically in an evident act of awareness. Husserl called this 'a distinctive state of affairs' in *Ideas I*.[6] In Cassirer's view it is the self-givenness of consciousness which can neither be submitted to, nor is it in need of, causal analysis since the self-givenness of consciousness itself is the first basis of this analysis.

On the other hand, transcendental philosophy is at the same time forced of neglect this human being in its concrete factual reality although it is the ground of every rationality and of every understanding of the world in its capability to experience, in its reasonableness, and in its freedom. In Husserl's thinking this finds expression in his doctrine of the reduction to pure structures of consciousness; in Cassirer this shows in the exposition of pure functions of knowledge. Transcendental philosophy seems to thematize the human being as the starting point of analysis only in order immediately to leave behind the human being as a concrete being. What is at stake are pure structures and functions of consciousness as such—and not the concrete human being. At a first glance it is even plausible that reliable (transcendental) structures of truth cannot be derived epistemologically from a contingent fact, namely from the concretely existing human being who (moreover) appears very different in different cultures. Only if it would turn out that the human being—although a fact—is not a fact among others, but a fact *sui generis*, the relationship of transcendental philosophy to human reality could change.

And this is precisely the discovery which is made by Husserl and by Cassirer—in their characteristic ways.

Husserl sets forth the new conception of cultural anthropology by deepening his concept of intentionality and of reduction, and Cassirer by further developing the concept of function to the more precise concept of symbolic formation without giving up the claims of transcendental philosophy.

The double-sidedness of this new conception of a transcendental philosophy can be explained as developing out of two different interests which at a first glance seem to be contradictory:

1. The critical philosophy of Husserl and Cassirer starts from the insight that reality is a field of phenomena which is intentionally mediated, i.e., apprehended, and functionally mediated, i.e., apprehended, and functionally constituted. Consciousness is the non-derivable quintessence of apprehension. The pure structures of this apprehension are the criteria for every knowledge concerning reality. Pointing to merely ontical or ontological facts is of no help here, and turns out to be dogmatic; and moreover it already presupposes the effectiveness of subjectivity. In this sense, Cassirer refers to Kant's dictum: 'the proud name of an ontology . . . has to make way for the modest one of a mere analytics of the understanding'.[7] Accordingly, it is the meaning of the transcendental reduction in Husserl to focus on the pure structures of the apprehension of reality. And this means to bracket this reality including its ontological claims, and to regard it as a mere field of phenomena. The worldliness of consciousness, i.e. the usual ontological belief, turns out to be a kind of transcendental delusion.[8]

2. But we also have to ask whether those structures of the apprehending consciousness which are characterized as pure and fundamental are actually conceived adequately as pure structures in the transcendental analysis, since these structures are always performed by the individual concrete human being. And thus it could be possible that analysis arrives at these structures, as it were, precipitatingly, and fails to notice essential single features. Consequently, Husserl says in *Crisis*: 'Idealism always proceeded too hastily in its theories, and often could not liberate itself from hidden objectivistic presuppositions. Or, as a speculative one, it left out that task of investigating concretely and analytically the factual subjectivity, as it intuitively affirms the actual phenomenal world. This task is—properly understood—nothing else but the performance of phenomenological reduction and bringing into play transcendental phenomenology.[9] Thus it is the deepening of the idea of reduction itself which leads Husserl to investigate subjectivity in its concreteness in order to avoid arriving too hastily at a theory of the transcendental forms. The worldliness of consciousness is hence not only transcendental delusion but as much an unavoidable determination of this consciousness.

Kant's analytics of the understanding as it is taken up by Cassirer can be compared analogously to Husserl's reduction. Cassirer retains this Kantian analytics, but he explicitly extends it from the so-called understanding (*Verstand*, in the Kantian sense) to 'the whole range of the comprehension of the world', i.e. like Husserl he wants to deal with all aspects of the actuality of the subject in its concreteness.[10] Here Cassirer explicitly refers to the increase of knowledge about the effective subjectivity as we know it from the development of the human and social sciences since the nineteenth century which Kant could not take into consideration at his time. Also for Husserl the human sciences (*die Geisteswissenschaften*) gain a privileged function for their more differentiated and more concrete access to subjectivity. Thus Husserl formulates already in 1917. 'Not the natural sciences, but the human sciences are disciplines which lead into 'philosophical' depths'.[11]

The two above mentioned interests are connected by Husserl's doctrine of the cogitative types in the context of his method of reductions, and by Cassirer's theorem of the symbolic forms.

Herewith Husserl and Cassirer corroborate Dilthey's thesis that the self-reassurance of consciousness in an evident 'becoming aware' (*inne-werden*) can only be effected by an actual human being as a member of a culture.[12] But, whereas Dilthey put this at the beginning of his analyses merely in the form of a thesis because he felt that the abstract epistemological subjects of Locke, Hume, and Kant were bloodless creatures,[13] Husserl and Cassirer substantiated this thesis in their comprehensive and detailed transcendental analyses. Initially, the transcendental philosophers, Husserl and Cassirer, had also taken into consideration only the pure structures and functions of subjectivity, disregarding the concrete acting human being. But Husserl's cogitative types and Cassirer's symbolic forms can be seen as configurations of consciousness-world relations according to which a mere consciousness as only an abstract aggregate of structures and functions is unthinkable. Consciousness is always intentionally connected with the world as it is meant or, in other words, it concretely exists in a symbolic form as a correlation of form and matter.

In the *Cartesian Meditations* Husserl at first conceives the cogitative types as the structures of intentional consciousness which are discovered by reduction, such as 'perceptions—the perceived'; 'recollection—the recollected'; 'assertion—the asserted'.[14]

Here, 'the ego is what it is solely in reference to intentional objectivities; it always possesses that which is and that which has the possibility of being. Consequently, the essential characteristics of the ego is persistently to form systems of intentionality, as well as to possess systems already formed . . . .'[15] In this context, the ego is the measure of being; 'its being is being for itself'. 'The ego's being-for-itself is being that is in a state of continual self-constitution' and thereby 'the foundation for all constitution of the so-called transcendent'.[16]

Two considerations are important here: on the one hand, there is the consideration that the so-called ego which is, as it were, the individual understanding centre of a reality, i.e., its own reality makes no sense at all without such a reality. Therefore transcendent objectivities serve as guidelines to discover the ego. On the other hand, Husserl notices 'an ambiguity in the notion of the ego: it is a different ego on each of the various strata of phenomenological problems'.[17] There are 'degrees of relative immediacy and mediatedness' of the activity of the ego,[18] 'different degrees of distance from the background... of distance from and of nearness to the ego, where the actual pure ego living in the particular cogitations is the point of reference'.[19] Thus, 'not every evidence has the form of the specific ego-act'. There are 'variant formations'.[20] A cogitative type can be understood as a characteristic figuration of an ego-world-aggregate—and precisely in this sense it can be understood as a model for cultural realities.[21]

In question are reflections about the types of systems of intentionality that can actually exist. And here the 'phenomenological analysis is not at all analogon to any objective analysis of physical objects'[22] for the very fact that 'intentional implications' are involved.[23] It is characteristic of these systems to consist in a manifold variety of intentions, each particularly centred. And these intentions can be implicit and mediated; thus all intersubjectively mediated intentions also belong to these systems. These systems of intentionality moreover turn out to be concretely organized, i.e. they necessarily make use of certain hyletic and sensory possibilities; so that Husserl can even speak of a physiological *a priori*.[24] In this context I prefer to speak of a necessary *a priori* of manifestation of transcendental subjectivity.

Husserl connects his theorem of the cogitative types at first with his doctrine of reduction. In his view there are, as it were, some main types of certain structures of intentionality which are worked out by reductions in order to understand the meaning of intentional coherence. These main types comprise the following:

1. the pure structure of consciousness of the ego-cogito-cogitatum,
2. the pure temporality with its ego-pole,
3. the habitualized ego as a monad,
4. the life-world,
5. the concrete transcendental intersubjectivity.

All these are cogitative types, discovered by reductions, which are used, as it were, as corner-stones to organize the system of possible orders of intentionality. But also definite and specific cultural ways of living can be described and analyzed as cogitative types.

Only in his late philosophy did Husserl subsume this under the title of a universal anthropology. He uses the phrase 'universal *Geisteswissenschaft* as anthropology'.[25]

Cogitative types can also be interpreted as forms of projects of the world (*Weltentwurf*) which are each characterized by their styles of acting, of thinking, and of living, and also by their own forms of interaction. The difference between such types can be too great to allow any mutually intelligible exchange. From the standpoint of transcendental phenomenology it must nevertheless be possible to integrate such types into the system of intersubjectivity or, more precisely, into the system of inter-intentionality. Husserl provided two principal criteria for the estimation of intentional or cultural systems: on the one hand the *life-world*, and on the other hand the so-called *concrete transcendental intersubjectivity*. The life-world proves to be the model for the most elementary familiar intersubjective human understanding of the world. It is the smallest common multiple of actually possible human-cultural orientation. Although its structure is universal, each individual concrete realization of this structure is peculiarly restricted to a particular culture-group of human beings such that different groups of human beings can exist in very different life-worlds, in isolation from each other. According to Husserl concrete transcendental intersubjectivity is the name for the totality of all possible and imaginable intentions and of their coherence. It is characterized as concrete since by definition no other founding intention can exist apart from it. It is called transcendental because it serves as the ultimate frame within which specific systems of intentionality can be evaluated at all.

The question might be raised whether—at least in a phenomenological sense—the life-world as a universal structure and concrete transcendental intersubjectivity as the ultimate sense of transcendentality could ever be actually realized or whether they are merely ideas of possibilities which the human being can imagine and perhaps even must imagine for the sake of orientation, but which can never be realized adequately and authentically. Whenever we conceive the life-world we already conceive more than the mere life-world, and whenever we speak of concrete transcendental intersubjectivity we think of something we cannot realize. The normal human being of a culture lives within systems which are situated between these two aspects.

The later Husserl expresses this as follows: 'The human being is being within finitude such that it is continually in the awareness of the infinite.' 'The human being in the state of worldliness'—and that is the concrete cultural reality of human beings—'lives within the pre-givenness of itself and of its world . . . it lives in horizons, it lives in the awareness of finitude within the infinity of the world'.[26] Human consciousness is at the same time the awareness of finitude and of the infinite. This means: the human being realizes its situation as situatedness, and by this very realization it is—although within the situation—also already beyond the situation.[27]

Husserl gives a theoretical foundation to this position in *Crisis* where he states that the term *ego* is essentially equivocal when he discusses the relation between the ego, performing the epoché, and the ego which is reductively conceived in the epoché. He characterizes the ego as personally indeclinable and at the same time as transcendentally declinable.[28] In a cultural-anthropological sense this means that the human being always lives in particular cultural figurations, and that it at the same time can compare these figurations in considering (*Besinnung*) an idea of general humanity.[29] 'Every transcendental ego', as 'an ego within the transcendental intersubjectivity', and thereby participating in the constitution of the world, must 'necessarily be constituted as a human being within the world.' Transcendentality is not a particular stratum in the human being which could be hypostatized. It is rather only effective 'in so far the human being is the self-objectivation of the respective transcendental ego, a self-objectivation which can be shown by phenomenological self-consideration'.[30]

The 'in so far' of the self-consideration of a concrete human being is the same as its transcendentality. The self-consideration within the individual concrete connections of intentionality is its self-objectivation, its understanding of reality; that is its culture. This culture can appear in different formations, but here becomes manifest the spirituality or energy which constitutes the world and the self, and which unites all human beings.

The crucial point of human self-consideration is its basic characteristic of being in attitudes. The concept of attitude (*Einstellung*) plays a decisive role in Husserl. It is also to be connected with the theorem of the cogitative types. The cogitative types are each realized in the respective attitudes which can be determined as the particular forms of an original relation of the human being to itself and to the world. It is well known that Husserl distinguished several forms of 'attitudes'. It is of crucial significance that the human being, at a certain level of cultural development, finds an attitude even towards the phenomenon and the problem of being in attitudes; and this means that freedom is brought into play.[31] Whoever wants to investigate cultural phenomena in a cultural anthropological perspective must have discovered the problem of attitudes, and must be able to comprehend the different attitudes in concrete contexts if he does not want to lose sight of the phenomenon of culture, and if he does not want to misinterpret it naturalistically or objectivistically.

Whereas Husserl arrived at the theme of culture only in his late philosophy after long procedures of transcendental phenomenological analyses, this theme of culture is already vividly present at an early stage of Cassirer's work. It is true, his early works on the history of philosophy, as for example, the work '*Das Erkenntnisproblem in der Philosophie und Wissenschaft der neueren Zeit*[32] were designed to measure the history of philosophy by the standards of Kantianism. But at the same time the whole variety of the historical-cultural development comes thus into this kantianizing philosophy.[33] Thus the mere scholarly philosophy becomes a philosophy according to the world-concept of philosophy—in the sense of Kant's *Anthropology*. This means: Philosophy itself is seen as a cultural phenomenon among other cultural phenomena, and can only obtain its meaning in connection with these. Consequently, Cassirer in 1938 calls his philosophy of symbolic forms 'prolegomena to a future philosophy of culture'.[34] Already in 1923 he had stated that in the philosophy of symbolic forms the 'critique of reason' turns into a 'critique of culture'.[35] 'For the content of the concept of culture cannot be separated from the basic forms and the basic directions of mental production: here, 'being' cannot be seized anywhere else but in 'doing'. 'It is only here that the basic thesis of idealism finds its genuine and complete corroboration'—namely, in the fact that every content 'presupposes an original act of the mind'. But the 'philosophical contemplation' is no longer 'restricted' 'to the analysis of the pure form of knowledge', but is extended to the entire understanding or comprehension of the world.[36] The concept of world itself becomes a concept of culture.

This conception had become possible since Cassirer had connected the Kantian concept of constitution—according to which the understanding prescribes the laws to nature—with Vico's theorem concerning the historical, cultural productivity of the human being. According to Kant, the understanding meets itself and its laws when dealing with nature in the natural sciences, and similarly, according to Vico, the human being understands history because the human being itself produced it and its forms. Already the 'natural world-view',[37] i.e. the 'natural world-concept',[38] shares with elaborated scientific knowledge the characteristic of being the material which is already shaped consciously and functionally. There are no things in themselves, neither in a Kantian, nor in a positivistic sense. In all cases one has to presume the establishing of structures, and above all also the 'pre-logical establishing of structures', or 'forms which have been coined'. Cassirer refers to language, myth, and the arts as such forms.[39] Herewith the concept of symbolic form in its full meaning is obtained in Cassirer, and this concept can be compared to Husserl's concept of cogitative types.

According to Cassirer, the concept of a 'symbolic form' comprises 'every energy of the mind..., by means of which a mental or ideal content of meaning is attached to a concrete sensory sign, and is immanently appropriated to this sign. In this sense language, the mythical-religious world, and the arts each appear as a particular symbolic form. For in all of them becomes apparent the basic phenomenon that our consciousness is not contented with receiving the impression of something exterior, but that it attaches every impression to a free activity of expression, and penetrates it by that'.[40] Cassirer calls the immanent coherence of the representing consciousness 'intentional',[41] and characterizes it as 'symbolic pregnancy'. This is explained as 'the mode' 'in which an experience of perception, as a "sensory", experience, at the same time comprises a certain not directly intuitive "sense", and represents it immediately and concretely.'[42] Thus, 'the medium' is constituted in every particular case, 'the medium which enables us to seize and to understand any ideal being (sc. sense)'.[43] It is only possible to seize cultural reality if the apprehension of such kind of sense is admitted, and for this very reason the apprehension of cultural realities must be distinguished from the specific reductive methods of the natural sciences, and 'phenomenological analyses' have to be employed here.[44] In so far the concept of nature is a concept on the border-line of our human experience, and one can state that our concept of reality is always mediate, i.e., in each case it is a particular correlation of matter and form, of material content and spiritual penetration of this content. 'The bipartition: symbol or object here turns out to be impossible since the closer analysis shows that it is precisely the function of the symbolic which is the precondition of every apprehension of "objectivities" or of circumstance'.[45]

Of course, the media may be of a great variety, and this is the reason why there is a plurality of cultural appearances; but the basic energy of symbolic formation is common to all these appearances, and this constitutes the functional unity of cultural reality. The basic forms of such 'media' are the 'symbolic forms'; as Cassirer called them, such as language, myth, the arts, science, technology, economy.

Although a transcendental theory of consciousness remains the basis of Cassirer's reflections, he as well as Husserl in his late works warns against a mere hypostatization of the concept of the ego, and, accordingly, of the concept of world. 'Ego' and 'world' differentiate only within the process of symbolic formations, as it were, within or as cultural history. This process of differentiation is called '*Auseinandersetzung*' by Cassirer[46] which might be translated as 'dissociation', the connotation 'confrontation' is remarkable. Thus he shows in the second valume of *Philosophy of Symbolic Forms* how, on the basis of mythical magic, techniques as forms of objectivation gradually arise from merely fanciful manipulation. The unavoidable mediatedness of human thought cannot be discovered before these techniques are developed. It is only on this basis that types of ego and types of world can be confronted. Similarly, Cassirer tries to show how, in the development of monotheistic religions and their sublimation of the conceptions of sacrifice, something like a concept of ego and of mind appears which is capable of self-discipline. This concept can then be taken up and can be further developed by philosophy.

In Cassirer as well as in Husserl a problem arises: whether particular symbolic forms—i.e., particular cogitative types in Husserl—are arbitrarily and unfoundedly privileged, or a philosophical relativism of cultures really turns up. Cassirer tried at least to take this problem into account by working out something like basic functions or basic dimensions of symbolic formation. Since 1927[47] he has distinguished three symbolic functions: Expression (*Ausdruck*), representation (*Darstellung*), the pure meaning (*reine Bedeutung*). For Cassirer, expression is an original phenomenon belonging to every kind of orientation; it stands for the fact that we always apprehend what is sensorily given with regard to sense (i.e. meaning), and do so from the respective viewpoints of such apprehension even before we are aware of a difference between sensation and meaning. Therefore, Cassirer holds that the so-called mind-body relation is the most elementary symbolic relation.[48]

Cassirer thus attaches every culture to the concretely and physically existing human being. This original apprehension of expression is called phenomenological by Cassirer.[49] In contrast to this, in the function of *representation* an ontological difference is consciously made between sense and substratum. Thereby that which we call constitution of ideas becomes possible. This function or dimension is decisive for objective orientation as well as for artistic creation. The function of meaning, i.e., of *pure meaning*, as it is called by Cassirer, denotes the capability of an abstract handling of symbols which are totally disconnected from the sense of any concrete content (as in mathematics or symbolical algorithms).

The structure of Cassirer's main work, *Philosophy of Symbolic Forms*, suggests the misinterpretation that there is a definite cultural progress from myth to exact sciences. But this contradicts Cassirer's opinion. In his essay "*Form and Technik*" (1930) Cassirer explains that all culture oscillates between the extremes 'expression' and 'pure meaning', and that the arts produce an ideal equilibrium between them.[50] It is true that the exact sciences represent an optimum of emancipation of the human mind from the state of merely being bound to expression. But sciences in the strict sense are, for Cassirer forms of orientation which are reduced to definite conditions. Philosophy is not identical with them. It only makes use of them in order to understand the different 'idioms' of symbolic formation and their 'grammar',[51] for symbolic forms are kinds of languages, each of them contributing to the constitution of a 'common world'.[52] Thus Cassirer in 1942 characterizes 'science' as only 'an element and a component in the system of 'symbolic forms'.' In a certain sense it may be seen as the keystone in the edifice of these forms; but it does not stand alone, and it could not achieve its specific results if there were not other energies which contribute to the task of a 'synopsis', of a mental 'synthesis.'[53] Cassirer is concerned with the understanding of the 'abundance of the human mind' without the hypostatization of things in themselves or of a background beyond the world of appearances. The 'immanent diversity of the "appearing itself"' is to be understood.

In this respect a 'philosophy of symbolic forms' can maintain the claims to unity and to universality which metaphysics in its dogmatic form had to give up. It is not only able to unite the different modes and directions of knowledge of the world, but can also evaluate the respective legitimacy of every attempt to understand the world, of every interpretation of the world which the human mind is capable of, and it can understand them all in their peculiarity. Only in this way the problem of objectivity can become visible in its wideness, and if it is conceived in this way it not only comprises the cosmos of nature, but also that of culture.[54]

Cassirer tries to avoid the relativism of the concept of truth by a reflection reminiscent of the theory of systems. He refers the truth claim of a particular symbolic form to the entire system of symbolic forms, thereby introducing a kind of relativity similar to what Husserl does with his theorem of concrete transcendental intersubjectivity. In his work on Einstein's theory of relativity (1920), Cassirer explains: systematic philosophy...

...must apprehend the entirety of the symbolic forms, and must assign to each particular symbolic form a steady position within this entirety, because the concept of a structured reality arises for us by the application of particular symbolic forms, and it is by means of these forms that subject and object, ego and world are distinguished and come to confront each other in certain figurations. If we assume that this task was solved,[55] then only the legitimacy of particular forms of concepts and of knowledge as well as the legitimacy of the general forms of theoretical, ethical, esthetical and religious modes of world understanding would be confirmed, and their respective limits would be defined. Of course in this conception every particular form would be conceived as only relative with respect to other forms;—but since this relativity is throughout a mutual one, since none of the particular forms could count as the expression of 'truth' or 'reality' but only the systematic entirety of all of these forms, thus the limitation which would result would appear, after all, an immanent limitation, as a limitation which ceases to be relevant the very moment the particular is again related to the entirety, and is considered within the coherence of the whole.'[56]

This task turns out to be a task of determining the human being himself, and it is the core of philosophy which is now essentially understood as an anthropological one. Notes concerning philosophical anthropology which date back to the year 1929 can be found in Cassirer's remains in the context of his discussions with Heidegger in Davos: The 'problem of a philosophical anthropology moves again into the centre of modern philosophical problems.' It turns out to be 'a focus of philosophical research and of philosophical questions—which is approached from very different directions.'

> But it cannot at all be seen as a specifically 'modern' problem, it does not at all belong to any determined epoch, to a particular step in the development of philosophical thinking—but it appears in all situations where philosophical reflection has grown to a certain maturity and height, and where it finds itself confronted with the necessity of ultimate decisions. The great epochs of distinction and decision (*Scheidung and Entscheidung*), of 'crisis' in the proper meaning of the word—they always lead to the problem of philosophical anthropology. It belongs to the essence of philosophy not to be only and not even in the first place consideration about the world, about the cosmos, but to be essentially self-consideration—and this self-consideration finds as the first, the essential problem the question concerning the essence of the human being.[57]

Here it becomes apparent how close Cassirer's philosophy of culture as a philosophy of symbolic forms is to Husserl's late philosophy as an universal anthropology of cogitative types. A presupposition of this concept of philosophy is the assumption that a certain development of culture authorizes considerations which corroborate the unity of the culture of humankind, and which as well respect the plurality of cultural forms of existence of the concrete human being. This means that the consideration does not presuppose a determined culture which is formed in this or that way and which then would be declared absolute in order to measure other cultures by its standards. It rather seems that Husserl and Cassirer assume the possibility of a consideration concerning the meaning of the whole in very different forms of culture, if these have reached a respective degree of maturity. As a philosophical consideration it has to make use of all the methods (e.g., also of those of the sciences) which have developed during the process of culture without being totally absorbed by these methods in single questions.

It cannot be overlooked that in Husserl as well as in Cassirer the personal and individual concept of freedom is constitutive for the human being and for human culture. Freedom is the capability of autonomous view of and attitude towards the world, view and attitude which first of all constitute world as a meaningful, and which, therewith, make the world a world of human beings.

One might suspect that this conception is too idealistic and thus unrealistic. Is it really possible to apprehend cultural reality and the reality of cultures if one sees them to be founded exclusively on freedom? To this one has to reply if anyone would apprehend cultural reality without taking into account freedom and personal competence of attitudes, then the concept of culture itself would disappear, and culture would be reinterpreted as an indifferent—as, as it were, a natural process without a self. Cassirer critically analyzed this problem in his essay '*Naturalistische und humanistische Begründung der Kulturphilosophie*' from 1939.[58]

But Husserl and Cassirer never took a freely floating concept of freedom as the measure of cultural reality. They rather show that freedom, creativity, personal attitude, etc. are always already situated in cultural reality and formed in determined and concrete ways. There is not so much a free attitude towards reality but rather within reality. So human beings and cultures are related to each other in ways which often appear as natural contingent processes, and which can also be evaluated as such processes. But the possibility of evaluating these processes, and of assigning a meaning to them within the economy of one's own culture elevates them beyond the character of being merely natural processes. With the assumption that all cultural relations are merely natural processes, the phenomenon of culture itself would be denied. In contrast to this, the acknowledgement of cultural intentionality not only lends significance to the merely natural processes but also enables us to evaluate them. In this sense in Husserl as well as in Cassirer even natural science is a product of human cultural achievements which is highly appreciated by these two philosophers who maintain a scientific and rational attitude.

NOTES AND REFERENCES

1. Erich Rothacker: Probleme der Kulturanthropologie. In: Nicolai Hartmann (ed.): *Systematische Philosophie*, Stuttgart, 1942.
2. Helmuth Plessner: Die Stufen des Organischen und der Mensch. Einleitung in die philosophische Anthropologie (1928). In: *Gesammelte Schriften*, Bd. IV, ed. Günter Dux, Frankurt, 1981.
3. Ernst Cassirer: *Philosophie der symbolischen Formen*, 3 Vols. (in the following footnotes: PSF) (1923/25/29). Erster Teil: Die Sprache, Darmstadt 1956; Zweiter Teil: Das mythische Denken, Darmstadt 1958; Dritter Teil: Phänomenologie der Erkenntnis, Darmstadt, 1958.
4. Edmund Husserl: *Formale und transzendentale Logik*, Halle 1929 (= FtL), 155. (Hua XVII).
5. E. Cassirer: *Zur Einsteinschen Relativitätstheorie*. Erkenntnistheoretische Betrachtungen, Berlin, 1920, p. 166.
6. Hua III, 107.
7. Immanuel Kant: *Kritik der reinen Vernunft*, A, 273/B, 303; cf. E. Cassirer: *Wesen und Wirkung des Symbolbegriffs*, Darmstadt/Oxford, 1956 (in the following footnotes: WWS), p. 228.
8. Cf. Hua XV, 389
9. Hua VI, 272.
10. WWS, 228.
11. Hua VI, 366.
12. Wilhelm Dilthey: *Ideen über eine beschreibende und zergliedernde Psychologie* (1894). In: GS V, 152; cf. also I, p. XVIII.
13. Dilthey, op. cit., I, p. XVIII.
14. Hua I, 27.
15. Hua I, 25.
16. *Ibid*.
17. Hua I, 26.
18. Hua VIII, 175.
19. Hua III, 205.
20. FtL, 253.
21. Cf. Hua I, 180.

22. Hua VIII, 125.
23. Hua VII, 125.
24. Cf. Hua IX, 326; VI, 482; IV, 155.
25. Cf. Hua XV, 460 pp., 480 pp. Texts from the years 1932–35; cf. also the Berlin lecture from 1931: Phenomenology and Anthropology, published in: *Philosophy and Phenomenological Research*, No. 2, 1941, 1–14.
26. Hua XV, 389.
27. Cf. Hua XV, 390.
28. Hua VI, 188.
29. Cf. also the conception of limes-forms in Hua VIII, 162.
30. Hua VI, 190.
31. Hua IV, 179 pp. cf. Hua III/1, 62.
32. E. Cassirer: *Das Erkenntmisproblem in der Philosophie und Wissenschaft der neueren Zeit*, Vol. I, Berlin 1906; Vol. II, Berlin 1907; Vol. III, Berlin 1920; Vol. IV, Darmstadt, 1975.
33. Cf. also: E. Cassirer: *Freiheit und Form. Studien zur deutschen Geistesgeschichte*, Berlin, 1916.
34. WWS, 227 pp.
35. PSF, Vol. I, pp. 10.
36. *Ibid.*
37. "natürliche Weltsicht", in: E. Cassirer: *Zur Logik der Kulturwissenschaften* (1942), Darmstadt, 1961 (in the following footnotes: LKW), p. 45.
38. PSF, Vol. III, p. 329.
39. LKW 18, 39 pp.
40. WWS, p. 175.
41. PSF, Vol. III, 185.
42. PSF, Vol. III, 235.
43. WWS, p. 176.
44. LKW, 39 pp.
45. LKW, 31.
46. *Ibid.*
47. In his essay 'Das Symbolproblem und seine Stellung im System der Philosophie' (1927). In: E. W. Orth/J. M. Krois (ed.): *Ernst Cassirer-Symbol, Technik, Sprache*, Hamburg, 1985, pp. 1–21.
48. PSF, Vol. III, 117.
49. PSF, Vol. III, 110.
50. Erst Cassirer: Form und Technik (1930). In: E. W. Orth/J. M. Krois (ed.): Ernst Cassirer—*Symbol, Technik, Sprache*, Hamburg 1985, p. 86.
51. PSF, Vol. I, 19.
52. KW, 42; cf. also Cassirer's London lecture delivered in 1936 'Critical Idealism as a Philosophy of Culture'. In: Donald Phillip Verene (ed.): *Symbol, Myth and Culture.* Essays and Lectures of Ernst Cassirer 1935–1945. New Haven/London (Yale U.P.), 1979, 64–91.
53. LKW, 18.
54. LKW, 19 pp.
55. It has to be noted that the formula 'If we assume that this task was solved' indicates the constructive character of these considerations, it cannot be interpreted as an actual verification; it must rather be interpreted as a methodical idea. In Husserl's concrete transcendental intersubjectivity we find a similar problem.
56. Cassirer: *Zur Einsteinschen Relativitätstheorie*, *op. cit.*, 119.
57. Cf. the remains of Cassirer in the Beinecke Rare Book Library, Yale University, No. 94.

58. E. Cassirer: Naturalistiche und humanistische Begründung der Kulturphilosophie. In: *Göteborgs Kungl. Vetenskaps- och Vitterhets-Samhälles Handlingar.* 5[e] följden, Ser. A, Bd. 7, No. 3 (1939), p. 1–28. Reprint in *Der Bogen*, Bd. 2., Nr. 4 (Wiesbaden 1947), p. 11–15, 21–26.

Human Scientific Propositions

LESTER EMBREE

This essay has the aim of clarifying a species of scientific propositions. As such it is planned as a contribution to epistemology, but that requires several comments. By *epistemology* is intended philosophical reflection on knowledge. Knowledge is not confined to scientific knowledge because there are also everyday knowledge, technological knowledge, and philosophical knowledge. Nevertheless, scientific knowledge has been of central concern in Western epistemology and this centrality does not need to be examined here. Hence the present concern specifically pertains to the philosophy of science or science theory. But where moden Western epistemology has been focused on the natural sciences, the focus here, which will be on the human sciences, is different.

Furthermore, if knowledge is justified belief and if not all such belief involves propositions, then not all knowledge is propositional. Historically, however, the emphasis in epstemology and science theory has been on propositional knowledge and, again, that is something that does not need to be disputed here. Morever, Western philosophy of science has been preoccupied with the formal or logical analysis of propositions or rather their combinations into arguments and, in contrast to that thrust, the present effort is focused on content rather than the form. In other words, it is a reflection on propositions in relation to the matters themselves that they refer to.

In the light, then, of the pertinent matters, two theses will be offered for consideration: (1) that human scientific propositions are about cultural objects and (2) that cultural objects are properly intelligible only in reference to the persons or communities in which they are originally constituted.

Besides the primary consideration of the matters referred to, the genus of propositions can be related to the kind of science they pertain to. Since the genus designated by the expression *human science* is not yet universally recognized, it is also worth inserting as an introductory remark that there are three species of human sciences: (a) the *psychological* disciplines focusing on individual or personal human life, (b) the *social scientific* disciplines, which are focused on collective or communal life in synchronic perspective, and (c) the *historical sciences* which focus on communal or group life in diachronic perspective. Furthermore, it deserves mention that the human sciences arose from a prescientific status mostly in the 19th century and soon came under the influence of the earlier arisen and relatively more developed natural sciences. De facto, the human sciences, especially the psychological sciences, are currently quite naturalized. No dispute is here intended with the scientific aim of explanation or with the recourse to mathematization as a means, for these are accepted. But an opposition to naturalism is sometimes more than implicit. And if the view of the human sciences appears idealized, this is appropriate for their stage of development.

The following exposition begins with some remarks about propositions in everyday life and then proceeds to consider how matters in general present themselves to theoretical, natural scientific, and human scientific attitudes.

I

Whether or not science and hence scientific propositions are present in a given case of human life, humans live and speak in what can be called *everyday life*, which is chiefly practical. Most of speech is for practical purposes. It may be that the imperative is the original form. Some of the propositions in everyday life are value judgements and even some are of a chiefly cognitive sort. Everyday life, like ordinary language, is amazingly complex. Nevertheless, if the expression 'object' is taken broadly enough, it can be asserted generally that the objects of everyday concern are objects that somehow exist, have value, and are useful. Against the tendency to focus on knowledge and existence in most epistemology, the emphasis here will be on value and use, which tend to be ignored in the naturalizing attitude.

One of the events of personal and communal maturation is the recognition that there are other individual and collective outlooks. Thus humans eventually learn that other persons value and use objects differently, as do other social classes, age and ethnic groups, genders, etc. Then again, how objects are valued and used can be understood to change from period to period within a tradition. And when there are vastly different cultures, just about everything is at least subtly different.

The reaction to the recognition of cultural diversity is often *relativism*. When in Rome, one does as the Romans. Different groups, different values, different ontologies, different purposes. Relativism may be a more personal than communal reaction. Another reaction is *cultural imperialism*. In this reaction to cultural diversity, the weaker are forced to conform to how objects exist, have value, and are useful for the stronger. This reaction is probably more frequent in history than relativism and tends more to occur for groups.

Seemingly the most rare response to the fact of cultural diversity within and between individuals, societies and historical eras is a movement towards science and philosophy. The false absolutism of the cultural imperialist and the shallowness of the cultural relativist are seen. One seeks more deeply for beings, goods, and purposes that do or at least ought to hold for all subjects, which would be genuine absolutes. For some reason, values seem the most variable of the sorts of cultural characteristics. But, *prima facie*, physical health would seem a matter of definite positive value in all societies and eras and if it is not so as a matter of fact perhaps it ought to be. If there were but one absolute value, relativism would be vanquished. At the core of the rare response that is science and philosophy is a standing back and seeking to understand apart from action. It may be fostered more by some cultural situations than others but at base involves attempting to gain results that are not culturally relative. This is of course *theory*.

II

Once the theoretical attitude is taken up, the decision can be made to focus on knowledge of *nature*, to seek natural scientific knowledge. Such a decision can have vast consequences. One is often concerned with building a model of sensuously perceivable things, properties, and relations. (Even if unobservables are included, as they are in modern physics, knowledge of observable things plays a role in the foundations of knowledge of unobservables). For example, the Occident has seen two main systematizations of astronomical objects. In first one there is (a) the earth, (b) the planets that include the sun and the moon, and (c) the stars. In the second one there are (a) the stars, which include the sun, (b) the planets, which include the earth, and (c) satellites, which include the moon. In the earlier propounded system, the stars and planets (including the sun and moon) rotate in various ways around the earth, which is not a planet, which is in the centre of the system, and which does not move. In the more recently propounded system, satellites (including the moon) go around planets, (the earth included) go around stars (including the sun), and it seems that there is no centre and nothing that does not move.

What is of importance for present purposes is that both the Ptolemaic and the Copernican astronomical systems, at least as we tend to understand them, presuppose some sort of *disregarding of the values and uses that the items under discussion might have in everyday life*. For example, while there is a seeming gain with respect to an ontological absolute that can be called nature, part of the price for the Copernican system is the status of the earth as divinely ordained home for humans. That view of the world, which modern Western astronomy struggled against, is culturally specific. The use of the sun and moon in the measurement of time into morning and afternoon, day and night, months, seasons, years, etc., for practical purposes in everyday life, i.e., as clock and calendar, is very likely part of all cultures. The chronometric use of sun and moon would even today be set aside when the two astronomical systems are discussed. Yet even the most sophisticated people constantly use these impressive objects for this purpose in everyday life.

The question of the difference between natural scientific and human scientific propositions is central for the philosophy of the human sciences. The objects of these two sorts of propositions can be called *natural objects* and *cultural objects*. The present contention is that one species of object, namely cultural objects, have values and uses for people in everyday life and the objects of another species, namely natural objects, have these characteristics somehow modified. How cultural objects are cultural can be examined a bit more closely.

Once thinkers have been impressed by how promising if not successful the natural sciences are with respect to determining nature as something that exists for everybody in the same way regardless of differences in how the cultural world varies for individuals, societies, and eras, the question of cultural diversity can be answered by saying that cultural objects are preexisting natural objects upon which different cultural characteristics are bestowed according to the historical era, society, ethnic group, age, class, gender, etc. Then the one nature is absolute, but the various cultural worlds are relative.

In this facile but widespread view, the ever so varying cultural characteristics are accidental and the invariant natural determinations essential. Whether something is a letter opener or a hunting knife, it is still of a determinate length, weight, colour, hardness, etc. Indeed, it might even seem that one could forget about cultural characteristics entirely. Reflection upon objects as they present themselves shows, however, that objects always have some sort of existence, value, and purpose for people in everyday life. These characteristics of objects correlate with what may be generally called the positional components in conscious life. Husserl emphasized the characteristics that objects can be reflectively seen to have correlative to believing, which are modes of existence, but he also recognized the place for investigation of values in correlation with the affective-emotional components and of ends and means in correlation with volitional components. Thus, if an individual or a group dislikes something, that something has negative intrinsic value for that subject and if an individual or group uses a means to prevent or destroy something, that something is a negative means. Obviously, much more can be said about values, uses, and even modes of existence, but enough has probably been said to suggest that these characteristics of objects as they present themselves to subjects or, equivalently, as they are posited by subjects, can in general be called *cultural characteristics*.

The extreme variability of cultural characteristics, especially values, is a strong motive for considering cultural characteristics accidental. A brief comparison may weaken the grip of this motive. Sensuously perceived objects are perceived in spatial relations. The pencil, for example, is in the pocket, then it is out of the pocket and on the desk, then it rolls across the desk, falls to the floor, and rolls under the chair. The spatial relations of *inside* and *outside*, *on* and *under*, *still* and *moving*, etc., can change enormously, but the object is nevertheless always in spatial relations. Analogously, a cultural object may have this value or that for these people or those in the present, past, or future, but everyday objects always have value.

If all objects are fundamentally and concretely cultural objects, a position mentioned earlier is reversed. A cultural object is not a natural object with something added. Rather a natural object is a cultural object with something subtracted. This is not the place for a full discussion of whether that 'subtraction' is neutralization of the cultural characteristics, an abstraction from them, or some third procedure. But it may be suggested that learning to view objects as natural rather than as originally cultural is part of training in a natural scientific discipline.

Some may imagine that objects of natural science remain cultural objects except that their values and uses are transformed into those posited by the communities of natural scientists. To a degree, this is correct, so that how objects are valued and used by scientists ought to be considered by historians and sociologists of science. But since the natural sciences are cultivated in the theoretical attitude and cultural character is originally constituted in everyday practical life, the values and uses of objects for natural scientists, who as such are in the theoretical attitude, is at best derivative and the point intimated above, namely that natural scientific objects are cultural objects that have have their original, i.e. everyday, cultural characteristics somehow disregarded, remains unaffected.

Furthermore, humanity increasingly lives in cultural worlds that can be said to be 'scientific' due to the effects of education and technology. This does not signify that there are groups that have come to live their lives in the theoretical attitude but rather that results obtained in the theoretical attitude have affected how objects have come to be believed in, valued, and used in everyday life.

In sum, once the theoretical attitude is taken up, the natural scientific specification of it may be tempting as establishing nature as an absolute being that can be known through natural science, but it is an error to think that objects as they originally present themselves in everyday life do not include values and uses for individuals and groups in history.

III

Another attitude is possible. One can theorize humanistically rather than naturalistically. One does not disregard cultural characteristics but rather focuses upon cultural objects as such. This may be a more difficult attitude to maintain because one is constantly attracted back out of the theoretical attitude into practical participation in one's own everyday cultural life. This is no doubt one of the factors behind the human sciences being less developed than the natural. Positively put, one needs to keep distinct how objects exist, have value, and are useful for the scientific researcher from how they do so, i.e., how they have cultural character, for the personal or communal social or historical cases of everyday human life being researched. Consider, for example, the historian of religion. It is probable that all cultural worlds have religious aspects that can be analyzed in terms of how objects are believed in, valued, and used, but the historian of religion does not need to subscribe to the religions he/she studies; indeed it may be best if he/she does not do so.

Propounded and examined from a theoretical standpoint, human scientific propositions are true or false with respect to cultural objects. The human-scientific psychological propositions are true or false concerning individual life within socio-historical worlds, social-scientific propositions are true or false concerning contemporaneous group life within a culture, and historical-scientific propositions are true or false concerning group cultural life diachronically considered. There are very interesting epistemological questions concerning how propositions that refer to absent objects, e.g., those in the past, are rendered true or false, but those questions are beyond the modest scope of the present essay.

Against the background that has been sketched, two claims can now be offered again about human scientific propositions:

(A) Human scientific propositions are about cultural objects, and
(B) Human scientific propositions at least tacitly refer to some person or community in everyday life for whom the cultural objects exist, have value, and are useful, and are thus understandable only if those subjects are taken into account.

Human scientific propositions are different from natural scientific propositions and nevertheless they are scientific propositions, which it is the science-theoretical purpose of this epistemological essay to clarify. The present essay is successful to the degree that these propositions are now clearer for the reader.

Phenomenology of Human Relations: Some Reflections

S. P. BANERJEE

As a social being born in a particular society with a given set of circumstances and situations, it appears a bit odd to be sceptical about the 'other'. The concept of the atomistic individual disconnected from/and doubtful about the other's existence, is difficult though not impossible. To maintain this sort of philosophical scepticism, one perhaps is constrained to admit, like Hume, that one can afford to be a philosopher in the 'Sundays of one's thought, but not on other days'. The practical impossibility of doubting the other's existence has never been seriously denied nor can be denied inasmuch as the person so denying lives in a soceity where he encounters the other/alter ego almost as a condition of his own social existence.

However, one may choose to be a philosopher with his Sunday thoughts and may cherish genuine doubts about the other's existence. He has already guarded himself by accepting the practical/actual situation of his social reality while persisting in his philosophical doubt about it. The question is: (1) Is it possible? Can we completely divorce actuality from our thoughts? or, (2) Do we not find the other as given in our philosophical reflection also? If we have to answer Hume, we have to ponder over these questions. Otherwise, we have to admit that even Kant, through all his genius, could not properly answer Hume on this question. Leibniz's was a novel experiment in maintaining the individuality of each monad while still retaining the relationship of one with the other but only at the ideal level where this relationship was made an ontological condition. For the very conception of a monad without the 'mirroring' capacity is not just possible. Phenomenologically, nothing was given and as such the relationship of one with many remained only an ontological presupposition.

We may restate our position by admitting that Humean type of scepticism in regard to the existence of other selves is not an acceptable position. We do not doubt the existence of other selves—neither practically nor philosophically. The social reality forces itself on us and we are compelled both actually and philosophically, if we do not have recourse to solipcism, to accept the fact of the *existence of other selves*, our diverse social relations and relationships, our moral world, our very communicative structure and so many other things. I experience around me the presence of a world which does not owe its existence to me; I always realize that my world is continually related to this transcendent totality. I came into existence into an already-existing-world and every moment of my existence is conditioned by its relation to this already-existing-world where things and persons are present and my life-history is constituted by my relationship with the world. There can be a genuine philosophical problem, apparently paradoxical though, regarding the *knowledge of other selves as distinguished from the existence of other selves.*

To my mind it appears that if one starts with the primacy and privacy of one's knowledge of one's own self/mind, it becomes next to impossible to achieve knowledge of other selves. Neither the theory of inference nor that of empathy can be of much help in this matter. Briefly stated, the theory of inference for knowing other minds/selves would be like this: Mind knows itself directly in a unique way; it has a 'rational insight' or 'privileged access' to itself. Here the subject knows itself as subject. I am not sure if the Nyāya theory of *anuvyavasāya* is something like this. Anyway, only one's own self/mind knows itself as a subject; but the same is not claimed for the other mind. The mind may know it directly, too, but only as an object. So, the other subject is known to me only as an object and, then, the problem is: how can I ascribe subjectivity to it?

The inferential argument is one of a weak type—that of analogy. J.S. Mill[1] has perhaps stated the argument most clearly. He argues that my own feeling, my own experience obliges me to ascribe these experiences to other beings like me in so far as they are alive and they are not automata. As a true empiricist, Mill's anticipation of structuralist conception of mind (inasmuch as he speaks of 'feeling as the intermediate link between the modifications of the body' on the one hand and outward demeanour' on the other) is appreciable but the weak form of inferential argument he presents is not perhaps acceptable or logical. I do not suggest that bodily modifications are totally irrelevant, but what I contend is that they are neither the only nor the sole datum of any such inference, if such an inference is really there. Secondly, it seems that as a piece of inference it is totally illogical. If Mill is in genuine difficulty of identifying 'the walking and speaking figure' he can never do it by my personal experience of 'feeling'. It is difficult to decipher the existence of feeling in others for there is not a single datum obtained by direct perception for any such inference.

Hampshire[2], Malcom[3], and Price[4] have offered variations of this argument. Ledger Wood also speaks interestingly of two types of inter-subjective cognition: primary and secondary. In primary inter-subjective cognition 'two minds to be mutually cognizant must establish between themselves a sympathetic rapport such that each is a cognitive object for the other as are lovers engrossed in each other's subjectivity'.[5] But this is not an analogical argument while his secondary type is. Without any detailed discussion on all the varieties of analogical argument, the basic difficulty may be pointed out. The argument starts with an implicit acceptance of what is supposed to be inferred as the conclusion. If I do not somehow presume the other as already a being like me, the other-ascription of the mental predicates becomes illegitimate. On the basis of analogy all I can do is to conclude that it is my own self that is present there as well—and not some other or alien self. The real difficulty is regarding the starting-point. If we start with the primacy of self-knowledge and its privacy, it becomes impossible to ascribe subjectivity to others. Inference theory has to work under serious handicaps because for its justification, it has to refer, at some stage or other, to direct experience.

Such an experience involves not only cognitive relations but, perhaps, more significantly and fruitfully, noncognitive relations also, e.g. the affective relations, relations through communication and moral relations like trust and obligations. Moreover, it is supposed in the inference theory that I perceive my own bodily states objectively. This is indeed a wrong assumption. When I am angry, I do not observe my bodily states as marks of my mental states. What really happens is that my bodily states are experienced, not objectively, not as distinct marks of mental states, but as undistinguished from, in fact, as one with, perhaps, as saturated with, the mental state. Under such circumstances the entire pattern of inference becomes inapplicable. So, the conclusion that emerges is that should one start from one's own cases of experience, it becomes very difficult, frankly impossible, to arrive at the existence of other *subjects*, other minds. Nothing can act as the proper criterion for such an inference and thus the argument from analogy fails to prove anything.

P. F. Strawson has offered some innovative arguments in his *Individuals* on this matter. For him, the concept of 'Person' is a basic particular in our actual conceptual structure and it is not further analyzable. To this concept both the M-predicates (e.g., weight, height, location, etc.) and P-predicates (feeling, being tired, performing duties, etc.) are ascribed. And in this ascription there is no distinction of primacy between self-ascription and other-ascription. Rather, a basic condition of my ascribing them to me is that I am also capable of ascribing them to others. 'To learn their use is to learn both aspects of their use. In order to have this type of concept, one must be both a self-ascriber and an other-ascriber of such predicates and must see every other as a self-ascriber'.[6]

Strawson's theory takes care of the linguistic asepct of the problem and he solves the problem by ruling out the question of primacy of self-ascription or of other-ascription. He does it within the linguistic framework, our actual conceptual structure, which obliges us to use our language the way we do. But is there this compulsion? What are the roots of such obligations? To answer such problems, one, perhaps, has to search the *lebenswelt*, the given in our primacy of experience, which in a way determines the 'actual conceptual structure'. So, the basic problem remains: How can the other be given to me not as an object but as a subject? Are there experiences which present to me the other's facticity as a subject? I believe one may go a step further and assert that there must be such experiences otherwise how would our social existence be constituted by interpersonal relationship as it is. So, we have actually to examine the way we encounter the other without transforming it into an object.

Even though we have not discussed here the problem of one's knowledge of one's own self which is taken as the primary fundamental datum in the theory of inference, it may be pointed out that the problem of one's own self is separately connected with that of otherselves. I am given to myself only in association with an other. 'Pure' self-consciousness may.be a myth.

And, again, the notion of intention and activity is basic to any theory of self-consciousness. Knowledge is in a very important sense intentional and without action (through intention) knowledge may not be an actuality.

Knowledge is action—action of living through intention. This gives knowledge its personal touch without affecting its universality and rules out any purely non-personal or secular approach to it.

II

In the history of the treatment of the problem of the alter ego/the other/inter-subjectivity we come across many illustrious names, e.g., Hegel, Husserl, Sartre, Buber, Scheler etc. and in a brief context it is not possible nor necessary to discuss their theories, however originial and meritorious they may be. But it is also true that all the aspects of the problem have been thoroughly discussed by these thinkers. We may only draw our lessons from them.

In Husserl's treatment, it has perhaps been clearly evident that if one starts with the Cartesian theory of primacy of one's knowledge of one's own self, the relationship between *I* and *thou* is insoluble, at least on the transcendental level. I do not claim adequate competence to pronounce any judgement but I give vent only to my hunch, even though in the absence of detailed arguments, it might appear sermonic.

Heidegger feels the necessity of admitting (a) the relation between 'human realities' as a relation of being and (b) the relation causing 'human realities' to depend on one another as their essential being. Heidegger has thus tried to overcome the difficulty faced by his predecessors through his attempt to establish a relationship of being between the *I* and *other*. According to him, human reality is 'being-in-the-world' and as such, from the outset, 'being-with' (Mitsein) i.e. being-with-other. This being-with is an essential structure of one's own being.

Heidegger does not take his departure from Cartesian *cogito*. From the very outset, he is convinced of the transcendental relation of the (my) self to the other as constituting my own being, just as the being-in-the-world measures my own human reality. So, the problem of the other is a false problem. The type of connection with the other has changed from Husserl to Heidegger. With Husserl and others, it was a *being-for*. With Heidegger it is *being-with*.

In Heidegger's theory, as Sartre thinks, the original relationship between myself and the other is not between you and me; it is the *we*. This is certainly a progress over the theory of *being-for*. But it is an indication and not the solution of the problem. It cannot explain any concrete case of my being-with, say, being-with my friend Debi. The other in Heidegger remains an abstract term and does not have the power of breaking the barrier and to become the concrete Debi. Thus the problem of the alter ego is not satisfactorily solved.

Sartre's ego encounters his other rather as an alien/enemy who objectifies me through his look, through whose supposed detection I feel ashamed, etc. According to Sartre, (a) the other is that being towards whom I do not turn my attention. (b) The other is one who objectifies me by his look, makes me experience shame, jealousy, hate, etc. The other by objectifying me reveals to me my new dimension of objectness which by myself I cannot do. (c) By looking at the same object like me, the other limits my possibilities and freedom. But again, (d) the other's presence without intermediatory is the necessary condition of all my thought which I would attempt to form concerning myself. (e) It is through the objectivization of the other that I regain my subjectivity, myself, my freedom. The other is thus presented to me both as a subject-totality and as an object-totality. I perceive the subjectivity of the other insofar as he objectifies me. But I cannot perceive the other as a subject as he is for-himself.

With all its brilliance, Sartre's theory of the alter ego cannot satisfactorily solve the problem. We feel like agreeing with de Wailhens[7] that Sartre renders impossible a relationship between the I-subject and the other-subject. Either I am the subject and the other is the object or the other is the subject and I am the object. This is the ultimate basis of Sartre's subtle analysis of human relationship such as love, hatred, sexual desire etc. This is why Sartre is so fond of Hegel's 'Master-slave' concept. In each of the attitudes mentioned, Sartre tries to show that these can be reduced to either my masochistic submission to the alienation of my freedom by the other or my sadistic transformation of the other's subjectivity into my instrument. This 'instrumentalism' or appropriation of myself by the other or of the other by myself is fundamental in Sartre's theory of the alter-ego or intersubjectivity. Proper intersubjectivity is impossible on such a basis with the insoluble dialectics of 'we-subject' and 'we-object', 'Being' and 'Nothingness', 'Being-in-itself' and 'Being-for-itself'. And the source of the major part of the difficulty may rest in Sartre's ambiguous use of 'subject' and 'object'—as also his notion of 'freedom' and 'action'. But it is not possible for us to discuss in details all these in the present context.

Both Buber and Max Scheler in their treatment of the problem of intersubjectivity (in *I* and *Thou* and the *Nature of Sympathy*) have developed very interesting and highly insightful theories from which we gather much in solving the problem. We may also bring to focus some of our common experiences which present us with the given in the intersubjective relationship. I shall briefly discuss here a few of such human phenomena, e.g. (a) communication, (b) emotions like love and hate, sympathy and jealousy, (c) moral experience, (d) action and body.

Communication through language or otherwise (sometimes silence may be very communicative) seems possible only on the assumption of the existence of other persons. The entire language-system is an evolute in the context of society (intersubjective intercourse) and social need. This capacity of verbal communication marks off human beings from other animals and it is this sort of communication that clearly manifests the reality of the 'other' whom I address on the assumption that he/she is capable of understanding me and responding to me in an appropriate way. In the experience of dialogue, there is constituted between the other person and myself as common ground: my thoughts and his are interwoven into a single fabric...[8]

This communication, through language or through silence or through bodily gestures and postures is parasitical on the assumption of the prior existence of a kingdom of persons who understand, react and reciprocate to such communication. Scepticism, to be logical, must here be totally silent and would thus destroy itself. The reality of communication proves beyond doubt the reality of the person communicated to. It further implies a closeness and mutuality of relation based on mutual understanding. Many of our social ruptures are due to failure of communication or misunderstanding, generated by faulty communication. But all these prove the reality of the related persons involved in communication, faulty or perfect.

LOVE AND HATE, SYMPATHY AND JEALOUSY

A phenomenological study of these emotions exhibits the implicit assumption of the existence of the other (person). These emotions are common experiences of human life and are beyond the scope of logical doubt. Love is the *concrete mutuality* of two or more persons (I am not considering here the possibility of my loving my pet dog or my parker 51) each reaching out towards the other. In genuine love two persons experience an inseparable union, a rapport which unfolds a vast scope of their *united existence*. Buber thinks that in marriage love has its fruition for in it two hearts meet in the closest way possible. According to Vaiṣṇava thinkers, true love exists between the *bhakta* (worshipper) and the *Bhagawān* (Lord) and it can have five types of expression. Whatever it is, love reveals the realm of inter-subjective participation beyond any sort of reasonable doubt. And love at its highest must also be accompanied by the most intimate and successful type of communication.

It has to be admitted that in the case of intense love a relationship between *persons* alone is indicated. The highest degree of intensity of love is possible only between persons and is inter-personal. The reaching out of one heart to another is the deepest communication which a person makes to another. Love in this sense is the deepest, sincerest and most private communication of one person to another and there is no mystery here. It indicates both a duality and a close relationship. The *Vaiṣṇava* wants union with his God but detests the idea of losing his identity in Him. For the most intense relation duality is a prerequisite.

Whatever is applicable to love is, in a reverse way, applicable to hate. In experiencing hate, the hater experiences, so to say, a sort of shrinking from the object of hate. Hate asserts the emphatic rupture of the relation between the hater and the hated and this primarily implies a human situation. And we may conclude that love and hatred are intrinsically social relations and dispositions and are elementary acts which cannot be analyzed or defined any further.

Contrary to general belief, it is a phenomenological finding that both love and hate are acts, acts of elementary type, not acts of conation. The core of love and hatred is constituted by this elementary act. And again, notwithstanding such expressions as 'self-love' and 'self-hatred' love and hatred are essentially social dispositions. They necessarily presuppose the 'other'. Self-love' or 'self-hatred' is a case of transference from others. In a sense, love and hatred have a moral bearing and we may agree with Scheler that they appertain to value. The fundamental point, however, remains that (i) love and hatred as elementary acts cannot be defined. They can only be experienced. (ii) They are essentially social dispositions and presuppose the reality or social existence i.e. the polarity between myself and the other.

Some thinkers might feel some uneasiness about accepting love and hate as social dispositions, but there should be no such objection regarding acceptance of sympathy and jealousy as social. Sympathy implies a partaking of/a sharing in, the joy or sorrow of the 'other'. Without the 'other' sympathy is meaningless. It is a form of emotional identification which might, though not necessarily, end in love. Sympathy expresses more of the activity of the sympathizer than that of the sympathized. Like sympathy, its reverse jealousy also is explicitly social or interpersonal. We do not ordinarily come across such expressions as 'I am jealous of myself'. One can be jealous of somebody for having something which the agent lacks. It implies a lack, a negation, an absence of an attribute or something else in the agent while he/she is conscious of the other possessing it. This implicit comparison forms the core of jealousy which is essentially of interpersonal character and cannot be branded as totally private.

MORAL EXPERIENCE

It has never been challenged that moral life and moral obligations point to a field of interpersonal relationship. Moral values may be intrinsic. But the admission of this fact does not imply that these values are meaningful even without a social context. Moral obligation is primarily an obligation to an other, a fellow-being. Kant was evidently anxious not to lose sight of this other directedness of the moral situation when he formulated his 'categorical imperative' as a universal maxim for *being a person*, and treating *everybody* (either in his own self or in *others*) as a person. The exact nature of the other may be determined by the extent to which we extend the notion of morality. The theory of *karma* in traditional Indian thinking takes the entire universe as forming the moral background where, depending on the past stock of actions, species become interchangeable. Thus men may be reborn as animals and animals as men. Anyway, moral experience is essentially an other-bound experience where the intrinsic character of the values are determined by social-contexts. Moral life is not surely identical with social life but it is not possible without the interpersonal background. Moral obligation is an obligation to an other, a person, a fellow-being. The feeling of obligation is not generally directed to one's own self; it is directed towards the other and toward a person—except in exceptional cases or cases of figurative use of language (e.g. 'you are morally obliged to give sufficient food to your faithful dog').

The facts of moral life and moral obligation not only suggest the existence of the 'other' (person) but also the reality and actuality of the partnership between a man and the 'other'. Moral obligation is also living upto the expectation of the 'other'. The 'other' stands over and above me and in fulfilling the obligation I live up to the expectation I take him to have of me. Scepticism can never be allowed on these counts and I do not think it has ever been advocated in the history of philosophy in this context.

BODY

The (human) body is not just a thing. It facilitates my participation in the being and life of the alter ego, the 'other' and the other's in my being and life. It is a level of subjectivity which may be degraded into just an object depending on the loss of relation that exists between two persons. The body has a profound significances in the course of our participation in the being and life of our fellow-beings. We cannot, however, share our being equally with all bodies; the depth of sharing varies in degrees depending on the nature of intimacy and communication that exists between two persons. A man can participate more in the body of his beloved than that of a prostitute which is more a thing than a living, human 'body'.

Anyway, this participation has a limit. However deeply a man may love his wife, he cannot identify his body with hers. Every body has a boundary of its own which helps us in demarcating one person from the other. The difference enables one to love or hate the other. But the importance of the body in interpersonal relationship should not lead us to equate the body with the *person*. The basic point that is being stressed is that the body can be both thing-like and person-like and only as the latter does it help in constituting personal identity.

Descartes was perhaps mistaken in taking the body as a thing standing apart from consciousness. I am not sure about Strawson's position who seems to repeat the same mistake, despite his contrary pronouncements, in taking the body as the prime 'particular' in terms of which personal identity has been construed. One might gratefully recall in this context the important Aristotelian thesis that the body is the mind in preparation.

The arid rationalism of the Cartesian kind can be avoided only when we realize the significance of will and intention. Our knowledge is not a lone adventure of reason. Our will animates and also regulates it. The non-fulfilment of our intention is the cause of our embarking upon knowing. It is the fulfilment of our intention that makes us call off, at least overtly, our cognitive adventure.

The inmost *core* of our consciousness is *will*. It is not a mad and impatient nucleus. Will is the pulse-beat of our consciousness. Without will, consciousness will be rendered immobile. The fact that we live and let others live has to be understood as our response to an inherent urge of our lived consciousness. To live I cannot live alone. Living is an encounter—continuous encounter with the other. I do not live in a void. I do not suffer or enjoy a Nihil. I am not lost in a supportless, timeless and spaceless Nothing. My existence, as I know and live it, is always supporting and supported by the other. And when I unpack the box of others, it is found to contain other humans, wills, lives and things. It is amidst these that I live my life and know my object and thus enjoy the fulfilment of my intention, or suffer the frustration of its non-fulfilment. I live my life among others and for this reason, it is not entirely mine. I am continuously engaged in a dialogue of being and nothing.

I know my object; yet my object is not entirely mine. The other of my knowledge is not brought into being by a legislation of my decision or by arbitrary fiat of my will. But it is also not there in spite of me. It is there, at least partly, because of me. My consciousness is carrying a compass, as it were, within it whereby I know the direction of my knowledge and the possible objects which I may encounter on the way. My object is in an important sense both epistemic and personal. The object is not objective in its own right. It is in relation to my knowledge or your knowledge that something or some being is an object. What is more interesting to note is that a being can turn into a thing, i.e., almost a dead object because of my or your indifference to it or our refusal to participate in its being. But even while I so refuse, I cannot legislate the object out of existence even though its continuance loses all meaning for me. This may happen in interpersonal relationship too.

Without an 'other' I cannot even know myself. To be what I *am* I *need* to confront an '*other*'. To know I must know an other. To be I must be with an other. To use my language meaningfully I primarily start with 'we' from which I is, so to say, abstracted. Knowledge is necessarily knowledge *of*—. This brings out the intentional character of knowledge. Knowledge is also in an important sense interpersonal and there cannot be rational no-owner theory of knowledge. Person owns knowledge.

I cannot own myself in the way I intend to. For I cannot confront myself directly. I cannot know myself *qua* pure self. In other words, as already pointed out, I discount the possibility of direct self-knowledge of myself, it is necessarily accompanied with my knowledge either of an other self or at least of an other thing. But in company with a human being, I know myself better and clearer than I know myself in the company of an animal or a thing. The degree of my active participation in the life of a thing or person measures my success or failure in knowing my self. I know my self best in the company of the person who answers my intentions best. Perhaps it is having this principle in view that the religionist says that when I am in company or in communion with the Eternal Thou, the Perfect Person, I know my self best.

NOTES AND REFERENCES

1. An examination of William Hamilton's Philosophy, N.Y., 6th edn. pp. 243–44.
2. S. Hampshire "The Analogy of feeling", Mind, 1952, pp. 1–12.
3. N. Malcom, Knowledge and Certainty, N.Y., 1963, pp. 132–33.
4. H. H. Price, 'Our Evidence for the Existence of Other Minds' Philosophy', (XIII), 1938, pp. 425–56.
5. Ledger Wood, Analysis of Knowledge, London, 1940, pp. 103–29.
6. P. F. Strawson, Individuals, London, Methuen, p. 108.
7. See, Schutz, A. 'Sartre's Theory of the Alter Ego', in Journal of Philosophy and Phenomenological Research, December, 1948.
8. M. Merleau-Ponty, *Phenomenology of Perception*, London, Routledge & Kegan Paul, 1962, p. 354.

Object, Objective Phenomenon and Objectivating Act According to the 'Vijñaptimātratāsiddhi' of Xuanzang (600–664)

ISO KERN

The Indian Buddhist School of Yogācāra or Vijñānavāda has developed, from a subjective or immanent point of view, an extremely rich theory of the structure of knowledge and consciousness in general. For an occidental phenomenologist, this philosophical theory formulated in a foreign culture is of great interest: he may find here some intercultural control and 'universal' verification of his own insights and he may be stimulated to consider new questions and answers.

The principal founders of this School, the brothers Asanga and Vasubandhu, were born in Puruṣapura, today Peshavar in Pakistan, and lived probably in the fourth century. However, I shall here not investigate their writings, but a work of a Chinese monk, Xuanzang (600?–664), and a commentary to this work by a pupil of Xuanzang, Kuiji (632–682). Both of these Chinese Buddhist thinkers lived in the seventh century—three centuries after Asanga and Vasubandhu. They spent most of their time in the city of Changan (today Xian) which at that time was the capital of the Chinese Tang-Empire, and which was situated several thousand miles to the east of Puruṣapura.

I am studying the Yogācāra or the Vijñānavāda in geographically and culturally so remote a perspective, i.e., in the light of a Chinese text, because Indian philosophy and Indian culture are very far away from, and strange to me. Moreover, I have became somewhat acquainted with Chinese language and thinking during the last fourteen years. However, in trying to understand some fundamentals of Chinese thought, I was directed also towards Indian Buddhist sources. I was directed to them by the fact that Chinese thinking, not only Buddhist but also Daoist and Confucian, stretches one of its most nourishing roots to those sources from about the 4th century onward.

Xuanzang, an eminent Chinese Buddhist thinker, started a voyage from Changan through Central Asia and Bactria to India in the year 629, probably at the age of 29. Here he spent some 15 years, studying, travelling, collecting Buddhist texts, before he returned to China with a rich intellectual harvest in 645. In India he listened to many teachers at different places, teachers of different Buddhist schools of both the Hīnayāna and the Māhāyāna persuasions, but the place he stayed the longest at was Nālandā, then the most flourishing Buddhist university in India. The Yogācāra school then prevailed at this university, and Xuanzang attended the lectures of *Sīlabhadra*. Sīlabhadra was at that time more than 100 years old. In his youth he had been a pupil of *Dharmapāla* (530–561).[1] Dharmapāla was the leading figure in the Nālandā of the 6th century. He continued and developed the philosophical work of *Dignāga* (about 480–540), the great logician and epistemologist of the Yogācāra school. Xuanzang presents his own thinking always as the thinking of Dharmapāla and when, in his works, he quotes different opinions he allies himself always with Dharmapāla's view as the right one. Yet it cannot always be taken for granted that the opinions he attributes to Dharmapāla were necessarily Dharmapāla's opinions. Some of the views Xuanzang attributes to Dharmapāla may not actually be his but those of his followers. It may be noted that Dharmapāla lived 100 years earlier than Xuanzang.

As the works of Dharmapāla and of other thinkers of the Yogācāra school that Xuanzang quotes are mostly lost in the original Sanskrit language (there are some works of Dharmapāla preserved in a Chinese translation, e.g., his commentary to Vasubandhu's *Viṃśatikā* (T. 31, Nr. 1591) and his commentary to the *Ālambana-parīkṣā* of Dignāga (T. 31, Nr. 1625). Xuanzang's work is very important for the historiography of Indian philosophy. Moreover, it is fascinating to observe how the thoughts of India are mirrored and transformed in a different language and culture.

The textual base of my considerations are the *Cheng wei shi lun* ('Doctrine of Mere-Consciousness', '*Vijñapti-mātratā-siddhi*'), written in the winter of 659/60 by Xuanzang, and the *Cheng wei shi lun shu ji* ('Recorded explanations of the *Cheng wei shi lun*') by Xuanzang's pupil Kuiji (632–682). Xuanzang's *Cheng wei shi lun* is a very extensive commentary on and further elaboration of Vasubandhu's small work *Triṃśika Vijñapti-mātratāsiddhi*. This small text of only thirty verses is a condensation of Vasubandhu's Vijñānavāda-philosophy. Generally, it is considered to be his last work. In his commentary to Vasubandhu's *Triṃśika*, Xuanzang relied on ten Indian commentaries of this work. These commentaries stemmed from Dharmapāla and his pupils but also from other traditions of the Yogācāra-philosophy, such as the commentary by Sthiramati (about 510–570)[2]. Sthiramati was an older contemporary of Dharmapāla and the intellectual head of the university of Valabhī in Kathiavar (in West India), after Nālandā the second main centre of the Yogācāra. Kuiji's 'Recorded explanations of the *Cheng wei shi lun*' is a sub-commentary to Xuanzang's commentary. It records Xuanzang's oral explanations of his work.

Like a phenomenologist, Xuanzang considers knowledge from an immanent or subjective point of view: he does not accept any things separate from or outside of consciousness. Again, just as in phenomenology, this point of view does not mean to Xuanzang that everything is produced by my consciousness. In his commentary Kuiji gives the following explanation of the expression 'mere consciousness' *wei shi, vijñapti mātra*), which is the label of this school:

> One speaks of mere consciousness because of the non-separatedness from consciousness. This means that there are not other real things separate from and outside of consciousness. . . . As to the Absolute (*zhen ru*, *bhūtatathatā*), although it is not

evolved (*bian*, *pariṇāma*) by consciousness, it is nonetheless nothing separate from and outside of consciousness. Therefore one speaks of mere consciousness. This term merely excludes things (*fa*, *dharma*) considered to be outside the mind (*xin*, *citta*). (T. 43, Nr. 1830, p. 323b9–12).

If we speak here of an *immanent* or *inner* point of view, we do not give a genuine characterization, because from this point of view there is nothing external in contrast with which consciousness could be called internal.

In his commentary (in the Chinese version by Yijing (635–713)) to the *Ālambanaparīkṣā* by Dignāga, Dharmapāla says: 'The look (form) of the object (*jing xiang*) is originally not separate from consciousness. Therefore it is called the *inner* look of the object. The word 'inner' means here: not separate from consciousness. But if there is nothing outside of consciousness in respect to what do we speak of "inner"?..'.(T. 31, Nr. 1625, p. 891c14–16). In Husserl's work we could find similar reflections on the term immanent, by which he characterizes the phenomenological point of view.

My question is now the following: How does Xuanzang, given the above reflections, explain the relation between knowledge and the object of knowledge? What does become the object of knowledge from his subjective point of view? More specifically let me ask this question with regard to physical objects, such as stones, plants, animals.

In the line of the realistic Hīnayāna, Xuanzang continues to conceive of the object as a *condition* for the arising of the knowledge (or consciousness) of it. In this causal explanation of knowledge the object is called 'the base-condition (of knowledge or consciousness)' (*suo yuan yuan*, *ālambana-pratyaya*). The Hīnayāna definition of this objective support of consciousness runs, in the quotation of Xuanzang, as follows: 'That which produces (*yin sheng*) a consciousness which resembles it, is called the base-condition (*suo yuan yuan*, *ālambanapratyaya*) < of that consciousness >. (*Cheng wei shi lun*, edition of the *Jinling ke jing chu*, Nanking 1896, I, p. 12b10). However, Xuanzang adopts the immanent, 'idealistic' point of view. The base-condition can therefore not be a thing outside of consciousness. He declares: 'There are not real atoms outside of consciousness. We know therefore definitely that that which consciousness itself evolves (*bian*) as a look (*xiang* < *fen* >, *nimitta* < *bhāga* >) resembling matter (*se*, *rūpa*) and so on, is the base-condition. The objectivating act (*jian* < *fen* >, *darśana* < *bhāga* >) relies on it (*tuo*) and arises (*sheng*) since it bears its look (i.e., of the base-condition) (*dai ji xiang*)' (I, p. 13b4–6). The more general definition of the objective base-condition (*suo yuan yuan*, *ālambanapratyaya*) of consciousness in Xuanzang's work is this: 'The base-condition is a real element (*fa*, *dharma*) which the mind (and its associates), bearing the look (form) of it (*dai ji xiang*), intends (thinks, means) and on which it relies (*suo lü*, *suo tuo*)'. (VII, p. 19b4–5; completed by *Shuji* T. 43, Nr. 1630, p. 501a3–4).

Xuanzang's '*idealistic*' view of the object as a *condition* for the arising of knowledge or consciousness of that object seems to contain a difficulty in the form of a contradiction. This difficulty is already mentioned in Dignāga's

Ālambanaparīkṣa: "How can the inner look (form) of the object (*nei jing xiang*) which is not separate from consciousness simultaneously arise with consciousness and be a condition of consciousness?" (*vritti* to the sixth *kārikā*, T. 31, Nr. 1624, p. 888c20–21). In other words: How can the object on one side be evolved by consciousness and on the other side be a condition for the arising of consciousness?

Dignāga in the seventh verse and in its explanation of his *Ālambanaparīkṣa* proposes two solutions of this difficulty. First he says: 'The look (form) of the object (*jing xiang*) and consciousness definitely follow each other. Although the look (form) arises simultaneously with the consciousness of it, it can nevertheless be a condition of consciousness. The logicians say: If existence and nonexistence of two things follow each other, they have the character of cause and effect, despite the fact that they arise simultaneously.' (l.c. p. 888c24–25). According to Erich Frauwallner, this first solution based on the simultaneousness of cause and effect (if A then B; if not A, then not B) was adopted and elaborated by the followers of Dignāga, specifically by Dharmakīrti (*Dignāga's Ālambanaparīkṣā*, Kl. Schriften, p. 190).

The second solution Dignāga gives is more complicated: 'The look (form) < of the object > of a former consciousness is the condition of a later consciousness. It brings about in the root-consciousness (*ben shi*, *mūlavijñāna*) the production of an effect (*guo, phala*) which is similar to that <look>; and < this > potentiality (*gong neng*) causes the arising < of the later actual consciousness>.' (p. 888c16–17). This solution makes use of the notion of root-consciousness, the *mūlavijñāna*, which is another name for the eighth consciousness or storehouse-consciousness (*ālayavijñāna*). This deepest level of consciousness, which is subconscious, contains the history of a given stream of consciousness in form of potentialities or, more accurately, virtualities called seeds (*zhong zi*, *bīja*). These seeds are, as we could say in a Husserlian language, the sedimentation of the history of a given stream of consciousness, a sedimentation which influences (conditions) the future experience of that consciousness.

This second solution, which to me seems highly interesting, is elaborated by Xuanzang. In the chapter on the eighth consciousness in the section on the objective base (*ālambana*) and the act (*xing xiang*, *ākāra*), which is the act of knowledge or of discrimination (*liao bie yong*, *vijñaptikrīyā*), he says that the eighth consciousness by the power of its seeds as causes and conditions evolves (*bian*) the objective base (*ālambana*) and that the act of knowledge (*xing xiang*, i.e., *liao bie yong*) relies on it (*zhang*) and thereby arises. (16b4–6; *Shuji* 317a9–10).

Fortunately, the commentary of Kuiji records explanations to this passage given by Xuanzang. (p. 317a11ff). It distinguishes two different meanings of 'evolve' (*bian* pariṇāma). The first is: *produce* (*sheng bian*). According to this meaning, the seeds or *virtualities* of the eighth consciousness, which are, as we shall see, of two kinds, evolve, i.e., produce, the *actual* consciousness and also the objective base (*ālambana*) of that actual consciousness. The second meaning of 'evolve', according to the commentary, is: ' *to take as objective base* (*yuan*), which is the same as *to make appear* (*bian xian*)' (p. 317a21–22). According to this *second* meaning, the actual consciousness, in its aspect as objectivating or discriminating act (*jian fen*, *darśanabhāga*), evolves the appearance, i.e., it makes actually appear the object or objective base on which it relies. This actual *appearance* of the objective base evolved by the objectivating act is called 'the part of the *own* look (form) <of the object> (*zi xiang fen*)' or the 'evolved shadow image' (*suo bian ying xiang*) (p. 317a27–28, cf. 317a15).[3]

According to these explanations we get thus the following picture of our knowledge of material things: The seeds or virtualities of the subconsciousness (the eighth consciousness, *ālayavijñāna*) produce ('evolve' in the first sense) the object as objective base (*ālambana*) of our knowledge. The objectivating act (*jian fen*, *darśanabhāga*) as a part (*fen*, *bhāga*) of the actual consciousness relies on it (is based on it, is conditioned by it) and makes it actually appear ('evolve' in the second meaning) as an other part, the objective part of actual consciousness: This 'objective part' of actual consciousness is called its 'own look (form)' (*zi xiang fen*). This 'own look' or 'shadow image' (*ying xiang*) as a part (*fen*, *bhāga*) of actual consciousness is nothing else than the object *as it actually appears* in the actual stream of consciousness or the actual *objective phenomenon*.

The two kinds of 'evolution' (*bian*, *pariṇāma*) are, in the commentary of Kuiji, also called 'evolving on the level of cause' (*yin neng bian*, *hetu pariṇāma*) and 'evolving on the level of effect' (*guo neng bian*, *phala pariṇāma*) respectively. We find these two expressions also in Xuanzang's *Cheng wei shi lun* (II, p. 7b). The first expression signifies the evolving by seeds or virtualities and the second the evolving on the level of actual consciousness. I would like to remark in parenthesis that these two kinds of 'evolution' are very similar to the *two concepts of constitution* in Husserl, the *static* constitution and the *genetic* constitution: The analysis of the *static* constitution investigates, according to Husserl, the appearance of an object through the multiplicity of acts of an actual stream of consciousness, whereas the analysis of the *genetic* constitution investigates the becoming of mental habitudes (*Habitualitäten*), which as virtualities condition our experience of the world.

Let us go a step further and ask: what are precisely, according to Xuanzang, these potentialities or virtualities which are called *seeds* (*zhong zi*, *bīja*) and which produce the objective base (*suo yuan*, *ālambana*) of the act of knowledge or of actual consciousness in general? I mentioned already that they are of *two* kinds: The first kind is called 'seeds of similar continuation' (*deng liu*, *niṣyanda*) and the second is called 'seeds of different ripening' (*yi shu*, *vipāka*).

The *seeds of simlar continuation* are the virtualities whose causes are similar to the effects these virtualities produce. For instance, bad acts of stealing create or reinforce in us a disposition to steal and this virtuality manifests itself in new acts of stealing; or good acts of helping other people produce in us a disposition of helpfulness, a virtuality which then conditions a similar behaviour; also, actually playing an instrument creates or reinforces in us an aptitude to play this instrument. Consequently, this potentiality conditions the further actual playing of this instrument. I think everything that we call habit in our life, habit in a very broad sense that covers all kinds of acquired sensory-motor, intellectual and moral aptitudes and dispositions (cf. virtues in the Aristotelian sense) could be subsumed under this title 'seeds of similar continuation'. One does not need to be a pupil of Hume to be aware of the enormous power of these 'seeds' of habit in our experience and in our whole life. It makes sense, also from a phenomenological point of view, to say that these habitual acquisitions are a base conditioned by which actual consciousness makes its objects appear.

However, according to the theory Xuanzang defends these seeds are not the unique power by which our life is preconditioned. There are also the 'seeds of different ripening'. As their name indicates, the effects or fruits of these seeds are *different* from their causes. The causes of these seeds are, according to this conception, always morally qualified actions, good[4] or bad, they are *karma*; the fruits into which these 'karma-seeds'[5] ripen are different; they are no longer morally qualified as good or bad, but are more or less pleasant or unpleasant. They are the *retribution* of my former good and bad deeds. For instance, if I murder someone, this act creates in me a power which may lead to the fact that in my next life I shall be reborn as a tiger. To be an animal is considered unpleasant, but it is neither morally good nor bad.

The world I actually experience is thus not only conditioned by my habits but also by my 'karma seeds'. Xuanzang explains more precisely that these karma seeds condition the world in which I live *through my body*: Which kind of world I experience, a world of a tiger or of a humen being or a world of a god and so on, depends on my body which is produced by my karma seeds. He says: 'The root of the produced world is the body in its needs and its functions. What for a certain body serves as its support and its use is produced <as the corresponding world>' (II, 19b3–4). The commentary of Kuiji adds: 'The fundamental evolving is that of the body. There would be no reason to evolve what the body cannot use' (p. 322c13–14). That different sentient beings have evolved a *common* world they live in is explained by the similarity of their *karma* (p. 321c23–24). And this means also a similarity of their bodies.

This theory of karma seeds or seeds of different ripenings sounds to a phenomenologist not accustomed to Buddhist or Indian thinking very strange and obscure but also very familiar and illuminating. If we analyze phenomenologically the genetic constitution of the given world in our experience we can account for many aspects of it by concepts like association, associative inference, learning, acquisition, inductive formation of apperceptions and so on, concepts which could all be subsumed under a broad concept of *habitude* or *habit*. However, the fact that we have the body we actually have, this particular mortal body with this particular sensory-motor structure and these particular sensuous fields, cannot be accounted for by these concepts of habit. That we have these particular series of hyletic data and not others, that we have these particular fellow human beings, etc., all these aspects of our experience of the world we cannot account for by those concepts of habit. Phenomenology says here: That is *facticity*, and this means, that phenomenology has not further reason to offer.

I have the impression that it is exactly this aspect of facticity in our experience which is covered by the 'karma seeds' in the theory Xuanzang presents. These 'karma seeds' which make a link between morality and factual nature or between morality and natural happiness are not a phenomenological concept, just like Kant's concept of God in his *Critique of Practical Reason*, which makes a similar link, is not a phenomenological concept. Kant and also Husserl call this link a *postulate*.

As I attempt to give this interpretation, I have a feeling that phenomenological thinkers, conditioned by Western languages and culture, will find this philosophy something alien, different and unfamiliar. But they will also, I feel, find in it, in spite of different cultural presuppositions, insights with intercultural appeal—for the problems it deals with are universal problems of philosophy.

In this paper, I tried to understand, with the eyes of a phenomenologist, a small aspect of the very sophisticated theory of consciousness presented by Xuanzang, a Chinese monk who made a long pilgrimage to India. In doing so, I not only isolated a small aspect, which in this theory is interrelated with others, for instance with a very interesting conception of self-consciousness,[6] but I also neglected many elements of this theory which are proper parts of the aspect I studied here. I almost completely neglected, for instance, the different levels of consciousness elaborated in this theory, (i.e. the level of sensuous consciousness, intellectual consciousness, I-consciousness and subconsciousness). I also neglected the distinction between *own* or *immediate* objective base (*qin suo yuan yuan, sākṣāt?*) and *foreign* or *mediate* objective base (*shu suo yuan yuan*) (cf. VII, 19b4–20a10). This distinction is partly linked with the different levels of consciousness, because the theory explains, for instance, that sensuous consciousness and intellectual consciousness have their mediate (or foreign) objective base in the subconsciousness. This distinction also goes beyond those levels since the theory holds that the subconsciousness of *one* sentient being takes the sentient body, the consciousness and the world of *other* sentient beings as its mediate (or foreign) objective base, and so on. I could not deal with all these elements in this paper. My making a link here between phenomenology and the thinking of Vijñānavāda merely intended to let occidental phenomenologists guess that Vijñānavāda may be for them a treasure house to be explored and tapped. Indian phenomenologists and philosophers may clarify and correct many of the points I have referred to here.

NOTES AND REFERENCES

1. Cf. E. Frauwallner, *Landmarks in the History of Indian Logic*, WZKSO 5 (1961), p. 132 ff (*Kleine Schriften*, 1982, p. 854 ff.)
2. E. Frauwallner, l.c., p. 136 (858); Yuichi Kajiyama, *Bhāvaviveka, Sthiramati and Dharmapāla*, WZKSO 12/13 (1968/69), p. 193 ff.
3. So there are two meanings of 'the part of the look (form)' (*xiang fen, nimittabhāga*):

The look (form) as objective base produced by the seeds of the Ālaya-consciousness, and the *own* look (form), i.e., the appearance realized by the objectivating act (act of knowledge, act of discrimination), which relies on the look in the first sense. The *own* look is also called 'the *own* base condition' (*zi suo yuan*), which means the same as 'the immediate base condition' (*qin suo yuan*): *Shuji* 317b13–14. Of course, these two looks (forms) can also be identified, since it is the look in the first sense which the objectivating act, relying on it, brings to appearance; or the look in the second sense is the look in the first sense *qua* actually appearing.

4. Not transcendent good, but good in a manner which is still bound to the world, the *samsāra* (*you lou*, *āṣrava*).
5. The seeds of different ripening are also called 'karma seeds'.
6. Cf. my paper 'The Strucutre of Consciousness according to Xuanzang', *Journal of the British Society for Phenomenology*, Vol. 19, No. 3, October 1988.

Last Philosophy: Ideas for a Transcendental Phenomenological Metaphysics—Eugen Fink with Edmund Husserl, 1928–1938[1]

RONALD BRUZINA

The highest of all questions . . . are the 'metaphysical': they concern birth and death, the ultimate being of the 'I' and of the 'we' objectivated as humanity, the teleology that ultimately leads back to transcendental subjectivity and transcendental historicity, and naturally as highest item the being of God as the principle of this teleology, and the meaning of this being in contrast to the being of the first Absolute, the being of my transcendental I and the all-encompassing subjectivity that discloses itself in me—which together with the 'constitution' of the world as 'ours' pertain to the true locus of divine 'working'—speaking from God's viewpoint, the constant creation of the world in us, in our transcendental ultimately true being.

—Edmund Husserl to Gustav Albrecht, June 3, 1932.[2]

I. BACKGROUND TO AN OUTLINE OF A PHENOMENOLOGICAL METAPHYSICS

When Husserl wrote these lines to Albrecht, his lifelong friend, this was no mere occasional remark. In Husserl's programme of phenomenological labours in which 'first philosophy' was the explication of the transcendental roots of conscious life and experience in absolute subjectivity, questions of the 'highest' and 'last' things—among other matters—could only be addressed at the end of phenomenology, as the subject matter of *last* philosophy.[3] But even if Husserl's treatment of the questions belonging to a phenomenological metaphysics had to be withheld until phenomenology itself was sufficiently complete to provide the proper basis for it, this did not mean that the issues were out of mind. Particularly in the last period of his life, Husserl was profoundly aware that the final questions were pressing; they were to be encompassed by the works then being planned.

So, for example, in the revision of his 'Cartesian Meditations' that Husserl intended to make for a German audience, he meant for the exposition to reach 'to the highest "metaphysical" problematic'.[4] The first expansion of the original Sorbonne lectures that he had done in the spring of 1929 already sketched out what this metaphysics might be;[5] and three years later, in the same letter to Albrecht as is quoted above, he echoes the ideas he indicated in that 1929 version, speaking of metaphysics not as 'a field of vague speculation or a realm of entranced mysticism', but as 'the science that produces the final clarification of the world and of man, that thus has their final absolute meaning as its theme.'[6] Between these two statements of Husserl's, brief as they may be, lies another project however; and in that project, in addition to Husserl's own thinking on metaphysics there was another mind working with him to piece out the framework of a philosophy that would take up both first and last questions.

Soon after beginning a serious recasting of his 'Meditations' in such form as would address the philosophic context in Germany, Husserl began to reconsider whether the 'Cartesian Meditations' in the end would actually suit. As a result of this kind of doubt, for the next several years until he finally dropped work on the 'Cartesian Meditations' entirely in 1934, Husserl wavered between this revision task and a completely new exposition of phenomenology, a comprehensive systematic treatment of it that would simply replace those 'Meditation'. By mid-1930 this alternative project commanded his interest, as he explains in a letter to Dorion Cairns from September 23, 1930, which at the same times gives the basic pattern of the philosophic situation I wish to treat here. Husserl writes:

> With my excellent assistant, Dr. Fink, I am working on a new systematic outline of transcendental phenomenology (the problematic reaching up to ethical-religious and to 'metaphysical' issues). Hopefully it will appear in 1931. Read the fine prize essay of Dr. Fink in *Jahrbuch* XI and my Postscript to the English translation of *Ideen* (appearing in a few weeks).'[7]

Here we see it: in the project of a new systematic exposition, phenomenology opens out to include a treatment of metaphysics, to the extent that meaningfulness is made possible for it within phenomenology;[8] and Eugen Fink, whose work is highly esteemed and recommended to others by Husserl, is in the project with him. My intention here, now, is to sketch out, within this project, some specifics of that inclusion of the elements of a phenomenological metaphysics, and to base my sketch of this metaphysics precisely on the tentative ideas that Fink developed beyond the minimal indications that Husserl gave.

To justify this choice of method, there are a number of things that would have to be done first by way of both background and explanation. For example, one ought to review the documentation that describes the special place Fink held in Husserl's regimen of research and thinking, a place unique among the various research assistants Husserl had over the years. One ought to trace, too, the contribution Fink made to Husserl's plans and decisions regarding the direction phenomenology took in the last ten years of Husserl's life. Finally one would have to consider the character of thinking in a philosophic undertaking with respect to the way it is, or is not, the product exclusively of one human psyche, and therefore with respect to the way one would, or would not, identify 'a' philosophy as an 'individual' thing. I shall have to leave all this aside, however, in order to get to the matter at hand, viz., the ideas that were developed within the project of final, mature transcendental phenomenology to bring about at least the outlines of philosophic completeness in the form of a treatment of issues that could be spoken of as *metaphysical*.

II. A PLAN FOR METAPHYSICS WITHIN THE SYSTEM OF PHENOMENOLOGY

When Husserl wrote to Cairns in September of 1930 about the 'new systematic outline of transcendental phenomenology', he had something quite concrete in mind. Within the preceding month Fink had handed him a nine-page sketch for this 'System of Phenomenological Philosophy';[9] it is the fullest representation we have of the conception of a complete phenomenology in Husserl's final period.[10] The plan comprised two large divisions, a first book that would treat 'the Levels of Pure Phenomenology', and a second entitled 'Ontology and Phenomenology', Fink's nine-page sketch gave full detail on the first book, leaving the second with but three section headings. It is in the first book, as its final section, that we find the outline for a metaphysics:

Section 4: Basic Features of Phenomenological Metaphysics

A. Phenomenological idealism and the problem of transcendental historicity.
B. The transcendental necessity of the 'fact' of the *ego*. The centring of transcendental-historical intersubjectivity in the central egological monad.
C. The transcendental deduction of the 'uniqueness of the world'.
D. Restoration of the transcendental legitimacy of 'naïvité' (constitutive determination of the 'natural attitude' as a mode of existence of transcendental life itself).
E. The transcendental tendency to 'return-to-oneself' (prior forms in religion, wisdom, and in the ethical *authenticity* of life in the world). Philosophy as function of the Absolute: the philosopher as discloser of absolute subjectivity is the 'manager of the world-spirit.' Outlook upon a philosophy of history.—The philosopher as 'transcendental official' has the *possibility* of the highest authenticity, his responsibility as model: phenomenological restoration of the Platonic idea of the state.

Now, in point of fact, in view of how Husserl and Fink actually worked, there is nothing *definitive* about this plan for metaphysics; it was a preliminary sketch that not only was not realized, but was also subject to replacement by other arrangements of topics.[11] Moreover, it gives no hint either about the relative importance of the different themes given—not all of them are equally crucial to phenomenological philosophy—nor does it indicate where a number of commonly mentioned themes fit, such as some of the 'last things'—birth, death, and God—mentioned in Husserl's letter to Albrecht quoted at the beginning of this essay. Finally, it is not in the metaphysics as here sketched that one finds indicated any real treatment of the pivotal issue of the *being* of the *I* and the *being* of both the Absolute and 'God' (again mentioned in Husserl's letter to Albrecht). This question of being seems rather to be placed in the section *prior* to 'phenomenological metaphysics', namely in Section 3: 'Progressive Phenomenology', under the heading, 'D. Being as 'Idea', which comprised the following: the 'theory of levels of being; levels of pre-being and levels of worldly being (e.g., pretheoretical and theoretical being)'.

One might have supposed that it would be in the second book of the 1930 plan, viz., 'Ontology and Phenomenology', that treatment of being in the its various phenomenological levels would be located, but that does not seem to be the case. Instead of the question of being, 'Ontology and Phenomenology' seemed to be oriented more toward the explication of various important 'ontological regions', especially in confrontation with the treatment they would receive in non-philosophical sciences and in non-phenomenological treatment.[12] In fact, however, in probing the way the question of being in its various 'levels', on the one hand, and the issues for a 'last philosophy', a metaphysics, on the other, get thematized and located in the phenomenological enterprise as a whole, one begins to see certain crucial differences between Husserl and Fink coming out; and these differences must obviously be taken into account in regard to the whole idea of a phenomenological metaphysics.

A complete explication of these differences, however, cannot be undertaken here. Instead I wish to concentrate on tracing only the basics of the thinking *Fink* developed, during the period of his work with Husserl, about the character of metaphysics and ontology in phenomenology. For in Fink's work we find both a characterization of Husserl's ideas about these matters, and at the same time an insightful and broadly based critique of those ideas, which thereupon leads Fink to consider possibilities for a more adequate conception, precisely within a fully self-mastered transcendental phenomenology.

III. THE GENERAL PLAN FOR PHENOMENOLOGICAL METAPHYSICS AND ONTOLOGY IN FINK'S PERSPECTIVE

Fink's position on phenomenology, and on those components that would flesh out its full systematic, as he developed that position during his years with Husserl is visible to a certain extent in the essays he wrote during the period. Most of these were in fact read over by Husserl, though not all of them were published before Husserl's death.[13] The fact remains, however, that these essays were largely written as expositions and defences of Husserl's phenomenology. As a result Fink did not really display the central thinking from which his often startling recasting of Husserl's thought in those essays actually stemmed. More than that, one cannot see the extraordinarily broad context of philosophic critique and confrontation that Fink was bringing to phenomenology, nor follow the way he treated challenges to it not simply as external threats but as occasions for rethinking its bases and implications. For this it is necessary to study his personal notes from the years of his work with Husserl; and it is precisely on these notes that my study here is based.

The first thing that has to be done, now, is to place Fink's thinking out of Husserlian transcendental phenomenology in its context, namely, in regard to the challenges to it from other philosophic positions. There were two main 'external' opponent elements in that philosophic context, and one dominant alternative from within the phenomenological movement itself. The frist 'external' opponent was, as one might expect, Neo-Kantianism, the second the 'life-philosophies' that were so strong at the time. Fink addressed the work of the Neo-Kantians in his famous 1933 *Kantstudien* article, 'The Phenomenological Philosophy of Edmund Husserl and Contemporary Criticism.[14] But the Neo-Kantians were not the only then contemporary critics who had to be considered, so that Fink in fact at this same time had in mind to write a similar article directly on the question of 'life-philosophy and phenomenology'; and he characterized it precisely as 'Edmund Husserl's Phenomenological Philosophy in Contemporary Criticism, Part II'.[15] What this meant for Fink in fact was that Husserl's phenomenology had to be rethought in such a way as to take into account not simply the Neo-Kantians, but *Kant*, and to see how it did, or could, integrate what was valid in Kant's work within itself—and then to do the same not simply with Dilthey but, beyond Dilthey, with *Nietzsche* and *Hegel*. Finally, this rethinking of Husserl's philosophy had to take into account the radical questions set by that challenger within phenomenology, *Martin Heidegger*.

These are the philosophic powers, now, that had to be dealt with in order for Fink to be able to sketch out the way a transcendental phenomenology would consider within itself a place and legitimacy for metaphysics and ontology. And so we find a list of projects Fink outlined for himself for the year 1934 to include among other things the following:[16]

1. The 'System of Philosophy in its Basic Plan', again similar in comprehensive purpose as the earlier project Husserl had planned, but now conceived by Fink as a statement of *his own* position (more will be said about this in a moment);
2. 'World and Consciousness of World', which Fink here characterizes as '(my) first *philosophical* work', which from other indications we see he had projected, in one guise or another, for a *Habilitationsschrift*;[17]
3. 'Life-philosophy and Phenomenology', again the defence of phenomenology against a major criticism of the time;
4. 'Edmund Husserl's Phenomenology in Heidegger's Criticism' which he intriguingly entitles, after Hegel, 'Difference between the Husserlian and Heideggerian Systems of Philosophy.'

A great many of the notes that Fink wrote during his work with Husserl could in fact be organized around these broad topics; but for my purpose here I wish to select only one of these topics, the first, and draw from it the ideas that comprise Fink's elaboration of the elements needed for a phenomenological metaphysics and ontology.

For it is in a *systematic* plan for phenomenology, in a working out of its basics in such a way as to be both complete and self-critical, and at the same time to come to terms within itself with the valid issues of such major philosophers as Kant, Hegel, Nietzsche, and Heideger, that one would find the question of the possibility and character of a metaphysics and an ontology best explained. In this regard, then, we can best begin with the broadest outline of Fink's own plan for this 'system of philosophy'; and that is what we find in the following note from 1933, in the same period in which Fink produced the *Kantstudien* article spoken of earlier, namely, defending Husserl's phenomenology against

Neo-Kantianism. This, too, was the period between Fink's finishing what became the conclusion of his revision work on Husserl's 'Cartesian Meditations', and the burst of impetus on Husserl's part that resulted in the 'Krisis' writings. The plan for a 'system of philosophy' comprised four parts:

I. System as such, why it is needed, what function it serves in a philosophy in the first place;
II. Cosmology, dealing with existence;
III. Phenomenology, dealing with consciousness;
IV. Meontic, dealing with spirit.[18]

Setting aside the first question, regarding the nature and function of the system as such, despite its importance, we can concentrate on the remaining three parts—a 'streamlining' which Fink as well followed in other notes on the 'system'.[19]

IV. THE CENTRAL ISSUES IN FINK'S PLAN FOR A SYSTEM OF PHILOSOPHY

For Fink the whole key to the plan for a system of phenomenological philosophy, which, among other things, would establish the place and validity a metaphysics might have within it, lay in the determination of the meaning of *ontology* in the phenomenology enterprise. The only possibility for achieving this, as one might expect, was to find a way out of the deadlocked conflict between Husserl and Heidegger on how to understand *being* in phenomenology. Again from one of the principal collections of notes for illuminating the work of Fink with Husserl in 1933–34, here is Fink's representation of that deadlock:

> On the concept of *ontology* within the 'phenomenological movement' [there is] no unanimity.
>
> Husserl's intuitionist-'epistemological' entry: being = modality of positing. A being = an '*object*'. This intuitionism in the starting-point [provides] subjectivistic factors that in fact are only means for *blasting open* the 'natural attitude'. Husserl's real thesis on 'being' is the '*phenomenological reduction*': i.e., the thesis of the *constitutedness of a being* . Husserl's term *ontology* actually means only the *a prioristic* doctrine of material and formal 'regions' in a theory of objects; this, when viewed from the problem of ontology, is therefore only a *part of the problem*.
>
> Heidegger's centre is the concept of the *ontological difference*, the distinction between *a being and being*.[20]

There is, of course, more to Heidegger's standpoint *vis-à-vis* the Husserlian position than what is mentioned here. In particular, as frequent refections in Fink's notes show, the issue more pointedly was the charge that Husserl's concept of the subject was ontologically 'underdetermined', that is, conceived as standing in a worldless 'nowhere', utterly lacking that concreteness of the ecstatic relationship to being within a world-frame which was fundamental to the Heideggerian analysis of Dasein.[21] This was the position represented, for example, in the exchange of letters between Heidegger and Husserl on the occasion of their unsuccessful collaboration on the article on phenomenology for the *Encyclopaedia Brittanica*.[22] The outcome of that attempt at collaboration was a deadlock of irreconcilability between them. For Fink, now, to break this deadlock philosophically meant in effect to do what Heidegger demanded,[23] namely, to raise the question of the meaning of the being of that phenomenological stratum to which all else in phenomenology is referred, namely, absolute constituting subjectivity. But to raise this question meant as well that Fink had actually to develop a way of *handling* the question, a way of formulating it in terms of transcendental phenomenological procedures and themes, and therefore a way of critically *extending* and *modifying* transcendental phenomenology. The two crucial procedures for Fink, then, were a *critical reinterpretation* of central phenomenological moves, on the one hand, and, on the other, a *methodological analysis* of that new interpretative dimension of phenomenology. My treatment here, accordingly, will cover first, the essential elements of this criticial reinterpretation, and then, the methodological issues that Fink elicits from it and has to wrestle with. In the end, as I hope we shall see, it is the methodological question that will be the most intractable, and that raises the question whether Fink's whole endeavour can succeed. That, however, is a matter that shall have to taken up later.

To be most economical in a review of Fink's critical reinterpretation of phenomenology, let me simply offer a summary of the main steps taken in it, by way of a list of 'theses', as it were, each of which represented the focus of endlessly repeated reflections on Fink's part in his personal notes.

1. Phenomenology is regressive inquiry into *origins*; but the origin to be investigated has to be ultimately not simply the origin of *meaning* in its determinate constellations, in its constitution, but the origin of *being*. In this way phenomenology would move from its preliminary psychological stage, then past its epistemological concerns, and into its *final-philosophical* stage.[24]
2. To achieve this move to the final stage, however, the thrust to origins—i.e., the *reduction*—has to be critically reconceived beyond the framework of conceptual presuppositions that dominates respectively in each prior stage.
3. Thus, against persistence in the *psychological* stage, the apperceptions that the subject reflecting within the phenomenological reduction has of itself have to be considered not as *ipso facto* containing, and immediately displaying, the characteristics of the ultimate originating factor itself, but as the *transcendental semblances* which have to be interpretatively *passed through* in order to reach what is truly the origin.[25]
4. In addition, against persistence in the *epistemological* stage, the relationship to origins that is to be investigated regressively for the phenomena in question—which ultimately means phenomena *as being*, whether objects or subjects—can no longer be taken paradigmatically in terms of the *subject-object framework*.[26] Being does not mean simply to be the object for a subject.[27]
5. Ultimately the question of origins is the question of the origin *of the world*;

but when the world is taken precisely as the horizon of being, then the reductive move is a move of regress to the origins of being; for being is essentially a *constitutive result*.[28]

6. To investigate the origin of the world means precisely to negate essential containment within the world—which is precisely the point of the reduction. Accordingly, since being means in principle being within the horizon of the world, to negate essential containment within the world would mean to *negate belonging to the sphere of being*.
7. The basic meaning of the 'Absolute' is thus reached, namely, that which is absolved from intrinsic belonging in the world and in being.[29]
8. Therefore that which phenomenology would claim to reach as the origin of the world and of being, the Absolute, will have to be considered *beyond being*, in short, *meontic*.[30]
9. The formula for phenomenology radically reconsidered in terms of the question of being is, therefore, that it be, beyond ontology, 'a meontic metaphysics of the 'Absolute'.[31]

The core of the argument, that is, of the entire critical reinterpretation under the goad of the question Heidegger poses for Husserl's transcendental phenomenology, the question of the kind of being that is being reductively disclosed, can be seen in the following summary which Fink himself has given us:

The stage of beginning for phenomenology (Husserl) oriented the understanding of the world to the traditionally accepted subject-object relation. The method of phenomenological regressive inquiry thus became the inquiry into the 'living processes of constituting.' Primacy of the constitution of objects.—This made possible the great reversal of 'phenomenology': Heidegger grand 'ontology,' that once again transformed the problematic of 'idealism' into an ontological problem; inquiry into the subject became the *ontological grasp of the subject*. With that the apparent revolution in ontology: the break-up of the one-level concept of being! The kind of being had by subjectivity. In the impossibility of simply conceiving the 'subject' as 'confrontationally present' ['*vorhanden*'] the 'transcendental motive' showed through yet again. Cf. the autonomy in the concept of 'transcendence'!—Precisely the reversal of phenomenological philosophy into an ontology (one that no longer inquired into 'things,' but rather emphasized the internal difference in modes of being), wherein phenomenological explication of the subject was considered as a venture that was ontologically relevant, but one to be taken up only in totality structures. With the ontology of the subject playing the role of a fundamental ontology, this reversal is a retarding element that urges the speculative drive of phenomenology to renewed exertion and deeper probing: the ontologically graspable subject, Dasein, is the result of a 'constitution' (self-apperception!!!). Thereupon the concept of being is broken through in the concept of the Absolute: *meontic revolution*. 'Ego-ness' is broken through: Absolution. Philosophy as 'absolute knowing': which has to founder.

Shipwreck in God!![32]

This, of course, is a tightly compressed summary, that ends in a provocative and ominous suggestion that the whole effort to develop an ontology of the absolute constituting power for phenomenology has to fail, and that therefore a metaphysical clarification of final issues cannot succeed within phenomenology. Before drawing that conclusion, however, we have to learn a little more about this 'meontic' of Fink's, by following his 'meontic-phenomenological' explications of certain metaphysical issues. That done, we can then see his own methodological reflections on 'meontic' explication and what their outcome might be.

V. SPECIFIC ISSUES IN A MEONTIC METAPHYSICS

The letter Husserl wrote to Albrecht in mid-1932, which in the passage quoted at the beginning names important 'metaphysical' issues, no doubt reflects the work on the system of phenomenological philosophy that Husserl and Fink had already been intermittently working on for the two previous years; and we may surely draw from it to choose the themes to highlight in the 'meontic-phenomenological' interpretation Fink offers. Thus we have the following topics:

1. birth and death;
2. the ultimate being of the 'I' and the 'we';
3. the teleology of the regressive move that leads to both transcendental subjectivity and the coursing of that subjectivity in a concrete temporality, in a 'historicity';
4. the being of 'God' as teleological 'principle' of that regressive move;
5. the being of 'God' in contrast to the being of the transcendental 'Absolute';
6. the being of my own 'I' transcendentally considered, and the being of the 'all-encompassing subjectivity' disclosed in my 'I';
7. the constitution of the world as belonging to an 'us', coupled with the 'all-encompassing subjectivity' that lies in my 'I', together comprising the 'true locus of divine working'.

This is a weighty list, that can certainly not be exhaustively treated in a brief paper such as the present one. We need some pivotal principle, or principles, that will produce the interpretation to make in each case; for they all relate together.

Such a principle is indeed what we find expressed in one of Fink's working notes: 'We lay hold of the most decisive fundamental insight that is required for the understanding of phenomenological philosophy in the thesis, ***being is a result***'; to which Fink adds as a corollary that, therefore, 'substantially existent 'subjectivity' is constitutively a result' as well.[33] However, it is only by garnering additional details and filling out some of the implications of this principle that we will be able to see the decisiveness Fink credits it with.

To begin with, in another note close to the one just cited Fink offers a crucial clarification: 'All 'being' is a result, but it is not a deed done by 'some being'. *There is no 'analogia entis' between the transcendental and the substantially existent Subject*.'[34] The implication of this is clearly, therefore, that in some sense yet to be determined being is not the *final* matter for inquiry, but a stage in progress to that which is genuinely final. "Being" is an *abstract moment* in the speculative genesis of world-constitution.... What for dogmatic philosophy is ultimate and the final question is, for the "phenomenologist", simply the *exit* for thought to push into something that is *epekeina tês ousias*, beyond 'being' altogether, into the meontic dimension of the Absolute.'[35]

Fink, however, is acutely aware of the dangers that threaten here, specifically: first, the danger of devaluating those matters that lie on *this side* of what we may deem to be the 'meontic divide', to coin a term; and then, secondly, the methodological question regarding just how one could say anyting at all about what is on that *other side*. This methodological question is something we shall take up later. All in all what Fink does is to adopt a somewhat Hegelian strategy, and to try to conceptualize an intimate, indeed an unbreakable, relationship between the two sides of this 'divide', in fact, to *dissolve* the supposed division in a unity he could call *integration*.[36] The way Fink does this is to treat the whole realm of ontological meaning and validity, viz., the world and within it the human subject—or the human existent, if one prefers—, as the term and moment by which the 'meontic Absolute' realizes itself, as the term and moment by which 'non-being' comes to *be*. For example, regarding the *world*, first of all, Fink writes in one place:

> Meontic philosophy does not devaluate the world as only a semblance of being in contrast to that which is a 'being' properly speaking, the *ontos ôn* of the Absolute, but rather precisely lets the world be the *ontos ôn* in contrast to the nothingness of the Absolute. The world *is* the Absolute.[37]

Similarly, in regard to the human subject, meontic philosophy has to take it as the transformative realization of the Absolute in the form of finite conscious being, to the concealment of the Absolute's 'native' figure as 'no-being', as 'nothingness'. In this sense, human being is the simultaneous enfigurement and disfigurement of the absolute:

> Human subjectivity is the finite reflection of transcendental subjectivity. What makes the danger of anthropologism so great is that man always creeps into the transcendental subject, that on the other hand man even wears the features of the transcendental subject. Man is the disfigurement of the absolute subject.[38]

This, now, gives, a new dimension to the old phenomenological idea of the 'natural attitude'. In Fink's ontological-meontological rethinking of the reduction, the term 'natural attitude' sounds too much like a contingent psychological stance that human being in the world can easily overcome and alter, thus becoming radically philosophical. For Fink, a better term is 'encaptivation in the world' (*Weltbefangenheit*),[39] that is to say, a condition that, far from being negatable and removable, *makes up* the human situation. For Fink, 'encaptivation in the world' is the very 'horizon of being.'[40] It is not a contingent, alterable property, but 'the being of man itself.'[41] To break through 'encaptivation in the world', therefore, is to break out of humanness in the radical, meontic transformation worked by the reduction.[42] In sum,

> *The 'world' and the natural attitude are the same.* The world is not so much the wherein of objects, the concept of the totality of all beings, but at its deepest is ... the whole of the self-apperceptions in which the world-free transcendental subject binds itself to a world in order to be, in which the infinite finitizes and contingentizes itself.[43]

It is obvious, now, that this 'meontological' interpretation throws phenomenology into a whole new mould. For since 'the Absolute only *is* as its manifestation', and in no way exists beforehand and then afterwards performs an act of 'creation', constituting the world as its self-manifestation, since as well, therefore, constitution simply means, ultimately, the manifestation or appearance of the Absolute, phenomenology is simply 'the theory of the appearance of the Absolute'.[44] At the same time, the reduction serves precisely as the move that discloses this 'transcendental semblance' on the part of the human subject, inasmuch as it proposes in principle to 'un-world' and 'un-humanize' self-reflective action. As Fink puts it, 'only the action of *un-humanizing* makes the ontic-ontological standpoint convert into the meontic,[45] in a reversal of the thrust of origination, of constitution, by which the Absolute 'disfiguringly' realizes itself, ontologizes itself, in the manifestation of the world and of the subject in it.[46]

The effect of this recasting of phenomenology under the urging of the question of being, this recasting of a philosophy of origins into a meontic,[47] has now to be seen more directly in regard to the topics cited above for treatment in a phenomenological metaphysics. The basic idea for doing this can be stated fairly simply. To the extent that what is at issue in a particular topic properly pertains to the realm of being, i.e., to the realm of the world and of beings in it, it cannot be supposed as such to characterize the Absolute of transcendental origin itself. On the other hand, the only way anything pertaining at all to that originating Absolute itself can be affirmed is precisely in terms—appropriately interpreted—of some appearance in the realm of the world, and specifically in terms of reflective subjectivity as a 'transcendental semblance'. But this is simply because the world of being is the only realm of being there is; the Absolute simply *is not*, apart from the realm of being, apart from or outside the horizon of the world. The methodological question, thus, becomes all-important for determining the possibility of the meaningfulness of a meontic. But before turning to that in the final section of this paper, let me at least review rapidly the effect of Fink's meontic on the topics drawn from Husserl's letter to Albrecht and listed above.

To 1. For Fink, birth and death are ontic, not meontic determinations; there is no place for a beginning and end with respect to the ultimate constituting source, the Absolute—except, of course, that the Absolute only *is* in the traits of human subjectivity. In this restriction of beginning and end to the stream of being in the world Fink departs explicitly from Husserl's position.[48]

To 2. and 6. Ultimately the being of the 'I', and of many 'I's, of a multiplicity, is exclusively an in-the-world being. But this does not mean that ultimately the *meaning* of the 'I' and the 'we' is that of in-the-world being; their ultimate meaning lies in their relationship to the ultimate origin, which is the meontic Absolute.[49] For Fink this relationship does not entail transferring a 'monadological plurality' to the transcendental level, as it does for Husserl. In Fink's view there is no place in the meontic transcendental for either singularity or plurality.[50] In a word, the reduction is the 'meontic (not ontic) annulling of individuation.'[51]

To 3. The question of the temporality, and the historicity, of the regressive move (which is the reverse of constitutive origination) is one that is far too complex to be broached here. Nevertheless, suffice it to say that the analysis of temporality will be the deepest level of penetration to the process of origination that holds the meontic Absolute and the realm of the ontological together in an integration. The explication of this will have to wait for another occasion.

To 4. and 5. The question of God is not to be answered by positing some kind of 'primordial One' behind the appearances of things,[52] or a kind of 'first cause' in a chain of causes.[53] Rather, on the one hand, the distance between God and man is to be taken as indicating the absolution of the Absolute from the realm of man, i.e., from the world as the realm of being.[54] On the other hand, meontically considered, to ascend to God is to thrust beyond being; for the God of religion's conception is an idol with respect to the meontic Absolute.[55]

While this is, obviously, only the briefest indication of how these topics are handled, it is enough both to make the basic idea clear, and to allow us to move directly to the more serious *methodological question*, namely, how a determinacy and meaningfulness for assertions about the meontic origin, about the Absolute, is theoretically possible.

VI. THE METHODOLOGICAL ISSUES

The clearest way to enter this matter is to link up with the text that ended section IV above, where Fink, summarizing his line of thinking in transcendental phenomenology under the impact of Heidegger's question about the being of the transcendental subject, spoke of philosophy as 'absolute knowing' which 'has to *founder*'. The negativity of this assertion needs some explication. Two texts of Fink's will help to provide it, leading as they do so directly from the matters just considered in section V. The first passage is again from a rich collection dating largely from 1930–31:

> A philosophical interpretation of the world has not merely to follow the clue of the fundamental question of philosophy, the question of the origin of the world, and force itself away from the world toward the Absolute, it has not only to exit from encaptivation in the world, to achieve the act of liberating itself in God and of betraying the world; it has rather the central task of grasping the world from the direction of the Absolute, of grasping the ungodly...from the direction of the godly. The world is the wherein of the downfall of God in the world, his determination, his self-determination. The Absolute, however, *is* not the World. If the world, as the un-nihilating of the Absolute, is, the Absolute is not. The world, as condition of the not-being of the Absolute, is the first stage of self-realization. Only the *philosophical* un-nihilating of the nothingness of the Absolute is the proper ontification of the Absolute. The world thus becomes a mere *episode* in the self-realization of the Absolute. The world as episode is not something incidental, but is the absolute episode. In it lies the absolute ground for the nullity of the un-nihilating of the Absolute by philosophy: *foundering*.[56]

The question here is this. If the Absolute of origins *is* only in the manifestness of what has 'originated' out of it, namely, the sphere of being in the horizon of the world, and therefore if it *is* only there were *it itself* is *not*, then how does it become at all recognizable and knowable? And the answer is that in the regressive inquiry of reduction-sanctioned phenomenology that Absolute of origins is '*produced*' as the matter for inquiry, is given the form and figure precisely of that which is ultimate origin, but in such traits as, however, indicate at the same time that it is *not* any kind of *being* with those very same traits, i.e., that it literally *is not*. Hear Fink himself once more on this paradoxical idea:

> The *transcendental productivity* of phenomenological analysis is not ontic productivity, and therefore not a producing, a causing, a begetting. Ontic science is the demonstration of something *given beforehand*. Transcendental subjectivity is not given beforehand; it "is" not prior to the phenomenological reduction. On the other hand, it is not created in the phenomenological reduction. The ontic alternatives of givenness beforehand and creation do not apply to the transcendental sphere at all. The productivity of transcendental analysis, formally indicated, is determinable as *un-nihilating*. The transcendental origin of all beings is un-nihilated, i.e., pulled out of nothingness. Un-nihilating is a letting/making-be of being of a special sort-an ontification with a bad conscience and in continual protest, namely, an ontification by way of *me-ontifying*. [It is], therefore, not a letting-be that lets be being that already is, but rather a letting/making-be of that which is not: an *inserting into being* and not a leaving of it to its own being.[57]

To put this more simply, the product of the radical reflective turn in the phenomenological reduction, inasmuch as it reaches to that which is to be taken as the level of ultimate origins, beyond being, beyond the human, beyond the world, has to be given a status and appearance *like* something in being and in the world, at the same time in such a way that any belonging to being and the world is radically negated. And this appearance in *inappropriate* guise is, paradoxically, the *appropriate* appearance for that ultimate, for the Absolute.[58] In other words, there is a built-in *foundering* in the very conceptuality that is to be used 'properly' for the meontic Absolute. Here, then, is the critical pressure point in the problem of the legitimacy, indeed of even the theoretical possibility, of 'meontic' philosophical knowledge and assertions, which is the final matter for my paper.

First of all, the relationship of concepts as used properly in their proper realm, that is, within the horizon of the world and in reference to being, to their meontic usage is not that of a relationship between two referential instruments each of which relates to a distinct domain, one an ontic and ontological domain, the other a meontic. Rather, the two conceptualities are in *constant mutual transposition*,[59] exactly as the 'domains' they refer to are in fact but *one*, but with two 'values'. This constant mutual transposition, imposed by the meontic thesis of the exclusion of being from the Absolute of origins—better: the non-pertinence of being with respect to the latter—is the central relationship in terms of which that Absolute is deemed to be accessible *positively*, instead of entirely *negatively*.[60] Once again, the character of 'transcendental semblance' is pivotal; for precisely in the recognition of its 'semblance'-character, its function of provoking a 'foundering', lies the interpretative transposability of the ontic-ontological conceptuality that expresses that semblance into a meontic valuation.[61] To be kept in mind, however, is that the foundering that threatens here can only be deemed so to thought within the *ontic-ontological frame*.[62] Meontically speaking, the foundering in question is precisely the success aimed for!

The transcendental is in principle beyond the sphere of the applicability of ontology as such. In the realm of transcendental origins, one is dealing with the radically 'not': not-human, not-world, not-being. But the 'not' here is not the 'not' of contrariety or antithesis (the Greek 'ou-'), but rather the 'not' of *non-pertinence* or *non-applicability* (the Greek 'me-').[63] Consequently, since all characterization of subjective agency—i.e., of life as spirit—is drawn from the realm of being, i.e., from the realm of world-structured being, and specifically from the lived experience of that subjective being whose self-reflections are the action of this characterization itself, all conceptual articulations of the transcendental are *not-appropriate*, even if they are the only ones that can be made. They inevitably present the transcendental—the trans-ontological—in the conceptual guise of the ontological and mundane—i.e., finite human subjectivity in the world. They draw it out of its radical 'not'-status into the status of seeming-to-be something ontologically positive, they give it a constituted character and 'ontify' it.

For Fink, therefore, while the phenomenological reduction leads to *apparently* ontologically valued analysis and description, in the end it ultimately becomes the recognition of the radical 'not' of transcendental constituting subjectivity, the recognition that this radical sign of the meontic 'not' must govern the seemingly positive analysis and conceptualization thus produced within the reduction.

This situation, however, is not simply one of sheer negativity, because there is a structural *necessity in principle* that the Absolute of constituting agency take on the appearance it does both ontologically in the mundane form of the human subject, and reflectively and conceptually in terms of the analytic and descriptive characterizations drawn from the phenomena of that human subject. For that ontological, mundane human life and subjectivity is the very self-objectification of the Absolute of origins. It is its proper/not-proper appearance in the realm of being and knowability.

> As long as one in any way construes the Absolute under the concept of being, and treats it itself as a being, not only does it not stand as a philosohic thema, but it is in principle undisplayable. That the Absolute takes on the form of higher or more comprehensive being ("concretely"—"abstractly") in philosophical explication is itself an "*illusion*" that pertains necessarily to the essence of meontic explication. To fall victim to this illusion, to be deceived by it is the constant danger for every "absolute philosophy." It cannot escape, it can only "nullify/transcend" it: "*foundering*" *as* "*mirroring/counterillusion*".[64]

An appearance that has to be taken as non-proper semblance, an actual being that, transcendentally considered, is the 'illusury reflection' of some higher kind of being which can genuinely be no being at all, such is the meontic character of what one reaches via the reduction in the push of inquiry towards absolutely ultimate origins.[65]

We see here, too, why Fink rejects the notion of an *analogia entis* between ontic-ontological conceptuality and its meontic transposition.[66] The 'meontic analogy'[67] is not an analogy between realms of being. The analogy at most would be between two relationships, namely, between a) the relationship of an attitude blindly followed to that same attitude recognized as operative, and b) the relationship of encaptivation in the world as ontically lived to that same condition as meontically understood.[68] In the end, however, the question of the mutual transposability of the ontic-ontological and the meontic, and their radical inseparability is for Fink a *problem*, not a solution.[69] The search for a solution stemmed from his realization that the only way a meontic could work was to keep the 'originated' and the 'origin' integrally together, not despite, but *because of* the negative element of the *me*-ontic. What he also realized, however, was that phenomenology could not even attempt to work on this without a fundamental change taking place within it; it could at this point no longer be mere intuition-based description.

> Where phenomenology pushes forward into the meontic it itself removes the possibility of descriptive presentation, and justifies the speculative statement out of methodic insight into the relationship of tension between absolute meontic explication and language in the usual sense, encaptivated in the world and ensnared in the logic of the world.[70]

In short, the 'primordial relationship of origin and originated' (of Absolute and world), the 'Phenomenology of the Absolute', cannot be dealt with within the strictures of Husserl's own phenomenological method.[71] For Fink, the inner thrust of phenomenology itself, once the question of being is raised within it, carries it further. To put it simply, when phenomenology, in following the pursuit of the reduction as regression to origins, attempts seriously to work out its own implications for an ontology and a metaphysics, it puts itself again into question in a radical way, to be transformed and extended, and perhaps even to reach an inescapable critical turn, a crisis. Already in Fink's early work for Husserl this possibility was envisioned, and it haunted the next ten years of Fink's work with him, through the task of attempting to build a system of phenomenological philosophy that would be complete even in the domain of ontology and metaphysics. Let me end, then, with a provocative reflection of Fink's to this effect that was written already in the very first months of his work with Husserl.

> The origin is the me-on, is God. This the theme of metaphysics. Meontic philosophy (with its absolution and ekbasis) is the end of philosophy, is its own annihilation.[72]

NOTES AND REFERENCES

1. Acknowledgements: The research in 1985–86 on which this study is based was made possible by the support of the Alexander von Humboldt Foundation. In addition I wish to thank the Husserl–Archives, Louvain, for permission to quote from Husserl's correspondence in preparing this study. I owe a great debt of gratitude too to Guy Van Kerckhoven for having made freely available to me his own extensive research on the Husserl—Fink years. Finally, special thanks must go to Mrs. Susanne Fink both for permission to quote from the unpublished materials in the Nachlaß of Professor Fink, but above all for her tireless and generous help in my study of the unpublished materials themselves.
2. Letter in the Husserl Archives.
3. Rudolf Boehm explains Husserl's view on metaphysics as 'last' philosophy in contrast to phenomenology as 'first' philosophy in his Einleitung to Edmund Husserl, *Erste Philosophie (1923/24)*, Erster Teil: *Kritische Ideengeschichte*, Husserliana VII (Den Haag: Martinus Nijhoff, 1956), pp. xvi ff. Additional treatment can be found in his article, 'Husserl's Concept of the 'Absolute', in R.O. Elveton, ed., *The Phenomenology of Husserl*, (Chicago: Quadrangle, 1970), pp. 174–203; originally published as 'Zum Begriff des 'Absoluten' bei Husserl,' *Zeitschrift für philosophische Forschung*, 13 (1959) 214–242.
4. Letter to Ingarden, March 19, 1930, in Edmund Husserl, *Briefe an Roman Inqarden*, ed. Roman ingarden, Phaenomenologica 25, (Den Haag: Martinus Nijhoff, 1968), p. 59. The revision in question here was to have gone beyond the 1929 expansion of the original lectures spoken of next and which resulted in the basic text that was translated into French and finally published in 1931. It was this further revision that Husserl and Fink worked on in the following years.
5. Husserliana I, p. 182 (§ 64). Reference to the place of metaphysical questions as finding their proper place in phenomenology as laid out in his 'Cartesian Meditations' is also given in Husserl's 'Nachwort' to *Ideas*, Husserliana V, p. 141.
6. Letter from June 3, 1932, in the Husserl Archives.
7. Letter in the Husserl Archives. The first part of this quotation is cited in Karl Schuhmann, *Husserl Chronik*, Husserliana Dokumente I, p. 368. The work of Fink's to which Husserl refers is 'Vergegenwärtigung und Bild,' Fink's doctoral dissertation which Husserl had directed, and which, in initial briefer form, had received a philosophic essay prize in 1928. Husserl published it in his *Jahrubuch*, and often recommended it as fine piece of phenomenological work. It is reprinted in Eugen Fink, *Studien zur Phänomenologie, 1930–1939*, Phaenomenologica 21 (Den Haag: Martinus Nijhoff, 1966), pp. 1–78.
8. In his 'Nachwort', Husserl writes, referring to the 'Cartesian Meditations': 'Ein in Werk stehendes und voraussichtlich zu Anfang des nächsten Jahres erscheinendes Buch wird, hoffe ich, . . . erweisen, daß ein transzendentale Phänomenologie meines Sinnes . . . wirklich alle vom konkreten Menschen aus zu stellenden Fragen, darunter auch alle sogenannten metaphysischen, in ihrem Felde hat, soweit sie überhaupt einen möglichen Sinn haben—den allerdings erst diese Phänomenologie ursprünglich zu gestalten and kritisch zu begrenzen berufen ist.' Husserliana V, p. 141. In subsequent years Husserl may have shifted from seeing the 'Cartesian Meditations' as fit to achieve this, but his objective did not change; the thrust of this text remains regulative for him.
9. 'Disposition zu 'System der phänomenologischen Philosophie' von Edmund Husserl,' in *Ergänzungsband zur VI. Cartesianischen Meditation*, ed. Guy Van Kerckhoven, the accompanying volume that forms a set with Eugen Fink—Edmund Husserl, *VI. Cartesianische Meditation: Die Idee einer transzendentalen Methodenlehre*, ed. Hans Ebeling, Jann Holl, and Guy Van Kerckhoven, Husserliana Dokumente II, Den Haag:

Martinus Nijhoff, 1988. The text is also published in Kern's Einleitung to Husserliana XV (pp. xxxvi–xl), but without the marginal notes Husserl wrote on Fink's manuscript, which the new critical edition gives in their entirety. As Kern explains, Fink's full sketch is apparently based on a far briefer one of Husserl's own, which Kern also includes in his Einleitung (p. xxxvi).

10. This is in fact the very observation Kern makes on Fink's 'Disposition', Husserliana XV, p. xxxvi.
11. For example, another arrangement of these topics was done in Fink's sketches for revision of Husserl's 'Cartesian Meditations.' In the three or four years Fink worked on that revision—in alternation with work on the 'System of Phenomenological Philosophy—Husserl's original five 'Meditations' were to be complemented by two new ones, a sixth, a 'Kritik der phänomenologischen Erfahrung und Erkenntnis,' and a seventh, giving 'Ausblicke auf eine künftige Metaphysik' (Eugen-Fink-Archiv Z–VI LVI/4a). Fink's fully written '6th Meditation' of 1932 presumably would have been followed by a '7th Meditation', which, though never done, would have been a substitute for the treatment of metaphysics in the 'System of Phenomenological Philosophy.'
12. Here are the section headings that comprise the outline of the second book as Fink's sketch presents them:
    1. Abschnitt: Die Idee der universalen 'transzendentalen ästhetik
    2. Abschnitt: Natur und Geist
    3. Abschnitt: Von der reinen Innenpsychologie zur transzendentalen Phänomenologie.

    Kern's discussion of the sources or analogues to these topics in Husserl's own descriptions should be read (Husserliana XV, p. xl).
13. The principal collection of these essays is Eugen Fink, *Studien zur Phänomenologie, 1930–1939*, Phaenomenological 21 (Den Haag: Martinus Nijhoff, 1966). But three others from the same period are contained in Eugen Fink, *Nähe und Distanz* (Freiburg: Alber, 1976), pp. 7–97, as well as many others on Husserl's phenomenology that Fink prepared after the war years.
14. 'Die phänomenologische Philosophie Edmund Husserls in der gegenwärtigen Kritik,' reprinted in *Studien zur Phänomenologie*, pp. 79–156. An English translation has been published in Roy Elveton, ed., *The Phenomenology of Husserl* (Chicago, Quadrangle, 1970) pp. 73–147.
15. Eugen-Fink-Archiv Z–XI 25b. All indications are that this note is from 1933.
16. Eugen-Fink-Archiv Z–XIV II/1a-b.
17. One note (Eugen-Fink-Archiv Z–XV 105), roughly contemporary with the other texts referred to here, but difficult to date more exactly than as written sometime between 1930 and 1935, speaks explicitly of this Habilitation topic. Significantly, it deals with Kant as having made a crucial contribution to one of Fink's main topics, the analysis of world, and very much in metaphysical interest. In fact, Fink never wrote a *Habilitationsschrift* as such during this period, one main reason being that by continuing to work so closely with Husserl he was precluded from being acceptable to the academic authorities under National Socialism.
18. Eugen-Fink-Archiv Z–XI 10a.
19. A good example is the following outline, from 1934, with its obvious relevance to the original for the present paper, viz., the Conference on Phenomenology and Indian Philosophy organized by the Indian Council for Philosophis Studies and the Centre for Advanced Research in Phenomenology and held in New Delhi January 5–8, 1988. The note is from Eugen-Fink-Archiv Z–XIV V/3a, the same folder, and in the same period as the note cited above (footnote 16) giving Fink's plans for 1934 (Z-XIV 11/1a-b):

'Das System des sich vollendenden Geistes
I. Teil: Kosmologie (Demonstration)
II. Teil:: Phänomenologie des Geistes (Reduktion)
III. Teil:: Meontische Kosmogonie (Spekulation)
In der Sprache der alten Metaphysik I. Kosmologie II. Psychologie III. Theologie
In der Sprache des Buddhismus: I. Lehre vom Saṃsāra II. Der siebenfache Weg III. Lehre vom Nirvāṇa'

20. Eugen-Fink-Archiv Z-XI 7a–b.
21. Fink's texts on this point are too lengthy to cite. Typical examples are to be found in Eugen-Fink-Archiv Z-IV 129, Z-V VI/31, Z-VI 23, and Z-XV 19 and 29. The gist of Fink's response to this criticism, which can only be understood in terms of his overall position, is indicated in this portion of one of these notes: 'Das Mißverständnis von Seiten der ontologischen Philosophie unserer Tage gegenüber der "Phänomenologie" besteht darin, das konstitutive Subjekt in eins zu setzen mit der mundanen Objektivation desselben, also ihr zu supponieren, sie hätte es als Ontologie oder Ontik der Subjektivität mit einer bestimmten Region des Seienden zu tun und zwar täte sie dies so, daß sie gleichsam naiv und grobschlächtig mit der Analyse subjektiver Vorkommnisse begänne und sie roh, einfach im vulgären Verstand des Seins als bloßer Vorhandenheit, auslege und subtilen intentionalen Verflechtungen nachspüre, ohne zuvor die Seinsweise der ihr thematischen Seinsregion zu einem ontologisch zureichenden Verständnis gebracht zu haben. Keineswegs wird zuerst ein ontologisch unterbestimmtes Subjekt angesetzt und aus ihm die Welt konstitutiv-konstruktiv entwickelt, sondern das konstitutierende Subjekt *ist nicht*.' (Z-XV 29)
22. Cf. Walter Biemel, 'Husserl's *Encyclopaedia Brittanica* Article and Heidegger's Remarks Thereon', in Frederich Elliston and Peter McCormick, eds. *Husserl: Expositions and Appraisals* (Notre Dame: University of Notre Dame Press, 1977, pp. 286–303. The principal communications of Heidegger on this are published in Husserliana IX, pp. 600–603.
23. There is so far no documentary indication that Fink was acquainted with the actual correspondence between Husserl and Heidegger (though there is good reason to presume so), yet it is clear that he was perfectly acquainted with the *issue* that arises in that correspondence. A few snatches from Heidegger's communication in Husserliana IX will have to serve to indicate Heidegger's point: '... gerade das *Problem*: welches ist die Seinsart des Seienden, in dem sich "Welt" konstituiert? Das ist das zentrale Problem von "Sein und Zeit".... Das Konstituierende ist nicht Nichts, also etwas und seiend—obzwar nicht im sinne des Positiven. Die Frage nach der Seinsart des Konstituierenden selbst ist nicht zu umgehen.... Welches ist die Seinsart dieses absoluten ego—in welchem Sinn ist es *dasselbe* wie das je faktische Ich; in welchem Sinn *nicht* dasselbe?' (Husserliana IX, pp. 601–602.) The extent to which Fink's critical rethinking of phenomenology is structured in terms of this very problem of being I hope comes clear in the course of this paper. In fact, in one note (Eugen-Fink-Archiv Z-VI 15a) Fink does explicitly acknowledge Heidegger as the source of his coming to this understanding of the issue of ontology within phenomenology.
24. One of the fuller texts that explicate this position is the pair of texts Eugen-Fink-Archiv Z-VI 15a and Z-IV 94a, but Z-IV 18b also speaks directly to this point and more concisely.
25. There are, once again, many texts that treat this point, of which two of particular pertinence are Eugen-Fink-Archiv Z-V VII/11a and Z-XI 78.
26. Cf. Eugen-Fink-Archiv V-VII XVIII/9b.
27. Cf. the text quoted above on p. 275. Other texts (among many) to refer to here would be, for example, Z-XVI VIII/2b–3b; Z-XVII 5b; Z-XIX II/2a–b; Z-XX 10a–b, 19a–b.
28. Cf. Eugen-Fink-Archiv Z-IX 50a.

29. Cf. Eugen-Fink-Archiv Z–IV 78a and Z–V VII/12a–b.
30. Cf. Eugen-Fink-Archiv Z–VX 39a.
31. Cf. Eugen-Fink-Archiv Z–XX 7a and Z–X 24a.
32. Eugen-Fink-Archiv Z–XV 102a–b.
33. Eugen-Fink-Archiv Z–XV 95a.
34. Eugen-Fink-Archiv Z–XV 109a–b.
35. Eugen-Fink-Archiv Z–XV 38b–39a.
36. Eugen-Fink-Archiv Z–V VII/7a.
37. Eugen-Fink-Archiv Z–XV 127a.
38. Eugen-Fink-Archiv Z–VII XVII/31b.
39. Another rendering could be 'prejudice in favour of the world'. Maurice Merleau-Ponty's '*préjugé du monde*' captures the force neatly, and, indeed, may well be a borrowing directly from Fink.
40. Eugen-Fink-Archiv Z–XV 37b.
41. Eugen-Fink-Archiv Z–XI XCIII/2a.
42. Cf. Eugen-Fink-Archiv Z–XIII XVIII/5a.
43. Eugen-Fink-Archiv Z–VII XVII/23a–b.
44. Eugen-Fink-Archiv Z–XV 92b.
45. Eugen-Fink-Archiv Z–VII XVIII/9b.
46. Cf. Eugen-Fink-Archiv Z–XV VII/17b.
47. Cf. Eugen-Fink-Archiv Z–VII XXI/15a,
48. Cf. Eugen-Fink-Archiv OH–1 28.
49. Here, too, is the basis for Fink's turning of Heidegger's criticism of Husserl away as missing the mark: 'Wenn der meontische Grundcharakter des transzendentalen Subjekts eingesehen ist, so wird der Einwand Heideggers von der Unterbestimmtheit der Subjektivität, der transzendentalen Subjektivität, nichtig, sie hat ja gar kein Sein, sondern einzig die vorgegebene Subjektivität hat Sein: *Mensch* .' (Z-V VI/31a)
50. Cf. Eugen-Fink-Archiv Z–XIII 69a–b, 70a.
51. Eugen-Fink-ArchivZ-XIX II/8a, which contains notes from a discussion with Landgrebe from March 29, 1935. To be noted in this connection is the explanation of differences between Husserl and himself that Fink makes in regard to this '6th Cartesian Meditation', in Husserliana Dokumente II, 'Entwurf eines Vorwortes.' The last difference mentioned is precisely this question of individuation and multiplicity.
52. Cf. Eugen-Fink-Archiv Z–XIII 69a–b.
53. Cf. Eugen-Fink-Archiv Z–VII 2a.
54. Cf. Eugen-Fink-Archiv Z–VII XVII/32a.
55. Cf. Eugen-Fink-Archiv Z–XV 128a.
56. Eugen-Fink-Archiv Z–XV 55a–b.
57. Eugen-Fink-Archiv Z–V VI/19a–b.
58. A helpful distinction which Fink makes in another context is expressed thus: 'Entstellung und der transcendentale Schein: nicht nur auf der Endstufe der Entstellung: dem Sein des Menschen in der Welt inmitten der Natur, finden wir den echten und unechten transzendentalen Schein (echter transzendentaler Schein ist z.B. Tod, Geburt, Ohnmächtigkeit, bloße Zugänglichkeit des Erfahrens, Preisgegebenheit an die Natur, die kosmogonischen Auffassungen u.s.w.; unechter transzendentaler Schein ist die anthropologische, biologische, sociologische Behandlung der Philosophie, das Ernstnehmen der Masken)—sondern auf jeder konstitutiven Stufe finden wir den transzendentalen Schein, insofern die Rückschleppung der konstituierten Stufe auf die konstituierende (unechte Rücklage) statt hat.' (Eugen-Fink-Archiv Z–XVI XXIV/5b.
59. Cf. Eugen-Fink-Archiv Z–XV 31a–b.
60. Cf. Eugen-Fink-Archiv Z–XV 80a and Z–X 9b.

61. Cf. Eugen-Fink-Archiv Z–IX 12a.
62. In a Nietzschean vein, Fink writes: 'Wir kennen die Lehre: "der Mensch ist etwas, das überwunden werden muß," noch klingt sie uns in den Ohren, der brausende Gesang Zarathustras. Die überwindung des Menschen ist die *Absolution*. Den Menschen absolut verstehen: d.i. ihn als Inbegriff des Weltsturzes Gottes, als das Außersichgehen (Emanation des Absolution) zu begreifen, ist philosophieren.... Eingängig ins 'Nichts' (Meon) nichtet sich das Eingehen selbst, es "scheitert" (mundan gesprochen!).' (Eugen-Fink-Archiv Z–XV 62a)
63. Cf. Eugen-Fink-Archiv Z–VII XXI/9a.
64. The double translation in the last expression is needed to convey something of the word-play Fink exploits here to make the conceptual point: 'Solange man das Absolute unter dem Begriff des Seins überhaupt faßt, also es selbst als ein Seiendes behandelt, steht es nicht nur nicht im Thema der Philosophie, sondern ist prinzipiell nicht zu entfalten.–Daß das Absolute in der philosophischen Explikation die Form des höheren oder umfassenderen Seins annimmt ('konkret'-'abstrakt') ist selbst ein im Wesen der meontischen Explikation notwendig liegender '*Schein*'. Diesem Schein zu verfallen, durch ihn geblendet zu sein ist die ständige Gefahr für jede 'absolute Philosophie'. Ihm entrinnen kann sie nicht; aber ihn 'aufheben': '*Scheitern*' *als* '*Widerschein*'. Emphasis Fink's. (Eugen-Fink-Archiv Z–IX 12a)
65. A fuller statement of this, especially in the sense of 'Schein' in reference to Kant, can be found in Eugen-Fink-Archiv Z–VI 78a–b.
66. Cf. the text quoted above on p. 279 above.
67. In a short list of topics for a meontic philosophy this phrase, 'analogia entis und 'analogia meontica', occurs. (Eugen-Fink-Archiv Z–XI 90a)
68. Cf. Eugen-Fink-Archiv Z–IX 10a.
69. On a page used to write a new brief note, the following earlier fragment is found: 'Das tiefste philosophische Problem ist das der Ontifikation d.h. das Verhältnis von Ursprung und Welt' (Eugen-Fink-Archiv Z–VII 5b). Fink then jotted down this new point: 'Die These: das Absolute ist das Nichts ist preiszugeben zugunsten dieser: Das Absolute ist der Ursprung.' (Z–VII 5a)
70. Eugen-Fink-Archiv Z–XI 87a–b.
71. Cf. Eugen-Fink-Archiv Z–XV 22a–b.
72. Cf. Eugen-Fink-Archiv Z–IV 66a–b. The term 'ekbasis' here, which occurs frequently in Fink's notes from the earlier years with Husserl, is a Greek word he adapts to express the 'exit' from the world-situation that the phenomenological reduction is in principle supposed to open up to. The way in which the 'exit'-character of the reduction either becomes reconciled with the strong rational positivity of Husserl's transcendental phenomenology, or, alternatively, acquires a more corrosively critical force, will have to wait for another occasion to be examined.

Hermeneutics in Indian Philosophy

KRISHNA ROY

In contemporary philosophical world the hermeneutic movement has proved very influential. The transition to phenomenology through existentialism to phenomenological hermeneutics is historically quite evident. This trend, though neither very recent nor very novel, has been received renewed attention of recent Euro-American philosophers and human scientists. Some of the leading philosophers of the period like Ricoeur and Gadamer attach great importance to hermeneutics. The present paper proposes to show that this hermeneutic attitude is not peculiar to the Euro-American world and that such hermeneutic trend may be noticed in all other countries and cultures. This paper mainly intends to indicate the interpretative tendency as obtained in the Indian philosophical tradition.

This interpretative tendency, in fact, is rooted in the very human nature. Man is a self-interpretative being; he interprets himself as he articulates himself, actualises his potentialities and, in the process, creates himself anew. But man interprets not only himself; he also construes the world and his fellow beings. In his encounter with the milieu he is born in, man knows it, adapts himself to it and re-creates it at the same time. Though all men share the same physiological structure, this does not impair their uniqueness and individuality. Such individuality, creativity and ceaseless search are the qualities that make a person not only different from everybody else but also show in some significant way one's uniqueness. Each one of these innumerable human being has a unique way of understanding and interpreting the world. This paves the way for different philosophies or *Weltanschauungen*.

Thus, all the discourses that we have, whether scientific, philosophic, literary or artistic, are the expressions of man's receptivity and imagination. In knowing the world man creates it; his knowing is nothing but a way of interpreting. For man is not a mere passive recorder of events and ideas. He experiences them, becomes involved in them and evaluates them from his own specific perspective. The attempt of philosophising without a bias or prejudice is itself a bias or prejudice and we feel that man is perpetually condemned to espouse some values or disvalues. Of course, when I assert it I do it with a prejudice and when you object to it you too do it with a prejudice. There can be no absolute freedom from all prejudices or biases. Everybody, every mind has its own situatedness and unique orientation. And yet, in a big way we, all human beings, share 'the same world'. Though the world, as text, lends itself to multiple interpretations, it affirms and retains its own identity.

It appears then that any account of man's existential involvement with the world, whether scientific or phenomenological, culminates in what is described as the hermeneutics of man. To many human studies such as literary criticism, art, history and cultural anthropology, this technique of interpretation is inalienably present. From the inception to the conclusion, these discourses can never take a single step without relying on the art of interpretation. This is true in all countries and in all ages. This art of interpretation is as old as mankind itself. But if we trace the academic genesis of hermeneutics, we notice that it arose as the interpretation of texts that were incomplete, ambiguous, indistinct and yet seminal. In this sense hermeneutics goes back to the ancient or classical period where we find various interpretations of Greek, Latin and Sanskrit texts. The need of philology and exegetical studies was recognised by most of the philosophers and speculative thinkers of all ages.

Ordinarily, hermeneutics has two primary intentions: first, to ascertain the exact meaning-content of text, word or sentence; secondly, to discover the messages and significations contained in symbolic forms. Gradually, as its scope extended, its task also became multifarious. Gadamer thinks that 'the universality of the hermeneutic problem ... has to do with the universe of the reasonable, that is, with anything and everything about which human beings can seek to reach agreement.'[1]

The various supporters and exponents of hermeneutics, thus, explore various dimensions from their own specific point of view revealing progressively new meanings of our encounter with the world, natural as well as cultural. Hermeneutics, in general, presupposes the ideas of estrangement (between language and reality) and unfamiliarity (with the literal linguistic meaning) and tries to overcome them on the basis of understanding. Whenever reality is not so obvious or evident to us and the object in question seems abstruse and ambiguous, interpretation becomes an imperative for understanding. In this connection Gadamer observes: 'Should there be no direct understanding, interpretative ideas are drawn on, as needed, out of a linguistic storeroom in which they are lying ready. Rather, language is the universal medium in which understanding itself is realised. The mode of realization of understanding is interpretation. Understanding and interpretation are indissolubly bound up with each other'.[2]

Though it is true that hermeneutics does not create anything new in the object or text to be understood, it rather uncovers what was originally present but has not yet been discovered and grasped by man, yet, in the process of discovery, hermeneutics often reveals or points out some undisclosed dimensions, which may appear new and illuminating. It is further marked by some sort of 'openness' which indicates that a particular interpretation may not be acceptable or even may be falsified if it is not corroborated by experience in a different socio-cultural milieu.

Hermeneutics, thus, is neither passive nor static reception of a text or precept, it is a creative and dynamic response to what is revealed through language or a text. It reveals how experience and understanding are inalienably connected in language or a text. It further seeks to bridge the gap between the writer and the interpreter, the speaker and the hearer. Hence it attempts at, in the words of Gadamer, 'a fusion of horizons'.

Without going into the history of the development of hermeneutics since the ancient times we propose to focus our attention only on some of its important characteristics: (1) Hermeneutics primarily arose as the interpretation of classical, seminal, ambiguous, cryptic texts. (2) Gradually it became 'general' (from 'regional' in Ricoeur's word), exploring the meaning and milieu of all human actions and intentions. (3) Hermeneutics as the foundation of the human sciences mainly makes use of understanding, intuition and inner experiences of human beings. (4) It presupposes familiarity with, concern for, and involvement in the social and cultural contexts. And (5) finally, all hermeneutic endeavour is inevitably anthropocentric. However, the term 'anthropocentric' is not to be construed in its pejorative sense as often found in analytic philosophy. How and to what extent these said characteristics figure in Indian philosophical tradition would be briefly investigated in the following pages.

As we follow the evolution of Indian philosophy and culture, we notice an un-ending hermeneutic trend. This sub-continent is well-known for its diverse languages, religions and cultures—yet an underlying unity can never be missed by any discerning scholar. The same is the picture with the Indian philosophic development. Diverse philosophic interpretations reveal diverse reflections and attitudes towards life, truth and reality without losing their common spiritual core. In fact, the various philosophical systems and developments in India, both ancient and modern, may be regarded as the product or bye-product of creative interpretation of classical Indian texts. Re-interpretations and reassessment of the Vedas (and of the Upaniṣads), since the ancient (to the present) days, constitute the basic structure of Indian thought, religion and culture. And in all these hermeneutic projects man occupies the central position. For it is man who is the author of all these interpretations and it is man's encounter with life and reality that becomes the object of interpretation. Hence like all other Western hermeneutics, Indian philosophy too is both hermeneutic and anthropocentric. Man is both the subject and the object of hermeneutics. Its bipolarity, i.e., reflective or self-interpretative character is undeniably transparent.

It is said that the foundation of Indian philosophy goes back to the Vedic period. Since the Vedic period two fundamental aspects of Indian culture, the performative and the contemplative, took definite shape as is found in the Vedas and in the Upaniṣads. The Vedas and the Upaniṣads establish the basic principles which most of the Indian philosophers accept, and they also contain certain degree of authoritativeness. But this in no way forecloses the possibility of newer insights and ideals. Rather in the Vedas themselves we can notice a transition from polytheism to monotheism and then from monotheism to philosophical monism. This shows the openness of the Vedic 'seers', who admitted the possibility of reviewing differently their views over the period.

The Vedas are the best known of the early available records of Indian literature and are believed to have been revealed to 'the superconsciousness of the seers'. The four Vedas represent the thought of successive generations of reflective thinkers containing different strata of ideas, closely knit and expressed in cryptic lines, safe and suitable for oral transmission from generation to generation. Sri Aurobindo, a modern scholar in the Vedic literature, thinks that the Vedas are replete with suggestions of secret doctrines and mystic philosophies which the later thinkers wanted to clarify, explain and interpret from their own changing perspectives. He recognizes that in that great scripture of the mystics there are two different types of significance, an exoteric—for the many, and esoteric—for the few. The Vedic hymns, being couched as they are in ancient, cryptic language, are open to varied interpretations. In order to exemplify their esoteric significance Sri Aurobindo fixes the import of certain Vedic terms, deciphers a number of the Vedic symbols, elaborates the psychological functions of the Vedic Gods and reconciles through explanation the seeming inconsistencies obtained in between the Vedic texts. Thus the Vedas become a consistent and coherent corpus. The symbolic and figurative language of the Vedas partly encloses and partly discloses their psychological implication and esoteric import. That the worlds of ideas and objects are not picturesquely available in any human language is made abundantly clear in the Vedas.

In fact, all the four Vedas have greatly influenced the Indian philosophical thought, either positively or negatively. Some of the major systems accept the Vedic authority, while others do not. Six major schools—Sāṅkhya, Yoga, Nyāya, Vaiśeṣika, Mīmāṃsā and Vedānta, accept the authority of the Vedas and are called *āstika* or orthodox systems. In India we notice the development of all these systems simultaneously, not one after another. This is so because they reflect the diverse attitudes and interactions of the Indian people to the fundamental problems of human life. Even after accepting the Vedic authority in a general way the authors of these systems have given us the dynamic interpretations of the concerned classical texts. These various schools address themselves to the diverse aspects of reality, ontological and epistemological, without being indifferent to the axiological, spiritual and religious issues.

Even the history (*itihāsa*) and *Purāṇas* are to be regarded as commentaries on the 'sacred' Vedas. Manu, the most authoritative law-giver of India, has explicitly stated that these should be considered as elaboration and interpretation of the Vedas.

The need of hermeneutics or the art of interpretation was felt because some of the Vedic principles are found to be contradictory. But these contradictions are only apparent and they cease to appear as when we rightly interpret them. Interpretations, though in a sense freely framable, are not arbitrary. It is chiefly in this connection that the Mīmāṃsā system lays down the canons of interpretation which are of great value not only to those who want to understand the Vedas aright but also to all who are engaged in the work of finding out the exact import of the important texts like legal and moral treaties (*dharmaśāstra*). Jaimini's Mīmāṃsā-Sūtra may be regarded as the comprehensive and prevailing authority on the subject of interpretation. According to the Mīmāṃsakas, the whole procedure of interpretation consists of five steps:

(a) The first step is the text or passage which is the subject of interpretation (*viṣaya*), it being capable of having two or more meanings.

(b) The second step is the doubt regarding its meaning, the doubt being as to which of the two or more meanings is the correct meaning. This is called *samasyā*.
(c) The third is the postulation of some one probable meaning with a view to test how far that meaning stands the test of reasoning. This is called *pūrva-pakṣa*.
(d) The fourth is the refutation of the suggested meaning. If is called *uttaram*.
(e) The fifth and last is the establishment of the true meaning. This is called *nirṇaya*. The whole of the process is called an *adhikaraṇa*, signifying a complete process. '*Viṣayaḥ Viṣayaścaiva pūrvapakṣaḥ tathottaram; Nirṇayaśceti pancāngaṃ śāstre adhikaraṇaṃ smṛtam*.'[3]

A close study of Mīmāṃsā system further shows discussions regarding such principles of textual interpretation, called *nyāyas*. Such *nyāyas* are laid down and scattered in the writings of both Jaimini and Śabara. These interpretive principles, though primarily linguistic and grammatical, do contribute to the enrichment of the meaning of the textual exegesis and may be compared to what Ricoeur calls 'regional hermeneutics'. The basic aim of Pūrva Mīmāṃsā system is the proper knowledge of *dharma*, i.e., prescribed or injuncted action(s), which is indicated in all statemens that we find in the Vedas and in ordinary language. As the Vedas are the only source and authority for our knowledge of the details of all sacrificial procedures comprised under *dharma*, determination of this procedure is not possible without a correct interpretation of the Vedic texts. *Śabda*, in the form of Vedic injunction, is the authentic source of understanding *dharma*:

Śabda pramāṇaka vākyaṃ yacchabda āha tasmākam pramāṇam
(Śābara Bhāṣya 1.1.2)

And as a corollary of such interpretation of ritualistic texts, Pūrva Mīmāṃsā develops a systematic *Vākyabodha*, understanding of the sense of sentences and speech acts. Hence, the Pūrva Mīmāṁsā Śāstra may be regarded as the hermeneutics for clarification and correct understanding of the various rituals. Like the Śrauta-Sūtras, which deal with the complicated procedure of the sacrificial rites, the Pūrva Mīmāṃsa attempts at a judicious interpretation of the texts pertaining to the sacrificial performances. But, unlike the Śrauta-Sūtras, Jaimini discusses in the own *sūtras*, the basic problems related with the cult of sacrifice that dominated the Aryan society in his time and even centuries thereafter. Thus, he is very much concerned with the socio-cultural and philosophical implications of the various problems connected with the *adhikārins* (or persons entitled of) of Vedic sacrifice. In a way this highlights the importance of man and his milieu in interpreting various maxims and rituals. Out of their contexts the latter appear meaningless and bizarre.

The presence of hermeneutics can be noticed from the various commentaries of the Mīmāṃsā Sūtras. The important *Bhāṣyakāras* of Jaimini Sūtras are Śabara, Kumārila and Prabhākara among others. I will confine my remarks only to the *bhāṣya* attributed to Śabara which is believed to be the oldest available commentary on the Mīmāṃsā Sūtra of Jaimini. Śabara's main concern seems to make plain the intended sense of valid speech acts in terms of *śabda* and Vedas and to bring out the underlying principles. To start with, he explicates his view on *dharma* with a concern for language and reality.

An enquiry into *dharma* is an enquiry for the sake of *dharma*, for it (the enquiry) consists in the desire to know it (*dharma*) '*Dharmasya jijñāsā sā hi tasya jñātum icchā* (Śābara Bhāṣya 1.1.1).

Since the term *jijñāsā* may be understood as the urge to investigate, to realize and to engage (here in *dharma*), Śabara's treatment may be regarded as hermeneutical as it concerns the desire (*icchā*) to know (*jñātum*), and its object (*tasya*), namely, *dharma*.

In his *bhāṣya* Śabara suggests that since there are various opinions regarding *dharma* it is not a matter of blindly accepting or rejecting an opinion. Proper interpretation and understanding becomes necessary in the implementation and performance of *dharma*. Proper understanding born out of interpretation not only rules out the alternative views but also positively provides the constitutive elements necessary for correct assessment and assimilation.

In his *bhāṣya*, Śabara gradually delineates how *śabda* as a signifying unit makes known something (1.1.5). Reality becomes presented and re-presented through *śabda* (i.e., language). This may be considered as the anticipation of the current hermeneutic trend which emphasizes the necessity of overcoming the ambiguity of language and its estrangement from reality. '*Jijñāsā* or hermeneutics... does not entertain statements allegedly leading towards truth as if they were signposts meant to lead towards what really was, is or can be. Language shows directly what is to be understood.... Śabara's approach calls for a hermeneutical awareness in which man participates fully and is entirely involved for the realisation of *satyam* (truth).... Hermeneutics is, for Śabara, a part of individual's concrete existence that is constituted by whatever he understands.'[4]

It is interesting to note that, like some contemporary hermeneuticians, Śabara does recognize the role of the interpreter or reader and his different socio-linguistic context from that of the text or scripture. *Jijñāsā*, according to Śabara, is not a mere reporting or recapitulation of a statement, it is to grasp its relevance and impact, sense and force also. Śabara admits that without distorting the meaning of a text one may even be required to go against the traditional teaching. He says: 'We shall transgress this tradition. For if we do not transgress it, we would make non-sensical the Veda, which is full of sense.'

'*Atikramiṣyāma imām āmnāyam anatikrāmanto Vedam arthavantaṃ santam anarthakaṃ kalpayema dṛṣṭo hi tasyārthaḥ karmāvabodhanaṃ nāma. na ca tasya adhyayanamātrāt tatrabhavanto yāñjikāḥ phalaṃ samāmananti*'. (Śābara bhāṣya 1.1.1).

Although the main principle of *dharma* is presented in the Vedas—it acquires its new meaning and form in different generations and ages. Further, it implies that '*dharma* rather is to be acquired anew at each instance of hermeneutical awareness.... The Veda... is not to be considered as a mere reference book;... any text... has an actualizing effect on the reader, as it has been pointed out by Śabara especially with reference to *Codanā* that it (an injunction of a text) incites one to action.'[5]

In fact, one of the primary aims of the Mīmāṃsā as a branch of learning may be described as getting back from the expression to the idea behind it, the solving of the important problem of the relation of speech and thought. Consequently, the system includes a great deal of discussion relating to social or folk psychology. This psychological inquiry contains much that is valuable for contemporary semantics or the branch of knowledge dealing with the meaning in relation to linguistic forms. The Mīmāṃsā in this respect serves as a necessary complement to *vyākaraṇa* or grammar. The Mīmāṃsā rather makes significant contribution to psychology and philology and may be regarded as a hermeneutical system.

The point that we want to emphasize here is that while the Western hermeneuticians began with different interpretations of the Biblical and exegetical literature, the roots of the Indian philosophic systems are to be traced to the varied interpretations of the seminal ideas of the Vedic and the Upaniṣadic texts. That such hermeneutics or art of interpretation developed in India can be established also by quoting the (usages of) *sūtras* or aphorisms and their commentaries at various levels. This is hardly surprising, for men are *naturally* self-interpreting irrespective of their cultural affiliation.

The term *sūtra* literally means thread, yarn, or string, which runs through and holds together different things and links up diverse interpretations within one tradition. *Sūtras* not only connect the basic teachings but also keep open the possibility of further interpretation and assessment. They are the cues, the seminal ideas, often expressed in concise and abstruse ways. Brief and cryptic, they often prove to be ambiguous and need further clarification, explanation, commentaries and glosses. In the case of every system (*darśana*), we have first of all a period of philosophical fermentation which is reduced to *sūtras* or aphorisms. This, then, is succeeded by the writings of commentaries on the aphorisms, which are followed by glosses (*ṭīkā*), expositions and explanatory compendia.

The systematic commentaries are known as *bhāṣyas* and there may be many *bhāṣyas* on the *sūtra*. For example, Śaṅkara, Rāmānuja, Madhva and many others have given their varied interpretations or *bhāṣyas* of the same *Brahma-sūtra*. The *bhāṣyas*, besides elucidating the *sūtras*, also offer expositions and interpretations which reflect the perspectives of the concerned *bhāṣyakāras* (commentators). Śaṅkara's commentary is not merely a literal elucidation of the aphorisms but is certainly marked by deep insight, originality and profound philosophic acumen. The availability of various *bhāṣyas* proves the freedom and open-mindedness of the Indian thinkers in understanding the perennial questions and problems of human life. The prevalence of different *bhāṣyas* of the same *sūtra* further exemplify that these different thinkers, offering different expositions and interpretations, are not totally opposed to one another and belong to the same tradition (e.g., Śaṅkara, Rāmānuja and Madhva are all Vedāntins). Without deviating from the same basic principle and without constituting a thoroughly new system, these different ingenious *bhāṣyakāras* thus prefer to give different hermeneutics from their different *Weltanschauunen*. One might say that they, like Hermes, are creative conveyers or messengers of (God's) one and the same message or text.

The *sūtras* of the six orthodox systems are the outcomes of a series of past efforts and 'occupy a strictly central position summarising, on the one hand, a series of early literary essays extending over many generations and forming, on the other hand, the head spring of an ever broadening activity of commentators as well as virtually independent writers, which reaches down to our days and may yet have some future before itself.'[6]

Though such presence of *sūtras* and *bhāṣyas* are quite common primarily in the six orthodox systems, the heterodox or *nāstika* systems also develop more or less in the same way. The Buddha, the Jaina and the Cārvāka Systems do not accept the authority of the Vedas, yet in the development of these systems, elaboration, interpretation and discussion play a very significant role. The classical Indian scholars, generally speaking, rely on the method of dialogue and discussion, giving much importance to oral tradition, in addition to the different interpretations of the written texts. It is interesting in this connection that *śruti* (verbal testimony) has been accepted as an independent *pramāṇa* (means or instrument of valid knowledge or *pramā*).

The method of dialectic or *Vādapaddhati* is necessary for the clarification of philosophic thought. Both the *sūtrakāras* (aphorists) and the *bhāṣyakāras* (interpreters) anticipated the arguments of their opponents and tried to refute them by taking recourse to reasoning. There are historical evidences that thinkers of different schools often met together and argued about the possible solutions of different intellectual and practical problems. *Vāda* consists of a number of interpretations put forward by various speakers purporting to be reasons in support of several hypotheses, leading ultimately to the acceptance of only one as true to the exclusion of the rest. The detailed discussion of the *Vādapaddhati* can be found especially in the Nyāya system. Here we find discussions regarding various steps of this method, e.g. *jalpa*, *vitandā*, etc.

Besides Nyāya, in some other Indian systems too, this art of dialectics and the method of interpretation have been given much importance. In Baladeva's commentary on the Vedānta-Sūtra of Bādarāyaṇa we find an important maxim of interpretation. While interpreting a text there are certain maxims to be observed. Some of the same are laid down in the following verse:

Upakramopasaṃharābhyāsāpūrvatā phalam
Arthavādopapattiśca liṅgaṃ tātparya nirṇaye[7]

The beginning (*upakrama*), the conclusion (*upasaṃhara*), the repetition (*abhyāsa*), peculiarity (*apūrvatā*), the object (*phalam*), the expectation of purpose (*arthavāda*) and suitableness (*upapatti*) are the six indications by means of which the purport of a cryptic text may be arrived at.

The present paper does not intend to go into the intricacies of all these various means or stages. It only seeks to point out that in Indian thought this art of interpretation, argumentation and discussion have been assigned a special role and this dialectical and 'hermeneutic' trends have sustained the Indian philosophy and prevented it from becoming stagnant and inefficacious.

From the foregoing account it may appear that the Indian philosophical systems develop mainly as commentaries on and interpretations of the Vedas (and of some other classical texts). This is only partly true. The propounders of the Indian philosophical schools have certainly offered different interpretations of the Vedic and the Upaniṣadic principles but the same reveal their distinct attitudes towards the human self and the life-world. The primary *telos* or goal of the original texts, as well as that of commentaries, are to explore the close relationship between practical life and theoretical philosophy. The dualism of reason and experience, of pure reason and practical reason, is rejected by most of the Indian philosophers. However, their distinction is understandably recognized. True philosophy is not to be taken merely as an 'intellectual exercise'—it must be accorded a distinct place in our practical life. This aim of integrating truth or knowledge with the excellence of life is the motto of the Indian thinkers in general. This ideal has transformed our philosophical tradition into 'passionate conviction, stirring the hearts of man . . . and completely [transforming] his nature'. From this bird's eye view of the hermeneutic trend of our culture, it is evident that the essence of this approach 'lies in the proper evaluation of their [humans'] basic position that realisation of the highest reality is identical with integrated self-experience, and the way to such experience lies through the guidance of the ancient and indigenous tradition of mystics and intuitive philosophers, and not through intricacies of logic and mutually interdependent arguments.[8] The logic of the finite, to quote Sri Aurobindo, is the magic in the infinite. This does not entail rejection but only subordination of logic to intuitive or non-discursive insight into the nature of life and reality.

As one turns towards the Upaniṣads, which have been regarded as the other basic source of inspiration of classical and contemporary Indian Philosophical thinkings, one realizes, that the ideas available there, because of their emphasis on inner search and contemplation, may be viewed either as a total break from the Vedic activism or as a hermeneutic elaboration of the later Vedic monistic attitude. In any case, the Upaniṣads are rich in intuitive experiences and spiritual ideas, restricting the role of reason as the method of unconcealing the truth of life and world. This Upaniṣadic tradition of philosophizing from our own deeper experience was carried over by many subsequent Indian thinkers and may even be taken to be one of the main distinctive features of the Indian thought. In this tradition, it is said, knowledge is required to pass through the three steps of *śravaṇa* (hearing), *manana* (examination of what is heard) and *nidhidhyāsana* (realization or assimilation of what is thus reflected upon). Deeper human experience (*upalabdhi*) is the source of our reflection and interpretation. It starts from our ordinary experience and proceeds further as it encompasses the whole of our being. Truth has to be attained not by discursive intellect, at least not primarily, but through many-sided life-experience. Such integral attitude towards life and man, together with a disavowal of intellectual exclusiveness' discloses the basic cast of the Indian mind. It shows how the Indian thinkers in those days could anticipate the contemporary existential-hermeneutic trend of viewing man in its complexity. Philosophy is not merely a rational discourse. Knowing and experiencing are not two separate compartments of human life. Philosophy springs from our whole being. Critical of the analytic tradition, and its trivial subtlety, many contemporary thinkers, echoing the traditional Indian thinkers, are raising the perennial issue: what is the ultimate source of philosophical knowledge? 'It is neither sense, nor reason, nor intuition, but the whole of man. Philosophy is the reaction of the whole of man to the whole of reality'. Man is a spirit, an integral whole, consisting of his body, mind, intellect, passion and will and his reason alone can no more exhaust him than his animality can encompass his reason. Reason or rational thought is a part of his being. Purely rational knowledge, therefore, militates against and contradicts the affirmations of the rest of a man's being and receives only by a corner of his self.'[9]

The primary telos of all Indian thought is to explore the mystery of human nature. 'Know Thyself' (*ātmānaṃ viddhi*) is the dictum of Indian philosophy. This dictum immediately reminds us of the Socratic maxim, despite the difference in the conceptions of the self found in these two different traditions. What the Upaniṣads mean by the word 'self' (*ātman*) is not the finite mind (of Socrates) but something deeper and higher. Yet this self is not a transcendent entity, dissociated from us completely. It is our own deeper self existing everywhere seemingly differentiating itself into subject and object, matter and form, and 'I' and 'thou'. Human nature consists of physical body, vital energy and psychic competences in addition to the primary self called *puruṣa* or *ātman*. Man is not a complex clock-work shut up into its mechanical immanence but a self-transcending articulation or expression of the ever-disclosive spiritual life. The organic aspect of man is only an accompaniment to the subtle self. It is true that, like many other concepts, the concept of self also has received diverse interpretations in different systems. Yet an inherent spirituality has been persisting all through. Even the Buddhist and the Jaina schools—though they do not accept the Vedic tradition—somehow belong to the spiritual tradition initiated by these ancient sages. The spirit is our own inmost being, not incomprehensible or mysterious.

There is a false but widespread view that Indian philosophical tradition, being primarily concerned as it is with esoteric spirituality and emancipation of the individual, is basically indifferent to, if not incompatible with, the ordinary practical life and the life-values of the common man. It is rooted in a superficial and scientistic understanding of Indian philosophy. It is true that the Indian thinkers do attach much importance to spirituality and liberation from the gross earth-bound sufferings but that is only a robust recognition of our somatic existence, of the stifling problems of our day-to-day life. The story of human life and thought as found in other cultures, rightly understood, is not quite different. The genesis of all Indian systems may be traced to a tragic sense, to the fact of suffering which man experiences in this earthly life. Mere intellectual pursuit is not the end of philosophy. It must help us to overcome the sufferings and turmoils of life and to make human life as authentic and as perfect as possible. Hence, though the diverse Indian systems give different interpretations of human nature and often suggest different means for achieving liberation either by knowledge (*jñāna*) or by devotion (*bhakti*) or by action (*karma*), they are basically humanistic and axiological in nature. They all emphasise how philosophic pursuit, besides satisfying our intellectual curiosity, can serve human ends—*puruṣārthas*—as well.

Perfection of the total, deeper nature of man can be achieved through self-knowledge, which enables man to liberate himself from all earthly follies and miseries. In our practical life, we always face an imbalance between what man is and what man wills to be. We are continuously being tormented by our own inner uneasiness, pangs of conscience and quest for peace, perfection and self-realization. True self-knowledge and disciplined life can perhaps overcome such tension of our nature, taking us close to our *telos* of truly integrated personality. The which sustains man, *dharma* (a synonym for religion) thus works as a parallel and complementary to the vision of reality, *darśana* (a synonym for philosophy). The Indian philosopher does not like to discover truth as an epistemic *telos*. He wills to live it, to realize it both in his own outer and inner experiences. *Tattva-jñāna*, knowledge of reality, opens up the possibility of *mokṣa* or liberation. The concepts of *tattva-jñāna and mokṣa*, however, have also received diverse interpretations in different philosophic systems. But admist all these diversities an underlying unifying note strikes us: it is the deep sense of awareness of the actual fleeting condition of man and an intense urge for self-transcendence and perfection. Indian philosophical hermeneutic is both homo-centric and value-oriented.

This hermeneutic note characterises not only classical Indian philosophy but such attitude also permeates in the contemporary Indian thought. Contemporary Indian thinkers like Tagore, Gandhi, Sri Aurobindo and even K. C. Bhattacharyya owe the origin and inspiration of their basic ideas to the rich tradition preserved in the classical Indian texts. That moving Upaniṣadic message which asks us to turn inwards, to our own deepest being, has certainly impressed these thinkers born in the nineteenth century. Yet they have not followed the ancient precept *in toto*; rather, they have reinterpreted the spiritual heritage from their contemporary and changed socio-cultural perspectives. They realized that if India is to play a worthy role in the contemporary world, she must not remain true only to her own great past (*svadhrama*); she must also move with the times (*yugadharma*). True freedom or self-rule (*swarāj*) of India is inseparable from, rather rooted in, our own individual freedom. The individual and the universal are identical, both essentially and historically.

These three leaders of the modern Indian Renaissance, Tagore, Gandhi and Sri Aurobindo, choṣe different ways of self-expression. Rabindranath chose literature as his primary mode. Gandhi preferred the mode of *praxis* (action). And Sri Aurobindo chose the path of meditation and contemplation. But none, it should be remembered, confined his self-expression to only one mode. All of them wrote extensively and left thousand of pages recording their creative and rich experiences.

Instead of giving the details of their diverse and unique ways of self-expression, the present paper only seeks to explore the basic similarity in their hermeneutics of classical spirituality. It is the fusion of sociality with spirituality, giving us a renewed concept of man.[10]

Though steeped in the rich classical heritage of India, all of them are equally perceptive of the growing impact of the Western tradition. Advancement of science, promotion of critical rationalism and resurrection of socialism are the three main ideals of the West which these Indian thinkers accepted for realization in the changed Indian contexts, without, however, being overwhelmed by their attending stereotypic or regimented characteristics. They detected even the darker sides of scientific civilization, mechanization and regimentation entailed by socialism, berating the value of the individual. Hence they felt the need for proper balance and harmony between the teachings of the East and of the West. They affirmed the unity of mankind despite its diverse historico-cultural articulations.

In their hermeneutics of classical Indian tradition, these thinkers, thus, initiate a tradition of social spirituality. I am deliberately using the term 'social spirituality' to connote the blend of socialism with spirituality. Traditional Indian spirituality has been reoriented to meet the needs of the modern society. This spirituality does not preach other-worldliness or orthodox revivalism. It affirms life, is not indifferent to the beauty and the joy of life, and does not encourage apathy toward the four-fold sustenance of life, the four-fold values,—religious, economic, hedonic and liberative. It is not devoid of historical sense either. This spirituality is aware of our inalienable involvement with the ordinary, socio-cultural milieu. It motivates us to transcend the trivialities of the daily life and to make our life and society more and more authentic, purposeful and perfect. Here spirituality is integral to socialism.

From the foregoing, it should become clear that the entire Indian philosophy, whether classical or contemporary, is truly humanistic. Man is the centre of all deliberation and interpretation. Even in the interpretation of sacred literature, text and context intermingle. Words and work, scripture and life, theory and practice, the transcendental and the historical merge into one another, giving us a broader, deeper hermeneutic understanding of man.

The present papers seeks to explore how, in different parts of the world, hermeneutic developments presuppose tradition and the latter, in its turn, accommodates and sustains the impact of hermeneutics—quietly yet continuously—through the passage of time, keeping the quest for man's being-in-the-world unended and undimmed.

No modern view (of a Christian, Mohammedan or Hindu) regarding man's encounter with his true being and society can be totally excluded from its relationship with the past images that we find in the Bible, the Koran, and the Upaniṣads (respectively). But these scriptures will undoubtedly lose their value and significance if they are not *re*viewed and *re*newed from the complex and perplexing perspective of our modern existence.

The hermeneuticians both of the East and of the West are historically called upon to bridge the gap between the past heritage and the present condition, keeping the road for future progress of man open and unending.

NOTES AND REFERENCES

1. H. Gadamer, *Philosophical Hermeneutics*, The MIT Press, 1985, p. 180.
2. ———, *Truth and Method*, London. Sheed & Ward, 1975, p. 360.
3. K. Sircar, *The Mīmāṃsā Rules of Interpretation*, Thacker, Spink and Co., 1909, p. 26.
4. O. Gachter, *Hermeneutics and Language in Pūrva Mīmāṃsā*, Delhi, Motilal Banarsidass, 1983, pp. 98–99.
5. *Ibid.*, p. 104.
6. M. Winternitz, *A History of Indian Literature*, Vol. I, p. 288.
7. *The Vedānta Sūtra of Bādarāyaṇa*, with the commentary of Baladeva, translated by S. C. Basu, New Delhi, Orient Books, 1979, p. 14.
8. P. D. Chandratre, *Methodology of the Major Bhāṣyas on the Brahmasūtra*, Nasik, 1958, pp. 240–241.
9. S. K. Saksena, '*Philosophical Theories and the Affairs of Man*' in *The Indian Mind*, edited by C. A. Moore, University of Hawaii Press, Honolulu, 1967, p. 25.
10. I have discussed this theme in 'The Socio-Spiritual Heritage of Modern India' in *Essays in Social and Political Philosophy*, edited by Krishna Roy and Chhanda Gupta, Allied/ICPR, New Delhi, 1989.

Reading the Ṛgveda: A Phenomenological Essay*

J. L. MEHTA

The following is an attempt at indicating how a broadly phenomenological approach to a reading of the Ṛgveda as a text is not only likely to prove rewarding at the present time but is imperative for anyone who is a participant, directly or indirectly, in the Indian philosophical and religious tradition. It is also a continuation of three earlier ventures in this field. The phenomenological background out of which this endeavour has emerged is in the first place the work of Martin Heidegger as a whole: the liberation from metaphysical conceptuality, the deep probing into the meaning of truth, the insistence on the primacy of language, the new, post-metaphysical way of thinking about man and his world, the basically religious drive behind Heidegger's work and the vision of life it holds out, all these made me turn towards the Ṛgveda as a text constitutive of the very horizon of the traditional Indian way of experiencing life, and worth exploring for its own sake as an *arche*-text. Secondly, Hans Gadamer's massive work, from his *magnum opus* to the continuing discussion with critics on the claims of philosophical hermeneutics opened my eyes to the role and nature of the activity of interpretation as integral to all philosophical thinking. Thirdly, the wide-ranging, many-faceted, ongoing writings of Paul Ricoeur, whose work not only brings his phenomenological predecessors into relation with his Anglo-Saxon contemporaries, but also exhibits a vital interest in literary theory and poetics, have proved no less stimulating than his concern with the interpretation of myths and symbols; his fruitful association with the Chicago History of Religions school and, above all, his contributions to Scriptural interpretation make his work directly relevant to similar endeavours in the Indian religious area. Fourthly, my own involvement with the Harvard Centre for the study of World Religions for about eight years has been a major influence at work in making me turn to interpretive thinking in relation to my own religious tradition. It will be inexcusable, finally, if I fail to mention the Indologist Heinrich Luders, whose posthumously published work *Varuṇa* fired my imagination and prompted me to come to close grips with the text of the Ṛgveda with eyes unclouded by the valuable but in many ways disputable work of earlier Vedists.

The Ṛgveda *saṃhitā* or collection, is a re-editing of hymns to various deities composed by different *ṛṣis* at different times, and the order in which

* The editors regret to say that the author of the paper passed away when the volume was under preparation for publication. Many of the quotations he translated from Sanskrit texts remain unidentified.—*Editors*

they are arranged, in ten Books, is presumably dictated by their use for ritual purposes. The composition of the earliest of these hymns goes back, according to scholarly opinion, to about 2000 B.C., and the mythology, which the hymns presuppose, goes still further back to an undetermined past. For a variety of reasons, the ten thousand odd *mantras* or verses which make up the text, do not seem to have been subjected to the kind of exegetical effort devoted later to the Upaniṣad portion of the extensive Brāhmaṇa literature which, together with three other 'collections', constitute the corpus called the Veda. There is evidence, it is true, of continued practice of Vedic exegesis since ancient times, the earliest extant text of an exegetical nature being no later than the 5th century B.C., and the Brāhmaṇa literature of a few centuries earlier itself includes a sizeable exegetical component. Although ritualist interpretation of the *Saṃhitā* was dominant, there seems to have been a general recognition of alternative principles or levels of interpretation. The last and most widely used commentary, that of *Sāyaṇa* belonging to the second half of the 14th century, contains clear evidence of a variety of schools of interpretation, although its own orientation is ritualistic. After centuries of concentration on Upaniṣadic exegesis, Indian scholars like Dayānanda Saraswati in the 19th century and Coomaraswamy, Aurobindo and Anirvana in the 20th felt the need for a modern, new interpretation of the Ṛgveda, untrammelled by the preconceptions of an outworn tradition and inspired by the faith that these Vedic *mantras* have something new and important to say to us even in our altered world of thought and sensibility. With the publication of Max Mueller's great edition of the complete Ṛgveda *Saṃhitā*, along with Sāyaṇa's commentary in six volumes (1849–73), a new era of Vedic studies began, to which Western Vedists have massively contributed. One may now 'read' it as a book—which it never was earlier—as a collection of sacred poems or as poetry presenting us with figures of the imagination, schemata for the production of new meanings, and make of it what we will, in the changed hermeneutic situation of today, pursuing modes of inquiry which are now open to us through our participation in the intellectual traditions of both India and the West.

What sort of a text is the Ṛgveda *Saṃhitā*? In view of the attention recently given to the concept of 'text' by literary theorists and philosophers, it may not be out of place to mention here that in this text, the very notion of 'text' is for the first time mentioned by the seer-poets who composed the hymns. Etymologically, a text is a piece of cloth: *textus*, from which the word derives, means 'woven', the Latin verb '*texo,—ere*' meaning weaving of cloth, intertwining or interlocking of any kind of material. As Roland Barthes said, 'Text means tissue; but whereas hitherto we have always taken this tissue as a product, a ready-made veil, behind which lies, more or less hidden, meaning (truth), we are now emphasizing, in the tissue, the generative idea that the text is *made*, is worked out in a perpetual interweaving'. The Vedic poets, while composing their *mantras*, were aware not only that they were weaving together a fabric but also what was involved in such activity and that in this process the subject 'lost in this tissue—this texture—unmakes himself', in Barthes' words, though not 'like a spider dissolving in the constructive secretions of the web', as he remarks, but rather as disappearing in favour of the fire burning within him. Addressing this fire within men, the *ṛṣi* says, 'I do not know how to stretch the thread and weave the cloth; he, Fire, is the one who knows how to stretch the thread and weave the cloth; we will speak the right words, for he is the immortal light within mortals, the light in the hearts of men, the one source of all thought.' Another *ṛṣi* prays to Varuṇa 'May we attain the fountainhead of the Truth that you guard. Do not let the thread break while I am still weaving this thought, nor let the measuring-stick of the workman shatter before its time'. The ritual offering of this fabric of words to the gods is the sacrifice and this, too, is conceived by these poets as a text 'woven out of seven threads'. A hymn describing the primordial creation of sacrifice by the Cosmic *Puruṣa* says, 'The sacrifice that is spread out with threads on all sides, drawn tight with a hundred and one divine acts, is woven by the fathers as they come near: 'weave forward, weave back ward', they say as they sit by the loom that is stretched tight. The Cosmic Man stretches the warp and draws the weft; the Man has spread it out upon the dome of the sky. These are the pegs that are fastened in place; they made the melodies into the shuttles for weaving. That was the model for the human sages, our fathers, when the primeval sacrifice was born. With the eye that is the mind, in thought, I see those who were the first to offer the sacrifice.' Sometimes, the verb *takṣa* is used to describe the poetic activity of making, fashioning or forming; both a poem and a sacrifice are 'made', with heart and mind, as a carpenter works with a chisel.

The commonest term used in the Ṛgveda to signify both the activity and its result, the poem made and the making of it is *brahman*, which means formulating, giving poetic form, a verbal formulation. The *ṛṣis* make a *brahman* in praise of or invoking a particular deity. Once made, the *brahman* can be recited, spoken, sung, heard and, according to the emphasis on its specific modality, it is variously termed *dhī, vāk, mantra, uktha, stoma, gir, manma* or just *ṛc*. The poet makes or fashions a *brahman*, but he is not its originator or creator, for it is god-given (*devattam*), something that 'comes' to him, but on which he has to work hard for giving it appropriate, new verbal form. All form-giving activity primarily resides in the deities, the primal makes of *brahman*, of whom Indra is the proto-typical *ṛṣi* and poet, and Bṛhaspati the master. A *brāhmaṇa* in the primary sense is one who is endowed with the gift of receiving, seeing or hearing a *mantra* and of giving poetic form to his thought; in the secondary sense, he is one who holds in his memory and is able to recite, an entire mass of *mantras* already created or produced, and make them heard—he is the holy book in which the whole body of *mantras* is inscribed; as belonging to a certain *varṇa* or class, he is a *brāhmaṇa* only in a tertiary or residual sense.

The hymn is a *mantra*, for it is an effective mental construct; it is *gir* because it is sung, *uktha* because it is spoken and recited, *manma* because it embodies a thought and *stoma* because it is said in praise of a deity. The *brahman* is a gift received by man, not under the ownership or command of human subjectivity, but when the poets' responsive labour turns it into a well-formed *sūkta*, it establishes a channel of communication between man and the deities, who are the source of what is given to him; it becomes a thread that binds them together. The *sūkta* not only invokes the presence of the god, drawing him near the mortal, but gives him pleasure and makes him grow in his divine effulgence, just as the god is the source from which the *brahman* is nourished and made to wax. (VI.38.4). As the veteran Vedist and Iranist Paul Thieme has pointed out in a brilliant article, 'Brahman in the proper sense denotes the activity which lies between the inspiration of a thought (*dhī*) and its utterance (*uktha*), the hard work of linguistic composition which is artistically appropriate. The deity is begged by the poet to vivify his *brahman* and his *dhī*. Thus brahman precedes the *uktha*'. Long practice and intense concentration of thought are needed; these the poet brings to bear upon his work through ascetic practices, and a kind of intoxicated rapture and excitement. Hence the poet so engaged is called a *vipra*, an ecstatic all aquiver with his *poiesis*. In the Atharvaveda there are even hints of the stages in this process, which is one of a 'progressive interior realisation', in Louis Renou's words, or that of poetic formation, as Thieme puts it (AV, VII, I, I). There is first the intuition or the inspiration (*dhiti*) by which the poet gets the germinal idea, the starting point of verbal articulation. This is followed by the silent speech in the mind. Then comes 'the third *brahman*', in which there takes place an accrual of words in explicit articulation. Finally, there is the fourth *brahman* (*turīyam brahma*) in which the thought finds its finished linguistic articulation. The poet succeeds in the discovery of 'the name of the milch-cow', that is, the formulation of a hidden truth, or like the seer Atri (5,40.6), in finding the Sun hidden within darkness. We will come back later to the 'cow' and 'the light hidden within darkness'.

In many ways, the Ṛgveda is a strange text, unique and *sui generis*. In its mode of being, it is in a sense revealed as well as revelatory and yet it is not scripture, not a book, in the ordinary sense. If it is *écriture* of any, its marks exist in the open space around us or in the equally invisible space within us, in our mind. Created in the mind, it took outward form as voice, in a texture of spoken words, which were then inscribed in the mind of the *brāhmaṇa*, who memorized it and thus became in his own person both the book and its custodian. In the composition, retention and reproduction, no material support except the voice was used, and the transmission was from mind to mind through the medium of the chanted word, without the slightest trace of textual aberrations to which all oral literature is normally subject. In the case of a few hymns one can identify the individual *ṛṣi* who authored them, very often they are identified by the school of the founder-*ṛṣi*, and quite a few are anonymous. And yet the entire text makes up one whole, with an intricate structure, both as to the division into ten books and to the arrangement of the hymns within each book. Not much has been done since Abel Bergaigne's great work in the late 19th century by way of investigating this structure, both in itself and in its relation to the three other *saṃhitās*, and the rest of the Vedic corpus. Fresh insights in our understanding of the form as well as content of the Ṛgveda text can certainly be gained by the application to its study of the procedures and strategies developed within the so called structuralist movement and semiotics. Since the hymns are arranged, in the text as we have it now, largely with a view to their ritual application, like the division into four Vedas, it is important that we destructure the text and so move a step further in approaching what W. O'Flaherty calls 'the molten centre of this rich and secret book,' by mastering the code of the work and so enabling its message to reach us today. Though we are separated from the Ṛgveda by a vast abyss of time, during which our cultural and spiritual world has altered several times over, and though we are now estranged from the language of the Veda by the emergence and long dominance of classical Sanskrit, we can take comfort and encouragement from the fact that such alienation is also an enabling condition for a re-appropriation of what was once said in the remote past, that the passage of time leads not just to a forgetting but can also mean a conservation, a keeping in reserve, in which time functions as a filter through which the message may reach us in a novel, perhaps in a more purified sense. Further, we are perhaps better situated today to take note of what Hans Gadamer calls the *Wirkungsgeschichte*, the consciousness of the effective history of the meaning of this text and seeing how it has entered into our subsequent literary heritage and our living, transformed and modified in changing cultural contexts in our history, yet with a voice which still murmurs in our ears, calling for understanding and fresh appropriation. For we in India still stand within that *Wirkungsgeschichte* and what we make of that text and how we understand it today will itself be a happening within that history. For students of subsequent major texts like the Mahābhārata and the Bhāgavatapurāṇa wide vistas open up for exploring the phenomenon of inter-textuality and for studying the Ṛgveda as the 'great code', alive and operative in these later works. Just as the text itself is an interpretation of lived experience, so its interpretation today must be a hermeneutics which, in Paul Ricoeur's words' is the very deciphering of life in the mirror of the text,... a matter of interiorizing the text's spiritual meaning, of actualizing it.'

What kind of a world is disclosed to us by this text, how is this world structured, and what is the vision of man's life it holds up before us? Keeping aside all notions of the so called 'world-picture of Vedic Aryans' or of a 'Vedic cosmology', we must understand 'world' itself as an *existentiable*, as an aspect of man's mode of being, of his being-in-the-world, or in Heidegger's later way of talking, as the unified play of the Fourfold of earth and heaven, gods and mortals, in which man dwells on earth as his home, under the heavens, in friendly commerce with the gods, with his fellowmen and with things, building and making, untiringly, with thoughts and words and things. Keenly and intensely aware of his finitude, man in this text is always 'the mortal' (*martaḥ*), exigent, desirous of earthly goods, needing help in the conduct of his life, unable to see clearly through the perils of living, to know the truth of what is within him or of things beyond. But he is aware of himself as a thinking being, and of a light within him, as also of a light that comes to him from beyond. He stands helpless on this impenetrable earth, as inscrutably earthy, but he is open to the heavens and responsive to the shining ones (*devas*) above, who are themselves eager to respond to his call, to enkindle a light in the darkness within, without and underneath him. The *ārya* is one who pursues the light (7.33.7); Agni produces a wide light for the *ārya* (7.5.6); the gods created this deity as the light for the *ārya* (1.59.2); the aśvins spread out the light for the *ārya* (1.117.21), they have made light for humankind; Indra discovered the light for the *ārya*. Man, if he is *ārya* (i.e., hospitable to the guest from beyond, open to transcendence), and a Brāhmaṇa dedicated to his creative vocation of 'wording the world', has but one all-consuming passion, the unceasing pursuit of light. It is this aspiration which gives meaning to life; this ardour of longing for the 'shining ones' that gives man a sense of his own mortality, that is, of the finite time he is given to fulfil himself on earth; it is in terms of this irresistible reaching out, 'leaping from peak to higher peak', as the text says, and to the uppermost heights possible to man, that we can understand how the space of his world is structured, as well as the regions of this space and the places in these regions, path where the divinities beckon to him. It is not the infinite spaces of such a world, one piled on top of another, that fills Vedic man with terror. If there is anything that does so, it is *Nirṛti*, inner disintegration, the falling apart that destroys the domain of possibility itself. (10.164.1). It is *abhvam*, the black abyss of darkness, '*das Schwarze Ungeheuer*', as Geldner felicitously renders it. It is *aṃhas*, the sense of being hemmed in and trapped, constriction, the anguish of space closing in. 'Light' is the key-word of the Great Code that is this text, the central concept that illumines the text immanently and holds it together as a unity, which unlocks its tropes, its symbolism and its mythic content. The existential, human world of the text has a three-tiered topography: the earth, the heavens and the space intervening, within which further articulation into regions is sometimes made. The topography does not define a static structure, which is rather an intensely dynamic field, with incessant transaction going on between the immortal 'shining ones' above and the mortals on earth below, the 'between' between the two, the intervening space, being the main area where this transaction is most concentrated, for it is the battle-ground between the power of 'shining ones' and the forces that cover up and obstruct, where victory is won over unyielding darkness. This is a space that must be cleared for an open channel of communication to be established between man and the gods, the message of invocation to be carried above and paths to be built for the divinities to reach man's dwelling place. Such clearing is done jointly by the weapon of *brahman*, forged by the *ṛṣis*, on the one hand, and the instrumentality of the power of shining forth that the gods possess.

The shining ones, of whom there are thirty-three, constitute a differentiated structure of light itself. The diffraction of the one Light generates 3340 sparkling points, reducible to thirty-three, or just three, take it as you fancy. The concern here is not the construction of a metaphysical or theological system but with the practice of human living, of which the longing for the utmost reaches of the divine is an integral, or integrative, dimension. The many divinities of the Veda, even the One God, are the bridge between mortal man and truth, transcendent, remote, generative of light itself. For each individual human being, what is given to begin with in his experience is multiplicity, the darkness of error, from where he can take off, as a task to be accomplished, and the very purpose of living, and reach out to unity, to more light, to truth. The entire topology of the Veda, with its ascending order of *lokas*, regions or 'clearings' (as Jan Gonda explains the term), from the earth to the third, highest heaven and beyond, is geared to this end. The Vedic seers' attention is turned towards the light itself, with its multitude of facets, rather than to the things illumined by it, as also to that in man which responds to lights, the power of seeing and the awareness of the shining forth, the *phainesthai* itself. The commonest word used for this ability is *dhī*, but the variety of terms for what the mind of man, of this son of Manu, is capable of, is as numerous as the words, symbols and metaphors for light. The Vedic seers never seem to tire of playing, beyond this, with the metaphors of light and the vocabulary of mentation, a gift of the gods to *all* children of Manu. As remarked earlier, the concern of this liturgical poetry is practical, namely the actualization in one's own person of what it means to be fully human, and not of a purely theoretical nature, for the sake of constructing a 'world-picture'. While interpreting an ancient text like the Ṛgveda, that is, translating its language into contemporary ways of speaking, the prevailing philosophical notions of terms of which this is bound to be done need reflective consideration, especially when it is a matter of the most general terms we call metaphysical. Philological knowledge and philosophical criticism cannot be kept apart, and both together must be taken as prerequisite for overcoming linguistic, cultural and historical distance. For example, Heinrich Luders has given what is to date the definitive account of the Vedic world-structure, of the three-layered heaven and the space beyond, the heavenly waters, ocean and rivers, from which the sacrality of the earthly waters derives. The philological work on which his conclusions are based is impeccable and even brilliant, as Paul Thieme acknowledges.

But both Vedists, among the most distinguished of them all, speak in terms of *Weltbild* and *Weltanschauung*, as though the Vedic *ṛṣis* were talking about nature in the modern sense, as an object confronting the human subject. For such a picture there cannot be any *sacred* fire (Agni), or the *sacred* waters here below, or a *sacred* plant. The Soma plant is reduced to the psychotropic mushroom amanita muscaria and the sacredness of the Ganga to a question of physical purity, i.e., relative absence of microbes and chemical pollutants. Once we move beyond philology to the task of understanding and interpretation, so that the horizons of the remote past and the present may fuse, can we afford to ignore the philosophical critique of the concept of world and the idea of a world-picture by Heidegger or by Wittgenstein and, more recently, Richard Rorty? In the interpretation of the Vedic text, it is not only religious and cultural-anthropological prejudices that have been at play during two centuries of Western Vedic scholarship; philosophical presuppositions too have wrought havoc here, through the unquestioning importation of Western conceptuality into another tradition.

Among the shining ones, the most important, because closest to man, is Agni, the divinity visible to the eyes on the sacrificial altar, present within his heart as the light by which man sees and knows and as the immortal lodged within the mortal. He is the burning flame of longing for self-transcendence, the vehicle which carries man's message to the gods and the servant of the gods who brings them to the mortal's home. He is a thing among earthly things and also a symbol for the transaction between the human and the divine, and a divinity in his own right, with a seat in each of the three worlds. As the sacrificial fire, he receives all man's oblations and is the mouth of all the deities to whom offerings are made. Another deity, Soma, represents the ultimate end of human spiritual endeavour, the fullness of awareness, potency and joy, in short, immortality. He dwells in the form of an inexhaustible reservoir of ambrosial waters in the highest heaven, nourishing the gods with its thousand streams, enabling them to shine forth in their specific virtue. Like Agni, Soma also dwells as the immortal among mortals, yet a thing among things, in the shape of the Soma plant, of which the juice is offered by men as the most precious oblation to the gods, the one offering for which the gods are always greedy and which establishes the firmest bond of friendship between man and the gods. The earthly Soma is both an embodiment and a symbol of the celestial deity. It is only when this deity shines forth in full majesty in the purified sacrificial Soma that it becomes a drink of immortality for mortals, as it is for the immortals in heaven. Soma bestows on the mortals this plenitude of being, this freedom from time in ecstatic joy because, as the celestial drink, it flows from the fountain-head of all sacrality, transcendent truth. One *ṛṣi* addresses Soma, while it is being purified for an offering, in the following words, 'You have been pressed with words of truth, truly and with faith and ardour . . . you speak the sacred truth, you shine with truth, you say the true, as yours are the true deeds, and you give utterance to faith. . . . There where the inextinguishable light shines, in the region of the Sun, in that immortal and unfading world, O Purifier, place me . . . where they move as they will, in the triple dome, in the third heaven of heaven, where the worlds are made of light, there make me immortal . . . there, where joy, gladness and delight are, where the desires of all desire are fulfilled, there, O drop of Soma, flow for Indra.'

Indra, insatiable in his thirst for Soma, is king of the gods, the most effulgent of all the shining ones. He is the lord of all that is, the performer of a hundred heroic deeds, master of the cows, power itself. His is the ability to execute an action, the power to carry it through, sheer force of will. Indra is the invincible power of breaking through, shattering obstacles, overcoming concealment. With him is associated the primal myth of the Indian tradition, the killing of the dragon Vṛtra, which names literally the force that covers and hides, blocks and thwarts. The poet sings in praise of Indra: 'He killed the dragon and pierced an opening for the waters, he split open the bellies of the mountains. . . . He drank the Soma and with his thunderbolt killed the first-born of the dragons and so brought forth the Sun, the sky and dawn. . . . He killed this Vṛtra-most Vṛtra and, over him as he lay there like a broken reed, the swelling waters flowed for the sake of mankind, waters that Vṛtra had enclosed with his power. . . . Indra is the king of all beings and rules over all peoples as their king, encircling all this as a rim encircles the spokes'. This myth, like others in Ṛgveda, is not invented by the poets but taken over and used as a vehicle for new thoughts in terms of which they are thus already interpreted in the text. As Wendy O'Flaherty very perceptively remarks, 'The Ṛgveda has no true mythology; it is written out of a mythology that we can only try to reconstruct from the Ṛgvedic jumble of paradox heaped on paradox, tropes heaped on tropes.' The important thing, it seems to me, is not so much to reconstruct the mythology as to try to see what the Ṛgvedic seer makes of what he has inherited, to what use he puts it. Similarly, references to natural processes or to what look like historical events are meaningful and important as vehicles employed to carry new meanings. Another myth with a metaphor at its core is that of the demon Vala, the enclosure, the cavity that shuts in. Here again we have a common noun turned into a proper name, what appears to us today as a mythologization of an abstract idea, in this case, that of enclosing or encaving. To quote the poet, 'The divine *ṛṣis* joined the challenger Indra; they brought forth great light out of darkness, the dawns recognized him and came to meet him; Indra became the only lord of the cow. . . . The killer of Vṛtra as lord of cows has shown us cows; he went among the dark one with his rosy forms. Revealing lovely gifts through truth, he has opened up all his own gates'. What are these cows imprisoned in the cavity of the mountain? What is the trope of a herd of cows in its enclosure meant to suggest? Throughout the Ṛgveda, the word functions as a polysemic signifier. Sometimes it means, or symbolizes, rain or the waters that are released from the cave of the clouds, most often rays of light, but also the inspired speech of the poet—its synonyms and their special forms adding further semantic complexity to the range of its symbolic value. An allied myth is that of the Paṇi demons who have hidden the cattle-treasure in the mountains. Literally, a *paṇi* is the hoarder of treasures, the miser who does not part with it without obtaining its price. The central image in all these myths is that of light encapsulated within a rock, which Indra liberates with his power of shattering the impenetrable, the thunderbolt, which in turn is often a symbol for poetic speech. Within the text itself one may observe interpretive operations on the symbols going on, moving from one level of meaning to another, beginning with the processes of nature such as cloud formation and rain-fall, and culminating explicitly in the disclosure of light from a covering darkness. This happens through the god-given *brahman*, or poetic work, of the seers, in which each level of interpretation provides a symbol for the next higher.

Among the greatest of the gods is Varuṇa, one of Aditi's seven sons. He is the all-powerful monarch who rules over mortals and gods, over heaven and earth. His throne rests on a thousand pillars, in the highest invisible heaven, his palace has a thousand doors. He looks down on all beings, keeping watch on their thoughts and actions, never deceived, seeing through the wrong-doing, the untruth in men, he vigilantly observes the truth and untruth in them, separating the one from the other. He is the guardian of truth or *Ṛta* and punisher of untruth in every form, of untruth in the relationship between man and the gods, and between man and man. In regard to his proper essence,

Paul Thieme has argued that Varuṇa represents the personified and deified concept of truth, that he is the god of truth, truth personified, just as the other ādityas associated with him represent the deification of other abstract ideas like contract, hospitality and sharing. His views (which follow a principle first adopted by A. Meillet and then further developed by H. Luders, the principle that many of the Vedic gods are deified abstract concepts) have generated a lot of controversy among leading Vedologists but appear to me to have strong philological grounding and to mark a major advance in Vedic studies. His interpretation of Varuṇa as 'god true-speech' or as the deification and personification of 'true speech, spoken truth', presupposes the interpretation of *Ṛta* offered with massive documentation by Luders. As against the commonly accepted translation, that is, interpretation, of this word as 'cosmic order', Luders has conclusively shown that in every single case where the word *Ṛta* occurs in this text it can, and should be, rendered as 'truth'. Thieme agrees emphatically with this conclusion, and remarks, 'that *ṛta* means truth and nothing but truth must be regarded as conclusively established by Luders.'

Ṛta or truth is the most important single word in the text, scattered all over it, enveloping and holding in its web, as it were, the entire text. From Roth to Renou, Vedic scholars have translated it as 'order' because they were captive to 'the vocabulary of modern European religiosity', Luders remarks, projecting into the Veda concepts alien to it. *Ṛta*, according to him, constitutes the central notion of Vedic religion, the highest power and the ultimate cause of all being for the Aryan Indians. As he comments, 'To have made truth into the highest principle of life, that is an achievement which perhaps even the moderns may perhaps envy those ancients.' He points out that the conception of *Ṛta* in the sense of truth goes back to Indo-Iranian times, for Asa in the Avesta incontrovertibly means truth; Plutarch renders it by the Greek *aletheia*, as Al Beruni later translates it with the Arabic for truth. In Iran, truth was personified as a goddess, like Aletheia in Parmenides' poem and was considered subservient to Ahura Mazda. The Vedic seers, on the contrary, never personified or deified *Ṛta*; for them *Ṛta* was the ultimate source and origin of all beings, including the gods, high above Being and Non-being. As Luders points out, the gods dwell in 'the highest seat of Ṛta, but they are themselves never spoken of as being themselves the seat of truth.' The almighty Varuṇa is the guardian god of truth, whether in the spoken word, or in the unspoken thought in the mind, in the invisible motives of human action or in their relationships to each other. All the other gods, too, subserve or mediate truth in their various cosmic functions and governance of human activities. As mentioned earlier, above the earth is sky or intervening space and beyond that is heaven with its three layers. Beyond these is 'the seat of truth', the eternal well-spring of life, the origin of gods and men. The mass of luminosity comprising the three heavenly regions, with the gods as its multiple focal points, has its origin there. Light itself is a symbol of their region, streaming down towards and for man in the shape of the many gods, or of the one and only, and in countless rays of benediction, promise and enabling condition of his existence and the way he constitutes his world. Here in this region is also the bubbling fountain-head of Soma, flowing out to form an ocean of heavenly waters, from which they gush down to the visible heaven and thence through the sky to the earth as the sacred river Saraswati. In Soma thus we have another, a 'thicker', more substantial symbol and embodied form of transcendent *Ṛta* than light, a more concrete image of the relationship between truth and the mode of being of a human being, the former reaching down with its claim on man, the latter reaching out in ecstatic response to truth as it takes on the form of a more tangible hold for man. The light-rays and heavenly streams are both 'cows', symbolic of the sacredness, the preciousness and the plenitude of the gift from beyond, as cattle are the earth's gift to agricultural man. Both are foot-holds for the shining forth of truth as the ultimate, sacred reality and the supreme condition of the possibility of being human for man and for all beings to *be*.

The explicitly and poetically designed semantic metaphoricity of the Ṛgveda, however, does not end here. Parallel to the division into *lokas*, or 'clearings' for the manifestation of the sacred in the earthly, to the diffraction of the primal mass of luminosity into the many-splendoured rays of light that illumine the darkness out of which man seeks to lift himself, and parallel to the phases in which Soma becomes available to ecstatic man as the gift of sacred truth, there is the phenomenon of *Vāk*, the word, and its epiphany on earth. As the imaginative vehicle on which these three are carried, *Vāk* may even be looked upon as the over-arching mode as well as medium in which the true and the sacred shore forth for the Vedic *ṛṣi*. The *brahman*, the verbal form-giving enterprise of the seer, which he makes, recites and sings, and puts to ritual use often, has already been mentioned. It carries the reality and weight of the entire sacrificial ritual, which is the form in which the whole process is dramatized and acted out. The goddess *vāk*, speech or language, personified in the Veda, as truth is not, has her origin in the same 'highest foot-step of *Viṣṇu*' or *Ṛta*, as light and Soma, and her manifestation and modes of being too are represented as 'cows'. It is she herself who is the thunderbolt (*vajra*) that destroys the *Vṛtra* that covers the truth of things, which releases the heavenly waters pent up in the rock-dragon. As *Bṛhaspati*, the master of speech, himself says, 'When the wise ones poetically fashioned speech, with their thoughts sifting it as grain is sifted through a sieve, then one friend recognizes another in it, a pleasing beauty is set in it (Thieme).... Many who can see, have not yet seen her; many who can hear, have not yet heard her. To a rare one, she reveals herself, as a loving bride, beautifully dressed, reveals her body to her husband.' And here is the great self-revelation of the goddess herself, in her own words: 'I move with the Rudras, with the Vasus, with the Adityas and all the gods. I carry both Mitra and Varuna, both Indra and Agni, and the two Aśvins. I carry the swelling Soma, and Tvaṣṭṛ and Pūṣan and Bhaga. I bestow riches on the pious sacrificer who presses the Soma and offers the oblation. Mine is the sovereignty, I am the confluence of riches, the skilful one who is first among those worthy of sacrifice. The gods divided me into many parts, for I dwell in many places and enter into many forms. One who eats, who sees, who breathes, who hears what is said, does so through me.

Though they do not realize it, they dwell in me. Listen, my learned friend, what I tell you deserves putting your faith in. I myself say this, which gods and men alike must find welcome. Whom I love I make awesome; I make him a *Brāhmaṇa*; one endowed with poetic creativity, I make him a *ṛṣi*, a sage. I stretch the bow for Rudra so that his arrow will strike down the hater of *brahman*. I incite conflict among peoples. I have pervaded heaven and earth. I gave birth to the father at the top of this world. My origin is in the waters, within the ocean. From there I spread out over all beings and touch the heavens with the crown of my head. I blow like the wind, embracing all the world. Beyond heaven, beyond the earth, such am I in my greatness.' The true and full epiphany of the goddess, *Vāk*, however, is the Ṛgveda text itself.

Vāk too is symbolized as a cow, as the primal cow. As a famous verse declares, 'The undying, inexhaustible, syllable of the song is the final abode where all the gods have taken their seat. What can one, who does not know this, do with the words of the poem? Only those who know it sit here together. The thousand-syllabled cow bowed as she fashioned the flowing waters. The quarters of the sky live on the oceans that flow out of her in all directions. The whole universe exists through the undying syllable that flows from her. Speech was divided into four parts that the wise poets know. Three parts, hidden in deep secret, humans do not have at their command; the fourth part of speech is what men speak.' In a remarkable lecture, 'On the way to language', Heidegger sought to think of language in such a way as 'to bring language itself to speech as language', language as it abides in its own manner of being, as language itself speaks in the speech of man. Heidegger also often pointed out that in disclosing to us things—whatever we speak *about*—language holds back the revelation of its own manner of being, conceals it. Although in all great poetry language in some measure thrusts itself into the forefront, so that it becomes its own subject-matter, in the case of Vedic poetry it does so pre-eminently. Multilayered webs of meaning are generated, pointing always to a transcendent origin in a secret place beyond, a place hidden, disclosed as hidden, and yet manifest in a nearness which bestows on man his very essence, a place where truth and the holy are one. The Vedic poets knew about the play of concealment and revealment from their own experience. Not only do Agni and Soma have their hidden aspects, their places of hiding, Indra's very existence needs a reassuring affirmation, and Varuṇa in his remote majesty remains unapproachable to all but the purest among Vedic seers, Vasiṣṭha. *Vāk* or speech itself remains concealed in its essence and even truth's true face is hidden by the light which streams forth from it, as by speech, which has its origin there, as it bursts forth in the song of the seers. As a Ṛgvedic verse says, 'The poets hide the paths of truth; they keep secret their hidden names' (10.5.2).

Historically also, this text has kept back, held in reserve, as Heidegger might say, much that it can tell us. This is largely due to the circumstance, as hinted earlier, that its exegesis was from the beginning geared to the perspective of the *use* of the Vedic mantras for ritual purposes, without much concern for the understanding of the text by itself, as autonomous and constituting a coherent world of meaning. Although it seems to have been recognized that it can be interpreted from alternative points of view and at many levels, the ritualist school prevailed. The other source of the stultification of endeavours to study the text was an excessive reliance on fanciful etymology and methodologically insecure foundations. For this reason, the philological work done by the best Western Vedists during the last hundred years or so remains an indispensable supplement to traditional Indian scholarship. Philological knowledge, however, is a necessary but not sufficient condition of interpretation, in the sense of a hermeneutic endeavour to which the present philosophical understanding of the interpreter and his situatedness in his present as well as in his tradition are vitally relevant. The interpreter's activity is determined, in large measure, by the contemporaneous state of thinking in linguistics and poetics, and in the study of religion, including that of myth, symbol and ritual, current in his time. Above all, his interpretation depends on the most general philosophical concepts available to him historically and currently, as well as his understanding of the meaning and nature of thinking itself. As Heidegger, Gadamer and George Steiner, not to mention Walter Benjamin, have made evident, all interpretation is a translation, an *Über-Setzung*, and all translation is an interpretation, irrespective of whether the translation is from one language to another or within the same language, where the appropriation of tradition in the present is a prime concern. Leaving aside the many hermeneutical and philosophical problems facing the present-day interpreter of an ancient text, I mention briefly one point each from the scholarly work of Luders and Thieme as examples of how philological understanding is sometimes bedeviled by the current philosophical idiom and outlook. Recognizing that *Ṛta* or truth was 'the highest principle of life for the Vedic seers', Luders yet says, '*Ṛta* exclusively signifies the truth of the spoken word or thought... that what is asserted corresponds with reality.' What is taken for granted by him and unquestioningly presupposed are the notions of truth and falsity as residing solely in statements and of the correspondence theory of truth, presuppositions which are constitutive of the Western metaphysical tradition, in terms of which he then inteprets the Vedic religio-poetic tradition. In his deconstructive critique of that Western tradition, Heidegger subjected the notion of truth to a penetrating life-long inquiry and found that the 'metaphysical' idea of truth as correctness of judgment presupposes something or some happening which is the condition of the possibility of the former. This he calls '*Lichtung*', which means a 'clearing', an open space, a prior opening up, through which a beam of light can traverse and so make anything shine forth. Without the free space of such an opening there can be neither light nor darkness, neither presence nor absence of anything, neither adequation or correspondence, nor certitude, as conceived in the ordinary sense of truth. Truth in this primordial sense, as *aletheia* or unconcealment, is an opening or clearing for presence and absence. When we consider, however, that concealment or *lethe* belongs to the very heart of *aletheia*, we reach the ultimate, basic, sense of truth as the opening for presence concealing itself, the opening of a 'self-concealing sheltering', and can see how the ordinary concept of truth as correctness of statement is derivable from it.

We must first experience, Heidegger says, '*aletheia* in a Greek manner as unconcealment and then, above and beyond the Greek, think it as the opening of self-concealing.' Might it not be helpful if the meaning of Ṛta is understood in this sense, 'above and beyond the Greek', and beyond the meanings attaching to it in the Western metaphysical tradition?

Despite my great admiration for Paul Thieme's philological acumen, I cannot help experiencing similar reservations about the language of some of his interpretations. Many of the Vedic gods are personifications of the forces and powers of nature, he says, whose origins go back to Indo-Iranian and proto-Indogermanic times. He does not take into account the possibility, it seems to me, that the Vedic seers might have been *using* this pre-given tradition for their own purposes and novel ends, as metaphors recognized as such. Further, Thieme thinks that there are ethical concepts which have been deified here, such as Mitra, who is contract personified, and Varuṇa, who is true speech personified, and Aryamana, who is hospitality personified—these are the gods who guard the sanctity of the corresponding ethical virtues, he also says. Yet he translates their names as God Contract, God True Speech, God Hospitality respectively, just as Indra for him is God Victory. I suppose one can, with some ingenuity, interpret all the Vedic deities thus, following Meillet's principle, already adumbrated half a century ago by Usener, that they are all deifications and personifications of abstract concepts. My trouble here is with these 'abstract concepts'. One advances, the Platonic tradition tells us, from the concrete to the abstract, from the multiplicity of facts to the Idea that subsumes them. Did the Vedic seers have a direct vision of such Ideas to begin with? Or, do we see here a process of moving from *logos* to *mythos* rather than the other way round? If these seers had already risen to such a level of abstraction, why would they go about re-entering the deifying, mythic darkness again? Isn't something seriously wrong with attempts to understand mythic-symbolic images in terms of concepts? What happens if one follows the deconstruction of the concept of 'concept' itself by Heidegger? In a tradition which knows nothing of the distinction between the pre-metaphysical beginnings and their post-metaphysical appropriation, how does one go about interpreting it in its origins?

Varuṇa is no deification of an abstraction, but a deity who serves an abstraction, if *Ṛta* can be called that. *Ṛta* itself is never called a god in the text, and is yet as little of an abstraction as Being in the Western philosophical tradition, as analysed by Heidegger. Varuṇa is a god-servant of truth. As Thieme himself translates the Vedic *mantra*, 'The thread of truth is stretched out in the straining-cloth, on the tip of the tongue through the potency of Varuṇa.' In him all poetry centres like the hub in the wheel (RV.8.41.6); he knows the hidden names of the cow, he opens the thought in the heart, enables truth to find expression in the 'formulation' of the poet, he mediates in the embodiment of truth, of the hidden word, in the poetic work of the poet's manifest speech. In what has gone above, I have by no means been trying to show that the Vedic poets were engaged in any sort of aletheiological inquiry. My intention was rather to suggest that they were 'doing' aletheio-poiesis. In recent poetic theory, the importance of the rhetorical or tropological dimension of language is being increasingly recognized. This involves paying attention to the way meaning is generated and conveyed rather than concentrating on the meaning produced, thus giving a certain priority to poetics over hermeneutics. In Paul de Man's words, 'When you do hermeneutics, you are concerned with the meaning of the work; when you do poetics, you are concerned with the stylistics or with the description of the way in which a work means.' The phenomenological-hermeneutical approach to texts, which is concerned with *what* is meant in the text, is not always compatible with the poetic's approach, which is concerned with the *how* or the manner in which that meaning is produced. Whether the latter necessarily subverts or undoes the former, as some theorists hold, or whether hermeneutics, that is, a phenomenology of understanding and interpretation, can be conceived broadly enough, as a phenomenology of reading, to comprehend poetics also, will have to be determined by a close reading of specific texts. The Ṛgveda, read as a text, would seem to offer ample scope for both kinds of exploration.

Speech and Writing in Heidegger's Philosophy

S. IJSSELING

In a footnote to the text of a lecture which Jacques Derrida held in 1968 under the title 'The Ends of Man', the following is asserted: 'Implicitly or explicitly, the privileged position of the spoken word is continually and solidly present in Heidegger.'[1] According to Derrida, Heidegger uncritically accepts the privileged position of the spoken word. The voice, or speaking, would always imply a greater proximity to the speaker and, on the contrary, the written word would carry with itself a distance and thereby also an absence. It is probable that at present Derrida would express himself in a more nuanced fashion. The appearance of Heidegger's *Gesamtausgabe* has brought about for Derrida extreme caution with regard to definitive assertions about Heidegger. At times, Derrida claims that everything he has to say has already been said by Heidegger. Still, it was in a different language and a different linguistic and historical context and thereby not really the same. However, at the same time, there remains in Derrida a certain reserve regarding Heidegger, for example regarding his interpretation of history. Nostalgic desire for a pure, unspoilt beginning and for an authentic presence to the origin is problematic for Derrida. For Derrida, this nostalgic desire appears as well in the interpretation of the history of speaking and writing, a history Heidegger frequently views in terms of a loss of proximity and 'originality'. Furthermore, Heidegger's view of history (i.e., history understood as a 'whole' which unfolds in different epochs) reminds Derrida too much of Hegel. Naturally, there is an essential difference, namely that in contrast to Hegel, Heidegger's discourse is one of withdrawal and dispossession (*Enteignis*). Everything depends upon how these differences are to be thought, particularly in connection with speech and writing.

There is no denying that for Heidegger, whose interest is in language *as* language and not as something else (e.g., as instrument of communication or system of signs), the spoken word is the point of departure. One reads in *On the Way to Language*: 'It belongs to our task to approach the specificity of language. Here also, language manifests itself above all as our speaking.' Heidegger adds, 'We pay attention now to everything that always and already, noticed or unnoticed, is implicated in our speaking.'[2] Spoken language is and remains the point of departure. However, this does not mean that Heidegger never dealt with the written word and the related acts of reading and writing. Perhaps these acts of reading and writing belong directly to that which always and already, noticed or unnoticed, is implicated in our speaking.

In a letter of 6-4-1955 to the graphic artist E. Pretorius, who had invited him to a lecture within a series 'on language', Heidegger writes: 'One theme appears to me to be inevitable: Speech and Writing; here become evident the essential questions of the East-West dialogue; questions of signification and image in the widest sense can be brought into the open.... The theme is too valuable and too essential to the present situation to be squandered by a premature or hasty treatment. It must disclose its own importance.[3] Thus, speech and text and the related reading and writing are inevitable themes, especially in the present situation of mankind. On the one hand, our culture is a written culture to a hitherto unknown extent. On the other hand, through the mechanisation of writing the relationship of man to language and subsequently his relationship to the world and to Being have been altered profoundly.

Secondly, Speech and Writing is a theme which concerns the dialogue between the European world and the Far East, a question of great interest to Heidegger. The West and the East are different for Heidegger, not in the last place because they have a completely different understanding of writing. European culture is characterized by the so-called letter-writing or alphabetical writing. Hegel called this form 'in-and-for-itself more intelligible,'[4] a statement which Heidegger would not maintain.[5] However, Heidegger would readily agree with Hegel that a different way of writing implies a different way of thinking. That the European way of thinking is in and for itself more perfect, as Hegel suggests, is something that Heidegger would never say. For Heidegger, the materialization of thought in writing is constitutive for philosophy as philosophy. We are of course accustomed to hearing that the birth of philosophy in Greece is linked to the structure of Greek language. Heidegger actually goes a step further and asserts that the origin of European as philosophy and as metaphysics, as well as the growth of the sciences from these, is in fact linked to the materialization of thought in writing. As is well known, Husserl expressed something similar in his *Origin of Geometry*. This work was translated into French by Derrida, and he added an extensive introduction and commentary. Husserl's argument is in many respects different from Heidegger's, and it would lead us too far to dwell on differences and convergences. Nevertheless, it is important to note that for both Husserl and Heidegger, writing is not only a medium, but actually constitutes philosophy and science, and that writing at the same is interwoven with the danger of a loss of meaning. A loss of meaning—for Husserl this can be overcome in principle through recollection, by retracing these steps which have led to the present situation of the sciences. For Heidegger, this loss belongs to the essence of language and the Sending of Being.

Thirdly, Speech and Writing is a theme which broaches questions of signification, image, design, the graphic, the 'grammata' and the grammatical. Heidegger understands writing as hand-work, more precisely it is 'handwriting', it is a way of graphic art or design. Heidegger plays with the fact that the Greeks had only one word for writing and drawing—*graphein*. And he asserts that in the mechanization of writing through type-writers and presses (and photo-copiers and word-processors), the essential origin, namely the hand itself, is eliminated. This brings with it an alteration in man's relation to language and in Being's relation to man.

Speech and Writing is an inevitable theme for Heidegger, and in no way does he try to avoid it. Already in *Being and Time*, one finds allusions to this topic. Along with the famous example of the hammer as 'equipment' (*Zeug*), there is mention of the writing-utensil, pen, ink and paper.[6] And along with the 'idle-talk' (*Gerede*), Heidegger also takes note of 'scribbling' (*das Geschreibe*)[7], in which speech is grounded not so much in hearsay, but rather is fed only by reading (*dem Angelesenen*). Heidegger comments: 'The average understanding of the reader will *never* be able to decide what has been drawn from primordial sources and how much is just idle-talk.'[8] Moreover, the dictatorship of the 'they' (*das Man*) can be illuminated by the example of reading: 'We take pleasure and enjoy ourselves as *they* take pleasure; we read, see and judge about literature and art as *they* see and judge.'[9] And finally, one of the most important tasks of philosophical research, as seen from the perspective of *Being and Time*, is precisely 'to ask what kind of being language as such has'.[10] Heidegger poses the question this way: Is language a kind of equipment ready-to-hand within the world, or has it *Dasein's* kind of being, or is it neither or these? And for our purpose, it is worthwhile to note that Heidegger continues: 'What kind of being does language have, if there can be such a thing as a 'dead' language?' We know of a dead language only in texts. And a related problem is precisely the manner of being of texts (i.e., written documents). To my knowledge, Heidegger did not bring the problem in this form to explicit discussion. Indeed, it was *Husserl* who did formulate the problem in this way, in the framework of the problem of Nature and Spirit, and he remains therefore always within the opposition between expression and significance. Let us turn briefly to Husserl's formulation of the problem.

In summary form, Husserl said:[11] Texts belong to the realm of cultural objects. Like all cultural objects, they have a material side, which could be called the physical, sensuous or bodily (*körperlich*), or incarnate (*leiblich*) aspect, as well as having a non-sensuous or spiritual side. The sensuous side of cultural objects belongs to the objective world, to spatio-temporal reality (*Realität*), like natural objects. However, the non-sensuous side of cultural objects, which Husserl also calls meaning (*Sinn*) or significance (*Bedeutung*), does not belong among the things of the spatio-temporal world. Both of these sides form a unity, and one of Husserl's main questions is precisely how this unity is to be conceived. This unity is not always homogeneous. For example, in a literary text, the sensuous side belongs to what is essential, namely the aesthetic merit. In scientific or non-literary texts, the sensuous side is 'non-essential'. In support of the non-essential character of the sensuous side, Husserl cites what has become the classic (although problematic) argument of the possibility of a *translation*, with the preservation of the complete identity of the theoretical contents or rather, the significance. The argument is problematic because a translation is always a rendering from one language into another. However, language is already and always presupposed, and with it the so-called sensible side.

Heidegger would not pose the question of the manner of being of texts in this way, and for many different reasons. One such reason is that for Husserl the point of departure is the opposition of expression (*Ausdruck*) and significance (*Bedeutung*). For Heidegger, language in its essence is not expression. Language cannot even be grasped in its essence when one focuses on its significance-character. Another reason is that Husserl carries out his analysis in the context of the distinction (if not the complete separation) of the sensible and the non-sensible as two regions. This division of the sensible and the non-sensible, physical and non-physical, of the *mundus sensibilis* and *mundus intelligibilis* is according to Heidegger a main feature or the basic structure of what he calls metaphysics, which is radically called into question by him.[12] This does not mean that Heidegger paid no attention to the sensuous to 'exterior' side of language, to the spoken and the written word. On the contrary, he writes at the close of *Hebel der Hausfreund*: 'The word of language sounds and resounds in the text; it appears and shines in written images. Sound and writing are sensuous, in which sense arises.'[13] And in the *Introduction to Metaphysics* Heidegger declares: 'When we perceive the word "Being", either hearing it as a phonetic unit or seeing it as a written sign, it immediately gives itself as something other than the succession of sounds and letters "abracadabra." This too is a succession of sounds, but we say at once that it is meaningless, though it may have its meaning as a magic formula. But "Being" is not meaningless in this way. Similarly, "Being", written and seen, is different from "kzomil." This too is a sequence of letters, but in connection with this sequence we cannot think anything.'[14] Here Heidegger gives attention to the written, to the face of the text in its materiality, in contrast to the spoken. Nevertheless, the question can be posed in view of what Heidegger says here, as to whether the specificity of writing really comes to be properly considered. Is there really a fundamental difference between that which Heidegger points out here, and what Husserl had already developed in relation to expression and significance in his *Logical Investigations*? Heidegger's framework also seems to be the opposition of meaning and significance. Moreover, the written word is ultimately thought in analogy and as a variant of the spoken word. Does the written word not occupy a wholly proper dimension, which remains unthought here by Heidegger?

It is perhaps true that Heidegger did not formulate the question of the way of being of a text in the same way as Husserl. But he did indeed talk about the essence of a 'work', most specifically in the *Introduction to Metaphysics* and in *The Origin of the Work of Art*. 'Work' is here above all the work of language—the work of poetry and of thought. The work of the thinker, which is often called hand-work, appears to us chiefly as the work of language, and even more as writing. 'The thought of the thinker is materialised in writing,'[15] claims Heidegger in *What is Called Thinking*? And in the *Parmenides*-lecture he asks: 'How could we know of Plato's Dialogues, if they had never been written?'[16] Only by means of texts, only by means of writing is philosophy preserved and made accessible to us. This fact is in my opinion seldom fully recognized or taken seriously, and even less are the implications and consequences of this fact brought to light.[17]

For Heidegger, work is 'the happening of truth at work'. A text is a place where discovery and covering-up, revelation and concealment occur—a text is a There (*Da*) of Being and Truth. In the work, the happening of truth is at work. This implies also that a philosophical text, a philosophical work according to Heidegger, ought never to be considered as a more or less adequate reproduction, presentation or expression of a pre-given meaning or pre-given reality that exists *outside* philosophy. Rather, philosophy is itself a work, that is, a place where truth as uncovering and covering-up takes place. When Heidegger reads a philosophical text, he asks therefore not so much about the meaning (*Sinn*) or significance (*Bedeutung*) of the text, but he asks rather about what *happens* in the text. A more concrete example: At the end of his Kant-book, Heidegger writes regarding his interpretation of Kant that 'we examine not what he says, but what happens in his laying of the foundation of metaphysics. The primordial explication of the *Critique of Pure Reason* as we have given it above has as its only objective the revelation of this happening.'[18] Heidegger says something similar with regard to his interpretations of Schelling and Hegel, of Leibniz or of Descartes, or of Nietzsche.

The thought of the thinker is written. To write down a thought is for Heidegger an extremely complicated state of affairs. In the same context as the just cited passage from the *Parmenides*-lecture, Heidegger claims: 'The Thinking and Saying in the Era of the completion of Greek thought in Plato has the form of Dialogues. It is as if at the apogee of Greek thought, this thought itself sought to clarify the essential role of 'the Word,' in an age when man comes to an immediate relation to *aletheia*. In his dialogue *Phaedros*, in the discussion of "the Beautiful" (near the end), Plato shows a very clear awareness of the privileged position of the spoken word over the *merely* written down. Still, how would we know of Plato's Dialogues, if they had not been written as well?'[19] It seems that Heidegger here considers the movement of the spoken word into the written as decline, deterioration, or decay. This view is confirmed by a paragraph concerning Socrates in *What is Called Thinking*? to which we will soon return. In the original Thinking and Saying there is still an immediate relation to being and Truth, a relation that is lost with the writing down of thought. The loss is linked with the completion, even with the end of Greek thought. A clearer example of what Derrida calls 'the privileged position of spoken language' would be difficult to find. Still, a number of comments can be made here. What Plato calls 'Dialogues', Heidegger sets not wholly unjustly between quotation marks. These are in fact written dialogues. Plato had worked for years on most of his dialogues. When one considers style, word-choice, puns, sentence-construction, rhythm, alliteration, allegory and analogy, and above all, when one senses the efficiency of these Dialogues, it is clear that they are as perfectly formed as possible. '*Plato scribens mortuus est*,'[20] one reads in Cicero. It is said that Plato died at his writing desk, while finishing his *Epinonis*. Despite the critique which Plato unleashes upon literature, he was dominated himself by the literary demon, and his writings belong to the best of Greek literature. How does it stand then with 'the clear awareness of the privileged position of the spoken word over the merely written down?' Can one speak here of decay or loss, or is it an insoluble tension that on the one hand is the condition of possibility for philosophy as philosophy and on the other hand forms the internal limitation for all philosophy whatsoever? Or is the situation even more complicated?

In *What is Called Thinking*? Heidegger talks about Socrates, whom he calls 'the purest thinker of the West, and who wrote nothing'.[21] The context here is a discussion of appearance and withdrawal. It is asserted of Socrates that throughout his entire life right up to and including his death he did nothing else than place himself in the draft of this appearance and withdrawal, and maintained himself therein. 'That is why he is the purest thinker of the west and wrote nothing.' Heidegger continues, 'he who begins to write what is thought, must unquestionably be linked to someone who in an all too strong draft takes refuge in a wind-shelter. It remains the mystery of a still hidden history that all of the thinkers after Socrates, notwithstanding their greatness, must be considered as such fugitives. This has determined the fate of Western science, from the *doctrina* of the Middle Ages to the *scientia* of Modern Times.'[22] Here as well, one hears an undertone of decay. The talk is of taking flight and of fugitives, of a purity that has been lost, and of a thinking that has become science and literature.

One can immediately pose the question whether this is the only possible interpretation. Could it not be the case that thought exists on the basis of a pre-given literature and that writing is a condition of possibility for thinking? Does thinking end in literature, or is it rather the case that literature becomes thought? Was the 'telling of stories' not interrupted by the question about the 'Essence'? Socrates is perhaps not the best example of this development, for he lived in a world in which writing already played an important role. Heidegger seems to presuppose a thinking which precedes every form of writing. But was there *ever* a thinking of this sort? Is this not a nostalgic desire for a past that in fact has never been present? Heidegger would probably agree that in fact it concerns a 'past' that has never been present, a return or step backwards towards a place where we have never been, for the beginning is not behind us, but lies in front of us. Yet the question still remains as to whether there is a thinking possible without some form of writing. A thinking without language Heidegger views as impossible. Only a few lines before the passage regarding Socrates, Heidegger writes: 'only in so far as man speaks does man think; the reverse, which metaphysics believes, is not the case.'[23] In my opinion, the essential relationship between writing and speaking remains unthought here by Heidegger.

The significance of these texts cited from *What is Called Thinking*? lies on another level. In writing down, in the materialization of thought in writing, is hidden a necessity, a destiny. It is the still hidden history, which reigns as the destiny or history of Being as withdrawal, here called 'flight into the wind-shelter'. This destiny or hidden necessity of the materialization of thought in writing is a condition of possibility for the philosophy of the Middle Ages and of Modernity, for science, and also for technology; without writing all these are unthinkable. This condition of possibility is as a withdrawal the way in which Being manifests itself.[24] Heidegger opposes philosophy, science and technology with the essential thinking, which reached its end and its completion in Plato.

A similar question is treated by Heidegger in *The Principle of Reason* (*Der Satz vom Grund*). In this text he contrasts the 'writings and works' of modern thinkers with the thought of the Greeks.[25] The former, claims Heidegger, are in their basic features far more difficult to approach than the Greeks, for these works of modernity are constructed differently, they are multi-layered, interwoven with the tradition and the discussion with Christianity. The texts of modern thinkers are more extensive and more fragmentary; and while this may seem to be merely a non-essential fact, it is for Heidegger the infallible sign that an alteration in thought has occurred and that modern thinking stands outside the realm of originary thinking.

Once again, the impression is one of decay, although the discourse here also includes the reign of the destiny of Being. The writings of the Greeks are less complex, more direct, closer to us, while those of modern times are full of reference to the tradition and to already available texts, that is, full of explicit and implicit quotations. Heidegger avoids the problem here as to whether a text—of any kind whatsoever—is possible at all without reference to other texts. For Heidegger, there should be a 'zero-point' of writing, an original writing, which in no way refers to or follows from the already written. Is there such a thing as an absolute, original writing, and what could it be? At the very least, everything that is written is written with words which are not just invented, but rather are pre-given. One always finds oneself within the domain and power of speech and writing, and were this not the case, then every form of speaking and writing would be impossible. Here too, especially here, one sees the reign of the flight of Being, of Being as withdrawal.

Despite all of his 'negative' comments about the written, Heidegger himself was a *reader*, someone who read and actually read a great deal. He was also someone who wrote, eagerly and profusely, as the *Gesamtausgabe* clearly attests. In his monograph on Heidegger, Walter Biemel recounts the weekly, silent walks which Heidegger took with Natorp in the woods in the region of Marburg. Biemel remarks that 'both Natorp and Heidegger lived not so much in the exchange of argument as in the written, carefully thought-out word, in contrast to someone like Scheler.'[26] Heidegger was a reader, much more so than for example Husserl, who considered much reading as a threat for philosophy. Heidegger had read almost all of the great works, not only of philosophy, but also of poetry and literature, and other sorts of texts as well. He considered it his task to learn how to read, and to teach how to read. In the *Zürcher* seminar of 1951, Emil Staiger wondered why Heidegger interwove the exposition of his thought with the interpretation of texts. Heidegger responded by saying, 'I have never held a so-called "systematic" lecture-course, because I wouldn't dare it; I believe that we first must learn again how to read. This simple affair, to learn to read the word of the thinker and the poet—this simple pre-school is that which in a more general view should be the preparation for everything I want to say'.[27] One could immediately add that in *Being and Time* the task of the destruction of the hitherto existing ontology, as well as the retrieval of metaphysics or the step backwards from metaphysics into its essence in the later writings, both of these are not only impossible without reading, but are in fact very specific *ways* of reading.

What Heidegger calls here 'a simple affair' is perhaps not so simple as one might think. Ultimately, one finds very little in Heidegger about what reading is precisely, about what it implies and what it presupposes. There exist only such remarks as 'Reading is gathering' and 'The ability to harken and to obey is the fundamental condition for true reading.'[28] Even in the very short text with the promising title *What is Called Reading*? (*Was heisst Lesen*?) not much more is said than that reading 'is the gathering of what is written, of what is said in the text'; and the 'gathering of what has already taken hold of our being, without our knowing'; and finally that 'without authentic reading we are unable to see what appears to us, to confront the appearing and the shining.'[29] As important as this may be, it is not much, especially when compared to what Heidegger says about thinking in *What is Called Thinking*? and in other writings. This is actually not so surprising, for 'reading' is not a typically philosophical theme. The word 'reading' is not even mentioned in J. Ritter's *Historical Dictionary of Philosophy*. A substantial, philosophical analysis of the act of reading is lacking. Perhaps it is a theme which is too dangerous and too threatening for philosophy and, as Derrida would say, has been 'suppressed'.[30]

There are many aspects to be considered when one attempts to pose the question of the essence of reading, what is constitutive of reading and what it means for *us* to read. To be able to read is a necessary condition for contemporary man to participate in the world, for modern society with its specific form of rationality cannot exist without some form of reading. Moreover, the majority of problems which confronts philosophy could only exist in a world in which writing has reached a certain level of perfection.

Reading is in no way a univocal activity. There are many different forms of reading. One can read quickly or slowly, read an entire text or only parts of it. Someone can read because he is in some way forced to do so, or he can do it out of interest. One can read for pleasure, for diversion; one can read to escape, or to forget, or to survive. Someone might read in order to be informed, to develop a strategy for action, or to discover the meaning and structure of things. The reader can look for the apparent meaning of a text, or he can search for some underlying meaning. In reading, attention can be paid to the style, the sound, the power of persuasion, or the effects of a text. Someone might read in order to find the truth, another might read for edification, while yet another for consolation. There are texts which are exhausted after one reading, and others which can be read again and again without ever fully surrendering their secrets. Moreover, every different sort of text requires its own way of reading; and there are many different sorts of text. Thus, a novel is read differently than a poem, a philosophical text is read differently than a scientific text, and a work by Hegel is read differently than one by Nietzsche, and a work by Heidegger is read differently than a work about Heidegger. Whoever reads all of these texts in the same way has never learned how to read well.

The way to read is always co-determined by the situation, which is a textual network of author, text and reader, and this situation is never permanently fixed, it is continually changing. Reading by its very nature inserts itself into a fluctuating matrix of relationships that extends limitlessly in all directions. Furthermore, there is the so-called 'para-text',[31] to which belong the title, name of the author and publisher, the year of the text's appearance, the table of contents, the preface, the footnotes, the bibliography, the dedication (written or printed), and so on. All of this is read as well and determines the way in which a text is read. For philosophers, who are normally idealists when it comes to the textual field, the 'materiality' of the text appears to have little importance and belongs solely to the realm of mere externals. However, is not the so-called meaning or significance always an effect of all these contingencies and externals? That Heidegger never considered these aspects of reading no doubt goes together with the fact that his discussion of language is rooted in the question about *the* spoken language (*the* said) and *the* written (*the* read). But is there something like *the* spoken language or *the* written?

Heidegger was not only a reader, but someone who wrote, and wrote with great eagerness. Despite his call for silence and economy of words, he wrote a great deal. He wrote with the hand and was also very proud of his hand-writing, as can be seen by the fact that he was pleased to see his signature printed by means of a block-press and that he published for Hildegarde Feick a written text in facsimile. Heidegger expressed himself in a more detailed way on the act of writing in its materiality or externality than he did on the act of reading.

Speaking and writing are two fundamentally different possibilities of language. In the *Letter on Humanism*, Heidegger writes to Beaufret that 'surely the questions raised in your letter could have been better answered in direct conversation. In written form thinking easily loses its flexibility. But in writing it is difficult above all to retain the multidimensionality of the realm peculiar to thinking.... On the other hand, written composition exerts a wholesome presence toward deliberate linguistic formulation.'[32] Derrida recognizes here the priority of the spoken word, but I find this not so readily apparent. Rather, the emphasis is more on the difference between the spoken and the written word. This is clear as well from an earlier letter to Beaufret on 23-11-1945 and which concludes: 'Fruitful thinking not only requires writing and reading, but also the *synousia* of dialogue and of the work of teaching and learning.'[33]

In dealing with writing, Heidegger spoke frequently about the 'hand-work of writing', which he felt 'was becoming a rarity.'[34] He spoke as well about the 'cultivation of letters' as opposed to literature,[35] and also about writing as 'hand-writing' and as 'drawing'. Speaking was more often placed in relationship to the mouth—'Speech is mouth-behaviour' (*Sprache ist Mund-Art*).[36]

Writing has a relation to the hand: 'Writing is hand-writing'.[37] Heidegger developed this last point in his *Parmenides*-lecture. Man is distinguishable from the animals by the word, and by the hand—'the hand is, along with the word, the essential mark of humanity.'[38] Animals don't speak and they have no hands, only paws, claws the talons,[39] or organs by which to snatch (*Greiforgane*)[40]; 'Only out of the word and along with the word the hand has arisen'.[41] In so far as man 'has' no speech, he also 'has' no hands. The hand, like the word, belongs to the essential elements of humanity. The hand is in a certain sense another name for *Dasein*. For Heidegger, speaking is a pointing-out, a 'letting-be-seen' or 'letting appear', a revealing that at the same time is also a concealing. The hand too points out, reveals the concealed—'The essential connection of the hand with the word shows itself therein—that the hand reveals the concealed.'[42] The writing hand produces something which displays itself for the human view: a text, Heidegger viewed writing as '*graphein*' and he saw the written as the graphic, the 'grammata'. The written is to be understood above all, as we have already seen in the letter to E. Pretorius, as graphic art or image.

This is of course already an interpretation of the genealogy of the written, but the history of the written is long and complicated. It can certainly not be understood as a continuous development, and the many dimensions of this history are only with great difficulty conceived as a unity. In his *Parmenides*-lecture Heidegger describes one aspect of this history, namely the drawing (*das Zeichnen*). In this lecture he treats the ultimate, or rather the penultimate stage of this history, that is, the discovery of the printing press. It is not mere coincidence, according to Heidegger, that this discovery concurs with the beginning of modernity and thereby also with the existence of technology. In this penultimate stage one also sees the discovery of the rotation press and the typewriter, wherein the triumph of the machine finds its expression. The last phase would then be the discovery of the computer and the world of informatica, which Heidegger dealt with later and very explicitly. Heidegger claims that with the typewriter, writing is removed from its essential origin, that is, the hand. Through this removal, an alteration has taken place *vis-à-vis* man's relation to language and the relation of Being to man. The typewriter is, so to say, for Heidegger *the* example of modern technology, which as a destiny determines all of man's relationships. With the advent of the machine, the word becomes a *means* of communication and the text becomes information which carries with it a uniformity: in mechanized writing, everybody becomes the same.[43]

Once again the discussion is of decay (*Verfall*) or loss, which Heidegger describes in detail and with his own rhetoric as the withdrawal of Being. It would of course be possible to consider this description as a romantic glorification of writing with the hand. Was not writing in Antiquity above all a work for slaves? Poets and thinkers seldom wrote themselves, but usually dictated. Was writing in the Middle Ages not the work of monks? Was not the work in the *Scriptorium* merely that of copying? Theologians, philosophers and princes had secretaries at their disposal. The present situation in which everyone has his own personal hand-writing appears only in Modern Times, in which man becomes a subject and an individual. Still, Heidegger has touched upon something essential when he says that our ways and means of handling a text have become totally different with the advent of technology, and especially of computer-technology. This different way of handling a text is already 'a determination of the relation of Being and the Word to man and thereby also of the relation of man to beings, as well as determining the way in which both men and things stand in unconcealment or retreat from it.'[44]

Without impunging the richness of Heidegger's insight into the essence of writing as graphic art or drawing and of the written as hand-written, one could still pose the question of whether other factors have played an essential role in the development of written culture. There is the fact that the Hebrews and the Semitic peoples were prohibited to establish images either of God or other beings. Writing could thereby be the opposite of image. Moreover, perhaps imaging is only one aspect of writing. Another aspect could be the trace (*Spur*) which is left behind, sometimes wished, but mostly undesired; a trace left behind by man *and* animals, and even water, wind, fire and stones. When one considers writing in connection with design then always presupposed in some way is an intention, a 'wanting to express and to signify'. Traces can be left behind without any form of desire, without intention or conscious design. With this notion of trace, which is so emphasized by Levinas and Derrida, writing can be seen in a completely new light. Writing then signifies that 'something has passed by'. Reading then becomes something like '*investigatio*', i.e., the seeking and following of traces (*vestigia*). Texts could then be read with a view towards what a poet or thinker says, without really knowing or fully understanding what they say. One always writes more than one knows or desires. It could be that when Heidegger spoke about draft (*Zug*) and cleft (*Riss*) in the context of writing, he had something similar in mind. It would be interesting to investigate once again the entire problematic of the trace in Heidegger.

Perhaps even more important is the fact that in his dialogue with the Japanese in *On the Way to Language*, Heidegger cites Plato's *Ion* in order to clarify his own point of view on hermeneutics. There it is said of the poets that they are the messengers of the gods'.[45] On the one hand, Plato commends the poets with the greatest praise; on the other hand he states explicitly that they actually do not know what they are saying. They are inspired. Their words come from far away and the gods or the muses allow them to say what they have to say. Although this is a point of criticism for Plato, it receives a positive significance in Heidegger. Language is more powerful than us. Inspiration or the muse, whom T. S. Eliot called 'The great memory', out of which the poets create, shows itself especially in the fact that poetry is continuously based upon an extremely complicated network of quotations.

What Heidegger says here about poets is equally valid for thinkers. They also say much more than they realize. What they write comes from afar, that is, just as with reading, there is no 'zero-point' of writing. Every text is always and necessarily based upon already existing texts. Every text arises in a network of implicit and explicit quotations from already available texts which have left behind their traces in the texts which man himself writes. Interpretation is thus an unending task and limitless analysis is possible because every trace refers further to other traces. When one takes seriously the fact that everyone who writes never fully understands what he writes and also is never fully understood, because the written is always also a trace, then there are naturally immeasurable consequences for philosophy. On the one hand, philosophy must attempt to control fully the texts which it writes; on the other hand, it will never succeed. That belongs to the greatness of philosophy, but also to its limitations, its finitude, which is not only the finitude of thinking, but also the finitude of Being itself.

NOTES AND REFERENCES

1. 'Implicitement ou explicitement, la valorisation du langage parlé est constante, massive chez Heidegger.' J. Derrida, 'Les fins de l'homme' dans *Marges de la philosophie*, Paris, 1973, p. 159. The English translation of this lecture appears under the title 'The Ends of Man' in *Margins of Philosophy*, transl. by A. Bass, Sussex, 1982, pp. 109–136. However, the cited footnote is not translated.
2. 'Es gilt dem Eigentümlichen der Sprache näherzukommen. Auch hier zeigt sich die Sprache zunächst als unsere Sprache. Wir achten jetzt darauf, was alles, und zwar immer schon, beachtet oder nicht, im Sprechen mitspricht. 'M Heidegger, *Unterwegs zur Sprache*, Pfullingen, 1959, p. 250.
3. The only available information regarding the existence of this letter comes from a catalogue of Erasmushaus, Haus der Bücher AG, Basel, Auction 62 from May 6th and 7th 1986, Books and Autographs. In this catalogue under number 212 (page 71) is listed: 'Heidegger, Martin, Philosoph, 1889–1976. L.a.s. Freiburg, 6.IV.1955. 4 S. 8°. (800.–)

   An den Graphiker Emile Pretorius, welcher ihn zu einem Vortrag innerhalb einer Reihe 'über die Sprache' in seiner 'Akademie' gebeten hatte. '... Ich brauchte einige Sammlung... für die Überlegung unseres Vorhabens... der mit Podewils durchgesprochene Plan ist, wie mir heute scheint, zu stark auf die Behandlung des Themas von Seiten der Wissenschaft abgestellt... Wir müssen vermeiden, dass es zu einer Art Philologenversammlung kommt, andererseits darf natürlich nicht aus dem Ärmel über die Sprache spekuliert und literarischer Essaystil vorgetragen werden... Ein Thema scheint mir unumgänglich: Sprache und Schrift; hier liessen sich wesentliche Fragen des West-Ost-Gesprärches, Fragen an Zeichnung und Bild im weitseten Sinn aufrollen... Sie haben durchaus recht, eine Ausdehnung der Vorträge auf einen ganzen Winter wäre für gesammelte Auffassen ungünstig. Das Thema ist zu kostbar und zu we-sentlich in der heutigen Lage der Menschheit, als dass es durch eine übereil-te Behandlung gleichsam verschleudert werden dürfte. Es muss sein eigenstes Schwergewicht of offenbaren.
4. G.W.F. Hegel, *Enzyklopädie der philosophischen Wissenschaften*, 1830; § 459. English translation of § 459 can be found in Hegel's *Philosophy of Subjective Spirit, vol. III, Phenomenology and Psychology*, transl. M. J. Petry, Dordrecht, 1979, pp. 179–199.
5. O. Pöggeler, 'Sprache—Haus des Seins? Sprachphilosophie im Kontext der Dichtung und Theologie' in *Evolution der Sprache. Über Entstehung und Wesen der Sprache*. Herausgegeb von W. Böhme. Karlsruhe, 1985, p. 109.
6. M. Heidegger, *Sein und Zeit*, Tübingen, 1953, p. 68 (= *SZ*). English translation as

Being and Time, transl. J. Macquarrie and E. Robinson, New York, 1962, p. 97 (=*BT*)
7. *SZ*, pp. 168–169; *BT*, p. 212
8. *SZ*, p. 169; *BT*, p. 212
9. *SZ*, p. 126–127: *BT*, p. 264
10. *SZ*, p. 166; *BT*, p. 209
11. See S. IJsseling, 'Lesen und Schreiben. Husserl über Texte' in *Distanz und Nähe: Reflexionen und Analysen zur Kunst der Gegenwart.* Herausgegeben von P. Jaeger und R. Lüthe, Würzberg, 1983, pp. 173–190.
12. M. Heidegger, *Der Satz vom Grund*, Pfüllingen, 1957, pp. 88–89.
13. 'Das Wort der Sprache tönt und läutet im Wortlaut, lichtet und leuchtet im Shcriftbild. Laut und Schrift sind zwar Sinnliches, aber Sinnliches, darin je und je ein Sinn verlautet und erscheint.' M. Heidegger, 'Hebel, der Hausfreund' in *Aus der Erfahrung des Denkens*, Gesamtausgabe Bd. 13, Frankfurt, 1983, p. 150.
14. 'Wenn wir das Wort 'Sein' vernehmen, indem wir es als Lautgebilde hören oder im Schriftbild sehen, dann gibt es sich doch sogleich anders als die Lautund Buchstabenfolge 'abracadabra'. Dies ist zwar auch eine Folse von Lauten, aber, so sagen wir hier unvermittelt, sie ist sinnlos, mag sie als Zauber-formel ihren Sinn haben. Dagegen ist 'Sein' in solcher Weise nicht sinnlos. Ebenso ist 'Sein', geschrieben und gesehen, sogleich anders als 'kzomil'. Diese Schriftgebilde ist zwar auch eine Abfolge von Buchstaben, aber eine solche, bei der wir uns nichts denken können.' M. Heidegger, *Einführung in die Metaphysik*, Tübingen, 1958, p. 60. English translation as *Introduction to Metaphysics*, transl. R. Mannheim, New Haven, 1959, p. 79.
15. M. Heidegger, *Was heisst Denken?*, Tübingen, 1971, p. 71. English translation as *What is Called Thinking?*, transl. J. G. Grey and F. Wieck, New York, 1968, p. 75.
16. 'Wo wären Platos Gespräche, wenn nicht auch sie zum Geschriebenen geworden wären?' *Parmenides*, Gesamtausgabe Bd. 54, Frankurt, 1982, p. 132.
17. S. IJsseling, 'Philosophie und Textualität. Über eine rhetorische Lektüre philosophischer Texte.' in *Zur Phänomenologie des philosophischen Textes Phänomenologische Forschungen*, Nr. 12, 1982, pp. 57–76.
18. 'Nicht dem nachfragen was Kant sagt, sondern dem, was in seiner Grundlegung der Metaphysik *geschieht*. Einzig auf die Freilegung dieses *Geschehens* zielt die oben durchgeführte Auslegung der *Kritik der reinen Vernunft*.' M. Heidegger, *Kant und das Problem der Metaphysik*, Frankfurt, 1973, p. 208. English translation as *Kant and the Problem of Metaphysics*, transl. J. Churchill, Bloomington, 1962, p. 221.
19. 'Das denkende Sagen gibt sich im Zeitalter der Vollendung des griechischen Denkens, im Denken Platons, die Gestalt des 'Gesprächs'. Es ist, als wollte vor dem Ende des griechischen Denkens noch einmal von diesem selbst durch seine eigene Art, zu sagen, bezeugt werden, welchen Wesensrang das Wort dort hat, wo der Mensch unmittelbar in den Bezug zum aletheia kommt. Aus Platons Dialog 'Phaidros', dem Gespräch über das Schöne (Schlusstück) erfahren wir überdies, dass Plato ein sehr klares Wissen vom Vorrang des unmittelbar gesprochen Wortes vor dem nur geschriebenen hatre. Doch wo wären Platons 'Gespräche', wenn nicht auch sie zum Geschriebenen geworden wären?, *Parmenides*, Gesamtausgabe Bd. 54, pp. 131–132.
20. Cicergo, *De senectute*, 13
21. 'den reinsten Denker des Abendlandes, der nichts geschrieben hat'. *Was heisst Denken?*, p. 52. *What is Called Thinking?*, p. 17.
22. *Was heisst Denken?*, p. 52. *What is Called Thinking?*, pp. 17–18.
23. *Was heisst Denken?*, p. 51. *What is Called Thinking?*, p. 16.
24. *Der Satz vom Grund*, p. 122.
25. *Der Satz vom Grund*, p. 123.
26. 'Denn sowohl Heidegger wie auch Natorp lebten nicht so sehr in der Diskussion als eher im *geschriebenen*, sorgfäfltig durchdachten Wort, im Gegensatz etwa zu Scheler'.

W. Biemel, *Martin Heidegger in Selbstzeugnisen und Bilddokumenten*, Hamburg, 1973, p. 33. English translation as *Martin Heidegger. An illustrated Study*, transl. J. L. Metha, London, p. 15.

27. M. Heidegger, *Seminare*, Gesamtausgabe Bd. 15, Frankfurt, 1986, pp. 426–427.
28. M. Heidegger, *Hölderlins Hymne 'Der Ister'*, Gesamtausgabe Bd. 53, Frankfurt, 1984, p. 81.
29. M. Heidegger, 'Was heisst Lesen?' in *Aus der Erfahrung des Denkens*, Gesamtausgabe Bd. 13, Frankfurt, 1983, p. 111.
30. J. Derrida, *L'écriture et la différence*, Paris, 1967, p. 293. English translation as *Writing and Difference*, transl. A. Bass, London, 1973, p. 196.
31. G. Genette, *Seuils*, Paris. 1987.
32. 'Diese Fragen Ihres Briefes liessen sinch wohl im unmittelbaren Gspräch eher klären. Im Schriftlichen büsst das Denken leicht seine Beweglichkeit ein. Vor allem aber kann es da nur schwer die ihm eigene Mehrdimensionalität seines Bereichs innehalten... Aber das Schriftliche bietet andererseits den heilsamen wang zur bedachtsamen sprachlichen Fassung.' M. Heidegger, 'Brief über den Humanismus' in *Wegmarken*, Gesamtausgabe Bd. 9, Frankfurt, 1976, p. 315. English translation as 'Letter on Humanism' in Martin Heidegger, *Basic Writings*, ed. D.F. Frell, London, 1978, p. 193.
33. This earlier letter can be found in M. Heidegger, *Lettre sur l'humanisme*, texte allemand traduit et présenté par R. Munier, Paris, 1964, p. 184.
34. 'Brief über den Humanismus', p. 344; 'Letter on Humanism', p. 223.
35. 'Brief über den Humanismus', p. 364; 'Letter on Humanism', p. 242.
36. 'Sprache ist Mund-art', *Unterwegs zur Sprache*, p. 244.
37. 'Schrift ist Hand-schrift', *Parmenides*, Gesamtausgabe Bd. 54, p. 119.
38. 'Die Hand ist in einem mit dem Wort die Wesensauszeichnung des Menschen.' *Parmenides*, Gesamtausgabe Bd. 54, p. 118.
39. *Parmenides*, Gesamtausgabe Bd. 54, p. 118.
40. 'Greiforgane', *Was heisst Denken?*, p. 51; *What is Called Thinking?*, p. 16.
41. 'Nur aus dem Wort und mit dem Wort ist die Hand entsprungen.' *Parmenides*, Gesamtausgabe Bd. 54, p. 119.
42. 'Der Wesenszusammenhang der Hand mit dem Wort zeigt sich darin, dass die Hand Verborgenes entbirgt.' *Parmenides*, Gesamtausgabe Bd. 54, p. 125.
43. *Parmenides*, Gesamtausgabe Bd. 54, p. 119.
44. 'schon ein Entscheid ist über den Bezug des Seins und des Wortes zum Menschen und damit über das Verhältnis des Menschen zum Seienden und die Art wie beide, Mensch und Ding, im Unverborgenen stehen oder ihm entzogen sind'. *Parmenides*, Gesamtausgabe Bd. 54, p. 125.
45. *Unterwegs zur Sprache*, p. 122.

Towards a Hermeneutic of Centrality in Indian Art

MARGARET CHATTERJEE

INTRODUCTION

What I shall try to do in this paper falls somewhere between phenomenological description and *Kulturkritik*. It seems to me that, *vis-à-vis* the context in which thinkers like Heidegger, Jaspers, Gadamer and Ricoeur have evolved their ideas, two characteristics stand out about the Indian situation; firstly, that it is not the case that linguistic worlds have priority, and secondly, that we exist in the midst of living traditions from which only recently a sense of alienation[1] begins to show itself. These two points require some defence. I shall take the matter of linguisticity first.

It is, I think, true to say that the contemporary practitioner of hermeneutics spends more time on literary texts[2] than on any other type of cultural expression. This itself is evidence of a stress on linguisticity. We owe this to a cluster of factors including the origin of the hermeneutic method in Biblical scholarship, the interest of the Romantics in philology, developments in linguistics and semiology, and the general proliferation of the written word since the Gutenberg revolution. Philosophy has yet to catch up with the revolution taking place in the audio-visual media. The fact remains that we are all still dominated by words, believing them to provide the most convenient nets in which to capture things and people.[3] The Naiyāyikas past and present are in this company, and no one would deny that Indian intellectual life over the centuries has thrown up texts in plenty. But he would be audacious indeed who tried to glean his understanding of Indian culture from written texts alone. In spite of the prevalence of *Śāstras*, canons and written documents of a daunting kind, it is, I believe, from other sources that we can learn most about the *Lebenswelt* of the Indian people. Of all these sources, two are of crucial importance—works of art and human behaviour. These constitute texts, in an extended sense if you will, in the sense that they need decoding, that people react to them differently and there is considerable differences between the insider's and the outsider's view. The *anonymity* of architecture, in particular, makes this a useful field for investigation, freeing us in large part from tangles regarding intentionality and the like. I have written elsewhere[4] on the importance of non-linguistic aspects of Indian culture and shall not enlarge on this general theme here.

The distinction which it seems to me needs to be made between traditions which are living, those which are well-nigh lost in antiquity, and those which may be alive but are unfamiliar to us, triggers off reflection. Many have suggested that the hermeneutic task begins with a sense of alienation, or alternatively, in reaction to a decline in the binding power of tradition. Back of such a view, once more, lurks a concern with textuality, whence stems the problem of construal. This very way of putting it echoes the Romantic task of recovery of the classics. But how much distancing takes place when it is the tradition which is familiar? The question is of some interest in a society which is only partly traditional and where it is common experience to be embedded in a particular traditional life-world, be aware of yet another tradition flourishing at one's doorstep, and be beckoned by yet another vaguely described as modernity. Indian attitudes to tradition (multiple as this is in a culturally diverse country) are currently deeply ambivalent. There have always been multiple mirrors in which we could look at ourselves with resultant nostalgia/envy/xenophobia or whatever.

We might at this point ask why distancing is deemed to be integral to the hermeneutic starting point. Helmut Plessner has suggestions to make in this regard. His plea for seeing with other eyes[5] goes further than stressing the importance of distance in *time* and highlights the role of alienated *situations* in promoting understanding. It seems to me that such a view flows from two sources. The first is the general perception of the role of crises which we find in the *Existenz philosophie* and *Existenz theologie* of the thirties and forties. The second source has deeper roots and stems from a perspectivism which can be dated from Newton's *Optics*, runs through Leibniz's monadology and reappears as non-spatial perspectivism in twentieth century hermeneutics. The visual root metaphor dies hard. In Newton and Leibniz it is 'redeemed' by the Divine point of view which was believed to provide the *correct* horizon. Notably it was thought that God was capable of being in more than one place at a time. Vision is the distance sense which is concerned with spatial awareness. Transfer vision from space to time and we find 'point of view', the perspective appropriate to consciousness turned on history. The visual root metaphor however continues. The perspectives hopefully converge; indeed the phenomenon investigated is believed to be precisely the point of convergence.[6] The irony is that the model this gives us is analogous to the one provided by Russell's theory of perception, a theory intended to rescue sensible perception from subjectivity, that is to say, it amounts to an avowed attempt to reinstate objectivity from a field in which it had almost been lost.

The crux quite clearly is how to deal with the scandal of the subject and how to deal with time. But this cannot be dealt with by reintroducing objectivity of a kind which those who deal with the human sciences after Husserl's *Krisis* have presumably left behind. I suspect that the metaphors of convergence of horizon still trail clouds from visual experience, and experiences moreover of a linear kind, in spite of the fact that these metaphors have been employed most of all in the interpretation of literary texts. In what follows I shall offer for consideration some hypotheses relevant to Indian art. *Inter alia* I shall suggest that convergence can be replaced by an image that goes in the opposite direction, i.e. movement from a centre outwards and for which initially kinaesthetic experience[7] and then vegetative growth provide paradigms.

PERSPECTIVISM AND CENTRALITY

Indian art forms (and here I refer to the indigenously Indian, i.e., Hindu, Jain, Buddhist) often puzzle the observer with their rich profusion. There is much to take into account, the apparent lack of perspective (I say apparent, because perspective certainly shows itself in some of the paintings), the abundance of detail on the exterior of temples rather than on the interior, the bustle and noise around them, the flatness of much of the paintings, the repetitiveness of the music. The features which strike those coming to Indian art forms with a familiarity with something different could be multiplied. Presumably an Indian art work 'makes sense' of the world in its own way. The anonymity of Indian art until the modern era lends support to the view that the key to it lies not so much in a personal vision as in broad cultural patterns which are to be found outside the sphere of art as well. We can therefore hunt for the clues to an interpretation of Indian art throughout the tapestry of multiple Indian *Lebenswelten*. The *Vorurteile* are often gestural, ways of comporting oneself in the world. Greeting with folded hands, taking the dust of a senior's feet are 'environed by the unexpressed'.[8] In saying this I am stressing the non-linguistic character of Indian *Zugehoerigkeit.*[9]

Elsewhere[10] I have suggested that the Indian life-world (speaking generally) bears the mark of a sense of the surrounding—the forest, the plains—a primeval experience which gave birth to a 'circular' set of metaphors of which the wheel, the lotus, the mandala, the cycle of seasons and the cycle of births and deaths are notable examples. Nature, rather than mathematics, is the matrix out of which the root ideas spring. This being so, we do not have to choose between space and time as an axis for our metaphysical thinking (we do not have to choose, say, between Descartes and Heidegger) for nature is so obviously spatio-temporal and so also is man's existence within it. Matters concerning diet and clothing, activities proper to different stages in life, rites of passage—all are carefully regulated in accordance with the principle of recurrence for which nature herself is the matrix. Change is assimilated within a kaleidoscoptic pattern, and what appears at first sight as an absence of historical sense shows itself as historical in an idiosyncratic way, where change is chronicled not in distinct succession so much as in a palimpsest where earlier forms are not completely obliterated but can be glimpsed through what earlier generations have left behind. The metaphor of sedimentation provides another equally useful clue. The strata lie on top of each other, but as in the case of geological formation, what lies beneath is often visible in the form of an upthrust.

Now one cannot have the surroundings, the circular, without a centre and we do indeed find the phenomenon of centrality well illustrated in Indian architecture and sculpture[11]—an expansion from world to cosmos whose leitmotif is celebration. This celebratory context involves both nature and history, and in so doing, I venture to suggest, enables us to avoid the *Erklaeren/ Verstehen* controversy. The thatness, the monumentality of architectural art-works, (I overlook for the moment the fact that monumentality as a quality is something a building may or may not possess) brings us back to the total *Gestalt* in whatever light, for example, we may view the sculptured facade (say, of the temples of Khajuraho). We scarcely run the risk, as appreciators, of a Schilleresque free aesthetic play. I would also hazard to say that the historical consciousness does not serve us too falsely in the understanding and appreciation of Indian temple architecture. The reason is this. Temples continue to be 'used' as they have for centuries. In watching the crowds at the temple of Jagannath, Puri, we are not up against the insurmountable otherness of the past but witnessing something which is *continuous* with the past. (I do not deny that one may observe it with a sense of its being utterly alien to one's own aesthetic/religious/cultural traditions).

Let us take a Jain temple as an example. As far as perspectivism in epistemology is concerned, there is no system of Indian philosophy which provides this to the extent that Jainism does. It was Jainism that inspired Gandhi's belief that all visions of the truth are fragmentary. In Jaina shrines, ceilings, walls, door-frames and pillars show an exuberance of scenes from Jaina mythology. There are voids in elevation, window openings, and circumambulatory paths on which light shines from the window above. An interesting example of an aggregation of shrines around a central one is found in the Tribhuvana-Dīpaka-Caturmukha-Jinālaya at Ranakpur in old Jodhpur State. Direct and reflected light make this interesting architecturally, and it also serves to illustrate my point about centrality.

The *siddha-cakra* (circle of the sacred ones) also illustrates this principle. A bronze tablet worshipped by the *Śvetāmbara* Sect is in the form of an eight-petalled lotus. The eye falls on the *arhat* (enlightened one) in the centre, surrounded by other emancipated souls. The postures of each are significant, but the focus is on the qualities each is believed to embody. The projection at the bottom allows ablution water to drain out.

Now it so happens that those who go to Jaina temples/shrines are usually Jainas (cf. those who visit cathedrals, and even Hindu temples, such being the nature of the tourist industry). Perambulations, mounting of staircases etc., are therefore, for the most part, in the context of religious exercises. The unseeing eyes of the *Tīrthaṅkaras* speak of the one who has succeeded in overcoming external distraction. Jaina architecture and sculpture certainly seem to survive in a context where religious symbolism still functions in a religious context and where the objects concerned do not serve as museum pieces but still 'make sense' for those who experience them participatively.

So far our Jaina examples have illustrated the principle of profusion stemming from a centre, a vegetative metaphor of growth the source of which is the seed. I put this forward as a hermeneutic tool which pulls in a different way from the optically-grounded metaphor of convergence. Before we leave this point, the role of intersubjectivity, of community, in each, needs to be mentioned. The idea of expansion from a centre is already rooted in the community whose *Lebenswelt* is given expression to in the temple. The community is the matrix and the temple is the focus of the communicative network which already exists. Arthitecture, I have already suggested, has an advantage over the text with respect to its physical location, the way it anchors us to the world, and its limited hospitality to multiple meanings (the *Spielraum* of these meanings has a particular *range*). Interpretations of a literary text, however, as it were, jostle for consensus, each set of meanings (this is particularly the case in the case of Protestant sects associated with the interpretation of scripture) giving birth to a communicative network among those who agree with that particular set of meanings.

I next wish to turn to the problem of 'misunderstanding', using, *en passant*, the Jaina example mentioned already.

MISUNDERSTANDING[12]

Probably the first person to discuss the notion of misunderstanding in the context of the theory of interpretation was Chladenius.[13] His chair being in theology, rhetoric and poetry, his concerns were with textuality, and he believed 'complete understanding' to be possible. He drew a distinction between wilful misrepresentation and misunderstanding or false interpretation, but also made room for cases where an interpretation falls short of certainty, the requisite evidence being lacking. We would, I imagine, these days set a question mark against the notion of 'complete understanding'. Once it is granted that the art object is open to multiple interpretations we tend to resist the idea of a 'correct interpretation' and 'complete understanding' alike. But we also face interesting puzzles about 'getting things wrong', 'not being quite on target' and so on.[14] If to admit multiple meanings is not to permit that 'anything goes', we seem to need a principle of exclusion which will serve to delimit a reasonable *Spielraum* of interpretations. Quite evidently there can be no such *general* principle. Even the appeal to 'competent judges' will not do, for there can be radical difference of opinion among those deemed competent to judge, and these days, quirky viewpoints often pass muster as legitimate criticism in the arts.

We need also to distinguish between 'misunderstanding' and 'understanding incompletely'. The arts apart, there are plenty of analogies for this in everyday life. Take the case of the overseas visitor, in search of a 'quiet restaurant' in the States, who enters what he imagines to be an ideal place and orders a meal from the very superior sort of 'waiter' who asks him what he would like. Alas, he has made a radical mistake, for he has entered a funeral parlour. He hasn't got any bit of it 'right'. It is not that he needs to know 'more' but that he is totally mistaken about where he is.

We also need to distinguish between misunderstanding and radical criticism. There might be contemporary criticis who find Rāma's treatment of Sītā incompatible with what we these days recognize as women's dignity, or who deplore the stereotype of females as creatures that twine and cling, a stereotype portrayed both in classical Indian sculpture and dance. I would call this *Kulkurkritik* and not misunderstanding. The very antiquity of Jainism raises teasing considerations. Some Jaina images look very much likes *yakṣas*,[15] while others resemble the Buddha. No doubt, for example, the artists of ancient Magadh had to hand images of *yakṣas* to serve as models. This is a matter of artistic exigency rather than religious sensibility. I suspect it is only the art historian who will find that the *yakṣa* idea is encapsulated in many Jaina figures. The devotees' sights will be set on other matters, and perhaps properly so. The Jain worshippers are distanced in time from the worshippers of centuries ago. However, in so far as they participate in a live tradition, they cannot be said to be distanced from it, still less alienated. There will always be more to know, more to understand. For the traditional worshipper the epistemic element, the knowing, is embedded in a whole cluster of affective, evaluative and other modalities of consciousness, and, as importantly, in ritual behaviour which expresses all these. If he or she is unaware of the artistic tradition which through the *yakṣa* idea roots Jain iconography in a world of earth gods and goddesses this is not a *Missverstaendnis* so much as an unknowing or even a forgetting. Such a forgetting is, in some contexts, even a benefit. The devout communicant might be disturbed if he recalled the significance of totemic participatory meals at the moment of participating in the Eucharist.

IN CONCLUSION

What do I tentatively conclude from the above? That participant-understanding of a live tradition may be partial; it may show differences from the participant-understanding of an earlier generation (I do not know how one would determine this difference) but, as far as I can see, it would illustrate neither 'distancing' nor fusion of horizons, but a continuity which would accommodate both change and encapsulation of the experience of earlier generations. I think we can find examples of where distance in time helps and also of where it presents obstacles. The advantage of distance in time is felt, tangentially, as it were, when contemporary art works strike us as opaque. We imagine, for example, that we are better able to evaluate Cézanne than his contemporaries were. But temporal distance is not necessarily an aid to understanding. Collingwood's analysis of the process of question and answer grew out of the instrinstic *difficulty* of interpreting archaeological data.

In choosing temple architecture for comment I have admittedly chosen a complicated example where the 'object' is viewed aesthetically by the outsider, and religiously or aesthetico-religiously[16] by the participant. At any rate we can glean the following—the art-buff or art-historian may well 'know' more than the worshipper, but the worshipper is not at disadvantage in his/her worship by being inadequately conversant with his/her own tradition. Does it make sense to speak of someone 'misunderstanding' his own tradition? One answer to this is that sometime the tradition itself accommodates such deviance. What is more to the point is to recognize that tradition can contain much that is monstrous. This is something that Jaspers, Raja Rammohun Roy and Gandhi in their various ways were very sensitive to.

To the extent that a hermeneutic awareness is developing in the cultural sciences in India today it witnesses to a sense that the sedimented meanings of the past need to be approached selectively. Now the sedimented experience of generations amounts to something very like an *a priori*, provided we take *a priori* to mean 'determining condition' and not, à la Kant, 'free from any empirical element'. It is also worth recalling another use of *a priori* mentioned by Ras Vihari Das, *avidyā as a priori*. He wanted to draw attention, I think, to the *Zusammenhang* between phenomenality and bondage. I would myself consider that *avidyā* was illumined by the shaft of light that comes from aesthetic, moral and religious experience. To say, as I have, that contemporary consciousness recognizes the need to *choose* among sedimented meanings makes the latter similar to what Habermas called 'transitory *a prioris*' a phrase he uses with reference to history and language.[17]

But the problem is that whenever we speak of tradition we are referring to what has *grown*, to processes which were not always the result of choice. Consequently, when we pick and choose at will, we are engaging in an activity which although natural to the reformer, policy-maker, or artist, may have little impact on society as a whole.

The way in which meanings are 'trailed' willy-nilly has a linguistic parallel which might be mentioned here. Diverse conceptual structures are 'carried over' historically through the use of the 'same' words from generation to generation. In his review of Kittel's *Theological Dictionary*[18] James Barr critized the editors for summing up diverse meanings drawn from a word's usage in various contexts, and for assuming that whenever the word occurs it contains within it all its other meanings. His shorthand for the 'defect' is illegitimate totality transfer'.

Words, practices, indeed the manifold 'expressions' of cultural life, have their resonances. Of course we cannot hear them all. I had intended to develop this with reference to the Indian concept of *dhvani* which has importance both in music and in the role of suggestion in literature. It occurred to me that this concept might parallel that of horizon. But this must remain a theme for another occasion. Suffice it to say that the musician often has to *control* resonance, and the writer needs to *control* suggestion, in the interest of protecting overall intention.

One residual question might still tantalize. What is this centrality which I have suggested is the source of so many Indian cultural expressions? There are those who will maintain that it is a metaphysical core of a rarefied kind, the Self understood in a monistic way. This is what you find in Abhinavagupta's image of the needle which penetrates successive layers of lotus leaves in the pursuit of *Brahmavidyā*. It is also the main tenor of Coomaraswamy's understanding of Indian art. But for my own part, I tend to find the source of the metaphor of expansion from a centre in the life-experience of India's agricultural people—the simple experience of growth. This *Lebenswelt* encapsulates *Bewusstseinslagen* which are shared by village communities, whether or not they ever reach the level of conceptuality. The agricultural year with its manifold 'messages' of seed-time and harvest, aging and decay, adverse seasons and calm weather, the celebration of festivals, the canny local criticism built into the *jātrā* (village open-air drama)—all witness to the changing tonalities of a life in which the centre still holds.

When Gandhi takes over the metaphor and speaks of the oceanic circle with the individual at the centre, but the individual in relation to others, *Gemeinschaft* rippling out in concentric circles to cover the whole world, what has happened is that recognition of the compatibility of individuality with increasingly wide areas of social allegiance has been built into a metaphor which was originally vegetative in inspiration. It speaks for the potency of the metaphor, I think, that it is capable of relating the cosmic to the social, something which, heaven knows, in our day and generation, needs doing.

NOTES AND REFERENCES

1. Cf. Gadamer's definition of hermeneutics as: 'The theory and practice of understanding and bringing to language, the alien, the strange, and whatever has become alien.' *Reason in the Age of Science*, trans. F. G. Lawrence, Cambridge, MS, & London, the M.I.T. Press, 1982, p. 149.
2. 'Texts' actually have a wide range—including scripture, laws, musical scores, choreographic designs etc.
3. George Steiner has written on this most convincingly.
4. Vide my *The Religious Spectrum*, Delhi, Allied Publishers, 1984 and 'The Phenomenology of Circumstance' in *Communication, Identity and Self-expression*, ed. by S. P. Banerjee and Shefali Moitra, Delhi, Oxford University Press, 1984.
5. H. Plessner, "Mit anderen Augen", *Zwischen Philosophie und Gesellschaft*, Berne, Francke, 1953, pp. 204; 17.
6. The spatial archetype of convergence seems to me to be the Gothic spire. Compare this with the *stūpa*, which is not pointed. It tapers but never fails to incorporate diversity. The message of growth from *loka* to *loka* is indicated cannily.
7. Cf. Husserl's reference to the '... practical kinaesthetic horizon', *Husserliana*, Vol. XI, p. 15.
8. An expression used by Hans Lipps with reference to words. Cf. *Untersuchungen zu einer hermeneutischen Logik*, Frankfurt, 1938, p. 71.
9. This is in contrast to Gadamer's stress on the *Zusammenhang* of language with this. Vide WM, pp. 123 ff. 153, 247; and TM pp. 115 ff, 142, 232.
10. 'Towards a phenomenology of circumstance' in *Communication, Identity and Self-expression*, op.cit.
11. It can also be found in the strong tonality of Indian classical music, where the elaboration of themes centres round the tonic and never fails to return to it.
12. Schleiermacher defined hermeneutics as the art of overcoming misunderstanding.
13. *Introduction to the Correct Interpretation of Reasonable Discourses and Writings*, *Leipzig*, 1942.
14. I have touched on this in my 'Some philosophical problems arising in the arts', *The Journal of Aesthetics and Art Criticism*, Wayne University, Vol. XXVIII, Spring, 1969.
15. Earth deities, massive in aspect, sculpted frontally, and not in the round. A *yakṣa* and a *yakṣiṇī* stand outside the Reserve Bank building in New Delhi, it so happens.
16. This last possibility may not be true for the Jaina, for Jainism enjoins in a particularly stringent manner the leaving behind of the sensuous. Temple architecture in India, as mentioned earlier, symbolizes what is to be left behind, by providing highly decorated *exteriors*.
17. Vide his *Towards a Rational Society*, trans. Jeremy J. Shapiro, Boston, 1970, p. 84. For the need to recognize a meshing of the transcendental, empirical and ontological *vide*

my *Our Knowledge of Other Selves*, Asia Publishing, Bombay, 1963 and article on 'The grounds and horizons of philosophical imagination', in *Philosophes sur eux-mêmes*, Berne, Vol. 10, 1983.

18. Ed. G. Kittel and G. Friedrich's *Theologisches Woerterbuch zum Neuen Testament*, Stuttgart, 1933–73. I have discussed this point in my book *The Concept of Spirituality*, Delhi, Allied Publishers.

Reflections on Papers

D. P. CHATTOPADHYAYA

I

Unanimity of conclusions is not perhaps the most important thing in philosophy. One wonders if unanimity in the modes of reasoning is at all achievable. These two points can be cited both to support the creative character of philosophizing and to butteress some thesis or other of relativism. Whether a philosopher is pro-relativist or anti-relativist does not make much difference to matters of life and experience with which he is concerned. For our theoretical attitude, unless it is passionately espoused and followed in life, remains more or less distant from our actual practice. Whatever definition of man one opts for, viz., 'rational animal', 'sign-using animal', 'tool-using animal', 'social animal', it is difficult to deny his concerns with what he is and what he does in terms of his rationality as well as animality. In the life-world our rationality and animality interact and, in effect, are interfused. The well-known distinctions between theory and practice, reason and experience, inner and outer, etc., appear to lose their sharp edges in the world as we live it. Consequently, the theoretical distinction drawn between realism and idealism, between psychologism, logicism and constructionism, and the like turn out to be suspect. To say that consciously or unconsciously we are 'committed' to regional ontology and socio-historically circumscribed praxiology is not to rule out the possibility of their 'unity' at a higher level.

In the light of this observation, one has the right to raise the question: what is the real interesting import of studying the relation between Phenomenology and Indian Philosophy? For it can rightly be pointed out that neither 'Indian Philosophy' nor 'Phenomenology' has a very definite and unified meaning. This becomes clearly evident from the essays in this volume. There are not only different schools or systems of Indian Philosophy but also subschools and sub-systems under each one of them. On the theory of *pramāṇas*, ways of proving/establishing *pramā* or valid knowledge, the diversity of Indian philosophers is bewildering. Even on the question of what 'Indian Philosophy' connotes philosophers are divided. One points out that philosophy, rightly understood, does not belong to any geographical unit, India or Europe. Only philosophers have their national or historical affiliations. Extending this point it is similarly argued that phenomenology is not peculiar to Europe or such European philosophers as Hegel and Husserl.

The workings of the human mind all over the world exhibit some *general* features. This can also be said of man's linguistic and other forms of cultural articulations. Since the natural-causal environments of the human mind are *not* found inconsistent with these common cultural features, one has good reason to assume that the supposed dichotomy between the natural and the cultural is untenable. Their relation may be differently graded but certainly it is not antagonistic. This explains the possibility of man's knowing both himself and the nature environing him. On the question whether this cognitive capacity is *a priori*, philosophers may, and in fact do, differ. But that it is more or less built there in the human mind itself is hardly deniable. Therefore, it is not at all surprising that even those who recognize naturalism as a respectable form of knowledge do not question the possibility of constituting 'higher' forms of it. For example, the materialist does not deny the efficacious superiority of consciousness. He only questions its ontological primacy. Access to reality, matter or consciousness (whatever it might be), is provided by human experience, different forms of human experience, common-sensical, artistic, scientific and mathematical. Even the so-called presuppositions of experience are disclosed in experience and could be meaningfully discussed only in terms of experience. In this broad sense, a heavy dose of phenomenology is present not only in Indian or European thought but also in all forms of human thought.

The Eurocentric thinkers like Hegel and Husserl often give the impression that the systems of thought developed in Europe have a superiority about them. And that superiority is said to be due to its formal or mathematical orientation. Often the Pythagorean-Platonic tradition is said to have laid the original foundation of this *form* of thought. One feels uneasy with this mode of presentation of the history of human thought. It is perplexing—both historically and conceptually. Are we to believe that the European thought before the advent of Pythagorus and Plato did not have any *formal* features? The affirmative answer to this question goes against the very basic idea of phenomenology, the native (if not *a priori*) capacity of the human mind itself. No human mind, Indian or European, can be operative or practically successful without its formal structure. It will be naive to believe that there was a *time* when human mind was there but its workings did not exhibit some or other formal features. Equally naive would it be to believe that there are or were some *places* where people could think or experience but without any underlying formal structure.

So the important point is not to raise some such questions as whether phenomenology or transcendentalism or formalism appeared first in the West or in the East. Comparably puzzling seems to be the assertion that the Indian mind is typically given to illusionism, other-worldliness and/or anti-historical disposition. This sort of generalizations is not only misleading but also stands in the way of raising those very questions which are relevant enough to invite meaningful answers.

Like all human activities, philosophical activity is marked by an irremediable element of creativity. This creativity is rooted in the freedom of consciousness. From this realm of freedom even the *human* body is not excluded. Whether one philosophizes in the Indian tradition or in the European tradition, one never ceases to be free. This mark of freedom and the resulting creativity are evident from endless diversity of modes of thought and of conclusions available within each tradition. The pro-pluralist philosopher goes to the extent of asserting that when we say 'a tradition' what we mean is 'several kindred and inter-acting traditions'. As against this view the anti-relativist highlights what 'a kindred' character of different traditions is like and what makes this kinship (in the realm of thought) possible. Instead of talking in terms of 'Westernization of Indian thought' or 'Indianisation of Western thought', we would be well-advised to try to understand one tradition from the stand point of another and *vice versa*. This does not even remotely preclude the possibility of studying a tradition from within. In fact, Indians have been studying their thought both from their own, internal, multiple points of view and, particularly in the last two hundred years or so, also from external multiple points of view. The same may be said of the European thought. Both Europeans and non-Europeans have been studying and inter-acting in their thought forms down the centuries. Interestingly enough, collateral attempts have been made to bring together these points of view as well as the resulting conclusions of their authors. This is a strategic anti-relativist and anti-sceptical move. In this way some philosophers like Hegel have developed a history of philosophy wherein *regional* histories of culture, including philosophy, do feature but only to be sublated by the Universal Spirit. The one way of combating relativism is to defend *open-ended* absolutism, conceding in the process autonomy of regional ontologies and histories. One could say that in different ways both Hegel and Husserl have followed this strategy.

II

Karl Schuhmann has brought to our notice a hitherto largely unknown fact that Husserl had some familiarity with Indian thought, particularly Buddhism. In spite of his exposure to Buddhism, it does not, however, appear that he gave up his Eurocentric orientation. One may straightaway criticize this approach. Another way of appreciating it is that in the process of formulating his universal view of philosophy as a science he has taken due note of Indian thought.

Some contributors to this Volume (J. N. Mohanty's, for example) are opposed to the idea that Indian philosophy and Western philosophy are entirely different. The practical orientation of Indian philosophy does not mean that it is theoretically different from the spirit of Western philosophy. This point gains strength when we recall Schutz's arguments in support of the view that theory itself is a form of practice. Theorization may be practical in two different but related senses. Firstly, while constructing his theory, the theoretician as a human being is putting himself into work and reappropriating the world he lives in. Secondly, theory has a practical orientation in it. The Advaita Vedāntin, for example, not only develops a monistic metaphysics but also tries to realize within himself the unity of mankind as a whole, the unity of all things and beings. Somewhat similarly, one may point out, Hegel's philosophy of history, besides being a theoretical undertaking, has its obvious practical implication, namely, to show the unity and culmination of all philosophies in his own philosophy and how to bring about the unity of Germany as a nation.

About the very nature of universal history of philosophy, all philosophers are not unanimous. For example, it has been argued by S. Bhattacharyya that while phenomenology exhibits a sort of family resemblance, it is not to be found within the different schools and sub-schools of Indian philosophy. Besides, he claims, rather unconventionally, that while Indian philosophy has influenced the cultures of neighbouring countries, there is no evidence that 'Indian philosophy was ever influenced by foreign philosophies.' Whatever be the truth-value of this view in historical terms, one feels impressed by his arguments purported to show how the concept of intentional consciousness has been differently understood and interpreted by different schools of Indian philosophy, Nyāya, Advaita Vedānta and Kāsmīr Śaivism. From his study one thing becomes abundantly clear that *fundamental* philosophical concepts may appear in different philosophical systems without ascertainable external causes. If, for instance, the concept of freedom of consciousness is taken as a basic concept, that is, if it is strictly adhered to, the possibility of external causation is bound to get diluted, if not actually ruled out. Incidentally, it may be mentioned that though as a *method* phenomenology is not very old, its *substantive* theses like intentionality of mental phenomena, the constitutive orientation of consciousness and anti-presuppositionalism are traceable to all historical periods of philosophy. This can be shown from the history of Western thought and also that of Indian thought.

In fact, R. Balasubramanian, an expert in Advaita Vedānta, himself characterizes this system of philosophy as 'transcendental phenomenology' and 'metaphysics of experience'. Through these characterizations he proposes to show that, like the phenomenologist, the Advaita Vedāntin (a) spells out his basic *problem* of enworlded subjectivity, (b) a *method* of explicating the problem, (c) a transcendental principle for ensuring the definitive character of evidence, and (d) a metaphysical theory to which it is committed. By following rigorously the method of transcendental phenomenology, it is claimed that the Advaita Vedāntin reaches the 'end' of non-dualistic metaphysics, *Brahman*.

Even coming to the recent past, the same thesis, of course in a different way, is reiterated by K. Bagchi in his new interpretation of the philosophy of K. C. Bhattacharyya. Quoting from Bhattacharyya's monograph, *Subject as Freedom*, he tries to show how the Advaita Vedāntic mode of philosophizing 'can interact with Husserl's phenomenology and how, on the basis of his understanding of the Advaita Vedānta, Bhattacharyya makes a genuine contribution to the general philosophical issue . . . of the relationship . . . between phenomenology and ontology'. Also like Balasubramanian, he finds a methodological affinity between Husserl (1859–1938) and Bhattacharyya (1875–1948), who, it may be recalled, were contemporaries. In this connection it is interesting to note Bagchi's observation that Bhattacharyya, like Heidegger, locates the demand for self-transcendence 'within the inner boundaries of knowledge'. This shows, among other things, how thinkers may independently arrive at strikingly similar conclusions, without any contact with each other. And this discloses the native cognitive similarity of the human minds separated by time and space.

III

A supporting parallel argument is to be found in David Carr's paper, 'Phenomenology and Philosophy of History', where he argues that individual's life-experience contributes not only to the shaping of local histories but also in promoting the global history. In this connection, he refers to Husserl's concept of 'consciousness' (*Bewusstsein*), Dilthey's concept of 'life' (*Leben*) and Heidegger's concept of 'being-there' (*Dasein*). Carr basically makes use of the concept of time-consciousness developed by human beings and used by historians. Though situated in the present, man is influenced by, and is open to, both the past and the future. Though he lives in a particular locality, his horizons of life are open-ended. What is true of man is also true of human culture as a totality. And, therefore, world history shows an expanding fusion of different cultures. One may view it as a product of different cognitive inquiries and also as a convergence of different individual and cultural lives.

A related point has been argued by D. P. Chattopadhyaya. He tries to establish the point that individual human beings, smaller social aggregates and larger social aggregates are different forms of articulations of a consciousness which is bipolar, that is, which has both an individualistic mooring and also a free and growing social character. Man's creative freedom and meaning-bestowing capacity enable him to constitute different forms of social life, community, society, nation, and international community. The same capacities explain his idea of the unity of mankind.

The issue of temporality underlying that of historicality has been gone into deeply by V. C. Thomas with reference to Sartre and Husserl. Time is said to be present and active in the being of every man. Husserl tries to show that human consciousness is to be grasped in terms of the temporal structures of 'now', 'retention' and 'protention'. Phenomenologically speaking, these structures are like fused 'horizons', i.e., continuous in nature. While Husserl speaks of equiprimordiality of consciousness and temporality, Sartre radicalizes the thesis by asserting that man cannot even have consciousness unless he is temporal. Existential being, time and consciousness are inseparable. Husserl views time in and around the transcendental ego, whereas Sartre discusses time around the concept of 'for-itself'. Sartrean time is measurable and this view goes against Husserl's denial of the measurability of time. In this respect Sartre stands closer to Heidegger. Another thing which brings Heidegger and Sartre close to each other is the concept of historical life-world. This enables both of them to underplay the role of rigorous transcendental reduction and highlights the importance of different historical situations or life-worlds and their inter-related changing structure.

Man's self-understanding, his I-consciouness, phenomenologically analyzed, exhibits different levels. Egology, the philosophy of I-consciousness, in spite of its different theories, remains central to all types of philosophy, Indian and European. In this connection, A. N. Balslev plausibly argues that both in Advaita Vedānta and Transcendental Phenomenology of Husserl comparable attempts have been made to show how different levels of the constitution of 'I' are established. The transcendentalist, contrary to popular belief, does recognize the importance of the physical-physiological 'I'. The phenomenologist, whether he is like Madhusūdana Sarasvatī (a Vedāntin) or like Husserl, cannot fail to take note of the empirical ego. There cannot be a *pure* I-consciousness which negates the phenomenal ego. In between the transcendental ego and the empirical ego works what may be called the eidetic ego. These levels of ego are not sharply separated. In and through the general form of time all experiences of ego are brought together and structured. Our fleeting sensory life, relatively stable habitual life and concretely unified. monadic life are hierarchically related and organized.

It is pointed out by Balslev that the Vedāntic view of I-consciousness ingenuously reconciles the seemingly opposite views of the world of objects developed by the Yogācāra Buddhist, on the one hand, and by the Naiyāyika, on the other. The fleeting objects of *adhyāsa* and the relatively durable objects of experience, *vyavahārika*, are all compresent in and before our *independent* I-consciousness. In a sense, 'I' takes the form (*ākāra*) of fleeting objects as well as the forms of the empirical-conventional ones. But in a more important sense it, i.e., 'I', does not cease to be formless (nirākara). Without positing the 'I' as a transcendental metaphysical entity, Advaita Vedānta shows the constitution of I-consciousness. This constitution is neither mere manifestation nor pure creation. In the process of constitution the 'individual I' and the 'universal I' are both effective partakers. And the process of constitution is phenomenological, gradually disclosive and not instantaneous.

That I-consciousness exhibits different levels and, in particular, orientations has been argued persuasively by, besides Balslev, Gregorios. He takes his cues from the 'speculative' ideas of Hegel, shows how Husserl makes use of them in his multilevelled I-phenomenology and how Heidegger situates *Dasein* in time and in-between time and beyond. Hegel's spirit is worldly and human being enworlded. If Hegel's project of philosophy is very speculative, Husserl's orientation one-sidedly pro-scientific, i.e., objectivistic. Heidegger's criticism of Husserl along this line had to be met by the latter in his works.

IV

In different ways both Kant and Hegel tried to defend natural science in terms of some principle of transcendental consciousness and not in terms of scientific method as ordinarily understood. In order to make philosophy a rigorous science Husserl first favours suspension (*epoche*) of the recognition of the external sense-objects. Unencumbered by the findings and abstract laws of empirical sciences, relatively free human consciousness starts reflecting upon itself. The life-world is sought to be recaptured in the intentional depth of 'subjective' consciousness through *ego*, *cogitatio* and *cogitatum*. In this second phenomenological-psychological reduction the world of scientific objects exhibits its two aspects: in relation to the external world it is subjective but in relation to the transcendental ego it is objective. This self-and-world consciousness is *in principle* universal and not *exclusively* peculiar to this or that person. The universal consciousness in I, You and He/She, however, does not negate our individuality. In it, together with life-world and science-world, we are also present. Otherwise it would have been relatively poor and abstract. At the same time, the point to be emphasized here is that our presence is consciousness of its *limits* as well as its *need* of expansion (towards universal unitary horizon).

P. M. Greogorias's main concern is the nature of human transcendence. It is a unique all-round transcendence. 'Can the Husserlian methodology deal adequately with this transcendence?' Through meaning-giving acts of various types man's self-transcendence as per Husserlian view succeeds only in showing the provisional or growing character human knowledge. That in God lies man's fullest possible self-transcendence is not available from his phenomenology. To him even God is one among endless appearences and itself constituted by man as 'an idealized human being'. Husserl pro-scientific *bias*, Gregorios feels, prevents him not only from finding out what is truly Transcendent, i.e. God, but also many crucial scientific findings of today, viz., Special Theory of Relativity, Quantum Mechanics and Probability theory.

In the Indian tradition, Gregorios reminds us, transcendence of consciousness, i.e., of consciousness-of, into consciousness-in-itself is taken as real transcendence. When he speaks of the Indian tradition in this way, Gregorios seems to have Advaita Vedānta primarily in the back of his mind. But it may be pointed out here that even the Advaitin has to recognize the practical-ontological status of scientific objects as constructions of I-consciousness under the influence of *vṛtti*. If self-contained consciousness, consciousness-in-itself, is taken to be the paradigm of transcendence, *real* transcendence, that does not necessarily mean the annulment or negation of other 'pre-*real*' modes of transcendence. For in that case commonsensical and scientific paradigms of knowledge would be left unrecognized and unexplained.

The possibility of different forms of knowledge, including science, depends, to a large extent, on how man's relation to the world is defined. While Greogorios highlights the basic character of Transcendent-oriented transcendence, T. M. Seebohm, paving the way for the vindication of the religious mode of consciousness within the phenomenological framework, addresses himself to 'The Paradox of Subjectivity' which deserves our serious consideration in order to demonstrate the possibility of man's knowledge *of* the world. Situated *in* the world of objects, how can man as subject know those objects? As the correlates of consciousness the latter, paradoxically enough, have *in* and *among* them the knowing subject itself. The interplay of objects and the (enworlded) subject (as object, as one among many) is context-bound (in terms of space-time), i.e., relative. Consequently, context-bound scientists author different sciences, giving rise to the problem of relativism and necessitating unificatory reduction.

To this problem Husserl's attention was particularly drawn by Heiddeger. Both were engaged, of course in different ways, in exploring the *foundation* of science, of natural science, in philosophical science. Science, claims Husserl, is grounded in the nature of man. Heidegger argues that this claim about the ground of science is a mere presupposition and as such will not do—for science has to be *shown* as so grounded. Husserl's way of reduction was initially the way of descriptive psychology but later on he favoured the eidetic and transcendental phenomenological varieties. Following the lines of Dilthey and Scheler, Heidegger opposes and criticizes Husserl's method and reduction. For, he thinks, Husserl did not adequately realize the importance of mundane situatedness of the subject. It seems to Seebohm that Heidegger is primarily concerned with expounding a view of the subject which is engaged in making scientific knowledge possible. The being of man is emphasized as the ground of scientific knowledge and the idea of Husserlian transcendental reduction is rejected for this particular purpose.

Husserl finds gaps in Heidegger's contention. He points out that temporal or historically given objects of nature are internally structured. Besides, other subjects knowing the 'same' world of fleeting objects are also available to the knowing subject. The intersubjectivity of my consciousness, though available in me, is not exclusively my individual constitution. Passive presence of the intersubjective world precedes its active constitution by the subject. Seebohm seems to be convinced by Husserl's arguments offered against his position by Heidegger. The ontologial ground of science delineated by the early Heidegger remains somewhat shaky because of its relative indifference to the concept of temporality as intersubjective cementing factor. Later on he tries to correct the position in terms of the ontological meaning of care, a promising way out of originary privacy and relativism to other-oriented futurity and public time, i.e., true transcendence. Husserl's phenomenological way of establishing the ultimate ground of science does recognize Heidegger's ontological concern with the being of the knowing subject but he is firm on the necessity of going beyond to the question of being itself,—being that grows horizonally in internal time-consciousness.

Nothing, no subject, no object, falls outside the enworlded human being. To think of the world as something out there-and-then in space-time with objects or phenomena in it is pre-scientific or naturalistic in the perjorative sense of the term. When man reflects on the nature of objects, cultural as well as scientific, he becomes increasingly conscious of their subject-rootedness, as correlates of cognitive consciousness. However, this does not take away the 'realistic' ontological implication of scientific objects. These objects lend themselves to different modes of comprehension, perceptual and conceptual, experimental and theoretical, etc. This point has been argued both by Heelan and Compton in their contributions to this volume.

P. A. Heelan convincingly clarifies the related roles of theorization and experimentation in scientific research. Scientific phenomena are not given to the scientist as raw or completely uncooked. They are gradually processed and increasingly structured in the corpus of science. The seemingly abstract scientific theories, rightly understood, are found to be grounded in the 'concreteness' of perception, historical evidence and social co-sharability. If theory is purported to explain phenomena, the latter may be regarded as fulfilment of the former. To avoid the mistake of naive naturalism the scientist is obliged to recognize phenomena as representations, the given as interpreted. The content (what) of interpretation and the mode (how) of it are complementary and gradedly related. According to Heelan, scientific theory has to take its data as phenomena available in consciousness and not as postulated external entities. That Heelan takes his own form of realism seriously is evident from his opposition to the Duhem-Quine-Hesse thesis. But, at the same time, he cautions us against identifying the representing field (of objects) with the represented object itself. One must not mistake nerve-irritations as objects which are causally responsible for them. In between are active interpretative representations. The objects of science are both given and constituted,—'given' in the sense that the phenomena which beg explanation are not created by the scientist but received (though not passively) by him, and 'constituted' in the sense that different perspectives of phenomena or objects as available to the working scientist as well as others are meaningfully brought together by the scientist himself, by the constitutive acts of his transcendental subjectivity.

To what is due scientific objectivity, its possible conditions and limitations? How best to understand this crucial concept of the philosophy of science? In terms of 'anti-realism' of Kuhn and Feyerabend? Or, within the epistemological and ontological critiques of Gadamer, Foucault and Rorty? J.J. Compton proposes to construct answers to these questions primarily keeping Merleau-Ponty's phenomenology of perception in view.

As we have seen, both Husserl and Heidegger tried, from different standpoints, the close relation between theoretical and pre-theoretical situations, between the life-world and the transcendental subjectivity, in the context of science. Compared to their approaches, Compton finds Merleau-Ponty's appraoch more concretely suggestive. He is persuaded that in understanding the correct meaning of natural science what proves of immense importance is the pre-scientific life of perception. True, in making science possible, besides body's interaction with the world, many other factors,—mythic, aesthetic, mathematical, mechanical, etc., are found to be effectively present. But the universe of science rests primarily on perception, direct experience.

The main problem which the proposed perceptualist account of science raises is whether it can explain the objectivity of abstract and theoretical entities and laws. Compton's response to this issue is affirmative. He tries to show that proto-objectivity lies hidden in and under my body's interaction with the world. This interaction, additionally, informs me what other bodies know of the world through their interactions with it. Perceptual perspectives of different individuals tend to converge indicating the existence of actual unitary objects. This relational account of objectivity is inseparable from intersubjectivity. Perspectival unity of object is not passively received but actively achieved.

Objectivity of science is achieved by individuals in community (as situated in the world) and not in insolation. The perspectival unity underlying scientific objectivity is both synchronic and diachronic, i.e., historical. By bringing in the time-dimension, i.e., historical perspective, of science, in indicating its objective character. Merleau-Ponty discloses the inter-subjective character of scientific objects and laws. Nothing scientific comes out instantly. Scientific objects are perspectivally disclosed through a time which is perceivable by all of us. Perspectivality, intersubjectivity and temporality are the related aspects of scientific objectivity. In terms of perspectivality one can grasp the context-bound character of science. But this synchronic contextuality must not be construed in a discontinuous manner. On the contrary, it is embedded in history, i.e., temporally instituted and transformed. Further, different research traditions exhibit their convergent trend. And this convergence is born out of different researchers' encounter with the world, primarily, perceptually and practically.

Pressing these points together Compton wants to demonstrate that Kuhn's paradigm-based account of objectivity, in its extant form, is inadequate and needs perspectival and historical supplementation. Even higher-level laws and theories can be shown to be rooted in perception, perceptual perspectives. To say this is not to advocate a form of psychological reductionism. What it means is that the truth of theoretical conjectures is in need of perceptual accountability. Born out of perception, pre-theoretical construction, theories for their fulfilment and establishment are obliged to return to perception.

Compton takes pains to show that the perceptual scientific objectivity, rightly understood, is fair also to realistic ontological insights. For, in and through perception we are intimated of the *real* world, the world which is there not only for me but also for others. The true image of science, carefully analyzed, exhibits its personal, cultural, historical and ontological rootedness.

V

That the world of science is not *there* (in the physical space-time framework) on its own right was forcefully brought out by Kant in his theory of scientific knowledge. Using the principle of Copernicus he tried to show how our knowledge of things conform to our consciousness. R. K. Sinari in his paper, 'The World as the Ontological Project of Man', tries to establish the point that to describe scientific knowledge primarily, if not exclusively, in terms of subject-object bipolarity, is naive and simplistic. Certainly Kant, notwithstanding his commitment to *noumena*, did not intend to depict the world of science as something which has nothing to do with human consciousness. On the contrary, he emphasized the 'mechanism of subjectivity' as 'most relevant' to the understanding of scientific knolwedge. The subjective and the objective are two inseparable 'poles', not antagonistic extremities of ontology. To recognize the subjective foundation and contribution of knowledge is not to deny the objectivity of the universe. What the phenomenologist brings pointedly to our notice is the inadequacy and untenability of the naturalistic mode of understanding of science. Even what is called naturalistic mode draws its meaning from the meaning-giving acts of the knowing mind. In this connection, Sinari notices Husserl's method of phenomenological reduction purported to suspend the proclaimed ultimacy of the empirical world.

Empirical meanings stand somewhat abstract and discrete unless they are viewed under the aspect of eidetic reduction. The multi-dimensional reductive disposition of the subject is the expression of how we constitute the world. Our consciousness of the objective world of science is the projection of our quest for structurable and essential meanings. In the world we seek what we have in us as pre-given. We do so actively, not passively, i.e., as articulation and constitution of our transcendental subjectivity. By following this line of argument Sinari tries to show that the world of pure objectivity is a chimera.

In this connection he tries to refute the concept of 'epistemology without the knowing subject' defended by Popper, Bunge and their followers. In fact in an inarticulate form this anti-subjectivist account of knowledge is traceable to Bolzano and Frege. As opposed to this 'ultra-realistic' construal of knowledge, Sinari claims that 'all scientific knowledge is basically creation of man'. This fundamental nature of knowledge is ordinarily forgotten by the scientist in his preoccupation with the naturalist image of *objects* of knowledge. He forgets to raise and answer the questions 'what is knowledge', 'how it is acquired', and 'how its validity could be established'. In other words, the scientist in his search for scientific knowledge becomes oblivious of the conditions and limitations of knowledge itself.

The pre-critical character of scientific knowledge and resulting technological civilization draw Sinari's critical comments. Dazzled by the so-called success of science and technology, he argues, we tend to forget their underlying subjectivity, the freedom of the human self which stands behind marvels. Popperian realism and Skinnerian behaviourism are targets of Sinari's pointed attack. Positively speaking, he turns his gaze on the 'inner space', and meaning-giving acts of transcendental subjectivity. He recalls both Kant and Husserl in showing how consciousness' intuitive and organizing acts make scientific objects possible and bring out their structural laws. In this connection Sinari also indicates the inadequacies of causalism and suggests how the causal account of the world needs supplementation by the acts of our free and purposive consciousness. Otherwise, one fears that the world of nature and that of culture will fall apart and we would be condemned to a fragmented view of reality and of our human situation in it. While he highlights the role of our free self in the constitutions of our shared world-view, Sinari recalls particularly the contributions of Śaṅkara, Husserl, Heidegger, and Sartre. In them he finds the affirmation that a misconception of science must not be allowed to engulf our most cherished world of values and freedom. Our constitutive and cognitive enterprises are being sustained by an ever creative *elan* behind them.

If *epistémé* (knowledge) is deemed to be once removed from creative consciousness, *tekhné* (art) is taken to be twice removed from it. Don Ihde in his paper, 'Technology as Cultural Instrument', argues to the effect that technology, rightly viewed, i.e., phenomenologically understood, is an essential expression of socio-historically situated human nature. It is basically cultural articulation of man and not an external adjunct.

Materiality of technological culture does not negate its cultural or human underpinnings. Therefore whenever some form of technology, agricultural or metallurgical, is transferred by way of import of export it carries with it a whole set of human relationships. It does not move in isolation and through social vacuum. Technology transfer is in effect a sort of culture transfer. Unlike some old-fashioned Marxists, one must not understand it purely in terms of economics. In his analysis of the issue Ihde takes his cues from Heidegger.

The basic three theses defended by him are purported (i) to vindicate the non-neutral, i.e., relational, character of technology, (ii) to show the error of judgement involved in reifying technology, and (iii) to point out the cultural and existential inter-change that accompanies technology transfer. In fact these three theses are closely inter-related. When technology is negatively described as non-neutral its positive counterpart obliquely hinted at is its concrete and relationally ensembled character. Strictly speaking, technology has no abstract and isolated character of its own. Its character, value or disvalue, consists in the relations in which it stands to the concerned human beings. Use and experience of technology determines its nature. Therefore, Ihde argues, it is to be understood phenomenologically, pairing it with its human situation. In this connection Ihde recalls Husserl's 'variational theory' of interpretation now extensively used by historians and anthropologists. The point is sought to be clarified by analyzing the case of encounter between Australian Gold Prospectors and new Guinean Highlanders. When a cultural group migrates from one area to another it takes with it not only its technology but its whole life-world, language, mode of production, food habits, art forms and other forms of value. Technology moves inseparably with people who experience and use it. It is environed by a gestalt-type cultural milieu.

Technological objects are like diversely interpretable texts and not *bare* ontological posits. A cultural identity of a hammer or sickle or an axe is to be discovered from how it is used, interpreted and to what uses it is put to.

Transfer of technology is to be understood as a sort of inter-cultural encounter and gradual accommodation, not confrontation. Difference of culture promotes and provides for mutual learning and not necessarily entailing clash and conflict. Even where inter-cultural encounter leads to violent confrontation its fall-out invariably proves to be mutually accommodating. Sooner or later, cultural gestalts, however different and distant they might be, show up their mutually recognizable human faces.

What makes technology interculturally sharable also in a way accounts for the intersubjective availability of science as a mode of knowledge. If Kant could be credited with the transcendental character of natural science, to Dilthey goes the credit of formulating a life-worldly critique of cultural science. Apparently Kant worked under the assumption that unless the transcendental, a sort of other-worldly, critique is worked out, the threat of relativism and scepticism would continue to pursue natural science. Dilthey undertook the responsibility of showing that life-world as captured in descriptive pyschology can save all forms of science, social as well as natural, free from the said threat. Dilthey's descriptive pyschology is not to be understood exactly in the empiricist Humean tradition. It is structural, not atomistic, in character and anticipates Husserl's transcendental phenomenology as rooted in and answerable to life-world.

In his paper, 'Nature and Life-World: Towards a Hermeneutics of Nature', R. Sundara Rajan's main aim is to reconcile the insights of Kant and Dilthey, relying mainly on the works of Husserl and his followers like Schutz and Gurwitsch. To grasp the true character of the objectivity of science we are required to appreciate phenomenological description of the modes of intersubjectivity. The point has been pursuasively argued by Schutz. The human way of knowing nature is environed by nature itself. In a manner of speaking, one might say that we know nature naturally. Our life-world, our practical world, our pre-theoretic and theoretic worlds and their different strata influence our understanding not only of the objects of science but also of the subjects knowing those objects. Sundara Rajan emphasizes the importance of the pre-theoretic life-world in our understanding of nature.

He wants to show, among other things, that the importance that is accorded today to scientific methodology in the pro-positivist circles is unwarranted and cannot stand phenomenological scrutiny. Without exploring the conditions which make science possible, it would, according to him, be inadvisable to rely on the methodological procedures used to test the validity of its findings. First it has to be realized that science itself is sustained by life-world and its intersubjectively sharable interpretations. In addition, it has also to be realized that uncritical respect for scientific method rests on its pre-reflectively shared character. Delved deeply, i.e., phenomenologically, it is found that science, both susbtantially and methodologically, is pre-given in us. What is pre-given is reconstituted and restructured by transcendental subjectivity. And this lifts the relative or local views of science from their seemingly scattered limitations. Consequently, in and through transcendental reduction we can reach an idealized and unified picture of science. Rightly understood, there is no incompatibility between ideal unity of science, philosophy as science, and its life-worldly moorings. Through *my* life-world I can get into others' life-worlds. My internal cognitive horizon provides me access to an intersubjective and an ever growing horizon. This shows that what I know within me is not peculiarly mine and that it is cognitively available to others as well through their own internal horizons. Nature transcends life-world. In life-world nature is shared, shared differently, even creatively, not identically by all of us. Natural objects cannot be internalized completely, they are experienced to be related among themselves and the relations thus experienced exhibit homological coherence and predictability. But all the perspectives of natural unity are not given to our human understanding. In that sense it remains transcendental for ever. Even in its mode of transcendence nature shapes our cognitive and evaluative consciousness. But nothing natural or transcendental can totally take away man's unique privacy or self-intimacy. Laying emphasis on the last point of life-world, Sundara Rajan tries to make out a case for diverse images of ecology, natural as well as cultural. In the process the causal account of man-nature relationship (at bottom) and the strong thesis of transcendental reduction (at top) are consciously underplayed by him.

VI

Whatever might be the domain of knowledge, empirical science or transcendental philosophy, man continues to occupy its centre as its main author. His authorship goes generally unnoted, if not totally forgotten, by the working scientist because of his primary preoccupation with external data and empirical methodology. Even in philosophy his role is often viewed as pre-suppositional and not constitutive.

In modern age, it is mainly Kant who in terms of his Copernican Revolution drew our attention to the fact that the certainty of scientific knowledge, its *a priori* character, is rooted in the understanding capacity of the scientist as knower. Vico anticipated Kant when he said that man knows the world of culture (consisting of epics, myths, history etc.) best because he 'creates' it. The world of culture taken as a whole is the concern of the anthropologist. However, the discipline has been construed in two different ways, empirical and philosophical. This is not to suggest that the philosophical anthropologist is required to be indifferent to empirical findings of the working anthropologists.

In his essay, 'Unity and Plurality of Cultures in the Perspectives of Edmund Husserl and Ernst Cassirer', E. W. Orth proposes to establish the thesis that human being and culture must be viewed in close inter-relationship. In this connection he refers to Scheler, Heidegger and Helmuth Plessner. Unlike their predecessors, Kant Husserl and neo-Kantians, they show the *centrality* of the concept of man not only to the understanding of culture but also to one of its specific domains, epistemology. In order to answer the question 'what man can possibly know', we must, Kant reminds us, have a definite notion of man himself. The neo-Kantian Cassirer finds that all *symbols*, the basic cultural stuff, are articulations of the very nature of man. In other words, cultural phenomena are different forms of representations of human consciousness. Orth tries to relate Cassirer's thematization of man and culture to Dilthey's view that 'every knowledge about the world is knowledge within human consciousness, and that this consciousness is itself the only entity which human being can assure himself of authentically is an evident act of awareness.' The affinity of this view with Husserl's own on the subject is transparent. The self-givenness of consciousness and its accompanying sense of certitude needs no causal foundation. It is only when the causally explained nature, lends itself to this self-givenness, that its structure can get related to culture. Unless man-culture relation is properly or transcendentally thematized, the dichotomy between nature and culture, science and anthropology, cannot be done away with. This cue left behind by Husserl and Cassirer is steadfastly followed by Orth in his contribution.

Neither Husserl nor Cassirer denies the importance of empirical findings of science but both of them find that it is only human sciences which enable one to go into the philosophical depth and unity of different cognitive domains. In this respect, following Dilthey, they want to get out of the abstract notions of epistemological subject espoused by Locke, Hume and Kant. Whether Kant should be bracketed with Locke and Hume on this point seems to be a debatable issue. For, as a philosopher particularly concerned with feeling and willing, Kant tries to grapple with the relation that obtains between nature and culture in terms of his theory of (harmonic) teleology. To start with, perhaps Husserl and Cassirer were also somewhat inclined toward a notion of the abstract knowing subject. But, later on, it is clear that Husserl through his concept of intentionality and Cassirer through his concept of symbolic forms have tried to concretize the relation between the knowing subject and the plurality of objects. If Cassirer's subject articulates itself in and through the multiplicity of symbolic forms, Husserl's (transcendental) subject expresses itself in and through different types of intentionality and their objective correlates. From the standpoint of transcendental phenomenology all these types are elements of intersubjectively sharable transcendental reduction. Even at the so-called lower cogitative types, temporalized ego-pole, the habitualised ego and the life-world, we find intentional coherence. While the intersubjective sharability of meaning is said to be highest at the level of concrete transcendentality, it is not altogether absent at the lower level, in the life-world, either. Human situations have their different horizons of meaningfulness. But this multiplicity of situational reality is no road-block to achieve their unity cognitively. Husserl shows that the ego, though situated at one place, is in a position to understand other situations and egos therein in terms of its transcendenal subjectivity. This is how he conceives universal anthropology wherein regional or local anthropologies are coherently organized.

Whereas Husserl grapples with the problem of defining the relation between unity and plurality of cultures only in his late philosophy, Cassirer takes it up rather early in his philosophical career. Influenced by Kant's views on anthropology and philosophy of history, Cassirer himself has done a lot of work on history of philosophy. To him, both history and philosophy are forms of culture taken in a broad sense. His philosophy of symbolic forms is intended as an introduction to a future philosophy of culture. Both abstract and concrete forms of knowledge, as found in different cultures, can be meaningfully organized and unified. In the unified philosophy of culture the positivist pairs of contrasting concepts like scientific/pre-scientific, logical/pre-logical, etc., do not figure at all. Cassirer draws no sharp distinction between the epic, the mythic, the metaphysic and the scientific. To him, these are different media or symbolic forms of man's self-articulation.

That both Husserl and Cassirer are seriously engaged in overcoming the problems of cultural relativism has been clearly brought out by Orth's painstaking analysis. The concept of human freedom understandably plays an important role in their construction of a sort of universal anthropology in which the empirical findings of working anthropologists are duly recognized.

If human knowledge is irretrievably confined to cultural relativism, even the claim that scientific propositions are universal is by implication seriously compromised. In our naturalistic zeal most of us tend to forget this important point. That even the propositions of natural science are not totally unrelated to their cultural context has been brought out by Lester Embree in his paper, 'Human Scientific Propositions'. The very title of the contribution hints at the human roots and cultural moorings of scientific proposition.

Nature as nature is nor mirrored in any system of science, old or new, Indian or Euro-American. Science bears the imprints of both the individuality of the scientist and of the cultural community to which he belongs. Uses and values attached to science are of serious consequence in determining its acceptance or rejection. Thus, it has been argued, cultural diversity leads to a sort of relativism or cultural imperialism. However, this does not rule out the third *theoretical* possibility of espousing one *absolute* value and of avoiding, from that standpoint, both relativism and cultural imperialism. But practically speaking, we find that even the Ptolemic and Copernican paradigms of hard astrophysical science are culture-specific and epoch-bound. Embree's analysis shows that by assimilating natural objects under a particular culture we are not automatically committed to any form of superficial relativism. The theoretical attitude which gives rise to science is itself rooted in some or other practical life-world.

To say this is not to commit ourselves to naturalistic mode of theorization. We can theorise otherwise, humanistically. True, objects could be understood without making reference to values and uses attending them. One might say that it is a transcendental or culture-invariant way of understanding objects. Embree's analysis purports to show, though obliquely, that even this transcendental construal is practically rooted in some or other cultural milieu. He draws our attention to the fact that scientific propositions need not be naturalistic in order to be recognized as scientific. His analysis aims at showing that human scientific propositions, notwithstanding their cultural affiliation, are scientific in a serious sense of the term. That science cannot be delinked from human nature is itself a part of a more comprehensive human reality. In that reality, human nature, on analysis, is found to be an inseparable part of the existence, actions and dispositions of human beings.

It is well known that man is not atomic or windowlessly monadic. His actions, dispositions and even existence are relational. This relational identity of man has been highlighted in S.P. Banerjee's contribution, 'Phenomenology of Human Relations: Some Reflections'. Referring to several classical thinkers like Leibniz, Hume and Kant and contemporary philosophers like Husserl, Heidegger, Hampshire and Strawson, he wants to show that scepticism, regarding otherselves is incoherent and untenable. Positively speaking, he tries to establish the point that man cannot be what he is without the relations in which he stands to other human beings.

Both Kant and Hegel highlight the significance, epistemological as well as ethical, of each for all and all for each. Otherwise, neither epistemic intersubjectivity nor the possibility of a conflict-free moral community could be envisaged. A somewhat similar point is sought to be established by Husserl in his universal anthropology—constitution of mankind by man in terms of his transcendental subjectivity. Scheler's emphasis on sympathy, Buber's accent on interhuman relational ontology and theology and Sartre's concept of *being-for-itself* clearly show why absolute privacy, undisturbed solitude, epistemological solipsism and the like concepts are all self-stultifying. Basically, the same point is positively highlighted in Heidegger's concept of *being-with, mit-sein*. Man's being is not only inseparable from, but in a way, constituted by the beings of others. By appropriating the world around him and the society to which he belongs, man lives, moves and sustains his being. In brief, one's being derives its sustenance from others' being(s).

Such concepts as sympathy, jealously, love and hate make no sense unless the relational nature of man is duly recognized. Love both presupposes and sustains partnership. It would be wrong to think that partnership makes love possible. For, it can be affirmed with equal plausibility that partnership itself derives its existence from love. To buttress the point it can be further mentioned that unloving, antipathic and even hating relationships are not unknown phenomena. In brief, ontologically speaking, human beings are relational complexes and not isolated terms. Even to speak of isolation itself commits us to pre-isolative relational complexes.

In this connection, Banerjee analyzes the concept of love as developed by the *Vaiṣṇava* schools of devotionalism. The relation of love tacitly presupposes a sort of dualistic ontology, difference between the lover and the beloved, between the worshipper and the worshipped (God, for instance). In connection with the concept of love, Banjerjee also makes good use of Merleau-Ponty's phenomenology of bodily perception. Man's self-transcendence starts with body but goes gradually beyond it. Body is more than an ontic posit; it is an expressive presence and communicative force.

The self-transcending character of human consciousness is evident from different aspects of human being, somatological, ontological and epistemological. The relation between knowledge and consciousness, though well-known, has been formulated in a number of ways. In his paper, 'Object, Objective Phenomena and Objectivating act according to *Vijñaptimātratā-siddhi* of Xuanzang (600–664)', Iso Kern analyses the phenomenological insights of the *Yogācara* of the *Vijñānavāda* school of Buddhism. Xuanzang, a Chinese monk-scholar, came to India to study the teachings of Dignāga and his distinguished followers like Dharmapāla and Śīlabhaḍra.

The basic thrust of Xuanzang's work, following the cues of Vasubandhu's thought, is to highlight the total untenability of subject-object duality. There is nothing outside consciousness and independent of it. External objects, rightly understood, cannot causally induce our knowing consciousness to recognize them as they appear to us. In a sense object works on consciousness from without but at the same time is constituted by it. The form of object and its identity are inter-relational. But underlying the seeming simultaneity of subject and object there lies deep in consciousness a disposition of self-articulation in the form of object. The objective base (*ālambana*) which is said to be responsible for causal activation of consciousness is, strictly speaking, a potentiality contained within consciousness itself. Consciousness is self-activating. To say that consciousness is self-activating is not to deny the appearance-character of the object. The 'seeds' of *saṃsakāras* lodged in consciousness are not there in a purely passive way. Results of one's habits, these seeds of karma are active, effective and account for the appearance of the objective world.

It seems from Kern's analysis that he is understandably not satisfied with the *facticity* of the 'karma seeds'. If these seeds are given in a causally compulsive way, it becomes difficult to explain moral enterprise, i.e., free will, and moral actions. If, on the other hand, the efficacy of karma seeds is denied, the question of moral enterprise or, for that reason, any sort of enterprise makes no sense. In that case man could be effortlessly or naturally moral. This problem of the Vijñānavādi reminds Kern of Kant's problem of defining the relation between causal nature and moral world. Without *postulating* God, the problematic relation between nature and culture cannot be satisfactorily tackled. But at this stage Husserl intervenes and points out that to postulate God in the Kantian way is to offend the principle of antipresuppositionalism which is so central to the phenomenological mode of thinking. The main point of Kern is that the phenomenological modes of thought are not peculiar to any particular culture or historical epoch. The basic structure and functions of human consciousness are more or less similar at all times and in all places. Though veiled, this is an imaginative way of vindicating transcendentalism.

One of the recurring themes of many papers of this Volume, it will be seen, pertains to the necessity and limits of relativism in the realms of both knowing and doing. On the one hand, empirical sciences give diverse and apparently inconsistent accounts of what is believed to be knowledge and what is deemed to be morally advisable action. On the other hand, dissatisfied with the inconsistency found in diverse views on knowledge and morals, man wants to arrive at a consistent view on the subject. This view, rather worldview, has two aspects, metaphysical and methodological. Ronald Bruzina's essay in this Volume is concerned mainly with the 'Ideas for a Transcendental Phenomenological Metaphysics' as developed by Fink and Husserl. This is often regarded as the 'Last Philosophy' of Husserl. In its formulation he was ably assisted by Eugen Fink (1928–1938). This last phase of Husserl's thought has at times been described as practical or practice-oriented.

Husserl's last project purports to give a new systematic form to his thought on both theoretical and practical issues. He wants to defend phenomenological idealism and to tackle the problem of transcendental historicality within its framework. Within this framework, relativism of knowledge, plurality of cultures and unity of the world are sought to be reconciled. Also in it is shown the inadequacy of naturalism and the necessity of transcendentalism. This transcendentalism is simultaneously human and God-oriented. That phenomenology as a method can, and in fact does, progressively discover an ever enlarging world of phenomena is what Husserl and Fink seek to establish in clear and unambiguous terms.

Fink takes up the cues Husserl had left behind. In its comprehensiveness it reminds one of Husserl's own project. Transcendental excesses are corrected by and reconciled with life-world. Fink also wants to defend Husserl's ontology against the criticism of Heidegger. While Heidegger harps on the ontological distinction between *being* and *a being*, the Husserlian programme emphasizes the transcendental unity of all beings, of all regional ontologies. In his regressive analysis the phenomenologist discovers the originary unity of different areas and levels of what is real. To take this regressive movement back to higher and higher levels, he has to carry on the process of transcendental reduction. From psychology and epistemology one is taken to the height of transcendental subjectivity which is the most comprehensive constitutive principle of meanings. Even the highest unity of meanings is not enclosed or finalistic. It has always a Beyond behind and before it.

This phenomenology of Beyond has been named as Meontic Metaphysics. According to Fink, it is concerned with such fundamental issues as birth and death, 'I' and 'we', teleological structure of time and history, God as a teleological principle, the relation between 'I', 'we' and God.

Fink shows, through careful analysis, that the meontological interpretation of phenomenology opens up a hitherto undisclosed horizon of human reality. Transcendental phenomenology does not merely take stock of what is already there. Its creativity and productivity are unbounded. It is in this respect that its ability to deal with the issues of values, creation of new values and meanings, re-creation of old meanings, transvaluation of old values remains boundless for ever.

Man and *meaning* are two inseparable concepts. That partly explains why man has often been defined as a semiotic being. He creates meaning and intepprets his experience as a text. When he does so he also interprets himself. His self-interpretation and other-interpretation are interwoven by his meaning-creating capacity. The hermeneutic disposition of man is universal. True, in different cultures it is developed differently. But its universal traits are unmistakable. In her paper, 'Hermeneutics In Indian Philosophy', Krishna Roy has indicated the Indian way of interpreting classical texts. On her own admission she has been influenced both by classical Indian philosophers and modern European thinkers like Gadamer and Ricoeur.

The main characteristics of hermeneutics on which she focuses her attention are five-fold. Firstly, ambiguity and aphoristic characters of classical texts demand interpretation for their understanding. Secondly, regional hermeneutics, deeply explored, exhibits some general forms. Thirdly, it is the foundation of all human sciences. Fourthly, successful interpretation requires the interpreter to be intimately familiar with and involved in the concerned cultural milieu. Finally, all hermeneutic exercises are invariably anthropocentric in the good sense.

Roy tries to make out her point by referring to different interpretations of the Vedas as found in six different orthodox (*āstika*) Indian systems of philosophy, Sāṅkhya, Yoga, Nyāya, Vaiśeṣika, Mīmāṃsā, and Vedānta. How it is so that the authors of *different* systems claim that the texts which they take as most authoritative are the *self-same* Vedas? The only plausible answer under the circumstance is that the same text may, in fact does, lend itself to different interpretations. This further suggests that the difference between the interpreters' self-interpretation enters into the very acts of their interpretation.

To concretize her point Roy refers to the Mīmāṃsā *sutras* of the Jaiminī, who, among the Indian classical thinkers, paid perhaps the most serious attention to the problems of interpretation. Jaiminī enumerates five distinct steps in the process of interpretation, viz., (i) *viṣaya*, the ambiguity of the subject of interpretation, (ii) *saṃaśya*, the doubt attending the said ambiguity, (iii) *purva-pakṣa*, to postulate one probable (alternative) meaning and show its untenability, (iv) *uttaram*, to refute the *purva-pakṣa*, and (v) *nirṇaya*, the discovery and establishment of true meaning.

To recognize the importance of the interpreter, *bhāṣyakāra*, in Indian philosophical tradition, *bhāṣyas* (interpretations) on *sūtras* (aphoristic texts) have been accorded a pride of place. For example, even famous thinkers like Śaṅkara and Rāmānuja, are known as *bhāṣyakāras*, interpreters, and not authors of seminal texts, *sūtrakāras*.

The point of *critical* interest to which Roy draws our attention is that relying on the same texts different interpreters cannot only logically develop and establish their different understandings of texts but also refute those of the opponents. The point has been illustrated also by referring to the contemporary thinkers like Tagore, Gandhi, Sri Aurobindo and K. C. Bhattacharyya. All of them claim, though in different forms, to have relied on the classical texts of the Vedas and Upaniṣads in developing their own thoughts.

The theme of Roy's paper and that of J. L. Mehta's are instructively similar. Both propose to show how the same text can be diversely interpreted and what is the originary source of this creative diversity. While Roy concentrates on the theoretical aspects of the issue, Mehta gives us a detailed and concrete case study. This is evident from the title of the latter's paper, 'Reading the Ṛgveda: A Phenomenological Essay'. His basic aim is to indicate 'how a broadly phenomenological approach to a reader of the Ṛgveda as a text is not only likely to prove rewarding at the present time, but is imperative for anyone who is a participant, directly or indirectly, in the Indian philosophical and religious tradition'. In his work, Mehta, like Roy, has been deeply influenced by Heidegger, Gadamer and Ricoeur. In this connection, he recalls not, only the classical works of Sāyaṇa and others, but also the recent ones of Dayānanda Saraswatī, Coomarswamy, Sri Aurobindo and Anirvana.

That the Ṛgveda Saṃhitā is a finely woven texture of different threads is clear from the internal evidence of the text itself. We are told that addressing the Fire the *ṛṣi* pronounces, 'I do not know how to stretch the thread and weave the cloth; he, Fire, is the one who knows how to stretch the thread and weave the cloth; we will speak the right words, for he is the immortal light within mortals, the light in the hearts of men, the one source of all thought.'

The *ṛṣi* of the Ṛgveda is both a poet and a seer. He makes poetry, formulates philosophy and is himself secretly present *in* what he makes, poetry and formula. Therefore, from his *mantras*, words and hymns one can discover and rediscover his identity and work. These are both revealed and revelatory. These are both self-shining and, at the same time, strangely enough, hold back some of their own meanings to be disclosed or discovered gradually.

This deities of the *Ṛgveda*, viewed both in their multiplicity and unity, are spanning the entire region between mortal man and truth, the earthly and the transcendent. The whole region is full of *lokas*, spheres and layers, which even the mortal man, with immortal fire within him, *can* gradually explore. These *lokas* may be viewed as and expressed in naturalistic idioms. In that case man is deemed to be naturalist. If his language is faithfully descriptive and characterized by law-like orderliness, he is called scientist. When his language is symbolic and metaphorical, he is considered a poet. The *same* man is called *ṛṣi*, the seer, when his expressions convey the sense of the Beyond behind and beyond the sensible objects of nature. The poet-seer of the *Ṛgvedā* draws our attention, on the one hand, to the deities of light, liquor, inspiration, and aspiration and, on the other, to the obstructive and negative forces, *asuras*, inhabiting the different nether *lokas*. In his quest for knowledge and bliss man has to pass through both the regions, *asuraloka* and *suraloka*, the region of darkness and the region of divinity.

Mehta takes immense pains to show that the seemingly abstract concepts of the Veda are felt truths of existence and that the symbolic deities are perceived reals. He gives one the impression that *conceptual* thinking is not required to go back to the perceptual worlds in a reverse journey; perhaps it may be taken as a journey from *logos* back to *mythos*. The *ṛṣi's* deep involvement in poetic language need not induce us to believe that he was involved in conceptual thinking about the ultimate reality. On the other hand, Mehta suggests, following Heidegger, that we should take the *ṛṣi* as one involved in reading the text of the concrete life-world marked by colour and cadence. We must not telescope our own abstract conceptual cast of mind into the intuitive, imaginative and plastic mind of the *ṛṣi*.

The debate over the question whether speech precedes writing or the converse is the case is very old and still going on. Some thinkers are of the view that speech acts are more efficacious than written words. The opposite view defended by others is that unless there is something available in writing or in some other durable form, speech acts by themselves could not have served their purposes. Closely connected is the case of the relation between, and the relative primacy claim of, oral tradition and the literary tradition. Equally relevant to this issue is the validity or otherwise of the Saussurian distinction between *la lingua* (language) and *la parole* (speech).

Heidegger's view on this delicate and complex issue is very interesting. He is of the view that in Far Eastern countries like China and Japan writing is itself like a picturing or depictive activity. In that cultural region written words are picture-like but this is not the case in European countries. Inscribed words in the latter cultural tradition are still, static and clear. Referring to the Vedic language one might say that its symbolism and rhetoricity impart a highly imagistic character to it.

Heidegger's interest in language as language and in the forms of speech and writing is well-known. Once he proposed that this very theme may be taken as an interesting point of dialogue between the East and the West. While the Eastern peoples accord primacy to language as speech, the Western peoples are inclined to reduce their experience into writing. This view of Heidegger has been enthusiastically espoused, among others, by Derrida. Writing exhibits a formalistic cast of mind, which gives rise to philosophical, scientific and mathematical modes of thinking. The rise of European science and philosophy is sought to be explained by Heidegger in terms of the European's propensity to write out his thought and even feelings in words. In contrast, the average Japanese man lives mainly in his oral tradition.

In India, for example, spoken words are taken very seriously even in the abstract disciplines like philosophy and theology. *Śruti* (words heard from the reliable persons like *gurus*) is often recognized as a *pramāṇa* (method of establishing a knowledge-claim as knowledge). In fact, in India some modes of learning, philosophical, musical and dancing, for example, are said to be *gurugamya* (that which is to be learnt directly from the guru). This highlights the importance of oral tradition, personal communication and an intimacy of direct conversational interaction. Reading lectures in book is a poor substitute for hearing it directly from the teacher. In its written form language seems to be dead, whereas in its uttered form it is lively and effectively communicative.

In his perspective paper, 'Speech and Writing in Heidegger's Philosophy', S. IJsseling tries to clarify the differences between speech and writing as painstakingly worked out by Heidegger. To start with, Heidegger rejects the instrumentalist view of language. Language is *not* an instrument or means of communication or expression. It is itself expressive. While Husserl emphasizes the distinction between the corporality and the meaningfulness of language, Heidegger sees no opposition between expression and how it is expressed. Language itself is expressive. If its spoken form is found to be more expressive than its written form, that does not mean language *qua* language is not meaningful. In a different way the Heideggerian insight has been used by later Wittgenstein and Merleau-Ponty.

It is because he believes the spoken words and conversation to be of primary importance, that Heidegger regards Socrates to be the purest thinker in the European tradition. For he speaks his philosophy and by speaking it he gives life to it and succeeds in 'perpetuating' its life. The same success cannot be ascribed to any other philosopher or thinker. For, from Plato onwards, one finds that the European thought in its different written forms has become more and more inflexible and stereotypic. A comparable point has been made out by Mehta when he affirms that the poetic plasticity of the Vedic language is not to be found in the written language of the subsequent Indian interpreters, commentators and annotators. The being of *mantras* consists in their being chanted. Hymns are nothing if these are not sung. The inspired and picturesque language of the poet-seer understandably proves more influential than the clear-cut formula of the philosopher and the scientist. However, this is not to deny the merit of the philosophical thought which succeeds in containing the excessive sensuousness of the poetic language. Poetry articulates .ıe mode of being, whereas philosophy does another. The precision and formulability of the latter are not to be sought and found in the former. But both, in different ways, articulate human nature.

While the importance of written and uttered words has been found to be undoubtedly relevant to understand a particular culture, the question remains whether their primacy as *kulturkritic* is beyond dispute. For example, to understand culture of India must one get into its linguistic worlds and literary texts? Notwithstanding the well-known views of Heidegger, Jaspers, Gadamer, and Ricoeur, Margaret Chatterjee has something new and interesting to say on the subject in her paper, 'Towards a Hermeneutic of Centrality in Indian Art'. From the models of Biblical and Vedic hermeneutics, stressing the importance of language, Chatterjee proposes to depart consciously. She believes that we can learn most about the life-world of the Indian people from their behaviour and works of art. Her preference for studying architectural art forms is insightful. For, she maintains, rightly or wrongly, that *anonymity* of architecture allows us to skirt the problem of intentionality. Perhaps it is worth remembering that even the works of 'unknown' authors helps us to discover or to find out later on who they were. Even if the individual authorship of art works cannot be known we can at least find out their cultural identity from their style and other internal evidences.

How we understand some particular art form or tradition largely depends on how we are situated in relation to it. To understand a tradition must we identify ourselves with it? Or, an element of alienation or disengagement from it is called for? Often we are told that one and the same culture may be viewed from different perspectives or points of view. Chatterjee is suspicious of the metaphors of the convergence of different perspectives of horizons. Instead of the metaphors of convergence abundantly found in the literary texts she proposes to follow an opposite approach, i.e., centrifugal approach, for the purpose of understanding the architectural form of art. In this connection she has in mind the Hindu, Jain and Buddhist forms of architecture.

In the Indian life-world Chatterjee finds a perceptive sense of surroundings, 'a primeval experience which gave birth to a 'circular' set of metaphors of which the wheel, the lotus and *maṇḍala*, the cycle of seasons and the cylce of births and deaths are notable examples'. The root of these ideas is to be found in nature and not mathematics. Linearity is assimilated in circularity and change within some kaleidoscopic pattern. However, this does not entail denial of any historical sense. Only it takes an idiosyncratic form in the perception of the Indian life-world. Circularity presupposes some centre. The centre of temple architecture, for example, is celebration, some congregative acts like worship and prayer. The concreteness of meaning of every form of art is to be gathered from its actual use and behavioural aspect.

Another notable point of interest highlighted by Chatterjee is to relate the centrifugal view of art form with the problem of 'misunderstanding' with special reference to the issue of meanings. Unlike the meanings of literary texts aiming at convergence, the multiple meanings of a work of art are primarily purported to hold together the behavioural meanings of the members of a cultural community. For example, the priest and the dancing girl (devadāsi), the resident monk and the visiting 'sinner' cannot possibly have the same perception of meanings of a temple. When people understand meanings by participating in a life-form, their participation can never be complete or total, ensuring unanimity in their understanding of the concerned cluster of meanings. The art historian finds the meaning of the form, for example, of temple architecture from without, while the worshipper gathers it by participating in a congregation there. Distant or disengaged view of the art historian at times may be more authentic than the view of the participant. Because deeply involved in a life-form one may fail to see its all facets and grasp its diverse meanings. Immersed in a culture one may fail to know where it has gone deviant or monstrous. A comparable mistake may be committed by an alien critic who fails to grasp the meanings of the behaviour of the people belonging to a particular life-world. It is not that only Europeans fails to understand the intended meanings of some of our rituals; some of the more modern among us, too, find them odd or bizarre. So it is interesting that extreme proximity and extreme distance both stand in the way of correct understanding of meanings.

VII

We are conscious that to generalize in human sciences like philosophy is hazardous. Even then it seems to us that it would not be misleading if we indicate some positive outcomes of the 'meeting of the minds' of Indian philosophers and phenomenologists. Firstly, the very definitions of 'Indian philosophers' and 'phenomenologists' are far from clear-cut. And, therefore, the resulting distinction, though differently drawn, between Indian philosophers and phenomenologists, appears at times rather arbitrary. One common point that some of the contributors to this Volume (Mehta, Mohanty, Balslev and Roy) make out, either substantively or parenthetically, is that as a method phenomenology is so native to human nature that philosophers, irrespective of their group or cultural affiliations, often exhibit its traits in their writings. No self-conscious man can help interpreting his experience, be it of subject or of object. When the experience 'awaiting interpretation' is described as text and also as contextured, the point that is highlighted is the rejection of the myth of the pure given. Experience is a gradually disclosive phenomenon situated in the life-context of the individual in question. It is also situated within and oriented by the larger life-world in which the individual himself is situated. The effective mutuality of the inter-relation between the knowing mind and its cultural milieu has been dealt with in a number of papers (Seebohm, Orth, Banerjee, Chattopadhyaya, Embree and Kern).

Secondly, the said mutuality purported to solve the relation between *practical* individuality of every culture and proclaimed theoretical universality of all cultures itself gives rise to another set of problems. Is relativism a necessary part or *basically* antithetical to the very possibility of transcendental unity of the different forms of both knowledge and values? Must Euro-centricity of Hegel and Husserl (see Schuhmann) or Indo-centricity (see Bhattacharyya and Chatterjee) be taken as a sort of provincialism of human thought and action or a perceptive affirmation of the uniqueness of every culture, its forms of art, theorisation and practice? That the answers to these questions can be coherently brought together has been argued in many papers of this Volume (Mohanty, Carr, Bruzina and Sinari).

The last point has been argued both from a very 'earthly' i.e. empirical/ scientific, point of view (Compton, Heelan and Sundara Rajan) and also from the more ambitious transcendental point of view (Sinari, Gregorios and Bruzina). In fairness, it may again be pointed out that these two points of view need not be viewed as incompatible. Positively speaking, these are, perhaps, complementary and the complementarity becomes only gradually or historically evident through research and on reflection.

Thirdly, to determine the complementarity or otherwise between the elements of theory and practice one has to examine carefully the relation between *central* elements and *circumferential* elements. True, what is central in one context is circumferential in another. But the point remains that in different ways they continue to be complementary to each other. In phenomenological, and particularly existential, forms of writings the centrality of man and his different modes of experience are given the highest importance. Now this point lends itself to diverse, at times even paradoxical, interpretations. Is man self-contained or atomic or, transcendentally viewed, harmoniously monadic? Bypassing the suggested answers to the above two questions, positive in the former case and negative in the latter, man and his experience have also been phenomenologically described as articulation of Being or God (Balasubramanian, Gregorios and Seebohm). The process of transcendence may be viewed as inverse to the process of articulation. But rightly understood man is the confluence of both self-transcendence and self-articulation. This has been illustrated by referring to both Indian and Western thinkers (Bagchi, Balslev, Compton, Sinari and Kern). One can look at the phenomena both ways, man as enworlded and world as creation of man's meaning-giving capacity. Strictly speaking, these are not the *ways of living* but rather ways of *being*. This very important point has been persuasively argued with reference to linguistic aspect of human experience (Mehta, IJsseling and Chatterjee). Enworldedness of man may be illustrated also by the technological, apparently a very abstract, situation of man's way of being and perhaps a way of being as well.

Contributors

KALYAN KUMAR BAGCHI: Professor of Philosophy, Visva-Bharati, Santiniketan.

R. BALASUBRAMANIAN: Chairman, Sri Aurobindo School of Eastern and Western Thought, University Pondicherry.

ANINDITA NEOGI BALSLEV: Fellow, Indian Institute of Advanced Study, Shimla.

S.P. BENERJEE: Acharya B.N. Seal Professor of Philosophy, University of Calcutta, Calcutta.

SIBAJIBAN BHATTACHARYYA: Fellow Emeritus, University Grants Commission, Calcutta.

RONALD BRUZINA: Professor of Philosophy, University of Kentucky, Lexington.

DAVID CARR: Professor of Philosophy, University of Ottawa, Ottawa.

MARGARET CHATTERJEE: Professor of Philosophy, University of Delhi, Delhi.

D.P. CHATTOPADHYAYA: Chairman, Indian Council of Philosophical Research, New Delhi.

JOHN J. COMPTON: Professor of Philosophy, Vanderbilt University.

LESTER EMBREE: Willian F. Deitrich Eminent Scholar in Philosophy; and President, The Center for Advanced Research in Phenomenology, Florida Atlantic University, Boca Raton.

PAULOS MAR GREGORIOS: President, World Council of Churches, The Delhi Orthodox Centre, Tughlaqabad, Delhi.

PATRICK A. HEELAN: Professor of Philosophy, The State University of New York, Stony Brook.

DON IHDE: Professor of Philosophy, The State University of New York, Stony Brook.

S. IJSSELING: Professor of Philosophy, Catholic University, Louvain; and Director of the Husserl-Archives, Louvain.

ISO KERN: Professor of European and Chinese Philosophy, University of Bern; and Professor, Department of Far Eastern Studies, Zurich.

J.L. MEHTA: Formerly of Harvard University and National Fellow, Indian Council of Philosophical Research, New Delhi.

JITENDRANATH MOHANTY: Professor of Philosophy, Temple University, Philadelphia.

ERNST WOLFGANG ORTH : Professor of Philosophy, Universität Trier.

R. SUNDARA RAJAN : Professor of Philosophy, University of Poona, Pune.

KRISHNA ROY : Reader in Philosophy, Jadavpur University, Calcutta.

KARL SCHUHMANN : Professor of History of post-Medieval Philosophy, University of Utrecht and Husserl-Archives, Louvain.

THOMAS M. SEEBOHM : Professor of Philosophy, Johannes Gütenberg-Universtität, Mainz.

RAMAKANT SINARI : Professor of Philosophy, Goa University, Goa.

V.C. THOMAS : Reader in Philosophy, Pondicherry University, Pondicherry.

Index

Absent 159; *see also* negation; nothing
Absolute 21, 102, 138, 146, 149, 270, 272, 277–84; *see also* being; god; *puruṣa*
Act 147, 222–3, 225–8, 258, 265–6
Action 10, 17, 50, 56, 62, 64, 72, 74, 89, 109, 112, 115–16, 118, 120–21, 125, 131, 216, 228, 255–7, 267–8, 280, 292, 294, 296, 300, 365; *see also karma*
Adhyāsa 102, 136–7, 169, 346
Advaita 12, 47–9, 51–2, 70–71, 73–6, 79–81, 83–5, 87, 89, 92–4, 96, 102, 133, 136–9, 343–4, 346–7; *see also monism*; Vedānta
Agent 86, 133, 170, 175, 283
Aggregate 121–4; *see also* group
Agni 309–10, 313
Ahaṅkāra 60–1, 64, 134; *see also* ego
Ālambana 11, 265–6, 268, 357
Ālambanaparīkṣā 263–5
Albrecht, Gustav 270, 277, 278, 280
Alienation 205, 230, 334–5, 363
Antaḥkaraṇa 61, 76, 90–91; *see also* sense (organs)
Anthropologism 154–5, 234, 279
Anthropology 209, 223, 233–4, 237, 239, 242–3, 356, 359; cultural anth. 233, 235, 238–9, 242–3, 291, 309; philosophical anth. 123, 138
Anthropologist (s) 352, 354
Anumāna; *see* inference
Apodicity 156, 158, 161–3
Apoha 11
Archaeology; *see* arts
Architecture *see* arts
Aristotle 8–9, 29, 164, 175, 191, 219, 260, 267
artifact(s) 207–8, 210–11, 213–5
art(s) 222, 229, 240, 291, 321, 327, 332, 334–8, 363–4; *see also* sculpture(s)
Asaṅga 262
astronomy 249 *see also* science
āstika 293, 359
atheism 21–2, 26; *see also* theism
ātman 82; *see also* being; *brahman*; *jīva*; *puruṣa*; self
Aurobindo, Sri 12, 90, 117, 121–5, 293, 298, 300, 304, 360
autobiography 108–11, 113–14
Avenarius, Richard 21–2
avidyā 12, 138, 338; *see also* ignorance
axe 207–10, 212–13; *see also* technology

Bādarāyaṇa 297
Bagchi, K. 344, 365
Baladeva 297
Balasubrahmanian, R. 344, 365
Balslev, A.N. 346, 364–5
Banerjee, S.P. 356–7, 364
being 10, 12–14, 117–18, 124–5, 129, 138–9, 144, 146, 148–9, 156–7, 161, 163–7, 186, 188, 192, 195, 203, 256–7, 279–80, 282, 284, 312–13, 319–21, 327–9, 357, 359, 365; *see also ātman, brahman*; Dasein; phenomenon; *puruṣa; reality;* sattva
Being and Nothingness 129
Being and Time 164–5, 185, 320, 325
bhakti; see devotion
bhāṣya(s) 294–8, 360; *see also śūtra(s)*; text(s); word(s)
Bhattacharya, S. 344, 365
Bhattacharyya, K.C. 96–103, 124, 300, 344, 360
birth 65–6, 278, 359, 363
body 45, 47–8, 52–6, 59–61, 65–6, 71–2, 74, 82, 90–91, 96, 102, 115–19, 122, 125, 133, 137, 148–9, 160, 170, 187–8, 229, 241, 254–5, 257, 260, 267, 299, 342, 357
Brahma-Sūtra; see Brahmasūtra
brahman 12, 55, 76, 82, 305–6, 311, 313–14, 344; *see also ātman*; being; *puruṣa;* self
Brāhmaṇa (Literature) 304–5; *see also* Veda(s)
Brahmasūtra 79; 102
Brentano, Franz 11, 21, 23, 134, 141–2
Bruzina, Ronald 6, 358, 365
Buddha 26, 29–30, 297, 337
Buddha, Sein Leben . . . 24
buddhi 57–9, 61, 64–5; *see also* ego
Buddhism 12, 21–2, 26–8, 30–31, 33–4, 61, 73, 343; *see also* Asaṅga; Dharmakīrti; Dharmapāla; Diṅnāga; Hinayāna; Śīlabhadra; Sthiramati; Vasubandhu; Vijñānavāda; Xuanzang; Yogācāra; Yijing

Buddhist(s) 9, 13–14, 19, 25, 31, 51, 120, 136, 151, 262, 267, 299

Cairns, Dorion 29, 271–2
Carr, David 345, 365
Cartesian 82, 154, 202, 256, 260
Cartesian Meditation 133, 135, 159, 162, 227, 236, 270–1
Cārvāka 61, 65, 297
Cassirer, Ernst 234–6, 239–44, 354–5
cause 20, 120, 122, 174, 176, 191–2, 195, 199, 265, 344, 351
centrality 335, 338–9, 363; *see also* circle
Chatterjee, Margaret 363, 365
Chattopadhyaya, D.P. 1–2, 4–5, 345, 364
Cheng wei shi lun 263–4, 266; *see also Vijñaptimātrata-siddhi*
China 32–5, 262
Christianity 20–3, 26–7, 324
Chladenius 336
Cicero 322
circle 334, 339, 363; *see also* centrality
cit; see consciousness
citta; see mind
cogitata 83, 144, 236–7, 347–8
cogitatio (or cogito) 70, 83, 144, 256, 347
cognition 10–11, 13–18, 21, 31–3, 57, 64, 72, 74, 80, 85–6, 119, 153, 179–80, 189, 216–19, 228–9, 254–5, 343, 355
commentary; *see bhāṣya(s)*
communication 115, 117–19, 188, 190, 208, 229, 255, 257–8, 260, 306, 308, 335–6, 362
Compton 5, 348–50, 365
(The) Concept of Philosophy 96–7
confusion 47–8; *see also* illusion
consciousness 10–13, 17–20, 45–6, 48–9, 51–9, 67–77, 79–81, 83–92, 98–9, 105–6, 115–16, 123, 125–31, 133–9, 142–50, 154–5, 158–63, 186, 198, 200–201, 204–5, 219, 222–3, 227, 229, 234–7, 239, 260–8, 274–5, 300, 337–8, 342, 344–51, 354, 357–8; *see also* - consciousness
craft; *see* artifact(s)
(The) Crisis of European Sciences and Technology 32, 143, 153, 155, 185, 220, 222, 230, 235, 238, 333
Critique of Pure Reason 198, 216, 322
culture 9–10, 26–7, 30, 32–5, 37, 70, 169–70, 176, 180, 188, 192–3, 207–9, 211–6, 222–3, 229–30, 233–44, 247–52, 268, 291–2, 296, 300–1, 309, 319–20, 332, 334, 337–8, 341–4, 351–6, 360–1, 363–4; *see also* Kulturkutik; relativism
cycle *see* centrality

D.P. *see* Chattopadhyaya, D.P.
Dasien 105, 108, 164–5, 275, 320, 327, 345; *see also* being
De Man, Paul; *see* Paul de Man
death 65–6, 108–9, 145, 279, 359, 363
deity *see* god
Derrida, Jacques 157, 318–19, 322, 325–6, 328, 362
Descartes 143, 214, 234, 260, 322, 334
devolion 30, 67, 357
dharma 294–5, 300; *see also* religion
Dharmakīrti 265
Dharmapāla 263–4, 359
dhi 305–6, 309; *see also* thought
dhvani 338; *see also śabda*
Dignāga; *see* Diṅnāga
Dilthey, Wilhelm 105, 107–9, 113, 143, 153, 155, 216–17, 223, 234, 236, 274, 345, 348, 352–5
Diṅnāga 149, 151, 263–5, 357
drawing 319, 326–7, 361
dream 48–9, 52, 73, 85–6
dṛṣṭi see seeing 93
dualism 48, 76, 202, 258, 298; *see also* Sāṅkhya
Duhern-Quine-Hesse thesis 170, 178, 349

economy 207–8, 215
ego 9, 20, 48, 54–61, 64–6, 74, 77, 81–9, 91–2, 127, 129–30, 133–9, 144, 146, 148–51, 157–61, 220, 236–8, 240–2, 253, 256–7, 260, 277, 345–7, 355; *see also ahaṅkāra*; *buddhi*; transcendental ego
eidos 72, 145, 147–50, 154, 161–2, 200, 223, 228; *see also* reduction, eidetic
Embree, Lester 356, 364
emotion(s) 50, 53, 65–6, 72–3, 77, 257–9; *see also* love
epistemology 13, 58, 80, 100–101, 147, 150, 153–4, 161, 163–5, 180, 198–200, 217–8, 233, 236, 247–8, 275–6, 293, 335, 354, 356
epoché 80, 91, 134–5, 142–5, 149, 163, 238, 346
ethics 22, 25–6, 29–30, 125, 271; *see also* morality

event(s) 110–12; *see also* history
existence 44, 72, 74, 93, 105, 115, 119, 129, 139, 143, 145, 148, 155–6, 161, 164–5, 173–4, 179, 193, 195, 198–9, 203–5, 217, 229, 253–4, 258, 261, 272, 275, 299, 334
existentialism 48, 67, 122, 126, 130–31, 290
experience 9, 17, 45, 57, 77, 79, 85–6, 93, 105–8, 118, 128–31, 133–5, 137, 143–5, 147–50, 154, 161–2, 170, 186–8, 191–3, 200–201, 205, 211, 219, 223–7, 229–30, 240, 257–9, 267–8, 291–2, 295, 298–300, 309, 315, 333, 341, 344–6, 365
Experience and Judgement 221, 223

Fink, Eugen 271–84, 358–9
Flaherty, W.O.; *see* O'Flaherty, W. Flux 51, 144, 158
Formal and Transcendental Logic 15, 223
foundationalism 17, 111, 208
freedom 96–8, 100–103, 115–19, 122–5, 202, 204–5, 234, 239, 243, 257, 300, 342–5, 351
Frege 67, 225, 351
function 100–101, 103

Gadmer, Hans 290–1, 303, 307, 310, 332, 349, 359–60, 363
Gauḍapāda 64
General Introduction to Pure Phenomenology 142
ghost 209, 212; *see also* spirit
god 5, 12, 26, 55–6, 67–8, 121–2, 147–8, 193, 209, 258, 268, 270, 272, 278, 281, 284, 293, 305–8, 311–14, 316, 328, 333, 347, 357–9, 365; *see also* deity
god(s), Vedic; *see* Agni; Indra; Rudra; Soma; Varuṇa
graphic; *see* drawing
Greek(s) 9, 17, 29–34, 316
Greogorias, P.M. 347, 365
group 68–9, 110–13, 243, 250; *see also* aggregate; plurality
Grundprobleme 156–7, 164, 166
guṇa; see quality
Gurwitsch 137–9, 220, 222–4, 353

hallucination 45–6, 73, 179; *see also* illusion
heaven 70, 308
Heelan, Patrick 6–7, 193, 348–9, 365
Hegel 17, 20, 35–6, 120–23, 141–2, 145, 149–50, 256–7, 274, 318, 322, 326, 341–3, 346, 356, 365
Heideggar, Martin 103, 105, 108–9, 111, 113, 121, 123–4, 129–31, 141–3, 148, 150–51, 153, 155–7, 161, 164–6, 199, 205, 207, 211, 233, 242, 256, 274–7, 281, 303, 307, 309, 314–16, 318–28, 332, 334, 344–6, 348–9, 351–2, 354, 356–7, 359–63
hermeneutics 156, 177, 179–80, 216–7, 220, 227, 230, 290–3, 295–99, 301, 303–4, 315, 317, 328, 332, 335, 337, 353, 359; *see also* interpretation
Hesse *see* Duhem...
Hinayana 262–4; *see also* Buddhism
Historical Dictionary of Philosophy 325
history 105, 109–14, 120–1, 123, 138, 153–4, 170, 176, 189–90, 209, 229, 240, 270, 272, 278, 281, 291, 338, 345
human (being) 116–21, 123, 138–9, 145–6, 188, 203–4, 219–20, 233–5, 238–40, 242–4, 256–7, 261, 267, 279, 291–3, 308, 313, 347, 351
 humanity 32, 35, 105, 115, 120, 251, 270, 326; *see also* man
Hume, David 50–51, 80, 120, 139, 192, 236, 253, 267, 353, 355
Husserl, Edmund 8–18, 21–38, 72, 79–83, 85, 91, 96–101, 103, 105–6, 108–9, 112–13, 126–31, 133–7, 141–5, 264–6, 268, 270–5, 277–8, 280, 284, 319–21, 333, 341–49, 351–9, 362, 365
Hussert Archives 28
hylectic (data) 83, 159–61, 267
hymn(s) 305–6, 362; *see also mantra*

I-consciousness 133, 135–7, 146, 346–7; *see also* self-consciousness
I-Philosophy 68–70; *see also* individualism
(The) Ideal of Human Unity 123
idealism 12, 20, 48, 103, 120, 136, 141, 157, 162, 169, 235, 264, 341
Ideas I 8, 12, 24, 133–5, 142, 147, 219, 234, 271
identity 10, 45–7, 50, 59–60, 66, 71, 79, 124–5, 135–6, 204, 258, 260, 363
ignorance 92; *see also avidyā*
Ihde, Don 6, 351–2
IJsseling, S. 362, 365
illusion 51, 71, 73, 99, 102, 139, 151, 283 *see also* hallucination; *māyā*
impression 158, 192, 199, 201; *see also* memory
incarnation 53, 55; *see also* reincarnation
individual(ism) 52, 66, 73–4, 110–14, 116,

121–5, 129, 202, 239, 253, 255, 301, 339, 345, 364; *see also* I-philosophy
Indra 310, 313–4, 316
indriya(s) see sense (organs)
industrialization 20, 207; *see also* technology
inference 14–16, 92, 151, 254–5, 267
intentionality 11, 83–5, 89, 91, 122, 127–9, 131, 135, 144–5, 150, 158, 161, 163, 193–4, 200–201, 235–40, 244, 255–7, 260–61, 292, 332, 338, 344, 355, 363
internal organ; *see antaḥ-karaṇa*
interpretation 116, 172, 216, 220, 222, 290–301, 303–4, 307, 309, 311–12, 315, 317–8, 329, 333, 336, 349, 353, 359–60, 364; *see also* hermeneutics
intersubjectivity 159, 161, 187–8, 190, 217–9, 237–8, 242, 254, 258, 272, 335, 348, 350, 352–3, 355–6; *see also* subjectivity
Introduction to Metaphysics 321
intuition 147, 149, 200, 204, 240, 299, 351, 361

J.N.; *see* Mohanty, Jitendranath
Jaimini 293–4, 360
Jain(ism) 13, 136, 297, 299, 334–7
James, William 45, 66, 92
Jiten; *see* Mohanty, Jitendranath
jiva 53, 138; *see also self ātman*; person; *puruṣa*; self
judgement 218–9, 221, 223

Kant 8, 13, 19–20, 27, 35, 56, 80, 98–9, 103, 105, 117, 122, 142, 144–5, 147–8, 156–7, 166, 191, 198–200, 204, 216–7, 225, 235–6, 239–40, 253, 259, 268, 322, 338, 346, 350–6, 358; *see also Kant*
Karma 65, 259, 358; *see also* action
Kāśmīra Śaivism 51–2, 75–6, 344
Kaviraj, Gopinath 70
Kern, Iso 6, 357–8, 364–5
Kittle 338
knowledge 1, 15–16, 19, 30–33, 35, 56–7, 61, 71, 73–5, 80–82, 86, 92, 97–100, 103, 112, 118–19, 122, 143–5, 147–9, 151, 161, 198–202, 217–8, 225, 234–6, 242, 247, 249, 255–6, 261–3, 265, 297–8, 301, 341, 343, 345, 347–8, 350–8, 362, 365
Kockelmans, Joseph 156, 164
Krishna; *see* Roy, Krishna
Krisis see; (The) Crisis...
Kuhn, Thomas 189–90, 218, 349–50
Kuji 262–3, 265–7
Kulturkutik 332, 336, 363; *see also* culture
Kumārila 294

Laben *see;* Life
language 9, 67, 166, 203, 208, 240, 242, 248, 255, 257, 259, 291–3, 295–6, 303, 309, 314–15, 317–21, 323, 326, 328, 332, 341, 361–3, 365
Letter on Humanism 326
liberation 53, 65–8, 70–71, 74, 300; *see also nirvāṇa*; renunciation; salvation
life 105, 107–8, 110, 117, 124, 229, 273–4, 283, 345
life-world 130–31, 143–4, 188–9, 194, 216–7, 219–24, 227–30, 236, 238, 298, 333–4, 341, 345, 347, 349, 353, 359, 361, 363–4
logic 9, 14–15, 19, 28, 30–31, 33, 50–51, 74, 123, 141, 151, 164, 166, 200–201, 223, 298, 343; *see also tarka*
Logical Investigations 12, 133–4, 142, 154, 321
love 50, 137, 257–9, 357; *see also* emotion(s)
Luders, Heinrich 309, 312, 315

Madhusūdana Sarasvatī 133, 137, 346
man 32, 34, 50, 115, 121–5, 202–5, 259–60, 299–301, 305, 308, 327, 341–3, 345–6, 354, 356–7, 365
manas 60–61, 64–5; *see also* mind
mantra 314, 316, 361; *see also* hymn
Marx 34, 121–202, 352
Marxist 122
Masaryk, Thomas 21–23, 26
materialism 179, 200
mathematics 23, 143, 164, 166, 170, 172, 178, 198, 203, 224, 342, 362; *see also* science
matter 56, 65, 96, 240
Max Müller, F. 24
māyā 12, 20, 71, 75–6; *see also* hallucination; illusion
meaning 16, 100–101, 103, 107, 110, 112, 116, 125–7, 136, 146–7, 165–6, 186, 188, 200, 204, 217, 225–7, 229, 240–41, 243–4, 276, 291–4, 296, 307, 314–5, 317, 319–20, 322, 325–6, 336, 338, 345, 351, 355, 359, 363–4; *see also* sense; *sphoṭa*
measurement 171–9, 193, 200, 202
meditation 9, 11, 17, 98, 133, 135, 159, 162,

190, 227, 270–1, 300, 334; *see also* *samādhi*
Mehta, J.L. 360–2, 364–5
Meillet, A. 312
memory 46–9, 65, 106; *see also* impression; remember; *saṃkārā(s)*
meontology 275, 277–84, 360; *see also* ontology
Merleau-Ponty 175, 185–8, 190–4, 227, 229, 349–50, 357, 362
metaphysics 81, 134, 138, 141, 157, 165, 199–201, 270–74, 277–8, 280, 309, 321, 343, 358–9
metempsychosis 22, 45, 53
Mill, J.S. 254
Mīmāṃsā 11, 15, 136, 293–4, 296; *see also* Jaimini; Kumārila; Prabhākara; Śabara
Mīmāṃsāsūtra 293–4, 360
mind 13, 15, 45, 53, 55, 57–9, 71, 73, 80–81, 85–6, 90, 92, 96, 102, 109, 111, 116–7, 133, 138, 148, 150–51, 198–9, 240–42, 260, 263, 299, 309, 341–2, 361–2; *see also* *manas*
Mind and Matter 96
misunderstanding 336–7, 363; *see also* understanding
model(s) 120–21
modification 56, 58–9, 190, 254
Modus Tolles 98
Mohanty, Jitendranath 1–2, 4–7, 138, 343, 364–5
monad 45, 70, 133, 135, 253, 272; *see also* transcendental ego
monism 48, 73, 120, 292, 338, 343; *see also* Advaita
monotheism 292; *see also* theism
morality 259, 267; *see also* ethics
mysticism 270, 293
myth 29, 111, 240–41, 303, 311, 315, 361

Naiyāyika *see* Nyāya
Nalanda 262–3
nature 116, 122, 147, 155, 191–3, 195, 216–17, 219–22, 224, 227–30, 239, 242, 248–51, 334, 349, 353–4, 357, 358
negation 93, 117–18; *see also* absent; nothing
neo-Kant(ism) 105, 234, 273–5, 354; *see also* Kant
Neumann, Karl Eugen 25–7, 29, 31
nirvāṇa 20–21; *see also* liberation; salvation
noema/noemata 9, 98–9, 144–8, 150, 170–72, 176, 224–6
noesis/noetic 9, 98–9, 145–7, 150, 170, 175–6, 178, 222, 224–5
nothing 129, 260–61, 279, 281; *see also* absent; negation
Nozick, Robert 46, 50
nune stans 158–9, 162–3
Nyāya 11, 14–15, 17, 19, 71, 76, 136, 254, 297, 332, 344, 346

object 11–12, 35, 50, 52, 56–9, 61, 64, 67, 72–3, 75–7, 79–80, 82, 84–91, 93, 99–100, 102, 106–7, 109, 119, 127, 133, 136–7, 141–2, 144–5, 147–51, 155, 159–61, 165, 170–2, 190, 198, 200–201, 204, 220–21, 224–8, 237, 240, 242, 247–52, 255–7, 260–61, 264–7, 275–7, 291, 348–9, 357–8
objectivism 125, 201, 217
objectivity 97–98, 101, 103, 118, 125, 135, 143, 153, 185–90, 194, 199–201, 205, 218–19, 224, 226, 236, 240, 242, 265–6, 333, 349–51, 353
O'Flaherty, Wendly 311
On the Way to Language 328
ontology 13, 15, 19–20, 47, 49, 57–8, 60, 84, 96, 116, 124, 127, 129–31, 141, 144, 156–7, 163–5, 199–201, 204–5, 211, 235, 273–5, 277, 279, 281, 283–4, 293, 348, 350, 357, 359; *see also* meontology
organ(s) 61, 89, 187; *see also* sense (organs)
Origin of Geometry 319
Origin of the Work of Art 321
Orth, E.W. 7, 354–5, 364

Pantheism; *see* theism
Parfit 46–7
Paul de Man 317
perception 6, 11, 13–14, 16, 19, 47, 50–52, 61, 64, 92, 98, 106, 109, 118–19, 127, 147–8, 151, 159–61, 185–90, 192–5, 219, 223, 226–8, 230, 236, 240, 333, 357; *see also pratyakṣa*
person 49, 53, 58, 71–2, 74, 133, 154, 255, 259–61; *see also jīva*; *puruṣa*; self
Phaenomenologie des Geistes 141
phenomenology *see* reduction, phenomenology
(The) Phenomenology of Internal Time-Consciousness 106, 126–7, 130

Phenomenology of Spirit and Philosophy of Right 123
phenomenon 8, 109, 169–80, 191, 193, 198–9, 203, 206, 216–17, 219, 235, 266, 349; *see also* being; reality; *sattva*
Philosophical Investigations *53*
Philosophy as a Rigorous Science *143, 145, 223*
Philosophy of Arithmetic *23–4*
Philosophy of Symbolic Forms *241*
picture; see *drawing*
place 87, 164, 187; see also *space*
Plato 20–21, 29, 33–7, 103, 198, 321–4, 328, 342; Platonic 145; 148, 150, 272, 316, 342; Platonism 38
Plessner, Helmuch 231, 354
plurality 87; see also *gross*
politics 111, 124–5, 215
polytheism 292; see also *theism*
Popper 351
Prabhākara 294
pramā see *knowledge; truth*
pramāṇa *10, 13, 15–19, 151, 297, 341, 362*
pratyakṣa *151, 264;* see also *perception*
praxis (human) 207–8, 210, 213–14
(The) Principle of Reason *324*
Prolegomena *15, 153*
psychology 13, 15, 102–3, 134, 138–9, 144, 153–5, 187, 217, 234, 247, 276, 279, 296, 359; psychologism 15, 19, 153–4, 217, 234, 341
puruṣa *117, 124, 299;* see also jīva*; person; self*

quality 57, 60–61, 65, 85–7, 89

Rāmānuja 83, 360
rationalism 30, 260, 301
retionality 9–10, 17–18, 37, 120, 180, 187, 189, 195, 234, 298, 325, 341
reading 318–20, 324–6, 328; see also word(s)
realism 11, 136, 169, 171, 179–80, 186, 193, 221, 341, 349, 351
reality 11, 18, 26, 73–4, 82, 93, 103, 107, 109, 137, 139, 141–5, 147, 149–50, 155, 163, 169, 180, 188, 198–9, 204, 221–2, 224, 226–8, 235, 291–3, 295, 299–300, 313, 328; *see also* being; phenomenon; *sattva*
reason 29, 32–3, 36, 38, 56, 119, 141–2, 144, 165–6, 198–9, 216, 298–9, 322, 324, 341
rebirth; *see* reincarnation
recognition 174, 243
recollection 107, 128, 236; *see also* memory
reduction 133–4, 139, 145, 155, 159, 161, 163, 165–6, 208, 234–7, 276–7, 280–2, 347–8, 353; eidetic 72, 135, 149, 351; phenomenology 72, 101–2, 126, 129, 134–5, 142, 144, 156–8, 244–9, 345, 351, 354–5, 359
reflection 46, 48, 57, 71, 74–6, 85, 88–91, 97–8, 100, 102, 108–9, 116–17, 134, 141, 144, 154, 158–9, 161, 164–5, 186, 240, 242, 247, 250, 283, 332, 365; *see also* replica
reincarnation 56, 65; *see also* incarnation
relativism 9–10, 17–18, 32, 153–5, 170, 223, 242, 248–9, 341, 343, 348, 352, 355–6, 358, 364; *see also* culture
religion 9, 20–22, 25–6, 30, 149, 229, 241, 272, 292–3, 303, 315, 335
remember 106–7, 145; *see also* memory
renunciation 30–31; *see also* liberation
replica 46–47; *see also* reflection
retention 126–8, 130, 158
Ṛgveda 303–7, 309, 311, 313–4, 317, 360–61
Ricoeur, Paul 290, 292, 303, 307, 332, 359–60, 363
Rorty, R. 309
Roy, Krishna 1, 359–60, 364
ṛsi(s) 303, 305–6, 308–9, 311, 313–14, 360–61; *see also* seer(s); word
ṛta 312–3; 315–6; *see also* truth
Rudra 313–14
Russell 189, 333

Śabara 294–6
śabda 15–16, 18–19, 294–5; *see also dhvani*; scripture(s); sentence; speech; *sphoṭa* word
Śaivism 12; *see also* Kaśmīra Śaivism
Śākta 68
salvation 28–30; *see also* liberation
samādhi 55; *see also* meditation
Saṃhita 303–4, 306, 360; *see also* Veda(s)
saṃskāra(s) 359; *see also* memory
Śaṅkara 75, 79–81, 92–3, 205, 296, 351, 360
Sāṅkhya 13, 48, 51–2, 56, 58, 60–61, 64–5, 68, 76, 117
Satre 82–5, 88–90, 105, 121, 123–4, 126–31, 205, 256–7, 345, 351, 357

sattva 61; *see also* being; phenomenon; reality
Satz vom Grund 166
Sāyaṇa 304, 360
scepticism 17, 19, 51, 143, 253, 258, 260, 343, 356
Scheler, Max 155, 233, 256–8, 348, 354, 357
Schleirmacher 216
Schopenhauer 20–23, 26–7
Schuhmann, Karl 343, 365
Schutz, Alfred 219, 343, 353
Science 29–34, 36–37, 141–4, 153, 155, 164–6, 169–78, 180, 185–92, 194, 198–204, 216–22, 229–30, 235–6, 238, 240–42, 247, 270, 301, 319, 323–4, 333, 348–52, 354, 362; human sc. 115, 119, 247–9, 251–2, 292, 333, 355–6, 364; natural sc. 20, 193, 195, 244, 249–52, 346, 349, 356; social sc. 110–11, 116, 119, 180, 202–3, 233, 247
scripture(s) 16, 92, 295, 336; *see also śabda*
sculpture(s) 211, 335; *see also* art(s)
Seebohm, T.M. 6, 347–8, 364–5
seeing 14, 81–2, 92; *see also* vision
seer(s) 292, 309, 314; *see also ṛṣi(s)*; word
self 45–9, 51–2, 54, 56, 61, 64, 67, 71, 79–83, 90–91, 93, 102, 109, 118, 143, 145–6, 149–50, 239, 243, 253–4, 299, 338, 347, 351, 357; -consciousness 45, 48, 54–5, 64, 74–5, 109, 126, 216, 255; -control 52; -engagement 97–8; -identification 46–9; -realization 48–9, 52, 68, 70, 76, 300; -surrender 49, 67; *see also* ātman; *jiva*; person; *puruṣa*; soul; spirit
sense; *see* meaning; *śabda*
sense (organs) 5, 9, 11, 13, 60–61, 64–5, 72, 82, 90–91, 137, 175, 191, 226, 299, 346; *see also antaḥkaraṇa*
sentence 291; *see also* word
SF see (The) Subject of Freedom
Siddhāntabindu 137
Śilabhadra 262
Sinari, R.K. 350–51, 365
Skinner, B.F. 118, 203, 351
society (or social) 118–25, 138, 176, 202–3, 212, 248, 253, 255, 259, 296, 300–1
Socrates 29–31, 33, 35, 299, 322–3, 362
solipsism 157, 159, 254
Soma 309–10, 313–14,
soul 52, 72, 138; *see also* self
space 10, 22, 107, 120, 122, 124, 144, 146, 148, 188, 195, 202–3, 224, 227, 308–9, 320, 333–4, 348
speaking 67, 318, 326–7; *see also* word
speech 61, 67, 296, 314, 319, 361–2; *see also* word
sphoṭa 11; *see also* meaning; śabda
spirit 56, 127, 141, 149, 209, 212, 275, 283; *see also* ghost; self
spiritualism 47, 102, 150, 293
spirituality 239, 301
Śruti 17, 362; *see also* Veda(s)
Sthiramati 263
Studies in Philosophy 96
subject 9, 50, 52, 56–7, 67, 73, 75–6, 79–80, 82, 87, 99, 100, 134–5, 138, 141, 145, 148–9, 151, 154, 156–7, 163, 166–7, 170, 220, 236, 242, 255, 257, 276–9, 344; empirical sub. 56–9; subjective 89, 97, 102, 136, 139, 144, 146, 175, 199, 262–4
(The) Subject of Freedom 96–8, 100, 103
subjectivism 124–5
subjectivity 18, 26–7, 54, 79–80, 90–91, 99–103, 118, 124–5, 129, 137, 144, 153–7, 161, 163–4, 166, 169, 198–205, 235–6, 254, 257, 260, 272, 276, 278, 344, 347, 351, 353; *see also* intersubjectivity; transcendental subjectivity
succession *see* flux
Sundara Rajan, R. 353, 365
superimposition; *see adhyāsa*
Sureśvara 91
sūtra(s) 296–7, 360; *see also* bhāsya(s); text(s); word(s)
Suttapiṭaka 25, 27
symbol 228–9, 234, 236, 240–43, 291, 293, 303, 309–11, 313, 315, 335, 354, 361

tanmātra(s) 60–61
tarka 15; *see also* logic
technology 20, 37, 122–3, 166, 175–6, 180, 202, 204–5, 207–15, 247, 251, 270, 324, 327–8, 351–2, 365; *see also* industrialisation
teleology 32, 36, 121–3, 270, 278, 299–300
temporality 11–12, 105–6, 108–10, 112–13, 120, 126–7, 129–31, 157–61, 163–5, 188–9, 202, 224, 278, 281, 320; *see also* time
text(s) 216, 291–4, 296–8, 300–1, 303–4, 307–8, 311–12, 315, 317, 319–29, 332–3, 336, 359–60; *see also bhāṣya(s); sūtra(s)*; word(s)

theism 21 *see also* athesim; monotheism; pantheism; polytheism
Theological Dictionary 338
Theime, Paul 307, 309, 312, 315–16
thinking; *see* thought(s)
Thomas, V.C. 345
thought(s) 50, 66, 71–2, 74, 296, 321–6, 362, 365; *see also dhi*
time 12, 17, 19, 47, 87, 90, 106–8, 122, 126–7, 129–31, 135, 146, 148, 158–9, 164–5, 177, 185, 187–8, 195, 320, 325, 333–4, 337, 345–6, 348, 350; *see also* temporality
tradition 136, 139, 248, 332–3, 337–8, 342–3, 353, 362
transcendence 9, 12–13, 18, 20, 26–7, 51, 85–6, 89, 91–4, 98, 103, 125, 144–50, 157, 159–64, 192, 203, 205, 216–17, 223–30, 234–6, 238–9, 277, 280, 299, 308, 310, 345–48, 353–4, 357, 359, 361, 365
(The) Transcendence of the Ego 128
transcendental ego 127–9; 131; *see also* ego; monad
transcendental phenomenology 27, 79, 84, 133, 138–9, 142, 145, 150, 153–7, 237, 271, 274, 277, 344, 353
transcendental subjectivity 51–2, 80, 82, 134, 270, 282, 349, 351, 355, 357, 359; *see also* subjectivity
transcendentalism 30, 35, 356
translation 166, 315, 320
Triṃśikā 253
truth 10–11, 15, 17, 30, 218, 228, 295, 298, 303, 305–6, 308, 310–13, 315–16, 321, 325, 335, 361

understanding 209, 216–17, 219–2, 234–5, 239, 240, 258, 291–2, 295, 309, 315, 317, 328, 333, 336–8; *see also* misunderstanding
upādhi 11
Upanishad(s) 21, 82, 86, 93, 292, 298–301, 304, 360

Vācaspati Miśra 61, 64
Vaiśeṣika 71
vāk 313–14; *see also* word
Vaiṣṇava 67–8, 258, 357
value 250–1, 259, 351, 359
Varuna 303, 305, 311–13, 316
vastu see object
Vasubandhu 262–3, 357
Vedanta 12–13, 18, 21, 99–100, 102–3, 136, 297, 346; *see also* Advaita, Vedanta; Bādarāyaṇa; Baladeva; Gauḍapāda; Madhusūdana Sarasvatī; Rāmānuja; Śaṅkara; Sureśvara
Vedāntasāra 72
Veda(s) 21, 55, 292–5, 297–9, 304–9, 313–16, 359–61; *see also* Brahmana (Literature); Ṛgveda; Saṃhita(s); Śruti
verbal instruction; *see* śabda
Vico 239–40, 354
vijñāna see consciousness
Vijñānabhairavam 59
Vijñānavāda 73, 262–3, 357–8
Vijñapti-mātrata-siddhi 263, 357
Viṃśatikā 263
vision 179; *see also* seeing

What is called Reading 325
What is called Thinking 321–3, 325
will 115–16, 118, 260–61, 299
William *see* James, William
Wittgenstein 53, 118, 309, 362
word(s) 243, 291, 309, 313, 318, 321, 327–8, 338, 361–2; *see also bhāṣya(s)*; reading; *ṛṣi(s)*; *śabda*; sentence; speech; *sūtra(s)*; text(s); *vāk*; writing
Writing 318–28, 361–2; *see also* word(s)

Xuanzang 262–3; 265–8, 357

Yijing 264
Yoga 12–13, 68, 70
yogācāra 11, 136, 262–3, 346, 357

Zöllner, Johann 21